The Tomes of Delphi™
Win32 Core API
Windows 2000 Edition

John Ayres

Wordware Publishing, Inc.

Library of Congress Cataloging-in-Publication Data

Ayres, John.
 Tomes of Delphi: Win32 Core API Windows 2000 edition / by John Ayres.
     p. cm.
 Includes bibliographical references and index.
 ISBN 1-55622-750-7 (pbk.)
 1. Microsoft Win32.   2. Delphi (Computer file).   I. Title.
 QA76.76.O63 A97   2001   2001046842
 005.265--dc21   CIP

Copyright © 2002, Wordware Publishing, Inc.

All Rights Reserved

2320 Los Rios Boulevard
Plano, Texas 75074

No part of this book may be reproduced in any form or by
any means without permission in writing from
Wordware Publishing, Inc.

Printed in the United States of America

ISBN 1-55622-750-7
10 9 8 7 6 5 4 3 2 1
0110

Delphi is a trademark of Borland Software Corporation in the United States and other countries.
Windows is a registered trademark of Microsoft Corporation in the United States and/or other countries.
Other product names mentioned are used for identification purposes only and may be trademarks of their respective companies.

All inquiries for volume purchases of this book should be addressed to Wordware Publishing, Inc., at the above address. Telephone inquiries may be made by calling:

(972) 423-0090

Praise for The Tomes of Delphi 3: Win32 Core API

"*The Tomes of Delphi* is the definitive reference for the Win32 API expressed in the Object Pascal language. It's a must-have for application and component developers looking to extend their reach beyond the capabilities of the Visual Component Library."

    Steve Teixeira, Director Core Technology
    Zone Labs, Inc. and co-author of *Delphi 6 Developer's Guide*

****

"*The Tomes of Delphi 3: Win32 Core API* is an excellent resource for Delphi programmers needing to go beyond drag and drop development. This book not only discusses the API in depth, but also provides solid examples of using Delphi to access the power of Windows provided through the API."

    Xavier Pacheco, President and CEO
    Xapware Technologies, Inc and co-author of the best-selling
    Delphi 6 Developer's Guide

****

"One of the features I liked most when I first approached Delphi was its power to go down to the Windows API-level, something most other visual tools still lack. But this is not an easy task, and no book like *The Tomes of Delphi 3: Win32 Core API* can help you understand Windows from the Delphi perspective."

    Marco Cantu, author of the best-selling *Mastering Delphi 6*

****

"Delphi lets developers work 'under the hood' with the Win32 API. *The Tomes of Delphi 3: Win32 Core API* gives every Delphi developer the knowledge to use the Win32 API powerfully, creatively, and effectively."

    Michael Swindell, Director of Product Management
    RAD Tools Group, Borland Software Corporation

****

"*The Tomes of Delphi 3: Win32 Core API* is my number one resource when looking for information about how to use the Win32 core API in Delphi. I especially enjoy the helpfile that contains the complete text from the book and can be accessed directly when programming."

    Bob Swart (a.k.a. "Dr. Bob"), Author, trainer, consultant

****

"Not only were these the first Delphi books to concentrate on API-level programming, they set the standard for all future Delphi API books."

    Alan C. Moore, Contributing Editor
    Delphi Informant Magazine

Dedication

I would like to dedicate this book to the following people and/or deities who have had a profound influence in my life: First, to God, whom I've been growing much closer to these last few years, for giving me the intelligence to wade through the confusing and sometimes maddening sea of Windows API documentation and make sense of it all; second, to my family, for putting up with my lack of participation in family activities during this project; and finally, but most of all, to my wife and soulmate, Marci, who made sure I had clothes to wear in the morning and food in the evening, fixed my lunches, and generally took up all of my housework responsibilities so I could concentrate on the book. She encouraged me and prodded me along when the weight of this project became unbearable, and because of this she is directly responsible for this work being completed. She is a very inspiring task master; cracking the whip to bring me in line when I would have rather been playing *X-Wing vs. Tie Fighter*. I am unworthy of such a devoted and loving wife, and I thank God every day for providing me with such a perfect companion. Baby, this one's for you.

Contents

	Foreword	xvi
	Acknowledgments	xviii
	Introduction	xix
Chapter 1	**Delphi and the Windows API**	1
	Windows Data Types	1
	Handles	3
	Constants	4
	Strings	4
	Importing Windows Functions	4
	Incorrectly Imported Functions	5
	Callback Functions	5
	Function Parameters	6
	Unicode	6
	Delphi vs. the Windows API	7
Chapter 2	**Window Creation Functions**	9
	Creating Windows: The Basic Steps	9
	Window Attributes	10
	The Window Procedure	13
	Hardcore Windows Programming	13
	Window Types	15
	Multiple Document Interface	17
	Extending Functionality	23
	Delphi vs. the Windows API	25
	Window Creation and Registration Functions	26
	CreateMDIWindow	26
	CreateWindowEx	29
	DestroyWindow	45
	MessageBox	46
	RegisterClass	49
	RegisterClassEx	53
	UnregisterClass	55
Chapter 3	**Message Processing Functions**	57
	The Message Queue and Message Loop	57
	Windows Hooks	58
	Interprocess Communication	61
	Delphi vs. the Windows API	61
	Message Processing Functions	62

v

BroadcastSystemMessage. 63
CallNextHookEx 65
CallWindowProc 66
DefFrameProc. 68
DefMDIChildProc 73
DefWindowProc. 74
DispatchMessage 75
GetMessage 76
GetMessageExtraInfo 79
GetMessagePos 80
GetMessageTime 81
GetQueueStatus 81
InSendMessage 83
PeekMessage 84
PostMessage. 86
PostQuitMessage 89
PostThreadMessage 89
RegisterWindowMessage 91
ReplyMessage. 93
SendMessage 94
SendMessageCallback 95
SendMessageTimeout. 97
SendNotifyMessage 100
SetMessageExtraInfo 102
SetWindowsHookEx 103
WH_CALLWNDPROC Hook Function 105
WH_CALLWNDPROCRET Hook Function 106
WH_CBT Hook Function 107
WH_DEBUG Hook Function 110
WH_FOREGROUNDIDLE Hook Function 111
WH_GETMESSAGE Hook Function 111
WH_JOURNALPLAYBACK Hook Function 112
WH_JOURNALRECORD Hook Function 114
WH_KEYBOARD Hook Function 115
WH_MOUSE Hook Function 116
WH_MSGFILTER Hook Function 117
WH_SHELL Hook Function 118
WH_SYSMSGFILTER Hook Function 120
TranslateMessage 122
UnhookWindowsHookEx 123
WaitMessage. 123

Chapter 4 **Memory Management Functions. 125**
The Win32 Virtual Memory Architecture 125
Categories of Memory Allocation Functions 126
Heaps 126
The 16-Bit Memory Functions 127
Virtual Memory 127

Three States of Memory	127
How Much Memory is Really There?	128
Multiple Heaps	128
Error Trapping	129
Thread Access	129
Speed	130
Delphi vs. the Windows API	130
Memory Management Functions	131
CopyMemory	132
FillMemory	133
GetProcessHeap	134
GlobalAlloc	135
GlobalDiscard	136
GlobalFlags	137
GlobalFree	138
GlobalHandle	138
GlobalLock	139
GlobalMemoryStatus	140
GlobalReAlloc	142
GlobalSize	145
GlobalUnlock	145
HeapAlloc	146
HeapCreate	148
HeapDestroy	150
HeapFree	150
HeapReAlloc	151
HeapSize	152
IsBadCodePtr	153
IsBadReadPtr	154
IsBadStringPtr	155
IsBadWritePtr	156
MoveMemory	157
VirtualAlloc	159
VirtualFree	163
VirtualProtect	164
VirtualQuery	166
ZeroMemory	168
Chapter 5 Dynamic-Link Library Functions	**169**
Importing/Exporting Functions	169
Calling Conventions	170
The Dynamic-Link Library Entry Point Function	170
Delphi vs. the Windows API	171
Dynamic-Link Library Functions	171
DLLMain	171
DisableThreadLibraryCalls	172
FreeLibrary	173
FreeLibraryAndExitThread	174

GetModuleFileName 178
GetModuleHandle 179
GetProcAddress 179
LoadLibrary 180
LoadLibraryEx 183

Chapter 6 Process and Thread Functions 187
Important Concepts 187
    Processes 188
    Threads 188
    Priority Levels 188
Synchronization and Coordination 188
    Deadlocks 189
    Synchronization Objects 190
        Critical Sections 190
        Semaphores 190
        Mutexes 190
        Events 191
    Synchronizing Processes with a Mutex 191
Delphi vs. the Windows API 192
Process and Thread Functions 192
    CreateEvent 194
    CreateMutex 197
    CreateProcess 200
    CreateSemaphore 206
    CreateThread 210
    DeleteCriticalSection 211
    DuplicateHandle 211
    EnterCriticalSection 214
    ExitProcess 215
    ExitThread 216
    GetCurrentProcess 217
    GetCurrentProcessId 217
    GetCurrentThread 218
    GetCurrentThreadId 218
    GetExitCodeProcess 219
    GetExitCodeThread 220
    GetPriorityClass 221
    GetThreadPriority 223
    GetWindowThreadProcessId 225
    InitializeCriticalSection 226
    InterlockedDecrement 228
    InterlockedExchange 230
    InterlockedIncrement 231
    LeaveCriticalSection 232
    OpenEvent 232
    OpenMutex 233
    OpenProcess 234

Contents ■ **ix**

        OpenSemaphore 236
        PulseEvent 237
        ReleaseMutex 238
        ReleaseSemaphore 239
        ResetEvent 240
        ResumeThread 240
        SetEvent 241
        SetPriorityClass 241
        SetThreadPriority 243
        Sleep 244
        SuspendThread 244
        TerminateProcess 245
        TerminateThread 246
        TlsAlloc 247
        TlsFree 250
        TlsGetValue 250
        TlsSetValue 251
        WaitForInputIdle 251
        WaitForSingleObject 253

Chapter 7   **Timer Functions 255**
    Emulating a Timer 255
    Precise Timing 257
    Delphi vs. the Windows API 259
    Timer Functions 259
        GetTickCount 259
        KillTimer 260
        QueryPerformanceCounter 262
        QueryPerformanceFrequency 263
        SetTimer 264

Chapter 8   **Error Functions 267**
    Error Descriptions 267
        Audible Error Cues 268
    Delphi vs. the Windows API 269
    Error Functions 270
        Beep 270
        ExitWindows 271
        ExitWindowsEx 272
        FatalAppExit 273
        GetLastError 274
        MessageBeep 275
        SetLastError 276

Chapter 9   **Graphical Device Interface Functions 279**
    Device Independence 279
    Device Contexts 280
        Device Context Types 280
        Screen, Window, and Client Area Device Contexts 282

	Coordinate Systems. 283
	Mapping Logical Coordinates into Device Coordinates 284
	Mapping Modes. 284
	Problems with Logical Coordinate Mapping 288
	Delphi vs. the Windows API. 289
	Graphical Device Interface Functions 289

        ChangeDisplaySettings 290
        ClientToScreen. 294
        CreateCompatibleDC 296
        DeleteDC. 299
        DPtoLP. 299
        EnumDisplaySettings 300
        GetDC 303
        GetDCOrgEx. 304
        GetDeviceCaps 305
        GetMapMode 313
        GetSystemMetrics 314
        GetViewportExtEx. 319
        GetViewportOrgEx 320
        GetWindowDC. 320
        GetWindowExtEx 322
        GetWindowOrgEx 323
        LPtoDP. 323
        MapWindowPoints. 324
        OffsetViewportOrgEx 326
        OffsetWindowOrgEx 327
        ReleaseDC. 328
        RestoreDC. 329
        SaveDC 329
        ScaleViewportExtEx. 330
        ScaleWindowExtEx 334
        ScreenToClient. 335
        ScrollDC 336
        SetMapMode. 338
        SetViewportExtEx 339
        SetViewportOrgEx. 340
        SetWindowExtEx 341
        SetWindowOrgEx. 342

Chapter 10   Painting and Drawing Functions 345
    Graphical Objects. 345
        Pens and Brushes. 346
    Delphi vs. the Windows API. 346
    Painting and Drawing Functions 347
        Arc 348
        BeginPaint 351
        Chord. 352
        CreateBrushIndirect 354

CreateHatchBrush 357
CreatePatternBrush. 358
CreatePen. 360
CreatePenIndirect 362
CreateSolidBrush. 364
DeleteObject 365
DrawCaption 366
DrawEdge 367
DrawFocusRect 370
DrawFrameControl. 371
DrawState 375
Ellipse 379
EndPaint 380
EnumObjects 381
ExtCreatePen 383
ExtFloodFill 387
FillPath 388
FillRect 389
FillRgn 391
FrameRect 391
FrameRgn 392
GetBkColor. 394
GetBkMode 395
GetBoundsRect. 395
GetBrushOrgEx 397
GetCurrentObject 398
GetCurrentPositionEx 399
GetMiterLimit 400
GetObject. 401
GetObjectType 405
GetPixel 406
GetPolyFillMode 407
GetROP2 409
GetStockObject. 411
GetUpdateRect 413
GetUpdateRgn 413
GrayString 414
InvalidateRect 417
InvalidateRgn 419
LineDDA 421
LineTo 423
LockWindowUpdate 424
MoveToEx 425
PaintDesktop 425
PaintRgn 426
Pie 427
PolyBezier 429
PolyBezierTo. 431

	Polygon 432
	Polyline 433
	PolylineTo 434
	PolyPolygon 435
	PolyPolyline 437
	Rectangle. 438
	RoundRect 440
	SelectObject 442
	SetBkColor. 443
	SetBkMode 444
	SetBoundsRect. 444
	SetBrushOrgEx 446
	SetMiterLimit 446
	SetPixel 447
	SetPixelV 449
	SetPolyFillMode 449
	SetROP2 450
	StrokeAndFillPath 452
	StrokePath 453

Chapter 11 Region and Path Functions 455

Regions and Paths 455
    Regions 455
    Paths. 458
Special Effects 458
Delphi vs. the Windows API 460
Region and Path Functions 461
    AbortPath 462
    BeginPath 463
    CloseFigure 463
    CombineRgn 465
    CopyRect. 468
    CreateEllipticRgn 469
    CreateEllipticRgnIndirect 469
    CreatePolygonRgn 471
    CreatePolyPolygonRgn 474
    CreateRectRgn 476
    CreateRectRgnIndirect. 477
    CreateRoundRectRgn 478
    EndPath 480
    EqualRect 480
    EqualRgn. 481
    ExcludeClipRect 482
    ExtCreateRegion. 485
    ExtSelectClipRgn 487
    FlattenPath 489
    GetClipBox 489
    GetClipRgn 490

GetPath	491
GetRegionData	494
GetRgnBox	494
InflateRect	495
IntersectRect	496
InvertRect	497
InvertRgn	498
IsRectEmpty	498
OffsetClipRgn	499
OffsetRect	501
OffsetRgn	505
PathToRegion	507
PtInRect	509
PtInRegion	509
PtVisible	510
RectInRegion	511
RectVisible	511
SelectClipPath	512
SelectClipRgn	516
SetRect	519
SetRectEmpty	520
SetRectRgn	521
SetWindowRgn	522
SubtractRect	525
UnionRect	526
WidenPath	527

Chapter 12 Bitmap and Metafile Functions 529

Bitmaps	529
Device-dependent Bitmaps	530
Device-independent Bitmaps	530
Bitmap Operations	530
Metafiles	537
Enhanced Metafiles	537
Delphi vs. the Windows API	537
Bitmap and Metafile Functions	538
BitBlt	539
CloseEnhMetaFile	541
CopyEnhMetaFile	541
CopyImage	542
CreateBitmap	545
CreateBitmapIndirect	548
CreateCompatibleBitmap	550
CreateDIBitmap	552
CreateDIBSection	556
CreateEnhMetaFile	562
DeleteEnhMetaFile	565
EnumEnhMetaFile	566

Contents

GetBitmapBits 569
GetBitmapDimensionEx 571
GetDIBits 571
GetEnhMetaFile 575
GetEnhMetaFileDescription 578
GetEnhMetaFileHeader 579
GetStretchBltMode 581
LoadBitmap 582
LoadImage 585
PatBlt 588
PlayEnhMetaFile 590
PlayEnhMetaFileRecord 591
SetBitmapBits 592
SetBitmapDimensionEx 594
SetDIBits 594
SetDIBitsToDevice 599
SetStretchBltMode 601
StretchBlt 602
StretchDIBits 604

Chapter 13 **Text Output Functions** **609**

Fonts 609
    Font Families 609
    Character Sets 610
    Character Dimensions 611
The Windows Font Table 611
Font Embedding 612
Delphi vs. the Windows API 617
Text Output Functions 618
    AddFontResource 619
    CreateFont 619
    CreateFontIndirect 626
    CreateScalableFontResource 632
    DrawText 634
    DrawTextEx 638
    EnumFontFamilies 642
    EnumFontFamiliesEx 647
    GetCharABCWidths 653
    GetCharWidth 655
    GetFontData 656
    GetGlyphOutline 657
    GetKerningPairs 662
    GetOutlineTextMetrics 664
    GetRasterizerCaps 679
    GetTabbedTextExtent 680
    GetTextAlign 681
    GetTextCharacterExtra 682
    GetTextColor 683

GetTextExtentExPoint 683
GetTextExtentPoint32 686
GetTextFace 687
GetTextMetrics 688
RemoveFontResource 694
SetTextAlign 694
SetTextCharacterExtra 697
SetTextColor 698
SetTextJustification 699
TabbedTextOut 700
TextOut 702

Appendix A **Bibliography** 705

Appendix B **Virtual Key Code Chart** 707

Appendix C **Tertiary Raster Operation Codes** 711

Index 719

Foreword

The Windows API is the foundation upon which most contemporary programs are built. It is the heart and soul of database applications, multimedia applications, even many network based applications. Every Windows application relies on the Windows API to perform everything from the most mundane to the most esoteric task.

All of the good programmers I know have a solid foundation in the Windows API. It is the language in which the architecture of the Windows operating system is most eloquently expressed, and it holds the secrets programmers need to know if they want to develop powerful, well tuned applications.

There are at least three reasons why most serious programmers need to know the Windows API:

1. It is occasionally possible to write strong, robust applications without having a good understanding of the Windows API. However, there comes a time in the course of most application development projects when you simply have to turn to the Windows API in order to solve a particular problem. Usually this happens because a tool you are using does not have a feature you need, or because the feature is not implemented properly. In such cases, you have to turn to the Windows API in order to implement the feature yourself.

2. Another reason to use the Windows API surfaces when you want to create a component or utility that others can use. If you want to build a component, ActiveX control, or simple utility that will perform a useful function needed by other developers or power users, then you probably will need to turn to the Windows API. Without recourse to the Windows API, such projects are usually not feasible.

3. The final and best reason for learning the Windows API is that it helps you see how you should architect your application. We have many high-level tools these days that let us build projects at a very remote, and powerful, level of abstraction. However, each of these tools is built on top of the Windows API, and it is difficult, if not impossible, to understand how to use them without understanding the architecture on which they are founded. If you understand the Windows API then you know what the operating system can do for you, and how it goes about providing that service. With this knowledge under your belt, you can use high-level tools in an intelligent and thoughtful manner.

I am particularly pleased to see the publication of Wordware's books on the Windows API because they are built around the world's greatest development tool: Delphi. Delphi gives you full access to the entire Windows API. It is a tool designed to let you plumb the depths of the operating system, to best utilize the features that have made Windows the preeminent operating system in the world today.

Armed with these books on the Windows API, and a copy of Delphi, you can build any type of application you desire, and can be sure that it is being constructed in the optimal possible manner. No other compiler can bring you closer to the operating system, nor can any other compiler let you take better advantage of the operating system's features. These books are the Rosetta stone which forms the link between Delphi and the Windows API. Readers will be able to use them to create the most powerful applications supported by the operating system. My hat is off to the authors for providing these books as a service to the programming community.

> Charles Calvert
> former Borland Developer Relations Manager

Acknowledgments

Teamwork. This abstract concept leads one to think of other abstract concepts such as victory, accomplishment, and conquest. Teamwork is the secret ingredient behind innumerable triumphs throughout history, and so it was with this book. Writing this book took many long, hard hours, but this project would not have been completed without the help of so many generous, caring people. In an effort to give credit to those who deserve so much more, I would like to thank the following people, in no particular order, for their contributions to the book:

Marian Broussard, who was the front line proofreader. She ruthlessly pointed out grammar mistakes and spelling errors, and helped correct a lot of inconsistencies in the book. She selflessly volunteered her time to help a new writer accurately and clearly transcribe his thoughts to paper.

Joe Hecht, my mentor and idol. Joe was always eager to answer any questions, looked at code, pointed out mistakes when I was having problems, and pointed me in the right direction when Microsoft's API documentation became a little confusing.

Jim Hill and all the good people down at Wordware Publishing, who took a chance on an eager, enthusiastic, greenhorn writer. He kept me in line and on track, and even took me out for dinner once in a while.

Marci Ayres, who performed a lot of code testing, grayscale image conversion, document formatting, and other support functions.

Lisa Tobin, for performing additional proofreading duties.

Rusty Cornet, for introducing me to this new development environment called Delphi.

Debbie Vilbig and Darla Corley, for giving me the time to learn Delphi and write a call tracking application when I should have been doing real work.

Sarah Miles, for providing me with a short-term loan that allowed me to buy the machine that this book was written on.

Suzy Weaver and Brian Donahoo for trusting a former employee and providing a nice, quiet place to work on the weekends.

Of course, no acknowledgment would be complete without thanking the Delphi development staff at Borland for giving all of us such an awesome development tool.

Introduction

The Windows programming environment. No other operating system in history has caused so much controversy or confusion among the programming industry. Of course, no other operating system in history has made so many millionaires either. Like it or not, Windows is here to stay. It's hard to ignore such a large user base, and there are few job opportunities anymore that do not require the programmer to have knowledge of the Windows environment.

In the beginning, a programmer's only choice of tools for creating Windows applications was C/C++. The age of this language has resulted in a wealth of Windows API documentation, filled with abstract and incomplete information, and examples that are as esoteric and arcane as the C language itself. Then along came Delphi. A new era in Windows programming was born, with the ability to easily create complex and advanced Windows applications with a turnaround time unheard of previously. Although Delphi tries its best to insulate the programmer from the underlying Windows architecture, Delphi programmers have found that some programming obstacles simply cannot be overcome without using low-level Windows API functions. Although there have been a few books that touched on the subject of using Windows API functions in Delphi, none have ever discussed the issue in depth. There are numerous magazine articles that describe very specific subsets of the API, but unless the Delphi programmer had a background in C, and the time to convert a C example into Delphi, there was simply no recourse of action. Thus, this book was born.

This book is a reference manual for using Windows 32-bit API functions in the Delphi environment. As such, it is not a Windows or Delphi programming tutorial, nor is it a collection of Delphi tricks that solve specific problems. To date, this book is the most complete and accurate reference to the Windows API for the Delphi programmer. It is not a complete reference, as the Windows API includes thousands upon thousands of functions that would fill many volumes much larger than the one you are holding. However, this book covers the most common and important cross section of the Windows API. Additionally, every function in this book is available under both Windows 95/98/Me and Windows NT/2000. Most of these functions will also work under Windows NT prior to the new version.

The Chapters

Chapter 1: Delphi and the Windows API

This chapter introduces the reader to *The Tomes of Delphi: Win32 Core API—Windows 2000 Edition*. It covers general Windows programming concerns and techniques, and explains various nuances of programming with the Win32 API in the Delphi environment.

Chapter 2: Window Creation Functions

Creating a window is the most fundamental part of any Windows application. Chapter 2 covers the low-level window creation and class registration functions. Examples include techniques for creating windows and windowed controls using low-level API functions, and how to extend the functionality of existing Delphi windowed controls.

Chapter 3: Message Processing Functions

Windows allows applications to communicate with each other and with the system through the use of messages, and this chapter covers the functions used to manipulate and send them. Examples include interprocess communication using registered, user-defined Windows messages, and how to install Windows hooks.

Chapter 4: Memory Management Functions

Only the most simplistic of programs will not need access to dynamically allocated memory. This chapter covers functions used to allocate and release system and virtual memory. Examples demonstrate heap management routines, virtual memory allocation, and retrieving information about allocated memory blocks.

Chapter 5: Dynamic-Link Library Functions

Dynamic-link libraries are at the core of the Windows operating system architecture, and Windows could not run without them. This chapter covers functions that allow an application to load and import functions from a DLL. Examples include explicitly loading a DLL and importing its functions at run time, and providing a user-defined DLL entry point.

Chapter 6: Process and Thread Functions

Multitasking environments allow an application to spawn other applications, or even another thread of execution within itself. This chapter covers the functions used to create and manage threads and processes. Examples include creating and destroying a thread, launching an external process, creating a mutex, and using thread events.

Chapter 7: Timer Functions

Setting up a timer to repeatedly call a function is the only solution for some programming issues. This chapter covers essential functions used to create a low-level Windows timer. Examples include utilizing the high-resolution timer to measure code performance.

Chapter 8: Error Functions

Error management is always an issue with any programming project. This chapter covers functions used in debugging and error management. Examples include displaying system-defined error strings, and user-defined error values.

Chapter 9: Graphical Device Interface Functions

The basic Graphical Device Interface functions are integral to any graphics programming in Windows. This chapter covers functions used to manipulate and create device contexts. Examples include creating various types of device contexts, retrieving device capabilities, and changing the display mode.

Chapter 10: Painting and Drawing Functions

Basic graphical output starts with drawing lines, circles, squares, and other geometrical primitives. This chapter covers functions for all types of geometrical drawing and painting. Examples include drawing lines and shapes, creating brushes and pens, and a quick and dirty bitmap fade technique.

Chapter 11: Region and Path Functions

Region and path functions are almost ignored by most graphical programming references, yet these functions allow the developer to perform some amazing special effects. This chapter covers the functions used to create and manipulate regions and paths. Examples include clipping graphical output to a region or path, and using paths to produce special text effects.

Chapter 12: Bitmap and Metafile Functions

Bitmaps and metafiles are the two graphics formats that are natively supported by Windows. The bitmap functions are essential to almost any graphics programming in Windows, and this chapter covers the functions used to create and manipulate bitmap and metafile graphics. Examples include creating device-dependent and device-independent bitmaps, creating metafiles, and parsing metafile records.

Chapter 13: Text Output Functions

Outputting text to the screen is the most commonly performed graphical operation in almost any Windows application. No program can get by very well without displaying some kind of text, and this chapter covers the functions used to manipulate fonts and display text on the screen. Examples include enumerating fonts, retrieving font information, font embedding, and various methods of text output.

Conventions

Certain writing conventions have been used throughout this book to convey specific meanings. All example code throughout each chapter appears in a monotyped font, such as the following:

```
function HelloThere(Info: string): Integer;
begin
  ShowMessage(Info);
end;
```

In order to be consistent with other works on Delphi programming, the example code follows the Borland coding conventions, which include using mixed case for variable names and identifiers, lowercase for reserved words, and nested code indented two spaces per level. Any constants used in the code will appear in all capitals, such as TRUE and FALSE. Also, notice that the name of the unit that contains an individual function is located on the same line as the function name. This unit must be included in the Uses clause of any unit in which this function is used. However, most of the functions covered in this series are located in the Windows.pas file, which is automatically added to the Uses clause by Delphi. In addition, when the text refers to a window, as in a visual object on the screen, the word "window" will begin with a lowercase letter. When the text refers to Windows, as in the operating system, the word "Windows" will be capitalized.

Function Descriptions

The Windows API function descriptions have been laid out in a format that provides an increasing amount of detail to the reader. This should allow the reader to quickly glance at a function description for a simple reminder of required parameters, or to read further for a detailed explanation of the function, an example of its use, and any acceptable constant values used in a parameter.

Each function description includes the exact syntax found in the Delphi source code, a description of what the function does, a detailed list and description of the function's parameters, the value returned from the function, a list of related functions, and an example of its use. Any defined constants used in a function parameter are found in tables that follow the example, so that the descriptive text of the function is not broken by a distraction, and all of the constants are available in one place for easy perusal. Some tables may be repeated under various functions that use the same parameters. This was done to eliminate the need to flip back and forth between several pages while perusing the function descriptions. An asterisk (*) indicates the function is covered in *The Tomes of Delphi: Win32 Shell API—Windows 2000 Edition*.

Sample Programs

Although every book reaches a point where the authors are frantically hacking away at the text trying to meet deadlines, I did not want the example code to suffer due to time restraints. Unlike some other books, I wanted to make sure that the example code worked in every case. Therefore, I have taken every effort to ensure that the source code on the CD works as expected and that the code found in the book is the exact code found on the CD. This should guarantee that code entered straight from the text will work as described. However, most of the code examples rely on buttons, edit boxes, or other components residing on the form, which may not be apparent from the code listing. When in doubt, always look at the source code included on the CD. Also, bear in mind that some examples may only work under certain conditions; for example, many of the examples demonstrating graphical API calls will only work correctly under a 256-color video mode.

Who This Book is For

Due to the nature of reference manuals, and the lack of any involved explanations into general Windows or Delphi programming, this book is intended for use by experienced Delphi programmers with a working knowledge of Windows programming. This is not to say that intermediate or even beginning Delphi programmers will not benefit from this book; in fact, there are quite a few example programs included that solve a number of everyday programming conundrums. The heavily documented examples should provide enough explanation for even the most neophyte Delphi programmer to gain some understanding of the API function being demonstrated. As a reference manual, the book is not intended to be read sequentially from cover to cover. However, the chapters have been laid out in a logical order of progression, starting with the most fundamental Windows API functions and working towards the more specialized functions.

If you are looking for an introduction to Delphi programming, or a step-by-step Windows programming tutorial, there are plenty of other fine books out there to get you started. However, if you've got a nasty problem whose only hope of salvation is using the Windows API, if you want to extend the functionality of Delphi components and objects, or you want a down-and-dirty, no-holds-barred collection of Delphi Win32 API programming examples, then this book is for you. You will not find a more complete and accurate guide to the Win32 API for the Delphi programmer.

Chapter 1

Delphi and the Windows API

When Delphi was introduced, it brought a new era to Windows programming. Never before had it been so easy to create robust, full-featured applications for the Windows environment with such short development times. Now in its sixth incarnation, Delphi has been the development tool for innumerable shareware and freeware applications, internal business and proprietary system applications, several well-known commercial applications, even a commercial game or two. Delphi's power and ease of use make it a wonderful choice for a development platform that can stand up to C++ and Visual Basic in almost every situation.

One of Delphi's strengths is the Visual Component Library, Borland's object model. This object model has allowed the Delphi development team to encapsulate the vast majority of Windows programming tedium into easy-to-use components. Earlier Windows programming languages required the developer to write large amounts of code just to squeeze a minimal amount of functionality out of Windows. The mere act of creating a window and accepting menu selections could take pages of code to create. Delphi's excellent encapsulation of this dreary requirement of Windows programming has turned what once was a chore into a fun, exciting experience.

Windows Data Types

Windows API functions use a number of data types that may be unfamiliar to the casual Delphi programmer. These data types are all taken from the original C header files that define the Windows API function syntax. For the most part, these new data types are simply Pascal data types that have been renamed to make them similar to the original data types used in legacy Windows programming languages. This was done so that experienced Windows programmers would understand the parameter types and function return values, and the function prototypes would match the syntax shown in existing Windows API documentation to avoid confusion. The following table outlines the most common Windows data types and their correlating Object Pascal data type.

Table 1-1: Windows data types

Windows Data Type	Object Pascal Data Type	Description
LPSTR	PAnsiChar	String pointer
LPCSTR	PAnsiChar	String pointer

Windows Data Type	Object Pascal Data Type	Description
DWORD	LongWord	Whole number
BOOL	LongBool	Boolean value
PBOOL	^BOOL	Pointer to a Boolean value
PByte	^Byte	Pointer to a byte value
PINT	^Integer	Pointer to an integer value
PSingle	^Single	Pointer to a single (floating-point) value
PWORD	^Word	Pointer to a 16-bit value
PDWORD	^DWORD	Pointer to a 32-bit value
LPDWORD	PDWORD	Pointer to a 32-bit value
UCHAR	Byte	8-bit value (can represent characters)
PUCHAR	^Byte	Pointer to an 8-bit value
SHORT	Smallint	Signed 16-bit whole number
UINT	LongWord	Unsigned 32-bit whole number
PUINT	^UINT	Pointer to an unsigned 32-bit whole number
ULONG	Cardinal	Unsigned a 32-bit whole number
PULONG	^ULONG	Pointer to an unsigned 32-bit whole number
PLongint	^Longint	Pointer to a 32-bit value
PInteger	^Integer	Pointer to a 32-bit value
PSmallInt	^Smallint	Pointer to a 16-bit value
PDouble	^Double	Pointer to double (floating-point) value
LCID	DWORD	A local identifier
LANGID	Word	A language identifier
THandle	LongWord	An object handle. Many Windows API functions return a value of type THandle, which identifies that object within Window's internal object tracking tables.
PHandle	^THandle	A pointer to a handle
WPARAM	Longint	A 32-bit message parameter. Under earlier versions of Windows, this was a 16-bit data type.
LPARAM	Longint	A 32-bit message parameter
LRESULT	Longint	A 32-bit function return value
HWND	LongWord	A handle to a window. All windowed controls, child windows, main windows, etc., have a corresponding window handle that identifies them within Window's internal tracking tables.
HHOOK	LongWord	A handle to an installed Windows system hook
ATOM	Word	An index into the local or global atom table for a string
HGLOBAL	THandle	A handle identifying a globally allocated dynamic memory object. Under 32-bit Windows, there is no distinction between globally and locally allocated memory.

Windows Data Type	Object Pascal Data Type	Description
HLOCAL	THandle	A handle identifying a locally allocated dynamic memory object. Under 32-bit Windows, there is no distinction between globally and locally allocated memory.
FARPROC	Pointer	A pointer to a procedure, usually used as a parameter type in functions that require a callback function.
HGDIOBJ	LongWord	A handle to a GDI object. Pens, device contexts, brushes, etc., all have a handle of this type that identifies them within Window's internal tracking tables.
HBITMAP	LongWord	A handle to a Windows bitmap object
HBRUSH	LongWord	A handle to a Windows brush object
HDC	LongWord	A handle to a device context
HENHMETAFILE	LongWord	A handle to a Windows enhanced metafile object
HFONT	LongWord	A handle to a Windows logical font object
HICON	LongWord	A handle to a Windows icon object
HMENU	LongWord	A handle to a Windows menu object
HMETAFILE	LongWord	A handle to a Windows metafile object
HINST	THandle	A handle to an instance object
HMODULE	HINST	A handle to a module
HPALETTE	LongWord	A handle to a Windows color palette
HPEN	LongWord	A handle to a Windows pen object
HRGN	LongWord	A handle to a Windows region object
HRSRC	THandle	A handle to a Windows resource object
HKL	LongWord	A handle to a keyboard layout
HFILE	LongWord	A handle to an open file
HCURSOR	HICON	A handle to a Windows mouse cursor object
COLORREF	DWORD	A Windows color reference value, containing values for the red, green, and blue components of a color

Handles

An important concept in Windows programming is the concept of an object handle. Many functions return a handle to an object that the function created or loaded from a resource. Functions like CreateWindowEx return a window handle. Other functions, like CreateFile, return a handle to an open file, or, like HeapCreate, return a handle to a newly allocated heap. Internally, Windows keeps track of all of these handles, and the handle serves as the link through the operating system between the object and the application. Using these handles, an application can easily refer to any of these objects, and the operating system instantly knows which object a piece of code wants to manipulate.

Constants

The Windows API functions declare literally thousands upon thousands of different constants to be used as parameter values. Constants for everything from color values to return values have been defined in the Windows.pas, Types.pas, and System.pas files. The constants that are defined for each API function are listed with that function within the text. However, the Windows.pas file may yield more information concerning the constants for any particular function, and it is a good rule of thumb to check this Delphi source code file when using complicated functions.

Strings

All Windows API functions that use strings require a pointer to a null-terminated string type. Windows is written in C, which does not have the Pascal string type. Earlier versions of Delphi required the application to allocate a string buffer and convert the String type to a PChar. However, Delphi 3 introduced a string conversion mechanism that allows a string to be used as a PChar by simply typecasting it (i.e., PChar(MyString), where MyString is declared as MyString: string). For the most part, this conversion will work with almost all Windows API functions that require a string parameter.

Importing Windows Functions

The Windows API is huge. It defines functions for almost every kind of utility or comparison or action that a programmer could think of. Due to the sheer volume of Windows API functions, some functions simply fell through the cracks and were not imported by the Delphi source code. Since all Windows API functions are simply functions exported from a DLL, importing a new Windows API function is a relatively simple process if the function parameters are known.

Importing a new Windows API function is exactly like importing any other function from a DLL. For example, in earlier versions of Delphi, the BroadcastSystemMessage function described in Chapter 3 was not imported by the Delphi source code (it is now imported and available for use, but we'll use this function as an example). In order to import this function for use within an application, it is simply declared as a function from within a DLL as:

```
function BroadcastSystemMessage(Flags: DWORD; Recipients: PDWORD;
    uiMessage: UINT; wParam: WPARAM; lParam: LPARAM): Longint; stdcall;

implementation

function BroadcastSystemMessage; external user32 name 'BroadcastSystemMessage';
```

As long as the parameters required by the function and the DLL containing the function are known, any Windows API function can be imported and used by a Delphi application. It is important to note that the stdcall directive must be appended to the prototype for the function, as this defines the standard mechanism by which Windows passes parameters to a function on the stack.

> **Note:** Use the stdcall directive, appended to the end of the function prototype, when importing Windows API functions.

Incorrectly Imported Functions

Some functions have been incorrectly imported by the Delphi source code. These exceptions are noted in the individual function descriptions. For the most part, the functions that have been imported incorrectly deal with the ability to pass NIL as a value to a pointer parameter, usually to retrieve the required size of a buffer so the buffer can be dynamically allocated to the exact length before calling the function to retrieve the real data. In Delphi, some of these functions have been imported with parameters defined as VAR or CONST. These types of parameters can accept a pointer to a buffer, but can never be set to NIL, thus limiting the use of the function within the Delphi environment. As is the case with almost anything in Delphi, it is a simple matter to fix. Simply reimport the function as if it did not exist, as outlined in the previous section. Functions that have been imported incorrectly are identified in their individual function descriptions throughout the book.

Callback Functions

Another very important concept in Windows programming is that of a callback function. A callback function is a function within the developer's application that is never called directly by any other function or procedure within that application, but is instead called by the Windows operating system. This allows Windows to communicate directly with the application, passing it various parameters as defined by the individual callback function. Most of the enumeration functions require some form of application-defined callback function that receives the enumerated information.

Individual callback functions have specific parameters that must be declared exactly by the application. This is required so that Windows passes the correct information to the application in the correct order. A good example of a function that uses a callback function is EnumWindows. The EnumWindows function parses through all top-level windows on the screen, passing the handle of each window to an application-defined callback function. This continues until all top-level windows have been enumerated or the callback function returns FALSE. The callback function used by EnumWindows is defined as:

```
EnumWindowsProc(
hWnd: HWND;             {a handle to a top-level window}
lParam: LPARAM;         {the application-defined data}
): BOOL;                {returns TRUE or FALSE}
```

A function matching this function prototype is created within the application, and a pointer to the function is passed as one of the parameters to the EnumWindows function. The Windows operating system calls this callback function for each top-level window, passing the window's handle in one of the callback function's parameters. It is important to note that the stdcall directive must be appended to the prototype for the callback function, as this defines the standard mechanism by which Windows passes parameters to a function on the stack. For example, the EnumWindows callback function would be prototyped as:

```
EnumWindowsProc(hWnd: HWND; lParam: LPARAM); stdcall;
```

Without the stdcall directive, Windows will not be able to access the callback function. This powerful software mechanism, in many cases, allows an application to retrieve information about the system that is only stored internally by Windows and would otherwise be unreachable. For a complete example of callback function usage, see the EnumWindows function, and many other functions throughout the book.

Function Parameters

The vast majority of Windows API functions simply take the static parameters handed to them and perform some function based on the value of the parameters. However, certain functions return values that must be stored in a buffer, and that buffer is passed to the function in the form of a pointer. In most cases, when the function description specifies that it returns some value in a buffer, null-terminated string buffer, or a pointer to a data structure, these buffers and data structures must be allocated by the application before the function is called.

In many cases, a parameter may state that it can contain one or more values from some table. These values are defined as constants, and they are combined using the Boolean OR operator. The actual value passed to the function usually identifies a bitmask, where the state of each bit has some significance to the function. This is why the constants can be combined using Boolean operations. For example, the CreateWindowEx function has a parameter called dwStyle, which can accept a number of constants combined with the Boolean OR operator. To pass more than one constant to the function, the parameter would be set to something like "WS_CAPTION or WS_CHILD or WS_CLIPCHILDREN." This would create a child window that includes a caption bar and would clip around its child windows during painting.

Conversely, when a function states that it returns one or more values that are defined as specific constants, the return value can be combined with one of the constants using the Boolean AND operator to determine if that constant is contained within the return value. If the result of the combination equals the value of the constant, then that constant is included in the return value.

Unicode

Originally, software only needed a single byte to define a character within a character set. This allowed for up to 256 characters, which was more than plenty for the entire alphabet, numbers, punctuation symbols, and common mathematical symbols. However, due to the shrinking of the global community and the subsequent internationalization of Windows and Windows software, a new method of identifying characters was needed. Many languages have well over 256 characters used for writing, much more than a single byte can describe. Therefore, Unicode was invented. A Unicode character is 16 bits long, and can therefore identify 65,535 characters within a language's alphabet. To accommodate the new character set type, many Windows API functions come in two flavors: ANSI and Unicode. When browsing the Windows.pas source code, many functions are defined with an A or W appended to the end of the function name, identifying them as an ANSI function or Wide character (Unicode) function. The functions within this book cover only the ANSI functions. However, the Unicode functions usually differ only in the type of string information passed to a function, and the text within this book should adequately describe the Unicode function's behavior.

Delphi vs. the Windows API

The Delphi development team did a world-class job of encapsulating the majority of important Windows API functionality into the VCL. However, due to the vastness of the Windows API, it would be impossible and impractical to wrap every API function in an Object Pascal object. To achieve certain goals or solve specific problems, a developer may be forced to use lower level Windows API functions that are simply not encapsulated by a Delphi object. It may also be necessary to extend the functionality of a Delphi object, and if this object encapsulates some part of the Windows API, it will be the API that the developer will likely have to use to extend the functionality by any great amount.

Indeed, there are literally hundreds of APIs out there that dramatically extend Windows' functionality, and due to the sheer numbers of API functions and the ever-changing, ever-expanding functionality being introduced by Microsoft, it would be near impossible to actively import every last function from every available API. Therefore, it is important that the well-prepared and capable Delphi programmer is familiar with hardcore Windows programming, as it is highly likely that you'll be called upon sometime in your Delphi career to make use of some Windows API functionality that is not encapsulated by the VCL.

There may even be situations where it is impractical to use the Delphi components that encapsulate Windows functionality. The VCL makes Windows programming easy, but by their very nature, Delphi applications tend to be 350KB in size at a minimum. Bypassing the VCL and using direct Windows API calls, on the other hand, can yield a Delphi application as small as 10KB. Every situation is different, and fortunately, as Delphi programmers, we have a lot of flexibility in this area. Using direct Windows API calls may not always be necessary, but when it is, it's good to know that we have that option available to us.

Chapter 2

Window Creation Functions

Window creation is a fundamental part of any Windows program. Almost every user interface element is a window, such as the application window itself and controls that accept input from the mouse and keyboard. Even the desktop is a window. The window creation functions are some of the most complex and error-prone functions in the entire Windows API. Fortunately, Delphi does a very good job of hiding the details of creating a window. However, knowing the steps required to create a window the hard way can give the developer the knowledge needed to extend Delphi's basic functionality and accomplish things that are not encapsulated by the VCL.

Creating a window requires the developer to follow a complex and detailed sequence of steps. In general, creating a window involves registering a class with the operating system, followed by a complex function call to actually create the window based on this class. A window class is a set of attributes that define the basic look and behavior for a window. These attributes are used as a template from which any number of windows can be created. There are predefined classes for every common Windows user interface control, such as edit boxes, buttons, etc. However, to create a new type of window, such as the main window for an application, the developer must register a window class. Delphi's encapsulation of the Windows API makes all of this transparent to the developer. However, there may be certain instances when the developer needs to create a window the old-fashioned way.

Creating Windows: The Basic Steps

Creating a window using low-level Windows API functions is a detailed but straightforward task. There are three steps the developer generally must follow when creating a window:

1. A new window class must be registered. If the developer is creating a window based on one of the predefined Windows classes, this step is omitted.
2. The window is then created using one of the window creation functions.
3. Finally, this window is displayed on the screen. This step is omitted if the WS_VISIBLE style flag is used in the dwStyle parameter.

Window Attributes

An application must provide several attributes to the Windows API functions that describe the desired window in both appearance and behavior. These attributes include the window class, window name, styles, parent or owner window, size, position, z-order, child window identifier or menu handle, instance handle, and creation data.

Window Class Every window belongs to a window class. A window class must be registered with the system before any windows of that class can be created. The window class describes most aspects of a window's appearance and behavior. Indeed, many of the attributes listed here are described in the window class. Of particular interest is the window procedure, a callback function that is responsible for the actual behavior of the window (more on this a bit later).

Window Name Also known as the window text, the window name identifies the window to the user. The display of the window name attribute depends on the class of window. Windows with title bars, such as the main window and dialog boxes, will display the window name in the title bar itself (if present). Other windows, such as edit boxes and buttons, display the window name within the area occupied by the window. Some windows, such as list boxes and combo boxes, do not display the window name.

Window Style Every window has one or more styles. The window style defines certain aspects of a window's behavior and appearance that are not specified in the window class. Window styles are specified by combining constants that identify the desired behavior or appearance with the Boolean OR operator. Some window styles apply to all windows, while others are used only with specific window classes.

Parent/Owner Window If a window has a parent, it is known as a child window, and its position and display are somewhat dependent on its parent window. An owned window, by contrast, always appears in front of its owning window, and disappears when its owner is minimized. This is discussed in more detail below.

Window Size Every window has dimensions (unless it is a hidden window). The window's size is specified in pixels, and merely determines how much space the window takes up either on the screen or within its parent window.

Window Position The window location is also specified in pixels. A window's location is interpreted as the horizontal and vertical position of its upper-left corner in relation to either the screen or its parent window.

Window Z-Order A window's z-order determines its vertical position in the stack of overlapping windows on either the desktop or its parent window. By changing a window's z-order, a window can be moved on top of or behind other windows.

Child Window Identifier/Menu Handle Each child window can have a unique, application-defined identifier with which it is associated. Conversely, every window except child windows can have a menu. The CreateWindowEx function (used to create a window) interprets a specific parameter as either a child window identifier or a menu handle based on the window style.

Instance Handle Every Windows application has an instance handle, which is provided to the application by the operating system when the application starts. The instance handle is a unique identifier that is used internally to distinguish between all of the running applications. The applications of such a unique identifier become especially apparent when one realizes that more than one copy of the same application can be running simultaneously. The instance handle is used in many of the window manipulation functions, especially the window creation functions.

Creation Data Every window can have application-defined creation data associated with it. This data is in the form of a pointer, and can be used to define a single value or point to a complex collection of data. When the window is first created, a message is sent to its window procedure (described in the next section), which contains a pointer to this creation data. This is an application-defined value, and is not required to make the window creation functions behave properly.

If a window is successfully created, it returns a handle that uniquely identifies the window. This window handle is used in a variety of API functions to perform tasks on the window associated with that handle. Any control that descends from TWinControl is a window created with one of the window creation functions and therefore has a window handle, accessible as the Handle property of that particular control. This handle can be used in any Windows API function that requires a window handle as a parameter.

The following example demonstrates how to create a window using the basic steps.

Listing 2-1: Creating a window

```
{Register the Window Class}
function RegisterClass: Boolean;
var
  WindowClass: TWndClass;
begin
  {setup our new window class}
  WindowClass.Style := CS_HREDRAW or CS_VREDRAW;    {set the class styles}
  WindowClass.lpfnWndProc := @DefWindowProc;        {point to the default
                                                     window procedure}
  WindowClass.cbClsExtra := 0;                      {no extra class memory}
  WindowClass.cbWndExtra := 0;                      {no extra window memory}
  WindowClass.hInstance := hInstance;               {the application instance}
  WindowClass.hIcon := 0;                           {no icon specified}
  WindowClass.hCursor := 0;                         {no cursor specified}
  WindowClass.hbrBackground := COLOR_WINDOW;        {use a predefined color}
  WindowClass.lpszMenuName := nil;                  {no menu}
  WindowClass.lpszClassName := 'TestClass';         {the registered class name}

  {now that we have our class set up, register it with the system}
  Result := Windows.RegisterClass(WindowClass) <> 0;
end;

procedure TForm1.Button1Click(Sender: TObject);
var
  hWindow: HWND;
begin
```

```
    {Step 1: Register our new window class}
    if not RegisterClass then
    begin
      ShowMessage('RegisterClass failed');
      Exit;
    end;

    {Step 2: Create a window based on our new class}
    hWindow := CreateWindowEx(0,                    {no extended styles}
                              'TestClass',          {the registered class name}
                              'New Window',         {the title bar text}
                              WS_OVERLAPPEDWINDOW,  {a normal window style}
                              CW_USEDEFAULT,        {default horizontal position}
                              CW_USEDEFAULT,        {default vertical position}
                              CW_USEDEFAULT,        {default width}
                              CW_USEDEFAULT,        {default height}
                              0,                    {no owner window}
                              0,                    {no menu}
                              hInstance,            {the application instance}
                              nil                   {no additional information}
                              );

    {Step 3: If our window was created successfully, display it}
    if hWindow <> 0 then
    begin
      ShowWindow(hWindow, SW_SHOWNORMAL);
      UpdateWindow(hWindow);
    end
    else
    begin
      ShowMessage('CreateWindow failed');
      Exit;
    end;

end;
```

Figure 2-1:
The new
window

The Window Procedure

Each window class has a function associated with it known as the window procedure. It is a callback function that Windows uses to communicate with the application. This function determines how the window interacts with the user, and what is displayed in its client area. Windows created from a particular class will use the window procedure assigned to that class. See Listing 2-2 for an example of using a window procedure.

Delphi automatically creates window procedures that provide the appropriate functionality based on the window type. However, a developer may want to modify or extend this behavior. Subclassing the window procedure and providing a new one can alter a window's functionality.

The window procedure is little more than a large Case statement, checking for specific messages that the developer wants to provide functionality for. Each message that will have an action associated with it has a line in the Case statement. In Delphi, this manifests itself as the events for any particular control, such as OnKeyPress or OnResize. Any messages that are not specifically handled must be passed to the DefWindowProc procedure. MDI child windows use the DefMDIChildProc procedure, and MDI frame windows use the DefFrameProc procedure. These procedures provide the basic behavior for any window, such as resizing, moving, etc.

Hardcore Windows Programming

Delphi is fully capable of bypassing the functionality provided by the VCL, allowing a developer to write an entire Windows program in nothing but Object Pascal. The following example demonstrates how such a program is written. Note that the main unit must be removed from the project, and the following code is typed directly into the project source file.

Listing 2-2: A Windows application written entirely in Object Pascal

```
program HardCore;

uses
    Windows, Messages;

{$R *.RES}

{The window procedure for our hardcore API window}
function WindowProc(TheWindow: HWnd; TheMessage, WParam,
                    LParam: Longint): Longint; stdcall;
begin
  case TheMessage of
    {upon getting the WM_DESTROY message, we exit the application}
    WM_DESTROY: begin
                  PostQuitMessage(0);
                  Exit;
                end;
  end;
```

```
    {call the default window procedure for all unhandled messages}
    Result := DefWindowProc(TheWindow, TheMessage, WParam, LParam);
end;

{ Register the Window Class }
function RegisterClass: Boolean;
var
  WindowClass: TWndClass;
begin
  {setup our new window class}
  WindowClass.Style := CS_HREDRAW or CS_VREDRAW;      {set the class styles}
  WindowClass.lpfnWndProc := @WindowProc;             {our window procedure}
  WindowClass.cbClsExtra := 0;                        {no extra class memory}
  WindowClass.cbWndExtra := 0;                        {no extra window memory}
  WindowClass.hInstance := hInstance;                 {the application instance}
  WindowClass.hIcon := LoadIcon(0, IDI_APPLICATION);  {load a predefined logo}
  WindowClass.hCursor := LoadCursor(0, IDC_UPARROW);  {load a predefined cursor}
  WindowClass.hbrBackground := COLOR_WINDOW;          {use a predefined color}
  WindowClass.lpszMenuName := nil;                    {no menu}
  WindowClass.lpszClassName := 'TestClass';           {the registered class name}

  {now that we have our class set up, register it with the system}
  Result := Windows.RegisterClass(WindowClass) <> 0;
end;


var
  TheMessage: TMsg;
  OurWindow: HWND;
begin
  {register our new class first}
  if not RegisterClass then
  begin
    MessageBox(0,'RegisterClass failed',nil,MB_OK);
    Exit;
  end;

  {now, create a window based on our new class}
  OurWindow := CreateWindowEx(0,                      {no extended styles}
                       'TestClass',                   {the registered class name}
                       'HardCore Window',             {the title bar text}
                       WS_OVERLAPPEDWINDOW or         {a normal window style}
                       WS_VISIBLE,                    {initially visible}
                       CW_USEDEFAULT,                 {horizontal position}
                       CW_USEDEFAULT,                 {vertical position}
                       CW_USEDEFAULT,                 {default width}
                       CW_USEDEFAULT,                 {default height}
                       0,                             {no parent window}
                       0,                             {no menu}
                       hInstance,                     {the application instance}
                       nil                            {no additional information}
                       );

  {if our window was not created successfully, exit the program}
  if OurWindow=0 then
  begin
    MessageBox(0,'CreateWindow failed',nil,MB_OK);
```

```
    Exit;
end;

{the standard message loop}
while GetMessage(TheMessage,0,0,0) do
begin
  TranslateMessage(TheMessage);
  DispatchMessage(TheMessage);
end;

end.
```

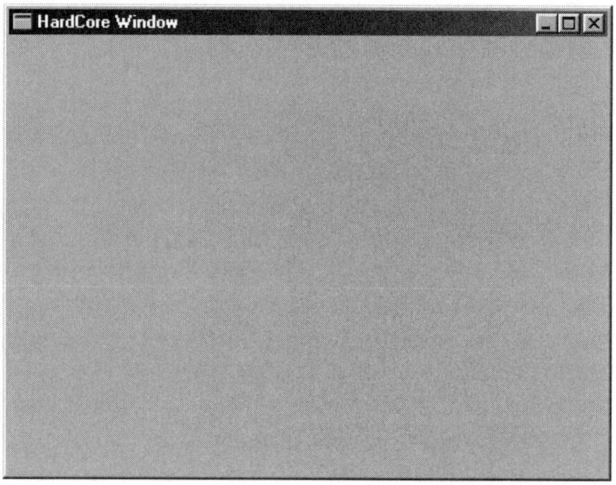

Figure 2-2:
The hardcore
window

Window Types

The style flags available for the dwStyle and dwExStyle parameters of the CreateWindow-Ex function provide an almost infinite variety of window types. In general, all windows can be classified under three categories:

- Overlapped: This is the most common type of window, and is generally the style used by the main window of the application. This type of window includes the WS_OVERLAPPED style flag in the dwStyle parameter, can be resized by the user at run time, and includes a caption bar, system menu, and minimize and maximize buttons. This type of window will appear on the taskbar.
- Pop-up: Common dialog boxes and property sheets fall into this category. Pop-up windows are considered a special type of overlapped window that appears outside of an application's main window; they are basically a standard window of the WS_OVERLAPPED style, except that title bars are completely optional. This type of window includes the WS_POPUP style flag in the dwStyle parameter. The parent window of a pop-up window is always the desktop window. The hWndParent parameter is used to specify an owner for pop-up windows. An unowned pop-up window will remain visible even when the main window of an application is minimized, and will appear on the taskbar. If a window handle is provided in the hWndParent parameter, the window associated with that handle becomes the

owner of the pop-up window. The owned pop-up window will hide when the owner is minimized, reappear when the owner is restored, stay on top of the owner window even when the owner window is maximized or has focus, and does not appear on the taskbar. This type of window is perfect for toolbar or palette windows.

- Child: This is the second most common style. All windowed controls and MDI child windows fit into this category. This window type includes the WS_CHILD style flag in the dwStyle parameter. MDI child windows will include the WS_EX_MDICHILD style flag in the dwExStyle parameter. The window whose handle is provided in the hWndParent parameter of the window creation function becomes the parent window to this child window. The parent window provides the surface upon which the child window displays itself. Conversely, a child window is completely contained within the parent. Child windows are not always clipped to the edges of the parent window; if a child window is not clipped (i.e., the parent window does not contain the WS_CLIPCHILDREN style), drawing will take place in the same position as the child window. However, if the WS_CLIPCHILDREN style is included in the parent window, the parent window will not be able to draw over it, and the child window is always shown on top of the parent window's client area. Child windows do not appear on the taskbar. When the parent window of a child window is destroyed, the child windows are also destroyed.

Note: A parent window can have multiple child windows, but a child window can only have one parent window.

Any window can have the WS_OVERLAPPED style flag, but the WS_CHILD and WS_POPUP flags are mutually exclusive. If the hWndParent parameter of an overlapped window contains the handle to another window, this window acts as the owner for the overlapped window, which takes on the characteristics of an owned pop-up. Since the parent window is responsible for providing a display area for its child windows, whenever the parent window of any window is destroyed, all related windows belonging to that parent are also destroyed. Figure 2-3 illustrates the various types of windows.

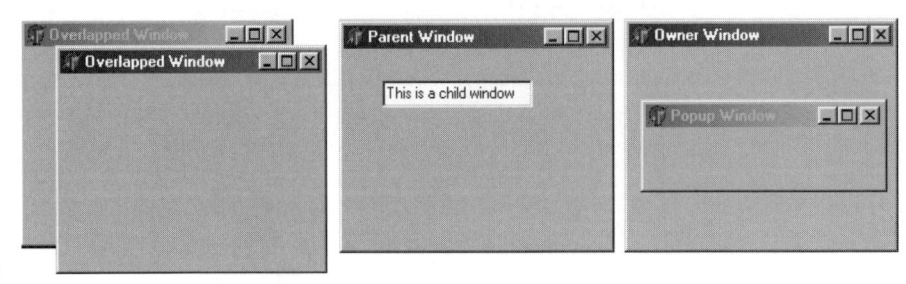

Figure 2-3: Window types

Multiple Document Interface

Multiple document interface applications consist of a frame window, which acts as the main application window, a client window, the workspace where all of the child document windows are displayed, and one or more MDI child windows. The MDI child windows are where users perform their work. Delphi encapsulates most of this functionality through the FormStyle property of a form. Simply setting this property to fsMDIForm can create an MDI frame and client window; setting the property to fsMDIChild creates MDI child windows. However, there may be certain times when a developer needs to create an MDI application using conventional Windows API functions. Developers should follow these steps when creating an MDI application using the Windows API:

1. A new window class must be registered. This class is used to create the frame window, and cannot be one of the predefined Windows classes.
2. The frame window is then created using one of the window creation functions.
3. Display the frame window on the screen. This step is omitted if the WS_VISIBLE style flag is used in the dwStyle parameter.
4. Create a variable of type TClientCreateStruct, and fill in the members of the structure with the appropriate information.
5. The client window is created using one of the window creation functions. Use the predefined Window class name MDICLIENT, and pass the handle to the frame window in the hWndParent parameter. Use the WS_CLIPCHILDREN and WS_CHILD style flags in the dwStyle parameter, and pass a pointer to the TClientCreateStruct variable in the lpParam parameter.
6. Display the client window on the screen. This step is omitted if the WS_VISIBLE style flag is used in the dwStyle parameter.
7. Register the classes that will be used for the MDI child windows.
8. Create the MDI child window. This is done by creating a variable of type TMDICreateStruct, filling out the members of the structure, and sending a WM_MDICREATE message to the MDICLIENT window, passing a pointer to the TMDICreateStruct variable in the lParam member of the message or by using the CreateMDIWindow API function.
9. Display the new MDI child window on the screen. This step is omitted if the WS_VISIBLE style flag is used in the dwStyle parameter.

Note: Microsoft is now discouraging the use of MDI, although it will continue to be supported in the near future for backward compatibility.

The following example shows how to create an MDI application using hardcore Windows programming techniques. It must be created in the same fashion as the example in the earlier section titled "Hardcore Windows Programming."

Listing 2-3: Creating an MDI application in Object Pascal

```pascal
program MDIApp;

uses
    Windows, Messages;

var
  TheMessage: TMsg;
  FrameWindow, ClientWindow, ChildWindow: HWND;

const
  {the ID for the first MDI child window}
  IDCHILDWND = 100;

{$R *.RES}

{this defines the window procedure for our frame window}
function FrameWindowProc(TheFrameWindow: HWnd; TheMessage, WParam,
                         LParam: Longint): Longint; stdcall;
var
  {this is used when creating an MDI client window}
  ClientStruct: TClientCreateStruct;
begin
  case TheMessage of
    {The frame window will be created first. Once it is created, the
     WM_CREATE message is sent to this function, where we create the
     MDI client window}
    WM_CREATE: begin
        {Step 4: Fill in the appropriate information about the client window}
        ClientStruct.hWindowMenu:=0;
        ClientStruct.idFirstChild:= IDCHILDWND;

        {Step 5: Create the MDI client window}
        ClientWindow := CreateWindowEx(0,              {no extended styles}
                            'MDICLIENT',               {registered class name}
                            NIL,                       {no window text}
                            WS_CHILD or                {a child window}
                            WS_CLIPCHILDREN or         {clip its child
                                                        windows}
                            WS_VISIBLE,                {initially visible}
                            0,                         {horizontal position}
                            0,                         {vertical position}
                            0,                         {width}
                            0,                         {height}
                            TheFrameWindow,            {handle of the parent
                                                        window}
                            0,                         {no menu}
                            hInstance,                 {application instance}
                            @ClientStruct              {additional creation
                                                        information}
                            );

        {Step 6 was taken care of by including the WS_VISIBLE flag in the
         dwStyle parameter. Now we check to see if it was created}
```

```pascal
            if ClientWindow=0 then
                begin
                     MessageBox(0,'CreateClientWindow failed',nil,MB_OK);
                     Exit;
                end;
      end;
      {upon getting the WM_DESTROY message, we exit the application}
      WM_DESTROY: begin
                     PostQuitMessage(0);
                     Exit;
                  end;
   end;

   {call the default frame window procedure for all unhandled messages}
   Result := DefFrameProc(TheFrameWindow, ClientWindow, TheMessage, WParam,
                         LParam);
end;

{ Register the frame window Class }
function RegisterFrameClass: Boolean;
var
   WindowClass: TWndClass;
begin
   {setup our frame window class}
   WindowClass.Style := CS_HREDRAW or CS_VREDRAW;     {set the class styles}
   WindowClass.lpfnWndProc := @FrameWindowProc;       {point to our frame window
                                                       procedure}
   WindowClass.cbClsExtra := 0;                       {no extra class memory}
   WindowClass.cbWndExtra := 0;                       {no extra window memory}
   WindowClass.hInstance := hInstance;                {the application instance}
   WindowClass.hIcon := LoadIcon(0, IDI_WINLOGO);     {load a predefined logo}
   WindowClass.hCursor := LoadCursor(0, IDC_ARROW);   {load a predefined cursor}
   WindowClass.hbrBackground := COLOR_WINDOW;         {use a predefined color}
   WindowClass.lpszMenuName := nil;                   {no menu}
   WindowClass.lpszClassName := 'FrameClass';         {the registered class name}

   {now that we have our class set up, register it with the system}
   Result := Windows.RegisterClass(WindowClass) <> 0;
end;

{ Register the child window Class }
function RegisterChildClass: Boolean;
var
   WindowClass: TWndClass;
begin
   {setup our child window class}
   WindowClass.Style := CS_HREDRAW or CS_VREDRAW;     {set the class styles}
   WindowClass.lpfnWndProc := @DefMDIChildProc;       {point to the default MDI
                                                       child window procedure}
   WindowClass.cbClsExtra := 0;                       {no extra class memory}
   WindowClass.cbWndExtra := 0;                       {no extra window memory}
   WindowClass.hInstance := hInstance;                {the application instance}
   WindowClass.hIcon := LoadIcon(0, IDI_APPLICATION); {load a predefined logo}
   WindowClass.hCursor := LoadCursor(0, IDC_ARROW);   {load a predefined cursor}
   WindowClass.hbrBackground := COLOR_WINDOW;         {use a predefined color}
```

```
    WindowClass.lpszMenuName := nil;                  {no menu}
    WindowClass.lpszClassName := 'ChildClass';        {the registered class name}

  {now that we have our class set up, register it with the system}
  Result := Windows.RegisterClass(WindowClass) <> 0;
end;

{this begins the main program}
begin
  {Step 1: Register our frame class first}
  if not RegisterFrameClass then
  begin
    MessageBox(0,'RegisterFrameClass failed',nil,MB_OK);
    Exit;
  end;

  {Step 2: Create the frame window based on our frame class}
  FrameWindow := CreateWindowEx(0,              {no extended styles}
                        'FrameClass',           {the registered class name}
                        'Frame Window',         {the title bar text}
                        WS_OVERLAPPEDWINDOW or  {a normal window style}
                        WS_CLIPCHILDREN,        {clips all child windows}
                        CW_USEDEFAULT,          {default horizontal position}
                        CW_USEDEFAULT,          {default vertical position}
                        CW_USEDEFAULT,          {default width}
                        CW_USEDEFAULT,          {default height}
                        0,                      {handle of the parent window}
                        0,                      {no menu}
                        hInstance,              {the application instance}
                        nil                     {no additional information}
                        );

  {Step 3: If our frame window was created successfully, show it}
  if FrameWindow <> 0 then
  begin
    ShowWindow(FrameWindow, SW_SHOWNORMAL);
    UpdateWindow(FrameWindow);
  end
  else
  begin
    MessageBox(0,'CreateFrameWindow failed',nil,MB_OK);
    Exit;
  end;

  {For steps 4-6, see the FrameWindowProc procedure above}

  {Step 7: Register the child window class}
  if not RegisterChildClass then
  begin
    MessageBox(0,'RegisterChildClass failed',nil,MB_OK);
    Exit;
  end;

  {Step 8: Create the MDI child window}
  ChildWindow := CreateMDIWindow('ChildClass',    {the registered class name}
```

Window Creation Functions   21

```
                              'Child Window',   {the title bar text}
                              WS_VISIBLE,       {initially visible}
                              CW_USEDEFAULT,    {default horizontal position}
                              CW_USEDEFAULT,    {default vertical position}
                              CW_USEDEFAULT,    {default width}
                              CW_USEDEFAULT,    {default height}
                              ClientWindow,     {handle of the parent window}
                              hInstance,        {the application instance}
                              0                 {no application-defined value}
                              );

{Step 9 was taken care of by including the WS_VISIBLE flag in the
 dwStyle parameter. Now we check to see if it was created}
if ChildWindow <> 0 then
begin
  ShowWindow(ChildWindow, SW_SHOWNORMAL);
  UpdateWindow(ChildWindow);
end
else
begin
  MessageBox(0,'CreateChildWindow failed',nil,mb_ok);
  Exit;
end;

{the standard message loop}
while GetMessage(TheMessage,0,0,0) do
begin
  TranslateMessage(TheMessage);
  DispatchMessage(TheMessage);
end;
end.
```

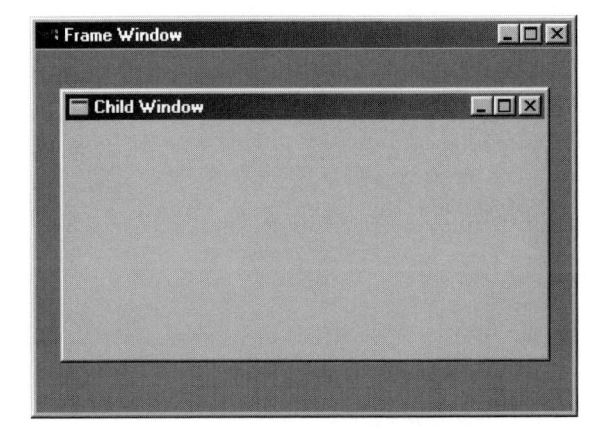

Figure 2-4:
The Object
Pascal MDI
application

The conventional way to create MDI child windows is to send the WM_MDICREATE message to the MDICLIENT window. However, this message cannot be used to create MDI child windows from a different thread. Use the CreateMDIWindow function to get around this limitation. A developer can use this function to allow each MDI child window to have its own thread.

22 ■ Chapter 2

It is possible to combine the functionality of the VCL with the power of low-level Windows API functions. The following example demonstrates how to use low-level Windows API functions to create MDI child windows with a Delphi form as the MDI frame window. Note that the main form must have the FormStyle set to fsMDIForm, and the ClientHandle property contains a handle to the MDICLIENT window.

Listing 2-4: Using the WM_MDICREATE message with a Delphi form

```
{ Register the MDI Child Window Class }
function RegisterClass: Boolean;
var
  WindowClass: TWndClass;
begin
  {setup our new window class}
  WindowClass.Style := CS_HREDRAW or CS_VREDRAW;       {set the class styles}
  WindowClass.lpfnWndProc := @DefMDIChildProc;         {point to the default MDI
                                                        child window procedure}
  WindowClass.cbClsExtra := 0;                         {no extra class memory}
  WindowClass.cbWndExtra := 0;                         {no extra window memory}
  WindowClass.hInstance := hInstance;                  {the application instance}
  WindowClass.hIcon := LoadIcon(0, IDI_WINLOGO);       {load a predefined logo}
  WindowClass.hCursor := LoadCursor(0, IDC_APPSTARTING); {load a predefined cursor}
  WindowClass.hbrBackground := COLOR_WINDOW;           {use a predefined color}
  WindowClass.lpszMenuName := nil;                     {no menu}
  WindowClass.lpszClassName := 'TestClass';            {the registered class name}

  {now that we have our class set up, register it with the system}
  Result := Windows.RegisterClass(WindowClass) <> 0;
end;

procedure TForm1.FormCreate(Sender: TObject);
begin
  {register our child window class}
  if not RegisterClass then
  begin
    ShowMessage('RegisterClass failed');
    Exit;
  end;
end;

procedure TForm1.CreateChild1Click(Sender: TObject);
var
    ChildWnd: HWND;
    MDICreate: TMDICreateStruct;
begin
    {note that the main form has the FormStyle
     property set to fsMDIForm}

    {fill in the members of the MDICreate structure}
    with MDICreate do
    begin
      szClass:='TestClass';                            {our registered class name}
      szTitle:='MDI Child window';                     {caption bar test}
```

```
            hOwner:=hInstance;                        {the application instance
                                                       handle}
         X:=CW_USEDEFAULT;                            {default horizontal position}
         Y:=CW_USEDEFAULT;                            {default vertical position}
         CX:=CW_USEDEFAULT;                           {default width}
         CY:=CW_USEDEFAULT;                           {default height}
         style:=WS_OVERLAPPEDWINDOW OR WS_VISIBLE;    {standard, visible window}
         lParam:=0;                                   {no extra information}
      end;

      {now, create the MDI child window using the WM_MDICREATE message}
      ChildWnd:=SendMessage(Form1.ClientHandle, WM_MDICREATE, 0,
                     Longint(@MDICreate));
   end;
```

Extending Functionality

When Delphi creates a control that encapsulates one of the predefined Windows classes, such as an edit box or button, the code for that object calls the CreateWindowEx function to create the actual window. The CreateParams method is called prior to calling CreateWindowEx. In this method, a data structure of type TCreateParams is initialized with information that will eventually be used as the parameters in the CreateWindowEx call. The TCreateParams structure is defined as:

```
TCreateParams = record
     Caption: PChar;                      {the window text}
     Style: Longint;                      {the style flags}
     ExStyle: Longint;                    {the extended style flags}
     X: Integer;                          {the initial horizontal position}
     Y: Integer;                          {the initial vertical position}
     Width: Integer;                      {the initial width}
     Height: Integer;                     {the initial height}
     WndParent: HWND;                     {a handle to the parent window}
     Param: Pointer                       {additional creation data}
     WindowClass: TWndClass;              {window class information}
     WinClassName: array[0..63] of Char;  {the registered class name}
end;
```

The WindowClass member is of type TWndClass and contains information used in the parameters to the RegisterClass function. Please see the CreateWindowEx, RegisterClass, and RegisterClassEx functions for a full description of what these parameters affect.

The developer can override the CreateParams method, specifying the appropriate information to be used when creating that control or window. In this way, a developer can extend the functionality of standard Delphi controls at the API level.

The following example shows how a developer can create a button that supports multiple lines of text, wrapping to fit within the confines of the control borders, from a TButton control by modifying the flags in the Style member.

Listing 2-5: Overriding CreateParams to extend the functionality of a TButton control

```
unit MultiLineButton;

interface
uses
  Windows, Messages, SysUtils, Classes, Controls, StdCtrls;

type
  TMultiLineButton = class(TButton)
  private
    { Private declarations }
  protected
    { Protected declarations }
  public
    { Public declarations }
    procedure CreateParams(var Params: TCreateParams); override;
  published
    { Published declarations }
  end;

procedure Register;

implementation

procedure TMultiLineButton.CreateParams(var Params: TCreateParams);
begin
  {call the inherited procedure to fill in the default values}
  inherited CreateParams(Params);

  {create an edit box...}
  Params.Style:=Params.Style or      {that has default button properties plus}
              BS_MULTILINE;          {multiple lines}
end;


procedure Register;
begin
  RegisterComponents('Samples', [TMultiLineButton]);
end;
```

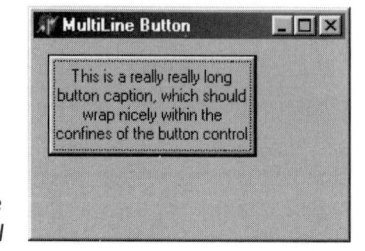

Figure 2-5:
The multi-line button control

This technique can be used with forms as well. The following example shows how to create a form with a raised edge.

Listing 2-6: Creating a form with a raised edge

```
type
  TForm1 = class(TForm)
  private
    { Private declarations }
  public
    { Public declarations }
    procedure CreateParams(var Params: TCreateParams); override;
  end;

var
  Form1: TForm1;

implementation

{$R *.DFM}

procedure TForm1.CreateParams(var Params: TCreateParams);
begin
  {call the inherited function to create the default parameters}
  inherited CreateParams(Params);

  {this form will have an edge with a ridge}
  Params.ExStyle:=Params.ExStyle or WS_EX_OVERLAPPEDWINDOW;
end;
```

Figure 2-6: The raised edge form

Delphi vs. the Windows API

For the most part, Delphi developers will not typically have to resort to calling window creation API functions. It is extremely easy to create main windows and dialog boxes using Delphi, which is all that is required in 99% of programming situations. However, by understanding the window creation process, Delphi developers can get a better understanding of the inner workings of an application, which may be helpful when some advanced techniques are required.

Additionally, by creatively using various style flags in certain combinations, it is very easy to extend the functionality of windowed controls. We've already seen an example of a multiline button; it is just as easy to extend other controls by using the same technique (i.e., creating a multiline, right-aligned edit control that accepts only numeric input uses almost the exact same code, just with a few different style parameters). By using the styles already available within the operating system, we can easily extend the functionality of the common controls without writing hundreds of lines of code.

Also, if you are writing DLLs that will be interacting with C applications, it may be necessary to define windows using these basic API functions. This also bypasses the VCL, and will result in applications and DLLs that are only 10-20KB in size, as opposed to the 100-200KB footprint of a standard Delphi application using the VCL.

Window Creation and Registration Functions

The following window creation and registration functions are covered in this chapter:

Table 2-1: Window creation and registration functions

Function	Description
CreateMDIWindow	Creates MDI child windows.
CreateWindowEx	Creates windows.
DestroyWindow	Destroys a window.
MessageBox	Creates a temporary dialog box displaying a message.
RegisterClass	Registers a new window class.
RegisterClassEx	Registers a new window class using extended style flags.
UnregisterClass	Unregisters a registered window class.

CreateMDIWindow   *Windows.pas*

Syntax

```
CreateMDIWindow(
  lpClassName: PChar;        {a pointer to the child class name string}
  lpWindowName: PChar;       {a pointer to the window name string}
  dwStyle: DWORD;            {window style flags}
  X: Integer;                {initial horizontal position}
  Y: Integer;                {initial vertical position}
  nWidth: Integer;           {initial width of the window}
  nHeight: Integer;          {initial height of the window}
  hWndParent: HWND;          {a handle to the parent MDI client window}
  hInstance: HINST;          {a handle to the module instance}
  lParam: LPARAM             {an application-defined value}
): HWND;                     {returns a handle to the new window}
```

Description

This function creates multiple document interface child windows, and is similar to sending a WM_MDICREATE message to an MDI client window. For more information on creating windows, see the CreateWindowEx function. This function is intended to be used for creating MDI child windows in a separate thread.

> **Note:** Windows 95 can support a maximum of 16,364 window handles.

Parameters

lpClassName: A pointer to a null-terminated, case-sensitive string specifying the window class for the MDI child window. This class is registered by calling the RegisterClass function.

lpWindowName: A pointer to a null-terminated, case-sensitive string. This string is displayed in the title bar of the MDI child window.

dwStyle: A 32-bit number that specifies what styles this window uses. If the MDI client window is using the MDIS_ALLCHILDSTYLES window style flag, this parameter can be any combination of the styles from the window styles section of Table 2-5 in the CreateWindowEx function. Otherwise, it can be any combination of styles from Table 2-2. Two or more styles are specified by using the Boolean OR operator, i.e., WS_MINIMIZE OR WS_HSCROLL.

X: The initial horizontal position for the upper-left corner of the MDI child window. This position is relative to the client area of the MDI client window. Using the CW_USEDEFAULT constant causes Windows to choose the default horizontal position for the window.

Y: The initial vertical position for the upper-left corner of the MDI child window. This position is relative to the client area of the MDI client window. Using the CW_USEDEFAULT constant causes Windows to choose the default vertical position for the window.

nWidth: The initial width of the MDI child window. If the CW_USEDEFAULT constant is used, Windows gives the MDI child window an internally defined default width.

nHeight: The initial height of the MDI child window. If the CW_USEDEFAULT constant is used, Windows gives the MDI child window an internally defined default width.

hWndParent: A handle to the MDI client window that becomes the parent of the child window.

hInstance: The instance handle of the application or module creating this window.

lParam: A 32-bit application-defined value.

Return Value

If this function succeeds, it returns a handle to the newly created MDI child window; otherwise, it returns zero.

See Also

CreateWindowEx, WM_MDICREATE

Example

Listing 2-7: Creating an MDI child window

```
{ Register the MDI Child Window Class }
function RegisterClass: Boolean;
var
  WindowClass: TWndClass;
begin
  {setup our new window class}
  WindowClass.Style := CS_HREDRAW or CS_VREDRAW;    {set the class styles}
  WindowClass.lpfnWndProc := @DefMDIChildProc;      {point to the default MDI
                                                     child window procedure}
  WindowClass.cbClsExtra := 0;                      {no extra class memory}
  WindowClass.cbWndExtra := 0;                      {no extra window memory}
  WindowClass.hInstance := hInstance;               {the application instance}
  WindowClass.hIcon := LoadIcon(0, IDI_WINLOGO);    {load a predefined icon}
  WindowClass.hCursor := LoadCursor(0, IDC_APPSTARTING); {load a predefined
                                                          cursor}
  WindowClass.hbrBackground := COLOR_WINDOW;        {use a predefined color}
  WindowClass.lpszMenuName := nil;                  {no menu}
  WindowClass.lpszClassName := 'TestClass';         {the registered class name}

  {now that we have our class set up, register it with the system}
  Result := Windows.RegisterClass(WindowClass) <> 0;
end;

procedure TForm1.CreateChild1Click(Sender: TObject);
var
  hWindow: HWND;
begin
  {register our new class first. Note that the FormStyle property of the main
   form in this example is set to fsMDIForm.}
  if not RegisterClass then
  begin
    ShowMessage('RegisterClass failed');
    Exit;
  end;

  {now, create a window based on our new class}
  hWindow := CreateMDIWindow('TestClass',       {the registered class name}
                             'API Window',      {the title bar text}
                             WS_VISIBLE OR      {the MDI child window is
                                                 visible,}
                             WS_CAPTION OR      {has a caption bar,}
                             WS_SYSMENU OR      {a system menu,}
                             WS_MINIMIZEBOX OR  {and minimize and}
                             WS_MAXIMIZEBOX,    {maximize boxes}
                             CW_USEDEFAULT,     {default horizontal
                                                 position}
                             CW_USEDEFAULT,     {default vertical position}
                             CW_USEDEFAULT,     {default width}
                             CW_USEDEFAULT,     {default height}
                             Form1.ClientHandle, {handle of the MDI client
                                                  window}
```

```
                            hInstance,             {the application instance}
                            0                      {no additional information}
                            );

    {if our window was created successfully, show it}
    if hWindow <> 0 then
    begin
      ShowWindow(hWindow, SW_SHOWNORMAL);
      UpdateWindow(hWindow);
    end
    else
    begin
      ShowMessage('CreateWindow failed');
      Exit;
    end;

end;
```

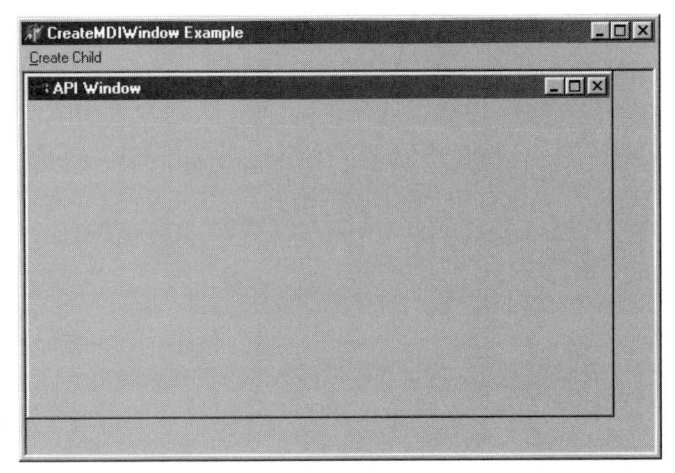

Figure 2-7:
The MDI child
window

Table 2-2: CreateMDIWindow dwStyle values

Value	Description
WS_MINIMIZE	The MDI child window is initially minimized.
WS_MAXIMIZE	The MDI child window is initially maximized.
WS_HSCROLL	The MDI child window has a horizontal scroll bar.
WS_VSCROLL	The MDI child window has a vertical scroll bar.

CreateWindowEx   Windows.pas

Syntax

CreateWindowEx(
dwExStyle: DWORD;   {extended window style flags}
lpClassName: PChar;   {a pointer to the class name string}
lpWindowName: PChar;   {a pointer to the window name string}
dwStyle: DWORD;   {window style flags}

X: Integer;	{initial horizontal position}
Y: Integer;	{initial vertical position}
nWidth: Integer;	{initial width of the window}
nHeight: Integer;	{initial height of the window}
hWndParent: HWND;	{a handle to the parent window}
hMenu: HMENU;	{a handle to the menu, or a child window identifier}
hInstance: HINST;	{a handle to the module instance}
lpParam: Pointer	{a pointer to additional information}
): HWND;	{returns a handle to the new window}

Description

The CreateWindowEx function creates an overlapped, pop-up, or child window based on either one of the predefined window classes or a new window class created with the RegisterClass or RegisterClassEx function. This function is used when creating any type of window, including the main window of the application and any child windows or user interface controls that are used in the application. The initial size and position of the window may be set, and an owner, parent, or menu may be specified.

Before this function returns, it sends a WM_CREATE message to the window procedure. For overlapped, pop-up, and child windows, this function will also send the WM_GET-MINMAXINFO and WM_NCCREATE messages. If the WS_VISIBLE style is specified, CreateWindowEx will send all of the messages necessary to activate and show the window.

Note: In the Windows.pas source code, the CreateWindow function is not imported from the User32.DLL. Instead, the function calls the CreateWindowEx function, passing a zero for the dwExStyle parameter. Internally, the CreateWindow API function calls CreateWindowEx, so the CreateWindow API function will not be documented.

Note: Windows 95 can support a maximum of 16,364 window handles.

Parameters

dwExStyle: A 32-bit number that specifies what extended styles this window uses. Available extended style constants are listed in Table 2-3. Multiple styles are specified by using the Boolean OR operator, i.e., WS_EX_ABSPOSITION OR WS_EX_CONTROLPARENT. Using the WS_EX_RIGHT extended style for static or edit controls is equivalent to using the SS_RIGHT or ES_RIGHT styles, respectively. Using this style with button controls is the same as using BS_RIGHT and BS_RIGHTBUTTON styles.

lpClassName: A pointer to a null-terminated, case-sensitive string, or an integer atom. It describes a valid, predefined class name or one created with the RegisterClass function. See Table 2-4 for valid predefined window classes. If this specifies an atom, the atom must have been created with a call to GlobalAddAtom. The atom, a 16-bit value less than

$C000, must be in the low-order word of ClassName and the high-order word must be zero.

lpWindowName: A null-terminated string containing the name for this window. This is displayed on the title bar of the window. If this window is a control, this is the text displayed on the control.

dwStyle: A 32-bit number that describes what styles this window uses. Available style constants are listed in Table 2-5. Multiple styles are combined by using the Boolean OR operator; i.e., WS_HSCROLL OR WS_VSCROLL.

X: The initial horizontal position of the upper-left corner of the window. For overlapped or pop-up windows, this coordinate is relative to the screen. For child windows, this coordinate is relative to the upper-left corner of the parent window's client area. If the constant CW_USEDEFAULT is used, Windows selects the default position for the upper-left corner, and the Y parameter is ignored. The CW_USEDEFAULT constant is only valid for overlapped windows. If it is specified for any other window type, the X and Y parameters are set to zero.

Y: The initial horizontal position of the upper-left corner of the window. For overlapped or pop-up windows, this coordinate is relative to the screen. For child windows, this coordinate is relative to the upper-left corner of the parent window's client area. If an overlapped window is created with the WS_VISIBLE style set and the X parameter is set to CW_USEDEFAULT, the Y parameter is ignored.

nWidth: The initial width of the window. Overlapped windows can use the CW_USEDEFAULT constant, in which case the nHeight parameter is ignored. If this constant is used, Windows selects a default width and height for the window. The default width will extend from the initial X coordinate to the right edge of the screen; the default height will extend from the initial Y coordinate to the top of the icon area. If CW_USEDEFAULT is specified for child or pop-up windows, the nWidth and nHeight parameters are set to zero.

nHeight: The initial height of the window. If the nWidth parameter is set to CW_USEDEFAULT, the nHeight parameter is ignored.

hWndParent: A handle to the window's parent or owner. A valid window handle must be specified if the window to be created is a child or owned window. Child windows are confined to the client area of the parent window. An owned window is an overlapped or popup window that is destroyed when its owner is destroyed and hidden when its owner is minimized; it is always displayed on top of its owner window. This can be set to 0 if the window does not have an owner. If no parent window is specified, the window will not automatically be destroyed when the application ends. The DestroyWindow function is used to remove the window in this instance. This parameter must have a valid window handle if the WS_CHILD style is used; it is optional if the WS_POPUP style is used.

Windows 2000 or later: To create a message-only window, use HWND_MESSAGE.

hMenu: A handle to a menu object. For an overlapped or pop-up window, this parameter can be NIL if the class menu should be used. For controls, this is set to an integer value that is the ID of the control being created. All WM_COMMAND messages will reference this ID when an action has occurred with the control. The child window identifier must be unique among all child windows with the same parent window.

hInstance: The instance handle of the application or module creating the window.

Windows NT/2000 or later: This parameter is ignored.

lpParam: A pointer to application-defined data that is used during the window creation process. The window procedure receives a WM_CREATE message when the CreateWindowEx function is called. The lParam member of this message contains a pointer to a TCreateStruct data structure. The lpCreateParams member of the TCreateStruct structure contains the pointer to the application-defined data. For MDICLIENT windows, pass a pointer to a TClientCreateStruct structure in this parameter. If no extra creation information is needed, set this parameter to NIL.

The TClientCreateStruct structure contains additional information that is needed to create an MDICLIENT window. Delphi defines the TClientCreateStruct as:

```
TClientCreateStruct = packed record
    hWindowMenu: THandle;        {a handle to a menu}
    idFirstChild: UINT;          {the identifier of the first MDI child window}
end;
```

hWindowMenu: This is the handle to the MDI application's window menu.

idFirstChild: This specifies the identifier of the first MDI child window. Windows increments this identifier for every MDI child window created, and reassigns identifiers when child windows are destroyed so the range of identifiers are contiguous. These identifiers are used in the WM_COMMAND messages sent to the MDI frame window when a child window is chosen from the window menu, and should not conflict with other command identifiers.

The TCreateStruct structure contains all of the parameters that were passed to the CreateWindowEx function. The developer can use this information to perform any additional initialization at the time of window creation. The TCreateStruct data structure is defined as:

```
TCreateStruct = packed record
    lpCreateParams: Pointer;     {a pointer to application-defined data}
    hInstance: HINST;            {a handle to the module instance}
    hMenu: HMENU;                {a handle to the menu, or a child window identifier}
    hwndParent: HWND;            {a handle to the parent window}
    cy: Integer;                 {initial height of the window}
    cx: Integer;                 {initial width of the window}
    y: Integer;                  {initial vertical position}
    x: Integer;                  {initial horizontal position}
    style: Longint;              {window style flags}
    lpszName: PAnsiChar;         {a pointer to the window name string}
    lpszClass: PAnsiChar;        {a pointer to the class name string}
    dwExStyle: DWORD;            {extended window style flags}
end;
```

The lpCreateParams member is a pointer to application-defined data. The other members of this structure contain the information passed in the parameters to the CreateWindowEx function.

Return Value

If this function succeeds, it returns a handle to the new window; otherwise, it returns zero. To get extended error information, call the GetLastError function.

See Also

DestroyWindow, MessageBox, RegisterClass, WM_COMMAND, WM_CREATE, WM_GETMINMAXINFO, WM_NCCALCSIZE, WM_NCCREATE, WM_PAINT

Example

Listing 2-8: Creating a window with extended window styles

```
var
  hWindow: HWND;

{ Register the extended Window class }
function RegisterClassEx: Boolean;
var
  WindowClassEx: TWndClassEx;
begin
  {setup our new window class}
  WindowClassEx.cbSize := SizeOf(TWndClassEx);         {the size of the structure}
  WindowClassEx.Style := CS_HREDRAW or CS_VREDRAW;     {set the class styles}
  WindowClassEx.lpfnWndProc := @DefWindowProc;         {point to the default window
                                                        procedure}
  WindowClassEx.cbClsExtra := 0;                       {no extra class memory}
  WindowClassEx.cbWndExtra := 0;                       {no extra window memory}
  WindowClassEx.hInstance := hInstance;                {the application instance}
  WindowClassEx.hIcon := LoadIcon(0, IDI_APPLICATION); {load a predefined logo}
  WindowClassEx.hCursor := LoadCursor(0, IDC_WAIT);    {load a predefined cursor}
  WindowClassEx.hbrBackground := COLOR_WINDOW;         {use a predefined color}
  WindowClassEx.lpszMenuName := nil;                   {no menu}
  WindowClassEx.lpszClassName := 'TestClass';          {the registered class name}
  WindowClassEx.hIconSm := 0;                          {no small icon}

  {now that we have our class set up, register it with the system}
  Result := Windows.RegisterClassEx(WindowClassEx) <> 0;
end;

procedure TForm1.Button1Click(Sender: TObject);
begin
  {register our new class first}
  if not RegisterClassEx then
  begin
    ShowMessage('RegisterClassEx failed');
    Exit;
  end;
```

```
    {now, create a window based on our new class}
    hWindow := CreateWindowEx(WS_EX_CLIENTEDGE OR       {this window has a sunken
                                                         edge}
                             WS_EX_CONTEXTHELP,         {and a context sensitive
                                                         help button}
                             'TestClass',               {the registered class name}
                             'API Window',              {the title bar text}
                             WS_OVERLAPPEDWINDOW AND    {a normal window}
                             NOT WS_MAXIMIZEBOX AND     {without a minimize or
                                                         maximize button}
                             NOT WS_MINIMIZEBOX,        {so the help button is not
                                                         obscured}
                             CW_USEDEFAULT,             {default horizontal position}
                             CW_USEDEFAULT,             {default vertical position}
                             CW_USEDEFAULT,             {default width}
                             CW_USEDEFAULT,             {default height}
                             0,                         {no parent window}
                             0,                         {no menu}
                             hInstance,                 {the application instance}
                             nil                        {no additional information}
                             );

  {if our window was created successfully, show it}
  if hWindow <> 0 then
  begin
    ShowWindow(hWindow, SW_SHOWNORMAL);
    UpdateWindow(hWindow);
  end
  else
  begin
    ShowMessage('CreateWindow failed');
    Exit;
  end;

end;

procedure TForm1.Button2Click(Sender: TObject);
begin
  {first, destroy our window}
  DestroyWindow(hWindow);

  {now we can unregister our new class}
  Windows.UnregisterClass('TestClass', hInstance);
end;
```

Figure 2-8:
The new window

Table 2-3: CreateWindowEx dwExStyle values

Value	Description
WS_EX_ACCEPTFILES	Accepts files dragged and dropped from other applications, such as the Windows Explorer.
WS_EX_APPWINDOW	Forces a top-level window onto the taskbar when the window is minimized.
WS_EX_CLIENTEDGE	The window border has a sunken edge.
WS_EX_CONTEXTHELP	Causes the context-sensitive help button (a small button with a question mark) to appear in the title bar. When pressed, the mouse cursor changes to a pointer and a question mark. If the user clicks on a child window or control, it receives a WM_HELP message. The child should pass the message to the parent's window procedure, which should then call the WinHelp function using the HELP_WM_HELP command. The Help application displays a pop-up window that usually contains help information for the child window. The WS_MAXIMIZEBOX and WS_MINIMIZEBOX styles must not be included, or the context help button will be obscured by the minimize and maximize buttons.
WS_EX_CONTROLPARENT	Allows users to press the Tab key to move from child window to child window.
WS_EX_DLGMODALFRAME	This window has a double border. The WS_CAPTION style must be used to add a title to this style of window.
WS_EX_LAYERED	**Windows 2000 or later:** Creates a layered window (not covered in this text). This flag cannot be used for child windows, nor can it be used in conjunction with the CS_OWNDC or CS_CLASSDC styles.
WS_EX_LAYOUTRTL	**Windows 2000 or later, Arabic and Hebrew versions of Windows 98 and Me:** Creates a window with a horizontal origin on its right edge.
WS_EX_LEFT	Creates a window with left-aligned properties. This is the default style.
WS_EX_LEFTSCROLLBAR	If the shell's language is Hebrew, Arabic, or any other language that supports reading order alignment, the vertical scroll bar, if any, will be placed to the left of the client area. For other languages, this style is simply ignored.
WS_EX_LTRREADING	Text displayed in this window is in a left-to-right reading order. This is the default style.
WS_EX_MDICHILD	Creates an MDI child window.

Value	Description
WS_EX_NOACTIVATE	**Windows 2000 or later:** Any top-level window created with this style will not become the foreground window when it is clicked, nor will the window be brought to the foreground when the user minimizes or closes the foreground window. Windows with this style will also not appear on the taskbar by default.
WS_EX_NOINHERITLAYOUT	**Windows 2000 or later:** This style prevents the window from passing its window layout to its child windows.
WS_EX_NOPARENTNOTIFY	A window with this style does not send WM_PARENTNOTIFY messages to its parent when it is created or destroyed.
WS_EX_OVERLAPPEDWINDOW	Combines the WS_EX_CLIENTEDGE and WS_EX_WINDOWEDGE styles.
WS_EX_PALETTEWINDOW	Combines the WS_EX_WINDOWEDGE, WS_EX_TOOLWINDOW, and WS_EX_TOPMOST styles.
WS_EX_RIGHT	If the shell's language is Hebrew, Arabic, or any other language that supports reading order alignment, this window has generic right-aligned properties. For other languages, this style is simply ignored.
WS_EX_RIGHTSCROLLBAR	Places the vertical scroll bar, if present, on the right side of the client area. This is the default style.
WS_EX_RTLREADING	If the shell's language is Hebrew, Arabic, or any other language that supports reading order alignment, the window is displayed using right-to-left reading order properties. For other languages, this style is simply ignored.
WS_EX_STATICEDGE	Creates a window with a three-dimensional border style.
WS_EX_TOOLWINDOW	Creates a floating toolbar style window. The title bar is shorter than a normal title bar, and the window caption is drawn in a smaller font. This style of window will not show up on the taskbar or when the user presses Alt+Tab.
WS_EX_TOPMOST	This window stays above all other windows, even when deactivated. This style can be set using the SetWindowPos function.
WS_EX_TRANSPARENT	Any sibling windows that are beneath this window are not obscured by it, and will receive the WM_PAINT message first.
WS_EX_WINDOWEDGE	This window has a border with a raised edge.

Table 2-4: CreateWindowEx lpClassName values

Value	Description
BUTTON	Used when creating buttons, group boxes, check boxes, radio buttons, or icon windows. The BS_OWNERDRAW style can be used to control its visual look in various states. Button controls can either be alone or in groups, with or without text, and typically change appearance when the user clicks on them.
COMBOBOX	Creates a list box with a selection area similar to an edit box. The list selection area can be displayed at all times or enabled as a drop-down. Depending on the style, the user can or cannot edit the contents of the selection area. If the list box is visible, typing characters in the selection area highlights the first entry in the list that matches the characters typed. Similarly, selecting an item from the list displays it in the selection area.

Value	Description
EDIT	Creates a standard edit control, either single or multiline. This control will receive focus by either clicking on it or moving to it using the Tab key. This allows a user to input text from the keyboard. The WM_SETFONT message can be sent to this control to change the default font. Tab characters are expanded into as many space characters as needed to fill it to the next tab stop. Tab stops are assumed to be at every eighth character position.
LISTBOX	Creates a standard list box, a control with a list of strings that can be selected. The user selects a string by simply clicking on it. The selected string is highlighted, and a notification message is sent to the parent window. Single or multiple selections are supported, and the styles LBS_OWNER-DRAWFIXED or LBS_OWNERDRAWVARIABLE can be used to control how the strings are drawn.
MDICLIENT	Creates a multiple document interface client window. An MDICLIENT window must exist before creating MDI child windows. The WS_CLIP-CHILDREN and WS_CHILD styles should be specified when using this class.
RICHEDIT_CLASS	Creates a rich text version 2.0 control. This control allows the user to view and edit text, format individual characters or entire paragraphs, and embed COM objects. **Note:** Rich Text controls support all of the styles available for edit controls except for the ES_LOWERCASE, ES_OEMCONVERT, and ES_UPPERCASE styles.
SCROLLBAR	Creates a standard scroll bar control. This control sends a notification message to the parent window when it is clicked. The parent window is responsible for updating the position of the scroll bar thumb. This class also includes size box controls, a small rectangle the user can drag to change the size of the window.
STATIC	Creates a static text control, such as simple text fields, boxes, or rectangles. Static controls neither receive input nor provide output.

Table 2-5: CreateWindowEx dwStyle values

Window Styles	Description
WS_BORDER	Gives the window a thin line border.
WS_CAPTION	Gives the window a title bar, and includes the WS_BORDER style.
WS_CHILD	Creates a child window. The WS_POPUP style cannot be used if this style is specified.
WS_CHILDWINDOW	The same as the WS_CHILD style.
WS_CLIPCHILDREN	Clips around child windows during painting, and is used when creating parent windows.
WS_CLIPSIBLINGS	Clips windows relative to each other during painting. Without this style, the entire area of the window will be included in the update region, even if overlapped by a sibling window, making it possible to draw in the client area of the overlapping child window. When this style is used, the sibling's overlapping area is left out of the update region.
WS_DISABLED	The window is initially disabled and cannot receive user input.
WS_DLGFRAME	Creates a window with the dialog box border style, and cannot have a title bar.

Window Styles	Description
WS_GROUP	Marks the beginning of a group of controls. The next controls created will belong to this group, and when the WS_GROUP style is used again, it will end the grouping and create a new group. The user can change the focus from one control to the next in a group by using the cursor keys. This is commonly used when creating radio buttons.
WS_HSCROLL	Gives the window a horizontal scroll bar.
WS_ICONIC	This is the same as WS_MINIMIZE.
WS_MAXIMIZE	The window starts out maximized.
WS_MAXIMIZEBOX	Includes the maximize button in the title bar.
WS_MINIMIZE	The window starts out minimized.
WS_MINIMIZEBOX	Includes the minimize button in the title bar.
WS_OVERLAPPED	Gives the window both a title bar and a border. This is the same as the WS_TILED style.
WS_OVERLAPPEDWINDOW	Combines the WS_OVERLAPPED, WS_CAPTION, WS_SYSMENU, WS_THICKFRAME, WS_MINIMIZEBOX, and WS_MAXIMIZEBOX styles. This is a standard window, and is the same as the WS_TILEDWINDOW style.
WS_POPUP	Creates a pop-up window. The WS_CHILD style cannot be used with this style.
WS_POPUPWINDOW	Combines the WS_BORDER, WS_POPUP, and WS_SYSMENU styles. The WS_CAPTION style must be specified before the system menu becomes visible.
WS_SIZEBOX	The window has a sizing border. This is the same as the WS_THICKFRAME style.
WS_SYSMENU	The system menu box is present in the title bar. The WS_CAPTION style must also be specified.
WS_TABSTOP	Indicates that the control can receive the keyboard focus when the user presses the Tab key. Pressing the Tab key again will change the focus to the next control with this style.
WS_THICKFRAME	Gives the window a sizing border.
WS_TILED	This is the same as the WS_OVERLAPPED style.
WS_TILEDWINDOW	This is the same as the WS_OVERLAPPEDWINDOW style.
WS_VISIBLE	The window is initially visible.
WS_VSCROLL	Gives the window a vertical scroll bar.

Button Styles	Description
BS_3STATE	Creates a check box with three states: unselected, selected, or grayed. The grayed state is used to show that the state of the check box is undetermined.
BS_AUTO3STATE	The same as BS_3STATE, but the check box will change its state when selected by a user. The cycle will go through checked, grayed, and unchecked.
BS_AUTOCHECKBOX	The same as BS_CHECKBOX, but it will change its state when selected by the user.
BS_AUTORADIOBUTTON	The same as BS_RADIOBUTTON, but the button is selected when the user clicks on it, and any other buttons in its group are unselected.
BS_BITMAP	The button will display a bitmap.

Button Styles	Description
BS_BOTTOM	The title will be at the bottom of the button's rectangular area.
BS_CENTER	Centers the button title horizontally.
BS_CHECKBOX	Creates a check box control with the title displayed to the right, unless the BS_LEFTTEXT or BS_RIGHTBUTTON style is specified.
BS_DEFPUSHBUTTON	If this button is in a dialog box, it is clicked if the user presses the Enter key, even if it doesn't have focus. This causes the button to have a thick, black border.
BS_FLAT	Creates a button with a flat border. When pressed, the text moves like a normal button, but the borders do not reflect any movement.
BS_GROUPBOX	Creates a group box control with a title displayed in the upper-left corner.
BS_ICON	Creates a button that can display an icon.
BS_LEFT	Left justifies the title in a button. If the button is a radio button or check box and does not have the BS_RIGHTBUTTON style specified, the text will be left justified on the right side of the button.
BS_LEFTTEXT	Places the title on the left side of a check box or radio button. This is the same as the BS_RIGHTBUTTON style.
BS_MULTILINE	This button has multiple lines of text for its title. The text will wrap if the button is too narrow.
BS_NOTIFY	In addition to the BN_CLICKED message sent when a button is clicked, this style causes the BN_DBLCLK, BN_KILLFOCUS, and BN_SETFOCUS notification messages to be sent to the parent window.
BS_OWNERDRAW	Creates an owner-drawn button. The parent window receives a WM_MEASUREITEM message when the button is created, and a WM_DRAWITEM message when the button needs to be drawn. This style should not be used with any other styles.
BS_PUSHBUTTON	When the button is selected, it posts a WM_COMMAND message to the parent window.
BS_PUSHLIKE	Makes radio buttons and check boxes have a button-like look and feel. It will be sunken when it is checked, and raised when it is not checked.
BS_RADIOBUTTON	Creates a small circle with text to one side. The text is displayed to the right of the circle, unless the BS_LEFTTEXT or BS_RIGHTBUTTON styles are used. The circle can be clicked on or off, and this control usually groups a set of related but mutually exclusive choices.
BS_RIGHT	Right justifies the title in a button. If the button is a radio button or check box and does not have the BS_RIGHTBUTTON style specified, the text will be right justified on the right side of the button.
BS_RIGHTBUTTON	Places the check box or radio button on the right side of the text. This is the same as the BS_LEFTTEXT style.
BS_TEXT	Causes a button to display text.
BS_TOP	Displays the title at the top of the button.
BS_VCENTER	Centers the text vertically in the button.

Combo Box Styles	Description
CBS_AUTOHSCROLL	Allows the edit control of the combo box to scroll horizontally when text reaches the box boundaries. Without this style, only text that fits in the boundaries is allowed.

Combo Box Styles	Description
CBS_DISABLENOSCROLL	Forces a vertical scroll bar to be visible even when all items in the list are displayed. It will be disabled unless needed to show additional items.
CBS_DROPDOWN	Creates a drop-down combo box, with the list visible only when the user clicks on a down arrow button next to the edit box.
CBS_DROPDOWNLIST	Creates a drop-list combo box. The user is unable to type in the edit control, and can only select items in the list.
CBS_HASSTRINGS	Used in conjunction with an owner-drawn list box. The combo box maintains the memory and address for all of the strings, and the application can use the CB_GETLBTEXT message to retrieve a particular string.
CBS_LOWERCASE	Only lowercase characters can be entered; uppercase characters are automatically converted to lowercase.
CBS_NOINTEGRALHEIGHT	Forces a combo box to the exact size specified. By default, Windows will resize the combo box so no item is partially displayed.
CBS_OEMCONVERT	Windows will convert any entered text to the OEM character set and then back to the Windows character set so that the CharToOem function, if used, converts characters properly. This style is useful when the combo box contains file names, and is only valid with the CBS_SIMPLE or CBS_DROPDOWN styles.
CBS_OWNERDRAWFIXED	Creates an owner-drawn combo box control. The owner of this control is responsible for drawing the items, each of which will be the same height. The owner receives a WM_MEASUREITEM message when the control is created, and a WM_DRAWITEM message when an item needs to be redrawn.
CBS_OWNERDRAWVARIABLE	This is the same as the CBS_OWNERDRAWFIXED style, except that each item in the list can be different sizes. WM_MEASUREITEM is sent for each item in the combo box when it is created, and a WM_DRAWITEM message is sent when an item needs to be redrawn.
CBS_SIMPLE	Creates a combo box where the list of items is always visible, and the current selection is displayed in the edit control.
CBS_SORT	Sorts any string added to the list box when using the CB_ADDSTRING message.
CBS_UPPERCASE	Only uppercase characters can be entered; lowercase characters are automatically converted to uppercase.

Dialog Box Styles	Description
DS_3DLOOK	Gives dialog boxes a three-dimensional look by drawing three-dimensional borders around control windows in the dialog box. This style is included by default.
DS_ABSALIGN	Positions a dialog box relative to the upper-left corner of the screen. Without this style, Windows assumes the coordinates are client coordinates.
DS_CENTER	Centers the dialog box in the screen area that is not obscured by the taskbar.
DS_CENTERMOUSE	Causes the mouse cursor to be centered in the dialog box.
DS_CONTEXTHELP	Causes the WS_EX_CONTEXTHELP extended style to be defined for this dialog box. Please see Table 2-3 for a description of the WS_EX_CONTEXTHELP style.

Dialog Box Styles	Description
DS_CONTROL	Creates a dialog box that will work as a child window of another dialog box, like a page in a property sheet. This allows the user to tab among the child windows of this window, use its accelerator keys, etc.
DS_FIXEDSYS	The dialog box uses SYSTEM_FIXED_FONT instead of the SYSTEM_FONT.
DS_MODALFRAME	The dialog box has a modal dialog box frame, and can be combined with the WS_CAPTION and WS_SYSMENU styles to give it a title bar and system menu.
DS_NOFAILCREATE	**Windows 95/98/Me:** Creates the dialog box regardless of any errors encountered during creation.
DS_NOIDLEMSG	While the dialog box is displayed, no WM_ENTERIDLE messages are posted to the owner.
DS_SETFONT	Indicates that the dialog box template contains information specifying a font name and point size. This font is used to display text information inside the dialog box client area and its controls. The font handle is passed to each control in the dialog box with the WM_SETFONT message.
DS_SETFOREGROUND	Calls the SetForegroundWindow function to force the dialog box into the foreground.
DS_SHELLFONT	Forces the dialog box to use the system font. The WM_SETFONT message, containing a handle to the system font, is sent to the dialog box and each of its controls.
DS_SYSMODAL	Causes the dialog box to have the WS_EX_TOPMOST extended style. This has no other effect on any other windows in the system while the dialog box is displayed.

Edit Control Styles	Description
ES_AUTOHSCROLL	The control will scroll horizontally during editing by ten characters if the user reaches the end of the boundaries.
ES_AUTOVSCROLL	Scrolls text up one page when the user presses the Enter key on the last line.
ES_CENTER	**Windows 98/2000:** Centers the text in a single line or multiple line edit control. On earlier versions of windows, this works only on multiple line edit controls.
ES_LEFT	Left-aligns text.
ES_LOWERCASE	Only lowercase characters can be entered; uppercase characters are automatically converted to lowercase.
ES_MULTILINE	Creates a multiple line edit control. The ES_WANTRETURN style must be specified to use the Enter key as a carriage return. If the ES_AUTOVSCROLL style is not specified, the system will beep when the user presses the Enter key and no more lines can be displayed. If the ES_AUTOHSCROLL style is specified, the user must press the Enter key to start a new line. Otherwise, the text will wrap when it reaches the edge of the edit control box. If scroll bars are specified for edit controls, the control will automatically process all messages for them.
ES_NOHIDESEL	Selections in the edit control are shown after the control loses focus.
ES_NUMBER	This edit control only accepts numerical digits.
ES_OEMCONVERT	This style is the same as the CBS_OEMCONVERT combo box style.

Edit Control Styles	Description
ES_PASSWORD	Displays the password character, set using the EM_SETPASSWORDCHAR message, in place of any character typed. The default password character is an asterisk.
ES_READONLY	The edit control is read-only, and users cannot edit the text therein.
ES_RIGHT	**Windows 98/2000:** Causes text to be right aligned in single line or multiple line edit controls. On earlier versions of Windows, this works only on multiple line edit controls.
ES_UPPERCASE	Only uppercase characters can be entered; lowercase characters are automatically converted to uppercase.
ES_WANTRETURN	The Enter key inserts carriage returns in a multiple line edit control. Ctrl+Enter is used to insert carriage returns when this style is not specified. This style has no effect on single line edit controls.

List Box Styles	Description
LBS_DISABLENOSCROLL	Displays a vertical scroll bar, even when all items are displayed. The scroll bar is disabled unless needed to display additional items.
LBS_EXTENDEDSEL	Allows a range of items to be selected using the Shift key and the mouse.
LBS_HASSTRINGS	Specifies that the list box has items consisting of strings. The list box maintains the memory and addresses for the strings, and the application can use the LB_GETTEXT message to retrieve a particular string. By default, all list boxes except owner-drawn list boxes have this style.
LBS_MULTICOLUMN	Creates a multiple column list box. The list box can be scrolled horizontally, and the LB_SETCOLUMNWIDTH message can be used to set the width of the columns.
LBS_MULTIPLESEL	Allows multiple items to be selected with the mouse.
LBS_NODATA	Indicates that no data is in the list box. The LBS_OWNERDRAWFIXED style must be used when this style is specified. This style is used when the number of items exceeds 1,000, and the LBS_SORT and LBS_HASSTRINGS styles cannot be used. Commands to add, insert, or delete an item are ignored, and requests to find a string always fail. Windows sends a WM_DRAWITEM message to the owner when an item needs to be drawn. The itemID member of the DRAWITEMSTRUCT structure passed with the WM_DRAW-ITEM message specifies the line number of the item to be drawn. A no-data list box does not send a WM_DELETEITEM message.
LBS_NOINTEGRALHEIGHT	Forces the list box to be displayed at the specified size. Without this style, Windows resizes the list box so that no item is partially displayed.
LBS_NOREDRAW	The list box does not receive the WM_PAINT message when this style is specified. Use the WM_SETREDRAW message to change this style at run time.
LBS_NOSEL	The items in the list box can be viewed but not selected.
LBS_NOTIFY	Sends a notification message to the parent when a list box item is clicked or double-clicked.
LBS_OWNERDRAWFIXED	Indicates that the owner is responsible for drawing the contents of the list box, sending a WM_MEASUREITEM message to the owner when the list box is created, and a WM_DRAWITEM message when the list box has changed. All of the items will be the same height.

List Box Styles	Description
LBS_OWNERDRAWVARIABLE	This is the same as the LBS_OWNERDRAWFIXED style, except that each item in the list box can be different sizes. WM_MEASUREITEM is sent for each item in the list box when it is created, and a WM_DRAWITEM message is sent when an item needs to be redrawn.
LBS_SORT	Sorts alphabetically any string added to the list box when using the LB_ADDSTRING message.
LBS_STANDARD	Combines the LBS_SORT, LBS_NOTIFY, and WS_BORDER styles.
LBS_USETABSTOPS	Tabs are expanded when drawing strings, and the application can use the LB_SETTABSTOPS message to change tab positions.
LBS_WANTKEYBOARDINPUT	The list box parent receives WM_VKEYTOITEM messages when the user presses a key and the list box has focus, allowing the owner to perform any special processing on keyboard input.

MDI Client Styles	Description
MDIS_ALLCHILDSTYLES	Allows MDI child windows to use any window style listed in this table. If this style flag is not specified, MDI child windows are limited to the styles available in Table 2-2.

Rich Edit Styles	Description
ES_DISABLENOSCROLL	When scroll bars are not needed, they will be disabled instead of hidden.
ES_NOIME	**Asian languages only:** Disables the input method editor operation.
ES_SELFIME	**Asian languages only:** The rich edit control will let the application handle all IME operations.
ES_SUNKEN	Gives the appearance of a sunken border around the rich text control.
ES_VERTICAL	**Asian languages only:** Draws text and other objects in a vertical direction.

Scroll Bar Styles	Description
SBS_BOTTOMALIGN	Aligns the bottom of the scroll bar with the bottom edge of the rectangle specified in the CreateWindowEx function. Use this style with the SBS_HORZ style.
SBS_HORZ	Creates a horizontal scroll bar. If the SBS_BOTTOMALIGN or SBS_TOPALIGN styles are not used, the scroll bar has the width, height, and position specified by the parameters of the CreateWindowEx function.
SBS_LEFTALIGN	Aligns the left edge of the scroll bar with the left edge of the rectangle specified in the CreateWindowEx function. Use this style with the SBS_VERT style.
SBS_RIGHTALIGN	Aligns the right edge of the scroll bar with the right edge of the rectangle specified in the CreateWindowEx function. Use this style with the SBS_VERT style.
SBS_SIZEBOX	Creates a scroll bar with a size box. If the SBS_SIZEBOXBOTTOMRIGHTALIGN or SBS_SIZEBOXTOPLEFTALIGN styles are not used, the scroll bar has the width, height, and position specified by the CreateWindowEx parameters.
SBS_SIZEBOXBOTTOM-RIGHTALIGN	Aligns the size box with the lower-right corner of the rectangle specified by the CreateWindowEx function. Use this style with the SBS_SIZEBOX style.

Scroll Bar Styles	Description
SBS_SIZEBOXTOPLEFTALIGN	Aligns the size box with the upper-left corner of the rectangle specified by the CreateWindowEx function. Use this style with the SBS_SIZEBOX style.
SBS_SIZEGRIP	This is the same as the SBS_SIZEBOX style, but with a raised edge.
SBS_TOPALIGN	Aligns the top of the scroll bar with the top edge of the rectangle specified in the CreateWindowEx function. Use this style with the SBS_HORZ style.
SBS_VERT	Creates a vertical scroll bar. If the SBS_RIGHTALIGN or SBS_LEFTALIGN styles are not used, the scroll bar has the width, height, and size as specified in the CreateWindowEx function.

Static Control Styles	Description
SS_BITMAP	Creates a static control that displays the bitmap specified by the lpWindowName parameter, ignoring the nWidth and nHeight parameters as these are calculated according to the bitmap's width and height. The lpWindowName parameter specifies a bitmap name as defined in the resource file; it is not a filename.
SS_BLACKFRAME	Creates a box that is drawn using the same color as window frames, usually black.
SS_BLACKRECT	Creates a filled rectangle using the same color as window frames, usually black.
SS_CENTER	Creates a static text control that is centered and wrapped as necessary.
SS_CENTERIMAGE	Causes controls that have the SS_BITMAP or SS_ICON styles to keep the image centered vertically and horizontally when the control is resized. If the bitmap is smaller than the client area, the client area is filled with the color of the pixel in the bitmap's upper-left corner. This does not happen when an icon is used.
SS_ENDELLIPSIS	**Windows 2000 or later:** If a string is too long to be fully displayed in the bounding rectangle, it is truncated and ellipses are displayed.
SS_ENHMETAFILE	Displays an enhanced metafile. The metafile is scaled to fit the static control's client area. The lpWindowName parameter is the name of an enhanced metafile as defined in the resource file; it is not a filename.
SS_ETCHEDFRAME	Draws the frame of the static control using the EDGE_ETCHED style. See the DrawEdge function for more information.
SS_ETCHEDHORZ	Draws the top and bottom sides of the static control frame using the EDGE_ETCHED style. See the DrawEdge function for more information.
SS_ETCHEDVERT	Draws the left and right sides of the static control frame using the EDGE_ETCHED style. See the DrawEdge function for more information.
SS_GRAYFRAME	Creates a box that is drawn using the same color as the desktop, usually gray.
SS_GRAYRECT	Creates a filled rectangle using the same color as the desktop, usually gray.
SS_ICON	Creates a static control that displays the icon specified by the lpWindowName parameter, ignoring the nWidth and nHeight parameters as these are calculated according to the icon's width and height. The lpWindowName parameter is the name of an icon as defined in the resource file; it is not a filename.
SS_LEFT	Creates a static text control that is left aligned and wrapped as necessary.
SS_LEFTNOWORDWRAP	Creates a static text control that is left aligned. Tabs are expanded, but words are not wrapped and are clipped at the boundaries of the control.

Static Control Styles	Description
SS_NOPREFIX	The ampersand (&) character in the control's text is not interpreted as an accelerator.
SS_NOTIFY	When the user clicks or double-clicks the control, STN_CLICKED, STN_DBLCLK, STN_ENABLE, and STN_DISABLE messages are sent to the parent.
SS_OWNERDRAW	The window owning this control is responsible for its visual display, and will receive a WM_DRAWITEM message when the control needs to be drawn.
SS_PATHELLIPSIS	**Windows 2000 or later:** If the string is too long to be fully displayed within the bounding rectangle, characters from the middle of the string will be truncated and replaced with an ellipsis. If the backslash character (i.e., "\") is contained within the string, Windows will try to reserve as much of the text after the last backslash as is possible within the bounding rectangle.
SS_RIGHT	Creates a static text control that is right aligned and wrapped as necessary.
SS_RIGHTJUST	With this style, the lower-right corner of a static control with the SS_BITMAP or SS_ICON style flags set remains fixed when the control is resized. Only the top and left sides will be adjusted to accommodate a new icon or bitmap.
SS_SIMPLE	Creates a left-aligned static text control. The parent window or dialog must not process the WM_CTLCOLORSTATIC message when using this style.
SS_SUNKEN	Creates a box that has a perimeter resembling a lowered bevel.
SS_WHITEFRAME	Creates a box that is drawn using the same color as the window background, usually white.
SS_WHITERECT	Creates a filled rectangle using the same color as the window background, usually white.
SS_WORDELLIPSIS	**Windows 2000 or later:** Any word that cannot be fully displayed within the bounding rectangle will be truncated and replaced with an ellipsis.

DestroyWindow   Windows.pas

Syntax

```
DestroyWindow(
  hWnd: HWND           {a handle to a window}
): BOOL;               {returns TRUE or FALSE}
```

Description

This function is used to destroy windows created with the CreateWindowEx function, or modeless dialogs created with the CreateDialog function. Child windows of the specified window are destroyed first, then the window's menu is destroyed, the thread message queue is emptied, any active timers are destroyed, clipboard ownership is removed, and the clipboard viewer chain is broken if the window is at the top of the viewer chain. Using this function to remove the parent window of an application will end that application. The messages WM_DESTROY and WM_NCDESTROY are sent to the window before it is deleted to deactivate it and remove its focus. This function cannot be used to destroy a window created by a different thread. If the window to be destroyed is a child window and does not have the WS_EX_NOPARENTNOTIFY style specified, a WM_PARENT-NOTIFY message is sent to its parent.

> **Note:** A thread cannot use this function to destroy a window created by a different thread.

Parameters

hWnd: The handle to the window to be destroyed.

Return Value

If this function succeeds, it returns TRUE if the window is destroyed; otherwise, it returns FALSE. To get extended error information, call the GetLastError function.

See Also

CreateWindowEx, UnregisterClass, WM_DESTROY, WM_NCDESTROY, WM_PARENTNOTIFY

Example

See Listing 2-8 under CreateWindowEx.

MessageBox   Windows.pas

Syntax

```
MessageBox(
    hWnd: HWND;              {the handle of the owning window}
    lpText: PChar;           {the message text}
    lpCaption: PChar;        {the message box window caption}
    uType: UINT              {type and style flags}
): Integer;                  {returns a flag indicating the selected button}
```

Description

MessageBox is used when the application needs to display a simple message to the user, or receive a confirmation or feedback from the user. Common applications of this function are to alert the user to an error condition or to ask for confirmation of an action, such as asking the user if they want to close an application before saving all of their work.

> **Note:** If the MB_ICONHAND and MB_SYSTEMMODAL flags are used, the message box is displayed regardless of available memory. However, the lpText string will not be automatically broken to fit within the message box borders.

Parameters

hWnd: The handle to the window that owns the message box. If 0 is specified, the message box will have no owner.

Window Creation Functions 47

lpText: The text to be displayed as the message.

lpCaption: The text for the message box window caption. If NIL is passed, the caption will default to "Error."

uType: A series of flags affecting the appearance and behavior of the message box. This value can be a combination of one flag from each of the following tables.

Return Value

If the message box failed to create, the function returns 0; otherwise it returns one of the values from Table 2-11.

See Also

CreateWindowEx, MessageBeep, SetForegroundWindow*

Example

Listing 2-9: Creating a message box

```
procedure TForm1.Button1Click(Sender: TObject);
begin
  {Display a simple message box}
  MessageBox(Handle, 'This is a simple message box.', 'MessageBox Text',
             MB_OK or MB_ICONINFORMATION);
end;
```

Figure 2-9: The example message box

Table 2-6: MessageBox uType button styles

Button Styles	Description
MB_ABORTRETRYIGNORE	Displays three buttons: Abort, Retry, and Ignore.
MB_CANCELTRYCONTINUE	**Windows 2000 or later:** Displays three buttons: Cancel, Try Again, and Continue. This flag should be used in favor of MB_ABORTRETRYIGNORE.
MB_OK	Displays an OK button.
MB_OKCANCEL	Displays an OK and a Cancel button.
MB_RETRYCANCEL	Displays a Retry and a Cancel button.
MB_YESNO	Displays a Yes and a No button.
MB_YESNOCANCEL	Displays three buttons: Yes, No, and Cancel.

Chapter 2

Table 2-7: MessageBox uType icon styles

Icon Styles	Icon Graphic	Description
MB_ICONEXCLAMATION, MB_ICONWARNING	⚠	Displays an exclamation point symbol. Typically used to confirm an action.
MB_ICONINFORMATION, MB_ICONASTERISK	ⓘ	Displays a lowercase "i" icon. Typically used to display general information that may be of use to the user.
MB_ICONQUESTION	❓	Displays a question mark icon. Typically used in conjunction with Help systems.
MB_ICONSTOP, MB_ICONERROR, MB_ICONHAND	⊗	Displays a red stop sign icon. Typically used to confirm destructive actions or to indicate an error condition.

Table 2-8: MessageBox uType default button flags

Default Button Flag	Description
MB_DEFBUTTON1	Makes the first button displayed the default button. This flag is used by default.
MB_DEFBUTTON2	Makes the second button displayed the default button.
MB_DEFBUTTON3	Makes the third button displayed the default button.
MB_DEFBUTTON4	Makes the fourth button displayed the default button.

Table 2-9: MessageBox uType modality flags

Modality Flag	Description
MB_APPLMODAL	Displays the message box as a modal window relative to the window identified by the hWnd parameter. This means that the messagebox window must be closed before interaction with the owning window can resume, but the user can move to other windows in the system, or even in the application depending on window hierarchy. This flag is used by default.
MB_SYSTEMMODAL	Same as MB_APPLMODAL, except that the WS_EX_TOPMOST style is used when creating the message box window.
MB_TASKMODAL	Same as MB_APPLMODAL, except that all top-level windows of the current application are disabled if 0 is specified in the hWnd parameter.

Table 2-10: MessageBox uType optional flags (one or more of these flags may be used)

Optional Flag	Description
MB_DEFAULT_DESKTOP_ONLY	**Windows NT/2000 or later:** Same as MB_SERVICE_NOTIFICATION, except that the message box window is displayed only on the default desktop.
MB_HELP	**Windows 95/98 or later:** Displays a Help button. When the Help button is pressed (or the user presses F1) a WM_HELP message is sent to the window specified by the hWnd parameter.
MB_RIGHT	Right justifies all text in the message box.
MB_RTLREADING	**Arabic and Hebrew Versions:** Displays the message box text and caption in right-to-left reading order.

Optional Flag	Description
MB_SETFOREGROUND	Makes the message box the foreground window.
MB_TOPMOST	Creates the message box using the WS_EX_TOPMOST window style.
MB_SERVICE_NOTIFICATION	**Windows NT/2000 or later:** Used by services, this displays the message box on the currently active desktop, even in the absence of a logged in user. The hWnd parameter must be 0 when this flag is used.

Table 2-11: MessageBox return values

Return Value	Description
IDABORT	The Abort button was selected.
IDCANCEL	The Cancel button was selected.
IDCONTINUE	The Continue button was selected.
IDIGNORE	The Ignore button was selected.
IDNO	The No button was selected.
IDOK	The OK button was selected.
IDRETRY	The Retry button was selected.
IDTRYAGAIN	The Try Again button was selected.
IDYES	The Yes button was selected.

RegisterClass   Windows.pas

Syntax

```
RegisterClass(
  const lpWndClass: TWndClass          {a window class data structure}
): ATOM;                               {returns a unique atom}
```

Description

RegisterClass is used to create custom Windows controls and non-existing classes for new windows. This same class can be used to create any number of windows in an application. All classes that an application registers are unregistered when the application terminates.

> **Note:** Under Windows 95/98, any window classes registered by a DLL are unregistered when the DLL is unloaded. By contrast, on Windows NT/2000 this does not happen; when a DLL is unloaded, it must explicitly unregister any window classes it registered while it was loaded.

Parameters

lpWndClass: A variable of the type TWndClass data structure. The data structure is defined as:

```
TWndClass = packed record
    Style: UINT;                       {class style flags}
```

```
        lpfnWndProc: TFNWndProc;        {a pointer to the window procedure}
        cbClsExtra: Integer;            {extra class memory}
        cbWndExtra: Integer;            {extra window memory}
        hInstance: HINST;               {a handle to the module instance}
        hIcon: HICON;                   {a handle to an icon}
        hCursor: HCURSOR;               {a handle to a cursor}
        hbrBackground: HBRUSH;          {a handle to the background brush}
        lpszMenuName: PAnsiChar;        {the menu name}
        lpszClassName: PAnsiChar;       {the class name}
end;
```

Style: Defines some of the default behavior of the window. The style constants available are listed in Table 2-12, and can be combined using a Boolean OR operator, i.e., CS_DBLCLKS OR CS_NOCLOSE.

lpfnWndProc: The address of the application-defined callback function, known as the window procedure, that processes messages for this window. The syntax for this callback function is described below.

cbClsExtra: Specifies the number of extra bytes to allocate at the end of the window class structure. This space can be used to store any additional information required. Use the SetClassLong and GetClassLong functions to access this space. Windows initializes these bytes to zero.

Windows 95: The RegisterClass function fails if this parameter specifies more than 40 bytes.

cbWndExtra: Specifies the number of extra bytes to allocate at the end of the window instance. Windows initializes these bytes to zero. This space can be used to store any additional information required. Use SetWindowLong and GetWindowLong to access this space. If an application uses the TWndClass structure to register a dialog box created by using the CLASS directive in a resource file, this member must be set to DLGWINDOWEXTRA.

Windows 95: The RegisterClass function fails if this parameter specifies more than 40 bytes.

hInstance: The instance handle that contains the window procedure for this class.

hIcon: A handle to an icon resource that is used when a window of this class is minimized. If this member is set to zero, the window will use the Windows logo icon.

hCursor: A handle to a mouse cursor resource. If this member is set to zero, the application is responsible for setting the cursor when the mouse moves into the window. By default, the window uses the standard arrow cursor.

hbrBackground: A handle to a brush that will be used to paint the background of any window belonging to this window class. One of the system color values in Table 2-13 can be used in place of a brush handle. Background brushes are automatically deleted when the class is freed. If this member is set to zero, the application is responsible for painting its own background when requested to update its client area. To determine if the background must be painted, the application can either process the WM_ERASEBKGND message, or test the fErase member of the PAINTSTRUCT structure filled by the BeginPaint function.

lpszMenuName: A pointer to a null-terminated string with the default menu resource name for this class, as it appears in the resource file. If an integer was used to identify the menu, use MakeIntResource to convert it to a string. Set this member to NIL if this class does not have a default menu.

lpszClassName: Either a pointer to a null-terminated string that describes the class name, or an atom. If this specifies an atom, the atom must have been created with a call to GlobalAddAtom. The atom, a 16-bit value, must be in the low-order word of ClassName and the high-order word must be zero. This value is used in the lpClassName parameter of the CreateWindowEx function.

Return Value

If this function succeeds, it returns an atom that uniquely identifies the new window class. Otherwise, the return value is zero. To get extended error information, call the GetLastError function.

Callback Syntax

```
WindowProc(
hWnd: HWND;             {a handle to a window}
uMsg: UINT;             {the message identifier}
wParam: WPARAM;         {32-bit message information}
lParam: LPARAM          {32-bit message information}
): Longint;             {returns a 32-bit value}
```

Description

This is an application-defined callback function that processes messages sent to a window, usually in the form of a Case statement. This function can perform any required task.

Parameters

hWnd: The handle to the window receiving the message.

uMsg: The message identifier.

wParam: A 32-bit value that is dependent on the type of message received.

lParam: A 32-bit value that is dependent on the type of message received.

Return Value

The return value of the window procedure is dependent on the message received and the result of processing the message.

See Also

CreateWindowEx, GetClassInfo*, GetClassLong*, GetClassName*, RegisterClassEx, SetClassLong*, UnregisterClass

Example

See Listing 2-8 under CreateWindowEx.

Table 2-12: RegisterClass lpWndClass.Style values

Value	Description
CS_BYTEALIGNCLIENT	Aligns the window's client area to byte boundaries horizontally. This will improve drawing performance, but the width of the window and its horizontal positioning are affected.
CS_BYTEALIGNWINDOW	Aligns the entire window to horizontal byte boundaries. This will improve performance when moving or resizing a window, but the width of the window and its horizontal positioning are affected.
CS_CLASSDC	Allocates one device context (DC) to be shared by every window in this class. If multiple threads attempt to use this DC at the same time, only one thread is allowed to complete its drawing operations successfully.
CS_DBLCLKS	Sends the window procedure a double-click message when a double-click occurs within the window.
CS_GLOBALCLASS	Allows an application to create a window of this class regardless of the hInstance parameter passed to the CreateWindowEx function. If this style is not specified, the hInstance parameter passed to these functions must be the same hInstance parameter passed to the RegisterClass function. A global class is produced by creating a window class in a DLL. In Windows NT, the DLL must be listed in the registry under the key HKEY_LOCAL_MACHINE \Software\Microsoft\Windows NT\CurrentVersion\Windows\ APPINIT_DLLS. Whenever a process starts, Windows loads these DLLs in the context of the newly created process before calling the main function of that process. The DLL must register the class during its initialization procedure. Essentially, this will create a class that is available to every application while the application that created the class is running. A common example would be new custom controls implemented in a DLL.
CS_HREDRAW	Causes the entire window to be repainted when the width of the client area changes.
CS_NOCLOSE	Disables the Close command on the system menu.
CS_OWNDC	Allocates a unique device context for each window created with this class.
CS_PARENTDC	Any window created with this class uses the parent window's device context. This will improve an application's performance. When an application calls the GetDC function and passes it the handle of a window whose class has the CS_PARENTDC style, Windows searches for a device context that has been precalculated for the parent window. If all child windows have the CS_PARENTDC style, Windows does not have to recalculate a device context for any of them.
CS_SAVEBITS	When a portion of this window is obscured by another window, this style causes the window to save this hidden area as a bitmap, which is used to repaint the window when the hidden area reappears. Windows will redisplay this image at its original location, and will not send a WM_PAINT message to a window that was previously obscured, assuming that the memory used by the bitmap has not been discarded and that other screen actions have not invalidated the image. This is useful for small windows that are displayed briefly, but will decrease performance as Windows must allocate memory to store the bitmap before displaying the window.
CS_VREDRAW	Causes the entire window to be repainted when the height of the client area changes.

Table 2-13: RegisterClass lpWndClass.hbrBackground values

Value	Description
COLOR_3DDKSHADOW	The dark shadow color for three-dimensional display elements.
COLOR_3DLIGHT	The lighted edge color for three-dimensional display elements.
COLOR_ACTIVEBORDER	The active window border color.
COLOR_ACTIVECAPTION	The active window caption color.
COLOR_APPWORKSPACE	The background color used in multiple document interface applications.
COLOR_BACKGROUND	The desktop color.
COLOR_BTNFACE	The color of pushbutton faces.
COLOR_BTNHIGHLIGHT	The color of a highlighted pushbutton.
COLOR_BTNSHADOW	The shaded edge color on pushbuttons.
COLOR_BTNTEXT	The text color on pushbuttons.
COLOR_CAPTIONTEXT	The text color used in caption, size box, and scroll bar arrow box controls.
COLOR_GRAYTEXT	The color of disabled text. This will be set to zero if the display driver cannot support solid gray.
COLOR_HIGHLIGHT	The color used for selected items in a control.
COLOR_HIGHLIGHTTEXT	The color used for the text of selected items in a control.
COLOR_INACTIVEBORDER	The inactive window border color.
COLOR_INACTIVECAPTION	The inactive window caption color.
COLOR_INACTIVECAPTIONTEXT	The text color in an inactive caption bar.
COLOR_INFOBK	The background color for tooltip controls.
COLOR_INFOTEXT	The text color for tooltip controls.
COLOR_MENU	The menu background color.
COLOR_MENUTEXT	The text color used in menus.
COLOR_SCROLLBAR	The scroll bar gray area color.
COLOR_WINDOW	The window background color.
COLOR_WINDOWFRAME	The window frame color.
COLOR_WINDOWTEXT	The color of text used in a window.

RegisterClassEx *Windows.pas*

Syntax

```
RegisterClassEx(
  const WndClass: TWndClassEx    {an extended window class data structure}
): ATOM;                          {returns a unique atom}
```

Description

This function is identical to the RegisterClass function, except that there are two extra members added to the TWndClass data type. One specifies the size of the TWndClassEx structure in bytes, and the other allows a small icon to be specified that is used in the title bar of windows created with this class.

54 ■ Chapter 2

> **Note:** Under Windows 95/98, any window classes registered by a DLL are unregistered when the DLL is unloaded. By contrast, on Windows NT/2000 this does not happen; when a DLL is unloaded, it must explicitly unregister any window classes it registered while it was loaded.

Parameters

WndClass: A variable of the type TWndClassEx data structure. The data structure is defined as:

```
TWndClassEx = packed record
    cbSize: UINT;                     {the size of this structure}
    Style: UINT;                      {class style flags}
    lpfnWndProc: TFNWndProc;          {a pointer to the window procedure}
    cbClsExtra: Integer;              {extra class memory bytes}
    cbWndExtra: Integer;              {extra window memory bytes}
    hInstance: HINST;                 {a handle to the module instance}
    hIcon: HICON;                     {a handle to an icon}
    hCursor: HCURSOR;                 {a handle to a cursor}
    hbrBackground: HBRUSH;            {a handle to the background brush}
    lpszMenuName: PAnsiChar;          {the menu name}
    lpszClassName: PAnsiChar;         {the class name}
    hIconSm: HICON;                   {a handle to a small icon}
end;
```

Note that the TWndClassEx data structure is identical to the TWndClass structure, with the cbSize member added to the beginning and the hIconSm member added to the end. Refer to the RegisterClass function for a description of the other members of this data structure.

cbSize: Specifies the size of the TWndClassEx structure in bytes, and can be set with SizeOf(TWndClassEx). This is used when retrieving information about a class.

hIconSm: A handle to a small icon that will be displayed in the title bar of windows created with this class.

Return Value

If this function succeeds, an atom that uniquely identifies the new window class is returned; otherwise, it returns zero. To get extended error information, call the GetLastError function.

See Also

CreateWindowEx, GetClassInfoEx*, GetClassLong*, GetClassName*, RegisterClass, SetClassLong*, UnregisterClass

Example

See Listing 2-8 under CreateWindowEx.

UnregisterClass   Windows.pas

Syntax

```
UnregisterClass(
  lpClassName: PChar;        {a pointer to the class name string}
  hInstance: HINST           {a handle to the module instance}
): BOOL;                     {returns TRUE or FALSE}
```

Description

This function removes a class that was previously registered with the RegisterClass or RegisterClassEx functions. The memory that was allocated by these functions is freed. This function is used while a program is still running. An application must destroy any windows that were created with the specified class before calling this function. Any classes that an application registers are automatically removed when the application terminates.

> **Note:** Under Windows 95/98, any window classes registered by a DLL are unregistered when the DLL is unloaded. By contrast, on Windows NT/2000 this does not happen; when a DLL is unloaded, it must explicitly unregister any window classes it registered while it was loaded.

Parameters

lpClassName: Either a pointer to a null-terminated string that contains the name of the class, or an integer atom. If this specifies an atom, the atom must have been created with a call to GlobalAddAtom. The atom, a 16-bit value less than $C000, must be in the low-order word of ClassName and the high-order word must be zero. System global classes, such as dialog box controls, cannot be unregistered.

hInstance: The instance handle of the module that created the class.

Return Value

If the function succeeds, it returns TRUE; otherwise it returns FALSE. This function will fail if the class could not be found or if there are windows still open that are using this class. To get extended error information, call the GetLastError function.

See Also

RegisterClass, RegisterClassEx

Example

See Listing 2-8 under CreateWindowEx.

Chapter 3

Message Processing Functions

Modern programming techniques have evolved far beyond the old DOS procedural programming metaphors. In today's world, we develop event-driven applications. An event-driven application is one that is oriented toward responding to events, such as user input or a notification from the system. This event-driven architecture takes the form of messages that are sent between the operating system and the application. A message signals the application or the operating system that something has happened, and some sort of processing should take place as a result of this event. Messages are quite literally the lifeblood of Windows; hardly anything occurs within the Windows operating system or a Windows application without unleashing a flurry of messages. Fortunately, Delphi developers rarely have to deal with the tedium of responding to all of these messages, but understanding how Windows applications process and dispatch messages will be necessary when an application is called upon to handle something out of the ordinary.

The vast majority of messages are sent to an application as a direct result of user input, such as moving the mouse, clicking a button or scroll bar, or activating another application, but system events can also trigger a message, such as when hardware configuration has changed as a result of inserting or removing an expansion card. At the heart of every Windows program is a small loop that retrieves these messages and dispatches them to their destination window procedures. Fortunately, Delphi automatically takes care of this message management through the TApplication object.

The Message Queue and Message Loop

Each thread has its own message queue. This can be thought of as a first in/first out structure, where messages are processed in the order in which they were received. This takes place in the message loop, located in the WinMain function of a traditional Windows application. This message loop is implemented in Delphi as the ProcessMessages method of the TApplication object. This function spins in a tight loop, continually retrieving messages from the message queue and, after filtering out and handling specific message types, dispatching them to their destination window procedures. From the Forms unit, the message loop in every Delphi application is implemented as:

Listing 3-1: The application message loop

```
procedure TApplication.ProcessMessages;
var
```

```
  Msg: TMsg;
begin
  while ProcessMessage(Msg) do {loop};
end;

function TApplication.ProcessMessage(var Msg: TMsg): Boolean;
var
  Handled: Boolean;
begin
  Result := False;
  if PeekMessage(Msg, 0, 0, 0, PM_REMOVE) then
  begin
    Result := True;
    if Msg.Message <> WM_QUIT then
    begin
      Handled := False;
      if Assigned(FOnMessage) then FOnMessage(Msg, Handled);
      if not IsHintMsg(Msg) and not Handled and not IsMDIMsg(Msg) and
        not IsKeyMsg(Msg) and not IsDlgMsg(Msg) then
      begin
        TranslateMessage(Msg);
        DispatchMessage(Msg);
      end;
    end
    else
      FTerminate := True;
  end;
end;
```

An application could set up its own message loop by simply creating a loop that continually called GetMessage or PeekMessage, TranslateMessage if needed, and DispatchMessage until a specific message was retrieved that signaled an end of the loop. This is, in fact, how Delphi implements modal dialog boxes.

Even though the main thread in an application automatically gets a message queue, each individual thread that an application creates can have its own message queue. A thread creates a message queue the first time it calls any of the functions in GDI32.DLL or USER32.DLL. Once a thread has created its own message queue, it must implement a message loop using GetMessage or PeekMessage, and it will receive messages sent to it via the PostThreadMessage function.

Windows Hooks

An application can intercept messages going to itself or other applications through the use of hook functions. A hook function is installed using the SetWindowsHookEx function, and uninstalled using the UnhookWindowsHookEx function. The same application can install multiple hook functions, forming a chain of hook functions intercepting messages for their specific hook type. The last hook function installed becomes the first hook function in the hook chain, and will receive messages before the other hook functions in the chain.

The installed hook function receives the indicated messages for its hook type before the destination window procedure. If a hook function does not handle a message that it has received, it should send it to the other hook functions in the chain by using the CallNextHookEx function. A hook that intercepts messages for only one application can reside in the source code for that application. However, a hook that intercepts messages for multiple applications or for the system must reside in a separate dynamic-link library.

In the case of a global hook DLL, calling UnhookWindowsHookEx will uninstall the global hook, but the DLL containing the hook procedure will not be unloaded. This is because the DLL will be called by every application in the system that has installed a hook in the DLL's particular hook chain. However, the system will eventually free the DLL after all processes explicitly linked to the DLL have terminated and all processes that have called the hook procedure inside the DLL have resumed processing outside of the hook procedure. The following example illustrates a DLL that implements a global mouse hook.

Listing 3-2: Setting a global mouse hook

The DLL containing the system-wide mouse hook:

```
library GMousehook;

uses
  SysUtils,
  Classes,
  WinTypes,
  WinProcs,
  Messages;

var
  {holds various global values}
  IsHooked: Boolean;
  HookHandle: HHook;
  DesktopWin: HWND;

{this is the procedure called every time a mouse message is processed}
function HookProc(Code: Integer; wParam: WPARAM; lParam: LPARAM): LRESULT;
                                                                  stdcall;
begin
  {if the user clicked the left mouse button, output a sound}
  if (wParam = WM_LBUTTONDOWN) then
    MessageBeep(MB_ICONASTERISK);

  {call the next hook in the chain. note that leaving this out would
   effectively remove this message}
  Result := CallNextHookEx(HookHandle, Code, wParam, lParam);
end;

function SetHook: Boolean; stdcall;
begin
  Result := FALSE;

  {make sure the hook is not already set}
  if IsHooked then
    Exit;

  {get a handle to the desktop window}
```

```
    DesktopWin := GetDesktopWindow;

    {set this hook as a system level hook}
    HookHandle := SetWindowsHookEx(WH_MOUSE, HookProc, HInstance, 0);

    {indicate if the hook was set right}
    Result := HookHandle <> 0;
end;

function RemoveHook: Boolean; stdcall;
begin
  Result := FALSE;

  {remove the hook}
  if (not IsHooked) and (HookHandle <> 0) then
    Result := UnhookWindowsHookEx(HookHandle);

  {reset the global variable}
  IsHooked := FALSE;
end;

exports
  SetHook name 'SetHook',
  RemoveHook name 'RemoveHook',
  HookProc name 'HookProc';

begin
   IsHooked := FALSE;
end.
```

The example that hooks and unhooks the system-wide mouse hook:

```
unit MouseHookDemoU;

interface

uses
  Windows, Messages, SysUtils, Variants, Classes, Graphics, Controls, Forms,
  Dialogs, StdCtrls;

type
  TForm1 = class(TForm)
    Label1: TLabel;
    Button1: TButton;
    Button2: TButton;
    procedure Button1Click(Sender: TObject);
    procedure Button2Click(Sender: TObject);
  private
    { Private declarations }
  public
    { Public declarations }
  end;

  function SetHook: Boolean; stdcall;
  function RemoveHook: Boolean; stdcall;

var
```

```
    Form1: TForm1;

implementation

{$R *.dfm}

function SetHook; external 'GMouseHook.dll' name 'SetHook';
function RemoveHook; external 'GMouseHook.dll' name 'RemoveHook';

procedure TForm1.Button1Click(Sender: TObject);
begin
  {set the hook}
  if SetHook then
    ShowMessage('Global Mouse Hook Set, Click on Desktop')
  else
    ShowMessage('Global Mouse Hook Not Set');
end;

procedure TForm1.Button2Click(Sender: TObject);
begin
  {remove the hook}
  if RemoveHook then
    ShowMessage('Global Mouse Hook Removed, Click on Desktop')
  else
    ShowMessage('Global Mouse Hook Not Removed');
end;
```

Interprocess Communication

Messages allow applications to communicate with each other through the use of PostMessage, SendMessage, and similar functions. Two applications can create a new message identifier simply by adding a constant value to WM_USER (i.e., WM_NEW-MESSAGE = WM_USER+1), using this new message identifier to send custom messages back and forth. However, be aware that PostMessage, SendMessage, and other functions can broadcast a message to every window in the system. If this user-defined message identifier is broadcast to all applications, it is possible that other applications may contain a handler for the same user-defined message identifier as defined by the sending application, which could produce unexpected results. For this reason, it is best if the developer registered a unique message for interprocess communication using the RegisterWindowMessage function. Given a unique string, this will ensure that only the applications that registered the same string with RegisterWindowMessage will receive the message.

Delphi vs. the Windows API

Delphi does not have any built-in functionality to support message hooks, so programmers must use the Windows API for this type of functionality. Setting message hooks is a very powerful technique, and can be used to create applications like computer-based training aids or even to override many system level functions and disable unwanted operations (i.e., disabling Ctrl+Alt+Del for applications running on a public kiosk).

Messages are an integral part of how Windows works, and understanding this complex system can provide developers with new opportunities for advanced functionality, especially in specialized applications. Delphi tries very hard to hide most of the complexity of message processing from the developer, and indeed this is one of its strengths, as it takes much of the tedium of message processing out of Windows programming. However, sometimes it is necessary to delve into the inner workings of message loops and the message processing system in order to provide advanced functionality, and when working at this level you'll be using many of the message processing API functions.

Message Processing Functions

The following message functions are covered in this chapter:

Table 3-1: Message processing functions

Function	Description
BroadcastSystemMessage	Sends a message to applications or drivers.
CallNextHookEx	Sends hook information to the next hook in the chain.
CallWindowProc	Passes a message to a window procedure.
DefFrameProc	Passes any unhandled messages to the default window procedure of a frame window for default processing.
DefMDIChildProc	Passes any unhandled messages to the default window procedure of an MDI child window for default processing.
DefWindowProc	Passes any unhandled messages to the default window procedure for default processing.
DispatchMessage	Dispatches a message to a window procedure.
GetMessage	Retrieves and removes a message from the message queue.
GetMessageExtraInfo	Retrieves extra message information.
GetMessagePos	Retrieves the coordinates of the mouse cursor when the last message was retrieved.
GetMessageTime	Retrieves the create time of the last message retrieved.
GetQueueStatus	Retrieves the types of messages found in the queue.
InSendMessage	Indicates if a message was sent via one of the SendMessage functions.
PeekMessage	Retrieves a message from the message queue, optionally removing it.
PostMessage	Posts a message to a message queue.
PostQuitMessage	Posts a WM_QUIT message to a message queue.
PostThreadMessage	Posts a message to the message queue of a thread.
RegisterWindowMessage	Retrieves a unique message identifier for an application-defined message.
ReplyMessage	Sends a message processing return value back to a SendMessage function.
SendMessage	Sends a message to a window procedure.
SendMessageCallback	Sends a message to a window procedure, and provides a callback function that is called when the message is processed.
SendMessageTimeout	Sends a message to a window procedure, returning after a specified timeout period.
SendNotifyMessage	Sends a message to the window procedure in another thread and returns immediately.

Message Processing Functions

Function	Description
SetMessageExtraInfo	Sets extra message information.
SetWindowsHookEx	Places a hook procedure into a hook procedure chain.
TranslateMessage	Translates virtual key messages into character messages.
UnhookWindowsHookEx	Removes a hook procedure from a hook chain.
WaitMessage	Yields control to other threads until the calling thread's message queue receives a message.

BroadcastSystemMessage   Windows.pas

Syntax

```
BroadcastSystemMessage(
Flags: DWORD;            {flags specifying message sending options}
Recipients: PDWORD;      {flags specifying message recipients}
uiMessage: UINT;         {the identifier of the message to send}
wParam: WPARAM;          {a 32-bit message specific value}
lParam: LPARAM           {a 32-bit message specific value}
): Longint;              {returns a 32-bit value}
```

Description

This function sends the specified message to all indicated recipients. Unlike the SendMessage functions, this function can send messages to applications, drivers, and system components. If the BSF_QUERY flag is not specified in the Flags parameter, the function ignores message processing return values from recipients.

Parameters

Flags: Specifies message sending options. This parameter can be one or more values from Table 3-2.

Recipients: A pointer to a DWORD variable that contains flags indicating the recipients of the message. When the function returns, this variable will contain flags indicating which recipients actually received the message. The variable can contain one or more values from Table 3-3. If this parameter is set to NIL, the message is sent to every component on the system.

uiMessage: The identifier of the message being sent.

wParam: A 32-bit value dependent on the message being sent.

lParam: A 32-bit value dependent on the message being sent.

Return Value

If the function succeeded, it returns a positive value; otherwise it returns –1. If the Flags parameter is set to BSF_QUERY and at least one recipient returns the BROADCAST_QUERY_DENY value upon receiving the message, the function returns 0.

See Also

RegisterWindowMessage, SendMessage, SendNotifyMessage

Example

See Listing 3-3 under CallWindowProc.

Table 3-2: BroadcastSystemMessage Flags values

Value	Description
BSF_ALLOWSFW	**Windows 2000 or later:** Allows the recipient of the message to set the foreground window while processing the sent message.
BSF_FLUSHDISK	Process any pending disk read/write operations after each recipient returns from processing the message.
BSF_FORCEIFHUNG	Continue broadcasting the message even if the timeout period has expired or one of the recipients is hung.
BSF_IGNORECURRENTTASK	The message will not be sent to any windows belonging to the current task.
BSF_NOHANG	Hung applications are forced to time out. If a recipient is hung and causes a timeout, message broadcasting is discontinued.
BSF_NOTIMEOUTIFNOTHUNG	The application waits for a response from a recipient as long as the recipient is not hung, and does not time out.
BSF_POSTMESSAGE	Posts the message to the recipient's message queue and continues broadcasting. Do not use this value in combination with BSF_QUERY.
BSF_QUERY	The message is sent to one recipient at a time, and is sent to subsequent recipients only if the current recipient returns TRUE. Do not use this value in combination with BSF_POSTMESSAGE.
BSF_SENDNOTIFYMESSAGE	**Windows 2000 or later:** Sends the message via the SendNotifyMessage function. Do not use this value in combination with BSF_QUERY.

Table 3-3: BroadcastSystemMessage Recipients values

Value	Description
BSM_ALLCOMPONENTS	The message is broadcast to all system components. This is the equivalent to setting the Recipients parameter to NIL.
BSM_ALLDESKTOPS	**Windows NT/2000 or later:** The message is broadcast to all desktops. This flag requires the SE_TCB_NAME privilege.
BSM_APPLICATIONS	The message is broadcast to all running applications.
BSM_INSTALLABLEDRIVERS	**Windows 95/98/Me only:** The message is broadcast to all installable drivers.
BSM_NETDRIVER	**Windows 95/98/Me only:** The message is broadcast to all Windows-based network drivers.
BSM_VXDS	**Windows 95/98/Me only:** The message is broadcast to all system level device drivers.

CallNextHookEx   Windows.pas

Syntax

```
CallNextHookEx(
    hhk: HHOOK;              {a handle to the current hook}
    nCode: Integer;          {the hook code}
    wParam: WPARAM;          {a 32-bit hook specific value}
    lParam: LPARAM           {a 32-bit hook specific value}
): LRESULT;                  {returns the return value of the next hook in the chain}
```

Description

This function passes the specified hook information to the next hook procedure in the current hook procedure chain. Unless otherwise specified, calling the CallNextHookEx function is optional. An application can call this function inside of the hook procedure either before or after processing the hook information. If CallNextHookEx is not called, Windows does not call any subsequent hook procedures in the chain (those that were installed before the current hook procedure was installed).

Parameters

hhk: A handle to the current hook. This is the value returned from the SetWindowsHookEx function.

nCode: Specifies the hook code passed to the current hook procedure. This code is used by the next hook procedure in the chain to determine how to process the hook information.

wParam: Specifies the wParam parameter value passed to the current hook procedure. The meaning of this value is dependent on the type of hook associated with the current hook procedure chain.

lParam: Specifies the lParam parameter value passed to the current hook procedure. The meaning of this value is dependent on the type of hook associated with the current hook procedure chain.

Return Value

If the function succeeds, it returns the value returned by the next hook procedure in the chain. This value must also be returned by the current hook procedure. The meaning of the return value is dependent on the type of hook associated with the current hook chain. If the function fails, it returns zero.

See Also

SetWindowsHookEx, UnhookWindowsHookEx

Example

See Listing 3-16 under SetWindowsHookEx.

CallWindowProc   Windows.pas

Syntax

```
CallWindowProc(
  lpPrevWndFunc: TFNWndProc;    {a pointer to the previous window procedure}
  hWnd: HWND;                    {a handle to a window}
  Msg: UINT;                     {the identifier of the message to send}
  wParam: WPARAM;                {a 32-bit message specific value}
  lParam: LPARAM                 {a 32-bit message specific value}
): LRESULT;                      {returns a message specific return value}
```

Description

This function passes the specified message and its associated parameters to the window procedure pointed to by the lpPrevWndFunc parameter. An application must use this function in the window procedure of a subclassed window to pass any unhandled messages to the previous window procedure.

Parameters

lpPrevWndFunc: A pointer to the previous window procedure of the subclassed window. This value is returned from the SetClassLong or SetWindowLong functions when a window is subclassed, or by calling the GetClassLong or GetWindowLong functions with the appropriate index value to retrieve a pointer to the window procedure.

hWnd: A handle to the window associated with the window procedure pointed to by the lpPrevWndFunc parameter.

Msg: The message identifier to send to the window procedure.

wParam: A 32-bit value dependent on the message being sent.

lParam: A 32-bit value dependent on the message being sent.

Return Value

The value returned from this function specifies the result of the message processing and is dependent on the message sent.

See Also

GetClassLong*, GetWindowLong*, SetClassLong*, SetWindowLong*

Example

Listing 3-3: Calling the previous window procedure in a subclassed window

This application sends a message:

```
procedure TForm1.Button1Click(Sender: TObject);
var
  Recipients: DWORD;  // holds the recipient flags
begin
```

```
  {set the recipients to all applications}
  Recipients := BSM_APPLICATIONS;

  {send the user-defined message to all applications on the system by
   posting it to their message queues}
  BroadcastSystemMessage(BSF_IGNORECURRENTTASK or BSF_POSTMESSAGE, @Recipients,
                         UserMessage, 0, 0);
end;

procedure TForm1.FormCreate(Sender: TObject);
begin
  {register a user-defined message}
  UserMessage := RegisterWindowMessage('CallWindowProc Test Message');
end;
```

and this application receives the message:

```
{the prototype for the new window procedure}
    function NewWindowProc(TheWindow: HWND; Msg: Integer; wParam: WPARAM;
                           lParam: LPARAM): Longint; stdcall;

var
  Form1: TForm1;
  UserMessage: UINT;          // holds a user-defined message identifier
  OldWindowProc: TFNWndProc;  // holds a pointer to the previous window procedure

implementation

function NewWindowProc(TheWindow: HWND; Msg: Integer; wParam: WPARAM; lParam:
LPARAM): Longint;
var
  iLoop: Integer;             // a general loop counter
begin
  {if the user-defined message has been received...}
  if Msg=UserMessage then
  begin
    {...turn on some user interface elements}
    Form1.ProgressBar1.Visible := TRUE;
    Form1.Label2.Visible := TRUE;
    Form1.Repaint;

    {animate the progress bar for a short period of time}
    for iLoop := 0 to 100 do
    begin
      Form1.ProgressBar1.Position := iLoop;
      Sleep(10);
    end;

    {turn off the user interface elements}
    Form1.ProgressBar1.Visible := FALSE;
    Form1.Label2.Visible := FALSE;

    {the message was handled, so return a one}
    Result := 1;
  end
  else
    {any other message must be passed to the previous window procedure}
```

```
      Result := CallWindowProc(OldWindowProc, TheWindow, Msg, wParam, lParam);
end;

procedure TForm1.FormCreate(Sender: TObject);
begin
  {register a user-defined message}
  UserMessage := RegisterWindowMessage('CallWindowProc Test Message');

  {subclass this window.  replace the window procedure with one of
   ours.  this window procedure will receive messages before the
   previous one, allowing us to intercept and process any message
   before the rest of the application ever sees it.}
  OldWindowProc := TFNWndProc(SetWindowLong(Form1.Handle, GWL_WNDPROC,
                              Longint(@NewWindowProc)));
end;

procedure TForm1.FormDestroy(Sender: TObject);
begin
  {reset the window procedure to the previous one}
  SetWindowLong(Form1.Handle, GWL_WNDPROC, Longint(OldWindowProc));
end;
```

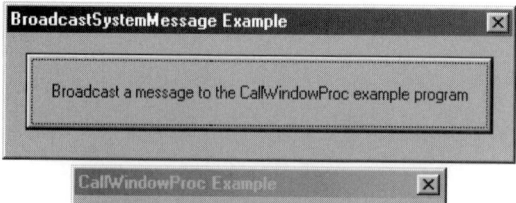

Figure 3-1:
The new window procedure received the message

DefFrameProc   Windows.pas

Syntax

```
DefFrameProc(
hWnd: HWND;                {a handle to the MDI frame window}
hWndMDIClient: HWND;       {a handle to the MDI client window}
uMsg: UINT;                {the identifier of the message to send}
wParam: WPARAM;            {a 32-bit message specific value}
lParam: LPARAM             {a 32-bit message specific value}
): LRESULT;                {returns a message specific return value}
```

Description

This function provides default message processing for any message not handled in the window procedure of a multiple document interface frame window. Any messages not explicitly handled by the MDI frame window procedure must be passed to the DefFrameProc function.

> *Note:* Non-MDI applications would send unhandled messages to the DefWindowProc function.

Parameters

hWnd: A handle to the MDI frame window.

hWndMDIClient: A handle to the MDI client window.

uMsg: The identifier of the message to send.

wParam: A 32-bit value dependent on the message being sent.

lParam: A 32-bit value dependent on the message being sent.

Return Value

The value returned from this function specifies the result of the message processing and is dependent on the message sent.

See Also

CallWindowProc, DefMDIChildProc, DefWindowProc

Example

Listing 3-4: Providing default message handling in an MDI frame window

```
program DefFrameProcExample;

uses
    Windows, Messages, SysUtils;

var
  TheMessage: TMsg;
  FrameWindow, ClientWindow, ChildWindow: HWND;

const
  {the ID for the first MDI child window}
  IDCHILDWND = 100;

{$R *.RES}

{this defines the window procedure for our frame window}
function FrameWindowProc(TheFrameWindow: HWnd; TheMessage, WParam,
                        LParam: Longint): Longint; stdcall;
var
    {this is used when creating an MDI client window}
    ClientStruct: TClientCreateStruct;
begin
  case TheMessage of
    {The frame window will be created first. Once it is created, the
```

```
              WM_CREATE message is sent to this function, where we create the
           MDI client window}
           WM_CREATE: begin
               {Fill in the appropriate information about the client window}
               ClientStruct.hWindowMenu := 0;
               ClientStruct.idFirstChild := IDCHILDWND;

               {Create the MDI client window}
               ClientWindow := CreateWindowEx(
                           0,                     {no extended styles}
                           'MDICLIENT',           {the registered class name}
                           NIL,                   {no window text}
                           WS_CHILD or            {this is a child window}
                           WS_CLIPCHILDREN or     {clip its child windows}
                           WS_VISIBLE,            {initially visible}
                           0,                     {horizontal position}
                           0,                     {vertical position}
                           0,                     {width}
                           0,                     {height}
                           TheFrameWindow,        {handle of the parent window}
                           0,                     {no menu}
                           hInstance,             {the application instance}
                           @ClientStruct          {additional creation information}
                           );

               {check to see if it was created}
               if ClientWindow = 0 then
                   begin
                       MessageBox(0, 'CreateClientWindow failed', nil, MB_OK);
                       Exit;
                   end;

               {indicate that the message was handled}
               Result := 1;
           end;
           {upon getting the WM_DESTROY message, we exit the application}
           WM_DESTROY: begin
                       PostQuitMessage(0);
                       Exit;
                   end;
      else
        {call the default frame window procedure for all unhandled messages}
        Result := DefFrameProc(TheFrameWindow, ClientWindow, TheMessage,
                          WParam, LParam);
      end;
end;

{this defines the window procedure for our MDI child window}
function MDIChildWindowProc(TheMDIChildWindow: HWnd; TheMessage, WParam,
                            LParam: Longint): Longint; stdcall;
begin
   case TheMessage of
     {upon getting the WM_DESTROY message, we exit the application}
     WM_LBUTTONDOWN: begin
                     SetWindowText(TheMDIChildWindow,PChar('Mouse Button '+
                                   'Clicked at '+IntToStr(LoWord(GetMessagePos
                                   ))+', '+IntToStr(HiWord(GetMessagePos))));
```

```
                              {indicate that the message was handled}
                              Result := 1;
                          end;
      else
        {call the default MDI child window procedure for all unhandled messages}
        Result := DefMDIChildProc(TheMDIChildWindow, TheMessage, WParam, LParam);
      end;
end;

{ Register the frame window Class }
function RegisterFrameClass: Boolean;
var
   WindowClass: TWndClass;
begin
   {setup our frame window class}
   WindowClass.Style := CS_HREDRAW or CS_VREDRAW;      {set the class styles}
   WindowClass.lpfnWndProc := @FrameWindowProc;         {point to our frame
                                                        window procedure}
   WindowClass.cbClsExtra := 0;                         {no extra class memory}
   WindowClass.cbWndExtra := 0;                         {no extra window memory}
   WindowClass.hInstance := hInstance;                  {the application instance}
   WindowClass.hIcon := LoadIcon(0, IDI_WINLOGO);       {load a predefined logo}
   WindowClass.hCursor := LoadCursor(0, IDC_ARROW);     {load a predefined cursor}
   WindowClass.hbrBackground := COLOR_WINDOW;           {use a predefined color}
   WindowClass.lpszMenuName := nil;                     {no menu}
   WindowClass.lpszClassName := 'FrameClass';           {the registered class name}

   {now that we have our class set up, register it with the system}
   Result := Windows.RegisterClass(WindowClass) <> 0;
end;

{ Register the child window Class }
function RegisterChildClass: Boolean;
var
   WindowClass: TWndClass;
begin
   {setup our child window class}
   WindowClass.Style := CS_HREDRAW or CS_VREDRAW;      {set the class styles}
   WindowClass.lpfnWndProc := @MDIChildWindowProc;      {point to the default MDI
                                                        child window procedure}
   WindowClass.cbClsExtra := 0;                         {no extra class memory}
   WindowClass.cbWndExtra := 0;                         {no extra window memory}
   WindowClass.hInstance := hInstance;                  {the application instance}
   WindowClass.hIcon := LoadIcon(0, IDI_APPLICATION);   {load a predefined logo}
   WindowClass.hCursor := LoadCursor(0, IDC_ARROW);     {load a predefined cursor}
   WindowClass.hbrBackground := COLOR_WINDOW;           {use a predefined color}
   WindowClass.lpszMenuName := nil;                     {no menu}
   WindowClass.lpszClassName := 'ChildClass';           {the registered class name}

   {now that we have our class set up, register it with the system}
   Result := Windows.RegisterClass(WindowClass) <> 0;
end;

{this begins the main program}
begin
   {Register our frame class first}
   if not RegisterFrameClass then
```

```
begin
  MessageBox(0,'RegisterFrameClass failed',nil,MB_OK);
  Exit;
end;

{Create the frame window based on our frame class}
FrameWindow := CreateWindowEx(
                    0,                        {no extended styles}
                    'FrameClass',             {the registered class name}
                    'DefFrameProc Example',   {the title bar text}
                    WS_OVERLAPPEDWINDOW       {a normal window style}
                    or WS_CLIPCHILDREN,       {clips all child windows}
                    CW_USEDEFAULT,            {default horizontal position}
                    CW_USEDEFAULT,            {default vertical position}
                    CW_USEDEFAULT,            {default width}
                    CW_USEDEFAULT,            {default height}
                    0,                        {handle of the parent window}
                    0,                        {no menu}
                    hInstance,                {the application instance}
                    nil                       {no additional information}
                    );

{If our frame window was created successfully, show it}
if FrameWindow <> 0 then
begin
  ShowWindow(FrameWindow, SW_SHOWNORMAL);
  UpdateWindow(FrameWindow);
end
else
begin
  MessageBox(0, 'CreateFrameWindow failed', nil, MB_OK);
  Exit;
end;

{Register the child window class}
if not RegisterChildClass then
begin
  MessageBox(0, 'RegisterChildClass failed', nil, MB_OK);
  Exit;
end;

{Create the MDI child window}
ChildWindow := CreateMDIWindow('ChildClass',    {the registered class name}
                    'Child Window',  {the title bar text}
                    WS_VISIBLE,      {initially visible}
                    CW_USEDEFAULT,   {default horizontal position}
                    CW_USEDEFAULT,   {default vertical position}
                    CW_USEDEFAULT,   {default width}
                    CW_USEDEFAULT,   {default height}
                    ClientWindow,    {handle of the parent window}
                    hInstance,       {the application instance}
                    0                {no application-defined value}
                    );

{check to see if it was created}
if ChildWindow <> 0 then
begin
```

```
    ShowWindow(ChildWindow, SW_SHOWNORMAL);
    UpdateWindow(ChildWindow);
  end
  else
  begin
    MessageBox(0,'CreateChildWindow failed',nil,mb_ok);
    Exit;
  end;

  {the standard message loop}
  while GetMessage(TheMessage,0,0,0) do
  begin
    TranslateMessage(TheMessage);
    DispatchMessage(TheMessage);
  end;
end.
```

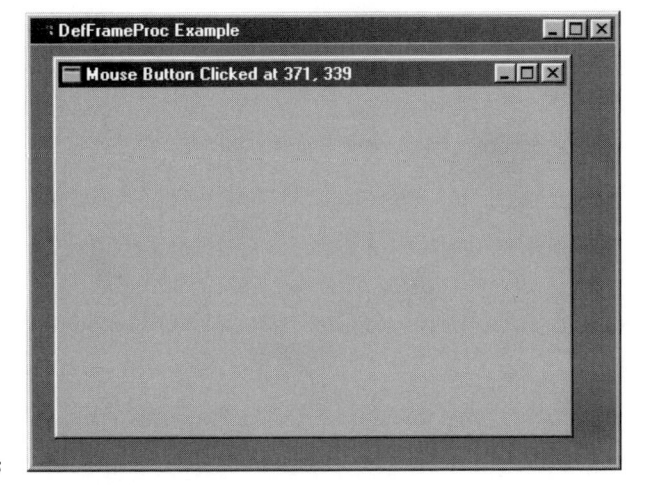

Figure 3-2:
The MDI frame and child windows

DefMDIChildProc   Windows.pas

Syntax

```
DefMDIChildProc(
hWnd: HWND;              {a handle to the MDI child window}
uMsg: UINT;              {the identifier of the message to send}
wParam: WPARAM;          {a 32-bit message specific value}
lParam: LPARAM           {a 32-bit message specific value}
): LRESULT;              {returns a message specific return value}
```

Description

This function provides default message processing for any message not handled in the window procedure of a multiple document interface child window. Any messages not explicitly handled by the MDI child window procedure must be passed to the DefMDI-ChildProc function. This function assumes that the parent window of the window identified by the hWnd parameter was created using the MDICLIENT class.

Parameters

hWnd: A handle to the child window.

uMsg: The identifier of the message to send.

wParam: A 32-bit value dependent on the message being sent.

lParam: A 32-bit value dependent on the message being sent.

Return Value

The value returned from this function specifies the result of the message processing and is dependent on the message sent.

See Also

CallWindowProc, DefFrameProc, DefWindowProc

Example

See Listing 3-4 under DefFrameProc.

DefWindowProc   Windows.pas

Syntax

```
DefWindowProc(
hWnd: HWND;              {a handle to a window}
Msg: UINT;               {the identifier of the message to send}
wParam: WPARAM;          {a 32-bit message specific value}
lParam: LPARAM           {a 32-bit message specific value}
): LRESULT;              {returns a message specific return value}
```

Description

This function provides default message processing for any message not handled in the window procedure of an application. Any messages not explicitly handled by the application's window procedure must be passed to the DefWindowProc function. This function ensures that all incoming Windows messages are processed.

Note: MDI applications would send unhandled messages to the DefFrameProc function.

Parameters

hWnd: A handle to the window.

Msg: The identifier of the message to send.

wParam: A 32-bit value dependent on the message being sent.

lParam: A 32-bit value dependent on the message being sent.

Message Processing Functions

Return Value

The value returned from this function specifies the result of the message processing and is dependent on the message sent.

See Also

CallWindowProc, DefFrameProc, DefMDIChildProc

Example

See Listing 3-5 under GetMessage.

DispatchMessage   Windows.pas

Syntax

```
DispatchMessage(
const lpMsg: TMsg         {a pointer to a TMsg message structure}
): Longint;               {returns a message specific return value}
```

Description

This function dispatches the specified message to a window procedure. The value specified by the lpMsg parameter is typically provided by the GetMessage function. The DispatchMessage function is used in the message loop of a Windows program.

Parameters

lpMsg: A pointer to a message information structure. This structure is typically passed as a parameter to the GetMessage or PeekMessage functions before the DispatchMessage function is called. The TMsg function is defined as:

```
TMsg = packed record
    hwnd: HWND;           {a handle to the window receiving the message}
    message: UINT;        {the message identifier}
    wParam: WPARAM;       {a 32-bit message specific value}
    lParam: LPARAM;       {a 32-bit message specific value}
    time: DWORD;          {the time when the message was posted}
    pt: TPoint;           {the position of the mouse cursor}
end;
```

hwnd: A handle to the window whose window procedure receives the message.

message: The message identifier.

wParam: A 32-bit message specific value.

lParam: A 32-bit message specific value. If the message member contains WM_TIMER and the lParam parameter of the WM_TIMER message is not zero, lParam will contain a pointer to a function that is called instead of the window procedure.

time: The time at which the message was posted.

pt: A TPoint structure containing the position of the mouse cursor at the time the message was posted, in screen coordinates.

Chapter 3

Return Value
This function returns the value returned from the window procedure, the meaning of which is dependent on the message being processed.

See Also
GetMessage, PeekMessage, PostMessage, TranslateMessage

Example
See Listing 3-5 under GetMessage.

GetMessage   Windows.pas

Syntax
```
GetMessage(
  var lpMsg: TMsg;           {a pointer to a TMsg message structure}
  hWnd: HWND;                {a handle to the window whose messages are retrieved}
  wMsgFilterMin: UINT;       {the lowest message value to retrieve}
  wMsgFilterMax: UINT        {the highest message value to retrieve}
): BOOL;                     {returns TRUE or FALSE}
```

Description
This function retrieves information about the next waiting message in a thread's message queue. The message information is stored in a TMsg structure pointed to by the lpMsg parameter. The retrieved message is removed from the queue unless it is a WM_PAINT message, which is removed after processing the message with the BeginPaint and EndPaint functions. GetMessage can be instructed to retrieve messages that lie only within a specified range, but if the wMsgFilterMin and wMsgFilterMax parameters are both set to zero, GetMessage will retrieve all available messages. The WM_KEYFIRST and WM_KEYLAST constants can be used to retrieve only keyboard input messages, and the WM_MOUSEFIRST and WM_MOUSELAST constants can be used to retrieve only mouse input messages. This function cannot retrieve messages for windows owned by other threads or applications, or for any thread other than the calling thread. This function will not return until a message has been placed in the message queue.

Parameters
lpMsg: A pointer to a message information structure. This structure receives the message information retrieved from the calling thread's message queue. The TMsg function is defined as:

```
TMsg = packed record
  hwnd: HWND;             {a handle to the window receiving the message}
  message: UINT;          {the message identifier}
  wParam: WPARAM;         {a 32-bit message specific value}
  lParam: LPARAM;         {a 32-bit message specific value}
  time: DWORD;            {the time when the message was posted}
  pt: TPoint;             {the position of the mouse cursor}
```

end;

Note that the hwnd member of messages posted to the calling thread by the PostThreadMessage function will be set to zero. See the DispatchMessage function for a description of this data structure.

hWnd: A handle to the window whose messages are to be retrieved. If this value is zero, GetMessage retrieves message information for any window owned by the calling thread, including thread messages sent to the calling thread by the PostThreadMessage function.

wMsgFilterMin: The message identifier of the lowest message value to be retrieved.

wMsgFilterMax: The message identifier of the highest message value to be retrieved.

Return Value

If the function succeeds and does not retrieve the WM_QUIT message, it returns TRUE. If the function fails, or it retrieves the WM_QUIT message, it returns FALSE.

See Also

PeekMessage, PostMessage, PostThreadMessage, WaitMessage

Example

Listing 3-5: A Windows API window with a normal message loop

```
program GetMessageExample;

uses
    Windows, Messages, SysUtils;

{$R *.RES}

{The window procedure for our API window}
function WindowProc(TheWindow: HWnd; TheMessage, WParam,
                   LParam: Longint): Longint; stdcall;
begin
  case TheMessage of
    {upon getting the WM_DESTROY message, we exit the application}
    WM_DESTROY: begin
                  PostQuitMessage(0);
                  Exit;
                end;
    WM_LBUTTONDOWN: begin
                  {show the message time and the mouse coordinates}
                  SetWindowText(TheWindow, PChar('Message Time: '+IntToStr(
                           GetMessageTime)+'   Mouse Coordinates: '+
                           IntToStr(LoWord(GetMessagePos))+', '+
                           IntToStr(HiWord(GetMessagePos))));

                  {indicate that the message was handled}
                  Result := 1;
                end;
    else
      {call the default window procedure for all unhandled messages}
      Result := DefWindowProc(TheWindow, TheMessage, WParam, LParam);
```

Chapter 3

```delphi
      end;
  end;

  { Register the Window Class }
  function RegisterClass: Boolean;
  var
    WindowClass: TWndClass;
  begin
    {setup our new window class}
    WindowClass.Style := CS_HREDRAW or CS_VREDRAW; {set the class styles}
    WindowClass.lpfnWndProc := @WindowProc;        {point to our window procedure}
    WindowClass.cbClsExtra := 0;                   {no extra class memory}
    WindowClass.cbWndExtra := 0;                   {no extra window memory}
    WindowClass.hInstance := hInstance;            {the application instance}
    WindowClass.hIcon := LoadIcon(0, IDI_APPLICATION); {load a predefined logo}
    WindowClass.hCursor := LoadCursor(0, IDC_ARROW);   {load a predefined cursor}
    WindowClass.hbrBackground := COLOR_WINDOW;     {use a predefined color}
    WindowClass.lpszMenuName := nil;               {no menu}
    WindowClass.lpszClassName := 'TestClass';      {the registered class name}

    {now that we have our class set up, register it with the system}
    Result := Windows.RegisterClass(WindowClass) <> 0;
  end;

var
  TheMessage: TMsg;    // holds a message
  OurWindow: HWND;     // the handle to our window
begin
  {register our new class first}
  if not RegisterClass then
  begin
    MessageBox(0,'RegisterClass failed',nil,MB_OK);
    Exit;
  end;

  {now, create a window based on our new class}
  OurWindow := CreateWindowEx(
                    0,                       {no extended styles}
                    'TestClass',             {the registered class name}
                    'GetMessage Example',    {the title bar text}
                    WS_OVERLAPPEDWINDOW or   {a normal window style}
                    WS_VISIBLE,              {initially visible}
                    CW_USEDEFAULT,           {default horizontal position}
                    CW_USEDEFAULT,           {default vertical position}
                    CW_USEDEFAULT,           {default width}
                    CW_USEDEFAULT,           {default height}
                    0,                       {handle of the parent window}
                    0,                       {no menu}
                    hInstance,               {the application instance}
                    nil                      {no additional information}
                    );

  {if our window was not created successfully, exit the program}
  if OurWindow=0 then
  begin
    MessageBox(0,'CreateWindow failed',nil,MB_OK);
    Exit;
```

```
      end;

      {the standard message loop}
      while GetMessage(TheMessage,0,0,0) do
      begin
        TranslateMessage(TheMessage);
        DispatchMessage(TheMessage);
      end;

    end.
```

Figure 3-3:
The time and position of the WM_LBUT-TONDOWN message

GetMessageExtraInfo   Windows.pas

Syntax

    GetMessageExtraInfo: Longint;   {returns an application-defined value}

Description

This function retrieves the 32-bit application-defined value associated with the last message retrieved by the GetMessage or PeekMessage functions. Use the SetMessageExtraInfo function to specify this value.

Return Value

If the function succeeds, it returns the 32-bit application-defined value associated with the last message retrieved by the GetMessage or PeekMessage functions that was set using the SetMessageExtraInfo function. If the function fails, it returns 0.

See Also

GetMessage, PeekMessage, SetMessageExtraInfo

Example

Listing 3-6: Retrieving extra message information

```
{define an application specific user message}
const
```

```
    UserMessage = WM_USER+1;

type
  TForm1 = class(TForm)
    Button1: TButton;
    procedure Button1Click(Sender: TObject);
  private
    { Private declarations }
  public
    {the handler for our user message}
    procedure DoMessage(var Msg: TMessage); message UserMessage;
  end;

var
  Form1: TForm1;

implementation

{$R *.DFM}

procedure TForm1.Button1Click(Sender: TObject);
begin
  {set the message extra information}
  SetMessageExtraInfo(12345);

  {send the user message to the window}
  Perform(UserMessage, 0, 0);
end;

procedure TForm1.DoMessage(var Msg: TMessage);
begin
  {the user message was retrieved, show the message extra info}
  Button1.Caption := 'User Message Received. Info: '+
                     IntToStr(GetMessageExtraInfo);
end;
```

*Figure 3-4:
The extra message information was retrieved*

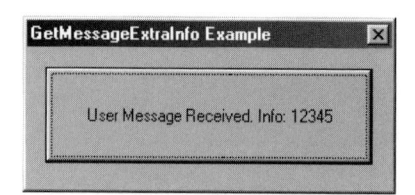

GetMessagePos   Windows.pas

Syntax

```
GetMessagePos: DWORD;          {returns the mouse position in screen coordinates}
```

Description

This function returns the horizontal and vertical position, in screen coordinates, of the mouse cursor at the moment when the last message retrieved by the GetMessage function occurred. The horizontal position of the mouse cursor is in the low-order word of the return value, and the vertical position is in the high-order word.

Return Value

If the function succeeds, it returns the horizontal and vertical position, in screen coordinates, of the mouse cursor at the moment when the last message retrieved by the GetMessage function occurred. If the function fails, it returns 0.

See Also

GetCursorPos*, GetMessage, GetMessageTime, PeekMessage

Example

See Listing 3-5 under GetMessage.

GetMessageTime   Windows.pas

Syntax

GetMessageTime: Longint;   {returns the time that the message was created}

Description

This function retrieves the elapsed time, in milliseconds, from the time that the system was started to the time that the last message that was retrieved by the GetMessage function was put into the thread's message queue.

Return Value

If the function succeeds, it retrieves the elapsed time, in milliseconds, from the time that the system was started to the time that the last message that was retrieved by the GetMessage function was put into the thread's message queue. If the function fails, it returns 0.

See Also

GetMessage, GetMessagePos, PeekMessage

Example

See Listing 3-5 under GetMessage.

GetQueueStatus   Windows.pas

Syntax

```
GetQueueStatus(
flags: UINT            {message queue status flags}
): DWORD               {returns message queue status flags}
```

Description

This function returns a series of flags indicating the types of messages found in the calling thread's message queue at the time the function was called. However, if the return value indicates that a message is currently in the queue, it does not guarantee that the GetMessage or PeekMessage functions will return a message as these functions perform some filtering that may process some messages internally.

Parameters

flags: Specifies the types of messages to check for in the calling thread's message queue. This parameter can be a combination of one or more values from the following table.

Return Value

If this function succeeds, it returns a DWORD value. The high-order word of this return value contains a combination of the flags values that indicate the types of messages currently in the message queue. The low-order word contains a combination of the flags values that indicate the types of messages that have been added to the queue since the last call to the GetQueueStatus, GetMessage, or PeekMessage functions. If the function fails, or there are no messages in the queue, it returns 0.

See Also

GetInputState*, GetMessage, PeekMessage

Example

Listing 3-7: Retrieving the current message queue status

```
procedure TForm1.Button1Click(Sender: TObject);
var
  CurrentMessage: DWORD;
begin
  {look for any message}
  CurrentMessage := GetQueueStatus(QS_ALLINPUT);

  {display the queue status}
  PrintStatus(HiWord(CurrentMessage), ListBox1);
  PrintStatus(LoWord(CurrentMessage), ListBox2);
  Label3.Caption := 'GetQueueStatus value: '+IntToHex(CurrentMessage, 8);
end;

{this simply converts the GetQueueStatus return value into a string}
function PrintStatus(Index: Integer; ListBox: TListBox): string;
begin
  ListBox.Items.Clear;

  if (Index and QS_KEY)=QS_KEY
    then ListBox.Items.Add('QS_KEY');
  if (Index and QS_MOUSEMOVE)=QS_MOUSEMOVE
    then ListBox.Items.Add('QS_MOUSEMOVE');
  if (Index and QS_MOUSEBUTTON)=QS_MOUSEBUTTON
    then ListBox.Items.Add('QS_MOUSEBUTTON');
  if (Index and QS_POSTMESSAGE)=QS_POSTMESSAGE
    then ListBox.Items.Add('QS_POSTMESSAGE');
  if (Index and QS_TIMER)=QS_TIMER
    then ListBox.Items.Add('QS_TIMER');
  if (Index and QS_PAINT)=QS_PAINT
    then ListBox.Items.Add('QS_PAINT');
```

```
      if (Index and QS_SENDMESSAGE)=QS_SENDMESSAGE
        then ListBox.Items.Add('QS_SENDMESSAGE');
      if (Index and QS_HOTKEY)=QS_HOTKEY
        then ListBox.Items.Add('QS_HOTKEY');
      if (Index and QS_ALLPOSTMESSAGE)=QS_ALLPOSTMESSAGE
        then ListBox.Items.Add('QS_ALLPOSTMESSAGE');
    end;
```

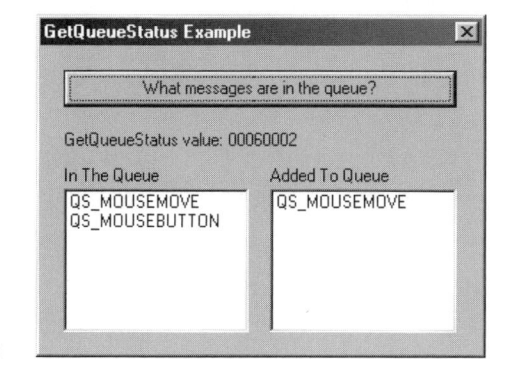

Figure 3-5:
The current queue status

Table 3-4: GetQueueStatus flags values

Value	Description
QS_ALLEVENTS	A user input message, the WM_TIMER, WM_PAINT, and WM_HOTKEY messages, or a posted message is in the queue.
QS_ALLINPUT	Any Windows message is in the queue.
QS_ALLPOSTMESSAGE	A posted message (excluding all messages listed in this table) is in the queue.
QS_HOTKEY	A WM_HOTKEY message is in the queue.
QS_INPUT	Any user input message is in the queue.
QS_KEY	A WM_KEYUP, WM_KEYDOWN, WM_SYSKEYUP, or WM_SYSKEYDOWN message is in the queue.
QS_MOUSE	A WM_MOUSEMOVE message or mouse button message (such as WM_LBUTTONDOWN) is in the queue.
QS_MOUSEBUTTON	A mouse button message (such as WM_LBUTTONUP) is in the queue.
QS_MOUSEMOVE	A WM_MOUSEMOVE message is in the queue.
QS_PAINT	A WM_PAINT message is in the queue.
QS_POSTMESSAGE	A posted message (excluding all messages listed in this table) is in the queue.
QS_SENDMESSAGE	A message sent by another thread or application via one of the SendMessage functions is in the queue.
QS_TIMER	A WM_TIMER message is in the queue.

InSendMessage   *Windows.pas*

Syntax

```
InSendMessage: BOOL;           {returns TRUE or FALSE}
```

Description

This function determines if the window procedure is currently processing a message sent to it by another thread via one of the SendMessage functions.

Return Value

If the function succeeds and the window procedure is processing a message sent to it from another thread by one of the SendMessage functions, it returns TRUE. If the function fails, or the window procedure is not processing a message sent to it from another thread by one of the SendMessage functions, it returns FALSE.

See Also

PostMessage, PostThreadMessage, ReplyMessage, SendMessage, SendMessageCallback, SendMessageTimeout

Example

See Listing 3-12 under RegisterWindowMessage and Listing 3-9 under PostMessage.

PeekMessage   Windows.pas

Syntax

```
PeekMessage(
var lpMsg: TMsg;          {a pointer to a TMsg message structure}
hWnd: HWND;               {a handle to the window whose messages are retrieved}
wMsgFilterMin: UINT;      {the lowest message value to retrieve}
wMsgFilterMax: UINT;      {the highest message value to retrieve}
wRemoveMsg: UINT          {message removal flags}
): BOOL;                  {returns TRUE or FALSE}
```

Description

This function retrieves information about the next waiting message in a thread's message queue. The message information is stored in a TMsg structure pointed to by the lpMsg parameter. Messages can optionally be removed from the queue. PeekMessage can be instructed to retrieve messages that lie only within a specified range, but if the wMsgFilterMin and wMsgFilterMax parameters are both set to zero, PeekMessage will retrieve all available messages. The WM_KEYFIRST and WM_KEYLAST constants can be used to retrieve only keyboard input messages, and the WM_MOUSEFIRST and WM_MOUSELAST constants can be used to retrieve only mouse input messages. This function cannot retrieve messages for windows owned by other threads or applications, or for any thread other than the calling thread. Unlike GetMessage, this function returns immediately and does not wait until a message has been placed into the message queue.

Parameters

lpMsg: A pointer to a message information structure. This structure receives the message information retrieved from the calling thread's message queue. The TMsg function is defined as:

```
TMsg = packed record
    hwnd: HWND;          {a handle to the window receiving the message}
    message: UINT;       {the message identifier}
    wParam: WPARAM;      {a 32-bit message specific value}
    lParam: LPARAM;      {a 32-bit message specific value}
    time: DWORD;         {the time when the message was posted}
    pt: TPoint;          {the position of the mouse cursor}
end;
```

Note that the hwnd member of messages posted to the calling thread by the PostThreadMessage function will be set to 0. See the DispatchMessage function for a description of this data structure.

hWnd: A handle to the window whose messages are to be retrieved. If this parameter is set to 0, PeekMessage retrieves message information for any window owned by the calling thread, including thread messages sent to the calling thread by the PostThreadMessage function. If this parameter is set to –1, PeekMessage retrieves messages posted to the thread only by the PostThreadMessage function.

wMsgFilterMin: The message identifier of the lowest message value to be retrieved.

wMsgFilterMax: The message identifier of the highest message value to be retrieved.

wRemoveMsg: A flag indicating if the message is to be removed from the message queue. If this parameter is set to PM_NOREMOVE, the message is not removed from the queue. If this parameter is set to PM_REMOVE, the message is removed. WM_PAINT messages cannot normally be removed, but if a WM_PAINT message indicates a null update region, PeekMessage can remove it from the queue.

Return Value

If the function succeeds and there is a message available in the queue, it returns TRUE. If the function fails, or there are no messages waiting in the queue, it returns FALSE.

See Also

GetMessage, PostMessage, PostThreadMessage, WaitMessage

Example

Listing 3-8: Retrieving messages using PeekMessage

```
procedure TForm1.FormMouseDown(Sender: TObject; Button: TMouseButton;
  Shift: TShiftState; X, Y: Integer);
var
  CurMouse: TPoint;       // identifies the mouse position in client coordinates
  TheMessage: TMSG;       // the message information structure
begin
  {if the left button was not clicked, don't start tracking the mouse}
  if Button <> mbLeft then Exit;

  {indicate that the mouse is being tracked}
  Caption := 'PeekMessage Example - Mouse is being tracked';
```

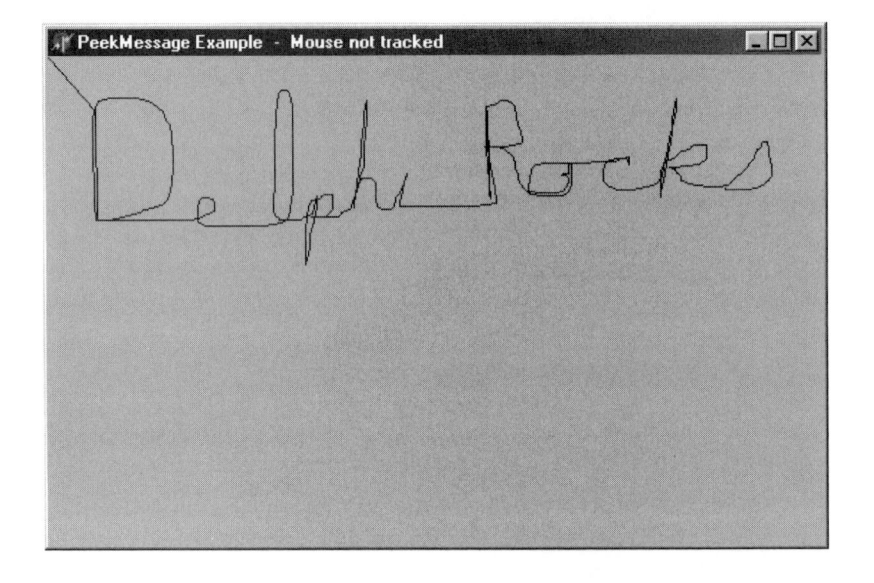

```
  {this causes the program to go into a tight loop that will exit
   only when the right mouse button is clicked}
  while not PeekMessage(TheMessage, Handle, WM_RBUTTONDOWN,
                        WM_RBUTTONDOWN, PM_NOREMOVE) do
  begin
    {get the current mouse cursor position in screen coordinates}
    GetCursorPos(CurMouse);

    {translate this into client coordinates}
    CurMouse := Form1.ScreenToClient(CurMouse);

    {draw a line to the new mouse position}
    Canvas.LineTo(CurMouse.X, CurMouse.Y);
  end;

  {the loop has ended, indicate that the mouse is no longer being tracked}
  Caption := 'PeekMessage Example  -  Mouse not tracked';
end;
```

Figure 3-6: A crude drawing example

PostMessage   Windows.pas

Syntax

```
PostMessage(
hWnd: HWND;               {a handle to a window}
Msg: UINT;                {the identifier of the message to send}
wParam: WPARAM;           {a 32-bit message specific value}
lParam: LPARAM            {a 32-bit message specific value}
): BOOL;                  {returns TRUE or FALSE}
```

Description

This function places the indicated message in the message queue of the thread that owns the specified window, returning immediately without waiting for the message to be processed. Caution is advised when sending a message whose parameters contain pointers, as the function will return before the thread associated with the specified window has a chance to process the message and the pointers could be freed before they are used.

Parameters

hWnd: A handle to the window whose window procedure is to receive the specified message. If this parameter is set to zero, PostMessage functions exactly like a call to the PostThreadMessage function with the idThread parameter set to the identifier of the calling thread. If this parameter is set to HWND_BROADCAST, the message is sent to all top level windows in the system, including disabled and invisible windows. The message is not sent to child windows. Applications that need to send a user-defined message to other applications using HWND_BROADCAST should use the RegisterWindowMessage to obtain a unique message identifier.

Msg: The identifier of the message to send.

wParam: A 32-bit value dependent on the message being sent.

lParam: A 32-bit value dependent on the message being sent.

Return Value

If the function succeeds, it returns TRUE; otherwise, it returns FALSE. To get extended error information, call the GetLastError function.

See Also

GetMessage, PeekMessage, RegisterWindowMessage, SendMessage, SendMessageCallback, SendMessageTimeout, SendNotifyMessage

Example

Listing 3-9: Posting a message to a window's message queue

This application posts the message:

```
procedure TForm1.FormCreate(Sender: TObject);
begin
  {register a user-defined message}
  UserMessage := RegisterWindowMessage('PostMessage Test Message');
end;

procedure TForm1.Button1Click(Sender: TObject);
begin
  {post the user-defined message to the specified window's
   message queue}
  PostMessage(FindWindow('TForm1','PostMessage Get Example'), UserMessage, 0,0);

  {this message box will pop up immediately, as PostMessage
   does not wait for the message to be processed.}
  ShowMessage('Returned');
end;
```

and this application receives it:

```
procedure TForm1.DefaultHandler(var Msg);
var
  iLoop: Integer;       // a general loop control variable
begin
  {allow default message handling to occur}
  inherited DefaultHandler(Msg);

  {if the message was our user-defined message...}
  if TMessage(Msg).Msg=UserMessage then
  begin
    {...turn on some user interface components}
    ProgressBar1.Visible := TRUE;
    Label2.Visible := TRUE;

    {indicate if the message was sent via one of the SendMessage functions}
    if InSendMessage then Label3.Visible := TRUE;

    {repaint the form}
    Form1.Repaint;

    {animate the progress bar for a short amount of time}
    for iLoop := 0 to 100 do
    begin
      ProgressBar1.Position := iLoop;
      Sleep(10);
    end;

    {turn off the user interface elements}
    ProgressBar1.Visible := FALSE;
    Label2.Visible := FALSE;
    Label3.Visible := FALSE;

    {indicate the message was handled}
    TMessage(Msg).Result := 1;
  end;
end;

procedure TForm1.FormCreate(Sender: TObject);
begin
  {register a user-defined message}
  UserMessage := RegisterWindowMessage('PostMessage Test Message');
end;
```

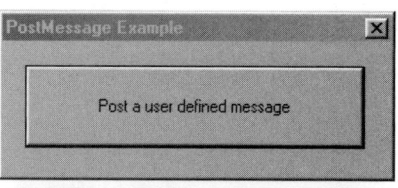

*Figure 3-7:
The
PostMessage
function posts
the message
and returns
immediately*

PostQuitMessage   Windows.pas

Syntax

    PostQuitMessage(
    nExitCode: Integer   {the application-defined exit code}
    );   {this procedure does not return a value}

Description

This function posts a WM_QUIT message to the calling thread's message queue, causing the application to terminate.

Parameters

nExitCode: An application-defined value that is passed to the wParam parameter of the WM_QUIT message. This value is returned to Windows when the application terminates.

See Also

GetMessage, PeekMessage, PostMessage

Example

Listing 3-10: Terminating an application

```
procedure TForm1.Button1Click(Sender: TObject);
begin
  {indicate to Windows that the application should terminate}
  PostQuitMessage(0);
end;
```

PostThreadMessage   Windows.pas

Syntax

    PostThreadMessage(
    idThread: DWORD;   {the identifier of the thread}
    Msg: UINT;   {the identifier of the message to send}
    wParam: WPARAM;   {a 32-bit message specific value}

lParam: LPARAM	{a 32-bit message specific value}
): BOOL;	{returns TRUE or FALSE}

Description

This function places the specified message into the message queue of the thread identified by the idThread parameter. The function returns immediately, without waiting for the thread to process the message. A thread creates a message queue the first time it makes a call to any Win32 user or GDI functions. When the thread retrieves messages by using the GetMessage or PeekMessage functions, the hWnd member of the returned message structure will be set to zero.

Parameters

idThread: The identifier of the thread to which the message is posted.

Msg: The identifier of the message to send.

wParam: A 32-bit value dependent on the message being sent.

lParam: A 32-bit value dependent on the message being sent.

Return Value

If the function succeeds, it returns TRUE; otherwise, it returns FALSE. To get extended error information, call the GetLastError function. GetLastError will return ERROR_INVALID_THREAD_ID if the idThread parameter does not contain a valid thread identifier, or if the thread it identifies does not have a message queue.

See Also

CreateThread, GetCurrentThreadId, GetMessage, GetWindowThreadProcessId, PeekMessage, PostMessage, SendMessage

Example

Listing 3-11: Posting a message to a thread

```
const
  NewMessage = WM_USER+1;    // a new user-defined message

implementation

function ThreadFunction(Parameter: Pointer): Integer; stdcall;
var
  DC: HDC;     // holds a device context
  Msg: TMsg;   // a message information structure
begin
  {create a message loop}
  while (GetMessage(Msg, 0, 0, 0)) do
  begin
    {if the retrieved message is our user-defined message...}
    if Msg.Message = NewMessage then
    begin
      {...retrieve a handle to the device context}
```

```
      DC := GetDC(Form1.Handle);

      {set the background mode to be transparent}
      SetBkMode(DC, TRANSPARENT);

      {display text indicating that the message was received}
      TextOut(DC, 10, 10, 'User message seen by thread', 27);

      {release the device context}
      ReleaseDC(Form1.Handle, DC);
    end;
  end;
end;

procedure TForm1.Button1Click(Sender: TObject);
var
  ThreadId: Integer;    // holds the new thread ID
begin
  {create a new thread}
  ThreadHandle := CreateThread(nil, 0, @ThreadFunction, nil, 0, ThreadId);

  {make sure that the thread was created correctly}
  if ThreadHandle = 0 then
  begin
    ShowMessage('New thread not started');
    Halt;
  end;

  {pause for 100 milliseconds}
  Sleep(100);

  {post the user-defined message to the thread}
  PostThreadMessage(ThreadId, NewMessage, 0, 0);
end;
```

RegisterWindowMessage   Windows.pas

Syntax

RegisterWindowMessage(
lpString: PChar   {a pointer to a message string}
): UINT;   {returns a unique message identifier}

Description

This function generates a new message identifier that is unique throughout the system. This new message identifier can be used by any of the PostMessage or SendMessage functions, and is typically used to provide a means of communication between two applications. If two different applications register the same message string, each application will receive an identical unique message identifier. This identifier remains valid until the current Windows session terminates.

Parameters

lpString: A pointer to a null-terminated string containing the message to be registered.

Return Value

If the function succeeds, it returns a unique message identifier in the range of $C000 through $FFFF. If the function fails, it returns zero.

See Also

PostMessage, PostThreadMessage, SendMessage, SendMessageCallback, SendMessageTimeout, SendNotifyMessage

Example

Listing 3-12: Communicating using a unique message identifier

This application sends the message:

```
procedure TForm1.FormCreate(Sender: TObject);
begin
  {register the user-defined message}
  UserMessage := RegisterWindowMessage('System Wide User-defined Message');
end;

procedure TForm1.Button1Click(Sender: TObject);
var
  ReturnValue: LRESULT;   // holds the result returned by SendMessage
begin
  {send the user-defined message to the specified window}
  ReturnValue := SendMessage(FindWindow('TForm1','RegisterMessage Get Example'),
                             UserMessage, 0, 0);

  {display the result of the message processing}
  Button1.Caption := 'SendMessage Result: '+IntToStr(ReturnValue);
end;
```

and this application receives it:

```
procedure TForm1.DefaultHandler(var Msg);
begin
  {allow default message handling to occur}
  inherited DefaultHandler(Msg);

  {if the user-defined message was recieved...}
  if (TMessage(Msg).Msg=UserMessage) then
  begin
    {...send a reply. this causes the message to return
     immediately if sent by one of the SendMessage functions}
    ReplyMessage(5);

    {enable the timer and turn on a user interface object}
    Timer1.Enabled := TRUE;
    Label2.Visible := TRUE;

    {indicate if the message was sent via one of the SendMessage functions}
    if InSendMessage then Label3.Visible := TRUE;
  end;
end;

procedure TForm1.FormCreate(Sender: TObject);
```

```
begin
  {register the system wide user-defined message}
  UserMessage := RegisterWindowMessage('System Wide User-defined Message');
end;

procedure TForm1.Timer1Timer(Sender: TObject);
begin
  {turn off the user interface elements after one second}
  Timer1.Enabled := FALSE;
  Label2.Visible := FALSE;
  Label3.Visible := FALSE;
end;
```

Figure 3-8:
Using the unique message identifier

ReplyMessage   Windows.pas

Syntax

ReplyMessage(
lResult: LRESULT   {a message processing result value}
): BOOL;   {returns TRUE or FALSE}

Description

This function is used to reply to a message sent to the calling thread by another thread or process through one of the SendMessage functions. This causes the thread sending the message to return from the SendMessage function immediately as if the thread receiving the message had completed the message processing. If the message was not sent through one of the SendMessage functions, or was sent by the same thread, this function has no effect.

Parameters

lResult: A value specifying the result of the message processing. This is used as the return value from the SendMessage function for which this function is replying, and can specify an application-defined value.

Return Value

If the function succeeds and the calling thread was processing a message sent to it from another thread or process via one of the SendMessage functions, then it returns TRUE. If the function fails, or the calling thread was not processing a message sent to it from another thread or process via one of the SendMessage functions, then it returns FALSE.

See Also

InSendMessage, SendMessage, SendMessageCallback, SendMessageTimeout

Example

See Listing 3-12 under RegisterWindowMessage.

SendMessage   Windows.pas

Syntax

```
SendMessage(
hWnd: HWND;              {a handle to a window}
Msg: UINT;               {the identifier of the message to send}
wParam: WPARAM;          {a 32-bit message specific value}
lParam: LPARAM           {a 32-bit message specific value}
): LRESULT;              {returns a message specific result}
```

Description

This function sends the specified message to the window procedure of the indicated window, and does not return until the called window procedure has processed the message. If the specified window belongs to the calling thread, that window's window procedure is called immediately as a subroutine. However, if the window belongs to a different thread, Windows switches to that thread, sending the message to the appropriate window procedure, and the thread sending the message is blocked until the receiving thread processes the message.

Parameters

hWnd: A handle to the window whose window procedure is to receive the specified message. If this parameter is set to HWND_BROADCAST, the message is sent to all top-level windows in the system, including disabled and invisible windows. The message is not sent to child windows. Applications that need to send a user-defined message to other applications using HWND_BROADCAST should use RegisterWindowMessage to obtain a unique message identifier.

Msg: The identifier of the message to send.

wParam: A 32-bit value dependent on the message being sent.

lParam: A 32-bit value dependent on the message being sent.

Return Value

If the function succeeds, it returns a message-specific value indicating the result of the message processing. If the function fails, it returns zero.

See Also

InSendMessage, PostMessage, RegisterWindowMessage, ReplyMessage, SendMessageCallback, SendMessageTimeout, SendNotifyMessage

Example

See Listing 3-12 under RegisterWindowMessage.

SendMessageCallback   Windows.pas

Syntax

```
SendMessageCallback(
hWnd: HWND;                              {a handle to a window}
Msg: UINT;                               {the identifier of the message to send}
wParam: WPARAM;                          {a 32-bit message specific value}
lParam: LPARAM                           {a 32-bit message specific value}
lpResultCallBack: TFNSendAsyncProc;      {a pointer to an application-defined callback
                                          procedure}
dwData: DWORD                            {an application-defined value}
): BOOL;                                 {returns TRUE or FALSE}
```

Description

This function sends the specified message to the window procedure of the window indicated by the hWnd parameter. Unlike SendMessage, this function returns immediately. After the window procedure in the receiving thread has finished processing the message, the system calls the application-defined callback procedure specified by the lpResultCallBack parameter, passing the message sent, the result of the message processing, and an application-defined value. The callback procedure will only be called when the receiving thread calls the GetMessage, PeekMessage, or WaitMessage functions. Caution is advised when sending a message whose parameters contain pointers, as the function will return before the thread associated with the specified window has a chance to process the message and the pointers could be freed before they are used.

Parameters

hWnd: A handle to the window whose window procedure is to receive the specified message. If this parameter is set to HWND_BROADCAST, the message is sent to all top-level windows in the system, including disabled and invisible windows. The message is not sent to child windows. Applications that need to send a user-defined message to other applications using HWND_BROADCAST should use RegisterWindowMessage to obtain a unique message identifier.

Msg: The identifier of the message to send.

wParam: A 32-bit value dependent on the message being sent.

lParam: A 32-bit value dependent on the message being sent.

lpResultCallBack: A pointer to the application-defined callback procedure. If the hWnd parameter is set to HWND_BROADCAST, this procedure is called once for every top-level window receiving the message.

dwData: An application-defined value sent to the callback function pointed to by the lpResultCallBack parameter.

Return Value

If the function succeeds, it returns TRUE; otherwise, it returns FALSE. To get extended error information, call the GetLastError function.

Callback Syntax

```
SendMessageCallbackProc(
hWnd: HWND;            {a handle to the receiving window}
Msg: UINT;             {the identifier of the received message}
dwData: DWORD;         {an application-defined value}
lResult: LRESULT       {the result of the message processing}
);                     {this procedure does not return a value}
```

Description

This callback procedure is called once for every window receiving the sent message, and may perform any desired task.

Parameters

hWnd: A handle to the window whose window procedure received the message.

Msg: The identifier of the message that was sent to the window procedure associated with the window identified by the hWnd parameter.

dwData: An application-defined value. This is the value specified by the dwData parameter of the SendMessageCallback function.

lResult: The result of the message processing as returned by the receiving window's window procedure. This value is dependent on the type of message processed.

See Also

PostMessage, RegisterWindowMessage, SendMessage, SendMessageTimeout, SendNotifyMessage

Example

Listing 3-13: Sending a message with a callback function

```
{the callback function}
  procedure MessageCallback(Window: HWND; Msg: UINT; Data: DWORD;
                    LResult: LRESULT); stdcall;
```

```
var
  Form1: TForm1;

implementation

procedure TForm1.Button1Click(Sender: TObject);
begin
  {send the message, specifying a callback function}
  SendMessageCallback(Form1.Handle, WM_SYSCOMMAND, SC_MAXIMIZE, 0,
                      @MessageCallback, 12345);
end;

procedure MessageCallback(Window:HWND; Msg:UINT; Data:DWORD; LResult:LRESULT);
begin
  {when the message is received, this function is called}
  ShowMessage('The message callback function was called: '+IntToStr(Data));
end;
```

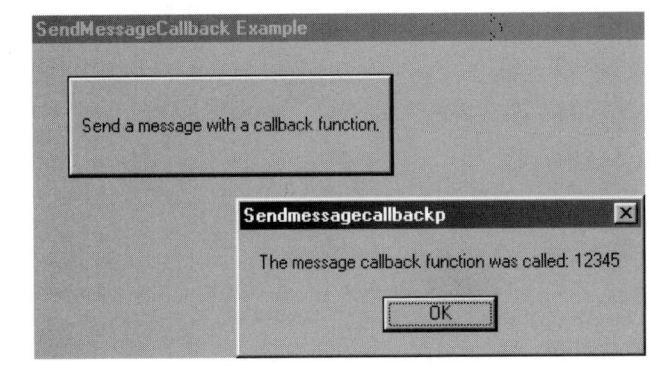

Figure 3-9:
The callback function was called

SendMessageTimeout   Windows.pas

Syntax

SendMessageTimeout(
    hWnd: HWND;   {a handle to a window}
    Msg: UINT;   {the identifier of the message to send}
    wParam: WPARAM;   {a 32-bit message specific value}
    lParam: LPARAM   {a 32-bit message specific value}
    fuFlags: UINT;   {send message behavior flags}
    uTimeout: UINT;   {the timeout period in milliseconds}
    var lpdwResult: DWORD   {a variable to receive the result of message processing}
): LRESULT;   {returns a non-zero number on success}

Description

This function sends the specified message to the window procedure associated with the window indicated by the hWnd parameter. If this window belongs to another thread, the function does not return until the message has been processed or the specified timeout period has elapsed. If the window specified by the hWnd parameter belongs to the calling thread, this function behaves exactly like SendMessage, calling the window procedure directly and ignoring the uTimeout parameter.

Parameters

hWnd: A handle to the window whose window procedure is to receive the specified message. If this parameter is set to HWND_TOPMOST, the message is sent to all top-level windows in the system, including disabled and invisible windows. The message is not sent to child windows. Applications that need to send a user-defined message to other applications using HWND_TOPMOST should use RegisterWindowMessage to obtain a unique message identifier.

Msg: The identifier of the message to send.

wParam: A 32-bit value dependent on the message being sent.

lParam: A 32-bit value dependent on the message being sent.

fuFlags: A series of flags indicating how the message is to be sent. This parameter can be set to one value from Table 3-5.

uTimeout: Specifies, in milliseconds, the amount of time to wait before the function returns.

var lpdwResult: A pointer to a variable receiving the result of the message processing. This value is dependent on the type of message processed.

Return Value

If the function succeeds, it returns a non-zero number; otherwise, it returns zero. To get extended error information, call the GetLastError function.

See Also

InSendMessage, PostMessage, SendMessage, SendMessageCallback, SendNotifyMessage

Example

Listing 3-14: Sending a message and returning before it is processed

This application sends the message:

```
procedure TForm1.FormCreate(Sender: TObject);
begin
  {register the user-defined Windows message}
  UserMessage := RegisterWindowMessage('SendMessageTimout Test Message');
end;

procedure TForm1.Button1Click(Sender: TObject);
var
  MsgResult: DWORD;
begin
  {send the message, and time out after 300 milliseconds}
  SendMessageTimeout(HWND_TOPMOST, UserMessage, 0, 0,
                     SMTO_NORMAL, 300, MsgResult);

  {indicate that the SendMessageTimeout function has returned}
```

```
  ShowMessage('Returned');
end;
```

and this application receives it:

```
var
  Form1: TForm1;
  UserMessage: UINT;   // holds our user-defined message identifier

implementation

procedure TForm1.DefaultHandler(var Msg);
var
  iLoop: Integer;     // general loop counter
begin
  {process message normally}
  inherited DefaultHandler(Msg);

  {if this is our user-defined message...}
  if TMessage(Msg).Msg=UserMessage then
  begin
    {...display some user interface objects}
    ProgressBar1.Visible := TRUE;
    Label2.Visible := TRUE;
    Form1.Repaint;

    {animate the progress bar for a short time}
    for iLoop := 0 to 100 do
    begin
      ProgressBar1.Position := iLoop;
      Sleep(10);
    end;

    {turn off the user interface objects}
    ProgressBar1.Visible := FALSE;
    Label2.Visible := FALSE;

    {indicate that the message was handled}
    TMessage(Msg).Result := 1;
  end;
end;

procedure TForm1.FormCreate(Sender: TObject);
begin
  {register the user-defined Windows message}
  UserMessage := RegisterWindowMessage('SendMessageTimout Test Message');
end;
```

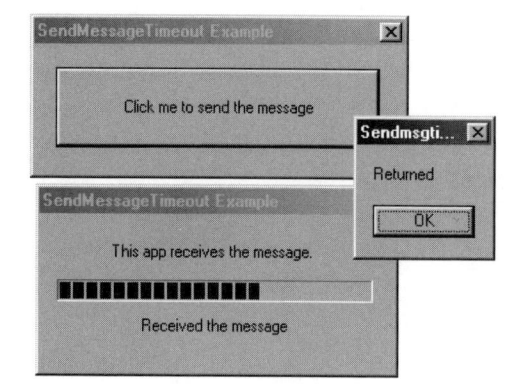

*Figure 3-10:
The function
timed out*

Table 3-5: SendMessageTimeout fuFlags values

Value	Description
SMTO_ABORTIFHUNG	The function will return before the timeout period has elapsed if the receiving process is hung.
SMTO_BLOCK	The calling thread is blocked and stops execution until the function returns.
SMTO_NORMAL	The calling thread is not blocked while waiting for the function to return.
SMTO_NOTIMEOUTIFNOTHUNG	**Windows 2000 or later:** Does not return when the timeout period has elapsed if the receiving thread is not hung.

SendNotifyMessage   Windows.pas

Syntax

```
SendNotifyMessage(
hWnd: HWND;          {a handle to a window}
Msg: UINT;           {the identifier of the message to send}
wParam: WPARAM;      {a 32-bit message specific value}
lParam: LPARAM       {a 32-bit message specific value}
): BOOL;             {returns TRUE or FALSE}
```

Description

This function sends the specified message to the window procedure of the window indicated by the hWnd parameter. If this window belongs to another thread, the function returns immediately without waiting for the message to be processed. If the window specified by the hWnd parameter belongs to the calling thread, this function behaves exactly like SendMessage. Caution is advised when sending a message whose parameters contain pointers to a window in another thread, as the function will return before the thread associated with the specified window has a chance to process the message and the pointers could be freed before they are used.

Parameters

hWnd: A handle to the window whose window procedure is to receive the specified message. If this parameter is set to HWND_BROADCAST, the message is sent to all top-level windows in the system, including disabled and invisible windows. The message is not sent to child windows. Applications that need to send a user-defined message to other applications using HWND_BROADCAST should use RegisterWindowMessage to obtain a unique message identifier.

Msg: The identifier of the message to send.

wParam: A 32-bit value dependent on the message being sent.

lParam: A 32-bit value dependent on the message being sent.

Return Value

If the function succeeds, it returns TRUE; otherwise, it returns FALSE. To get extended error information, call the GetLastError function.

See Also

PostMessage, PostThreadMessage, RegisterWindowMessage, SendMessage, SendMessageCallback, SendMessageTimeout

Example

Listing 3-15: Sending a message via SendNotifyMessage

This application sends the message:

```
procedure TForm1.Button1Click(Sender: TObject);
begin
  {send a message. this function will return immediately}
  SendNotifyMessage(HWND_BROADCAST, WM_CLEAR, 0, 0);

  {indicate that the function has returned}
  ShowMessage('Returned');
end;
```

and this application receives it:

```
{we override the WM_CLEAR message handler to do
 something special when received}
procedure TForm1.WMClear(var Msg: TWMClear);
var
  iLoop: Integer;    // general loop control variable
begin
    {turn on some user interface objects}
    ProgressBar1.Visible := TRUE;
    Label2.Visible := TRUE;
    Form1.Repaint;

    {animate the progress bar for a short time}
    for iLoop := 0 to 100 do
    begin
      ProgressBar1.Position := iLoop;
```

```
        Sleep(10);
    end;

    {turn off the user interface objects}
    ProgressBar1.Visible := FALSE;
    Label2.Visible := FALSE;

    {indicate that the message was processed}
    Msg.Result := 1;
end;
```

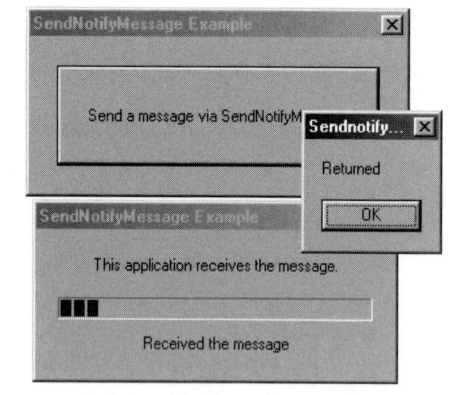

Figure 3-11: The SendNotify-Message function returned immediately

SetMessageExtraInfo   Windows.pas

Syntax

SetMessageExtraInfo(
lParam: LPARAM   {a 32-bit application-defined value}
): LPARAM;   {returns the previous 32-bit application-defined value}

Description

This function sets the 32-bit application-defined value associated with the calling thread's message queue. This 32-bit value can be retrieved by calling the GetMessageExtraInfo function.

Parameters

lParam: A 32-bit application-defined value.

Return Value

If the function succeeds, it returns the previous 32-bit application-defined value associated with the calling thread's message queue; otherwise, it returns zero.

See Also

GetMessageExtraInfo

Example

See Listing 3-6 under GetMessageExtraInfo.

SetWindowsHookEx   Windows.pas

Syntax

```
SetWindowsHookEx(
  idHook: Integer;           {hook type flag}
  lpfn: TFNHookProc;         {a pointer to the hook function}
  hmod: HINST;               {a handle to the module containing the hook function}
  dwThreadId: DWORD          {the identifier of the associated thread}
): HHOOK;                    {returns a handle to a hook function}
```

Description

This function installs an application-defined function into a hook chain. This hook function can be used to monitor events in either the thread identified by the dwThreadId parameter or all threads in the system. A popular use of hooks is to intercept and process specific messages before the system or a window procedure ever sees them. The hook function can pass the hook information to the next function in the hook chain by calling the CallNextHookEx function. This function can be called before or after any processing occurs in the called hook function. Calling the next hook in the chain is completely optional; however, if the next hook function in the chain is not called, other applications that have installed hooks will not receive hook notifications and could behave erratically. Hooks can be scoped to either a single thread or to the system, depending on the hook type. For a specific hook type, thread hooks are called first, then system hooks. A system hook is a shared resource, affecting all applications when installed. All system hooks must be located in a dynamic-link library. Before an application terminates, it must call UnhookWindowsHookEx for every hook function it installed to free system resources associated with installing a hook.

Parameters

idHook: A flag indicating the type of hook function to install. This parameter can be set to one value from the following table.

lpfn: A pointer to the hook function. If the dwThreadId parameter is set to zero or specifies the identifier of a thread created by another process, this parameter must point to a function located in a dynamic-link library; otherwise, this parameter can point to a function in the code associated with the current process. The idHook parameter identifies the type of hook function to which this parameter should point. See below for a detailed description of each type of hook function.

hmod: A handle to the module (a dynamic-link library) containing the hook function pointed to by the lpfn parameter. This parameter must be set to zero if dwThreadId identifies a thread created by the current process and lpfn points to a hook function located in the code associated with the current process.

dwThreadId: The identifier of the thread to which the installed hook function will be associated. If this parameter is set to zero, the hook will be a system-wide hook that is associated with all existing threads.

Return Value

If the function succeeds, it returns a handle to the newly installed hook function; otherwise, it returns zero.

See Also

CallNextHookEx, UnhookWindowsHookEx

Table 3-6: SetWindowsHookEx idHook values

Value	Description
WH_CALLWNDPROC	Installs a hook function that intercepts messages before they are sent to the destination window procedure. This hook can be either a system- or thread-level hook.
WH_CALLWNDPROCRET	Installs a hook function that receives messages after they have been processed by the destination window procedure. This hook can be either a system- or thread-level hook.
WH_CBT	Installs a hook function that receives hook notifications useful in providing computer-based training functionality. This hook can be a system-level hook only.
WH_DEBUG	Installs a hook function that is used to debug other hook functions. This hook can be either a system- or thread-level hook.
WH_FOREGROUNDIDLE	Installs a hook function that is called when the application's foreground thread is about to become idle. This hook can be either a system- or thread-level hook.
WH_GETMESSAGE	Installs a hook function that intercepts messages posted to a message queue. This hook can be either a system- or thread-level hook.
WH_JOURNALPLAYBACK	Installs a hook function that replays messages previously recorded by a WH_JOURNALRECORD hook. This hook can be a system-level hook only.
WH_JOURNALRECORD	Installs a hook function that records all input messages sent to the system message queue, and is useful in providing macro functionality. This hook can be a system-level hook only.
WH_KEYBOARD	Installs a hook function that intercepts keystroke messages. This hook can be either a system- or thread-level hook.
WH_MOUSE	Installs a hook function that intercepts mouse messages. This hook can be either a system- or thread-level hook.
WH_MSGFILTER	Installs a hook function that intercepts messages generated as a result of user interaction in a dialog box, message box, menu, or scroll bar. This hook can be a thread-level hook only.
WH_SHELL	Installs a hook function that receives notifications as a result of shell interaction. This hook can be either a system- or thread-level hook.
WH_SYSMSGFILTER	Installs a hook function that intercepts messages generated as a result of user interaction in a dialog box, message box, menu, or scroll bar throughout the entire system. This hook can be a system-level hook only.

WH_CALLWNDPROC Hook Function

Syntax

CallWndProcProc(
nCode: Integer;   {the hook code}
wParam: WPARAM;   {was message sent by current process flag}
lParam: LPARAM   {a pointer to a TCWPStruct structure}
): LRESULT;   {this function should always return zero}

Description

This hook function is called when a message is sent via one of the SendMessage functions. Before the message is sent to the destination window procedure, it is passed through this hook function. The hook function can examine the message, but cannot modify it. Otherwise, this function can perform any desired task. This hook function must be associated with the thread calling the SendMessage function, not the thread receiving the message.

Parameters

nCode: Indicates if the hook function should process the message or pass it to the next hook in the chain. If this parameter is set to HC_ACTION, the hook function must process the message. If it is less than zero, this hook function should pass the message to the next hook by calling the CallNextHookEx function without further processing, and should return the value returned by CallNextHookEx.

wParam: Indicates if the message was sent by the current process or a different process. If this parameter is set to zero, the message was sent by another process; a non-zero value indicates that the message was sent by the current process.

lParam: A pointer to a TCWPStruct data structure that contains information about the message. The TCWPStruct data structure is defined as:

TCWPStruct = packed record
    lParam: LPARAM;   {a 32-bit message specific value}
    wParam: WPARAM;   {a 32-bit message specific value}
    message: UINT;   {the identifier of the message}
    hwnd: HWND;   {a handle to the window receiving the message}
end;

lParam: A 32-bit value dependent on the message being sent.

wParam: A 32-bit value dependent on the message being sent.

message: The identifier of the intercepted message.

hwnd: The handle of the window whose window procedure will receive the message.

Return Value

This hook function should always return zero.

WH_CALLWNDPROCRET Hook Function

Syntax

```
CallWndProcRetProc(
    nCode: Integer;          {the hook code}
    wParam: WPARAM;          {was message sent by current process flag}
    lParam: LPARAM           {a pointer to a TCWPRetStruct structure}
): LRESULT;                  {this function should always return zero}
```

Description

This hook function is called after a message is sent via one of the SendMessage functions. After the message is sent to the destination window procedure, it is passed through this hook function. The hook function can examine the message, but cannot modify it. Otherwise, this function can perform any desired task. This hook function must be associated with the thread calling the SendMessage function, not the thread receiving the message.

Parameters

nCode: Indicates if the hook function should process the message or pass it to the next hook in the chain. If this parameter is set to HC_ACTION, the hook function must process the message. If it is less than zero, this hook function should pass the message to the next hook by calling the CallNextHookEx function without further processing, and should return the value returned by CallNextHookEx.

wParam: Indicates if the message was sent by the current process or a different process. If this parameter is set to zero, the message was sent by another process; a non-zero value indicates that the message was sent by the current process.

lParam: A pointer to a TCWPRetStruct data structure that contains information about the message. The TCWPRetStruct data structure is defined as:

```
TCWPRetStruct = packed record
    lResult: LRESULT;        {message processing result}
    lParam: LPARAM;          {a 32-bit message specific value}
    wParam: WPARAM;          {a 32-bit message specific value}
    message: UINT;           {the identifier of the message}
    hwnd: HWND;              {a handle to the window receiving the message}
end;
```

lResult: The result of the message processing as returned by the window procedure that processed the message.

lParam: A 32-bit value dependent on the message that was sent.

wParam: A 32-bit value dependent on the message that was sent.

message: The identifier of the intercepted message.

hwnd: The handle of the window whose window procedure processed the message.

Return Value

This hook function should always return zero.

WH_CBT Hook Function

Syntax

```
CBTProc(
  nCode: Integer;          {a hook code}
  wParam: WPARAM;          {a value dependent on hook code}
  lParam: LPARAM           {a value dependent on hook code}
): LRESULT;                {returns 1 or 0}
```

Description

This hook function is used to provide computer-based training functionality for an application. It is called by the system before activating, creating, destroying, minimizing, maximizing, moving, or sizing a window, before completing a system command, before setting the keyboard input focus to a window, before removing a mouse or keyboard message from the system message queue, or before synchronizing with the system message queue. The return value from this hook function indicates if Windows prevents one of these events from taking place. This hook must not install a WH_JOURNALPLAYBACK hook except as described in the table below, but otherwise can perform any desired task. This is a system-level hook only and as such must reside in a dynamic-link library.

Parameters

nCode: Indicates how the hook function should process the message. If it is less than zero, this hook function should pass the message to the next hook by calling the CallNextHookEx function without further processing, and should return the value returned by CallNextHookEx. Otherwise, this parameter will contain one value from the following table.

wParam: A 32-bit value dependent on the value of the nCode parameter. See the following table for possible values.

lParam: A 32-bit value dependent on the value of the nCode parameter. See the following table for possible values.

Return Value

For the following nCode values, the hook function should return 0 to allow the operation to continue; it should return 1 to prevent it: HCBT_ACTIVATE, HCBT_CREATEWND, HCBT_DESTROYWND, HCBT_MINMAX, HCBT_MOVESIZE, HCBT_SETFOCUS, HCBT_SYSCOMMAND. For the HCBT_CLICKSKIPPED, HCBT_KEYSKIPPED, and HCBT_QS nCode values, the return value is ignored.

Table 3-7: CBTProc nCode values

Value	Description
HCBT_ACTIVATE	A window is about to be activated.
	wParam: Specifies the handle of the window being activated.
	lParam: Contains a pointer to a TCBTActivateStruct structure containing information about the window being activated.

Value	Description
HCBT_CLICKSKIPPED	A mouse message has been removed from the system message queue. When this hook code is received, the CBTProc function must install a WH_JOURNALPLAYBACK hook function in response to the mouse message. This value is sent to the CBTProc only if a WH_MOUSE hook function is installed.
	wParam: The identifier of the mouse message removed from the message queue.
	lParam: Contains a pointer to a TMouseHookStruct structure containing information about the mouse message.
HCBT_CREATEWND	A window has been created, but the hook function is called before the window receives the WM_CREATE or WM_NCCREATE messages, and before its final size and position have been established. If the hook function returns zero, the window will be destroyed, but it will not receive a WM_DESTROY message.
	wParam: Contains a handle to the newly created window.
	lParam: Contains a pointer to a TCBTCreateWnd structure containing information about the newly created window.
HCBT_DESTROYWND	A window is about to be destroyed.
	wParam: Contains a handle to the window being destroyed.
	lParam: This value is undefined and will contain zero.
HCBT_KEYSKIPPED	A keyboard message has been removed from the system message queue. When this hook code is received, the hook function must install a WH_JOURNALPLAYBACK hook function in response to the keyboard message. This value is sent to the CBTProc only if a WH_KEYBOARD hook function is installed.
	wParam: The virtual key code of the keyboard message removed from the message queue.
	lParam: Contains a value indicating the repeat count, scan code, key transition code, previous key state, and context code of the keyboard message removed from the message queue.
HCBT_MINMAX	A window is about to be minimized or maximized.
	wParam: Contains a handle to the window being minimized or maximized.
	lParam: A 32-bit value whose low-order word specifies the show window value used for the operation. The high-order word is undefined.
HCBT_MOVESIZE	A window is about to be repositioned or sized.
	wParam: Contains a handle to the window being repositioned or sized.
	lParam: Contains a pointer to a TRect structure containing the new coordinates of the window.
HCBT_QS	A WS_QUEUESYNC message has been retrieved from the message queue.
	wParam: This value is undefined and will contain zero.
	lParam: This value is undefined and will contain zero.
HCBT_SETFOCUS	A window is about to receive input focus.
	wParam: Contains a handle to the window receiving the keyboard input focus.
	lParam: Contains a handle to the window losing the keyboard input focus.

Value	Description
HCBT_SYSCOMMAND	A system command message has been retrieved from the message queue. wParam: Contains a system command value indicating the system command. Set the WM_SYSCOMMAND message for a list of possible values. lParam: Contains the value of the lParam parameter of the WM_SYSCOMMAND message.

The TCBTActivateStruct data structure is defined as:

```
TCBTActivateStruct = packed record
    fMouse: BOOL;           {mouse click activate flag}
    hWndActive: HWND;       {a handle to the active window}
end;
```

fMouse: A Boolean value indicating if the window was activated by a mouse click. A value of TRUE indicates that a mouse click activated the window.

hWndActive: A handle to the active window.

The TMouseHookStruct data structure is defined as:

```
TMouseHookStruct = packed record
    pt: TPoint;             {the screen coordinates of the mouse cursor}
    hwnd: HWND;             {a handle to the window receiving the message}
    wHitTestCode: UINT;     {a hit test value}
    dwExtraInfo: DWORD;     {message defined information}
end;
```

pt: A TPoint structure containing the horizontal and vertical coordinates of the mouse cursor, in screen coordinates.

hwnd: A handle to the window receiving the mouse message.

wHitTestCode: A value indicating the part of the window where the mouse cursor was at the time of the event. See the WM_NCHITTEST message for a list of possible values.

dwExtraInfo: A value containing extra information associated with the mouse message.

The TCBTCreateWnd data structure is defined as:

```
TCBTCreateWnd = packed record
    lpcs: PCreateStruct;        {a pointer to a TCreateStruct structure}
    hwndInsertAfter: HWND;      {a handle to the preceding window in the z-order}
end;
```

lpcs: A pointer to a TCreateStruct data structure containing information about the window being created. See the CreateWindowEx function for a description of this data structure.

hwndInsertAfter: A handle to the window preceding the newly created window in the z-order.

WH_DEBUG Hook Function

Syntax

DebugProc(
nCode: Integer;   {the hook code}
wParam: WPARAM;   {the type of hook being called}
lParam: LPARAM   {a pointer to a TDebugHookInfo structure}
): LRESULT;   {returns a non-zero value to block the hook}

Description

This hook function is used to debug other hook functions. The system calls this hook function before calling the hook functions for any other hook, passing it information about the hook to be called. This function can instruct Windows to call the destination hook function or to skip it, and can perform any desired task.

Parameters

nCode: Indicates if the hook function should process the message or pass it to the next hook in the chain. If this parameter is set to HC_ACTION, the hook function must process the message. If it is less than zero, this hook function should pass the message to the next hook by calling the CallNextHookEx function without further processing, and should return the value returned by CallNextHookEx.

wParam: Specifies the type of hook being called. This parameter can contain one value from the SetWindowsHookEx idHook values table.

lParam: A pointer to a TDebugHookInfo data structure containing the parameters being passed to the hook function about to be called. The TDebugHookInfo data structure is defined as:

TDebugHookInfo = packed record
    idThread: DWORD;   {a thread identifier}
    idThreadInstaller: DWORD;   {a thread identifier}
    lParam: LPARAM;   {the lParam parameter being passed to the hook}
    wParam: WPARAM;   {the wParam parameter being passed to the hook}
    code: Integer;   {the nCode parameter being passed to the hook}
end;

idThread: The identifier of the thread containing the hook procedure to be called.

idThreadInstaller: The identifier of the thread containing the debug hook function.

lParam: The lParam parameter that will be passed to the hook procedure being called.

wParam: The wParam parameter that will be passed to the hook procedure being called.

code: The nCode parameter that will be passed to the hook procedure being called.

Return Value

To prevent the destination hook from being called, the hook function should return a non-zero value. Otherwise, the hook procedure must pass the hook information to the CallNextHookEx function, returning the value returned from CallNextHookEx.

WH_FOREGROUNDIDLE Hook Function

Syntax

```
ForegroundIdleProc(
NCode: Integer;            {the hook code}
WParam: WPARAM;            {not used}
Lparam: LPARAM;            {not used}
): DWORD;                  {returns zero or the return value from the next hook}
```

Description

This hook function is called when the foreground thread is about to become idle.

Parameters

nCode: Indicates if the hook function should process the message or pass it to the next hook in the chain. If this parameter is set to HC_ACTION, the hook function must process the message. If it is less than zero, this hook function should pass the message to the next hook by calling the CallNextHookEx function without further processing, and should return the value returned by CallNextHookEx.

wParam: Not used.

lParam: Not used.

Return Value

This hook function should return zero if this message is processed.

WH_GETMESSAGE Hook Function

Syntax

```
GetMsgProc(
nCode: Integer;            {the hook code}
wParam: WPARAM;            {message removal flag}
lParam: LPARAM             {a pointer to a TMsg structure}
): LRESULT;                {this function should always return zero}
```

Description

This hook function is called when the GetMessage or PeekMessage functions are called to retrieve a message from the message queue. The retrieved message is passed through this hook function before being passed to the destination window procedure. This hook function can modify the message parameters, sending the modified message to the destination window procedure when the hook function returns, and can perform any desired task.

Parameters

nCode: Indicates if the hook function should process the message or pass it to the next hook in the chain. If this parameter is set to HC_ACTION, the hook function must process the message. If it is less than zero, this hook function should pass the message to the next hook by calling the CallNextHookEx function without further processing, and should return the value returned by CallNextHookEx.

wParam: Indicates if the message has been removed from the queue. A value of PM_REMOVE indicates that the message has been removed from the queue; a value of PM_NOREMOVE indicates that the message has not been removed from the queue.

lParam: A pointer to a TMsg data structure containing information about the message. The TMsg data structure is defined as:

```
TMsg = packed record
    hwnd: HWND;              {a handle to the window receiving the message}
    message: UINT;           {the message identifier}
    wParam: WPARAM;          {a 32-bit message specific value}
    lParam: LPARAM;          {a 32-bit message specific value}
    time: DWORD;             {the time when the message was posted}
    pt: TPoint;              {the position of the mouse cursor}
end;
```

See the DispatchMessage function for a detailed description of this data structure.

Return Value

This hook function should always return zero.

WH_JOURNALPLAYBACK Hook Function

Syntax

```
JournalPlaybackProc(
    nCode: Integer;          {a hook code}
    wParam: WPARAM;          {this parameter is not used}
    lParam: LPARAM           {a pointer to a TEventMsg structure}
): LRESULT;                  {returns a wait time in clock ticks}
```

Description

This hook procedure is used to insert a mouse or keyboard message into the system message queue by copying the message information to the TEventMsg structure pointed to by the lParam parameter. Its most common use is playing back a series of mouse and keyboard messages recorded by a previous use of the WH_JOURNALRECORD hook function. While this hook function is installed, mouse and keyboard input are disabled. The JournalPlaybackProc function is always called in the context of the thread that initially set the WH_JOURNALPLAYBACK hook. If the user presses the Ctrl+Esc or Ctrl+Alt+Del key combinations while a WH_JOURNALPLAYBACK hook is installed, the system stops the message playback, unhooks the hook function, and posts a

WM_CANCELJOURNAL message to the application. Otherwise, this function can perform any desired task.

Parameters

nCode: A code specifying how the hook function should process the message. This parameter can contain one value from the following table. If it is less than zero, this hook function should pass the message to the next hook by calling the CallNextHookEx function without further processing, and should return the value returned by CallNextHookEx.

wParam: This parameter is not used and is set to zero.

lParam: A pointer to a TEventMsg structure containing information about the message being processed. This parameter is only used when the nCode parameter is set to HC_GETNEXT. The TEventMsg data structure is defined as:

```
TEventMsg = packed record
     message: UINT;      {a message identifier}
     paramL: UINT;       {additional message specific information}
     paramH: UINT;       {additional message specific information}
     time: DWORD;        {the time the message was posted}
     hwnd: HWND;         {a handle to the window receiving the message}
end;
```

message: The identifier of the message.

paramL: Additional message specific information. If the message is between WM_KEYFIRST and WM_KEYLAST, this member contains the virtual key code of the key that was pressed.

paramH: Additional message specific information. If the message is between WM_KEYFIRST and WM_KEYLAST, this member contains the scan code of the key that was pressed.

time: The time at which the message was posted to the message queue of the window identified by the hwnd member.

hwnd: A handle to the window whose window procedure received the message.

Return Value

The hook function should return the amount of time, in seconds, that the system should wait before processing the next message, if a pause is desired. When the application continues, the hook function will be called again with an nCode value of HC_GETNEXT. The hook function should return a zero after this second call or this loop will continue and the application will appear to be hung. If the next message should be processed immediately, the function should return zero. If the nCode parameter is not set to HC_GETNEXT, the return value is ignored.

Table 3-8: JournalPlaybackProc nCode values

Value	Description
HC_GETNEXT	The hook function must copy the current mouse or keyboard message to the TEventMsg data structure pointed to by the lParam parameter. The same message can be retrieved repeatedly by continuing to specify HC_GETNEXT without specifying HC_SKIP.
HC_NOREMOVE	An application called the PeekMessage function using a PM_NOREMOVE flag.
HC_SKIP	The hook function should prepare to copy the next mouse or keyboard message to the TEventMsg data structure.
HC_SYSMODALOFF	A system modal dialog box has been destroyed, indicating that the hook function must resume message playback.
HC_SYSMODALON	A system modal dialog box has been displayed, indicating that the hook function must suspend message playback.

WH_JOURNALRECORD Hook Function

Syntax

```
JournalRecordProc(
  nCode: Integer;         {a hook code}
  wParam: WPARAM;         {this parameter is not used}
  lParam: LPARAM          {a pointer to a TEventMsg structure}
): LRESULT;               {the return value is ignored}
```

Description

This hook procedure is used to record messages that have been removed from the system message queue. The hook function must not modify the messages being copied. These messages can be replayed later by using the WH_JOURNALPLAYBACK hook function. The hook function should watch for a VK_CANCEL message to be recorded, which is sent to the system when the user presses the Ctrl+Break key combination. This indicates that the user wishes to stop message recording, and the record sequence should be halted and the WH_JOURNALRECORD hook should be removed. If the user presses the Ctrl+Esc or Ctrl+Alt+Del key combinations while a WH_JOURNALRECORD hook is installed, the system stops the message playback, unhooks the hook function, and posts a WM_CANCELJOURNAL message to the application. The JournalRecordProc function is always called in the context of the thread that initially set the WH_JOURNALRECORD hook. Otherwise, this function can perform any desired task.

Parameters

nCode: A code specifying how the hook function should process the message. This parameter can contain one value from the following table. If it is less than zero, this hook function should pass the message to the next hook by calling the CallNextHookEx function without further processing, and should return the value returned by CallNextHookEx.

wParam: This parameter is not used and is set to zero.

lParam: A pointer to a TEventMsg structure containing information about the message being processed. The TEventMsg data structure is defined as:

```
TEventMsg = packed record
     message: UINT;          {a message identifier}
     paramL: UINT;           {additional message specific information}
     paramH: UINT;           {additional message specific information}
     time: DWORD;            {the time the message was posted}
     hwnd: HWND;             {a handle to the window receiving the message}
end;
```

See the WH_JOURNALPLAYBACK hook function for a description of this data structure.

Return Value

The return value from this hook function is ignored.

Table 3-9: JournalRecordProc nCode values

Value	Description
HC_ACTION	The lParam parameter contains a pointer to a TEventMsg structure containing information on the message removed from the system message queue. This structure should be copied to a buffer or file for later playback by the WH_JOURNALPLAYBACK hook.
HC_SYSMODALOFF	A system modal dialog box has been destroyed, indicating that the hook function must resume message recording.
HC_SYSMODALON	A system modal dialog box has been displayed, indicating that the hook function must suspend message recording.

WH_KEYBOARD Hook Function

Syntax

```
KeyboardProc(
nCode: Integer;          {the hook code}
wParam: WPARAM;          {a virtual key code}
lParam: LPARAM           {a bitmask containing keystroke information}
): LRESULT;              {indicates if the message is to be discarded}
```

Description

This hook function is called when the application calls the GetMessage or PeekMessage function and a keyboard message is retrieved. This function can perform any desired task.

Parameters

nCode: A code specifying how the hook function should process the message. This parameter can contain one value from Table 3-10. If it is less than zero, this hook function should pass the message to the next hook by calling the CallNextHookEx function without further processing, and should return the value returned by CallNextHookEx.

wParam: Contains the virtual key code of the key generating the message.

lParam: A 32-bit bitmask that indicates the repeat count, scan code, extended key flag, context code, previous key flag, and transition flag for the keyboard message. The values represented by the bits in this parameter are described in Table 3-11.

Return Value

To prevent the keyboard message from being passed to the destination window procedure, the hook function should return a non-zero value. To pass the message to the destination window procedure, the hook function should return zero.

Table 3-10: KeyboardProc nCode values

Value	Description
HC_ACTION	The wParam and lParam parameters contain information about a keyboard message.
HC_NOREMOVE	The wParam and lParam parameters contain information about a keyboard message. This message has not been removed from the message queue.

Table 3-11: KeyboardProc lParam bitmask values

Bits	Description
0-15	Specifies the number of times the keyboard message has been repeated due to the user holding down the key.
16-23	Identifies the original equipment manufacturer scan code.
24	A value of 1 in this bit indicates that the key is an extended key such as a function or a numeric keypad key.
25-28	These bits are reserved and their value is undefined.
29	A value of 1 in this bit indicates that the Alt key is down.
30	A value of 1 in this bit indicates that the key was down before the message was sent; 0 indicates that the key was up.

WH_MOUSE Hook Function

Syntax

```
MouseProc(
  nCode: Integer;           {the hook code}
  wParam: WPARAM;           {a mouse message identifier}
  lParam: LPARAM            {a pointer to a TMouseHookStruct structure}
): LRESULT;                 {indicates if the message is to be discarded}
```

Description

This hook function is called when the application calls the GetMessage or PeekMessage function and a mouse message is retrieved. This hook function must not install a WH_JOURNALPLAYBACK hook. Otherwise, this function can perform any desired task.

Parameters

nCode: A code specifying how the hook function should process the message. This parameter can contain one value from the following table. If it is less than zero, this hook function should pass the message to the next hook by calling the CallNextHookEx function without further processing, and should return the value returned by CallNextHookEx.

wParam: Contains the identifier of the mouse message.

lParam: A pointer to a TMouseHookStruct structure containing information about the mouse message. The TMouseHookStruct is defined as:

```
TMouseHookStruct = packed record
    pt: TPoint;              {the screen coordinates of the mouse cursor}
    hwnd: HWND;              {a handle to the window receiving the message}
    wHitTestCode: UINT;      {a hit test value}
    dwExtraInfo: DWORD;      {message-defined information}
end;
```

See the WH_CBT hook function for a description of this data structure.

Return Value

To prevent the mouse message from being passed to the destination window procedure, the hook function should return a non-zero value. To pass the message to the destination window procedure, the hook function should return zero.

Table 3-12: MouseProc nCode values

Value	Description
HC_ACTION	The wParam and lParam parameters contain information about a mouse message.
HC_NOREMOVE	The wParam and lParam parameters contain information about a mouse message. This message has not been removed from the message queue.

WH_MSGFILTER Hook Function

Syntax

```
MsgFilterProc(
    nCode: Integer;          {a hook code}
    wParam: WPARAM;          {this parameter is not used}
    lParam: LPARAM           {a pointer to a TMsg structure}
): LRESULT;                  {indicates if the message was processed}
```

Description

This hook event is used to monitor messages generated from user interaction with a dialog box, message box, menu, or scroll bar. The system calls this hook function when an input event has occurred in one of these objects, but before the message generated by such an event has been dispatched to the destination window procedure. This hook function must reside in the code of the thread that installed the hook, and can perform any desired task.

Chapter 3

Parameters

nCode: A code specifying how the hook function should process the message. This parameter can contain one value from the following table. If it is less than zero, this hook function should pass the message to the next hook by calling the CallNextHookEx function without further processing, and should return the value returned by CallNextHookEx.

wParam: This parameter is not used and is set to zero.

lParam: A pointer to a TMsg data structure containing information about the message. The TMsg data structure is defined as:

```
TMsg = packed record
    hwnd: HWND;              {a handle to the window receiving the message}
    message: UINT;           {the message identifier}
    wParam: WPARAM;          {a 32-bit message specific value}
    lParam: LPARAM;          {a 32-bit message specific value}
    time: DWORD;             {the time when the message was posted}
    pt: TPoint;              {the position of the mouse cursor}
end;
```

See the DispatchMessage function for a detailed description of this data structure.

Return Value

If the hook function processed the message, it should return a non-zero value. If the hook function did not process the message, it should return zero.

Table 3-13: MsgFilterProc nCode values

Value	Description
MSGF_DDEMGR	The input event happened while the dynamic data exchange management library was waiting for a synchronous transaction to be completed.
MSGF_DIALOGBOX	The input event happened in a dialog or message box.
MSGF_MENU	The input event happened in a menu.
MSGF_NEXTWINDOW	The input event was generated by the user pressing the Alt+Tab key combination to switch to a different window.
MSGF_SCROLLBAR	The input event happened in a scroll bar.

WH_SHELL Hook Function

Syntax

```
ShellProc(
    nCode: Integer;          {a hook code}
    wParam: WPARAM;          {additional hook specific information}
    lParam: LPARAM           {additional hook specific information}
): LRESULT;                  {this function should always return zero}
```

Description

This hook function is used by shell applications to receive notification about system events. It is used to monitor window activation and creation, and may perform any desired task.

Parameters

nCode: A code specifying how the hook function should process the message. This parameter can contain one value from the following table. If it is less than zero, this hook function should pass the message to the next hook by calling the CallNextHookEx function without further processing, and should return the value returned by CallNextHookEx.

wParam: Specifies information dependent on the nCode parameter. See the following table for a list of possible values. Unless otherwise specified, this parameter is ignored.

lParam: Specifies information dependent on the nCode parameter. See the following table for a list of possible values. Unless otherwise specified, this parameter is ignored.

Return Value

This function should always return zero.

Table 3-14: ShellProc nCode values

Value	Description
HSHELL_ACTIVATESHELLWINDOW	Indicates that the shell application should activate its main window.
HSHELL_GETMINRECT	Indicates that a window is being minimized or maximized and the system needs the new window position coordinates. The wParam parameter contains a handle to the window being resized, and the lParam parameter contains a pointer to a TRect structure that receives the new coordinates.
HSHELL_LANGUAGE	Indicates that the keyboard language has changed or that a new keyboard layout was loaded.
HSHELL_REDRAW	Indicates that the title of a window in the taskbar has been redrawn. The wParam parameter contains a handle to this window.
HSHELL_TASKMAN	Indicates that the user has activated the system task list.
HSHELL_WINDOWACTIVATED	Indicates that focus has changed to a different top-level, unowned window. The wParam parameter contains a handle to the newly activated window.
HSHELL_WINDOWCREATED	Indicates that a top-level, unowned window has been created. The window will already exist when the ShellProc hook function is called. The wParam parameter contains a handle to the newly created window.
HSHELL_WINDOWDESTROYED	Indicates that a top-level, unowned window has been destroyed. This window still exists when the ShellProc hook function is called. The wParam parameter contains a handle to the window about to be destroyed.

WH_SYSMSGFILTER Hook Function

Syntax

```
SysMsgFilterProc(
  nCode: Integer;              {a hook code}
  wParam: WPARAM;              {this parameter is not used}
  lParam: LPARAM               {a pointer to a TMsg structure}
): LRESULT;                    {indicates if the message was processed.}
```

Description

This hook event is used to monitor messages generated from user interaction with a dialog box, message box, menu, or scroll bar throughout the entire system. The system calls this hook function when an input event has occurred in one of these objects, but before the message generated by such an event has been dispatched to the destination window procedure. This hook function must reside in a dynamic-link library, and can perform any desired task.

Parameters

nCode: A code specifying how the hook function should process the message. This parameter can contain one value from the following table. If it is less than zero, this hook function should pass the message to the next hook by calling the CallNextHookEx function without further processing, and should return the value returned by CallNextHookEx.

wParam: This parameter is not used and is set to zero.

lParam: A pointer to a TMsg data structure containing information about the message. The TMsg data structure is defined as:

```
TMsg = packed record
  hwnd: HWND;              {a handle to the window receiving the message}
  message: UINT;           {the message identifier}
  wParam: WPARAM;          {a 32-bit message specific value}
  lParam: LPARAM;          {a 32-bit message specific value}
  time: DWORD;             {the time when the message was posted}
  pt: TPoint;              {the position of the mouse cursor}
end;
```

See the DispatchMessage function for a detailed description of this data structure.

Return Value

If the hook function processed the message, it should return a non-zero value. If the hook function did not process the message, it should return zero.

Table 3-15: SysMsgFilterProc nCode values

Value	Description
MSGF_DIALOGBOX	The input event happened in a dialog or message box.
MSGF_MENU	The input event happened in a menu.

Value	Description
MSGF_NEXTWINDOW	The input event was generated by the user pressing the Alt+Tab key combination to switch to a different window.
MSGF_SCROLLBAR	The input event happened in a scroll bar.

Example

Listing 3-16: Intercepting the Tab and Enter keys

```
{the prototype for the new keyboard hook function}
   function KeyboardHook(nCode: Integer; wParam: WPARAM;
                        lParam: LPARAM): LResult; stdcall;

var
  Form1: TForm1;
  WinHook: HHOOK;      // a handle to the keyboard hook function

implementation

{$R *.DFM}

procedure TForm1.FormCreate(Sender: TObject);
begin
  {install the keyboard hook function into the keyboard hook chain}
  WinHook:=SetWindowsHookEx(WH_KEYBOARD, @KeyboardHook, 0, GetCurrentThreadID);
end;

procedure TForm1.FormDestroy(Sender: TObject);
begin
  {remove the keyboard hook function from the keyboard hook chain}
  UnhookWindowsHookEx(WinHook);
end;

function KeyboardHook(nCode: Integer; wParam: WPARAM; lParam: LPARAM): LResult;
begin
  {if we can process the hook information...}
  if (nCode>-1) then
    {...was the TAB key pressed?}
    if (wParam=VK_TAB) then
    begin
      {if so, output a beep sound}
      MessageBeep(0);

      {indicate that the message was processed}
      Result := 1;
    end
    else
    {...was the RETURN key pressed?}
    if (wParam=VK_RETURN) then
    begin
      {if so, and if the key is on the up stroke, cause
       the focus to move to the next control}
      if ((lParam shr 31)=1) then
        Form1.Perform(WM_NEXTDLGCTL, 0, 0);
```

```
        {indicate that the message was processed}
        Result := 1;
    end
    else
      {otherwise, indicate that the message was not processed.}
      Result := 0
  else
    {we must pass the hook information to the next hook in the chain}
    Result := CallNextHookEx(WinHook, nCode, wParam, lParam);
end;
```

TranslateMessage   Windows.pas

Syntax

```
TranslateMessage(
const lpMsg: TMsg         {a structure containing the message to be translated}
): BOOL;                  {returns TRUE or FALSE}
```

Description

This function translates virtual key messages into character messages, posting the resulting message back into the calling thread's message queue. WM_CHAR messages are created only for those keys that are directly mapped to an ASCII character by the keyboard driver. Applications that process virtual key messages for special purposes should not call TranslateMessage.

Parameters

lpMsg: A pointer to a TMsg data structure containing information about the message to be translated. This data structure is retrieved by the GetMessage and PeekMessage functions, and is not modified by TranslateMessage. The TMsg data structure is defined as:

```
TMsg = packed record
    hwnd: HWND;           {a handle to the window receiving the message}
    message: UINT;        {the message identifier}
    wParam: WPARAM;       {a 32-bit message specific value}
    lParam: LPARAM;       {a 32-bit message specific value}
    time: DWORD;          {the time when the message was posted}
    pt: TPoint;           {the position of the mouse cursor}
end;
```

See the DispatchMessage function for a description of this data structure.

Return Value

If the function succeeds and a virtual key message was translated into a character message and posted to the calling thread's queue, this function returns TRUE. If the function fails, or a virtual key message was not translated into a character message, it returns FALSE. Note that under Windows NT, this function will return TRUE if the message is a function key or arrow key message.

See Also

GetMessage, PeekMessage

Example

See Listing 3-5 under GetMessage.

UnhookWindowsHookEx   Windows.pas

Syntax

```
UnhookWindowsHookEx(
hhk: HHOOK           {a handle to the hook being removed}
): BOOL;             {returns TRUE or FALSE}
```

Description

This function removes the specified hook that was installed into a hook chain by the SetWindowsHookEx function. The hook is not removed until all threads have finished their current call to the hook procedure. If no thread is calling the hook procedure at the time UnhookWindowsHookEx is called, the hook is removed immediately.

Parameters

hhk: A handle to the hook being removed.

Return Value

If this function succeeds, it returns TRUE; otherwise, it returns FALSE.

See Also

SetWindowsHookEx

Example

See Listing 3-16 under SetWindowsHookEx.

WaitMessage   Windows.pas

Syntax

```
WaitMessage: BOOL;        {returns TRUE or FALSE}
```

Description

This function suspends the calling thread, yielding control to other threads. This function will not return until a message is placed into the calling thread's message queue, at which time execution will resume.

Return Value

If the function succeeds, it returns TRUE; otherwise, it returns FALSE. To get extended error information, call the GetLastError function.

See Also

GetMessage, PeekMessage

Example

Listing 3-17: Waiting for a message

```
{this function places the application into a message loop
 that will break only when the left mouse button is clicked
 on the client area of the form.  the user will be unable to
 resize or move the form until then.}
procedure TForm1.Button1Click(Sender: TObject);
var
  TheMessage: TMSG;        // holds message info
  MouseClicked: Boolean;   // general loop control variable
begin
  {initialize the loop control variable}
  MouseClicked := FALSE;

  {place the application into a loop until a mouse button is clicked}
  while not MouseClicked do
  begin
    {empty the message queue}
    while PeekMessage(TheMessage, Handle, 0, 0, PM_REMOVE) do;

    {suspend the thread until a new message is placed in the queue}
    WaitMessage();

    {a new message has just dropped into the queue. retrieve it.}
    PeekMessage(TheMessage, Handle, 0, 0, PM_REMOVE);

    {if the new message was a mouse click, break out of the loop}
    if TheMessage.Message=WM_LBUTTONDOWN then
    begin
      MouseClicked := TRUE;
      {indicate that the message was a mouse click}
      ShowMessage('A message was received, resume execution');
    end;
  end;
end;
```

Chapter 4

Memory Management Functions

The Win32 API functions for memory management give the Delphi programmer effective tools for monitoring and managing memory resources. The Win32 API is designed to have a reasonable compatibility with 16-bit applications even though there are dramatic changes in the memory structure of the 32-bit operating systems. Knowing how to use memory resources effectively allows the developer to write code that is stable and efficient. Writing code for DLLs and threads places even more importance on the functions that are discussed in this chapter.

Delphi does a lot to hide the necessary steps of allocating and deallocating memory for objects, arrays, etc. Even dynamic arrays are easily implemented, and such objects as TList and TObjectList have made linked-list algorithms almost obsolete. However, while Delphi does a very good job of insulating the developer from most memory management practices, there are times when a developer needs more finite control over how the application handles memory. Indeed, Delphi's built-in memory management, while very functional, can be a bit slow when high performance is a priority. In these cases, a developer who understands how memory management functions work can write custom memory allocation and partitioning routines if necessary.

The Win32 Virtual Memory Architecture

Windows 95, NT, and later introduced a new memory design which differs remarkably from the memory model design of 16-bit Windows and DOS. The programmer is provided with a flat memory model that extends beyond the limits of physical memory. This "virtual" memory model contains a memory manager that maps a program's virtual memory reference to a physical address at run time. The swap file on a hard drive is used to swap pages of memory to disk when the system uses more virtual memory than is available in the physical RAM address space.

This memory design affords the Windows programmer room to operate. Data structures can be built in sizes under the virtual memory model that were previously impossible. Regardless of how much physical memory is installed in a target computer, the 2-gigabyte memory model is there for the developer to allocate as desired while the operating system performs mapping to disk. However, be aware that available disk space can limit the size of virtual memory availability.

Each program has its own 4-gigabyte virtual address space, with the lower 2 gigabytes available to the programmer for general use. The upper 2 gigabytes are reserved for system use. The API memory functions will allocate the requested amounts of memory from the lower 2 gigabytes of virtual address space.

Categories of Memory Allocation Functions

There are four types of memory allocation API calls. Virtual functions are for reserving and managing large memory buffers. Heap functions are for smaller memory allocations. Global and local functions are for smaller memory allocations, and are provided for 16-bit compatibility.

There are only private address spaces in a WIN32 environment. 16-bit Windows had both local (private) and global (shared) address spaces. The WIN32 API still maintains global and local versions of heap functions for compatibility, but they both allocate memory from the same local 2-gigabyte address space. All of the heap is local to a process and cannot be accessed by any other process.

Heaps

When a program needs buffer allocations of at least several kilobytes in size, it would be appropriate to use VirtualAlloc to get the memory block. VirtualAlloc gets memory in multiples of 4KB in size, with the exact amount rounded up to the nearest 4KB boundary. When the memory that the program allocates is to be used for small objects, arrays, or structures, calls to HeapAlloc would be most efficient. To use VirtualAlloc for a very small structure would be a waste of resources for typical memory fetches used in linked lists or construction of binary trees. This waste would also slow down the system due to disk swap file activity if all the memory allocation cannot fit into physical memory at once.

Each process has a default heap, but an application can allocate additional heaps for efficiency and management. Each heap has its own handle. An application can get the handle for the default heap with the GetProcessHeap API function.

Note: Threads within a process have access to the default heap of the process. The WIN32 memory manager serializes access to the heap. When a thread performs a heap function, other threads that want memory are held waiting until the function is finished. This results in a small delay that the application experiences. If a thread wants to have some heap space and will not be sharing that heap with other threads, it would be much faster for the thread to allocate its own heap and not use the default heap. When a thread uses its own heap there is optionally no serialization during heap allocations. The other threads that might also want heap space from other heaps are not delayed. The programmer has a choice when designing memory usage in threads: Use the default heap

> for convenience and slightly smaller code size, or use heaps that are private to threads for speed.

DLLs do not contain their own heap by default. A DLL shares heap space with the calling application. However, a DLL can allocate its own heap space and use it, just like the main thread of a process can allocate a heap in addition to the default heap.

It is very important to release heap memory when an application is through using it. Programs that do not do this are said to contain "memory leaks," and will produce errors if allowed to run indefinitely. The rule of thumb is, if an application allocated it, then it is responsible for freeing it.

The 16-Bit Memory Functions

16-bit Windows maintained a global heap that was common to the entire system and a local heap that was private to a process. The local heap was limited to a 64KB segment and was usually set by the programmer to be much less. Of the function calls in this chapter, only the Global and Local functions were available in the 16-bit Windows API.

The Global and Local memory calls in WIN32 perform the same function. The Global functions are not "global" as they are in 16-bit Windows. There is no shared memory except for the use of memory-mapped files. All the available memory in the lower 2 gigabytes of virtual address space is designed to be private to the application and is not seen by any other application, and the Global and Local memory allocation functions both allocate memory from this address space. Therefore, only the Global memory allocation functions will be covered by this text.

Virtual Memory

Memory allocations using VirtualAlloc are straightforward, with few options to confuse the issue. The main consideration is to request the correct amount of memory. Keep in mind that VirtualAlloc will grant memory in 4KB sizes. If this is too much memory, then consider using HeapAlloc instead. Although it is true that the application might not run out of virtual memory by using VirtualAlloc, it would create unnecessary work for the disk swapping routines if too much memory is wasted. If the application commits the block to physical memory, it will be swapped to disk when necessary because Windows thinks that committed memory is being used. An application should reserve memory to keep if from being used by other applications, then commit it when the memory is actually used. This will reduce disk swap file access drastically, resulting in performance improvements. Always release memory when the application is finished with it. It is easier and faster for the Windows virtual memory manager to keep the current memory pages mapped to physical memory when there are fewer of them to manage.

Three States of Memory

Memory can exist in three separate states. The state of a memory object will change as it is allocated, reallocated, and freed. These three states are:

Free: The page is neither committed nor reserved. It is not accessible to the process, but is available for allocation by one of the memory allocation functions.

Reserved: The memory has been reserved for use by the calling process, and cannot be used by other processes or threads. It is not being used, and is not committed to physical storage.

Committed: The memory object is committed to physical storage. It is marked as being used, and may contain volatile information. If the physical RAM memory needs to use the space for other virtual memory blocks, this page will be saved to the disk swap file. Only the process that allocated it can use this memory.

How Much Memory is Really There?

Theoretically there are 2 gigabytes of memory for the application to use in the virtual memory model. However, committing the memory to physical storage requires the support of the swap file on disk. Windows will use all of the available disk space on the system disk for swap file space as the default configuration, or will use less if configured to do so. As VirtualAlloc or other functions are used to commit virtual memory, the virtual memory manager will begin to consume available system (RAM) memory. When that physical memory comes close to being exhausted, it will begin to map memory pages to disk. When the available disk space is also exhausted, the allocation functions will report allocation failures. Therefore, the design limit is not really the 2-gigabyte limit of the theoretical design, but is, in fact, the size of available physical RAM memory plus swapfile space (less some reserve and overhead).

When making a request for memory allocation, it is wise to check the amount of memory available before making the request. Do not use all of the memory resources on the system because Windows or other software will need some of it. The 2 gigabytes of virtual memory is private to the process, but the swapfile is a resource that is shared by the operating system and all running tasks. Check this margin by calling the GlobalMemoryStatus function and checking the dwMemoryLoad or the dwAvailPageFile members that are provided in the returned structure. Leave several megabytes of virtual memory to provide elbowroom for the operating system and other applications. The dwMemoryLoad value will reach 100% well before the limit is reached.

Multiple Heaps

A program can perform all heap allocations from the default heap, getting the handle to the heap with the GetProcessHeap function call. However, this forces the program to deal with all the performance hits and issues that come with all the default error trapping and threads waiting in line for memory allocations.

Creating multiple heaps allows the developer to fine tune the system performance. Multiple heaps can be organized for separate purposes. If the application has several large linked lists and/or binary trees, then it might be more efficient to allocate a separate heap for each one. Separate heaps allow multiple threads to perform memory allocations from them while avoiding the conflicts that would be inherent with using only one heap.

Separate heaps also allow certain ones to have additional exception handling turned on. There are no disadvantages in creating multiple heaps.

Error Trapping

A solid software design would have tests after each memory allocation to be sure that the returned pointer was valid. In addition to the common pointer tests, there are the API options for turning Windows error trapping on or off. It is easiest and safest to leave all the error trapping options turned on. However, if the design is well tested, and if the application might be making thousands or perhaps even millions of calls for heap allocation, then the developer can avoid the performance hits by removing the Windows error trapping that involves exception handling. Windows will still, of course, return NIL pointer values so that the application can detect a failed API call.

The developer can fine tune the exception handling by specifying exactly which heap API calls will use the better (and somewhat slower) error trapping. By specifying the HEAP_GENERATE_EXCEPTIONS flag for the HeapCreate call, that error trapping will be in effect for every subsequent API call made to that heap without being further specified. By omitting that flag on HeapCreate, the developer can individually select which API calls will use the exception handling. However, keep in mind that the application can always detect the error by simply checking the return value of the function regardless of whether or not the HEAP_GENERATE_EXCEPTIONS flag was in effect.

Thread Access

Heap allocations might conflict with one another when more than one thread makes a request for memory from a shared heap. To prevent allocation conflicts in simultaneous requests, omit the flag HEAP_NO_SERIALIZE. This is indeed the default condition for heaps. When a thread performs a HeapAlloc request and another similar request is already in progress by another thread, one thread will be put to sleep until the heap system is available for another request. The heap allocation is said to be serialized. This involves a performance hit for the thread that is put to sleep. This performance hit can be significant when there are many threads making requests or when there are thousands or perhaps even millions of requests.

To eliminate this bottleneck on common heaps, create heaps that are private to the thread. Use a call to CreateHeap to establish a heap for each thread (or several heaps per thread if appropriate). Keep the heap handle, and then use that heap everywhere in that thread. This guarantees there will be no conflicts in memory allocation for the thread on that heap, and the developer can specify the HEAP_NO_SERIALIZE option for the allocation calls. This means that Windows will not even check to see if there are heap access conflicts since the programmer has claimed responsibility and risk for that issue. This speeds up the allocation, with performance gains that can be significant and measurable.

Speed

When an application has several heaps, or even several different uses for the same heap, try to get all of the memory for one purpose allocated as contiguous memory. Do this by performing all the HeapAlloc requests for each purpose together rather than interspersed with other code that might be making heap requests.

Consider the case of loading some huge databases into memory, perhaps into a linked list or binary tree. For several megabytes of data, the heap requests could exceed the physical memory available. This means that there will be much disk activity as the virtual memory manager tries to keep the currently addressed memory loaded into physical RAM. An application can reduce this disk activity by keeping all the memory being accessed clustered together rather than fragmented.

There are design tradeoffs here that can make or break a system. Suppose the application needs to read a large file that will exceed physical RAM, and the application needs two allocated structures for two purposes from the same file. It would be wise to use two heaps to keep the small memory allocations for each purpose clustered together. The virtual memory manager will manage the heaps in chunks of 4KB pages, so that when one set of data is active, those pages will be resident in physical memory. The inactive structure in the other heap will have its pages swapped off to disk. This will minimize disk thrashing while the application performs work on the individual heaps. Since each HeapAlloc request takes the heap handle as its first parameter, it requires no extra effort on the programmer's part to specify the correct heap. The application only has to create the necessary heaps at the beginning of the process and destroy them at the end.

Note that it does not matter in which order allocations are made from the heaps created. If the allocations are intermingled among several heaps, the system will still work effectively. Each heap will use its separate virtual memory pages for its own allocations. The application does not need to make all the allocations for one heap before beginning the allocations for another one. The only tuning the programmer needs to do to optimize heap usage is to provide a separate heap for each purpose or structure and to set the flags appropriately.

Delphi vs. the Windows API

In a strict sense it is not necessary to use any of the API memory allocation calls listed here. A program can use the Pascal New or GetMem functions, which allocate memory from the default memory space. However, using New or GetMem prevents the developer from controlling the allocation of additional heaps, selecting error trapping for Windows to use, or designing large buffers effectively. Windows provides a number of heap management functions for creating heaps and allocating memory from them, as well as the virtual memory functions. Delphi does not use any of the heap functions internally for allocating memory. Instead, Delphi uses the virtual memory functions. Although the Windows memory functions give the developer greater control over memory allocation and management, benchmarks have shown that Delphi's internal memory management functions are faster than using most of the Windows memory functions directly. However, these techniques ultimately use these Win32 API functions at some level, and understanding their usage allows developers to design custom memory management solutions to fill different requirements.

Memory Management Functions

The following memory management functions are covered in this chapter:

Table 4-1: Memory management functions

Function	Description
CopyMemory	Copies the values stored in one memory location to another memory location.
FillMemory	Fills a memory location with a value.
GetProcessHeap	Retrieves a handle to the process heap.
GlobalAlloc	Allocates memory from the process address space.
GlobalDiscard	Discards allocated memory.
GlobalFlags	Retrieves information about a memory object.
GlobalFree	Frees allocated memory.
GlobalHandle	Converts a pointer to memory into a handle.
GlobalLock	Converts a memory object handle into a pointer.
GlobalMemoryStatus	Retrieves information about available memory.
GlobalReAlloc	Reallocates an allocated memory object.
GlobalSize	Retrieves the size of a memory object.
GlobalUnlock	Unlocks a locked memory object.
HeapAlloc	Allocates memory from a heap.
HeapCreate	Creates a heap.
HeapDestroy	Destroys a heap.
HeapFree	Frees memory allocated from a heap.
HeapReAlloc	Reallocates memory allocated from a heap.
HeapSize	Retrieves the size of a memory object allocated from a heap.
IsBadCodePtr	Determines if a process has read access to a specific memory address.
IsBadReadPtr	Determines if a process has read access to a range of memory.
IsBadStringPtr	Determines if a process has read access to a range of memory stored as a string.
IsBadWritePtr	Determines if a process has write access to a range of memory.
MoveMemory	Moves the values stored in one memory location to another memory location. The memory locations may overlap.
VirtualAlloc	Allocates memory from the virtual address space.
VirtualFree	Frees allocated virtual memory.
VirtualProtect	Sets access protection on a range of virtual memory.
VirtualQuery	Retrieves information about a range of virtual memory.
ZeroMemory	Fills the values at a memory location with zero.

CopyMemory   Windows.pas

Syntax

```
CopyMemory(
  Destination: Pointer;     {address of the target memory block}
  Source: Pointer;          {address of memory block to copy}
  Length: DWORD             {size of memory block in bytes}
);                          {this procedure does not return a value}
```

Description

CopyMemory copies the requested number of bytes from one memory address to another memory address. This is similar to the Delphi Move procedure except that the source and destination parameters are in the reverse order. The memory blocks do not have to begin or end on any specific boundary or address, but all of the referenced addresses must be within the memory range assigned to the process by the memory manager. The range of memory pointed to by Source and Destination must not overlap. If there is a possible overlap in addresses of the memory blocks, then use the MoveMemory function. Overlapping blocks used with CopyMemory may produce unpredictable results.

Parameters

Destination: The target address to which the requested amount of memory will be copied.

Source: The source address from which the requested amount of memory will be copied.

Length: The number of bytes to copy.

See Also

FillMemory, MoveMemory, ZeroMemory

Example

Listing 4-1: Copying memory from one array to another

```
var
  Form1: TForm1;
  Info1, Info2: array[0..99] of byte;    // the copy from and copy to buffers

implementation

procedure TForm1.FormCreate(Sender: TObject);
var
  iLoop: Integer;
begin
  {fill the source buffer with information, and display this in the
   string grid}
  for iLoop := 1 to 100 do
  begin
    Info1[iLoop-1] := iLoop;
    StringGrid1.Cells[iLoop-1, 0] := IntToStr(Info1[iLoop-1]);
  end;
end;
```

```
procedure TForm1.Button1Click(Sender: TObject);
var
  iLoop: integer;
begin
  {copy the source buffer into the destination buffer}
  CopyMemory(@Info2, @Info1, SizeOf(Info1));

  {display the result in the second string grid}
  for iLoop := 1 to 100 do
    StringGrid2.Cells[iLoop-1, 0] := IntToStr(Info2[iLoop-1]);
end;
```

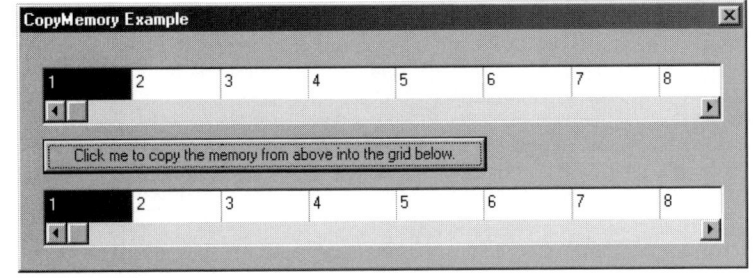

Figure 4-1:
The array was copied

FillMemory   Windows.pas

Syntax

FillMemory(
Destination: Pointer;   {address of memory block to initialize}
Length: DWORD;   {size of memory block in bytes}
Fill: Byte   {data to use for initialization}
);   {this procedure does not return a value}

Description

FillMemory initializes the requested block of memory to the given byte value. FillMemory is useful if every byte in a memory block needs to be initialized to the same value. The memory block does not have to begin or end on any specific boundary or address, but all of the referenced addresses must be within the memory range assigned to the process by the memory manager.

Parameters

Destination: The address of the block of memory to be initialized.

Length: The number of bytes of memory to be initialized.

Fill: The byte value used to initialize each byte of the memory block.

See Also

CopyMemory, MoveMemory, ZeroMemory

Example

Listing 4-2: Initializing buffer values

```
procedure TForm1.Button1Click(Sender: TObject);
var
  Info: array[0..199] of byte;     // the information buffer
  iLoop: integer;
begin
  {initialize the information buffer with a value}
  FillMemory(@Info, SizeOf(Info), 123);

  {display these values in the string grid}
  for iLoop := 1 to 200 do
    StringGrid1.Cells[iLoop-1 ,0] := IntToStr(Info[iLoop-1]);
end;
```

GetProcessHeap   Windows.pas

Syntax

GetProcessHeap: THandle;   {returns the handle of the default heap}

Description

This function gets the handle of the heap for the calling process. The function can be used with HeapAlloc, HeapReAlloc, HeapFree, and HeapSize to allocate memory from the process heap without having to first create a heap using the HeapCreate function.

Return Value

If the function succeeds, it returns a handle to the default heap for the current process; otherwise, it returns zero.

See Also

HeapAlloc, HeapCreate, HeapDestroy, HeapFree, HeapReAlloc, HeapSize

Example

Listing 4-3: Allocating memory from the process heap

```
procedure TForm1.Button1Click(Sender: TObject);
type
  BufferType = array[0..63] of byte;   // defines the buffer type
var
  Buffer: ^BufferType;                 // the buffer variable
  iLoop: Integer;                      // general loop control variable
begin
  {allocate memory from the heap of the calling process}
  Buffer := HeapAlloc(GetProcessHeap, HEAP_ZERO_MEMORY, sizeof(BufferType));

  {display the default values from the new buffer (should be all zeros)}
  for iLoop := 0 to 63 do
    StringGrid1.Cells[iLoop, 0] := IntToStr(Buffer^[iLoop]);

  {return the memory}
```

```
    HeapFree(GetProcessHeap, 0, Buffer);
end;
```

GlobalAlloc   Windows.pas

Syntax

```
GlobalAlloc(
uFlags: UINT;              {object allocation attributes}
dwBytes: DWORD             {number of bytes to allocate}
): HGLOBAL;                {returns a handle to a global memory object}
```

Description

The GlobalAlloc function allocates the requested number of bytes from the Windows heap. Memory allocated with this function will be double-word aligned, and may allocate a greater amount than specified to facilitate the alignment.

Parameters

uFlags: Specifies how the memory is to be allocated. GMEM_FIXED is the default value and is used if this parameter is set to zero. Except where noted, this parameter can be set to one or more values from the following table.

dwBytes: The number of bytes to be allocated.

Return Value

If the function succeeds, it returns a handle to the global memory block; otherwise, it returns zero. To get extended error information, call the GetLastError function.

See Also

GlobalFree, GlobalLock, GlobalReAlloc, GlobalSize

Example

Listing 4-4: Allocating global memory

```
procedure TForm1.Button1Click(Sender: TObject);
type
  Arrayspace = array[0..199] of integer;
var
  Arrayptr: ^Arrayspace;   // pointer to a dynamic array
  Arrayhandle: HGLOBAL;    // handle to the array object
  iLoop: Integer;          // loop counter
begin
  {allocate memory from the global heap}
  Arrayhandle := GlobalAlloc(GPTR, SizeOf(Arrayspace));
  if Arrayhandle = 0 then
    begin
      ShowMessage('Error getting memory block!');
      exit;
    end;

  {retrieve a pointer to the allocated memory}
```

Chapter 4

```
      Arrayptr := GlobalLock(Arrayhandle);
      if Arrayptr = nil then
        begin
          ShowMessage('Error getting pointer to memory!');
          exit;
        end;

      {initialize the allocated memory block with values,
       and display it}
      for iLoop := 0 to 199 do
      begin
        Arrayptr^[iLoop] := iLoop;
        StringGrid1.Cells[iLoop, 0] := IntToStr(Arrayptr^[iLoop]);
      end;

      {unlock the global memory...}
      GlobalUnlock(Arrayhandle);

      {...and free it}
      GlobalFree(Arrayhandle);
    end;
```

Figure 4-2:
The memory
was allocated
and initialized

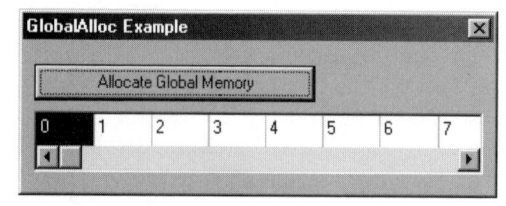

Table 4-2: GlobalAlloc uFlags values

Value	Description
GHND	Combination of the GMEM_MOVEABLE and GMEM_ZEROINIT flags.
GMEM_FIXED	Allocates a fixed memory block. Do not combine this flag with the GMEM_MOVEABLE flag. The return value can be typecast as a pointer to access the memory block. GlobalLock can also be used to acquire the pointer though no lock will be set.
GMEM_MOVEABLE	Allocates a moveable memory block. Do not combine this with the GMEM_FIXED flag.
GMEM_ZEROINIT	Initializes the contents of the allocated memory to zero.
GPTR	Combination of the GMEM_FIXED and GMEM_ZEROINIT flags.

GlobalDiscard Windows.pas

Syntax

```
GlobalDiscard(
  h: THandle          {handle of the global memory to be discarded}
): THandle;           {returns a handle to the global memory object}
```

Description

The GlobalDiscard function discards the memory block specified by the h parameter. The lock count for this memory object must be zero for this function to succeed. Once a global memory object has been discarded, its handle remains valid and can be used in subsequent calls to GlobalReAlloc.

Parameters

h: The handle to the memory object to be discarded.

Return Value

If the function succeeds, it returns a handle to the discarded global memory object; otherwise, it returns zero. To get extended error information, call the GetLastError function.

See Also

GlobalAlloc, GlobalReAlloc

Example

See Listing 4-6 under GlobalReAlloc.

GlobalFlags   Windows.pas

Syntax

```
GlobalFlags(
hMem: HGLOBAL          {a handle to the memory object}
): UINT;               {returns information flags and lock count}
```

Description

GlobalFlags provides information about the allocation flags and lock count for the specified memory object.

Parameters

hMem: A handle to the memory object for which information is to be retrieved.

Return Value

If the function succeeds, it returns a 32-bit value indicating the lock count and allocation flags of the specified memory object. The low-order byte of the low-order word contains the lock count of the specified memory object, and can be retrieved by combining the return value with the constant GMEM_LOCKCOUNT using the Boolean AND operator. The high-order byte of the low-order word contains either zero or GMEM_DISCARDED, indicating that the memory block has been discarded. If the function fails, it returns zero. To get extended error information, call the GetLastError function.

See Also

GlobalAlloc, GlobalDiscard, GlobalLock, GlobalReAlloc, GlobalUnlock

Example

See Listing 4-6 under GlobalReAlloc.

GlobalFree   Windows.pas

Syntax

```
GlobalFree(
hMem: HGLOBAL       {handle to the memory object to be deallocated}
): HGLOBAL;         {returns zero or the handle to the memory object}
```

Description

GlobalFree deallocates the memory block. It returns the memory to the heap and renders the handle invalid. This function will free a memory object regardless of its lock count.

Parameters

hMem: The pointer to the memory block to be returned to the system.

Return Value

If the function succeeds, it returns zero; otherwise, it returns a handle to the global memory object. To get extended error information, call the GetLastError function.

See Also

GlobalAlloc, GlobalFlags, GlobalLock, GlobalReAlloc, GlobalUnlock

Example

See Listing 4-4 under GlobalAlloc and Listing 4-6 under GlobalReAlloc.

GlobalHandle   Windows.pas

Syntax

```
GlobalHandle(
Mem: Pointer         {a pointer to the start of the memory block}
): HGLOBAL;          {returns zero or the handle to the memory object}
```

Description

GlobalHandle converts the pointer to a memory block specified by the Mem parameter into a global memory object handle. For memory objects allocated with the GMEM_FIXED flag set, the GlobalHandle and GlobalLock functions are not needed, because the handle and the pointer to memory are the same value. When GMEM_FIXED is used, the developer is responsible for being sure that all routines are finished with the memory object when it is freed.

Parameters

Mem: A pointer to the first byte of the memory block whose global memory handle is to be retrieved.

Return Value

If the function succeeds, it returns a handle to the global memory object; otherwise, it returns zero. To get extended error information, call the GetLastError function.

See Also

GlobalAlloc, GlobalLock, GlobalFree

Example

See Listing 4-6 under GlobalReAlloc.

GlobalLock Windows.pas

Syntax

```
GlobalLock(
hMem: HGLOBAL        {a handle to a memory object}
): Pointer;          {returns a pointer to the memory block}
```

Description

GlobalLock increments the lock counter for the given memory object by one, and forces the memory object to be maintained at a specific memory address. A memory object that is locked will not be moved to another address by the memory manager except for calls to the GlobalReAlloc function. The address that is returned will be a valid address for the memory object as long as the object has a lock count of at least one. Multiple routines can place lock counts on the object, so that the object cannot be moved as long as any routine is using the memory. The lock count can be decremented by calling the GlobalUnlock function. When a memory object is allocated with the GMEM_FIXED flag, it will always have a lock count of zero and will never be moved.

Parameters

hMem: A handle of the memory object whose pointer is to be retrieved.

Return Value

If the function succeeds, it returns a pointer to the first byte of the global memory block; otherwise, it returns zero. To get extended error information, call the GetLastError function.

See Also

GlobalAlloc, GlobalFlags, GlobalReAlloc, GlobalUnlock

Example

See Listing 4-4 under GlobalAlloc and Listing 4-6 under GlobalReAlloc.

GlobalMemoryStatus   Windows.pas

Syntax

GlobalMemoryStatus(
   var lpBuffer: TMemoryStatus   {a pointer to a TMemoryStatus structure}
);   {this procedure does not return a value}

Description

This procedure fills a TMemoryStatus structure with information regarding physical and virtual memory. However, due to the nature of Windows' memory management, two sequential calls to this function may yield different results.

Parameters

lpBuffer: A pointer to a TMemoryStatus structure that receives the information about physical and virtual memory status. The TMemoryStatus data structure is defined as:

```
TMemoryStatus = record
    dwLength: DWORD;            {the size of the structure in bytes}
    dwMemoryLoad: DWORD;        {estimated memory usage}
    dwTotalPhys: DWORD;         {the total amount of physical memory}
    dwAvailPhys: DWORD;         {the available amount of physical memory}
    dwTotalPageFile: DWORD;     {the total amount of swap file storage}
    dwAvailPageFile: DWORD;     {the available amount of swap file storage}
    dwTotalVirtual: DWORD;      {the total amount of virtual memory}
    dwAvailVirtual: DWORD;      {the available amount of virtual memory}
end;
```

dwLength: This member contains the size of the structure in bytes and must be set to SizeOf(TMemoryStatus) before the call to GlobalMemoryStatus is made.

dwMemoryLoad: Contains a value between 0 and 100 indicating the approximate percentage of memory in use.

dwTotalPhys: Indicates the total amount of physical RAM in bytes.

dwAvailPhys: Indicates the total amount of available physical RAM in bytes.

dwTotalPageFile: Indicates the maximum amount of storage space in the swap file in bytes, including both used space and available space. This number does not represent the actual physical size of the swap file.

dwAvailPageFile: Indicates the total amount of available space in the swap file in bytes.

dwTotalVirtual: Indicates the total amount of virtual address space for the calling process in bytes.

dwAvailVirtual: Indicates the total amount of unreserved and uncommitted space in the virtual address space of the calling process in bytes.

Example

Listing 4-5: Retrieving the memory status

```
procedure TGlobalMemoryStatusForm.ButtonGlobalMemoryStatusClick(
  Sender: TObject);
var
  GlobalMemoryInfo : TMemoryStatus;  // holds the global memory status information
begin
  {set the size of the structure before the call.}
  GlobalMemoryInfo.dwLength := SizeOf(GlobalMemoryInfo);

  {retrieve the global memory status...}
  GlobalMemoryStatus(GlobalMemoryInfo);

  {and display the information}
  Label1.caption := 'Results of GlobalMemoryStatus:';
  Label2.caption := 'Record structure size: '+IntToStr(
                    GlobalMemoryInfo.dwLength)+' bytes';
  Label3.caption := 'Current memory load: '+IntToStr(
                    GlobalMemoryInfo.dwMemoryLoad)+'%';
  Label4.caption := 'Total physical memory: '+Format('%.0n',[
                    GlobalMemoryInfo.dwTotalPhys/1])+' bytes';
  Label5.caption := 'Total available physical memory: '+Format('%.0n',[
                    GlobalMemoryInfo.dwAvailPhys/1])+' bytes';
  Label6.caption := 'Total paging file size: '+Format('%.0n',[
                    GlobalMemoryInfo.dwTotalPageFile/1])+' bytes';
  Label7.Caption := 'Total available paging file memory: '+Format('%.0n',[
                    GlobalMemoryInfo.dwAvailPageFile/1])+' bytes';
  Label8.caption := 'Total virtual memory: '+Format('%.0n',[
                    GlobalMemoryInfo.dwTotalVirtual/1])+' bytes';
  Label9.caption := 'Total available virtual memory: '+Format('%.0n',[
                    GlobalMemoryInfo.dwAvailVirtual/1])+' bytes';
end;
```

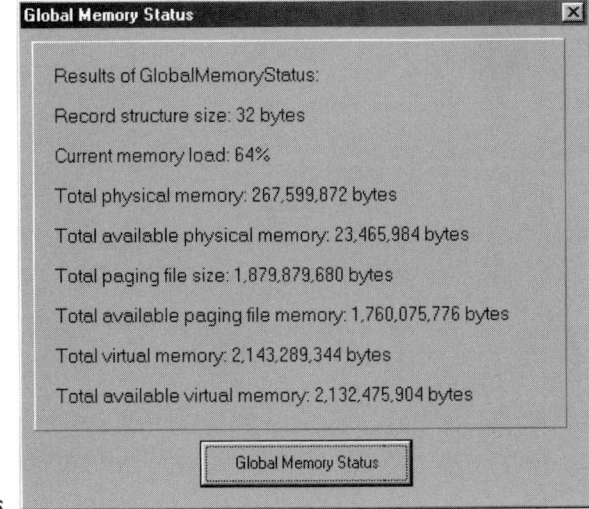

Figure 4-3: Displaying the memory status

GlobalReAlloc   Windows.pas

Syntax

```
GlobalReAlloc(
  hMem: HGLOBAL;          {a handle to a global memory object}
  dwBytes: DWORD;         {the size of the memory object}
  uFlags: UINT            {reallocation flags}
): HGLOBAL;               {returns a handle to a global memory object}
```

Description

This function is used to change the size or attributes of the specified global memory object. If this function reallocates a fixed memory object, the returned global memory handle can be used as a pointer to this memory block.

Parameters

hMem: A handle to the global memory object whose size or attributes are to be modified.

dwBytes: The new size of the global memory object in bytes. If the uFlags parameter contains the GMEM_MODIFY flag, this parameter is ignored.

uFlags: Specifies how the global memory object is to be modified. This parameter may contain one or more of the values from the following table. These values may be combined with the constant GMEM_MODIFY, which changes their behavior as outlined in the table.

Return Value

If the function succeeds, it returns a handle to the reallocated memory object; otherwise, it returns zero and the original handle remains valid. To get extended error information, call the GetLastError function.

See Also

GlobalAlloc, GlobalFree, GlobalLock

Example

Listing 4-6: Reallocating a global memory object

```
var
  Form1: TForm1;
  Arrayptr: ^Byte;          // pointer to a dynamic array
  Arrayhandle: HGLOBAL;     // handle to the array object
  PtrHandle: HGLOBAL;       // handle from GlobalHandle
  UnlockResult: Boolean;    // Unlock error checking
  ArrayFlags: integer;      // result of GlobalFlags call
  FreeResult: Hglobal;      // Free error checking
  FlagCount: integer;       // number of lock flags set
  Arraysize : integer;      // size of the memory object

implementation

procedure TForm1.Button1Click(Sender: TObject);
```

```
var
  iLoop: Byte;            // loop counter
  Baseptr: Pointer;       // temporary pointer
begin
  {allocate global memory}
  Arrayhandle := GlobalAlloc(GHND, 200);

  {retrieve a pointer to the global memory}
  Arrayptr := GlobalLock(Arrayhandle);

  {do something with the global memory block}
  Baseptr := Arrayptr;
  for iLoop := 0 to 199 do
  begin
    Byte(Baseptr^) := iLoop;
    StringGrid1.Cells[iLoop,0] := IntToStr(Byte(Baseptr^));
    BasePtr := Pointer(Longint(BasePtr)+1);
  end;

  {retrieve a pointer from the global memory handle}
  PtrHandle := GlobalHandle(Arrayptr);
  if PtrHandle <> Arrayhandle then
    ShowMessage('Memory Object Handle Error');

  {retrieve information on the global memory block}
  ArrayFlags := GlobalFlags(PtrHandle);
  Flagcount := ArrayFlags and GMEM_LOCKCOUNT;
  ShowMessage('# of global locks on Arrayhandle is '
              +IntToStr(Flagcount));

  {get the size of the global memory block}
  ArraySize := GlobalSize(PtrHandle);
  ShowMessage('Initial object size is ' + IntToStr(Arraysize));

  Button2.Enabled := TRUE;
  Button1.Enabled := FALSE;
end;

procedure TForm1.Button2Click(Sender: TObject);
var
  iLoop: Integer;
  Baseptr: Pointer;
begin
  {unlock the global memory block. this is not required
   if GMEM_FIXED was set on allocation.}
  if Flagcount > 0 then GlobalUnlock(Arrayhandle);

  {discard the memory block}
  Arrayhandle := GlobalDiscard(Arrayhandle);
  if Arrayhandle = 0 then
  begin
    ShowMessage('GlobalDiscard failed');
    exit;
  end;

  {our global memory handle is still valid}
  Arraysize := GlobalSize(Arrayhandle);
```

```
    ShowMessage('Discarded object size is ' + IntToStr(Arraysize));

    {reallocate global memory}
    Arrayhandle := GlobalReAlloc(Arrayhandle, 400, GMEM_ZEROINIT);
    if Arrayhandle = 0 then
    begin
      ShowMessage('Error in GlobalAlloc');
      exit;
    end;

    {retrieve the new size of the global memory block}
    ArraySize := GlobalSize(Arrayhandle);
    ShowMessage('ReAlloc''ed object size is ' + IntToStr(ArraySize));

    {do something with the new memory block}
    StringGrid1.ColCount := ArraySize;
    Baseptr := Arrayptr;
    for iLoop := 0 to 399 do
    begin
      StringGrid1.Cells[iLoop,0] := IntToStr(Byte(Baseptr^));
      BasePtr := Pointer(Longint(BasePtr)+1);
    end;

    {unlock the global memory block}
    SetLastError(NO_ERROR);            //Reset error trapping
    UnlockResult := GlobalUnlock(Arrayhandle);
    if UnlockResult then ShowMessage('Lock count is nonzero');
    if (not UnlockResult) and (GetLastError <> NO_ERROR) then
      ShowMessage('Error unlocking memory');

    {Free the global memory and invalidate its handle. Note
     that GlobalFree will free a locked memory block, and calling
     GlobalUnlock will not affect the behavior of GlobalFree.}
    FreeResult := GlobalFree(Arrayhandle);
    if (FreeResult <> 0)
      then ShowMessage('Error Freeing Memory');
end;
```

Table 4-3: GlobalReAlloc uFlags values

Value	Description
GMEM_MOVEABLE	If dwBytes is zero, this discards a previously moveable and discardable memory object. The function will fail if the lock count for the specified memory block is non-zero or if the block is neither moveable nor discardable.
	If dwBytes is nonzero, the block is moved to a new location (if necessary) to alter the size without changing the moveable or fixed status. For fixed memory objects the handle that is returned might be different than the hMem parameter. For moveable objects, the memory can be moved without the handle being changed even if the memory was locked with GlobalLock. This functionality is available only if the GMEM_MODIFY flag is not specified.
	Windows NT/2000 and later: Changes fixed memory to moveable memory only if the GMEM_MODIFY flag is also specified.

Value	Description
GMEM_ZEROINIT	If the memory object is set to a larger size, this specifies that the new memory contents are initialized to zero. This functionality is available only if the GMEM_MODIFY flag is not specified.

GlobalSize   Windows.pas

Syntax

```
GlobalSize(
  hMem: HGLOBAL          {a handle to the memory object}
): DWORD;                {returns the size of the memory object in bytes}
```

Description

This function returns the size of the specified memory object in bytes.

Parameters

hMem: The handle of the memory object whose size is to be retrieved.

Return Value

If the function succeeds, it returns the size of the specified global memory object in bytes; otherwise, it returns zero. To get extended error information, call the GetLastError function.

See Also

GlobalAlloc, GlobalFlags, GlobalReAlloc

Example

See Listing 4-6 under GlobalReAlloc.

GlobalUnlock   Windows.pas

Syntax

```
GlobalUnlock(
  hMem: HGLOBAL          {a handle to the memory object}
): BOOL;                 {returns TRUE or FALSE}
```

Description

GlobalUnlock decrements the lock count on moveable memory objects allocated with the GMEM_MOVEABLE flag, and has no effect on fixed memory objects allocated with the GMEM_FIXED flag.

Parameters

hMem: A handle to the memory object being unlocked.

Chapter 4

Return Value

If the function succeeds and the object is still locked after decrementing the lock count, it returns TRUE; otherwise, it returns FALSE. To get extended error information, call the GetLastError function. If GetLastError returns ERROR_SUCCESS, then the memory object is not locked.

See Also

GlobalAlloc, GlobalFlags, GlobalLock, GlobalReAlloc

Example

See Listing 4-4 under GlobalAlloc and Listing 4-6 under GlobalReAlloc.

HeapAlloc   Windows.pas

Syntax

```
HeapAlloc(
hHeap: THandle;          {a handle to a heap}
dwFlags: DWORD;          {allocation flags}
dwBytes: DWORD           {the requested size of allocation in bytes}
): Pointer;              {returns a pointer to allocated memory}
```

Description

HeapAlloc allocates the requested number of bytes from the specified heap.

Parameters

hHeap: A handle to the heap from which memory is allocated. This can be either a heap created with the HeapCreate function or the system heap as retrieved by the GetProcessHeap function.

dwFlags: Specifies how the allocation is made from the heap. If this parameter is set to zero, then the corresponding flags given as parameters to HeapCreate will be in effect; otherwise they will override the settings made in HeapCreate. If the hHeap parameter contains a handle to the system heap as returned by the GetProcessHeap function, this parameter is ignored. This parameter may be set to one or more of the values from Table 4-4.

dwBytes: Specifies the size of the requested memory block in bytes.

Return Value

If the function succeeds, it returns a pointer to the newly allocated memory block. If the function fails and the HEAP_GENERATE_EXCEPTIONS flag was not specified, the function returns NIL. If the function fails and the HEAP_GENERATE_EXCEPTIONS flag was specified, the function returns one of the values from Table 4-5.

See Also

GetProcessHeap, HeapCreate, HeapDestroy, HeapFree, HeapReAlloc, HeapSize

Example

Listing 4-7: Allocating memory from the heap

```
var
  Form1: TForm1;
  Arrayptr: ^Byte;         // pointer to byte array
  Baseptr: Pointer;        // a pointer to access the byte array
  MyHeap: THandle;         // private heap handle
  MySize: integer;         // heap size

implementation

procedure TForm1.Button1Click(Sender: TObject);
var
  iLoop: integer;          // loop counter
begin
  {Create a new private heap and test for errors}
  MyHeap := HeapCreate(HEAP_NO_SERIALIZE, $FFFF,0);
  if MyHeap = 0 then
  begin
    ShowMessage('Error creating private heap.');
    Exit;
  end;

  {Allocate memory for the array and test for errors}
  Arrayptr := HeapAlloc(MyHeap,HEAP_ZERO_MEMORY,200);
  if Arrayptr = nil then
  begin
    ShowMessage('Error Allocating memory');
    {release the heap if there was an error}
    if not HeapDestroy(MyHeap)
      then ShowMessage('Error destroying private heap');
  end;

  {fill memory}
  Baseptr := Arrayptr;
  for iLoop := 0 to 199 do
  begin
    Byte(Baseptr^) := iLoop;
    StringGrid1.Cells[iLoop,0] := IntToStr(Byte(Baseptr^));
    BasePtr := Pointer(Longint(BasePtr)+1);
  end;

  {How big is the heap?}
  MySize := HeapSize(MyHeap, 0, Arrayptr);
  Label1.Caption := 'HeapSize is ' + IntToStr(MySize);

  Button2.Enabled := TRUE;
  Button1.Enabled := FALSE;
end;

procedure TForm1.Button2Click(Sender: TObject);
begin
  {Extend the Array size}
  Arrayptr := HeapReAlloc(MyHeap, HEAP_ZERO_MEMORY, Arrayptr, 600);
  StringGrid1.ColCount := 600;
```

```
          if Arrayptr = nil then ShowMessage('Error expanding array.');

          {check the current (expanded) size}
          MySize := HeapSize(MyHeap, 0, Arrayptr);
          Label1.Caption := 'HeapSize is ' + IntToStr(MySize);

          {We're done, release the memory}
          if not HeapFree(MyHeap,0,Arrayptr)
            then ShowMessage('Error returning memory to heap.');

          {Destroy the heap}
          if not HeapDestroy(MyHeap)
            then ShowMessage('Error destroying heap.');
        end;
```

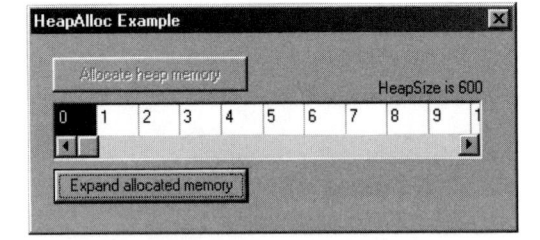

*Figure 4-4:
Memory was
allocated*

Table 4-4: HeapAlloc dwFlags values

Value	Description
HEAP_GENERATE_EXCEPTIONS	Indicates that Windows will generate an exception for an exception handler instead of returning a NIL.
HEAP_NO_SERIALIZE	Specifies that requests for heap will not be serialized. This should only be used for heaps that are created and used by a single thread. This flag removes the serialized locking feature that enables multiple threads to access the same heap.
HEAP_ZERO_MEMORY	The allocated memory will be initialized to zero.

Table 4-5: HeapAlloc return values

Value	Description
STATUS_ACCESS_VIOLATION	Indicates that the heap was corrupt or the function parameters were not accepted.
STATUS_NO_MEMORY	Indicates that the heap was corrupt or there was not enough memory to satisfy the request.

HeapCreate   Windows.pas

Syntax

HeapCreate(
flOptions: DWORD;   {allocation option flags}
dwInitialSize: DWORD;   {the starting heap size}

Memory Management Functions   149

```
    dwMaximumSize: DWORD        {the maximum heap size}
    ): THandle;                 {returns a handle to the new heap}
```

Description

This function reserves a block of memory from the virtual address space to be used as a heap by the calling processes. The initial size of the heap is allocated from available physical storage in the virtual address space.

Parameters

flOptions: Specifies heap attributes affecting all subsequent access to the new heap. This parameter can be one or more values from Table 4-6.

dwInitialSize: The initial size of the heap in bytes that is committed to physical memory. This value is rounded up to the nearest page boundary used by the virtual memory manager. The size of a page boundary can be determined by calling the GetSystemInfo function.

dwMaximumSize: The maximum size of the heap in bytes, rounded up to the nearest page boundary used by the virtual memory manager. This space will be marked as reserved in the virtual address space of the process. If this parameter is set to a non-zero value, the heap is non-growable, and memory can only be allocated up to the maximum size of the heap. If this parameter is zero, the heap is growable and the system will continue to grant memory allocations from the heap up to the available size of the virtual memory space.

Return Value

If the function is successful, it returns a handle to the newly created heap; otherwise, it returns zero. To get extended error information, call the GetLastError function.

See Also

GetProcessHeap, GetSystemInfo*, HeapAlloc, HeapDestroy, HeapFree, HeapReAlloc, HeapSize, VirtualAlloc

Example

See Listing 4-7 under HeapAlloc.

Table 4-6: HeapCreate flOptions values

Value	Description
HEAP_GENERATE_EXCEPTIONS	Indicates that Windows will generate an exception for an exception handler instead of returning a NIL.
HEAP_NO_SERIALIZE	Specifies that requests for access to the heap will not be serialized. This should only be used for heaps that are created and used by a single thread. This flag removes the serialized locking feature that enables multiple threads to access the same heap.
HEAP_ZERO_MEMORY	The allocated memory will be initialized to zero.

HeapDestroy   Windows.pas

Syntax

```
HeapDestroy(
  hHeap: THandle       {a handle of the heap being destroyed}
): BOOL;               {returns TRUE or FALSE}
```

Description

This function decommits and releases all pages from a heap created with the HeapCreate function, destroys the heap object, and invalidates the specified heap handle. A heap can be destroyed without first calling the HeapFree function to deallocate its memory.

Parameters

hHeap: The handle of the heap that is to be destroyed. This parameter must not be set to the value returned by the GetProcessHeap function.

Return Value

If the function succeeds, it returns TRUE; otherwise, it returns FALSE. To get extended error information, call the GetLastError function.

See Also

GetProcessHeap, HeapAlloc, HeapCreate, HeapFree, HeapReAlloc, HeapSize

Example

See Listing 4-7 under HeapAlloc.

HeapFree   Windows.pas

Syntax

```
HeapFree(
  hHeap: THandle;      {a handle to the heap}
  dwFlags: DWORD;      {option flags}
  lpMem: Pointer       {a pointer to the memory to be freed}
): BOOL;               {returns TRUE or FALSE}
```

Description

This function frees memory previously allocated from the heap by the HeapAlloc or HeapReAlloc functions. The freed memory will be available in the heap for the next heap allocation.

Parameters

hHeap: The handle of the heap from which the memory was originally allocated.

dwFlags: Specifies heap access behavior. This parameter can be either zero or HEAP_NO_SERIALIZE. See the HeapCreate function for a description of the HEAP_NO_SERIALIZE flag.

lpMem: A pointer to the memory block to be freed.

Return Value

If the function succeeds, it returns TRUE; otherwise, it returns FALSE. To get extended error information, call the GetLastError function.

See Also

GetProcessHeap, HeapAlloc, HeapCreate, HeapDestroy, HeapReAlloc, HeapSize

Example

See Listing 4-7 under HeapAlloc.

HeapReAlloc   Windows.pas

Syntax

```
HeapReAlloc(
hHeap: THandle;           {a handle to the heap}
dwFlags: DWORD;           {allocation option flags}
lpMem: Pointer;           {a pointer to the memory block being reallocated}
dwBytes: DWORD            {the requested size of reallocation in bytes}
): Pointer;               {returns a pointer to the memory block}
```

Description

This function resizes the memory allocated from a heap, and changes the memory block's attributes.

Parameters

hHeap: A handle to the heap from which memory is allocated. This can be either a heap created with the HeapCreate function or the system heap as retrieved by the GetProcessHeap function.

dwFlags: Specifies how the allocation is made from the heap. If this parameter is set to zero, then the corresponding flags given as parameters to HeapCreate will be in effect; otherwise they will override the settings made in HeapCreate. If the hHeap parameter contains a handle to the system heap as returned by the GetProcessHeap function, this parameter is ignored. This parameter may be set to one or more of the values from Table 4-7.

lpMem: A pointer to the memory block being reallocated.

dwBytes: Specifies the new size of the requested memory block in bytes.

Return Value

If the function succeeds, it returns a pointer to the reallocated memory block. If the function fails and the HEAP_GENERATE_EXCEPTIONS flag was not specified, the function returns NIL. If the function fails and the HEAP_GENERATE_EXCEPTIONS flag was specified, the function returns one of the values from Table 4-8.

See Also

GetProcessHeap, HeapAlloc, HeapCreate, HeapDestroy, HeapFree, HeapSize

Example

See Listing 4-7 under HeapAlloc.

Table 4-7: HeapReAlloc dwFlags values

Value	Description
HEAP_GENERATE_EXCEPTIONS	Indicates that Windows will generate an exception for an exception handler instead of returning a NIL.
HEAP_NO_SERIALIZE	Specifies that requests for heap will not be serialized. This should only be used for heaps that are created and used by a single thread. This flag removes the serialized locking feature that enables multiple threads to access the same heap.
HEAP_REALLOC_IN_PLACE_ONLY	Forces the memory manager to make any desired changes at the same location in virtual memory. If the request cannot be granted in place, the function fails and the original memory block is not modified.
HEAP_ZERO_MEMORY	The allocated memory will be initialized to zero.

Table 4-8: HeapReAlloc return values

Value	Description
STATUS_ACCESS_VIOLATION	Indicates that the heap was corrupt or the function parameters were not accepted.
STATUS_NO_MEMORY	Indicates that the heap was corrupt or there was not enough memory to satisfy the request.

HeapSize   Windows.pas

Syntax

```
HeapSize(
hHeap: THandle;          {a handle to the heap}
dwFlags: DWORD;          {option flags}
lpMem: Pointer           {a pointer to the memory block}
): DWORD;                {returns the size of the memory block in bytes}
```

Description

This function returns the size of a block of memory allocated from the specified heap in bytes.

Parameters

hHeap: A handle to the heap from which the memory was allocated. This can be either a heap created with the HeapCreate function or the system heap as retrieved by the GetProcessHeap function.

dwFlags: Specifies heap access behavior. This parameter can be either zero or HEAP_NO_SERIALIZE. See the HeapCreate function for a description of the HEAP_NO_SERIALIZE flag.

lpMem: A pointer to the memory block whose size is to be retrieved.

Return Value

If the function succeeds, it returns the size in bytes of the allocated memory block. If the function fails, it returns $FFFFFFFF.

See Also

GetProcessHeap, HeapAlloc, HeapCreate, HeapDestroy, HeapFree, HeapReAlloc

Example

See Listing 4-7 under HeapAlloc.

IsBadCodePtr   Windows.pas

Syntax

```
IsBadCodePtr(
lpfn: FARPROC          {pointer to possible code memory area}
): BOOL;               {returns TRUE or FALSE}
```

Description

This function determines if the address pointed to by the lpfn parameter contains code to which the current process has read access. Even if IsBadCodePtr is used before accessing memory at a given address, it is wise to use structured exception handling while accessing the memory. Rights can change by other processes in a preemptive multitasking environment. This function tests read access only at the specified memory address. For testing access to a memory block, use IsBadReadPtr instead.

Parameters

lpfn: A pointer to the memory address being checked.

Return Value

If the function succeeds and the process does not have read access to the specified memory address, the function returns TRUE. If the function fails, or the process has read access to the specified memory address, it returns FALSE. To get extended error information, call the GetLastError function.

See Also

IsBadReadPtr, IsBadStringPtr, IsBadWritePtr

Example

Listing 4-8: Testing for read access at a specific memory address

```
procedure TForm1.Button1Click(Sender: TObject);
var
  TestPtr: Pointer;   // an untyped pointer of questionable access
begin
  {try for a valid read address}
  Testptr := @TForm1.Button1Click;
  if IsBadCodePtr(Testptr)
    then ShowMessage('no read access')
    else ShowMessage('valid read access');
end;

procedure TForm1.Button2Click(Sender: TObject);
var
  TestPtr: Pointer;   // an untyped pointer of questionable access
begin
  {try for an invalid read address}
  TestPtr := Pointer($7FFFFFFF);
  if IsBadCodePtr(Testptr)
    then ShowMessage('no read access')
    else ShowMessage('valid read access');
end;
```

IsBadReadPtr   Windows.pas

Syntax

```
IsBadReadPtr(
lp: Pointer;              {a pointer to a memory block}
ucb: UINT                 {the size of the memory block in bytes}
): BOOL;                  {returns TRUE or FALSE}
```

Description

IsBadReadPtr tests the specified memory block for read access rights. Even if IsBadReadPtr is used before accessing memory, always use structured exception handling to trap errors resulting from dynamically changing memory rights in preemptive multitasking systems.

Parameters

lp: A pointer to the memory block whose read access rights are being checked.

ucb: The size of the memory block in bytes.

Return Value

If the function succeeds and the process does not have read access to every byte in the specified memory block, the function returns TRUE. If the function fails, or the process has read access to every byte in the specified memory block, it returns FALSE. To get extended error information, call the GetLastError function.

See Also

IsBadCodePtr, IsBadStringPtr, IsBadWritePtr

Example

Listing 4-9: Testing for read access to a range of memory

```
procedure TForm1.Button1Click(Sender: TObject);
var
  Testptr: Pointer;    // pointer to memory block of unknown access
  TestArray: array[1..64] of Integer;
begin
  {try for valid read access}
  Testptr := @TestArray;
  if IsBadReadPtr(Testptr, SizeOf(TestArray))
    then ShowMessage('no read access')
    else ShowMessage('valid read access');
end;

procedure TForm1.Button2Click(Sender: TObject);
var
  Testptr: Pointer;    // pointer to memory block of unknown access
begin
  {try for invalid read access}
  Testptr := nil;
  if IsBadReadPtr(Testptr, 9)
    then ShowMessage('no read access')
    else ShowMessage('valid read access');
end;
```

IsBadStringPtr   Windows.pas

Syntax

```
IsBadStringPtr(
lpsz: PChar;               {a pointer to a string}
ucchMax: UINT              {the maximum size of the string in bytes}
): BOOL;                   {returns TRUE or FALSE}
```

Description

IsBadStringPtr tests for read access to the entire range of memory occupied by the string pointed to by the lpsz parameter. The test will check the actual string area up to the null-terminating character, or up to the specified maximum size if no null terminator is found. This function can report a valid access if the memory block contains a null character near the beginning of the address range.

Parameters

lpsz: A pointer to a string whose read access is being checked.

ucchMax: The maximum size of the string, and the number of bytes to test for read access. Read access is tested for every byte up to the size specified by this parameter or until the null-terminating character is found.

Chapter 4

Return Value

If the function succeeds and the process does not have read access to every byte up to the null-terminating character, or to the size specified by the ucchMax parameter, the function returns TRUE. If the function fails, or the process has read access to every byte up to the null-terminating character, or to the size specified by the ucchMax parameter, it returns FALSE. To get extended error information, call the GetLastError function.

See Also

IsBadCodePtr, IsBadReadPtr, IsBadWritePtr

Example

Listing 4-10: Testing for read access to a string

```
procedure TForm1.Button1Click(Sender: TObject);
var
  Stringptr : PChar;     // a string pointer of unknown access
begin
  {allocate a string and initialize it}
  Stringptr := StrAlloc(20);
  Stringptr := 'Delphi Rocks';

  {Try for valid string access}
  If IsBadStringPtr(Stringptr, 20)
    then ShowMessage('no read access to string')
    else ShowMessage('Valid read access to string');
end;

procedure TForm1.Button2Click(Sender: TObject);
var
  Stringptr: PChar;      // a string pointer of unknown access
begin
  {try for invalid access}
  Stringptr := nil;
  if IsBadStringPtr(Stringptr ,10000)
    then ShowMessage('no read access to string')
    else ShowMessage('Valid read access to string');
end;
```

IsBadWritePtr   Windows.pas

Syntax

```
IsBadWritePtr(
  lp: Pointer;            {a pointer to a memory block}
  ucb: UINT               {the size of the memory block in bytes}
): BOOL;                  {returns TRUE or FALSE}
```

Description

IsBadWritePtr tests to see if the current process would be granted write access to all locations in the specified memory block.

Parameters

lp: A pointer to the memory block whose write access rights are being checked.

ucb: The size of the memory block in bytes.

Return Value

If the function succeeds and the process does not have write access to every byte in the specified memory block, the function returns TRUE. If the function fails, or the process has write access to every byte in the specified memory block, it returns FALSE. To get extended error information, call the GetLastError function.

See Also

IsBadCodePtr, IsBadReadPtr, IsBadStringPtr

Example

Listing 4-11: Testing for write access to a range of memory

```
procedure TForm1.Button1Click(Sender: TObject);
var
  Testptr: pointer;                     // a pointer of unknown access
  AnArray: array[1..100] of integer;    // test data
begin
  {test for valid write access}
  Testptr := @AnArray;
  if IsBadWritePtr(Testptr, SizeOf(AnArray))
    then ShowMessage('no write access')
    else ShowMessage('valid write access');
end;

procedure TForm1.Button2Click(Sender: TObject);
var
  Testptr: Pointer;                     // a pointer of unknown access
begin
  {test for invalid write access}
  Testptr := Pointer($3FFFFFFF);        // points to a random memory address
  if IsBadWritePtr(Testptr, 1000)
    then ShowMessage('no write access')
    else ShowMessage('valid write access');
end;
```

MoveMemory   Windows.pas

Syntax

```
MoveMemory(
  Destination: Pointer;      {a pointer to the target memory block}
  Source: Pointer;           {a pointer to the destination memory block}
  Length: DWORD              {the size of the memory block in bytes}
);                           {this procedure does not return a value}
```

Description

MoveMemory copies the requested number of bytes from one memory address to another memory address. This is similar to the Delphi Move procedure except that the source and destination parameters are in the reverse order. The memory blocks do not have to begin or end on any specific boundary or address, but all of the referenced addresses must be within the memory range assigned to the process by the memory manager. The address ranges identified by the Source and Destination parameters may overlap.

Parameters

Destination: The target address to which the requested amount of memory will be moved.

Source: The source address from which the requested amount of memory will be moved.

Length: The number of bytes to move.

See Also

CopyMemory, FillMemory, ZeroMemory

Example

Listing 4-12: Moving memory from one array to another

```
var
  Form1: TForm1;
  Array1,Array2: array[0..400] of Integer;   // holds the information to be moved

implementation

procedure TForm1.Button1Click(Sender: TObject);
var
  iLoop: Integer;    // general loop counter
begin
  {move the information from one array to the other}
  MoveMemory(@Array2,@Array1,SizeOf(Array1));

  {display the information}
  for iLoop := 0 to 400 do
  begin
    StringGrid1.Cells[iLoop,0] := IntToStr(Array1[iLoop]);
    StringGrid2.Cells[iLoop,0] := IntToStr(Array2[iLoop]);
  end;
end;

procedure TForm1.FormCreate(Sender: TObject);
var
  iLoop: Integer;    // general loop counter
begin
  {initialize the arrays}
  for iLoop := 0 to 400 do
  begin
    {set the values in this array to equal the loop counter}
    Array1[iLoop] := iLoop;
    StringGrid1.Cells[iLoop,0] := IntToStr(Array1[iLoop]);
```

```
      {set all values in this array to zero}
      Array2[iLoop] := 0;
      StringGrid2.Cells[iLoop,0] := IntToStr(Array2[iLoop]);
    end;
  end;
```

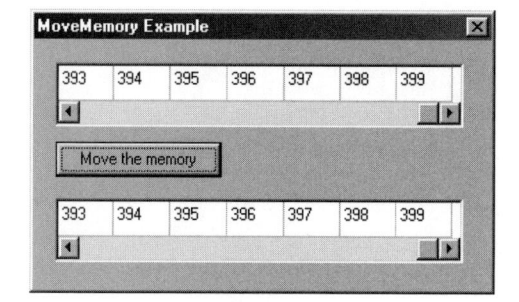

Figure 4-5:
The memory
was moved

VirtualAlloc   Windows.pas

Syntax

```
VirtualAlloc(
lpvAddress: Pointer;            {a pointer to the memory region to reserve or commit}
dwSize: DWORD;                  {the size of the memory region in bytes}
flAllocationType: DWORD;        {the type of allocation}
flProtect: DWORD                {the type of access protection}
): Pointer;                     {returns a pointer to newly allocated memory}
```

Description

VirtualAlloc is used for reserving or committing a region of pages in the virtual address space of the process. The memory committed by VirtualAlloc is initialized to zero. The region will be reserved or committed according to which flags are set in the flAllocationType parameter. To commit a region of memory to physical storage using the MEM_COMMIT flag, the application must first reserve it with the MEM_RESERVE flag. This can be done on two successive calls to VirtualAlloc for the same memory region. VirtualAlloc can be used to reserve a large block of pages, and then later commit smaller portions from the reserved block, allowing an application to reserve memory in its virtual address space without consuming physical memory until needed.

Parameters

lpvAddress: A pointer to the desired starting address of the virtual memory region to allocate. This parameter must be set to the return value from a previous call to VirtualAlloc if the virtual memory region has been reserved and is now being committed. A value of NIL allows Windows to determine the starting location of the region, which is the preferred method. If an address is specified, it will be rounded down to the next 64KB page boundary.

dwSize: Specifies the number of bytes to reserve or commit. The actual region of pages allocated includes all pages containing one or more bytes in the memory range of lpvAddress through lpvAddress+dwSize. Thus, a two-byte range of memory crossing a

64KB page boundary will cause both 64KB pages to be allocated. If the lpvAddress parameter is set to NIL, this value is rounded up to the next 64KB page boundary.

flAllocationType: Specifies the type of allocation to perform. This parameter can be one or more values from Table 4-9.

flProtect: Specifies the type of access protection applied to the allocated virtual memory. This parameter can be one value from Table 4-10.

Return Value

If the function succeeds, it returns a pointer to the base of the allocated memory region; otherwise, it returns NIL. To get extended error information, call the GetLastError function.

See Also

GlobalAlloc, HeapAlloc, VirtualFree, VirtualProtect, VirtualQuery

Example

Listing 4-13: Allocating virtual memory

```
procedure TForm1.Button1Click(Sender: TObject);
type
  ArrayType = array[0..6000] of integer;
var
  Arrayptr: ^ArrayType;                // pointer to buffer
  iLoop: integer;                      // loop counter
  MemInfo: TMemoryBasicInformation;    // query structure
  OldProt: Integer;
begin
  {allocate memory from the virtual address space for this array}
  Arrayptr := VirtualAlloc(NIL,SizeOf(ArrayType),
                      MEM_RESERVE or MEM_COMMIT, PAGE_READONLY);

  {check for errors}
  if Arrayptr = nil then
  begin
    ShowMessage('Error allocating array');
    Exit;
  end;

  {Examine the memory attributes}
  VirtualQuery(Arrayptr, MemInfo, SizeOf(TMemoryBasicInformation));

  {display information on the memory region}
  ListBox1.Items.Add('Base Address: '+IntToHex(Longint(MemInfo.BaseAddress),8));
  ListBox1.Items.Add('Allocation Base: '+IntToHex(Longint(
                    MemInfo.AllocationBase),8));
  ListBox1.Items.Add('Region Size: '+IntToStr(MemInfo.RegionSize)+' bytes');
  ListBox1.Items.Add('Allocation Protection:');
  DisplayProtections(MemInfo.AllocationProtect);

  ListBox1.Items.Add('Access Protection:');
  DisplayProtections(MemInfo.Protect);
```

Memory Management Functions

```
  case MemInfo.State of
    MEM_COMMIT:  ListBox1.Items.Add('State: MEM_COMMIT');
    MEM_FREE:    ListBox1.Items.Add('State: MEM_FREE');
    MEM_RESERVE: ListBox1.Items.Add('State: MEM_RESERVE');
  end;

  case MemInfo.Type_9 of
    MEM_IMAGE:   ListBox1.Items.Add('Type: MEM_IMAGE');
    MEM_MAPPED:  ListBox1.Items.Add('Type: MEM_MAPPED');
    MEM_PRIVATE: ListBox1.Items.Add('Type: MEM_PRIVATE');
  end;

  {Change the protection attributes on the memory block}
  if not VirtualProtect(Arrayptr,SizeOf(ArrayType),
                        PAGE_READWRITE,@OldProt)
     then ShowMessage('Error modifying protection');

  {Re-examine the memory attributes}
  VirtualQuery(Arrayptr, MemInfo, SizeOf(TMemoryBasicInformation));

  {display new access protection}
  ListBox1.Items.Add('New Access Protection:');
  DisplayProtections(MemInfo.Protect);

  {do something with the address space}
  for iLoop := 0 to 6000 do
  begin
    Arrayptr^[iLoop] := iLoop;
    StringGrid1.Cells[iLoop,0] := IntToStr(Arrayptr^[iLoop]);
  end;

  {decommit the memory and release the memory block}
  if not VirtualFree(Arrayptr, SizeOf(ArrayType), MEM_DECOMMIT)
     then ShowMessage('Error decommitting memory');

  if not VirtualFree(Arrayptr, 0, MEM_RELEASE)
     then ShowMessage('Error releasing memory');
end;

procedure DisplayProtections(ProtectFlag: DWORD);
begin
  case ProtectFlag of
     PAGE_READONLY:          Form1.ListBox1.Items.Add(' PAGE_READONLY');
     PAGE_READWRITE:         Form1.ListBox1.Items.Add(' PAGE_READWRITE');
     PAGE_WRITECOPY:         Form1.ListBox1.Items.Add(' PAGE_WRITECOPY');
     PAGE_EXECUTE:           Form1.ListBox1.Items.Add(' PAGE_EXECUTE');
     PAGE_EXECUTE_READ:      Form1.ListBox1.Items.Add(' PAGE_EXECUTE_READ');
     PAGE_EXECUTE_READWRITE: Form1.ListBox1.Items.Add(' PAGE_EXECUTE_READWRITE');
     PAGE_EXECUTE_WRITECOPY: Form1.ListBox1.Items.Add(' PAGE_EXECUTE_WRITECOPY');
     PAGE_GUARD:             Form1.ListBox1.Items.Add(' PAGE_GAURD');
     PAGE_NOACCESS:          Form1.ListBox1.Items.Add(' PAGE_NOACCESS');
     PAGE_NOCACHE:           Form1.ListBox1.Items.Add(' PAGE_NOCACHE');
  end;
end;
```

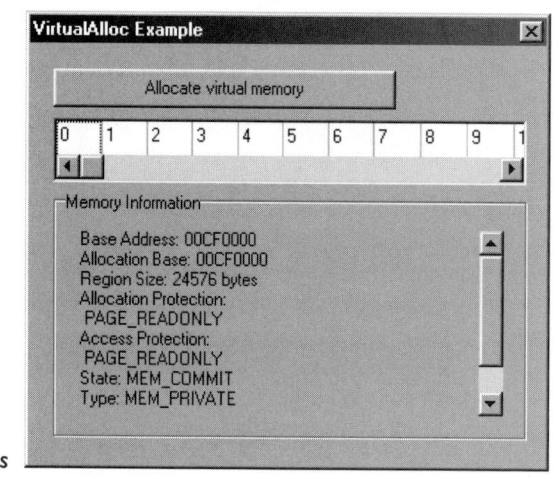

*Figure 4-6:
The allocated
memory status*

Table 4-9: VirtualAlloc flAllocationType values

Value	Description
MEM_COMMIT	Allocates the memory region to physical storage. This notifies the virtual memory manager that these pages are to be treated as active pages and should be swapped to disk if the memory space needs to be used for other purposes. A call to VirtualAlloc with this flag for a memory region that is already committed will not cause an error result.
MEM_RESERVE	Reserves the specified memory range so that calls to other memory allocation functions (such as GlobalAlloc, etc.) will not have access to that memory range.
MEM_RESET	**Windows NT/2000 and later:** Indicates that the memory range is no longer used. It will not be read from or written to the paging file, but will also not be decommitted.
MEM_TOP_DOWN	**Windows NT/2000 and later:** Attempts to allocate memory at the highest possible address.

Table 4-10: VirtualAlloc flProtect values

Value	Description
PAGE_EXECUTE	Specifies that the process may only execute code located in the memory region. Attempts to read or write to the committed region will result in an access violation.
PAGE_EXECUTE_READ	Specifies that execute and read access to the committed region of pages is allowed. Writing to the committed region will result in an access violation.
PAGE_EXECUTE_READWRITE	Specifies that execute, read, and write access to the committed region of pages is allowed.

Memory Management Functions

Value	Description
PAGE_GUARD	**Windows NT/2000 and later:** Specifies that pages in the region are guard pages. Reading from or writing to a guard page will cause the operating system to raise a STATUS_GUARD_PAGE exception and also turn off guard page status. This guard page status cannot be reset without freeing and recommitting the memory block. A violation is reported only once. PAGE_GUARD must be used in combination with at least one other flag except PAGE_NOACCESS. When the guard page becomes disabled due to an intrusion, the remaining page protection is still in effect with its normal error reporting.
PAGE_NOACCESS	All access to the page is prohibited. Any type of access will raise an access violation.
PAGE_NOCACHE	Specifies that the memory is not to be cached. This is not for general use, and is normally only applicable to device drivers or other system software requiring constant presence in memory. PAGE_NOCACHE must be used in combination with at least one other flag except PAGE_NOACCESS.
PAGE_READONLY	Specifies that the process can only read from the memory region. Attempts to write to this memory region will generate an access violation. Executing code within the read-only area on systems that differentiate code execution from memory reading will also generate an error.
PAGE_READWRITE	Specifies that both read and write access is allowed in the committed region of pages.

VirtualFree   Windows.pas

Syntax

```
VirtualFree(
  lpAddress: Pointer;        {a pointer to the memory region}
  dwSize: DWORD;             {the size of the memory region in bytes}
  dwFreeType: DWORD          {option flags}
): BOOL;                     {returns TRUE or FALSE}
```

Description

This function releases memory previously allocated by VirtualAlloc back to the virtual address space of the calling process. This memory is available for use by any subsequent calls to memory allocation functions. VirtualFree can also decommit a region of memory, marking it as reserved until recommitted by a subsequent call to VirtualAlloc. The state of all pages in the region of memory to be freed must be compatible with the type of freeing operation specified by the dwFreeType parameter.

Parameters

lpAddress: A pointer to the memory region to be decommitted or released. If the dwFreeType parameter is set to MEM_RELEASE, this parameter must be set to the return value from the VirtualAlloc function call that initially reserved the memory region.

dwSize: The size of the region to be freed in bytes. The actual region of pages freed includes all pages containing one or more bytes in the memory range of lpAddress through lpAddress+dwSize. Thus, a two-byte range of memory crossing a 64KB page boundary will cause both 64KB pages to be freed. If the dwFreeType parameter is set to MEM_RELEASE, this parameter must be set to zero.

dwFreeType: Specifies the type of freeing operation to perform. This parameter can be one value from the following table.

Return Value

If the function succeeds, it returns TRUE; otherwise, it returns FALSE. To get extended error information, call the GetLastError function.

See Also

GlobalAlloc, GlobalFree, VirtualAlloc

Example

See Listing 4-13 under VirtualAlloc.

Table 4-11: VirtualFree dwFreeType values

Value	Description
MEM_DECOMMIT	Decommits the specified region from physical storage, marking it as reserved. Decommitting a page that has already been decommitted will not cause a failure.
MEM_RELEASE	Specifies that the memory region is to be released back to the virtual address space of the calling process. The memory should be decommitted first if it has been committed to memory.

VirtualProtect Windows.pas

Syntax

```
VirtualProtect(
lpAddress: Pointer;        {a pointer to the memory region}
dwSize: DWORD;             {the size of the region in bytes}
flNewProtect: DWORD        {the requested access protection}
lpflOldProtect: Pointer    {a pointer to a variable receiving the previous protection}
): BOOL;                   {returns TRUE or FALSE}
```

Description

VirtualProtect modifies the protection attributes on the specified memory region. The entire memory region must be committed to physical storage.

Parameters

lpAddress: A pointer to the base of the memory region whose access protection attributes are to be changed. Every page in this region must have been allocated from a single call to VirtualAlloc.

dwSize: Specifies the size of the region pointed to by the lpAddress parameter in bytes. The actual region of pages whose access protection attributes are modified includes all pages containing one or more bytes in the memory range of lpAddress through lpAddress+dwSize. Thus, a two-byte range of memory crossing a 64KB page boundary will cause the access protection attributes of both 64KB pages to be modified.

flNewProtect: Specifies the new type of access protection applied to the specified virtual memory region. This parameter can be one value from the following table.

lpflOldProtect: A pointer to a variable that receives the previous access protection setting.

Return Value

If the function succeeds, it returns TRUE; otherwise, it returns FALSE. To get extended error information, call the GetLastError function.

See Also

VirtualAlloc

Example

See Listing 4-13 under VirtualAlloc.

Table 4-12: VirtualProtect flNewProtect values

Value	Description
PAGE_EXECUTE	Specifies that the process may only execute code located in the memory region. Attempts to read or write to the committed region will result in an access violation.
PAGE_EXECUTE_READ	Specifies that execute and read access to the committed region of pages is allowed. Writing to the committed region will result in an access violation.
PAGE_EXECUTE_READWRITE	Specifies that execute, read, and write access to the committed region of pages is allowed.
PAGE_EXECUTE_WRITECOPY	Specifies that execute, read, and write access to the committed region of pages is allowed. These pages have read-on-write and copy-on-write attributes.
PAGE_GUARD	**Windows NT/2000 and later:** Specifies that pages in the region are guard pages. Reading from or writing to a guard page will cause the operating system to raise a STATUS_GUARD_PAGE exception and also turn off guard page status. This guard page status cannot be reset without freeing and recommitting the memory block. A violation is reported only once. PAGE_GUARD must be used in combination with at least one other flag except PAGE_NOACCESS. When the guard page becomes disabled due to an intrusion, the remaining page protection is still in effect with its normal error reporting.
PAGE_NOACCESS	All access to the page is prohibited. Any type of access will raise an access violation.
PAGE_NOCACHE	Specifies that the memory is not to be cached. This is not for general use, and is normally only applicable to device drivers or other system software requiring constant presence in memory. PAGE_NOCACHE must be used in combination with at least one other flag except PAGE_NOACCESS.
PAGE_READONLY	Specifies that the process can only read from the memory region. Attempts to write to this memory region will generate an access violation. Executing code within the read-only area on systems that differentiate code execution from memory reading will also generate an error.

Value	Description
PAGE_READWRITE	Specifies that both read and write access is allowed in the committed region of pages.
PAGE_WRITECOPY	**Windows NT/2000 or later:** Specifies that the region of pages has copy-on-write access.

VirtualQuery   Windows.pas

Syntax

```
VirtualQuery(
  lpAddress: Pointer;                            {a pointer to the memory region}
  var lpBuffer: TMemoryBasicInformation;         {a pointer to TMemoryBasicInformation}
  dwLength: DWORD                                {the size of the information structure}
): DWORD;                                        {returns the number of bytes in info
                                                  structure}
```

Description

VirtualQuery provides information about a range of pages allocated from the virtual address space of the current process. VirtualQuery examines the first memory page specified by the lpAddress parameter, examining consecutive pages that have an exact match in attributes, until a page is encountered that does not have an exact attribute match or the end of the allocated memory range is encountered. It then reports the amount of consecutive memory found with the same attributes.

Parameters

lpAddress: A pointer to the base of the memory region from which to retrieve information. This value is rounded down to the next 64KB page boundary.

lpBuffer: A pointer to a TMemoryBasicInformation structure which receives the information on the specified range of pages. The TMemoryBasicInformation data structure is defined as:

```
TMemoryBasicInformation = record
  BaseAddress: Pointer;              {a pointer to the memory region}
  AllocationBase: Pointer;           {a pointer to the base address of the memory
                                      region}
  AllocationProtect: DWORD;          {initial access protection flags}
  RegionSize: DWORD;                 {the size of the region}
  State: DWORD;                      {state flags}
  Protect: DWORD;                    {access protection flags}
  Type_9: DWORD;                     {page type flags}
end;
```

BaseAddress: A pointer to the region of pages being queried.

AllocationBase: A pointer to the base of the memory region as returned by the VirtualAlloc call that initially allocated the region. The address pointed to by the BaseAddress member will be contained within this region.

AllocationProtect: Specifies the access protection attributes of the region when it was initially defined. See the VirtualAlloc function for a list of possible access protection attributes.

RegionSize: Specifies the size, in bytes, of the region of pages having identical attributes, starting at the address specified by the BaseAddress member.

State: Specifies the state of the pages within the examined region, and can be one value from Table 4-13.

Protect: Specifies the current access protection attributes of the region. See the VirtualAlloc function for a list of possible access protection attributes.

Type_9: Specifies the type of pages within the examined region, and can be one value from Table 4-14.

dwLength: Specifies the size of the TMemoryBasicInformation data structure in bytes, and should be set to SizeOf(TMemoryBasicInformation).

Return Value

If the function succeeds, it returns the number of bytes copied to the TMemoryBasicInformation data structure; otherwise, it returns zero.

See Also

GetSystemInfo*, VirtualAlloc, VirtualProtect

Example

See Listing 4-13 under VirtualAlloc.

Table 4-13: VirtualQuery lpBuffer.State values

Value	Description
MEM_COMMIT	Specifies that the pages within the region have been committed to physical storage.
MEM_FREE	Specifies that the pages within the region are free and available for allocation. The AllocationBase, AllocationProtect, Protect, and Type_9 members are undefined.
MEM_RESERVE	Specifies that the pages within the region are reserved and are not consuming physical storage space. The Protect member is undefined.

Table 4-14: VirtualQuery lpBuffer.Type_9 values

Value	Description
MEM_IMAGE	Specifies that the pages within the region are mapped into the view of an image section.
MEM_MAPPED	Specifies that the pages within the region are mapped into the view of a section.
MEM_PRIVATE	Specifies that the pages within the region are private, and are not shared with other processes.

ZeroMemory   Windows.pas

Syntax

```
ZeroMemory(
  Destination: Pointer;     {a pointer to a memory block}
  Length: DWORD             {the size of memory block}
);                          {this procedure does not return a value}
```

Description

ZeroMemory fills each byte in the specified memory block with the value zero.

Parameters

Destination: A pointer to the memory block whose values are to be set to zero.

Length: The size of the memory block pointed to by the Destination parameter.

See Also

CopyMemory, FillMemory, MoveMemory

Example

Listing 4-14: Initializing a memory block

```
procedure TForm1.Button1Click(Sender: TObject);
var
  iLoop: integer;
begin
  {initialize the array with some random values}
  for iLoop :=0 to 200 do
  begin
    TheArray[iLoop] := iLoop;
    StringGrid1.Cells[iLoop,0] := IntToStr(TheArray[iLoop]);
  end;

  {toggle button states}
  Button1.Enabled := FALSE;
  Button2.Enabled := TRUE;
end;

procedure TForm1.Button2Click(Sender: TObject);
var
  iLoop: integer;
begin
  {zero the memory}
  ZeroMemory(@TheArray, SizeOf(TheArray));

  {display the zeroed values}
  for iLoop :=0 to 200 do
  begin
    StringGrid1.Cells[iLoop,0] := IntToStr(TheArray[iLoop]);
  end;
end;
```

Chapter 5

Dynamic-Link Library Functions

A dynamic-link library is a compiled executable file containing functions that can be linked to an application on the fly at run time. The concept of DLLs is the core of the Windows architectural design; for the most part, Windows is simply a collection of DLLs. The core DLLs containing the majority of Win32 API functions are KERNAL32.DLL, USER32.DLL, and GDI32.DLL.

Using a DLL is a powerful way to implement code reusability and code sharing, and can result in smaller executables and better memory management. Bear in mind that DLLs do not have a message queue, and must rely on the calling application to process messages and events. A DLL also shares the calling application's stack.

Importing/Exporting Functions

In order to use a function located within a DLL, it must be exported. This is accomplished in the Exports section of the dynamic-link library project code. A function can be exported in four formats:

```
exports
  ShowAboutBox;
```

or

```
exports
  ShowAboutBox name 'ShowAboutBox';
```

or

```
exports
  ShowAboutBox index 1;
```

or

```
exports
  ShowAboutBox index 1 name 'ShowAboutBox';
```

An application can import a function from a dynamic-link library at run time or compile time. At compile time, the application can import a function from a dynamic-link library in three formats:

```
function ShowAboutBox(ExampleName, Comments: ShortString): Boolean;
  external 'EXAMPLE.DLL';
```

or

```
function ShowAboutBox(ExampleName, Comments: ShortString): Boolean;
  external 'EXAMPLE.DLL' name 'ShowAboutBox';
```

or

```
function ShowAboutBox(ExampleName, Comments: ShortString): Boolean;
  external 'EXAMPLE.DLL' index 1;
```

To import a function at run time, an application uses the LoadLibrary or LoadLibraryEx functions in conjunction with the GetProcAddress function. This allows a DLL to be loaded and unloaded at will, and can help an application manage resources in a more efficient manner. It also allows the application to fail more gracefully if a DLL is not available by checking for its existence first before importing its functions, an option unavailable if the DLL's functions are imported at compile time.

Calling Conventions

The nature of Windows and the dynamic-link library architecture allow an application written in one language to call a DLL written in another language. However, the developer must pay attention to the method by which the different languages pass parameters on the stack when calling a function, as this will vary from language to language and will come into play when calling a function in a DLL written in a language other than Delphi. There are four different standard methods by which parameters are passed on the stack: pascal, cdecl, fastcall or register, and stdcall. In exporting or importing functions, the calling conventions must match in both the exported and the imported code.

Table 5-1: Function calling conventions

Object Pascal	C ++	Description
pascal	PASCAL or _pascal	Parameters are passed from left to right.
cdecl	_cdecl	Parameters are passed from right to left.
stdcall	_stdcall	Parameters are pushed on the stack from right to left and retrieved from left to right. This is the Windows standard calling convention.
register	_fastcall	Places the first three parameters into CPU registers, and passes any other parameters on the stack from left to right.

The Dynamic-Link Library Entry Point Function

Dynamic-link libraries have the option of defining an entry point function that is called whenever the DLL is attached to a process or thread. When the DLL is linked in, either dynamically or explicitly, the entry point function receives a DLL_PROCESS_ATTACH notification. When the DLL is unloaded, the entry point receives a DLL_PROCESS_DETACH notification. If the calling process creates a thread, it will automatically attach itself to the DLL, and the DLL entry point function receives a DLL_THREAD_ATTACH notification. When the thread terminates, the DLL receives a DLL_THREAD_DETACH notification.

Delphi vs. the Windows API

If your application will statically link to its DLLs at compile time, there's not much use for most of these API functions. However, if you wish to dynamically load your DLLs at run time, there is simply no other way to accomplish this than to use the API functions described in this chapter. Additionally, there is no wrapper for the DLLMain callback, so you will need to work at the API level in order to detect process and thread attachment.

Dynamic-Link Library Functions

The following dynamic-link library functions are covered in this chapter:

Table 5-2: Dynamic-link library functions

Function	Description
DLLMain	A DLL-defined callback function that receives DLL notification messages.
DisableThreadLibraryCalls	Disables the DLL_THREAD_ATTACH and DLL_THREAD_DETACH DLL entry point notifications.
FreeLibrary	Decrements the reference count of a loaded module by one.
FreeLibraryAndExitThread	Decrements the reference count of a loaded module by one and terminates the calling thread.
GetModuleFileName	Retrieves the module path and filename from a module handle.
GetModuleHandle	Retrieves a module handle from a module name.
GetProcAddress	Retrieves the address of a function within a dynamic-link library.
LoadLibrary	Maps a dynamic-link library into the address space of the calling process.
LoadLibraryEx	Maps a dynamic-link library or an executable into the address space of the calling process.

DLLMain

Syntax

```
DLLMain(
   hinstDLL HINSTANCE;      {the handle of the DLL module}
   dwReason: DWORD;         {the DLL notification message}
   lpvReserved: LPVOID;     {initialization indication}
):BOOL;                     {returns TRUE or FALSE}
```

Description

This function is a callback function defined in a dynamic-link library for the specific purpose of receiving DLL notification messages. These messages are received when an application or thread loads the DLL into memory. It allows the DLL to initialize any dynamic memory allocations (such as thread local storage) or data structures according to the type of attachment occurring, or to clean up such objects upon detachment.

Parameters

hinstDLL: Specifies the handle to the DLL module. Incidentally, this value is the same as the DLL's module handle, and can be used in other API functions requiring a module handle (such as GetModuleFileName).

dwReason: Specifies the DLL notification message. This parameter will contain one value from the following table.

lpvReserved: Specifies more information concerning initialization and cleanup. If the dwReason parameter is DLL_PROCESS_ATTACH, lpvReserved is set to NIL for dynamic loads and non-NIL for static loads. If dwReason is DLL_PROCESS_DETACH, lpvReserved is NIL if the DLLMain function has been called by using FreeLibrary, and non-NIL if the DLLMain function has been called during process termination.

Return Value

The callback function should return TRUE to indicate that initialization has succeeded, or FALSE to indicate initialization failure. If the callback function returns FALSE when LoadLibrary was used, the LoadLibrary function will return 0. If the callback function returns FALSE when the DLL is opened during process initialization, the process will terminate with an error. The return value is ignored for any dwReason value other than DLL_PROCESS_ATTACH. To get extended error information, call the GetLastError function.

See Also

FreeLibrary, GetModuleFileName, LoadLibrary, TlsAlloc, TlsFree

Example

See Listing 5-1 under FreeLibraryAndExitThread.

Table 5-3: DLLMain dwReason values

Value	Description
DLL_PROCESS_ATTACH	Sent when the DLL is attaching to the process's address space.
DLL_PROCESS_DETACH	Sent when the DLL is detaching or being unmapped from process's address space.
DLL_THREAD_ATTACH	Sent when the current process creates a thread.
DLL_THREAD_DETACH	Sent when the current process terminates a thread.

DisableThreadLibraryCalls   Windows.pas

Syntax

```
DisableThreadLibraryCalls(
    hLibModule: HMODULE        {the handle to the module}
): BOOL;                       {returns TRUE or FALSE}
```

Description

This function disables the DLL_THREAD_ATTACH and DLL_THREAD_DETACH DLL entry point notifications for the DLL identified by the hLibModule parameter. This is useful in multithreaded applications where threads are created and destroyed frequently and the DLLs they call do not need the thread attachment notification. By disabling the thread attachment notifications, the DLL initialization code is not paged in when a thread is created or deleted, thus reducing the size of the application's working code set. This function should be implemented in the code servicing the DLL_PROCESS_ATTACH notification. Note that this function will automatically fail if the DLL identified by the hLibModule parameter has active static thread local storage.

Parameters

hLibModule: Specifies the handle of the dynamic-link library.

Return Value

If the function succeeds, it returns TRUE; otherwise, it returns FALSE. To get extended error information, call the GetLastError function.

See Also

DLLMain, FreeLibraryAndExitThread

Example

See Listing 5-1 under FreeLibraryAndExitThread.

FreeLibrary   Windows.pas

Syntax

```
FreeLibrary(
hLibModule: HMODULE    {specifies a handle to the module being freed}
): BOOL;               {returns TRUE or FALSE}
```

Description

The FreeLibrary function decrements the reference count of the loaded dynamic-link library. When the reference count reaches zero, the module is unmapped from the address space of the calling process and the handle is no longer valid. Before unmapping a library module, the system enables the DLL to detach from the process by calling the DLL entry point function, if it has one, with the DLL_PROCESS_DETACH notification. Doing so gives the DLL an opportunity to clean up resources allocated on behalf of the current process. After the entry point function returns, the library module is removed from the address space of the current process. Calling FreeLibrary does not affect other processes using the same DLL.

Parameters

hLibModule: A handle to the dynamic-link library whose reference count is to be decremented.

174 ■ Chapter 5

Return Value:

If the function succeeds, it returns TRUE; otherwise, it returns FALSE. To get extended error information, call the GetLastError function.

See Also

FreeLibraryAndExitThread, GetModuleHandle, LoadLibrary

Example

See Listing 5-4 under LoadLibrary.

FreeLibraryAndExitThread   Windows.pas

Syntax

```
FreeLibraryAndExitThread(
  hLibModule: HMODULE;        {a handle to the module being freed}
  dwExitCode: DWORD           {the exit code for the calling thread}
);                            {this procedure does not return a value}
```

Description

This function frees the dynamic-link library identified by the hLibModule parameter and terminates the calling thread. Internally, the function calls the FreeLibrary function to unload the DLL, passing it the value in the hLibModule parameter, and then calls the ExitThread function to exit the calling thread, passing it the value in the dwExitCode parameter.

Parameters

hLibModule: Specifies the dynamic-link library module whose reference count is to be decremented.

dwExitCode: Specifies the exit code to pass to the calling thread.

See Also

DisableThreadLibraryCalls, ExitThread, FreeLibrary

Example

Listing 5-1: The example dynamic-link library

Unit 1

```
library Example;

uses
  SysUtils,
  Classes,
  Windows,
  Dialogs,
  DLLAboutForm in 'DLLAboutForm.pas' {AboutBox};

{the exported functions}
```

```
exports
  ShowAboutBox name 'ShowAboutBox';

{the DLL entry point function.  this fires whenever a process or thread
 attaches to the DLL.  if a process has already loaded the DLL, any new
 threads created by the process will automatically attach themselves}
procedure DLLMain(AttachFlag: DWORD);
 begin
   {indicate attachement type}
   case AttachFlag of
     DLL_PROCESS_ATTACH: begin
                           MessageBox(0, 'Process: Attaching' , 'Alert', MB_OK);

                           {this function disables the DLL_THREAD_ATTACH and
                            DLL_THREAD_DETACH notifications. if the following
                            line is commented out, the DLL will receive
                            the thread attach/detach notification}
                           DisableThreadLibraryCalls(hInstance)
                         end;
     DLL_PROCESS_DETACH: MessageBox(0, 'Process: Detaching', 'Alert', MB_OK);
     DLL_THREAD_ATTACH:  MessageBox(0, 'Thread: Attaching' , 'Alert', MB_OK);
     DLL_THREAD_DETACH:  MessageBox(0, 'Thread: Detaching' , 'Alert', MB_OK);
   end;
end;

begin
  {initialize the DLL entry point function}
  DLLProc := @DLLMain;

  {call the entry point function on DLL initialization}
  DLLMain(DLL_PROCESS_ATTACH);
end.
```

Unit 2

```
unit DLLAboutForm;

interface

uses Windows, SysUtils, Classes, Graphics, Forms, Controls, StdCtrls,
  Buttons, ExtCtrls;

type
  TAboutBox = class(TForm)
    Panel1: TPanel;
    ProgramIcon: TImage;
    ProductName: TLabel;
    Version: TLabel;
    Copyright: TLabel;
    OKButton: TButton;
    Panel2: TPanel;
    Comments: TLabel;
  private
    { Private declarations }
  public
    { Public declarations }
```

```delphi
    end;

  {the exported prototype for displaying the about box}
  function ShowAboutBox(DLLHandle: THandle; ExampleName,
                       Comments: ShortString): Boolean; export;

var
  AboutBox: TAboutBox;

implementation

{$R *.DFM}

function ShowAboutBox(DLLHandle: THandle; ExampleName,
                     Comments: ShortString): Boolean;
begin
  {initialize the result value}
  Result := FALSE;

  {create the about box form}
  AboutBox := TAboutBox.Create(Application);

  {initialize the labels with the strings passed in}
  AboutBox.ProductName.Caption := ExampleName;
  AboutBox.Comments.Caption := Comments;

  {display a modal about box}
  AboutBox.ShowModal;

  {release the form}
  AboutBox.Release;

  {free the DLL and exit the thread from which it was called}
  FreeLibraryAndExitThread(DLLHandle, 12345);

  {indicate that the function completed}
  Result := TRUE;
end;
```

Listing 5-2: Calling the DLL from within a thread

```delphi
unit FreeLibraryAndExitThreadU;

interface

uses
  Windows, Messages, SysUtils, Classes, Graphics, Controls, Forms, Dialogs,
  StdCtrls;

type
  TForm1 = class(TForm)
    Button1: TButton;
    procedure Button1Click(Sender: TObject);
  private
    { Private declarations }
```

```
    public
      { Public declarations }
    end;

    {the thread function prototype}
    function ThreadFunc(Info: Pointer): Longint; stdcall;

var
  Form1: TForm1;
  hMod: THandle;            // holds the DLL module handle

  {the prototype for the imported DLL function}
  MyFunction: function(DllHandle: THandle; ExampleName,
                       Comments: ShortString): Boolean;

implementation

{$R *.DFM}

function ThreadFunc(Info: Pointer): Longint; stdcall;
begin
  {retrieve the address of the desired function}
  @MyFunction := GetProcAddress(hMod, 'ShowAboutBox' );

  {if an address to the desired function was retrieved...}
  if (@MyFunction<>nil) then
    {display the about box from the DLL}
    MyFunction(hMod, 'FreeLibraryAndExitThread Example',
           'This example demonstrates how to free a dynamic-link library '+
           'from within a thread via the FreeLibraryAndExitThread function.');
end;

procedure TForm1.Button1Click(Sender: TObject);
var
  TheThread: DWORD;         // holds the thread identifier
  ThreadHandle: THandle;    // holds a handle to the thread
  ExitCode: cardinal;       // holds the DLL exit code
begin
  {explicitly load the DLL}
  hMod := LoadLibrary('EXAMPLE.DLL');

  {create a thread that uses the function inside the DLL}
  ThreadHandle := CreateThread(nil, 0, @ThreadFunc, nil, 0, TheThread);
  if ThreadHandle=0 then
    ShowMessage('Thread not started');

  {wait until the thread has finished execution}
  WaitForSingleObject(ThreadHandle, INFINITE);

  {retrieve the exit code of the thread (returned from the DLL)}
  GetExitCodeThread(ThreadHandle, ExitCode);

  {display the exit code}
  ShowMessage(IntToStr(ExitCode));
end;
```

*Figure 5-1:
The About box displayed from a DLL called inside a thread*

GetModuleFileName   Windows.pas

Syntax

```
GetModuleFileName(
    hModule: HINST;         {a handle to the module}
    lpFilename: PChar;      {pointer to a null-terminated string buffer}
    nSize: DWORD            {the size of the lpFilename buffer}
): DWORD;                   {returns the number of characters copied to the buffer}
```

Description

This function retrieves the full path and filename of the module identified by the handle in the hModule parameter.

Windows 95 only: Returns a long filename only if the module's version number is 4.0 or greater and a long filename is available; otherwise, it returns the module filename in the DOS 8.3 format.

Parameters

hModule: A handle to the module whose full path and filename are to be retrieved. If this parameter is set to zero, the function returns the full path and filename of the calling process.

lpFilename: A pointer to a null-terminated string buffer that receives the path and filename.

nSize: Specifies the size of the buffer pointed to by the lpFilename parameter, in characters. If the returned path and filename is larger than this value, the string is truncated.

Return Value

If the function succeeds, it returns the number of characters copied to the buffer pointed to by the lpFilename parameter; otherwise, it returns zero. To get extended error information, call the GetLastError function.

See Also

GetModuleHandle, LoadLibrary

Example

See Listing 5-4 under LoadLibrary.

GetModuleHandle   Windows.pas

Syntax

```
GetModuleHandle(
lpModuleName: PChar        {the name of the module}
): HMODULE;                {returns a handle to the module}
```

Description

This function returns a handle to the module specified by the lpModuleName parameter if the module has been mapped into the calling process's address space. The returned handle cannot be duplicated, used by another process, or inherited by child processes. GetModuleHandle does not map a module into memory, and will not increment the reference count of a mapped module. Therefore, using a handle returned by this function in a call to the FreeLibrary function can cause a module to be prematurely removed from the process's address space.

Parameters

lpModuleName: A pointer to a null-terminated string containing the name of the loaded module whose handle is to be retrieved. This module can identify either a dynamic-link library or an executable. If the file extension is omitted, a default file extension of .DLL is assumed (include a dot (.) at the end of the filename to indicate no file extension). Name comparison is not case sensitive. If this parameter is set to NIL, the function returns a handle to the calling process.

Return Value

If the function succeeds, it returns a handle to the specified module; otherwise, it returns zero. To get extended error information, call the GetLastError function.

See Also

FreeLibrary, GetModuleFileName, GetProcAddress, LoadLibrary

Example

See Listing 5-4 under LoadLibrary.

GetProcAddress   Windows.pas

Syntax

```
GetProcAddress(
hModule: HMODULE;          {a handle to a module}
ProcName: LPCSTR           {a string identifying the name of the function}
): FARPROC;                {returns the function's address}
```

Description

The GetProcAddress function returns the address of the specified exported dynamic-link library function. The returned function can then be called like any other function within the application.

Parameters

hModule: A handle to a dynamic-link library. This handle can be retrieved by the LoadLibrary or GetModuleHandle functions.

ProcName: A null-terminated string specifying either the name of the function whose address is to be retrieved or its ordinal value. If this parameter identifies a function's ordinal value, the value must be in the low-order word, and the high-order word must be zero. The spelling and case of the function name pointed to by the ProcName parameter must be identical to that in the Exports clause of the DLL.

Return Value

If the function succeeds, it returns the address of the exported function within the dynamic-link library. If the function fails, it returns NIL. To get extended error information, call the GetLastError function.

See Also

FreeLibrary, GetModuleHandle, LoadLibrary

Example

See Listing 5-4 under LoadLibrary.

LoadLibrary   Windows.pas

Syntax

```
LoadLibrary(
lpLibFileName: PChar      {a string containing the name of the module}
): HMODULE;               {returns a handle to the loaded module}
```

Description

This function maps the module identified by the lpLibFileName parameter into the address space of the calling process. In the case of mapping an executable into the address space, this function returns a handle that can be used with the FindResource or LoadResource functions. Module handles are not global or inheritable, and cannot be used by another process. If the module specifies a DLL that is not already mapped into the calling process, the system calls the DLL's entry point function with the DLL_PROCESS_ATTACH notification.

Windows 95 only: LoadLibrary will fail if the specified module contains a resource with a numeric identifier greater than $7FFF.

Parameters

lpLibFileName: A pointer to a null-terminated string containing the name of the module to load. This module can identify either a dynamic-link library or an executable. If the file extension is omitted, a default file extension of .DLL is assumed (include a dot (.) at the end of the filename to indicate no file extension). If a module of the same name from within the same directory has already been mapped into the calling process's address space (name comparison is not case sensitive), the reference count for that module is incremented by one, and the function returns a handle to the previously loaded module. If the string specifies a path but the file does not exist, the function fails. If no path is specified, the function searches for the file in the following sequence:

1. The directory from which the calling application was loaded.
2. The current directory.
3. The Windows system directory.
4. The Windows directory.
5. The directories as listed in the PATH environment variable.

Return Value

If the function succeeds, it returns a handle to the loaded module. If the function fails, it returns NIL. To get extended error information, call the GetLastError function.

See Also

FindResource*, FreeLibrary, GetProcAddress, GetSystemDirectory*, GetWindowsDirectory*, LoadResource*, LoadLibraryEx

Example

Listing 5-3: The example dynamic-link library

Unit 1

```
library Example;

uses
  SysUtils,
  Classes,
  Windows,
  Dialogs,
  DLLAboutForm in 'DLLAboutForm.pas' {AboutBox};

{the exported functions}
exports
  ShowAboutBox name 'ShowAboutBox';

{the DLL entry point procedure.  this procedure will fire every time a
 process or thread attaches to the DLL.  if a process has attached to a DLL,
 any newly created threads will automatically attach themselves}
procedure DLLMain(AttachFlag: DWORD);
begin
  {display attachement type}
  case AttachFlag of
```

```
      DLL_PROCESS_ATTACH: MessageBox(0, 'Process: Attaching', 'Alert', MB_OK);
      DLL_PROCESS_DETACH: MessageBox(0, 'Process: Detaching', 'Alert', MB_OK);
      DLL_THREAD_ATTACH:  MessageBox(0, 'Thread: Attaching' , 'Alert', MB_OK);
      DLL_THREAD_DETACH:  MessageBox(0, 'Thread: Detaching' , 'Alert', MB_OK);
    end;
end;

begin
  {initialize the DLL entry function}
  DLLProc := @DLLMain;

  {call the entry function upon DLL initialization}
  DLLMain(DLL_PROCESS_ATTACH);
end.
```

Unit 2

```
var
  AboutBox: TAboutBox;

implementation

{$R *.DFM}

function ShowAboutBox(ExampleName, Comments: ShortString): Boolean;
begin
  {initialize the function results}
  Result := FALSE;

  {create the about box form}
  AboutBox := TAboutBox.Create(Application);

  {initialize labels from the supplied strings}
  AboutBox.ProductName.Caption := ExampleName;
  AboutBox.Comments.Caption := Comments;

  {show a modal about box}
  AboutBox.ShowModal;

  {release the form}
  AboutBox.Release;

  {indicate that the function completed}
  Result := TRUE;
end;
```

Listing 5-4: Loading the example dynamic-link library

```
procedure TForm1.Button1Click(Sender: TObject);
var
   hMod: THandle;                          // holds the DLL handle
   ModuleFileName: array[0..255] of char;  // holds the DLL name

   {this is the prototype for the function imported from the DLL}
   MyFunction: function(ExampleName, Comments: ShortString): Boolean;
```

```
begin
  {explicitly load the DLL}
  hMod := LoadLibrary('EXAMPLE.DLL');
  if (hMod=0) then Exit;

  {retrieve the address of the desired function}
  @MyFunction := GetProcAddress(hMod, 'ShowAboutBox' );

  {if the address was returned...}
  if (@MyFunction<>nil) then
  begin
    {call the function to display an about box}
    MyFunction('LoadLibrary Example','This example demonstrates loading '+
              'a dynamic-link library via the LoadLibrary function.');

    {retrieve the module filename}
    GetModuleFileName(GetModuleHandle('EXAMPLE.DLL'), @ModuleFileName[0],
                      SizeOf(ModuleFileName));

    {display the DLLs name}
    ShowMessage('The loaded DLL was: '+ModuleFileName);
  end
  else
    {indicate an error}
    ShowMessage('GetProcAddress Failed');

  {free the DLL}
  FreeLibrary(hMod);
end;
```

LoadLibraryEx   Windows.pas

Syntax

```
LoadLibraryEx(
  lpLibFileName: PChar;      {a string containing the name of the module}
  hFile: THandle;            {reserved for future use}
  dwFlags: DWORD             {extended optional behavior flag}
  ): HMODULE;                {returns a handle to the loaded module}
```

Description

The LoadLibraryEx function is equivalent to the LoadLibrary function in that it maps the module identified by the lpLibFileName parameter into the address space of the calling process. However, LoadLibraryEx can map the DLL without calling the DLL entry point function, it can use either of two file search strategies to find the specified module, and it can load a module in a way that is optimized for the case where the module will never be executed, loading the module as if it were a data file. These extended behaviors can be accomplished by setting the dwFlags parameter to a value listed in the following table. Module handles are not global or inheritable, and cannot be used by another process.

Windows 95 only: LoadLibrary will fail if the specified module contains a resource with a numeric identifier greater than $7FFF.

Parameters

lpLibFileName: A pointer to a null-terminated string containing the name of the module to load. This module can identify either a dynamic-link library or an executable. If the file extension is omitted, a default file extension of .DLL is assumed (include a dot (.) at the end of the filename to indicate no file extension). If a module of the same name from within the same directory has already been mapped into the calling process's address space (name comparison is not case sensitive), the reference count for that module is incremented by one, and the function returns a handle to the previously loaded module. If the string specifies a path but the file does not exist, the function fails. If no path is specified, the function searches for the file in the following sequence:

1. The directory from which the calling application was loaded.
2. The current directory.
3. The Windows system directory.
4. The Windows directory.
5. The directories as listed in the PATH environment variable.

hFile: Reserved for future use. Set this parameter to zero.

dwFlags: Specifies optional behavior when loading the module. This parameter can contain one value from the following table.

Return Value

If the function succeeds, it returns a handle to the loaded module. If the function fails, it returns NIL. To get extended error information, call the GetLastError function.

See Also

FindResource*, FreeLibrary, GetProcAddress, GetSystemDirectory*, GetWindowsDirectory*, LoadResource*, LoadLibrary

Example

Listing 5-5: The example DLL

```
library BitmapDLL;

{all this DLL does is provide a storage mechanism for a bitmap}

uses
  SysUtils,
  Classes;

  {link in the bitmap resource}
  {$R BitmapResources.res}
begin
end.
```

Listing 5-6: Retrieving resources from a loaded dynamic-link library

```
procedure TForm1.Button1Click(Sender: TObject);
var
   hMod: THandle;           // a handle to the DLL
   BitmapHandle: HBitmap;   // a handle to a bitmap
begin
   {explicitly load the DLL}
   hMod := LoadLibraryEx('BitmapDll.DLL', 0, 0);
   if (hMod = 0) then Exit;

   {retrieve a handle to the bitmap stored in the DLL}
   BitmapHandle := LoadBitmap(hMod, 'BITMAPEXAMPLE');
   If (Bitmaphandle = 0)then Exit;

   {assign the bitmap to the TImage component}
   Image1.Picture.Bitmap.Handle := BitmapHandle;

   {unload the DLL}
   FreeLibrary(hMod);
end;
```

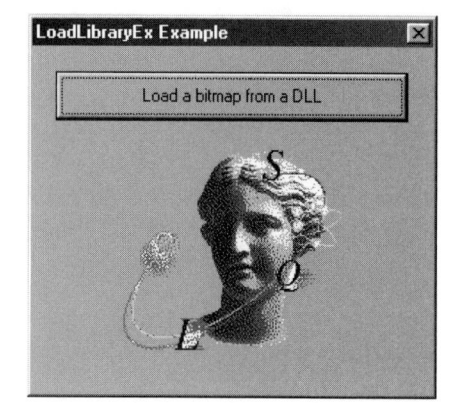

Figure 5-2:
The retrieved bitmap resource

Table 5-4: LoadLibraryEx dwFlags values

Value	Description
DONT_RESOLVE_DLL_REFERENCES	**Windows NT/2000 only:** The operating system does not call the DLL entry point function for DLL initialization and termination.
LOAD_LIBRARY_AS_DATAFILE	Maps the specified module into memory as if it were a data file. Functions within a DLL are not available, but the returned handle can be used to retrieve resources.
	Windows NT/2000 or later: The module handle can be used with any Win32 resource API functions.
	Windows 95/98: The module handle cannot be used with the LoadBitmap, LoadCursor, LoadIcon, or LoadImage API functions.
LOAD_WITH_ALTERED_SEARCH_PATH	Changes the search strategy. It is identical to the normal search strategy, except that the function will start its search in the directory of the module being loaded, as opposed to the directory of the calling application.

Chapter 6

Process and Thread Functions

Multithreaded applications allow the developer to divide an executable into many smaller tasks that will execute independently of one another. The Windows API provides a number of functions concerned with the creation and synchronization of threads. Delphi includes a very efficient encapsulation of some of these API functions through its TThread object. This object allows an application to create threads that can interact with other elements of the VCL in a thread-safe manner, and allows the thread to take advantage of Delphi's exception handling mechanism.

Multithreading an application can have several benefits. For example, processes that take a long time to complete, such as saving to disk, can be done in a separate thread, thereby providing the saving functionality in the background while leaving the user interface responsive. This technique can be used for all kinds of background or parallel processing, such as printing or Internet communication, and can make an application seem to run much faster. Indeed, multithreaded applications are truly at home on multiprocessor machines, and can run orders of magnitude faster in such environments than single-threaded applications. However, creating applications that launch multiple threads presents unique problems to the programmer, the most important of which is the synchronization of thread access to shared memory and resources. When multiple threads access a specific memory area or resource, it could cause widely varying problems, from simple unexplained changing of variable values to access violations and machine locks.

It is important to note that multiple threads accessing GDI objects simultaneously will result in general protection faults. In order for multiple threads to access GDI objects, they must be synchronized using various methods found throughout this chapter. Also of importance is the fact that not all operating systems implement true multiprocessing, even when it is supported by the underlying hardware. For example, Windows 9x only simulates multiprocessing, even if the underlying hardware supports it.

Important Concepts

Before embarking on a discussion of process and thread API functions and the various coordination and synchronization methods, it is important to define several concepts. This chapter deals with many API functions that operate on two entities: processes and threads.

Processes

A process consists of memory and resources. The memory in a process consists of three parts: stack, data, and code. The stack consists of all local variables and the call stack. Each new thread will have its own stack. Data consists of all variables that are not local and memory that is dynamically allocated. The code consists of the executable part of a program that is read-only. These three parts are available to all threads in a single process. The process cannot do anything except hold a thread and memory. The process has an identifier that can be retrieved by calling the GetCurrentProcessId function. This process identifier is unique throughout the system. You can think of a process as your application, and each application (or process) consists of one or more threads.

Threads

A thread of execution is started when the processor begins executing code. The thread is owned by a process, and a process can own one or more threads. Each thread has its own stack and message queue, and shares the virtual address space and system resources of its owning process.

In addition, a thread can use thread local storage to allocate a memory block that all threads can use for storage. The TlsAlloc function allocates the storage area, and the TlsGetValue and TlsSetValue functions are used to manipulate the stored value. When one thread allocates local storage, the memory area is available to all threads, but each thread will see its own unique value when accessing the memory. By using thread local variables, your thread does not need to wait for or lock out any other threads that use the thread local storage variables.

Priority Levels

The system determines when a thread gets a quantum of CPU time based on its priority level. Each process has a priority class, which determines that process thread's base priority level. Each thread in turn has its own priority level. Processes and threads with high priority levels take precedence over those with lower priorities. Low priority levels are used for threads that monitor system activity, such as screen savers. High priority threads should only be used for time-critical events or for threads that must communicate directly with hardware and cannot tolerate interruptions.

Synchronization and Coordination

When writing the code that runs when your thread is executed, you must consider the behavior of other threads that may be executing simultaneously. In particular, care must be taken to avoid two threads trying to use the same global object or variable at the same time. In addition, the code in one thread can depend on the results of tasks performed by other threads. There is no danger in multiple threads reading the same memory simultaneously, as long as no thread is writing to it. Fortunately, the Windows API provides a plethora of synchronization techniques to control access to resources by two or more processes or threads.

These techniques use what could be loosely termed as "objects" that represent different synchronization methods. There are several types available, each used to control synchronization in a slightly different manner. Each object has two states: signaled and non-signaled. These objects are used in a number of different wait functions, which are the gateways, or blocking points, of access to the shared resources to be protected. An object in a non-signaled state will cause the wait functions to suspend the execution of a thread until it enters the signaled state, at which point execution of the thread's code resumes.

Synchronization occurs by using wait functions (several of which are available) that block the execution of a thread until a specific condition is met. If that condition is not met, the thread will effectively enter into an idle state, consuming very little processor time. Once that condition is met, the thread will resume execution at the next instruction following the call to the wait function. There are two conditions that will cause a wait function to return: a timeout interval has elapsed or the object upon which the wait function acts enters a signaled state. If a finite timeout interval is specified, the wait function will return and the thread will resume execution when the synchronization object enters a signaled state or when the timeout interval is reached, whichever occurs first. However, when the timeout interval is defined as INFINITE, the wait function will not return until the object it is acting upon becomes signaled. Note that thread synchronization of access to shared resources can only occur if every thread uses the same synchronization techniques for accessing the same shared resource.

The wait functions come in two varieties: single object and multiple object. The single object wait functions take the handle to a single synchronization object, and return when the timeout interval has elapsed or the object enters a signaled state. Multiple object wait functions take an array of one or more synchronization object handles. These functions return either when the timeout interval elapses or when any one, or all, of the objects enters a signaled state (as determined by the function call).

Deadlocks

A deadlock can occur when two or more threads are waiting on each other indefinitely. For example, thread 1 begins execution and tries to access a shared resource used by thread 2. Thread 1 uses a wait function against a synchronization object and is suspended until the object enters a signaled state, expecting thread 2 to set the synchronization object to signaled when it is done with the resource. Thread 2 also tries to access the same shared resource, and uses a wait function against the same object. However, thread 2 is expecting thread 1 to set the synchronization object to signaled. If no other thread is able to set this synchronization object into a signaled state, threads 1 and 2 are deadlocked against each other, and will never resume execution. While this example may be a little simplistic, it demonstrates a common mistake made in multithreaded applications, one that the programmer should be aware of and watch out for, as debugging this type of problem can be difficult.

Synchronization Objects

There are a number of different objects that are available for synchronizing access to memory or resources. These objects are used in the aforementioned wait functions, and represent different synchronization techniques. These objects are critical sections, semaphores, mutexes, and events.

Critical Sections

A critical section acts as a gate, blocking other threads from entering a section of code. Unlike the other synchronization objects, critical sections are not used in wait functions, and can only be used by the threads within a single process. A critical section allows only one thread at a time to access the protected memory or resource. Caution must be used when employing critical sections since only one thread at a time is allowed access to the protected memory or resources. Critical sections can dramatically degrade the performance of an application if used incorrectly. Critical sections can be used to synchronize access to non-thread-safe code, such as calls to the GDI.

Semaphores

A semaphore object coordinates access to a resource that can support a limited number of clients. Essentially, it limits the number of threads that can access a resource, up to a specified number. When the semaphore object is created, the number of simultaneous accesses to the resource it protects is specified. Each time a wait function is used with a semaphore, the semaphore's count is decremented by one. Conversely, when the semaphore is released, its count is incremented by one. A semaphore is in a signaled state when its count is greater than zero, but becomes non-signaled when its count reaches zero. This count can never be less than one or greater than the initial value specified when the semaphore was created. Semaphores can be accessed across process boundaries. Threads can use wait functions against a semaphore multiple times, but each wait function will decrement the semaphore's count, and can result in the thread blocking its own execution if the semaphore's count reaches zero.

Mutexes

A mutex object coordinates mutually exclusive access to a resource (the name "mutex" coming from MUTual EXclusion) as only one thread at a time can own the mutex object. A mutex object's state is signaled when it is not owned by any thread, but becomes non-signaled when it is owned. Mutex objects can be accessed across process boundaries, so this can be used to coordinate access between multiple processes. A thread can use a wait function against the same mutex multiple times without blocking its own execution. However, each wait function must have an equal number of release functions to properly release the mutex object and set its state to signaled so that other waiting threads can access the shared resource.

Events

An event object is a synchronization object that is under the direct control of the application. Instead of changing state as a result of calling one of the wait functions (such as WaitForSingleObject), the application can use three different functions to control the state of the object. The SetEvent function sets the state of the event object to signaled, the ResetEvent function sets the state of the event object to non-signaled, and the PulseEvent function quickly sets the state of the event object to signaled and then non-signaled. When the event object is created, the application can determine if it will be a manual or automatic reset event. Manual reset events remain signaled until explicitly reset to non-signaled by a call to the ResetEvent function. Auto reset events remain signaled until a single waiting thread is resumed, at which point the system automatically sets the state back to non-signaled. A deadlock can occur when a thread is suspended in a permanent wait state as a result of a lost event object. If PulseEvent or SetEvent is used with an auto reset event and no threads are waiting, the event object is lost and a deadlock will occur. Events are especially useful in the situation where a thread must wait for another thread to complete its execution. The executing thread can simply set the event's state to signaled at the end of its execution, at which point the waiting thread will resume, guaranteed that the thread upon which it was waiting has successfully completed.

Synchronizing Processes with a Mutex

As an example of cross-process synchronization, let's examine a classic use of the mutex object. One typical application for using a mutex is to prevent two or more instances of the same application from running simultaneously. Since a mutex can be used across process boundaries, this is very easy to accomplish. We simply attempt to open a specific mutex name when the application starts; if we are successful, we know that the application is already running, and we can exit; otherwise, we create the mutex and continue processing. While not a hardcore thread synchronization example, it serves as a simple demonstration of using a synchronization object.

Listing 6-1: Preventing an application from running more than once

```
program RunOnceP;

uses
  Forms,
  Windows,
  Dialogs,
  RunOnceU in 'RunOnceU.pas' {Form1};

{$R *.res}

var
  MutexHandle: Integer;

begin
  {attempt to open a handle to the mutex. if this function is successful,
   we know that the application has already started, and we can terminate}
  if OpenMutex(MUTEX_ALL_ACCESS, FALSE, 'RunOnceMutex') <> 0 then
  begin
```

```
    ShowMessage('This application is already open!');
    Exit;
  end;

  {if we get here, we are the first instance of this application, so
   create the mutex and immediately acquire ownership of it}
  MutexHandle := CreateMutex(nil, TRUE, 'RunOnceMutex');

  Application.Initialize;
  Application.CreateForm(TForm1, Form1);
  Application.Run;

  {now that we are done, we must release the mutex}
  ReleaseMutex(MutexHandle);
end.
```

Delphi vs. the Windows API

Delphi encapsulates many of the concepts covered in this chapter. Delphi's TThread object provides an easy mechanism for creating and launching threads, and even includes the Synchronize method for processing non-thread-safe code. Critical sections are encapsulated by the TCriticalSection object, which makes using critical sections very easy. Additionally, there is a TEvent object that encapsulates the event object described in this chapter. All of this makes the job of writing multithreaded applications in Delphi much easier.

However, there are several additional API functions that are not encapsulated by native Delphi objects, and the functionality of these functions can greatly enhance a multi-threaded application. The semaphore functions are an example. Other functions, such as CreateProcess, don't have a Delphi equivalent, but are fortunately not very difficult to use. Even some of the Delphi objects don't fully encapsulate all of the functionality available (TEvent objects do not encapsulate the PulseEvent function, for example). Plus, sometimes it's easier and more practical to create a thread using API functions than to create an entire new TThread descendent.

Process and Thread Functions

The following process and thread functions are covered in this chapter:

Table 6-1: Process and thread functions

Function	Description
CreateEvent	Creates an event object.
CreateMutex	Creates a mutex object.
CreateProcess	Launches another application.
CreateSemaphore	Creates a semaphore object.
CreateThread	Creates and executes a thread.
DeleteCriticalSection	Deletes a critical section.
DuplicateHandle	Duplicates a handle.

Process and Thread Functions

Function	Description
EnterCriticalSection	Enters a critical section.
ExitProcess	Terminates a process.
ExitThread	Terminates a thread.
GetCurrentProcess	Retrieves a handle to the current process.
GetCurrentProcessId	Retrieves the current process's identifier.
GetCurrentThread	Retrieves a handle to the current thread.
GetCurrentThreadId	Retrieves the current thread's identifier.
GetExitCodeProcess	Retrieves the exit code from a terminated process.
GetExitCodeThread	Retrieves the exit code from a terminated thread.
GetPriorityClass	Retrieves the priority class of the process.
GetThreadPriority	Retrieves the priority level of a thread.
GetWindowThreadProcessId	Retrieves the specified window's process and thread identifiers.
InitializeCriticalSection	Initializes a critical section for use.
InterlockedDecrement	Decrements an interlocked variable.
InterlockedExchange	Exchanges the value of an interlocked variable.
InterlockedIncrement	Increments an interlocked variable.
LeaveCriticalSection	Leaves the critical section.
OpenEvent	Opens a handle to an existing event object.
OpenMutex	Opens a handle to an existing mutex object.
OpenProcess	Opens a handle to an existing process.
OpenSemaphore	Opens a handle to an existing semaphore object.
PulseEvent	Rapidly sets the state of an event object to signaled and unsignaled.
ReleaseMutex	Releases ownership of a mutex object.
ReleaseSemaphore	Releases ownership of a semaphore object.
ResetEvent	Resets an event object to an unsignaled state.
ResumeThread	Allows a previously suspended thread to resume execution.
SetEvent	Sets the state of an event object to signaled.
SetPriorityClass	Sets the priority class of the process.
SetThreadPriority	Sets the priority level of a thread.
Sleep	Suspends a thread for a specific period of time.
SuspendThread	Suspends a thread indefinitely.
TerminateProcess	Terminates the specified process and all of its threads.
TerminateThread	Terminates a thread without allowing it to perform cleanup routines.
TlsAlloc	Allocates a thread local storage index.
TlsFree	Frees an allocated thread local storage index.
TlsGetValue	Retrieves a value from a thread local storage index.
TlsSetValue	Set a value into a thread local storage index.
WaitForInputIdle	Suspends the calling thread until the specified process is waiting for user input.
WaitForSingleObject	Suspends the calling thread until the specified object becomes signaled.

CreateEvent   Windows.pas

Syntax

```
CreateEvent(
lpEventAttributes: PSecurityAttributes;    {pointer to security attributes}
bManualReset: BOOL;                        {flag for manual reset event}
bInitialState: BOOL;                       {flag for initial state}
lpName: PChar                              {name of the event object}
): THandle;                                {returns a handle of the event object}
```

Description

Creates an event object that is signaled or non-signaled. The handle returned by CreateEvent has EVENT_ALL_ACCESS access to the new event object and can be used in any function that requires a handle of an event object. An event object is under the direct control of the programmer, with the functions SetEvent, ResetEvent, and PulseEvent.

Parameters

lpEventAttributes: A pointer to a record that holds the security attributes information. If this parameter is set to NIL, the event object will have default security attributes. The TSecurityAttributes data structure is defined as:

```
TSecurityAttributes = record
  nLength: DWORD;                    {the size of the TSecurityAttributes structure}
  lpSecurityDescriptor: Pointer;     {the security descriptor}
  bInheritHandle: BOOL;              {handle inheritance flags}
end;
```

nLength: Specifies the size of the TSecurityAttributes parameter, in bytes. This member should be set to SizeOf (TSecurityAttributes).

lpSecurityDescriptor: A pointer to a security descriptor for the object that controls the sharing of the file. If this member is set to NIL, the file is assigned the default security descriptor for the process. If CreateFile is opening a file, this parameter is ignored.

Note: Under Windows 95/98/Me this member is always ignored.

bInheritHandle: Indicates if the returned handle is inherited when a new process is created. A value of TRUE indicates that new processes inherit the returned file handle.

bManualReset: Specifies whether a manual reset or auto reset event object is created. If TRUE, the ManualReset function must be used to reset the state to non-signaled. If FALSE, Windows automatically resets the state to non-signaled after a single waiting thread has been released.

bInitialState: Specifies the initial state of the event object. If TRUE, the initial state is signaled; otherwise, it is non-signaled.

lpName: A pointer to a null-terminated string specifying the name of the event. The name is limited to a maximum size of MAX_PATH characters and can contain any characters except the backslash (\).

> **Note:** Name comparison is case sensitive. If this parameter matches the name of any existing event object, the function requests EVENT_ALL_ACCESS access to the existing event object. If this occurs, the previous parameters of bInitialState and bManualReset are ignored because the creating process has already set them.

The lpName parameter can be set to NIL, in which case the event is created without a name. If the name matches an existing semaphore, mutex, or file mapping object, the function fails. In this instance, a call to GetLastError() will return ERROR_INVALID_HANDLE.

Return Value

If the function succeeds, it returns a handle to the event object. If the function fails, it returns zero. To get extended error information, call the GetLastError function.

See Also

CloseHandle*, CreateProcess, DuplicateHandle, OpenEvent, ResetEvent, SetEvent, WaitForSingleObject

Example

Listing 6-2: Creating an event and waiting for it

```
var
  Form1: TForm1;
  EventHandle: THandle;     // holds the event handle
  ThreadHandle: THandle;    // holds the thread handle

implementation

{$R *.DFM}

function ThreadFunction(Info: Pointer): Integer; stdcall;
var
  FormDC: HDC;           // holds a handle to the form device context
  Counter: Integer;      // general loop counter
  CounterStr: string;    // a string representation of the loop counter
  ObjRtn: Integer;       // wait function return value
begin
  {WaitForSingleObject will wait for the event to
   become signaled (ready to do something)}
  ObjRtn := WaitForSingleObject(EventHandle, INFINITE);

  {retrieve a handle to the form's device context}
  FormDC := GetDC(Form1.Handle);
```

```
      {begin a large loop}
      for Counter := 1 to 100000 do
      begin
        {display the counter value}
        CounterStr := IntToStr(Counter);
        TextOut(FormDC, 10, 10, PChar(CounterStr), Length(CounterStr));

        {process any pending messages}
        Application.ProcessMessages;

        {this causes the loop to pause, as the PulseEvent function
         rapidly sets the event's signaled state to signaled and
         then unsignaled}
        ObjRtn := WaitForSingleObject(EventHandle, INFINITE);
      end;

      {release the form's device context and exit the thread}
      ReleaseDC(Form1.Handle, FormDC);
      ExitThread(4);
   end;

   procedure TForm1.Button1Click(Sender: TObject);
   var
     ThreadID: DWORD;    // holds the thread identifier
   begin
     {create a new thread}
     ThreadHandle := CreateThread(nil, 0, @ThreadFunction, nil, 0, ThreadId);
   end;

   procedure TForm1.Button2Click(Sender: TObject);
   begin
     {indicate that the event is signaled.  this will cause the waiting
      thread to get past the WaitForSingleObject function, thus starting
      the loop}
     SetEvent(EventHandle);
     Label1.Caption := 'Event is signaled';
   end;

   procedure TForm1.Button3Click(Sender: TObject);
   begin
     {reset the event object to a non signaled state.  this will
      cause the thread loop to pause at the WaitForSingleObject
      function inside the loop}
     ResetEvent(EventHandle);
     Label1.Caption := 'Event is non signaled';
   end;

   procedure TForm1.Button4Click(Sender: TObject);
   begin
     {if the event has been reset (above), the thread's loop will be
      paused at the internal WaitForSingleObject function. PulseEvent
      will toggle the event's state from nonsignaled to signaled and back,
      causing the thread's loop to fire once.}
     PulseEvent(EventHandle); //Set to signaled and then nonsignaled
     Label1.Caption := 'signaled/nonsignaled';
   end;
```

```
procedure TForm1.Button5Click(Sender: TObject);
begin
  {create the event}
  EventHandle := CreateEvent(Nil, True, False, 'MyEvent');
end;
```

CreateMutex   Windows.pas

Syntax

```
CreateMutex(
lpMutexAttributes: PSecurityAttributes;   {a pointer to security attributes}
bInitialOwner: BOOL;                      {flag for the initial ownership}
lpName: PChar                             {mutex object name}
): THandle;                               {returns a handle of the mutex object}
```

Description

This function creates a named or unnamed mutex object. The mutex can be specified in any of the wait functions (i.e., WaitForSingleObject) across processes or within the same process. When a thread uses a wait function with a mutex, it owns the mutex until it calls ReleaseMutex. The thread that has ownership of the mutex can call wait functions with the same mutex specified more than once without fear of blocking its own execution. However, for each call to a wait function within the same thread and using the same mutex, the ReleaseMutex function must be called a like number of times. Multiple processes can call CreateMutex with the same name specified. This action will cause the second call to only open a handle to the existing mutex, not create a new one. Set bInitialOwner to FALSE in this situation. CloseHandle will close the handle to a mutex. The handle is automatically closed when the process that opened the handle is closed. When the last handle to the mutex is closed, the mutex is destroyed.

Parameters

lpMutexAttributes: A pointer to a TSecurityAttributes record that describes the security attributes of the mutex object. Please see the CreateEvent function for a description of this data structure. If this parameter is set to NIL, the mutex will have the default security attributes and the handle is not inheritable.

bInitialOwner: Specifies mutex ownership. If this parameter is set to TRUE, the calling thread requests immediate ownership of the mutex; otherwise, the mutex is not owned.

lpName: A pointer to a null-terminating string specifying the name of the created mutex.

Return Value

If the function succeeds, it returns the handle of the mutex that is created. The handle will have MUTEX_ALL_ACCESS access to the mutex. If the function fails, it returns zero. To get extended error information, call the GetLastError function. If the lpName parameter contains a mutex name that already exists, then GetLastError will return ERROR_ALREADY_EXISTS.

See Also

CloseHandle*, CreateProcess, DuplicateHandle, OpenMutex, ReleaseMutex, WaitForSingleObject

Example

Listing 6-3: Using a mutex to synchronize thread execution

```
function ThreadFunc0(Info: Pointer): Integer; stdcall
var
  ICount: Integer;        // general loop counter
  CountStr: string;       // holds a string representation of the counter
begin
  {wait for the mutex to become signaled. the mutex is created signaled so
   this thread gets ownership of the mutex and starts immediately}
  WaitForSingleObject(Form1.MutexHandle, INFINITE);

  {start a counter to display something}
  for ICount := 1 to 10000 do
  begin
    CountStr := IntToStr(ICount);
    Form1.Canvas.TextOut(10, 10, 'Thread 1 '+CountStr);
  end;

  {Release ownership of the mutex so the other threads can fire}
  ReleaseMutex(Form1.MutexHandle);
  ExitThread(1);
end;

function ThreadFunc1(Info: Pointer): Integer; stdcall
var
  ICount: Integer;        // general loop counter
  CountStr: string;       // holds a string representation of the counter
begin
  {wait for the mutex to become signaled. the mutex is created signaled so
   this thread gets ownership of the mutex and starts immediately}
  WaitForSingleObject(Form1.MutexHandle, INFINITE);

  {start a counter to display something}
  for ICount := 1 to 10000 do
  begin
    CountStr := IntToStr(ICount);
    Form1.Canvas.TextOut(110, 10, 'Thread 2 '+CountStr);
  end;

  {Release ownership of the mutex so the other threads can fire}
  ReleaseMutex(Form1.MutexHandle);
  ExitThread(2);
end;

function ThreadFunc2(Info: Pointer): Integer; stdcall
var
  ICount: Integer;           // general loop counter
  CountStr: string;          // holds a string representation of the counter
  LocalMutexHandle: THandle; // holds a handle to the mutex
```

```
begin
  {open a Handle to the mutex from this thread}
  LocalMutexHandle := OpenMutex(MUTEX_ALL_ACCESS, FALSE, 'MyMutex');

  {take ownership of the mutex. this will wait until the mutex is signaled}
  WaitForSingleObject(LocalMutexHandle, INFINITE);

  {start a counter to display something}
  for ICount := 1 to 10000 do
  begin
    CountStr := IntToStr(ICount);
    Form1.canvas.TextOut(210, 10, 'Thread 3 '+CountStr);
  end;

  {Release ownership of the mutex}
  ReleaseMutex(LocalMutexHandle);

  {close the mutex handle}
  CloseHandle(LocalMutexHandle);
  ExitThread(3);
end;

procedure TForm1.CreateThreadClick(Sender: TObject);
var
  ThreadId0, ThreadId1, ThreadId2: DWORD; // holds thread identifiers
begin
  {Create the mutex with the name MyMutex. the mutex is signaled
   so the first thread will start immediately}
  MutexHandle := CreateMutex(nil, False, 'MyMutex');

  {Create the first thread, and start it immediately}
  ThreadHandle := Windows.CreateThread(nil, 0, @ThreadFunc0, nil, 0, ThreadId0);

  {Create the second thread, and start it immediately}
  ThreadHandle1 := Windows.CreateThread(nil,0, @ThreadFunc1, nil, 0, ThreadId1);

  {Create the third thread, and start it immediately}
  ThreadHandle2 := Windows.CreateThread(nil,0, @ThreadFunc2, nil, 0, ThreadId2);

  {Stop the main thread for a short time so that the other threads get
   a chance to take ownership of the mutex before the main thread
   calls WaitForSingleObject}
  Sleep(1000);

  {Take ownership of the mutex; this will wait until the mutex is signaled}
  WaitForSingleObject(MutexHandle, INFINITE);

  {Close the mutexHandle so that this will work again}
  CloseHandle(MutexHandle);
end;
```

Figure 6-1:
The threads fire one at a time

CreateProcess   Windows.pas

Syntax

```
CreateProcess(
    lpApplicationName: PChar;              {pointer to the name of the application}
    lpCommandLine: PChar;                  {pointer to the command line of the application}
    lpProcessAttributes,                   {pointer to process security attributes}
    lpThreadAttributes: PSecurityAttributes; {pointer to the thread security attributes}
    bInheritHandles: BOOL;                 {inheritance flag}
    dwCreationFlags: DWORD;                {creation flag}
    lpEnvironment: Pointer;                {pointer to environment block}
    lpCurrentDirectory: PChar;             {pointer to the current directory}
    const lpStartupInfo: TStartupInfo;     {pointer to a TStartupInfo data structure}
    var lpProcessInformation: TProcessInformation   {pointer to a TProcessInformation
                                                     data structure}
): BOOL;                                   {returns TRUE or FALSE}
```

Description

This function will create a new process and its primary thread. The primary thread created will have an initial stack size that is specified in the header of the executable, and the thread will begin execution at the executable image's entry point. The entry point of a Delphi executable is set by choosing Project|Options, clicking on the Linker page, and modifying the image base setting. The default value for the image base should never need to be modified.

Parameters

lpApplicationName: A pointer to a null-terminated string that specifies the name of the executable. If this parameter is set to NIL, the lpCommandLine parameter must contain the path and executable name (i.e., C:\Windows\Wordpad.exe Readme.txt). In the case of long filenames that contain spaces, use quotes around the path and filename. If a filename is given with no path, the application will look in the current directory for the application, and will not search along the search path.

Windows NT/2000 and later: To start 16-bit processes, this parameter should be set to NIL and the lpCommandLine parameter should be used to specify the executable name and arguments.

lpCommandLine: A null-terminated string that specifies the command line for the executable. If this parameter is set to NIL, the lpApplicationName parameter can be used for the command line of the application. If neither of these parameters are set to NIL, the lpApplicationName parameter will indicate the path and name of the application, and the lpCommandLine parameter will indicate the command line of the application. If the lpApplicationName parameter is set to NIL, the first space-delimited portion of the lpCommandLine parameter will be the application name. If the .exe extension is not given, it will be appended unless there is a (.) in the filename or the filename contains the path.

lpProcessAttributes: A pointer to a TSecurityAttributes structure that specifies the security descriptor for the process.

Windows NT/2000 or later: If this parameter is set to NIL, the process will have the default security descriptor and is not inheritable. See the CreateEvent function for a description of this parameter.

lpThreadAttributes: A pointer to a TSecurityAttributes structure that specifies the security descriptor for the thread of the process.

Windows NT/2000 or later: If this parameter is set to NIL, the thread will have the default security descriptor and is not inheritable. See the CreateFile function for a description of this parameter.

bInheritHandles: Indicates if the new process will inherit handles opened by the calling process. If this parameter is set to TRUE, the created process will inherit all the open handles of the calling process. The inherited handles will have the same value and access privileges as the original handles.

dwCreationFlags: Specifies the creation of the process and control of the priority class. Priority class defaults to NORMAL_PRIORITY_CLASS. If the creating process has a priority class of IDLE_PRIORITY_CLASS, the child default priority class will be IDLE_PRIORITY_CLASS. This parameter can contain any combination of values from Table 6-2, and one value from Table 6-3.

lpEnvironment: A pointer to an environment block for the new process. If this parameter is set to NIL, the new process will use the environment of the calling process.

lpCurrentDirectory: A null-terminated string specifying the current drive and directory for the new process. If this parameter is set to NIL, the new process will have the same current directory as the calling process.

lpStartupInfo: A pointer to a TStartupInfo structure that specifies how the main window of the new process should appear. The TStartupInfo data structure is defined as:

```
TStartupInfo = record
  cb: DWORD;              {the size of the TStartupInfo record}
  lpReserved: Pointer;    {reserved}
  lpDesktop: Pointer;     {a pointer to the desktop}
  lpTitle: Pointer;       {the title for console applications}
  dwX: DWORD;             {the default column (left) position}
```

```
    dwY: DWORD;                {the default row (top) position}
    dwXSize: DWORD;            {the default width}
    dwYSize: DWORD;            {the default height}
    dwXCountChars: DWORD;      {the screen width for a console app}
    dwYCountChars: DWORD;      {the screen height for a console app}
    dwFillAttribute: DWORD;    {color settings for a console app}
    dwFlags: DWORD;            {flags to determine significant fields}
    wShowWindow: Word;         {the default show window setting}
    cbReserved2: Word;         {reserved}
    lpReserved2: PByte;        {reserved}
    hStdInput: THandle;        {the standard handle for input}
    hStdOutput: THandle;       {the standard handle for output}
    hStdError: THandle;        {the standard handle for error output}
end;
```

cb: Indicates the size of the TStartupInfo structure, in bytes.

lpReserved: This member is not used and should be set to nil.

lpDesktop: A pointer to a null-terminated string containing the name of the desktop and window station for this process.

lpTitle: A pointer to a null-terminated string containing the title displayed in the title bar of a console application. If no string is specified, the name of the executable is displayed instead.

dwX: Indicates the horizontal position of the upper-left corner of the window, in pixels. Valid only if STARTF_USEPOSITION is included in the dwFlags member.

dwY: Indicates the vertical position of the upper-left corner of the window, in pixels. Valid only if STARTF_USEPOSITION is included in the dwFlags member.

dwXSize: Specifies the width of the window, in pixels. Valid only if STARTF_USESIZE is included in the dwFlags member.

dwYSize: Specifies the height of the window, in pixels. Valid only if STARTF_USESIZE is included in the dwFlags member.

dwXCountChars: Windows NT/2000/XP only: Specifies the width of a console app window, in characters. Valid only if STARTF_USECOUNTCHARS is included in the dwFlags member.

dwYCountChars: Windows NT/2000/XP only: Specifies the height of a console app window, in characters. Valid only if STARTF_USECOUNTCHARS is included in the dwFlags member.

dwFillAttribute: Indicates the foreground and background text colors in a console app. Valid only if STARTF_USEFILLATTRIBUTE is included in the dwFlags member. This value can be a combination of flags from the following table. Including multiple flags in this member combines their color attributes (i.e. the flags BACKGROUND_RED, BACKGROUND_GREEN, and BACKGROUND_BLUE would combine to create a white background).

dwFlags: A series of flags indicating which TStartupInfo members contain values. This can be a combination of values from the following table.

wShowWindow: A flag indicating how the window is shown. This can be one value from the following table. Valid only if STARTF_USESHOWWINDOW is included in the dwFlags member.

cbReserved2: This value is reserved and should be set to zero.

lpReserved2: This value is reserved and should be set to nil.

hStdInput: Indicates a handle to be used as the standard input handle. Valid only if STARTF_USESTDHANDLES is included in the dwFlags member.

hStdOutput: Indicates a handle to be used as the standard output handle. Valid only if STARTF_USESTDHANDLES is included in the dwFlags member.

hStdError: Indicates a handle to be used as the standard error handle. Valid only if STARTF_USESTDHANDLES is included in the dwFlags member.

Table 6-2: CreateProcess lpStartupInfo.dwFillAttribute values

Value	Description
FOREGROUND_BLUE	Include blue in the foreground.
FOREGROUND_GREEN	Include green in the foreground.
FOREGROUND_RED	Include red in the foreground.
FOREGROUND_INTENSITY	Make the foreground color brighter.
BACKGROUND_BLUE	Include blue in the background.
BACKGROUND_GREEN	Include green in the background.
BACKGROUND_RED	Include red in the background.
BACKGROUND_INTENSITY	Make the background color brighter.

Table 6-3: CreateProcess lpStartupInfo.dwFlags values

Value	Description
STARTF_FORCEONFEEDBACK	Turns the feedback cursor on while the process is drawing.
STARTF_FORCEOFFFEEDBACK	Forces the feedback cursor off while the process is drawing (i.e. the default cursor is displayed).
STARTF_RUNFULLSCREEN	**Windows NT/2000/XP only:** Indicates that the process should run in full-screen mode. Valid only for console applications.
STARTF_USECOUNTCHARS	**Windows NT/2000/XP only:** Indicates that the dwXCountChars and dwYCountChars members contain values.
STARTF_USEFILLATTRIBUTE	Indicates that the dwFillAttribute member contains a value.
STARTF_USEPOSITION	Indicates that the dwX and dwY members contain values.
STARTF_USESHOWWINDOW	Indicates that the wShowWindow member contains a value.
STARTF_USESIZE	Indicates that the dwXSize and dwYSize members contain values.
STARTF_USESTDHANDLES	Indicates that the hStdInput, hStdOutput, and hStdError members contain values.

Table 6-4: CreateProcess lpStartupInfo.wShowWindow values

Value	Description
SW_SHOW	Displays the window in its current position and size.
SW_SHOWDEFAULT	Displays the window in the position and size as specified in the TStartupInfo structure.
SW_SHOWMAXIMIZED	Displays the window maximized.
SW_SHOWMINIMIZED	Displays the window minimized to the task bar.
SW_SHOWMINNOACTIVE	Displays the window minimized to the task bar, but does not activate the window.
SW_SHOWNA	Displays the window in its current position and size, but does not activate it.
SW_SHOWNOACTIVATE	Displays the window in its most recent position and size, but does not activate it.
SW_SHOWNORMAL	Activates and displays the window.

lpProcessInformation: A variable of type TProcessInformation that receives information about the new process. The TProcessInformation data structure is defined as:

```
TProcessInformation = record
    hProcess: THandle;         {the process handle}
    hThread: THandle;          {a handle to the primary thread}
    dwProcessId: DWORD;        {a global process identifier}
    dwThreadId: DWORD;         {a global thread identifier}
end;
```

hProcess: A handle to the newly created process.

hThread: A handle to the primary thread of the newly created process.

dwProcessId: A global process identifier used to identify a process.

dwThreadId: A global thread identifier used to identify a thread.

Return Value

If the function succeeds, it returns TRUE; otherwise, it returns FALSE. To get extended error information, call the GetLastError function.

See Also

CloseHandle*, CreateThread, ExitProcess, ExitThread, GetCommandLine*, GetEnvironmentStrings*, GetExitCodeProcess, GetFullPathName*, GetStartupInfo*, GetSystemDirectory*, GetWindowsDirectory*, OpenProcess, ResumeThread, TerminateProcess, WaitForInputIdle

Example

See Listing 6-17 under TerminateProcess.

Table 6-5: CreateProcess dwCreationFlags creation flag values

Value	Description
CREATE_DEFAULT_ERROR_MODE	The new process will get the current default error mode instead of the error mode of the calling process.
CREATE_NEW_CONSOLE	The new process will not inherit the parent's console; it will have its own. This flag cannot be used with the DETACHED_PROCESS flag.
CREATE_NEW_PROCESS_GROUP	The new process will be the root process of a new process group. A process group consists of the root process and all the descendents.
CREATE_NO_WINDOW	**Windows NT/2000 or later:** If the application is a console application, this flag causes the application to run without a console window.
CREATE_SEPARATE_WOW_VDM	**Windows NT/2000 or later:** This flag is only valid when starting a 16-bit application. The resulting process will run in its own private Virtual DOS Machine (VDM). By default, 16-bit Windows applications run in a shared VDM. Running a 16-bit application in a separate VDM has the advantage of letting one 16-bit application continue when another 16-bit application hangs during input.
CREATE_SHARED_WOW_VDM	**Windows NT/2000 or later:** This flag is only valid when starting a 16-bit application. This flag will cause the function to override the setting in the Win.ini for the DefaultSeparateVDM=TRUE and run the new process in the shared Virtual DOS Machine.
CREATE_SUSPENDED	The primary thread of the new process is created and suspended, and will not begin executing until the ResumeThread function is called.
CREATE_UNICODE_ENVIRONMENT	The block pointed to by lpEnvironment uses Unicode characters; otherwise, the environment uses ANSI characters.
DEBUG_PROCESS	The calling process will be treated as a debugger and the called process as a process being debugged. When this flag is used, only the calling process can call the WaitForDebugEvent function.
DEBUG_ONLY_THIS_PROCESS	If this flag is not set and the calling process is being debugged, the new process becomes another process being debugged by the debugger. If the calling process is not being debugged, no debugging occurs.
DETACHED_PROCESS	The new process will not have access to the console of the calling process. This flag cannot be used with the CREATE_NEW_CONSOLE flag.

Table 6-6: CreateProcess dwCreationFlags priority class values

Value	Description
ABOVE_NORMAL_PRIORITY_CLASS	**Windows 2000 or later:** The process has higher priority than NORMAL_PRIORITY_CLASS, but lower priority than HIGH_PRIORITY_CLASS.
BELOW_NORMAL_PRIORITY_CLASS	**Windows 2000 or later:** The process has higher priority than IDLE_PRIORITY_CLASS, but lower priority than NORMAL_PRIORITY_CLASS.

Value	Description
HIGH_PRIORITY_CLASS	Indicates time-critical tasks that must be executed immediately for it to run smoothly. The threads of a high-priority class process preempt the threads of normal or idle priority class processes. An example is the Windows Task List, which must be responsive to the user. HIGH_PRIORITY_CLASS can use nearly all cycles of a CPU, so use care when specifying this priority.
IDLE_PRIORITY_CLASS	All higher priority classes will preempt a process with this priority. A screen saver is a good example. Child processes inherit this priority class.
NORMAL_PRIORITY_CLASS	This priority class has no special scheduling needs, and is the default priority.
REALTIME_PRIORITY_CLASS	This is the highest possible priority class. The threads of this priority class will preempt any other threads of a lower priority class, including operating system processes performing important tasks. A real-time process that executes for a long interval (for a computer) can cause the mouse to be unresponsive or disk caches not to function. Be very careful when using this priority class.

CreateSemaphore   Windows.pas

Syntax

```
CreateSemaphore(
lpSemaphoreAttributes: PSecurityAttributes;   {pointer to a TSecurityAttributes structure}
lInitialCount: Longint;                       {initial count}
lMaximumCount: Longint;                       {maximum count}
lpName: PChar                                 {pointer to the name of the semaphore
                                                 object}
): THandle;                                   {returns the handle of the semaphore
                                                 object returned}
```

Description

This function creates a named or unnamed semaphore object. The handle returned by CreateSemaphore has SEMAPHORE_ALL_ACCESS access to the new semaphore object and can be used in any function that requires a handle to a semaphore object, such as the wait functions or DuplicateHandle. When the semaphore object is created, the number of simultaneous accesses to the resource it protects is specified. Each time a wait function is used with a semaphore, the semaphore's count is decremented by one. Conversely, when the semaphore is released, its count is incremented by one. A semaphore is in a signaled state when its count is greater than zero, but becomes non-signaled when its count reaches zero. This count can never be less than one or greater than the maximum value specified when the semaphore was created. The lInitialCount parameter specifies the initial count, and the lMaximumCount specifies the maximum count. Semaphores can be accessed across process boundaries. Threads can use wait functions against a semaphore multiple times, but each wait function will decrement the semaphore's count, and can result in the thread blocking its own execution if the semaphore's count reaches zero. If the lpSemaphoreAttributes parameter of CreateSemaphore is set to enable inheritance, the handle returned by CreateSemaphore may be inherited by a child process created with CreateProcess. The handle returned by the CreateSemaphore function can be duplicated with a call to DuplicateHandle.

Parameters

lpSemaphoreAttributes: A pointer to a TSecurityAttributes structure that specifies the security descriptor for the semaphore. If this parameter is set to NIL, the process will have the default security descriptor and is not inheritable. See the CreateEvent function for a description of this parameter.

lInitialCount: Sets the initial count for the semaphore; must be greater than or equal to zero. If this parameter is zero, the state of the semaphore is non-signaled. Whenever a wait function releases a thread that was waiting for the semaphore, the count is decreased by one.

lMaximumCount: Sets the maximum count of the semaphore, and must be greater than zero.

lpName: A null-terminated string containing the name of the semaphore. The name is limited to a maximum size of MAX_PATH characters. The name contained in this parameter is case sensitive and may contain any character except the backslash character. If this parameter is set to NIL, the semaphore object is created without a name. If the name matches another semaphore object, the function will request SEMAPHORE_ALL_ACCESS access to the object. Semaphore, mutex, event, and file mapping objects all share the same address space, so the function will fail if the name matches any other semaphore. In this situation, a call to GetLastError will return ERROR_INVALID_HANDLE.

Return Value

If the function succeeds, it returns a handle to the semaphore object. If there is an existing semaphore with the same name before the call to CreateSemaphore, a call to GetLastError will return ERROR_ALREADY_EXISTS. If the function fails, it returns zero.

See Also

CloseHandle*, CreateProcess, DuplicateHandle, OpenSemaphore, ReleaseSemaphore, WaitForSingleObject

Example

Listing 6-4: Creating a semaphore to synchronize multiple processes

```
procedure TForm1.ShowProgress;
var
  ICount: Integer;     // general loop counter
begin
  {wait for the semaphore, and get ownership. this decreases the
   semaphore's count by one. if the semaphore is currently at 0,
   this function will block until the semaphore's count increases}
  WaitForSingleObject(SemaphoreHandle, INFINITE);

  {display a visual indicator}
  for ICount := 1 to 1000 do
  begin
```

```
      Gauge1.Progress := ICount;
    end;

    {release the semaphore, and increase its count by 1}
    ReleaseSemaphore(Form1.SemaphoreHandle, 1, nil);
  end;

{you will want to click this button numerous times to get several child
 processes on the screen at once. the more you have, the better a demonstration
 of thread synchronization this example will be}
procedure TForm1.Button1Click(Sender: TObject);
var
  StartUpInfo: TStartUpInfo;         // holds startup information
  ProcessInfo: TProcessInformation;  // holds process information
  CurDir: string;                    // holds the current directory
begin
  {initialize the startup info structure}
  FillChar(StartupInfo, SizeOf(TStartupInfo), 0);
  with StartupInfo do
  begin
    cb := SizeOf(TStartupInfo);
    dwFlags := STARTF_USESHOWWINDOW;
    wShowWindow := SW_SHOWNORMAL;
  end;

  {launch the semaphore sibling program for the example}
  CurDir := ExtractFilePath(ParamStr(0))+'ProjectOpenSemaphore.exe';
  CreateProcess(PChar(CurDir), nil, nil, nil, False,
      NORMAL_PRIORITY_CLASS, nil, nil, StartupInfo, ProcessInfo);
end;

procedure TForm1.Button2Click(Sender: TObject);
var
  OldValue: DWORD;  // holds the previous semaphore count
begin
  {release the semaphore. this sets the semaphore's available count
   to 2 which will allow up to 2 threads access}
  ReleaseSemaphore(SemaphoreHandle, 2, @OldValue);

  {start the visual indication}
  ShowProgress;
end;

procedure TForm1.FormCreate(Sender: TObject);
begin
  {create the semaphore, with an initial count of 0 (non-signaled)
   and a maximum count of 2}
  SemaphoreHandle := CreateSemaphore(nil, 0, 2, 'TheSemaphore');
end;
```

Listing 6-5: The semaphore sibling program

```
{Whoops! Delphi does not include constant declarations for the desired
 access flags, although the constants for events could be used}
const
  SYNCHRONIZE = $00100000;
```

```
  STANDARD_RIGHTS_REQUIRED = $000F0000;
  SEMAPHORE_MODIFY_STATE = $0002;
  SEMAPHORE_ALL_ACCESS = (STANDARD_RIGHTS_REQUIRED or SYNCHRONIZE or $3);

{by performing this on a button click, it gives you the chance to move
 the window around and get several on the screen at once}
procedure TForm1.Button1Click(Sender: TObject);
var
  ICount: Integer;                // general loop counter
  SemaphoreHandle: THandle;       // holds the semaphore handle
  PrevCount: DWORD;               // holds the previous semaphore counter
begin
  {Open a handle to the semaphore}
  SemaphoreHandle := OpenSemaphore(SEMAPHORE_ALL_ACCESS, FALSE,
                                    'TheSemaphore');
  Button1.Caption := 'Semaphore opened and waiting';
  Button1.Enabled := FALSE;

  {wait to achieve ownership of the semaphore. this will decrease the
   semaphore's count by 1. if it is currently 0, this will block the
   thread until its count increases}
  WaitForSingleObject(SemaphoreHandle, INFINITE);

  {display a visual indication}
  for ICount := 1 to 100000 do
  begin
    Gauge1.Progress := ICount;
  end;

  {release the semaphore}
  ReleaseSemaphore(SemaphoreHandle, 1, @PrevCount);
end;
```

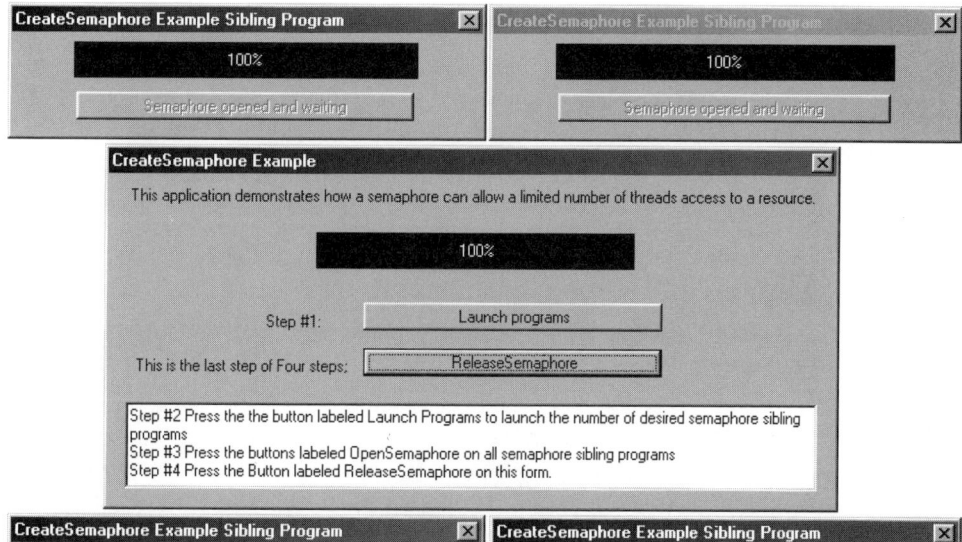

Figure 6-2: The processes were synchronized

CreateThread   Windows.pas

Syntax

```
CreateThread(
  lpThreadAttributes: Pointer;         {a pointer to a TSecurityAttributes
                                        structure}
  dwStackSize: DWORD;                  {initial stack size of the thread in bytes}
  lpStartAddress: TFNThreadStartRoutine; {address of the thread routine}
  lpParameter: Pointer;                {argument of the new thread}
  dwCreationFlags: DWORD;              {creation flags}
  var lpThreadId: DWORD                {address of the thread id}
): THandle;                            {returns the handle of the new thread}
```

Description

This function creates and executes a new thread. The resulting thread will occupy the same address space as the calling process. The thread execution begins at the address of the lpStartAddress parameter. The GetExitCodeThread function will return the exit code of the thread. The thread created has a THREAD_PRIORITY_NORMAL priority. To set the priority of the thread, call the SetThreadPriority function.

Parameters

lpThreadAttributes: A pointer to a TSecurityAttributes structure that specifies the security descriptor for the thread. If this parameter is set to NIL, the process will have the default security descriptor and is not inheritable. See the CreateEvent function for a description of this parameter.

dwStackSize: Specifies the initial stack size for the thread. If this parameter is set to zero, the thread will have the same stack size as the main thread of the process. The stack size of the thread may grow if necessary.

lpStartAddress: A pointer to a thread function. The function must use the stdcall calling convention. It must take a pointer parameter and return a Longint.

lpParameter: A pointer to the parameter that is passed to the function.

dwCreationFlags: Controls the creation of the thread. If CREATE_SUSPENDED is specified, the thread will not run until the ResumeThread function is called. If this parameter is set to zero, the thread will run immediately.

lpThreadId: A variable that receives the identifier of the new thread. This value is unique for the entire system.

Return Value

If the function succeeds, it returns the handle of the created thread. If the function fails, it returns zero. To get extended error information, call the GetLastError function.

See Also

CloseHandle*, CreateProcess, ExitProcess, ExitThread, GetExitCodeThread, GetThreadPriority, ResumeThread, SetThreadPriority

Example

See Listing 6-13 under InitializeCriticalSection and other examples throughout the chapter.

DeleteCriticalSection   Windows.pas

Syntax

```
DeleteCriticalSection(
  var lpCriticalSection: TRTLCriticalSection    {pointer to the critical section object}
);                                              {this procedure does not return a value}
```

Description

This function will delete the specified critical section object and free the resources associated with the object. Once the object is deleted, it cannot be used with EnterCriticalSection or LeaveCriticalSection.

Parameters

lpCriticalSection: A variable of type TRTLCriticalSection containing the critical section to delete. The TRTLCriticalSection structure should be treated by the application as a totally encapsulated object, and the members of the structure should never be directly manipulated.

See Also

EnterCriticalSection, InitializeCriticalSection, LeaveCriticalSection

Example

See Listing 6-13 under InitializeCriticalSection.

DuplicateHandle   Windows.pas

Syntax

```
DuplicateHandle(
  hSourceProcessHandle: THandle;    {handle of the process with the handle to duplicate}
  hSourceHandle: THandle;           {handle to duplicate}
  hTargetProcessHandle: THandle;    {handle of the process to duplicate to}
  lpTargetHandle: PHandle;          {pointer to the duplicate handle}
  dwDesiredAccess: DWORD;           {access flags for duplicate handle}
  bInheritHandle: BOOL;             {handle inheritance flag}
  dwOptions: DWORD                  {special action options}
): BOOL;                            {returns TRUE or FALSE}
```

Description

This function is used to duplicate a handle of an object. The duplicated handle refers to the same object as the original handle. The source and target process can be the same for this function. The duplicating process uses GetCurrentProcess to get the handle of itself. To get a handle outside of the current process, it may be necessary to use a named pipe or shared memory to communicate the process identifier to the duplicating process, then use the identifier in the OpenProcess function to open a handle. Duplicated handles can have more access rights than the original handle, in most cases.

Parameters

hSourceProcessHandle: Specifies the handle of the process that contains the handle to duplicate.

> **Note:** The handle must have PROCESS_DUP_HANDLE access before it can be duplicated.

hSourceHandle: The handle to duplicate. This handle can be the handle returned from one of the functions listed in Table 6-7.

hTargetProcessHandle: Specifies the handle of the process that is to receive the duplicate handle.

> **Note:** The handle must have PROCESS_DUP_HANDLE access before it can be duplicated.

lpTargetHandle: A variable that receives the duplicated handle.

dwDesiredAccess: Specifies access options for the new handle. If the dwOptions parameter specifies the DUPLICATE_SAME_ACCESS flag, this parameter is ignored. If this flag is not set, the access specification will depend on the type of object handle being duplicated. See the descriptions for the individual functions that created the object handle for more information about access options.

bInheritHandle: Specifies handle inheritance. If this parameter is set to TRUE, new processes created by the target process can inherit the duplicate handle. A value of FALSE indicates that the new handle cannot be inherited.

dwOptions: Specifies optional actions. This parameter can be set to zero or any combination of values from Table 6-8.

Return Value

If the function succeeds, it returns TRUE; otherwise, it returns FALSE. To get extended error information, call the GetLastError function.

See Also

CloseHandle*, CreateEvent, CreateFile*, CreateFileMapping*, CreateMutex, CreateProcess, CreateSemaphore, CreateThread, GetCurrentProcess, GetExitCodeProcess, GetExitCodeThread, GetPriorityClass, GetThreadPriority, OpenEvent, OpenMutex, OpenProcess, OpenSemaphore, RegCreateKeyEx*, RegOpenKeyEx*, ReleaseMutex, ReleaseSemaphore, ResetEvent, ResumeThread, SetEvent, SetPriorityClass, SetThreadPriority, SuspendThread, TerminateProcess, TerminateThread

Example

Listing 6-6: Use a duplicated thread handle to resume a thread

```
var
  Form1: TForm1;
  ThreadHandle: THandle;       // holds a handle to the current thread
  TargetHandle: THandle;       // holds a duplicated thread handle

implementation

{$R *.DFM}

function ThreadFunc(Info: Pointer): Integer;
var
  ICount: Integer;     // general loop counter
  FormDC: HDC;         // holds the form device context
begin
  {get a handle to the form's device context}
  FormDC := GetDC(Form1.Handle);

  {display something visual}
  for ICount := 1 to 10000 do
    TextOut(FormDC, 10, 50, PChar(IntToStr(ICount)), Length(IntToStr(ICount)));

  {pause the thread until ResumeThread is called, note SuspendThread
   is called with the duplicated handle}
  SuspendThread(TargetHandle);

  {display something visual}
  for ICount := 1 to 10000 do
    TextOut(FormDC, 110, 50, PChar(IntToStr(ICount)), Length(IntToStr(ICount)));

  {release the form's device context}
  ReleaseDC(Form1.Handle, FormDC);

  {end the thread}
  ExitThread(5);
end;

procedure TForm1.Button1Click(Sender: TObject);
var
  Duplicated: Bool;            // holds the result of handle duplication
  CurrentProcess: THandle;     // holds the current process handle
  CurrentThread: THandle;      // holds the current thread identifier
  ThreadId: DWORD;             // holds the created thread identifier
begin
  {Create The thread and start it immediately}
  ThreadHandle := CreateThread(nil, 0, @ThreadFunc, nil, 0, ThreadId);

  {retrieve the current process and thread}
  CurrentProcess := GetCurrentProcess;
  CurrentThread := GetCurrentThread;

  {duplicate the handle of the created thread into TargetHandle}
  Duplicated := DuplicateHandle(CurrentProcess, ThreadHandle, CurrentProcess,
                                @TargetHandle, 0, FALSE, DUPLICATE_SAME_ACCESS);
```

```
      {indicate if there was an error}
      if not(Duplicated) then
      begin
        ShowMessage('The duplication did not work');
      end;
    end;

    procedure TForm1.Button2Click(Sender: TObject);
    begin
      {Start the thread again after the pause, note ResumeThread is called with the
      duplicated handle}
      ResumeThread(TargetHandle);
    end;
```

Table 6-7: DuplicateHandle hSourceHandle values

Handle Type	Function
Console input	The CreateFile function will return the handle only when CONIN$ is specified.
Console screen buffer	The CreateFile function returns the handle when CONOUT$ is specified. A handle of a console can only be duplicated in the same process.
Event	The CreateEvent or OpenEvent function will return this handle.
File or communications device	The CreateFile function will return this handle.
File mapping	The CreateFileMapping function will return this handle.
Mutex	The CreateMutex or OpenMutex function will return this handle.
Pipe	The CreateNamedPipe or CreateFile function will return a named pipe handle. The CreatePipe function will return an anonymous pipe handle.
Process	The CreateProcess or OpenProcess function will return this handle.
Registry key	The RegCreateKey, RegCreateKeyEx, RegOpenKey, or RegOpenKeyEx function will return this handle. The DuplicateHandle function cannot use handles returned by the RegConnectRegistry function.
Semaphore	The CreateSemaphore or OpenSemaphore function will return this handle.
Thread	The CreateProcess, CreateThread, or CreateRemoteThread function will return this handle.

Table 6-8: DuplicateHandle dwOptions values

Value	Description
DUPLICATE_CLOSE_SOURCE	Closes the source handle. This will occur regardless of error status returned.
DUPLICATE_SAME_ACCESS	The duplicate handle has the same access as the source. Setting this will ignore the dwDesiredAccess parameter.

EnterCriticalSection   *Windows.pas*

Syntax

```
EnterCriticalSection(
var lpCriticalSection: TRTLCriticalSection      {pointer to the critical section object}
);                                              {this procedure does not return a value}
```

Description

The critical section object can be used to provide mutually exclusive access to a section of code within a single process. The object must be initialized before it can be used. Each thread requesting ownership of the protected resource will call EnterCriticalSection. Not more than one thread may gain access to the resource at a time and the current thread using the resource must call LeaveCriticalSection to release the code for the next thread. A thread may call EnterCriticalSection more than once after it has initial ownership of the critical section. This can help smooth the access to a critical section, as a thread may stop itself from gaining access to code it already owns. The thread must call LeaveCriticalSection for each time that it called EnterCriticalSection.

Parameters

lpCriticalSection: A variable of type TRTLCriticalSection containing the critical section to enter. The TRTLCriticalSection structure should be treated by the application as a totally encapsulated object, and the members of the structure should never be directly manipulated.

See Also

CreateMutex, DeleteCriticalSection, InitializeCriticalSection, LeaveCriticalSection

Example

See Listing 6-13 under InitializeCriticalSection.

ExitProcess   Windows.pas

Syntax

```
ExitProcess(
  uExitCode: UINT         {exit code for all threads}
);                        {this procedure does not return a value}
```

Description

This procedure will end a process and all of its threads, returning a common exit code. After a process is exited, its state and the state of all its threads become signaled.

A successful call to this procedure causes the following:

1. All object handles opened by the process are closed.
2. All threads in the process terminate.
3. The state of the process becomes signaled, satisfying any threads that have been waiting for the process.
4. The states of all threads within the process become signaled, satisfying any threads that have been waiting for the threads.
5. The termination status is changed from STILL_ACTIVE to the exit code specified by the uExitCode parameter.

Terminating the process might not remove it or any of its child processes from the system. Only when all the open handles of the process are closed is the process removed from the system.

Parameters

uExitCode: Specifies the exit code for the process, and for all threads that are terminated as a result of this call. Use the GetExitCodeProcess function to retrieve the process's exit value. Use the GetExitCodeThread function to retrieve a thread's exit value.

See Also

CreateProcess, CreateThread, ExitThread, GetExitCodeProcess, GetExitCodeThread, OpenProcess, TerminateProcess

Example

Listing 6-7: Exiting a process

```
procedure TForm1.Button1Click(Sender: TObject);
begin
  {exit the application}
  Windows.ExitProcess(10);
end;
```

ExitThread   Windows.pas

Syntax

```
ExitThread(
  dwExitCode: DWORD      {exit code for the thread}
);                       {this procedure does not return a value}
```

Description

This procedure will end a thread and clean up any associated DLLs. If this is the last thread of the process, the process will also end. Any threads that have been waiting for the thread in question to terminate will be released, and the thread in question will become signaled.

A successful call to this procedure causes the following:

1. All object handles opened by the thread are closed.
2. All threads started by the thread terminate.
3. The state of the thread becomes signaled, satisfying any threads that have been waiting for the thread.
4. The states of all threads within the thread become signaled, satisfying any threads that have been waiting for those threads.
5. The termination status is changed from STILL_ACTIVE to the exit code specified by the dwExitCode parameter.

Parameters

dwExitCode: Specifies the exit code for the process, and for all threads that are terminated as a result of this call. Use the GetExitCodeThread function to retrieve this value.

See Also

CreateProcess, CreateThread, ExitProcess, FreeLibraryAndExitThread, GetExitCode-Thread, TerminateThread

Example

See Listing 6-6 under DuplicateHandle, and various other examples throughout this chapter.

GetCurrentProcess   Windows.pas

Syntax

GetCurrentProcess: THandle;   {returns a handle to the current process}

Description

This function returns a pseudo-handle of the currently executing process. This handle is valid only in the context of the calling process. To use the handle in another process, create a duplicate of it using the DuplicateHandle function. This handle can also be used in the OpenProcess function to create a real handle. The returned handle is not inherited by child processes.

Return Value

If this function succeeds, it returns a handle to the current process; otherwise, it returns zero.

See Also

CloseHandle*, DuplicateHandle, GetCurrentProcessId, GetCurrentThread, OpenProcess

Example

See Listing 6-6 under DuplicateHandle.

GetCurrentProcessId   Windows.pas

Syntax

GetCurrentProcessId: DWORD;   {returns the identifier of the current process}

Description

This function retrieves the identifier of the current process. This value is unique for the entire system.

Return Value

If this function succeeds, it returns the identifier of the current process; otherwise, it returns zero.

See Also

GetCurrentProcess, OpenProcess, GetCurrentThreadId

Example

Listing 6-8: Retrieving the current process and thread identifiers

```
procedure TForm1.Button1Click(Sender: TObject);
begin
  Label1.Caption := 'Process Id: '+IntToStr(GetCurrentProcessId);
  Label2.Caption := 'Thread Id:  '+IntToStr(GetCurrentThreadId);
end;
```

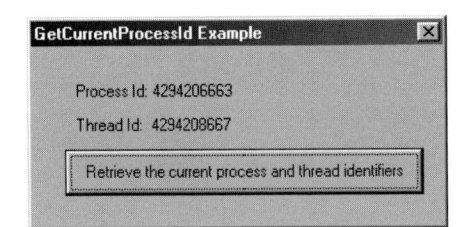

Figure 6-3: The process and thread identifiers

GetCurrentThread   Windows.pas

Syntax

GetCurrentThread: THandle;   {returns a handle for the current thread}

Description

This function returns a pseudo-handle of the currently executing thread. This handle is valid only in the context of the calling process. To use the handle in another process, create a duplicate of it using the DuplicateHandle function. The returned handle is not inherited by child processes.

Return Value

If this function succeeds, it returns a handle to the current thread; otherwise, it returns zero.

See Also

CloseHandle*, DuplicateHandle, GetCurrentProcess, GetCurrentThreadId

Example

See Listing 6-6 under DuplicateHandle.

GetCurrentThreadId   Windows.pas

Syntax

GetCurrentThreadId: DWORD   {the return value is the id of the current thread}

Description

This function returns the identifier for the current thread. This value will be unique for the entire system.

Return Value

If this function succeeds, it returns the identifier of the current thread; otherwise, it returns zero.

See Also

GetCurrentThread, GetCurrentProcessId

Example

See Listing 6-8 under GetCurrentProcessId.

GetExitCodeProcess   Windows.pas

Syntax

```
GetExitCodeProcess(
hProcess: THandle;          {handle to the process}
var lpExitCode: DWORD       {receives the termination status}
): BOOL;                    {returns TRUE or FALSE}
```

Description

This function is used to retrieve the value of the process exit code. If the process has not terminated, the function will return STILL_ACTIVE. If the process has terminated, the exit code can be one of the following:

1. The exit value specified in the ExitProcess or TerminateProcess function.
2. The return value from the main application function, known as WinMain in traditional Windows programming.
3. The exception value for an unhandled exception.

If the TerminateProcess function is called after the process code has run its course, GetExitCodeProcess may not return the correct exit code specified in TerminateProcess.

Parameters

hProcess: Specifies the handle for the process.

Windows NT/2000 or later: The handle must have PROCESS_QUERY_INFORMATION access.

lpExitCode: A variable that will receives the status of the process. This value is specified when the ExitProcess or TerminateProcess functions are called.

Return Value

If the function succeeds, it returns TRUE; otherwise, it returns FALSE. To get extended error information, call the GetLastError function.

See Also

ExitProcess, ExitThread, TerminateProcess

Example

See Listing 6-17 under TerminateProcess.

GetExitCodeThread   Windows.pas

Syntax

```
GetExitCodeThread(
hThread: THandle;              {handle of the thread}
var lpExitCode: DWORD          {receives the termination status}
): BOOL;                       {returns TRUE or FALSE}
```

Description

This function is used to retrieve the value of the thread exit code. If the thread has not terminated, the function will return STILL_ACTIVE. If the thread has terminated, the exit code can be one of the following:

1. The exit value specified in the ExitThread or TerminateThread function.
2. The return value from the thread function.
3. The exit value of the thread's process.

If the TerminateThread function is called after the thread code has run its course, GetExitCodeThread may not return the correct exit code specified in TerminateThread.

Parameters

hThread: A handle identifying the thread.

Windows NT/2000 or later: The handle must have THREAD_QUERY_INFORMATION access to the thread.

lpExitCode: A variable that receives the value of the exit code.

Return Value

If the function succeeds, it returns TRUE; otherwise, it returns FALSE. To get extended error information, call the GetLastError function.

See Also

ExitThread, GetExitCodeProcess, TerminateThread

Example

Listing 6-9: Retrieving a thread's exit code

```
function ThreadFunction(Info: Pointer): Integer; StdCall
var
  Count: Integer;          // general loop counter
  FormDC: HDC;             // holds the form device context
```

```
    CountStr: string;     // holds a string representation of the counter
begin
  {retrieve the form device context}
  FormDC := GetDC(Form1.Handle);

  {display something visual}
  for Count := 1 to 1000 do
  begin
    CountStr := IntToStr(Count);
    TextOut(FormDC, 10, 10, Pchar(CountStr), Length(CountStr));
  end;

  {release the device context and exit the thread}
  ReleaseDC(Form1.Handle, FormDC);
  ExitThread(4);
end;

procedure TForm1.Button_CreateThreadClick(Sender: TObject);
var
  ThreadId: DWORD;      // holds the thread identifier
begin
  {create and execute a thread}
  ThreadHandle := CreateThread(nil, 0, @ThreadFunction, nil, 0, ThreadId);

  if (ThreadHandle = 0) then
    MessageBox(Handle, 'No Thread Created', nil, MB_OK);
end;

procedure TForm1.Button_GetExitCodeClick(Sender: TObject);
var
  ExitCode: DWORD;      // holds the thread exit code
begin
  {retrieve and display the thread's exit code}
  GetExitCodeThread(ThreadHandle, ExitCode);
  ShowMessage('The exit code is ' + IntToStr(ExitCode));
end;
```

GetPriorityClass   Windows.pas

Syntax

```
GetPriorityClass(
hProcess: THandle            {a handle of the process}
): DWORD;                    {returns the priority class of the object}
```

Description

This function retrieves the priority class for the specified process. Every thread has a priority level based on a combination of the thread priority and the process priority. The system will determine when the thread gets a quantum of time on the CPU based on its priority.

Parameters

hProcess: The handle of the process in question.

Windows NT/2000 or later: The handle must have THREAD_QUERY_INFORMATION access to the process.

Return Value

If the function succeeds, it returns a priority class for the specified process, and can be one value from the following table. If the function fails, it returns zero. To get extended error information, call the GetLastError function.

See Also

GetThreadPriority, SetPriorityClass, SetThreadPriority

Example

Listing 6-10: Setting and retrieving the priority class

```
procedure TForm1.Button1Click(Sender: TObject);
var
  Process: THandle;       // holds a handle to the process
  PriorityClass: DWORD;   // holds the priority class
begin
  {retrieve the current process handle}
  Process := Windows.GetCurrentProcess;

  {retrieve the priority class}
  PriorityClass := GetPriorityClass(Process);

  {display the priority class}
  case PriorityClass of
    NORMAL_PRIORITY_CLASS:   Edit1.Text := 'NORMAL_PRIORITY_CLASS';
    IDLE_PRIORITY_CLASS:     Edit1.Text := 'IDLE_PRIORITY_CLASS';
    HIGH_PRIORITY_CLASS:     Edit1.Text := 'HIGH_PRIORITY_CLASS';
    REALTIME_PRIORITY_CLASS: Edit1.Text := 'REALTIME_PRIORITY_CLASS';
  end;
end;

procedure TForm1.Button2Click(Sender: TObject);
begin
  {set the selected priority class}
  case RadioGroup1.ItemIndex of
    0: SetPriorityClass(Windows.GetCurrentProcess, NORMAL_PRIORITY_CLASS);
    1: SetPriorityClass(Windows.GetCurrentProcess, IDLE_PRIORITY_CLASS);
    2: SetPriorityClass(Windows.GetCurrentProcess, HIGH_PRIORITY_CLASS);
    3: SetPriorityClass(Windows.GetCurrentProcess, REALTIME_PRIORITY_CLASS);
  end;
end;
```

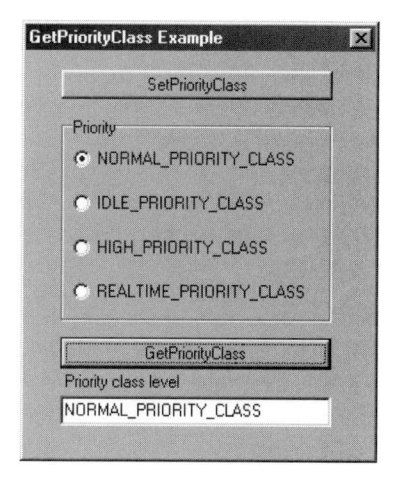

Figure 6-4:
The Priority class

Table 6-9: GetPriorityClass return values

Value	Description
HIGH_PRIORITY_CLASS	Indicates time-critical tasks that must be executed immediately for it to run smoothly. The threads of a high-priority class process preempt the threads of normal- or idle-priority class processes. An example is the Windows Task List, which must be responsive to the user. HIGH_PRIORITY_CLASS can use nearly all cycles of a CPU, so use care when specifying this priority.
IDLE_PRIORITY_CLASS	All higher priority classes will preempt a process with this priority. A screen saver is a good example. Child processes inherit this priority class.
NORMAL_PRIORITY_CLASS	This priority class has no special scheduling needs, and is the default priority.
REALTIME_PRIORITY_CLASS	This is the highest possible priority class. The threads of this priority class will preempt any other threads of a lower priority class, including operating system processes performing important tasks. A real-time process that executes for a long interval (for a computer) can cause the mouse to be unresponsive or disk caches not to function. Be very careful when using this priority class.

GetThreadPriority   Windows.pas

Syntax

```
GetThreadPriority(
hThread: THandle         {handle of the thread}
): Integer;              {returns the thread's priority level}
```

Description

GetThreadPriority will return the thread's priority based on the process's base priority class and the current thread's priority level. The system will use the priority level in scheduling the next thread to get a slice of CPU time.

Parameters

hThread: Specifies the handle of the thread in question.

Windows NT/2000 or later: The handle must have THREAD_QUERY_INFORMATION to the thread.

Return Value

If the function succeeds, it returns an integer value indicating the thread's priority level, and may be one value from the following table. If the function fails, it returns THREAD_PRIORITY_ERROR_RETURN. To get extended error information, call the GetLastError function.

See Also

GetPriorityClass, SetPriorityClass, SetThreadPriority

Example

Listing 6-11: Setting and retrieving the thread priority

```
procedure TForm1.Button1Click(Sender: TObject);
var
  ThreadPriority: Integer;   // holds the thread priority level
begin
  {retrieve the thread priority}
  ThreadPriority := GetThreadPriority(GetCurrentThread);

  {display the thread priority}
  case (ThreadPriority) OF
    THREAD_PRIORITY_LOWEST        : Edit1.Text :=
                                    'THREAD_PRIORITY_LOWEST (-2 to base)';
    THREAD_PRIORITY_BELOW_NORMAL  : Edit1.Text :=
                                    'THREAD_PRIORITY_BELOW_NORMAL (-1 to base)';
    THREAD_PRIORITY_NORMAL        : Edit1.Text :=
                                    'THREAD_PRIORITY_NORMAL (0 to base)';
    THREAD_PRIORITY_HIGHEST       : Edit1.Text :=
                                    'THREAD_PRIORITY_HIGHEST (+2 to base)';
    THREAD_PRIORITY_ABOVE_NORMAL  : Edit1.Text :=
                                    'THREAD_PRIORITY_ABOVE_NORMAL (+1 to base)';
    THREAD_PRIORITY_ERROR_RETURN  : Edit1.Text :=
                                    'THREAD_PRIORITY_ERROR_RETURN';
    THREAD_PRIORITY_TIME_CRITICAL : Edit1.Text :=
                                    'THREAD_PRIORITY_TIME_CRITICAL (base 15)';
    THREAD_PRIORITY_IDLE          : Edit1.Text :=
                                    'THREAD_PRIORITY_IDLE (base set to one)';
  end;
end;

procedure TForm1.Button2Click(Sender: TObject);
var
  ThreadHandle: THandle;   // holds the current thread handle
begin
  {retrieve the current thread}
  ThreadHandle := GetCurrentThread;

  {set the selected priority}
  case RadioGroup1.ItemIndex of
    0: SetThreadPriority(ThreadHandle, THREAD_PRIORITY_LOWEST);
```

```
    1: SetThreadPriority(ThreadHandle, THREAD_PRIORITY_BELOW_NORMAL);
    2: SetThreadPriority(ThreadHandle, THREAD_PRIORITY_NORMAL);
    3: SetThreadPriority(ThreadHandle, THREAD_PRIORITY_HIGHEST);
    4: SetThreadPriority(ThreadHandle, THREAD_PRIORITY_HIGHEST);
    5: SetThreadPriority(ThreadHandle, THREAD_PRIORITY_TIME_CRITICAL);
    6: SetThreadPriority(ThreadHandle, THREAD_PRIORITY_IDLE);
  end;
end;
```

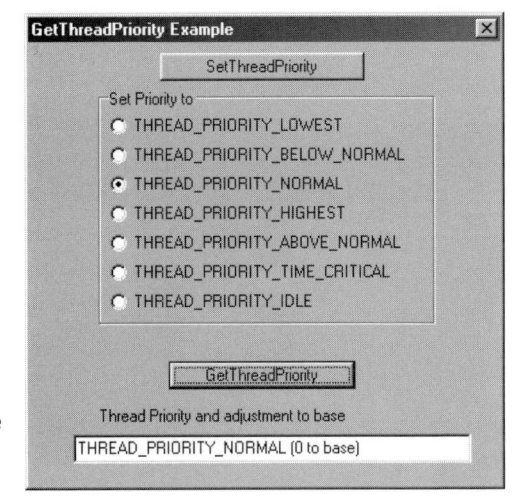

Figure 6-5: Displaying the thread's priority

Table 6-10: GetThreadPriority return values

Value	Description
THREAD_PRIORITY_ABOVE_NORMAL	One point above normal priority for the priority class.
THREAD_PRIORITY_BELOW_NORMAL	One point below normal priority for the priority class.
THREAD_PRIORITY_HIGHEST	Two points above normal priority for the priority class.
THREAD_PRIORITY_IDLE	Indicates a base priority level of one for IDLE_PRIORITY_CLASS, NORMAL_PRIORITY_CLASS, or HIGH_PRIORITY_CLASS processes, and a base priority level of 16 for REALTIME_PRIORITY_CLASS processes.
THREAD_PRIORITY_LOWEST	Two points below normal priority for the priority class.
THREAD_PRIORITY_NORMAL	Normal priority for the priority class.
THREAD_PRIORITY_TIME_CRITICAL	Indicates a base priority level of 15 for IDLE_PRIORITY_CLASS, NORMAL_PRIORITY_CLASS, or HIGH_PRIORITY_CLASS processes, and a base priority level of 31 for REALTIME_PRIORITY_CLASS processes.

GetWindowThreadProcessId   Windows.pas

Syntax

```
GetWindowThreadProcessId(
  hWnd: HWND;                    {a handle to a window}
  lpdwProcessId: Pointer         {a pointer to a buffer receiving the process identifier}
): DWORD;                        {returns the thread identifier}
```

Description

This function retrieves the identifier of the thread that created the window identified by the hWnd parameter. If the lpdwProcessId parameter is not set to NIL, it also returns the identifier of the process that created the window.

Parameters

hWnd: A handle to the window whose thread and process identifiers are to be retrieved.

lpdwProcessId: A pointer to a 32-bit buffer that receives the process identifier. This parameter can be set to NIL if the process identifier is not needed.

Return Value

If the function succeeds, it returns the identifier of the thread that created the specifier window; otherwise, it returns zero.

See Also

GetCurrentProcessId, GetCurrentThreadId

Example

Listing 6-12: Retrieving the window's thread and process identifiers

```
procedure TForm1.Button1Click(Sender: TObject);
var
  ProcessId: LongInt;    // holds the process identifier
begin
  {display the thread identifier}
  Label1.Caption:='Thread Id: '+IntToStr(GetWindowThreadProcessId(Form1.Handle,
                                                                  @ProcessId));

  {display the process identifier}
  Label2.Caption:='Process Id: '+IntToStr(ProcessId);
end;
```

Figure 6-6: The process and thread identifiers

InitializeCriticalSection   Windows.pas

Syntax

```
InitializeCriticalSection(
  var lpCriticalSection: TRTLCriticalSection    {pointer to the critical section}
);                                              {this procedure does not return a value}
```

Description

This function will initialize a critical section object. This object is used for synchronization of the threads within a single process. A critical section can only be used within a single process and will ensure that no thread will use the same section of code at the same time. After the initialization of the critical section object, the other threads of the process will use EnterCriticalSection and LeaveCriticalSection to provide mutually exclusive access to the same area of code.

Parameters

lpCriticalSection: A variable of type TRTLCriticalSection containing the critical section to initialize. The TRTLCriticalSection structure should be treated by the application as a totally encapsulated object, and the members of the structure should never be directly manipulated.

See Also

CreateMutex, DeleteCriticalSection, EnterCriticalSection, LeaveCriticalSection

Example

Listing 6-13: Using critical sections to synchronize a thread within the process

```
var
  Form1: TForm1;
  ThreadHandle: THandle;                  // holds the handles the threads
  ThreadHandle2: THandle;
  CriticalSection: TRTLCriticalSection;   // holds the critical section info

implementation

{$R *.DFM}

Function ThreadFunc(Info: Pointer): Integer; stdcall;
Var
  Count : Integer;     // general loop control variable
Begin
  {performing the EnterCriticalSection function prevents the second thread
   from executing until this thread leaves the critical section}
  EnterCriticalSection(CriticalSection);

  {show a visual display}
  for Count := 0 to 100 Do
  begin
    Form1.Edit1.Text := IntToStr(Count);
    Sleep(1);
  end;

  {display a message}
  Form1.Edit1.Text := 'Hello from the thread!';

  {pause for a second}
  Sleep(1000);
```

```
  {leave the critical section and exit the thread}
  LeaveCriticalSection(CriticalSection);
  ExitThread(4);
end;

procedure TForm1.Button1Click(Sender: TObject);
var
  ThreadId1, ThreadId2: DWORD;    // holds the created thread identifiers
begin
  {initialize the critical section information}
  InitializeCriticalSection(CriticalSection);

  {create and execute the first thread}
  ThreadHandle := CreateThread(nil, 0, @ThreadFunc, nil, 0, ThreadId1);

  {create and execute the second thread}
  ThreadHandle2 := CreateThread(nil, 0, @ThreadFunc, nil, 0, ThreadId2);
end;

procedure TForm1.FormDestroy(Sender: TObject);
begin
  {we are done, so destroy the critical section information}
  DeleteCriticalSection(CriticalSection);
end;
```

InterlockedDecrement   Windows.pas

Syntax

InterlockedDecrement(
   var Addend: Integer   {pointer to a 32-bit variable to decrement}
): Integer;   {returns a code indicating the resulting value's sign}

Description

This function will decrement a given 32-bit value. It will not allow more than one thread using any of the interlocked functions to access the same 32-bit value at the same time, thus resulting in a thread-safe mechanism for modifying an integer variable.

Parameters

Addend: A variable containing a 32-bit value that will be decremented by the function.

Return Value

If the resulting decremented value is zero, the function returns zero. The function returns a positive number if the result is positive, or a negative number if the result is negative. This function does not indicate an error upon failure.

See Also

InterlockedExchange, InterlockedIncrement

Example

Listing 6-14: Modifying a variable in a thread-safe manner

```
var
  Form1: TForm1;
  ThreadHandle: THandle;    // holds a thread handle
  ThreadHandle1: THandle;   // holds a thread handle
  MultiVar: Integer;        // the incrementing variable

implementation

{$R *.DFM}

Function ThreadFunc(Info: Pointer): Integer; stdcall;
var
  Count: Integer;           // general loop variable
begin
  {increment the variable by 10}
  for Count := 1 to 10 do
  Begin
    InterlockedIncrement(MultiVar);

    {slow it down a bit to insure that multiple threads will be
     accessing the interlocked variable simultaneously}
    Sleep(1);
  end;

  {exit the thread}
  ExitThread(4);
end;

procedure TForm1.Button1Click(Sender: TObject);
var
  ThreadId, ThreadId1: DWORD;    // holds the thread identifiers
begin
  {launch a thread, incrementing the variable by 10}
  ThreadHandle := CreateThread(nil, 0, @ThreadFunc, Nil, 0, ThreadId);

  {increment the variable again by 1}
  InterlockedIncrement(MultiVar);

  {increment the variable by 10 again. thanks to the InterlockedIncrement
   function, the variable will be exactly equal to 21, even though
   multiple threads have been incrementing it simultaneously}
  ThreadHandle1 := CreateThread(nil, 0, @ThreadFunc, Nil, 0, ThreadId1);
end;

procedure TForm1.Button2Click(Sender: TObject);
begin
  {show the variable}
  ShowMessage(IntToStr(MultiVar));
end;
```

```
procedure TForm1.Button3Click(Sender: TObject);
var
  RtnValue: Integer;      // holds the return value from InterlockedDecrement
begin
  {increment the variable}
  RtnValue := InterlockedDecrement(MultiVar);

  {display the return value}
  Label2.Caption := IntToStr(RtnValue);
end;

procedure TForm1.Button4Click(Sender: TObject);
var
  RtnValue: Integer;      // holds the return value from InterlockedExchange
begin
  {exchange the current variable's value with 50}
  RtnValue := InterlockedExchange(MultiVar, 50);
  {display the return value}
  Label2.Caption := IntToStr(RtnValue);
end;

procedure TForm1.Button5Click(Sender: TObject);
var
  RtnValue: Integer;      // holds the return value from InterlockedIncrement
begin
  {increment the variable}
  RtnValue := InterlockedIncrement(MultiVar);

  {display the return value}
  Label2.Caption := IntToStr(RtnValue);
end;

procedure TForm1.FormCreate(Sender: TObject);
begin
  {initialize the variable}
  Multivar := 0;
end;
```

InterlockedExchange   Windows.pas

Syntax

InterlockedExchange(
var Target: Integer;   {the 32-bit value to exchange}
Value: Integer   {new value for target}
): Integer;   {returns the prior value}

Description

This function will exchange the interlocked 32-bit value of the variable pointed to by the Target parameter with the 32-bit value identified by the Value parameter. This function will work across process boundaries as long as the variable to exchange is in shared memory.

Parameters

Target: A variable containing a 32-bit value that will be exchanged with the Value parameter.

Value: Specifies the new 32-bit value.

Return Value

The function returns the prior value of the variable identified by the Target parameter. This function does not indicate an error upon failure.

See Also

InterlockedDecrement, InterlockedIncrement

Example

See Listing 6-14 under InterlockedDecrement.

InterlockedIncrement   Windows.pas

Syntax

```
InterlockedIncrement(
  var Addend: Integer      {pointer to a 32-bit variable to increment}
): Integer;                {returns a code indicating the resulting value's sign}
```

Description

This function will increment a given 32-bit value. It will not allow more than one thread using any of the interlocked functions to access the same 32-bit value at the same time, thus resulting in a thread-safe mechanism for modifying an integer variable.

Parameters

Addend: A variable containing a 32-bit value that will be incremented by the function.

Return Value

If the resulting incremented value is zero, the function returns zero. The function returns a positive number if the result is positive, or a negative number if the result is negative. This function does not indicate an error upon failure.

See Also

InterlockedDecrement, InterlockedExchange

Example

See Listing 6-14 under InterlockedDecrement.

LeaveCriticalSection   Windows.pas

Syntax

```
LeaveCriticalSection(
var lpCriticalSection: TRTLCriticalSection    {pointer to the critical section}
);                                            {this procedure does not return a value}
```

Description

This function will release the critical section object for the next thread that needs access. If the same thread has called EnterCriticalSection more than once, it must call LeaveCriticalSection the same number of times. If a thread calls LeaveCriticalSection and the thread has not previously called EnterCriticalSection, it could lock the current thread of the section in question.

Parameters

lpCriticalSection: A variable of type TRTLCriticalSection containing the critical section to be released. The TRTLCriticalSection structure should be treated by the application as a totally encapsulated object, and the members of the structure should never be directly manipulated.

See Also

CreateMutex, DeleteCriticalSection, EnterCriticalSection, InitializeCriticalSection

Example

See Listing 6-13 under InitializeCriticalSection.

OpenEvent   Windows.pas

Syntax

```
OpenEvent(
dwDesiredAccess: DWORD;         {access flags}
bInheritHandle: BOOL;           {inheritance flag}
lpName: PChar                   {a pointer to the event object name}
): THandle;                     {returns the handle to the event object}
```

Description

This function will allow multiple processes to open a handle to an event object that has already been created. Use the DuplicateHandle function to make a duplicate of the handle and the CloseHandle function to close it. After all handles to the event object are closed, the event object is destroyed and all memory associated with the object will be freed. When a process terminates, any handles it may have had to the event object are automatically closed.

Parameters

dwDesiredAccess: Specifies the requested access to the event object. If the system supports object security and the security descriptor does not support the requested access, the function will fail. This parameter can contain one or more values from the following table.

bInheritHandle: Specifies handle inheritance. If this parameter is set to TRUE, a process created by CreateProcess can inherit the handle. If it is FALSE, the handle cannot be inherited.

lpName: A null-terminated string containing the name of the event object to be opened. Name comparisons are case sensitive.

Return Value

If the function succeeds, it returns the handle to the event object that was opened. If the function fails, it returns zero.

See Also

CloseHandle*, CreateEvent, CreateProcess, DuplicateHandle, PulseEvent, ResetEvent, SetEvent, WaitForSingleObject

Example

Listing 6-15: Opening an event created in another process

```
procedure TForm1.Button1Click(Sender: TObject);
begin
  {open the previously existing event}
  EventHandle := OpenEvent(EVENT_ALL_ACCESS, FALSE, 'MyEvent');
end;

procedure TForm1.Button2Click(Sender: TObject);
begin
  {set the event, which was opened from the other application}
  SetEvent(EventHandle);
end;
```

Table 6-11: OpenEvent dwDesiredAccess values

Value	Description
EVENT_ALL_ACCESS	Specifies all access flags for the event.
EVENT_MODIFY_STATE	Enables use of the SetEvent and ResetEvent functions with the given handle.
SYNCHRONIZE	**Windows NT only:** Enables any of the wait functions to specify the handle returned by OpenEvent.

OpenMutex   Windows.pas

Syntax

```
OpenMutex(
  dwDesiredAccess: DWORD;       {access flags}
  bInheritHandle: BOOL;         {inheritance flag}
```

234 Chapter 6

    lpName: PChar   {a pointer to the name of the mutex object}
    ): THandle;   {returns a handle of the mutex object}

Description

This function opens a previously created mutex, allowing a mutex to be opened across process boundaries. Use the DuplicateHandle function to make a duplicate of the handle and the CloseHandle function to close it. The handle is automatically closed when the calling process is closed. The mutex is destroyed when the last handle is closed.

Parameters

dwDesiredAccess: Specifies the desired access to the mutex object. This function will fail if the security descriptor does not permit the requested access for the calling process. This parameter can contain one or more values from Table 6-12.

bInheritHandle: Specifies handle inheritance. If this parameter is set to TRUE, a process created by CreateProcess can inherit the handle. If it is FALSE, the handle cannot be inherited.

lpName: A null-terminated string containing the name of the mutex object to be opened. Name comparisons are case sensitive.

Return Value

If the function succeeds, it returns the handle to the opened mutex object. If the function fails, it returns zero. To get extended error information, call the GetLastError function.

See Also

CloseHandle*, CreateMutex, CreateProcess, DuplicateHandle, ReleaseMutex, WaitForSingleObject

Example

See Listing 6-3 under CreateMutex.

Table 6-12: OpenMutex dwDesiredAccess values

Value	Description
MUTEX_ALL_ACCESS	All access for the mutex object.
SYNCHRONIZE	**Windows NT/2000 or later:** Enables the use of any of the wait functions to acquire ownership of the mutex with the given handle, or the ReleaseMutex function to release ownership.

OpenProcess   *Windows.pas*

Syntax

    OpenProcess(
    dwDesiredAccess: DWORD;   {access flags}
    bInheritHandle: BOOL;   {handle inheritance flag}

dwProcessId: DWORD	{the process identifier}
): THandle;	{returns the handle of the open process}

Description

OpenProcess will return the handle of an existing process object. This handle can be used in any function that requires a handle to a process where the appropriate rights were requested.

Parameters

dwDesiredAccess: Indicates the desired access privilege to the process. For a system that supports security checking, this parameter is checked against any security descriptor for the process. This parameter may contain one or more values from the following table.

bInheritHandle: Specifies if the returned handle may be inherited by a process created by the current process. If this parameter is set to TRUE, the handle may be inherited.

dwProcessId: Specifies the identifier of the process to open.

Return Value

If the function succeeds, it returns the handle of the specified process; otherwise, it returns zero. To get extended error information, call the GetLastError function.

See Also

CreateProcess, DuplicateHandle, GetCurrentProcess, GetCurrentProcessId, GetExitCodeProcess, GetPriorityClass, SetPriorityClass, TerminateProcess

Example

Listing 6-16: Launching and terminating a process

```
procedure TForm1.Button1Click(Sender: TObject);
const
  PROCESS_TERMINATE = $0001;    // OpenProcess constant
var
  ProcessHandle: THandle;       // a handle to the process
  ProcessId: Integer;           // the process identifier
  TheWindow: HWND;              // a handle to a window
begin
  {retrieve a handle to the window whose process is to be closed}
  TheWindow := FindWindow('TForm1', 'OpenProcess Example Window');

  {retrieve the window's process identifier}
  GetWindowThreadProcessId(TheWindow, @ProcessId);

  {retrieve a handle to the window's process}
  ProcessHandle := OpenProcess(PROCESS_TERMINATE, FALSE, ProcessId);

  {display a message}
  ShowMessage('goodbye');

  {terminate the spawned process}
  TerminateProcess(ProcessHandle, 0);
```

```
    end;

    procedure TForm1.Button2Click(Sender: TObject);
    var
      StartUpInfo: TStartUpInfo;          // holds startup information
      ProcessInfo: TProcessInformation;   // holds process information
      CurDir: string;                     // holds the current directory
    begin
      {initialize the startup info structure}
      FillChar(StartupInfo, SizeOf(TStartupInfo), 0);
      with StartupInfo do
      begin
        cb := SizeOf(TStartupInfo);
        dwFlags := STARTF_USESHOWWINDOW;
        wShowWindow := SW_SHOWNORMAL;
      end;

      {launch the spawned process}
      CurDir := ExtractFilePath(ParamStr(0))+'ProjectOpenProcess.exe';
      CreateProcess(PChar(CurDir), nil, nil, nil, False,
          NORMAL_PRIORITY_CLASS, nil, nil, StartupInfo, ProcessInfo);
    end;
```

Table 6-13: OpenProcess dwDesiredAccess values

Value	Description
PROCESS_ALL_ACCESS	All possible access flags for the given process.
PROCESS_CREATE_THREAD	Enables using the CreateRemoteThread function with the given handle to create a thread in the process.
PROCESS_DUP_HANDLE	Enables using the process handle as either the source or target process in the DuplicateHandle function to duplicate a handle.
PROCESS_QUERY_INFORMATION	Enables using the GetExitCodeProcess and GetPriorityClass functions to read information from the process object, using the given handle.
PROCESS_SET_INFORMATION	Enables using the SetPriorityClass function to set the priority class of the process with the given handle.
PROCESS_TERMINATE	Enables using the TerminateProcess function to terminate the process with the given handle.
PROCESS_VM_OPERATION	Enables using the VirtualProtectEx function to modify the virtual memory of the process with the given handle.
SYNCHRONIZE	**Windows NT/2000 or later:** Enables using any of the wait functions with the given handle.

OpenSemaphore *Windows.pas*

Syntax

```
OpenSemaphore(
dwDesiredAccess: DWORD;      {desired access rights}
bInheritHandle: BOOL;        {inheritance flag}
lpName: PChar                {the name of the semaphore object}
): THandle;                  {returns a handle of the open semaphore}
```

Description

This function will open multiple handles to the same semaphore object from a different process. The process that calls OpenSemaphore can use the handle returned for any function that requires a handle to a semaphore object. The handle may be duplicated with DuplicateHandle and should be closed with CloseHandle. When the last handle to the semaphore is closed, the semaphore object is destroyed. The handle will be automatically closed when the process is terminated.

Parameters

dwDesiredAccess: Indicates the desired access to the semaphore object. If the system supports object security, this function will fail if the security descriptor does not grant the requested access to the specified object from the calling process. This parameter may contain one or more values from the following table.

bInheritHandle: Specifies if the returned handle may be inherited by a process created by the current process. If this parameter is set to TRUE, the handle may be inherited.

lpName: A null-terminated string containing the name of the semaphore to be opened. Name comparisons are case sensitive.

Return Value

If the function succeeds, it returns the handle of the existing semaphore object. If the function fails, it returns zero. To get extended error information, call the GetLastError function.

See Also

CloseHandle*, CreateSemaphore, DuplicateHandle, ReleaseSemaphore, WaitForSingleObject

Example

See Listing 6-5 under CreateSemaphore.

Table 6-14: OpenSemaphore dwDesiredAccess values

Value	Description
SEMAPHORE_ALL_ACCESS	All possible access for the semaphore object.
SEMAPHORE_MODIFY_STATE	Enables use of the ReleaseSemaphore function to modify the semaphore's count with the given handle.
SYNCHRONIZE	**Windows NT only:** Enables use of any of the wait functions to wait for the semaphore's state to be signaled with the given handle.

PulseEvent   Windows.pas

Syntax

```
PulseEvent(
hEvent: THandle          {handle of the event object}
): BOOL;                 {returns TRUE or FALSE}
```

Description

The PulseEvent function sets the event object to a signaled state, then resets it to a non-signaled state after releasing the appropriate number of waiting threads. For manual reset objects, all waiting threads that can be released are immediately released. The event object is then reset to a non-signaled state and the function returns. For an auto event object, the function will reset the event to a non-signaled state and release only one waiting thread, even if multiple threads are waiting. If no threads can be released or if none are waiting, the function will set the event object to a non-signaled state and return.

Parameters

hEvent: Specifies the handle of the event object.

Windows NT/2000 or later: The handle must have EVENT_MODIFY_STATE access.

Return Value

If the function succeeds, it returns TRUE; otherwise, it returns FALSE. To get extended error information, call the GetLastError function.

See Also

CreateEvent, OpenEvent, ResetEvent, SetEvent, WaitForSingleObject

Example

See Listing 6-2 under CreateEvent.

ReleaseMutex   Windows.pas

Syntax

```
ReleaseMutex(
  hMutex: THandle          {handle of the mutex object}
): BOOL;                   {returns TRUE or FALSE}
```

Description

The ReleaseMutex function will release ownership of the specified mutex object. The calling thread must own the mutex object or the function will fail. A thread gets ownership of the mutex object by using it in one of the wait functions or by calling the CreateMutex function. ReleaseMutex will release the mutex for other threads to use. A thread can specify a mutex in more than one wait function if the thread owns the mutex in question, without blocking its execution. This will prevent a deadlock situation in a thread that already owns a mutex. The thread must call ReleaseMutex for each wait function in which the mutex object is specified.

Parameters

hMutex: Specifies the handle of the mutex object to be released.

Return Value

If the function succeeds, it returns TRUE; otherwise, it returns FALSE. To get extended error information, call the GetLastError function.

See Also

CreateMutex, WaitForSingleObject

Example

See Listing 6-3 under CreateMutex.

ReleaseSemaphore   Windows.pas

Syntax

```
ReleaseSemaphore(
hSemaphore: THandle;              {handle to the semaphore}
lReleaseCount: Longint;           {amount to add to the current count}
lpPreviousCount: Pointer          {pointer to the previous count}
): BOOL;                          {returns TRUE or FALSE}
```

Description

This function increases the count of the given semaphore object by the specified amount. The state of the semaphore is signaled when the count is greater than zero, and nonsignaled when the count is zero. The count of the semaphore is decreased by one when a waiting thread is released due to the semaphore's signaled state.

Parameters

hSemaphore: Specifies the handle of the semaphore object. This will be returned by the CreateSemaphore or OpenSemaphore functions.

Windows NT/2000 or later: This handle must have SEMAPHORE_MODIFY_STATE access.

lReleaseCount: Specifies the amount that the count of the semaphore object will be increased. This value must be greater than zero. The function will return FALSE if the specified count exceeds the maximum count of the semaphore after the increase.

lpPreviousCount: A pointer to a 32-bit value that receives the previous count of the semaphore. This parameter can be set to NIL if the previous count is not needed.

Return Value

If the function succeeds, it returns TRUE; otherwise, it returns FALSE. To get extended error information, call the GetLastError function.

See Also

CreateSemaphore, OpenSemaphore, WaitForSingleObject

Example

See Listing 6-4 under CreateSemaphore.

ResetEvent   Windows.pas

Syntax

```
ResetEvent(
  hEvent: THandle           {the handle of the event object}
): BOOL;                    {returns TRUE or FALSE}
```

Description

This function is used to set the state of an event object to non-signaled. The non-signaled state of the event object will block the execution of any threads that have specified the object in a call to a wait function. The event object will remain in the non-signaled state until set by the SetEvent or PulseEvent functions. This function is used for **manual reset** event objects as opposed to automatic reset event objects.

Parameters

hEvent: Specifies the handle of the event object.

Windows NT/2000 or later: The handle must have EVENT_MODIFY_STATE access.

Return Value

If the function succeeds, it returns TRUE; otherwise, it returns FALSE. To get extended error information, call the GetLastError function.

See Also

CreateEvent, OpenEvent, PulseEvent, SetEvent

Example

See Listing 6-2 under CreateEvent.

ResumeThread   Windows.pas

Syntax

```
ResumeThread(
  hThread: THandle          {the handle of the thread to start}
): DWORD;                   {returns the previous suspend count}
```

Description

This function will decrement the thread's suspend count by one. When the count is zero, the thread will resume execution. If the count is greater than one after the call to this function, the thread will still be suspended.

Parameters

hThread: A handle to the thread whose execution is being resumed.

Process and Thread Functions 241

Return Value

If the function succeeds, it returns the thread's previous suspend count; otherwise, it returns $FFFFFFFF. To get extended error information, call the GetLastError function.

See Also

SuspendThread

Example

See Listing 6-6 under DuplicateHandle.

SetEvent   Windows.pas

Syntax

```
SetEvent(
hEvent: THandle            {the handle of the event object to set}
): BOOL;                   {returns TRUE or FALSE}
```

Description

This function will set the state of the specified event object to signaled. Any number of waiting threads, or threads that subsequently begin wait operations, are released while the object state is signaled.

Parameters

hEvent: Specifies the handle of the event object to set. The CreateEvent or OpenEvent functions will return this handle.

Windows NT/2000 or later: The handle must have EVENT_MODIFY_STATE access.

Return Value

If the function succeeds, it returns TRUE; otherwise, it returns FALSE. To get extended error information, call the GetLastError function.

See Also

CreateEvent, OpenEvent, PulseEvent, ResetEvent, WaitForSingleObject

Example

See Listing 6-2 under CreateEvent.

SetPriorityClass   Windows.pas

Syntax

```
SetPriorityClass(
hProcess: THandle;         {the handle of the process}
dwPriorityClass: DWORD     {the priority class value}
): BOOL;                   {returns TRUE or FALSE}
```

Description

The SetPriorityClass function is used to set the priority class of a process, together with the priority value of any threads owned by the process. The priority class of a process is used to set the base priority of a thread. The threads will be scheduled in a round robin fashion based on their base priority level. Only when no other threads with a higher priority level are next in line will the threads of the next level get a slice of CPU time.

Parameters

hProcess: Specifies the handle of the process.

Windows NT/2000 or later: The handle must have PROCESS_SET_INFORMATION access.

dwPriorityClass: Specifies the priority class for the process. This parameter can be one value from the following table.

Return Value

If the function succeeds, it returns TRUE; otherwise, it returns FALSE. To get extended error information, call the GetLastError function.

See Also

CreateProcess, CreateThread, GetPriorityClass, GetThreadPriority, SetThreadPriority

Example

See Listing 6-10 under GetPriorityClass.

Table 6-15: SetPriorityClass dwPriorityClass values

Value	Description
HIGH_PRIORITY_CLASS	Indicates time-critical tasks that must be executed immediately for it to run smoothly. The threads of a high-priority class process preempt the threads of normal or idle priority class processes. An example is the Windows Task List, which must be responsive to the user. HIGH_PRIORITY_CLASS can use nearly all cycles of a CPU, so use care when specifying this priority.
IDLE_PRIORITY_CLASS	All higher priority class will preempt a process with this priority. A screen saver is a good example. Child processes inherit this priority class.
NORMAL_PRIORITY_CLASS	This priority class has no special scheduling needs, and is the default priority.
REALTIME_PRIORITY_CLASS	This is the highest possible priority class. The threads of this priority class will preempt any other threads of a lower priority class, including operating system processes performing important tasks. A real-time process that executes for a long interval (for a computer) can cause the mouse to be unresponsive or disk caches not to function. Be very careful when using this priority class.

SetThreadPriority   Windows.pas

Syntax

```
SetThreadPriority(
  hThread: THandle;      {the handle of the thread}
  nPriority: Integer;    {the priority level}
): BOOL;                 {returns TRUE or FALSE}
```

Description

This function will set the thread's priority level. This value, along with the value of the process priority, determines the thread's base priority level.

Parameters

hThread: Specifies the handle of the thread.

Windows NT/2000 or later: The handle must have THREAD_SET_INFORMATION access.

nPriority: Specifies the priority level for the thread. This parameter can be one value from the following table.

Return Value

If the function succeeds, it returns TRUE; otherwise, it returns FALSE. To get extended error information, call the GetLastError function.

See Also

GetPriorityClass, GetThreadPriority, SetPriorityClass

Example

See Listing 6-11 under GetThreadPriority.

Table 6-16: SetThreadPriority nPriority values

Value	Description
THREAD_PRIORITY_ABOVE_NORMAL	One point above normal priority for the priority class.
THREAD_PRIORITY_BELOW_NORMAL	One point below normal priority for the priority class.
THREAD_PRIORITY_HIGHEST	Two points above normal priority for the priority class.
THREAD_PRIORITY_IDLE	Indicates a base priority level of one for IDLE_PRIORITY_CLASS, NORMAL_PRIORITY_CLASS, or HIGH_PRIORITY_CLASS processes, and a base priority level of 16 for REALTIME_PRIORITY_CLASS processes.
THREAD_PRIORITY_LOWEST	Two points below normal priority for the priority class.
THREAD_PRIORITY_NORMAL	Normal priority for the priority class.
THREAD_PRIORITY_TIME_CRITICAL	Indicates a base priority level of 15 for IDLE_PRIORITY_CLASS, NORMAL_PRIORITY_CLASS, or HIGH_PRIORITY_CLASS processes, and a base priority level of 31 for REALTIME_PRIORITY_CLASS processes.

Sleep   Windows.pas

Syntax

```
Sleep(
dwMilliseconds: DWORD     {specifies the number of milliseconds to pause}
);                        {this procedure does not return a value}
```

Description

This function will pause a thread for a specified number of milliseconds.

Parameters

dwMilliseconds: This is the time in milliseconds to pause the thread. If this parameter is set to zero, the thread will relinquish the rest of its time to another thread of the same priority. If there is no other thread with the same priority, the function will return immediately and continue execution.

See Also

SuspendThread

Example

See Listing 6-3 under CreateMutex.

SuspendThread   Windows.pas

Syntax

```
SuspendThread(
hThread: THandle          {the handle of a thread}
): DWORD;                 {returns the previous suspend count}
```

Description

This function will suspend a thread and increment the thread's suspend count. If the suspend count is zero, the thread is eligible for execution. If the count is greater than zero, the thread is suspended. A thread's suspend count may be no larger than 127.

Parameters

hThread: Specifies the handle of the thread in question.

Return Value

If the function succeeds, it returns the previous suspend count of the thread. If the function fails, it returns $FFFFFFFF.

See Also

ResumeThread

Example

See Listing 6-6 under DuplicateHandle.

TerminateProcess *Windows.pas*

Syntax

```
TerminateProcess(
  hProcess: THandle;        {the process handle}
  uExitCode: UINT           {the exit code}
): BOOL;                    {returns TRUE or FALSE}
```

Description

TerminateProcess will end a process and all of its threads. This function will not check for or unload DLLs, so calling this function can cause memory leaks.

Parameters

hProcess: The handle to the process to terminate.

Windows NT/2000 or later: The handle must have PROCESS_TERMINATE access.

uExitCode: Specifies the process exit code. This value may be retrieved from the GetExitCodeProcess function.

Return Value

If the function succeeds, it returns TRUE; otherwise, it returns FALSE. To get extended error information, call the GetLastError function.

See Also

ExitProcess, GetExitCodeProcess, GetExitCodeThread, OpenProcess

Example

Listing 6-17: Creating and terminating a process

```
procedure TForm1.Button1Click(Sender: TObject);
var
  StartUpInfo: TStartUpInfo;    // holds startup information
begin
  {initialize the startup information}
  FillChar(StartupInfo, SizeOf(TStartupInfo), 0);
  with StartupInfo do
  begin
    cb := SizeOf(TStartupInfo);
    dwFlags := STARTF_USESHOWWINDOW;
    wShowWindow := SW_SHOWNORMAL;
  end;

  {launch a process}
  CreateProcess('c:\Windows\calc.exe', nil, nil, nil, False,
      NORMAL_PRIORITY_CLASS, nil, nil, StartupInfo, ProcessInfo);
end;

procedure TForm1.Button2Click(Sender: TObject);
var
  ExitCode: DWORD;              // holds the process exit code
```

```
begin
  {terminate the process and retrieve the exit code}
  TerminateProcess(ProcessInfo.HProcess, 10);
  GetExitCodeProcess(ProcessInfo.HProcess, ExitCode);

  {display the exit code}
  Label1.Caption := 'The exit code is '+Inttostr(ExitCode);
end;
```

TerminateThread   Windows.pas

Syntax

TerminateThread(
hThread: THandle;   {handle of the thread to terminate}
dwExitCode: DWORD   {exit code for the thread}
): BOOL;   {returns TRUE or FALSE}

Description

This function terminates a thread without allowing any normal clean-up code to fire. If the target thread owns a critical section, the critical section will not be released. The KERNEL32 state for the thread's process could be inconsistent, if the target thread is executing certain KERNEL32 calls when it is terminated. If the target thread is manipulating a shared DLL and changing its global state, its global state could be destroyed, affecting other users of the DLL. Threads cannot be protected against a call to TerminateThread, except by controlling access to its handle.

Parameters

hThread: Specifies the handle of the thread to terminate.

dwExitCode: Specifies the exit code of the thread. To retrieve this value, call the GetExitCodeThread function.

Return Value

If the function succeeds, it returns TRUE; otherwise, it returns FALSE. To get extended error information, call the GetLastError function.

See Also

CreateProcess, CreateThread, ExitThread, GetExitCodeThread

Example

Listing 6-18: Terminating a thread prematurely

```
var
  Form1: TForm1;
  ThreadHandle: THandle;   // holds a handle to the thread

implementation

{$R *.DFM}
```

```
function ThreadFunction(Info: Pointer): Integer; stdcall
var
  Count: Integer;      // general loop counter
  FormDC: HDC;         // holds a handle to the form device context
  CountStr: string;    // holds a string representation of Count
begin
  {retrieve a handle to the form's device context}
  FormDC := GetDC(Form1.Handle);

  {show something visual}
  for Count := 1 to 10000 do begin
    CountStr := IntToStr(Count);
    TextOut(FormDC, 10, 10, PChar(CountStr), Length(CountStr));
  end;

  {release the device context}
  ReleaseDC(Form1.Handle, FormDC);
end;

procedure TForm1.Button1Click(Sender: TObject);
var
  ThreadId: DWORD;     // holds the thread identifier
  ExitCode: DWORD;     // holds the thread exit code
begin
  {create and execute a thread}
  ThreadHandle := CreateThread(nil, 0, @ThreadFunction, nil, 0, ThreadId);
  if ThreadHandle = 0 then
    ShowMessage('Thread not Started');

  {pause for a very short period}
  Sleep(50);

  {discontinue the thread prematurely}
  TerminateThread(ThreadHandle, 4);

  {retrieve and display the thread's exit code}
  GetExitCodeThread(ThreadHandle, ExitCode);
  Label1.Caption := 'The Thread is Terminated with '+ IntToStr(ExitCode)+
                    ' as the Exit Code';
end;
```

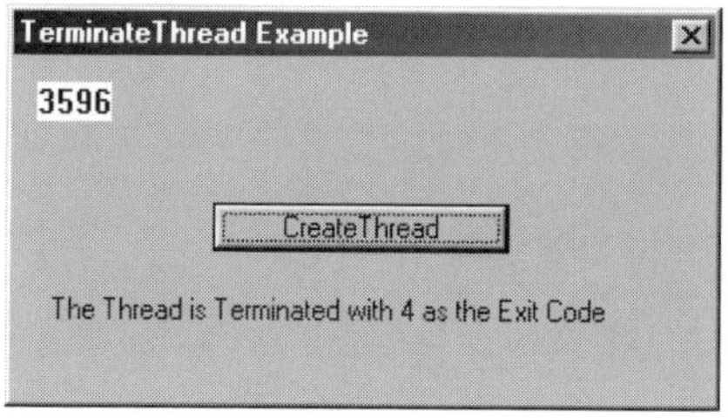

Figure 6-7: The prematurely terminated thread

TlsAlloc   Windows.pas

Syntax

TlsAlloc: DWORD;   {returns a thread local storage index slot}

Description

This function will allocate a thread local storage index. Any thread belonging to the calling process may use the created index to store and retrieve values local to that thread. Each thread of the process will use a thread local storage index to access its own storage slot. Use the TlsSetValue and TlsGetValue functions to set and get values from the index. Indexes cannot be seen across processes. The minimum number of indexes available on most systems is 64.

Return Value

If the function succeeds, it returns a thread local storage index. If the function fails, it returns $FFFFFFFF. To get extended error information, call the GetLastError function.

See Also

TlsFree, TlsGetValue, TlsSetValue

Example

Listing 6-19: Using thread local storage to store string information

```
var
  Form1: TForm1;
  ThreadHandle: THandle;    // holds a handle to a thread
  NDX: DWORD;               // holds the thread local storage index

implementation

{$R *.DFM}

Function ThreadFunc(Info: Pointer): Integer; stdcall;
Var
  FormDC: HDC;        // holds the forms device context
  AString: PChar;     // points to a string
Begin
  {retrieve a handle to the form's device context}
  FormDC := GetDC(Form1.Handle);

  {initialize the string}
  AString := 'Second thread';

  {place this value into the specified index of the thread local storage}
  if not(TlsSetValue(NDX, AString)) then
    ShowMessage('value not set');

  {display the value retrieved from the index of the thread local storage}
  TextOut(FormDC, 10, 50, TlsGetValue(NDX), 13);

  {display the thread local storage index}
  Form1.Label4.Caption := IntToStr(NDX);

  {release the form device context and exit the thread}
  ReleaseDC(Form1.Handle, FormDC);
  ExitThread(4);
end;
```

```delphi
procedure TForm1.Button1Click(Sender: TObject);
Var
  ThreadId: DWORD;      // holds a thread identifier
  Value: PChar;         // points to a string
  FormDC: HDC;          // holds the form device context
begin
  {allocate a thread local storage index slot}
  NDX := TlsAlloc;

  {retrieve a handle to the form's device context}
  FormDC := GetDC(Form1.Handle);

  {create a thread}
  ThreadHandle := CreateThread(nil, 0, @ThreadFunc, nil, 0, ThreadId);

  {initialize the string}
  Value := 'Main Thread';

  {place this value into the same index of the same thread local
   storage allocated slot. this value will be different than the
   one in the thread, although they are using the same index}
  if not(TlsSetValue(NDX, Value)) then
    ShowMessage('value not set');

  {display the value at the specified thread local storage slot}
  TextOut(FormDC, 300, 50, TlsGetValue(NDX), 11);

  {display the thread local storage index. note that it is the
   same as reported by the thread}
  Label3.Caption := IntToStr(NDX);

  {release the form's device context}
  ReleaseDC(Form1.Handle, FormDC);
end;

procedure TForm1.Button2Click(Sender: TObject);
begin
  {free the thread local storage slot}
  if not(TlsFree(NDX)) then
    ShowMessage('the TLS index was not freed')
  else
    ShowMessage('the TLS index was freed');
end;
```

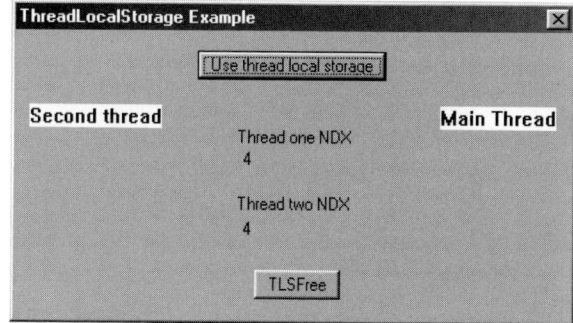

Figure 6-8:
The thread local storage variable in action

TlsFree   Windows.pas

Syntax

```
TlsFree(
    dwTlsIndex: DWORD      {the thread local storage index to free}
): BOOL;                   {returns TRUE or FALSE}
```

Description

The TlsFree function will release a thread local storage index. If the index contains a pointer to allocated memory, this memory should be freed before calling TlsFree.

Parameters

dwTlsIndex: A thread local storage index as returned by a previous call to the TlsAlloc function.

Return Value

If the function succeeds, it returns TRUE; otherwise, it returns FALSE. To get extended error information, call the GetLastError function.

See Also

TlsAlloc, TlsGetValue, TlsSetValue

Example

See Listing 6-19 under TlsAlloc.

TlsGetValue   Windows.pas

Syntax

```
TlsGetValue(
    dwTlsIndex: DWORD      {thread local storage index containing information}
): Pointer;                {returns the value in the specified index of the calling
                            thread}
```

Description

This function will retrieve the value stored in the specified thread local storage index of the calling thread.

Parameters

dwTlsIndex: The index to the thread local storage as returned by a previous call to the TlsAlloc function.

Return Value

If the function succeeds, it returns a pointer to the value stored at the specified index of thread local storage, and calls the SetLastError function to clear the last error value. If the function fails, it returns NIL.

See Also

GetLastError, SetLastError, TlsAlloc, TlsFree, TlsSetValue

Example

See Listing 6-19 under TlsAlloc.

TlsSetValue Windows.pas

Syntax

```
TlsSetValue(
  dwTlsIndex: DWORD;      {the thread local storage index}
  lpTlsValue: Pointer     {the value to be stored}
): BOOL;                  {returns TRUE or FALSE}
```

Description

This function stores a value in the calling thread's local storage at the specified index. The value stored is unique for each thread, even though the index may be the same.

Parameters

dwTlsIndex: Specifies the thread local storage index at which to store the value, as returned by a previous call to the TlsAlloc function.

lpTlsValue: A pointer to the value to be stored in the thread local storage index specified by the dwTlsIndex parameter.

Return Value

If the function succeeds, it returns TRUE; otherwise, it returns FALSE. To get extended error information, call the GetLastError function.

See Also

TlsAlloc, TlsFree, TlsGetValue

Example

See Listing 6-19 under TlsAlloc.

WaitForInputIdle Windows.pas

Syntax

```
WaitForInputIdle(
  hProcess: THandle;         {a handle to the process}
  dwMilliseconds: DWORD      {the timeout interval in milliseconds}
): DWORD;                    {returns a wait code}
```

Description

This function will wait until the given process has no more input pending and is waiting for user input, or until the timeout period specified by the dwMilliseconds parameter has elapsed. WaitForInputIdle can be used to suspend the execution of a thread that has created a process until that process is finished with all initialization and is ready for input. This function can be used at any time.

Parameters

hProcess: Specifies the handle of the process upon which to wait until it is ready for input.

dwMilliseconds: Specifies the timeout period in milliseconds. If this parameter is set to infinite, the function will not return until the specified process is idle.

Return Value

If the function succeeds, it returns one value from the following table. If the function fails, it returns $FFFFFFFF. To get extended error information, call the GetLastError function.

See Also

CreateProcess

Example

Listing 6-20: Waiting for a process to load

```
procedure TForm1.Button1Click(Sender: TObject);
var
  StartUpInfo: TStartUpInfo;            // holds startup information
  ProcessInfo: TProcessInformation;     // holds process information
begin
  {initialize the startup info structure}
  FillChar(StartupInfo, SizeOf(TStartupInfo), 0);
  with StartupInfo do
  begin
    cb := SizeOf(TStartupInfo);
    dwFlags := STARTF_USESHOWWINDOW;
    wShowWindow := SW_SHOWNORMAL;
  end;

  {launch another copy of Delphi}
  CreateProcess('c:\Program Files\Borland\Delphi6\Bin\Delphi32.exe', nil, nil,
                nil, False, NORMAL_PRIORITY_CLASS, nil, nil,
                StartupInfo, ProcessInfo);

  {this will cause the application to become unresponsive until Delphi
   has completely finished loading.  the application will not even
   accept focus}
  WaitForInputIdle(ProcessInfo.HProcess, infinite);

  {indicates that Delphi has finished loading}
  ShowMessage('Responsiveness Restored');
end;
```

Table 6-17: WaitForInputIdle return values

Value	Description
0	The wait was satisfied.
WAIT_TIMEOUT	The timeout interval elapsed and the wait was terminated.

WaitForSingleObject   Windows.pas

Syntax

```
WaitForSingleObject(
  hHandle: THandle;            {the handle of the object to wait for}
  dwMilliseconds: DWORD        {the timeout interval in milliseconds}
): DWORD;                      {returns an event code}
```

Description

This function will check the current state of the specified object. The current thread will enter an efficient wait state if the object is non-signaled. After the wait condition is satisfied (i.e., the object becomes signaled), the thread resumes execution. In some circumstances, a wait function can specify a handle of a file, named pipe, or communications device as an object to wait for.

Parameters

hHandle: Specifies the handle of the object for which to wait. The object type can be any one value from Table 6-18.

dwMilliseconds: Specifies the timeout period in milliseconds. The function will return after the specified timeout even if the object is non-signaled. If the parameter is set to zero, the function will test the object and return immediately. If this parameter is set to infinite, the timeout interval will never elapse.

Return Value

If the function succeeds, it returns one value from Table 6-19. If the function fails, it returns WAIT_FAILED. To get extended error information, call the GetLastError function.

See Also

CreateEvent, CreateFile*, CreateMutex, CreateProcess, CreateSemaphore, CreateThread, FindFirstChangeNotification*, OpenEvent, OpenMutex, OpenProcess, OpenSemaphore, PulseEvent, ResetEvent, SetEvent, Sleep

Example

See Listing 6-2 under CreateEvent.

Table 6-18: WaitForSingleObject hHandle values

Value	Description
Change notification	The FindFirstChangeNotification function will return this handle. The state of an object is signaled when a specified type of change occurs within a specified directory or directory tree.
Console input	The CreateFile function with CONIN$ specified will return this handle. When there is unread input in the console's input buffer, the state is signaled, and it is non-signaled when the input buffer is empty.
Event	The CreateEvent or OpenEvent function will return this handle. The SetEvent or PulseEvent function will explicitly set the event object to signaled. A manual reset event object's state must be reset explicitly to non-signaled by the ResetEvent function. For an auto reset event object, the wait function resets the object's state to non-signaled before returning. Event objects are also used in overlapped operations, in which the state is set by the system.
Mutex	The CreateMutex or OpenMutex function will return this handle. When a mutex object is not owned by any thread it is said to be signaled. One of the wait functions will request ownership of the mutex for the calling thread. The state of the mutex is said to be non-signaled when ownership is granted to a thread.
Process	The CreateProcess or OpenProcess function will return this handle. A process object is signaled when it is terminated.
Semaphore	The CreateSemaphore or OpenSemaphore function will return this handle. A semaphore object will maintain a count between zero and some maximum value. The state is signaled when the count is greater than zero and non-signaled when the count is zero. The wait function will decrease the count by one, if the object is signaled.
Thread	The CreateProcess or CreateThread functions will return this handle. The state of the thread is signaled when the thread terminates.

Table 6-19: WaitForSingleObject return values

Value	Description
WAIT_ABANDONED	The specified object is a mutex whose owning thread was terminated before the mutex was released. Ownership of the mutex object is granted to the calling thread, and the mutex is set to non-signaled.
WAIT_OBJECT_0	The state of the specified object is signaled.
WAIT_TIMEOUT	The state of the object is non-signaled, because the timeout interval elapsed.

Chapter 7

Timer Functions

Delphi's TTimer object provides an easy-to-use encapsulation of a Windows timer. However, the interval seems to have a limited resolution, and TTimer does not seem very reliable. The timeout value for a timer is only an approximation and is dependent on the system clock rate and how often the application retrieves messages from the message queue. The method by which Delphi encapsulates a Windows timer into an object tends to further reduce the reliability of the timeout interval.

Each TTimer object creates an invisible window. The window procedure for this window contains a message loop that calls the OnTimer event when it receives a WM_TIMER message. This method of encapsulation depletes from the maximum available window handles and from the maximum number of timers, making it slightly inefficient.

The API functions for creating and destroying a Windows timer are not complex. By using the SetTimer and KillTimer functions to create a standard Windows timer, the developer will save valuable sources. The other timer functions allow the developer to emulate a timer or perform precise timing measurements.

Emulating a Timer

The maximum amount of timers an application can have is only limited by the system configuration. However, it is a finite number and each timer takes a certain amount of Windows resources to maintain. To circumvent consuming additional resources, a developer can emulate a timer by using GetTickCount inside of a loop. A variable is initialized with a starting time retrieved from GetTickCount. Through each iteration of the loop, this starting time is subtracted from the current value of GetTickCount. If the value is greater than the timeout value specified, the application performs the desired actions and the process is started over. The following example demonstrates this technique.

Listing 7-1: Emulating a timer

```
var
  Form1: TForm1;
  Running: Boolean;     // the loop control variable

implementation

{$R *.DFM}
```

```
procedure FlashLoop;
var
  StartTick: DWORD;     // holds the start time
begin
  {get the current tick count}
  StartTick := GetTickCount;

  {if the loop is still running...}
  while Running do
  begin
    {...check the elapsed time. if a second has passed...}
    if (GetTickCount-StartTick)>1000 then
    begin
      {...update the label on the form}
      Form1.Label1.Visible := not Form1.Label1.Visible;

      {reinitialize the start time for the next round}
      StartTick := GetTickCount;
    end;

    {this is required so the loop doesn't lock up the machine}
    Application.ProcessMessages;
  end;
end;

procedure TForm1.Button1Click(Sender: TObject);
begin
  {set the loop control variable...}
  Running := TRUE;

  {...and start the loop}
  FlashLoop;
end;

procedure TForm1.FormClose(Sender: TObject; var Action: TCloseAction);
begin
  {the loop control variable must be set to FALSE
   so the loop will exit and the program can close}
  Running := FALSE;
end;
```

A similar method can be used to provide a pause within a loop or function. This approach is convenient when a standard timer may be inappropriate or difficult to implement. The following example demonstrates this technique.

Listing 7-2: Pausing a loop

```
var
  Form1: TForm1;
  Running: Boolean;    // the loop control variable

implementation

{$R *.DFM}

procedure FlashLoop;
var
```

```
    PacingCounter: DWORD;     // holds the reference start time
begin
  {if the loop is still running...}
  while Running do
  begin
    {...update the label on the form}
    Form1.Label1.Visible := not Form1.Label1.Visible;

    {pause the loop for one second}
    PacingCounter := GetTickCount;
    repeat
      {Let Windows process any pending messages}
      Application.ProcessMessages;
    until (GetTickCount-PacingCounter) > 1000;

  end;
end;

procedure TForm1.Button1Click(Sender: TObject);
begin
  {set the loop control variable...}
  Running := TRUE;

  {...and start the loop}
  FlashLoop;
end;

procedure TForm1.FormClose(Sender: TObject; var Action: TCloseAction);
begin
  {the loop control variable must be set to FALSE
   so the loop will exit and the program can close}
  Running := FALSE;
end;
```

Precise Timing

Most machines come equipped with a high-resolution timer. This timer fires several thousand times a second, making it very useful when precise timing information is required. This high-resolution timer is accessed with the QueryPerformanceCounter and QueryPerformanceFrequency functions. The QueryPerformanceCounter function returns the current value of the high-resolution timer, and QueryPerformanceFrequency returns the number of times the high-resolution timer fires every second. This frequency will vary from machine to machine depending on the hardware configuration.

A useful application of these two functions is measuring the amount of time a particular function call takes to complete. This information is very important when optimizing an application, and using this technique in every function highlights those functions that consume a gross amount of processor time. Use QueryPerformanceCounter at the beginning and end of the function to retrieve the starting and ending time. The difference of these two values is then divided by the frequency of the high-resolution timer retrieved from QueryPerformanceFrequency to arrive at the total elapsed time. Use the following formula to measure the total function time in seconds:

(Ending Time - Starting Time) / High Resolution Timer Frequency

The following example demonstrates this technique.

Listing 7-3: Measuring function time using the high-resolution timer

```
procedure TForm1.Button1Click(Sender: TObject);
var
  Loop1, Loop2: Integer;        // general loop control counters
  StartCount,                   // this holds the start and stop time for
  EndCount: TLargeInteger;      // the function
  Frequency: TLargeInteger;     // the frequency of the high resolution timer
  ElapsedTime: Extended;        // holds the total elapsed time
begin
  {retrieve the frequency of the high resolution timer}
  QueryPerformanceFrequency(Frequency);

  {begin timing the function by retrieving the current
   value of the high resolution timer}
  QueryPerformanceCounter(StartCount);

  {perform some function. in this example, we fill a 100 X 100
   cell string grid with numbers.}
  for Loop1 := 0 to 99 do
    for Loop2 :=0 to 99 do
      StringGrid1.Cells[Loop2, Loop1] := IntToStr((Loop1*100)+Loop2);

  {the function is complete. retrieve the current value
   of the high resolution counter as our end count}
  QueryPerformanceCounter(EndCount);

  {this formula computes the total amount of time the function
   took to complete}
  ElapsedTime := (EndCount - StartCount)/Frequency;

  {display the elapsed time, in seconds}
  Label1.Caption := 'Elapsed Time: '+FloatToStr(ElapsedTime)+' seconds.';
end;
```

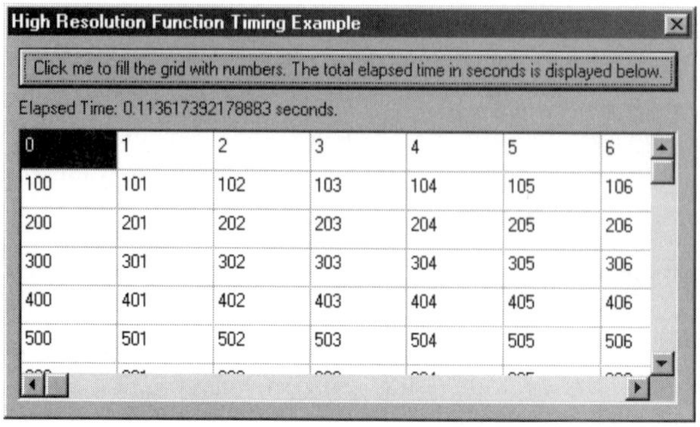

Figure 7-1: The result of timing the function

Delphi vs. the Windows API

As discussed in the introduction to this chapter, the TTimer object is convenient but isn't always the perfect solution. For a more reliable timer that does not eat up resources by allocating a window handle, use the SetTimer function. Additionally, Delphi does not provide a direct encapsulation of the high performance timer functions, although these functions are very simple and easy to use.

Timer Functions

The following timer functions are covered in this chapter:

Table 7-1: Timer functions

Function	Description
GetTickCount	Retrieves the number of milliseconds elapsed since Windows was started.
KillTimer	Deletes a timer.
QueryPerformanceCounter	Retrieves the current value of the high-resolution timer.
QueryPerformanceFrequency	Retrieves the frequency of the high-resolution timer.
SetTimer	Creates a timer.

GetTickCount Windows.pas

Syntax

GetTickCount: DWORD;   {returns a 32-bit number}

Description

This function returns the number of milliseconds that have elapsed since Windows was started. Since this time is stored in a DWORD, it will wrap to zero if Windows is left in operation for 49.7 days.

Windows NT/2000 or later: Applications should obtain the elapsed time since Windows was started by finding the System Up Time counter in performance data under the HKEY_PERFORMANCE_DATA registry key. This value will be an 8-byte number.

Return Values

If the function succeeds, the return value is the number of milliseconds that have elapsed since Windows was started; otherwise, it returns zero.

See Also

GetMessageTime, GetSystemTime*, SetSystemTime*, QueryPerformanceCounter

Example

Listing 7-4: Retrieving the number of milliseconds since Windows was started

```
procedure TForm1.Button1Click(Sender: TObject);
var
  Tick: DWORD;      // holds the number of milliseconds
begin
  {get the number of milliseconds since Windows was started}
  Tick:= GetTickCount;

  {display the number of milliseconds}
  Label1.Caption := 'Number of Milliseconds: ' + IntToStr(Tick);
end;
```

Figure 7-2: Displaying the number of milliseconds

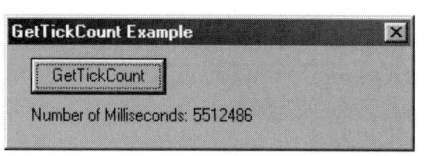

KillTimer   Windows.pas

Syntax

```
KillTimer(
hWnd: HWND;            {a handle to the window that installed the timer}
uIDEvent: UINT         {the timer identifier}
): BOOL;               {returns TRUE or FALSE}
```

Description

The KillTimer function destroys the specified timer.

Parameters

hWnd: This is a handle to the window associated with the timer. This must be the same window handle that was passed to the SetTimer function that created the timer. If the hWnd parameter of SetTimer is zero, this parameter must be set to zero.

uIDEvent: This identifies the timer to be destroyed. This parameter must be the same as the uIDEvent value passed to SetTimer if the window handle passed to SetTimer is valid. Otherwise, if the application calls SetTimer with hWnd set to zero, this parameter must be the timer identifier returned by SetTimer.

Return Values

If the function succeeds, it returns TRUE; otherwise, it returns FALSE. To get extended error information, call the GetLastError function.

See Also

SetTimer, WM_TIMER

Example

Listing 7-5: Setting and removing a timer

```
{our timer callback prototype. notice the export directive}
procedure TimerProc(hWnd:HWND;uMsg:UINT;idEvent:UINT;Time:DWORD);stdcall;export;

var
  Form1: TForm1;
  DemoCounter: Integer;    // a counter to demonstrate that a timer is running

const
  EXAMPLETIMER = 1;        // a timer identifier

implementation

{$R *.dfm}

{this function is run every time EXAMPLETIMER fires}
procedure TimerProc(hWnd: HWND; uMsg: UINT; idEvent: UINT; Time: DWORD);
begin
  {display a message to show that the timer is running}
  Form1.Label1.Caption := 'Timer1 is Now Running: ' + IntToStr(DemoCounter);

  {increment a counter to show that the timer is running}
  Inc(DemoCounter);
end;

procedure TForm1.Button1Click(Sender: TObject);
begin
  {reset our counter}
  DemoCounter:= 0;

  {create a timer to fire once per second}
  SetTimer(Form1.Handle, // handle of window for timer messages
           EXAMPLETIMER, // timer identifier
           1000,         // fire every 1000 milliseconds
           @TimerProc    // address of timer procedure
          );
end;

procedure TForm1.Button2Click(Sender: TObject);
begin
  {remove our example timer}
  KillTimer(Form1.Handle,    // handle of window that installed timer
            EXAMPLETIMER     // timer identifier
           );

  {clear the caption}
  Label1.Caption := '';
end;
```

QueryPerformanceCounter   Windows.pas

Syntax

```
QueryPerformanceCounter(
  var lpPerformanceCount: TLargeInteger    {points to the current counter value}
): BOOL;                                   {returns TRUE or FALSE}
```

Description

If the hardware supports a high-resolution performance timing counter, this function retrieves the current value of this counter.

Parameters

lpPerformanceCount: The address of a TLargeInteger that will be set to the current high-resolution performance counter value.

Return Values

If the function succeeds and the hardware supports a high-resolution performance counter, it returns TRUE. If the function fails, or the hardware does not support a high-resolution performance counter, it returns FALSE.

See Also

GetTickCount, QueryPerformanceFrequency

Example

Listing 7-6: Retrieving the current high-resolution performance counter value

```
procedure TForm1.Button1Click(Sender: TObject);
var
  PerformanceCount: TLargeInteger;
begin
  {if there is a high resolution performance counter in the hardware...}
  if QueryPerformanceCounter(PerformanceCount) then
    begin
      {...display its current counter...}
      Label1.Caption := 'Performance Counter Present';
      Label2.Caption := 'Hi-res counter value: '+
                        IntToStr(PerformanceCount);
    end
  else
    begin
      {...or display a message}
      Label1.Caption := 'Performance Counter Not Present';
      Label2.Caption := '';
    end;
end;
```

Figure 7-3:
The high-resolution timer count

QueryPerformanceFrequency   Windows.pas

Syntax

QueryPerformanceFrequency(
  var lpFrequency: TLargeInteger;   {points to the current frequency value}
): BOOL;   {returns TRUE or FALSE}

Description

If the hardware supports a high-resolution performance timing counter, this function retrieves the frequency of this counter in counts per second.

Parameters

lpFrequency: The address of a TLargeInteger structure that will be set to the high-resolution performance counter frequency in counts per second.

Return Values

If the function succeeds and the hardware supports a high-resolution performance counter, it returns TRUE. If the function fails, or the hardware does not support a high-resolution performance counter, it returns FALSE.

See Also

QueryPerformanceCounter

Example

Listing 7-7: Retrieving the high-resolution performance counter frequency

```
procedure TForm1.Button1Click(Sender: TObject);
var
  PerformanceFrequency: TLargeInteger;
begin
  {if there is a high resolution performance counter in the hardware...}
  if QueryPerformanceFrequency(PerformanceFrequency) then
    begin
      {...display its frequency...}
      Label1.Caption := 'Performance Frequency Present';
      Label2.Caption := 'Frequency: ' + IntToStr(PerformanceFrequency);
    end
  else
    begin
      {...or display a message}
      Label1.Caption := 'Performance Frequency Not Present';
```

```
         Label2.Caption := '';
      end;
   end;
end;
```

Figure 7-4: The high-performance timer frequency

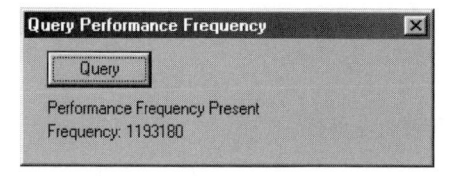

SetTimer   Windows.pas

Syntax

```
SetTimer(
hWnd: HWND;                      {a handle to the window receiving timer messages}
nIDEvent: UINT;                  {the timer identifier}
uElapse: UINT;                   {the timeout value, in milliseconds}
lpTimerFunc: TFNTimerProc        {a pointer to the callback procedure}
): UINT;                         {returns an integer identifying the new timer}
```

Description

This function creates a timer that fires at the specified timeout. When the timeout is reached, either the window procedure for the specified window receives a WM_TIMER message or the function pointed to by the lpTimerFunc parameter is called. If a WM_TIMER message is received, the wParam parameter of the message contains the value passed in the nIDEvent parameter.

Parameters

hWnd: This is a handle to the window associated with the timer, and must be owned by the calling thread. If this parameter is zero, the nIDEvent parameter is ignored and no window is associated with this timer.

nIDEvent: This is an integer that uniquely identifies this timer. If the hWnd parameter is set to zero, this parameter is ignored.

uElapse: Specifies the timeout value, in milliseconds.

lpTimerFunc: The address of the application-defined callback function. This function is called every time the timeout value is reached. If this parameter is set to NIL, the system posts a WM_TIMER message to the application queue, and the hWnd member of the message's MSG structure contains the value of the hWnd parameter passed into this function.

Return Value

If the function succeeds, it returns an integer identifying the new timer; otherwise, it returns zero. The KillTimer function can use this value to remove the timer.

Callback Syntax

TimerProc(
hWnd: HWND;   {a handle to the window associated with the timer}
uMsg: UINT;   {the WM_TIMER message}
idEvent: UINT;   {the timer identifier}
dwTime: DWORD   {the current system time}
);   {this procedure does not return a value}

Description

This function is called every time the timeout value for the timer is reached, if the lpTimerFunc parameter is set. This callback function can perform any desired task.

Parameters

hWnd: A handle to the window associated with the timer.

uMsg: This identifies the WM_TIMER message.

idEvent: This is the timer's identifier.

dwTime: This is the number of milliseconds since Windows was started, and is the same value returned by the GetTickCount function.

See Also

KillTimer, WM_TIMER

Example

See Listing 7-5 under KillTimer.

Chapter 8

Error Functions

We as developers strive to make software that is robust and easy to use, and one of our goals is to produce a software system where it is nearly impossible for a user to make a mistake. However, with the complex software systems in production today and in the future, it is getting more and more difficult to produce software that is totally idiot proof. Indeed, some actions taken by the application may fail due to no cause of the user, but instead due to an error in the system. Therefore, in order to make software as robust as possible, it is necessary to utilize functions that deal with errors.

Almost every Windows function returns a value from which the developer can determine if the function failed or succeeded. When some functions fail, they set a value in the thread local storage that gives more information on the cause of the failure. The developer can retrieve this information for assistance in debugging or to provide the user with a more detailed explanation of program failure.

It is very uncommon these days for a user to buy a machine that does not have some form of audio output device. Through the Control Panel, users can associate certain sounds with error messages, allowing users to set up their own sounds for certain events. Windows provides functions that allow the developer to use these familiar sounds to alert the user that an error has occurred.

Error Descriptions

When an API function fails, most only return a value of FALSE or zero, which may not be very helpful in determining the cause of the failure. Some functions indicate that the developer can call the GetLastError function to retrieve more information about the failure. This function, coupled with the FormatMessage function, can be very helpful in debugging an application or giving the user a more detailed explanation of an operating system error message. The following example will try to launch a nonexistent application. The operating system will display a message, and then the GetLastError and FormatMessage functions are used to retrieve a description of why the function failed. There are literally hundreds of error messages that can be retrieved by GetLastError, and they are all listed in the Windows.pas file.

Listing 8-1: Retrieving more information about a function failure

```
procedure TForm1.Button1Click(Sender: TObject);
var
  ExecInfo: TShellExecuteInfo;    // required for ShellExecuteEx
  ErrorMessage: Pointer;          // a pointer to the error message text
  ErrorCode: DWORD;               // holds the last error code
begin
  {prepare the data structure for the ShellExecuteEx function. this
   function will attempt to open a non existent file. this causes
   an error code to be set.}
  ExecInfo.cbSize        := SizeOf(TShellExecuteInfo);
  ExecInfo.fMask         := SEE_MASK_NOCLOSEPROCESS;
  ExecInfo.Wnd           := Form1.Handle;
  ExecInfo.lpVerb        := 'open';
  ExecInfo.lpFile        := 'c:\I_Do_Not_Exist.exe';
  ExecInfo.lpParameters  := '';
  ExecInfo.lpDirectory   := '';
  ExecInfo.nShow         := SW_SHOWNORMAL;

  {attempt to open and launch the non existent file}
  ShellExecuteEx(@ExecInfo);

  {get the last error code for the calling thread}
  ErrorCode := GetLastError;

  {retrieve the string describing this error code}
  FormatMessage(FORMAT_MESSAGE_ALLOCATE_BUFFER or FORMAT_MESSAGE_FROM_SYSTEM,
                nil, ErrorCode, 0, @ErrorMessage, 0, nil);

  {display the value of the last error code and its associated description}
  MessageDlg('GetLastError result: '+IntToStr(ErrorCode)+#13+
             'Error Description: '+string(PChar(ErrorMessage)),
             mtError, [mbOk], 0);

  {Windows allocated the memory for the description string,
   so we must free it.}
  LocalFree(hlocal(ErrorMessage));
end;
```

Figure 8-1:
The error string associated with the last error code

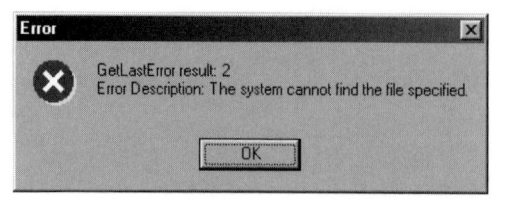

Audible Error Cues

When displaying an error message, it is sometimes useful to output a sound in conjunction with the error message display. When specific sounds are associated with different error events, it can help the user to quickly determine what type of error just occurred, even before reading the error message. The Sounds applet under the Control Panel allows users to associate sounds with certain events, including program or operating system errors such as the Exclamation or Asterisk events. The MessageBeep function allows a developer to alert the user of an error by playing the sounds they have associated for these events. See Listing 8-5 under MessageBeep for a demonstration of this functionality.

Delphi vs. the Windows API

Sometimes it is necessary to close an application or even shut down Windows, in the case of a necessary reboot after installation or a catastrophic failure. The Delphi Halt function can forcibly shut down an application, but using the FatalAppExit function allows the application to give some sort of feedback to the user, even in situations where memory has been corrupted and resources are extremely low. ExitWindows and ExitWindowsEx can close all programs and log the user off, or even forcibly reboot Windows, which may be useful in remote management applications. None of these functions are encapsulated in a higher level Delphi method or function.

When it's necessary to provide audible feedback in response to an error condition, the developer has several options. Both Beep and MessageBeep can produce sounds through the PC speaker or any installed sound card. However, under Windows 95/98, Beep ignores any parameters and outputs only the default sound on systems with sound cards or a default beep through the PC speaker on machines without a sound card. On the other hand, the developer does not have to be concerned about the existence of audio hardware, and under Windows NT/2000 Beep can be a very useful function when used on servers (which typically do not have sound hardware). By contrast, MessageBeep can play a specific alert sound. If this sound is not available, it tries to play the default sound; failing that, it outputs a default sound through the PC speaker. However, MessageBeep can be forced to output a standard sound through the PC speaker, but it does not have the options for PC speaker output available through the Beep function. This gives the developer flexibility when it is necessary to alert the user to an error condition through sound. The Delphi Beep function simply calls MessageBeep in an attempt to play the default system sound, and while useful, it does not give the developer as many options as are available through the API level functions.

Perhaps the most useful function in this chapter is the GetLastError function. While this function is not encapsulated in a higher level Delphi function, it is used throughout the VCL source code, and is extremely valuable when debugging code that uses low-level Windows API functions. Either the FormatMessage API function or the Delphi SysErrorMessage function can be used with the value returned from GetLastError to retrieve a text string describing the error for system error codes. Its sister function, SetLastError, is useful when a function needs to return both a value and an error code, and you do not want to pass values back through a parameter.

Error Functions

The following error functions are covered in this chapter:

Table 8-1: Error functions

Function	Description
Beep	Produces a standard beep.
ExitWindows	Closes all applications and logs off the user.
ExitWindowsEx	Shuts down the machine.
FatalAppExit	Forces the application to exit.
GetLastError	Retrieves the last error code.
MessageBeep	Plays a specific sound through the sound card.
SetLastError	Sets the error code.

Beep   Windows.pas

Syntax

```
Beep(
dwFreq: DWORD;            {the sound frequency}
dwDuration: DWORD;        {the sound duration}
): BOOL;                  {returns TRUE or FALSE}
```

Description

This function plays simple tones through the PC speaker. It is synchronous, and will not return control to the application until the sound has finished. Under Windows 95/98, this function simply plays the default sound event on machines with a sound card, and a default beep through the PC speaker on machines without one.

Parameters

dwFreq: The frequency of the sound in hertz. This value must be between 37 and 32,767.

Windows 95/98 only: This parameter is ignored.

dwDuration: The duration of the sound, in milliseconds.

Windows 95/98 only: This parameter is ignored.

Return Value

If the function succeeds, it returns TRUE; otherwise, it returns FALSE. To get extended error information, call the GetLastError function.

See Also

MessageBeep

Example

See Listing 8-5 under MessageBeep.

ExitWindows   Windows.pas

Syntax

```
ExitWindows(
  dwReserved: DWORD;      {reserved}
  Code: WORD              {reserved}
): BOOL;                  {returns TRUE or FALSE}
```

Description

This function causes Windows to close all applications, log the current user off, and present the login dialog box. Under Windows NT/2000, this function sends a WM_QUERYENDSESSION message to all running applications. Under Windows 95/98, this function sends a WM_QUERYENDSESSION message to all running applications except the one calling ExitWindows. Applications indicate they are shutting down by returning TRUE when receiving this message. If any application returns FALSE, the shutdown process is aborted. After the results of the WM_QUERYENDSESSION message have been processed, Windows sends a WM_ENDSESSION message to all running applications. The wParam parameter of the WM_ENDSESSION message is a non-zero value if the system is shutting down; otherwise, it is zero. New applications cannot be launched during this process.

Parameters

dwReserved: This parameter is reserved and must be set to zero.

Code: This parameter is reserved and must be set to zero.

Return Value

If the function succeeds, it returns TRUE; otherwise, it returns FALSE. To get extended error information, call the GetLastError function.

See Also

ExitWindowsEx, WM_ENDSESSION, WM_QUERYENDSESSION

Example

Listing 8-2: Exiting windows

```
implementation

const
  {an array of shutdown constants}
  ShutDownConst: array[0..3] of UINT = (EWX_LOGOFF, EWX_POWEROFF, EWX_REBOOT,
                                        EWX_SHUTDOWN);


procedure TForm1.Button1Click(Sender: TObject);
```

```
begin
  {shuts down the system according to the selection option}
  ExitWindowsEx(ShutDownConst[ComboBox1.ItemIndex], 0);
end;

procedure TForm1.Button2Click(Sender: TObject);
begin
  {logs off the current user}
  ExitWindows(0, 0);
end;
```

ExitWindowsEx   *Windows.pas*

Syntax

ExitWindowsEx(
uFlags: UINT;   {a flag indicating the type of shutdown}
dwReserved: DWORD   {reserved}
): BOOL;   {returns TRUE or FALSE}

Description

This function can log a user off, power the system off, and reboot the system. Like the ExitWindows function, this function causes a series of WM_QUERYENDSESSION and WM_ENDSESSION messages to be sent to all processes, dependent upon the uFlags parameter. However, ExitWindowsEx returns immediately after the function is called and the shutdown process happens asynchronously, so the application cannot assume that all processes have been closed when the function returns. During this process, applications are given a specific amount of time to respond to the shutdown request. If the applications do not respond in this time period, a dialog box appears giving the user the options of forcing the application to close, retrying the shutdown, or canceling the shutdown request. If the EWX_FORCE flag is specified, this dialog box does not appear and all processes are forced to shut down. Under Windows NT/2000, in order to shut down or restart the system the application must use the Windows API function AdjustTokenPrivileges to enable the SE_SHUTDOWN_NAME privilege.

Windows NT/2000 or later: If the EWX_FORCEIFHUNG flag is specified, it will forcibly shut down applications if they do not respond to the WM_QUERYENDSESSION or WM_ENDSESSION messages.

Windows 95/98 only: This function will not work from a console application.

Parameters

uFlags: A value indicating the type of shutdown. This flag can be one value from Table 8-2. Optionally, it can be combined with one flag from Table 8-3.

dwReserved: This parameter is reserved, and its value is ignored.

Return Value

If the function succeeds, it returns TRUE; otherwise, it returns FALSE. To get extended error information, call the GetLastError function.

See Also

ExitWindows, WM_ENDSESSION, WM_QUERYENDSESSION

Example

See Listing 8-2 under ExitWindows.

Table 8-2: ExitWindowsEx uFlags required values

Value	Description
EWX_LOGOFF	Shuts down all running processes and logs off the current user.
EWX_POWEROFF	Terminates all processes, logs the user off, shuts down the system, and turns off the power (if the power off feature is supported by the hardware).
	Windows NT/2000 or later: The calling process must have the SE_SHUTDOWN_NAME privilege set.
EWX_REBOOT	Terminates all processes, logs the user off, shuts down the system, and reboots the machine.
	Windows NT/2000 or later: The calling process must have the SE_SHUTDOWN_NAME privilege set.
EWX_SHUTDOWN	Terminates all processes, logs the user off, and shuts down the system to the point where Windows displays the screen informing the user that it is safe to turn off the machine.
	Windows NT/2000 or later: The calling process must have the SE_SHUTDOWN_NAME privilege set.

Table 8-3: ExitWindowsEx uFlags optional values

Value	Description
EWX_FORCE	Forces all processes to shut down. Windows does not send the WM_QUERYENDSESSION or WM_ENDSESSION messages to applications that are shut down. This can cause a loss of data.
EWX_FORCEIFHUNG	**Windows 2000 or later:** Forces a process to shut down if it does not respond to the WM_QUERYENDSESSION or WM_ENDSESSION messages.

FatalAppExit   Windows.pas

Syntax

```
FatalAppExit(
  uAction: UINT;           {reserved}
  lpMessageText: PChar     {a pointer to a string}
);                         {this procedure does not return a value}
```

Description

This function displays a message box with the specified text, and terminates the application when the message box is closed. If a kernel debugger is running, the user can choose to cancel the message box and return to the application that called the FatalAppExit function. Use this function to terminate an application only when there is no other way to shut it down. FatalAppExit may not free memory or close files, and can cause a general failure of Windows.

Parameters

uAction: This parameter is reserved and must be set to zero.

lpMessageText: A pointer to a null-terminated string that is displayed in the message box. This message is displayed on a single line, and typically should be no more than 35 characters long.

See Also

ExitProcess, ExitThread, TerminateProcess, TerminateThread

Example

Listing 8-3: Terminating an application

```
procedure TForm1.Button1Click(Sender: TObject);
begin
  {emergency termination of the application}
  FatalAppExit(0,'Terminating the application');
end;
```

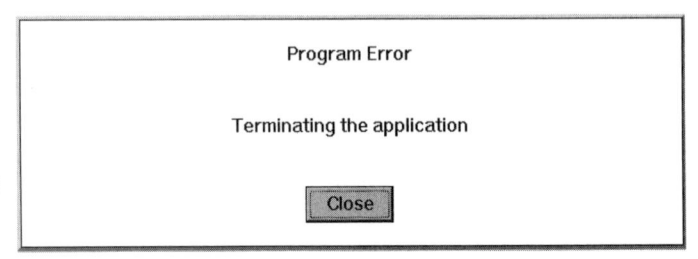

Figure 8-2: The dialog box presented by FatalAppExit

GetLastError   Windows.pas

Syntax

GetLastError: DWORD;   {returns the last error code}

Description

This function retrieves the last error code for the calling thread. Calling the SetLastError function sets this error code. The error code is a 32-bit value with the most significant bit as bit 31. Bit 29 is reserved for application-defined error codes, and will never be set by a Windows API function. If bit 29 is set, it indicates a custom error code defined by an application, and ensures that the error code does not conflict with any system-defined error codes. The developer should use GetLastError immediately when a function's return value indicates an error code is returned. Most API functions call SetLastError upon failure, but some call it upon success, setting the error code to zero and thus wiping out the error code from the function that last failed. Such cases are noted in the function reference. The error code is kept in thread local storage so multiple threads do not overwrite each other's error codes. The FormatMessage function can be used with the return value from GetLastError to retrieve a string describing the error for operating system error codes.

Return Value

If the function succeeds, it returns the last error code set by SetLastError. Individual function references list the conditions under which they use SetLastError to set the last error code. If the function fails, it returns zero.

See Also

FormatMessage*, SetLastError

Example

Listing 8-4: Setting and retrieving the last error code

```
procedure TForm1.Button1Click(Sender: TObject);
var
  ErrorCode: DWORD;    // holds our error code value
begin
  {set the last error code. bit 29 is set to indicate
   an application-defined error code, and the low order
   word is set to a decimal value of 100}
  SetLastError($20000064);

  {retrieve the last error code}
  ErrorCode := GetLastError;

  {display the code in the low order word}
  Button1.Caption := 'User-defined Error Code: '+IntToStr(LoWord(ErrorCode));
end;
```

MessageBeep   Windows.pas

Syntax

```
MessageBeep(
  uType: UINT             {the sound type}
): BOOL;                  {returns TRUE or FALSE}
```

Description

This function plays a wave through the sound card installed in the machine. This sound is played asynchronously, and control is immediately returned to the application. These sounds are assigned through the control panel, and are stored in the registry under the key HKEY_CURRENT_USER\AppEvents\Schemes\Apps\.Default. Individual sound events have their own key, and the current sound identified with the event is stored under its .Current key. If the specified sound could not be played, Windows attempts to play the system default sound. If the system default sound cannot be played, Windows outputs a standard beep sound through the PC speaker.

Chapter 8

Parameters

uType: An integer identifying the sound to play. This parameter can be one value from the following table.

Return Value

If the function succeeds, it returns TRUE; otherwise, it returns FALSE. To get extended error information, call the GetLastError function

See Also

Beep

Example

Listing 8-5: Playing sounds

```
implementation

const
  {an array of sound constants}
  Sounds: array[0..5] of UINT = ($FFFFFFFF,MB_ICONASTERISK,MB_ICONEXCLAMATION,
                                 MB_ICONHAND,MB_ICONQUESTION,MB_OK);

procedure TForm1.Button1Click(Sender: TObject);
begin
  {play the selected sound}
  MessageBeep(Sounds[ComboBox1.ItemIndex]);
end;

procedure TForm1.Button2Click(Sender: TObject);
begin
  {under Windows 95/98, the parameters are ignored, but under Windows NT/2000,
   this will produce a sound through the PC speaker}
  Windows.Beep(500, 500);
end;
```

Table 8-4: MessageBeep uType values

Value	Description
$FFFFFFFF	A standard beep using the computer speaker.
MB_ICONASTERISK	The sound associated with the Asterisk event.
MB_ICONEXCLAMATION	The sound associated with the Exclamation event.
MB_ICONHAND	The sound associated with the Critical Stop event.
MB_ICONQUESTION	The sound associated with the Question event.
MB_OK	The sound associated with the Default Sound event.

SetLastError   Windows.pas

Syntax

```
SetLastError(
  dwErrCode: DWORD       {the error code}
);                        {this procedure does not return a value}
```

Description

This function sets the last error code for the calling thread. The error code is a 32-bit value with the most significant bit as bit 31. Bit 29 is reserved for application-defined error codes, and will never be set by a Windows API function. Setting this bit indicates a custom error code defined by an application, and ensures that the error code does not conflict with any system-defined error codes. Most API functions call SetLastError upon failure, but some call it upon success and such cases are noted in the function reference. The error code is kept in thread local storage so multiple threads do not overwrite each other's error codes. Use the GetLastError function to retrieve this value.

Parameters

dwErrCode: A value indicating the last error code for the calling thread.

See Also

GetLastError

Example

See Listing 8-4 under GetLastError.

Chapter 9

Graphical Device Interface Functions

The Windows Graphical Device Interface (GDI) functions form the heart of the display system for Windows. This graphical system provides access to the display, printer, and plotter devices through a rich set of API functions.

Software that interacts with an output device must go through two major levels of abstraction: the Windows GDI kernel and the manufacturer's device driver. The device driver is a specific software interface for a hardware device, and the GDI provides the interface to the device driver for Windows applications. The GDI is capable of connecting to a variety of devices, even those that do not provide the sophisticated routines available in more advanced devices. In some areas, the GDI must take up the slack when the device driver does not provide high-level support.

The GDI is capable of supporting several kinds of devices simultaneously while maintaining a consistent interface to the application's program. The GDI must therefore be able to manage a collection of device drivers with varying capabilities and relate to them according to their functionality. It must do this while presenting to the application a consistent set of API functions that allow the programmer freedom from dealing with the devices directly.

The GDI functions operate at various levels depending on how specific the application needs to be with graphical output. At a low level, an application can manipulate an image on a pixel-by-pixel basis. At a higher level, an application can issue commands such as drawing ellipses or other device-independent graphical primitives. The GDI commands are processed by the GDI.EXE kernel in the Windows operating system and then passed to the device driver for that graphical output device according to the capabilities of the driver. Delphi encapsulates the majority of GDI functions through the TCanvas object. However, it is sometimes necessary to use lower level GDI functions to perform such tasks as drawing in non-client areas of windows or changing the window mapping mode. This chapter covers those functions used to manipulate device contexts and modify coordinate systems.

Device Independence

Windows supports a wide variety of output devices with varying capabilities. It is the task of the GDI to be able to understand the level of support that a particular device driver can provide, and issue commands to that driver based on that driver's individual capability.

If an application issues a command to draw an ellipse on a device, the GDI will determine whether that device is sophisticated enough to handle a high-level command for drawing an ellipse. If so, it will provide the most efficient set of commands to that device driver so that the image may be drawn under control of the driver. However, if the device has no such capability, the GDI must assume the drawing responsibility and issue lower level commands, perhaps on a pixel-by-pixel basis, to achieve the same results.

Regardless of the device driver that is supporting the output device, the GDI gives the high-level capability to the application. The programmer is generally not burdened with the task of knowing how to write code for formatting an image on a variety of output devices. That is the task of the GDI. There is a rich mixture of both high-level and low-level commands for presenting output from the Win32 API.

The programmer can generally choose how device independent the application will be. The API functions that reference hardware pixels will not be device independent, because devices of differing resolutions will show the images with their own capabilities. There would be no automatic scaling to account for the different resolutions. The functions that are given in terms of logical measurements instead of pixels are more device independent. The Win32 GDI system performs many internal tasks that map the API requests into device-specific commands, thereby giving the application a level of separation from the hardware.

Device Contexts

Windows contains an internal structure for images that are displayable or printable. These internal structures are known as device contexts, and contain information about how the image is to be presented. GDI functions need this handle because the device context structure contains information about presentation attributes, the coordinate system, clipping, graphics objects, and display modes. The graphics objects can include pens, brushes, bitmaps, palettes, regions, and paths. An application will not access a device context structure's information directly. The information in a device context is obtained and manipulated by using API calls. There are functions to get or create a device context, set or obtain device context attributes, and release a device context.

The GetDC and GetWindowDC functions will obtain device context handles representing the displayable surface of a window. These device contexts can be used in subsequent drawing functions to produce output directly on the window or form. A memory-based device context can be created with the CreateCompatibleDC function. This allows an application to prepare images offscreen that will later be copied to the surface of the window.

Device Context Types

A device context may be one of three types: common, class, or private. When the device context refers to a display, it may be called a display context and refer to a specific area on the screen, such as a window, the client area of a window, or the entire display.

Graphical Device Interface Functions

Display context types are created based on the class options for the window when the window is registered. The following table describes the display context type retrieved by a call to the GetDC function as a result of the applicable class styles registered by the window.

Table 9-1: Class flags and display contexts

Value	Description
none	A new device context must be obtained for each occurrence where one is needed. It is created with default values. The default clipping region is the client area. This is a common device context, and it is allocated from the application's heap space. There is no practical limit to the number of common device contexts that can be created other than memory limitations, but it is good practice to return the memory associated with a common device context by calling the ReleaseDC function when it is no longer needed.
CS_CLASSDC	A single display context is shared for all windows of the same class. Changes made to a display context will affect all other windows created from the same class. The use of class device contexts is not recommended.
CS_OWNDC	A private device context is created for the window. Each window will have its own device context, and the attributes of the device context are persistent. After the GetDC function is called the first time, any changes to the device context will be present when it is next retrieved. It is unnecessary to call the ReleaseDC function for private device contexts. This provides a boost in performance at the cost of approximately 800 additional bytes of memory per window.

In general, if the application will be performing few graphical output operations, common device contexts will provide all the functionality necessary. However, for graphically intense applications that will be drawing to the screen continuously, it is advisable to create a window with a private device context. The following example illustrates how to use the CS_OWNDC class style to create a window with a private device context.

Listing 9-1: Creating a window with a private device context

```
var
  Form1: TForm1;
  NewBrush,          // a handle to a new brush
  OldBrush: HBRUSH;  // holds the old brush

implementation

{$R *.DFM}

procedure TForm1.CreateParams(var Params: TCreateParams);
begin
  {initialize the parameters with default values}
  inherited CreateParams(Params);

  {indicate that this window should have its own device context. comment
   this line out to see the effects}
  Params.WindowClass.style := Params.WindowClass.Style or CS_OWNDC;
end;

procedure TForm1.FormActivate(Sender: TObject);
```

```
var
  TempDC: HDC;          // a temporary device context handle
begin
  {retrieve a handle to the private device context for this window}
  TempDC := GetDC(Form1.Handle);

  {create a new brush and select it into this device context}
  NewBrush := CreateHatchBrush(HS_DIAGCROSS, clRed);
  OldBrush := SelectObject(TempDC, NewBrush);

  {release the device context. note that since we are dealing with a private
   device context, the new brush will remain within the device context.}
  ReleaseDC(Form1.Handle, TempDC);
end;

procedure TForm1.FormPaint(Sender: TObject);
var
  TempDC: HDC;          // a temporary device context handle
begin
  {retrieve a handle to the private device context}
  TempDC := GetDC(Form1.Handle);

  {draw a rectangle. note that we are not creating a new brush, so the
   rectangle should be filled with the default brush selected in a device
   context.  since this is a private device context, it will use the brush
   previously selected to fill the rectangle}
  Rectangle(TempDC, 0, 0, ClientWidth, ClientHeight);

  {release the device context}
  ReleaseDC(Form1.Handle, TempDC);
end;

procedure TForm1.FormDestroy(Sender: TObject);
begin
  {delete the brush}
  SelectObject(GetDC(Form1.Handle), OldBrush);
  DeleteObject(NewBrush);
end;
```

Screen, Window, and Client Area Device Contexts

By default, display contexts relate to a window client area. This is where drawing is normally performed. It is also possible to obtain a device context for the entire window or for the display.

A device context for a window is obtained by using the GetWindowDC function. It obtains a device context for the window that includes the non-client area (borders, title bar, etc.). The device context is always a common device context and shares no properties with other device contexts regardless of type. Any changes to a device context retrieved from the GetWindowDC function will not affect private device contexts.

A device context for the entire screen is obtained by calling the GetDC function with zero as a window handle. This allows an application to perform drawing operations directly on the screen surface, drawing over windows or any other graphics. Drawing to the screen in this manner violates general Windows programming rules, however, and is not recommended.

Coordinate Systems

Windows provides several different coordinate systems for producing graphical output on display or print devices. The coordinate system can be based on device units, such as pixels, or it can be a logical measurement system, where one logical unit might translate into one or more pixels based on the method in which the logical units are mapped. A relative or logical coordinate system will allow an application to have a common set of commands that produce similar effects on different devices even when those devices have different display properties.

Graphical output is performed on a display or printing device that has its own units of measurement. The output device performs operations in pixels. The pixel is the single unit point of output on the device. It is sometimes called the device unit. The coordinate system at the device performs measurements in pixels (device units). Many of the graphical API functions use device units as a reference.

Location of pixels on a screen or printer is generally relative to an origin at the upper-left corner of the paper, screen, window, or client area of a window. In most cases the measurement values increase as the pixel point moves down or to the right of the origin. Device coordinate systems make the measurements in actual pixels, so that if the device has 100 pixels to the inch, then a point one inch down from the origin would have a vertical coordinate of 100.

The GDI provides some high-level functions that use logical coordinate systems. Such a system can provide the application with a logical representation of the drawing canvas that has measurements that are independent of that device's pixel resolution. The GDI functions that use logical coordinates will perform a translation on the coordinates and then issue commands to the device driver in its device coordinate system. This translation of measurements between logical and device coordinates is supported by a rich set of API function calls.

Some GDI functions support the higher level logical coordinates, and some functions apply only to pixel operations. The GDI functions that apply to logical coordinates are generally the drawing commands, which provide no mapping and seem, in effect, to be applied directly to pixel measurements. To obtain device-independent mapping of logical coordinates, an application must set a mapping mode and use the offset and scaling capabilities described below.

Each device context maintains a structure containing information needed to map logical coordinates to device coordinates. The device context for a display knows the hardware characteristics well enough to support the GDI calls that perform the coordinate mappings. The translations are performed at the device context level, and each creation of a device context needs its mapping mode set if it is to be able to convert from logical to display coordinates.

Mapping Logical Coordinates into Device Coordinates

The mapping of logical coordinates to display coordinates involves several possible GDI functions. There is an origin offset that can be applied to the logical coordinate reference, which is called the "window," and an offset that can be applied to the device coordinate reference, which is called the "viewport." Similarly, there are scaling factors that can be applied to the window and to the viewport. The point that is given in logical coordinates may make a mathematical transformation if it is allowed to do so by the mapping mode that is in effect for the display context. The MM_TEXT mode is the default mapping mode, which provides for a 1 to 1 mapping from logical to display coordinates.

The calculations for coordinate transformations take place for the horizontal and vertical components independently, and consist of the following mathematical operations:

```
xViewport = (xWindow - xWindowOrg) * (xViewportExt/xWindowExt) + xViewportOrg
yViewport = (yWindow - yWindowOrg) * (yViewportExt/yWindowExt) + yViewportOrg
```

The logical coordinate has the logical offset applied to it, and then is multiplied by the scaling factor between the logical and device extents, and then has the device offset applied to it. It would be simpler to apply the scaling factor and offset to only the logical system or to the device system, but these are whole numbers, not floating-point values. Also, the transformation can be designed with several devices in mind, where the applications of offset and scaling for logical (window) coordinates apply to all devices. Applications to the device (viewport) might be programmed to apply to different devices in a custom manner.

The org functions are concerned with a quantity being added or subtracted to a coordinate as it is changed from logical to device environments. The ext functions are concerned with the coordinate being scaled, made larger or smaller, as it is changed from logical to device environments. Each of these concepts has a property in both the logical and the device environment. The SetWindowOrgEx function, for example, sets the value for how much is subtracted from a coordinate as it leaves the logical coordinate system. The SetViewportOrgEx sets the value that is added to the coordinate as it reaches the device coordinate system. SetWindowExtEx sets a factor that is divided out of the coordinate as it leaves the logical coordinate system, and SetViewportExtEx sets a factor that is multiplied by the coordinate as it arrives at the device coordinate system. This is the behavior that is expressed in the mathematical formulas above.

Mapping Modes

The default mapping mode in a device context is MM_TEXT, which is a one-to-one translation, and therefore, no transformations take place. GDI functions that are specified to be in "logical units" are really also in device units when the MM_TEXT mode is in effect. For an application to use true logical coordinates, the mapping mode must be changed. The SetMapMode function is used for this purpose. The MM_ANISOTROPIC mode allows for complete flexibility in programming origin offsets and scaling. With this mode (and others except for MM_TEXT and MM_ISOTROPIC), it is possible to scale horizontal and vertical factors differently, resulting in skewed images. The basic unit of measurement stems from the pixel at the device level, with scaling and offsets applied as per settings by the programmer. MM_ISOTROPIC is similar to MM_ANISOTROPIC except that horizontal and vertical scaling is ensured to be maintained the same. The other mapping modes have built-in initial scaling factors based on the resolution of the device. They are initialized for specific units of measurement for logical coordinates. An application can place coordinates on a canvas based on actual physical measurements, while letting GDI figure out how many pixels it takes to produce that measured coordinate.

The example below illustrates how to move the origin and to apply a scaling factor to coordinate transformations. It allows the user to select a mapping mode, apply offsets to the logical (window) and device (viewport) systems, and apply scaling factors to the logical and device systems. The example displays the org and ext values currently in effect. The org values may be modified with the SetWindowOrgEx, SetViewportOrgEx, OffsetWindowOrgEx, and OffsetViewportOrgEx functions. The scaling or ext extents may be modified with the SetWindowExtEx, SetViewportExtEx, ScaleWindowExtEx, and ScaleViewportExtEx functions.

Listing 9-2: Modifying the viewport and window extents and origins

```
var
  Form1: TForm1;
  WOrigin: TPoint;         // holds the window origin
  VOrigin: TPoint;         // holds the viewport origin
  WExt: TPoint;            // holds the window extent
  VExt: TPoint;            // holds the viewport extent
  MyDisplayDC: HDC;        // holds the device context
  MyMapMode: Integer;      // holds the mapping mode

implementation

{$R *.DFM}

procedure TForm1.FormCreate(Sender: TObject);
begin
  {set the scale of the origin trackbars}
  TrackbarSWOX.Max := Panel1.Width;
  TrackbarSWOY.Max := Panel1.Height;
  TrackbarSVOX.Max := Panel1.Width;
  TrackbarSVOY.Max := Panel1.Height;

  {initialize the trackbars to their midpoints}
  TrackbarSWOX.Position := TrackbarSWOY.Max div 2;
  TrackbarSWOY.Position := TrackbarSWOX.Max div 2;
  TrackbarSVOX.Position := TrackbarSVOY.Max div 2;
  TrackbarSVOY.Position := TrackbarSVOX.Max div 2;
  TrackbarSWEX.Position := TrackbarSWEY.Max div 2;
  TrackbarSWEY.Position := TrackbarSWEX.Max div 2;
  TrackbarSVEX.Position := TrackbarSVEY.Max div 2;
  TrackbarSVEY.Position := TrackbarSVEX.Max div 2;
end;

procedure TForm1.ReportPosition;
var
  ReturnValue: TPoint;         // holds the window and viewport origins
```

```
      ReturnSize: TSize;          // holds the window and viewport extents
      ReadMapMode: Integer;       // holds the mapping mode
      ReadFinalOrigin: TPoint;    // holds the device origin
begin
  {display the window origin}
  GetWindowOrgEx(MyDisplayDC,ReturnValue);
  Label9.Caption := IntToStr(ReturnValue.x)
         + ', ' + IntToStr(ReturnValue.y);

  {display the viewport origin}
  GetViewportOrgEx(MyDisplayDC,ReturnValue);
  Label10.Caption := IntToStr(ReturnValue.x)
         + ', ' + IntToStr(ReturnValue.y);

  {display the window extents}
  GetWindowExtEx(MyDisplayDC,ReturnSize);
  Label11.Caption := IntToStr(ReturnSize.cx)
         + ', ' + IntToStr(ReturnSize.cy);

  {display the viewport extents}
  GetViewportExtEx(MyDisplayDC,ReturnSize);
  Label12.Caption := IntToStr(ReturnSize.cx)
         + ', ' + IntToStr(ReturnSize.cy);

  {display the current mapping mode}
  ReadMapMode := GetMapMode(MyDisplayDC);
  case ReadMapMode of
    MM_TEXT:        LabelGMMresult.Caption := 'MM_TEXT';
    MM_ANISOTROPIC:LabelGMMresult.Caption := 'MM_ANISOTROPIC';
    MM_ISOTROPIC:   LabelGMMresult.Caption := 'MM_ISOTROPIC';
    MM_HIENGLISH:   LabelGMMresult.Caption := 'MM_HIENGLISH';
    MM_HIMETRIC:    LabelGMMresult.Caption := 'MM_HIMETRIC';
    MM_LOENGLISH:   LabelGMMresult.Caption := 'MM_LOENGLISH';
    MM_LOMETRIC:    LabelGMMresult.Caption := 'MM_LOMETRIC';
    MM_TWIPS:       LabelGMMresult.Caption := 'MM_TWIPS';
  end;

  {display the final translation origin for the device context}
  GetDCOrgEx(MyDisplayDC, ReadFinalOrigin);
  LabelGetDCOrgExResult.Caption := IntToStr(ReadFinalOrigin.X) + ', ' +
                                   IntToStr(ReadFinalOrigin.Y);
end;

procedure TForm1.ReadUserRequest;
begin
  {retrieve the selected mapping mode}
  case RadioGroup1.ItemIndex of
    0: MyMapMode := MM_TEXT;
    1: MyMapMode := MM_ANISOTROPIC;
    2: MyMapMode := MM_ISOTROPIC;
    3: MyMapMode := MM_HIENGLISH;
    4: MyMapMode := MM_HIMETRIC;
    5: MyMapMode := MM_LOENGLISH;
    6: MyMapMode := MM_LOMETRIC;
    7: MyMapMode := MM_TWIPS;
  end;
```

```
  {set the origin and extent values according to the trackbar positions}
  WOrigin.x := TrackBarSWOX.Position;
  WOrigin.y := TrackBarSWOY.Position;
  VOrigin.x := TrackBarSVOX.Position;
  VOrigin.y := TrackBarSVOY.Position;
  WExt.x    := TrackBarSWEX.Position;
  WExt.y    := TrackBarSWEY.Position;
  VExt.x    := TrackBarSVEX.Position;
  VExt.y    := TrackBarSVEY.Position;
end;

procedure TForm1.PaintImage;
begin
  {retrieve a device context for the panel}
  MyDisplayDC := GetDC(Panel1.Handle);

  {erase the current image}
  Panel1.Repaint;

  {retrieve the user-defined values}
  ReadUserRequest;

  {set the mapping mode to the selected value}
  SetMapMode(MyDisplayDC, MyMapMode);
  if Checkbox1.Checked
    then SetWindowOrgEx(MyDisplayDC, WOrigin.x, WOrigin.y, nil);
  if Checkbox2.Checked
    then SetViewportOrgEx(MyDisplayDC, VOrigin.x, VOrigin.y, nil);
  if Checkbox3.Checked
    then SetWindowExtEx(MyDisplayDC, WExt.x, WExt.y, nil);
  if Checkbox4.Checked
    then SetViewportExtEx(MyDisplayDC, VExt.x, VExt.y, nil);

  {draw the image. note that the image is drawn to the same, hard coded
   coordinates. this demonstrates how changing the viewport and window
   origin and extents can affect drawn objects}
  Windows.Rectangle(MyDisplayDC,0,0,50,50);
  Windows.Rectangle(MyDisplayDC,-25,24,75,26);
  Windows.Rectangle(MyDisplayDC,24,-25,26,75);

  {display the current settings}
  ReportPosition;

  {release the device context}
  ReleaseDC(Panel1.Handle, MyDisplayDC);
end;

procedure TForm1.FormPaint(Sender: TObject);
begin
  {display the image}
  PaintImage;
end;
```

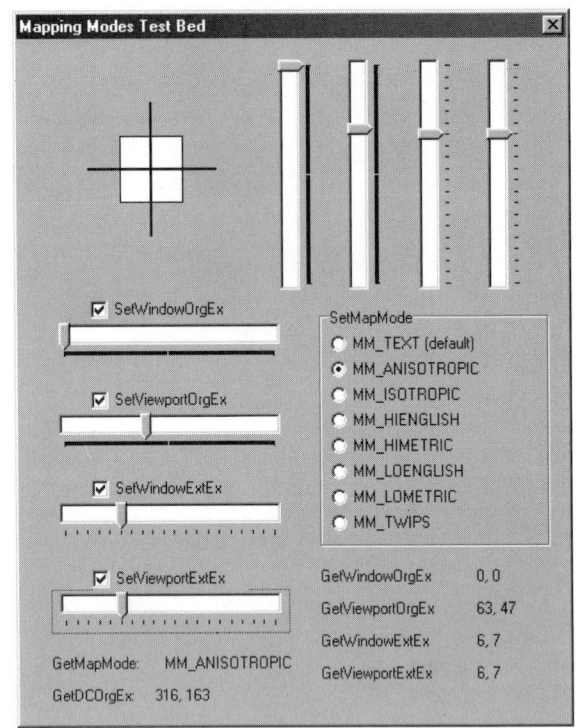

*Figure 9-1:
The viewport
and window
extent and
origin test bed
in action*

Problems with Logical Coordinate Mapping

An application that is not performing its translation of logical coordinates to device coordinates in the expected manner may have one of the following problems:

1. The device context may have a mapping mode that does not support the translation as expected. The mapping mode must be changed from the default value of MM_TEXT if any transformation is to take place.
2. The coordinates may be out of range. When possible, keep device and logical coordinates within 16-bit values. The transformations support up to 27 bits in size, but some display functions only support 16-bit coordinate sizes.
3. The image might be clipped (off the display area), or too small or large to be visible.
4. The scaling might not be as expected because the application is really placing the same number for the window and viewport extent, which produces a scaling factor of one (no effect).
5. The scaling factor might be producing no effect because the application is multiplying and dividing by the same number. To zoom the effective scaling factor, try setting only the multiplication or the division parameter, or be sure they are different factors.
6. The device context might be invalid. Test for errors when returning from GDI functions.

Delphi vs. the Windows API

Delphi encapsulates most of the GDI functionality in the TCanvas object. This releases the developer from dealing with the tedium of setting up and controlling device contexts. However, the TCanvas object does not encapsulate much of the advanced functionality offered by some of the GDI functions, in particular those controlling viewport and window extents, origins, etc. Using these GDI API functions, developers of graphical applications can create functionality allowing users to zoom or scroll the images they are creating while still using standard Delphi or Windows API drawing routines.

Graphical Device Interface Functions

The following graphical device interface functions are covered in this chapter:

Table 9-2: Graphical Device Interface functions

Function	Description
ChangeDisplaySettings	Changes the display mode.
ClientToScreen	Converts client coordinates to screen coordinates.
CreateCompatibleDC	Creates a memory device context.
DeleteDC	Deletes a device context.
DPtoLP	Converts device points to logical points.
EnumDisplaySettings	Enumerates available display modes.
GetDC	Retrieves a handle to a device context.
GetDeviceCaps	Retrieves device capabilities.
GetMapMode	Retrieves the current mapping mode.
GetSystemMetrics	Retrieves system element measurements.
GetViewportExtEx	Retrieves the viewport extents.
GetViewportOrgEx	Retrieves the viewport origin.
GetWindowDC	Retrieves a handle to a window device context.
GetDCOrgEx	Retrieves the final translation origin from the specified device context.
GetWindowExtEx	Retrieves the window extents.
GetWindowOrgEx	Retrieves the window origin.
LPtoDP	Converts logical points to device points.
MapWindowPoints	Converts multiple coordinates from one window coordinate system to another.
OffsetViewportOrgEx	Offsets the viewport origin.
OffsetWindowOrgEx	Offsets the window origin.
ReleaseDC	Releases a device context.
RestoreDC	Restores a saved device context state.
SaveDC	Saves the state of a device context.
ScaleViewportExtEx	Scales the viewport extents.
ScaleWindowExtEx	Scales the window extents.
ScreenToClient	Converts screen coordinates to client coordinates.
ScrollDC	Scrolls an area of a device context.

Function	Description
SetMapMode	Sets the mapping mode.
SetViewportExtEx	Sets the viewport extents.
SetViewportOrgEx	Sets the viewport origin.
SetWindowExtEx	Sets the window extents.
SetWindowOrgEx	Sets the window origin.

ChangeDisplaySettings   Windows.pas

Syntax

```
ChangeDisplaySettings(
  lpDevMode: PDeviceMode;      {points to TDeviceMode structure}
  dwFlags: DWORD               {display change options}
): Longint;                    {returns a result code}
```

Description

This function changes the graphics mode of the system display. The new device settings are contained in the TDeviceMode structure passed as the first parameter. It is common to place a call to EnumDisplaySettings prior to calling ChangeDisplaySettings to get a valid TDeviceMode structure. This helps toeinsure that the ChangeDisplaySettings function gets parameters that are compatible with the currently installed display driver.

A WM_DISPLAYCHANGE message is sent to all applications as notification that the display settings were changed. This is performed by Windows automatically and does not have to be explicitly performed by the caller.

Parameters

lpDevMode: A pointer to a TDeviceMode structure containing the information used to initialize the new graphics mode. If this parameter is set to NIL, the display mode values currently stored in the registry are used for the new display mode. Of the members in the TDeviceMode structure, only the dmSize, dmBitsPerPel, dmFields, dmPelsWidth, dmPelsHeight, dmDisplayFlags, and dmDisplayFrequency members are used by this function. The TDeviceMode structure is defined as:

```
TDeviceModeA = packed record
    dmDeviceName: array[0..CCHDEVICENAME – 1] of AnsiChar;   {not used}
    dmSpecVersion: Word;                                      {not used}
    dmDriverVersion: Word;                                    {not used}
    dmSize: Word;                                             {structure size}
    dmDriverExtra: Word;                                      {not used}
    dmFields: DWORD;                                          {valid fields}
    dmOrientation: SHORT;                                     {not used}
    dmPaperSize: SHORT;                                       {not used}
    dmPaperLength: SHORT;                                     {not used}
    dmPaperWidth: SHORT;                                      {not used}
    dmScale: SHORT;                                           {not used}
    dmCopies: SHORT;                                          {not used}
```

```
dmDefaultSource: SHORT;                                    {not used}
dmPrintQuality: SHORT;                                     {not used}
dmColor: SHORT;                                            {not used}
dmDuplex: SHORT;                                           {not used}
dmYResolution: SHORT;                                      {not used}
dmTTOption: SHORT;                                         {not used}
dmCollate: SHORT;                                          {not used}
dmFormName: array[0..CCHFORMNAME – 1] of AnsiChar;         {not used}
dmLogPixels: Word;                                         {not used}
dmBitsPerPel: DWORD;                                       {color depth}
dmPelsWidth: DWORD;                                        {screen width}
dmPelsHeight: DWORD;                                       {screen height}
dmDisplayFlags: DWORD;                                     {display mode}
dmDisplayFrequency: DWORD;                                 {frequency}
dmICMMethod: DWORD;                                        {not used}
dmICMIntent: DWORD;                                        {not used}
dmMediaType: DWORD;                                        {not used}
dmDitherType: DWORD;                                       {not used}
dmICCManufacturer: DWORD;                                  {not used}
dmICCModel: DWORD;                                         {not used}
dmPanningWidth: DWORD;                                     {not used}
dmPanningHeight: DWORD;                                    {not used}
end;
```

Only the following members are used by this function:

dmSize: Specifies the size of the TDeviceMode structure. This member must be set to SizeOf(TDeviceMode).

dmFields: A series of flags indicating which other members of the structure contain valid information. This member may be set to one or more values from Table 9-3.

dmBitsPerPel: Indicates the number of bits required to describe the color of one pixel (i.e., 4 bits for 16-color displays, 8 bits for 256-color displays, etc.).

dmPelsWidth: Specifies the width of the screen in pixels.

dmPelsHeight: Specifies the height of the screen in pixels.

dmDisplayFlags: A flag indicating the display mode. This member can be set to one value from Table 9-4.

dmDisplayFrequency: Specifies the vertical display refresh rate in hertz. A value of zero or one represents the hardware's default refresh rate.

dwFlags: A flag specifying how the graphics mode is to be changed. This parameter may be set to one value from Table 9-5. If the CDS_UPDATEREGISTRY flag is specified, the system attempts to make a dynamic graphics mode change and update the registry without a reboot. If a reboot is required, the DISP_CHANGE_RESTART return value is set and the application is responsible for rebooting Windows. The CDS_TEST mode can be used to see which graphics modes are available without performing the actual change.

Return Value

This function returns a flag indicating success or failure, and may be one value from Table 9-6.

See Also

EnumDisplaySettings, WM_DISPLAYCHANGE

Example

Listing 9-3: Changing the display mode

```
{Whoops! Delphi imports this function incorrectly, so we must manually
 import it}
function ChangeDisplaySettings(lpDevMode: PDeviceMode;
                               dwFlags: DWORD): Longint; stdcall;
var
  Form1: TForm1;
  DevModeArray: TList;    // holds a list of device mode information structures

implementation

uses Math;

{$R *.DFM}

{import the function}
function ChangeDisplaySettings; external user32 name 'ChangeDisplaySettingsA';

procedure TForm1.FormCreate(Sender: TObject);
var
  DevModeCount: Integer;           // tracks the number of display modes
  DevModeInfo: ^TDevMode;          // a pointer to display mode information
begin
  {create the list to hold display mode information structures}
  DevModeArray := TList.Create;

  {initialize the counter}
  DevModeCount := 0;

  {dynamically allocate memory to hold display mode information}
  GetMem(DevModeInfo, SizeOf(TDevMode));

  {begin enumerating display modes}
  while EnumDisplaySettings(NIL, DevModeCount, DevModeInfo^) do
  begin
    {add the information to the list}
    DevModeArray.Add(DevModeInfo);

    {increment the counter}
    Inc(DevModeCount);

    {display the resolution of the enumerated display mode}
    ListBox1.Items.Add(IntToStr(DevModeInfo^.dmPelsWidth)+'x'+
                       IntToStr(DevModeInfo^.dmPelsHeight)+', '+
```

```
                         IntToStr(Trunc(IntPower(2, DevModeInfo^.dmBitsPerPel)))+
                         ' colors');

    {allocate another slot for device mode information}
    GetMem(DevModeInfo, SizeOf(TDevMode));
  end;

  {the above loop always exits with one extra, unused block of memory,
   so delete it}
  FreeMem(DevModeInfo, SizeOf(TDevMode));

  {select the first item in the list box}
  ListBox1.ItemIndex := 0;
end;

procedure TForm1.FormDestroy(Sender: TObject);
var
  iCount: Integer;         // a general loop counter
begin
  {free all memory pointed to by each item in the list}
  for iCount := 0 to DevModeArray.Count-1 do
    FreeMem(DevModeArray.Items[iCount], SizeOf(TDevMode));

  {free the list}
  DevModeArray.Free;
end;

procedure TForm1.Button1Click(Sender: TObject);
var
  ModeChange: Longint;      // indicates if a Windows reboot is necessary
begin
  {change the display mode}
  ModeChange:=ChangeDisplaySettings(DevModeArray[ListBox1.ItemIndex],
                                    CDS_UPDATEREGISTRY);

  {indicate if a dynamic change was successful or if Windows must be rebooted}
  if ModeChange=DISP_CHANGE_SUCCESSFUL then
    ShowMessage('Dynamic display mode change successful.');
  if ModeChange=DISP_CHANGE_RESTART then
    ShowMessage('Change successful; Windows must be restarted for the changes '+
                'to take effect');
end;
```

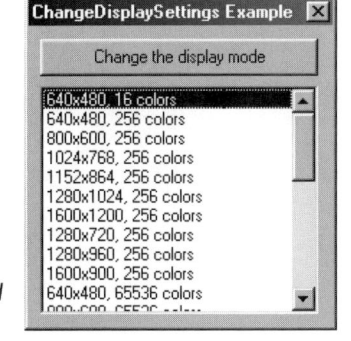

Figure 9-2:
The supported display modes

Table 9-3: ChangeDisplaySettings lpDevMode.dmFields values

Value	Description
DM_BITSPERPEL	The dmBitsPerPel member contains new data.
DM_PELSWIDTH	The dmPelsWidth member contains new data.
DM_PELSHEIGHT	The dmPelsHeight member contains new data.
DM_DISPLAYFLAGS	The dmDisplayFlags member contains new data.
DM_DISPLAYFREQUENCY	The dmDisplayFrequency member contains new data.

Table 9-4: ChangeDisplaySettings lpDevMode.dmDisplayFlags values

Value	Description
DM_GRAYSCALE	Indicates a non-color display.
DM_INTERLACED	Indicates an interlaced display.

Table 9-5: ChangeDisplaySettings dwFlags values

Value	Description
0	The change will be made dynamically.
CDS_UPDATEREGISTRY	The change is made dynamically, and the registry will be updated to reflect the new graphics mode under the USER key.
CDS_TEST	The change is not made, but the system is tested to see if it could be made. The function sets the same return values as if the change had been made.

Table 9-6: ChangeDisplaySettings return values

Value	Description
DISP_CHANGE_BADFLAGS	The caller passed invalid flags to the function.
DISP_CHANGE_BADMODE	The specified graphics mode is not supported.
DISP_CHANGE_FAILED	The display driver did not accept the newly specified graphics mode.
DISP_CHANGE_NOTUPDATED	**Windows NT/2000 or later:** Unable to write the new settings to the registry.
DISP_CHANGE_RESTART	Windows must be restarted for the changes to take effect.
DISP_CHANGE_SUCCESSFUL	The function was successful.

ClientToScreen   Windows.pas

Syntax

```
ClientToScreen(
  hWnd: HWND;              {the handle of a window}
  var lpPoint: TPoint      {a pointer to a TPoint structure}
): BOOL;                   {returns TRUE or FALSE}
```

Description

This function changes the coordinates of a point from client coordinates to screen coordinates. The point to be translated is in a TPoint structure pointed to by the lpPoint parameter. The function takes the coordinates pointed to by the lpPoint parameter and converts them into coordinates relative to the screen. The results are placed back into this TPoint structure. The coordinates of the point being passed use the upper-left corner of the client area of the specified window as the origin. The coordinates of the result use the upper-left corner of the screen as the origin.

Parameters

hWnd: The handle to the window that contains the point. The upper-left corner of the client area of this window is the origin of the coordinate system that defines the coordinates of the point being converted.

lpPoint: A pointer to a TPoint structure that contains the point to be converted. This TPoint structure receives the converted point when the function returns.

Return Value

If the function succeeds, it returns TRUE; otherwise, it returns FALSE. To get extended error information, call GetLastError.

See Also

MapWindowPoints, ScreenToClient

Example

Listing 9-4: Converting coordinates between coordinate systems

```
procedure TForm1.Memo1MouseDown(Sender: TObject; Button: TMouseButton;
  Shift: TShiftState; X, Y: Integer);
var
  Coords: TPoint;    // holds the point being converted
begin
  {indicate the clicked coordinates relative to the child window}
  Label1.Caption := 'Memo Coordinates: '+IntToStr(X)+', '+IntToStr(Y);

  {convert these coordinates into screen coordinates}
  Coords := Point(X, Y);
  Windows.ClientToScreen(Memo1.Handle, Coords);

  {display the clicked coordinates relative to the screen}
  Label2.Caption := 'Screen Coordinates: '+IntToStr(Coords.X)+', '+
                    IntToStr(Coords.Y);

  {convert the coordinates into window client coordinates}
  Windows.ScreenToClient(Form1.Handle, Coords);

  {display the clicked coordinates relative to the client area of the window}
  Label3.Caption := 'Form Coordinates: '+IntToStr(Coords.X)+', '+
                    IntToStr(Coords.Y);
end;
```

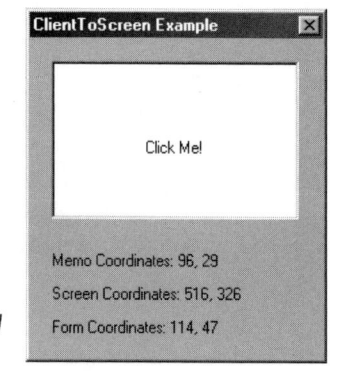

Figure 9-3:
The converted coordinates

CreateCompatibleDC   Windows.pas

Syntax

```
CreateCompatibleDC(
  DC: HDC              {the handle to a device context}
): HDC;                {returns a handle to a memory device context}
```

Description

This function creates a memory device context that is compatible with the specified device context. This is used with images that will be copied to the screen or to a printer. A bitmap must be selected into the device context returned by this function before the device context can be used with drawing operations. When an application is finished with the memory device context, it should be deleted by calling the DeleteDC function.

Parameters

DC: Specifies a handle to a device context for which the new device context will be compatible. This must be a device context that supports raster operations. The application can call the GetDeviceCaps function to determine if the device context meets this requirement. If this parameter is set to zero, the function creates a device context compatible with the screen.

Return Value

If the function succeeds, it returns a handle to the new memory device context. If it fails, it returns zero.

See Also

CreateCompatibleBitmap, DeleteDC, GetDeviceCaps

Example

Listing 9-5: Using memory device contexts for animation

```
var
  Form1: TForm1;
  OffscreenDC: HDC;        // an offscreen device context
```

Graphical Device Interface Functions   297

```delphi
    ANDMaskBitmap,           // used for holding the different parts of the
    ORMaskBitmap,            // circle graphic
    BackgroundBitmap,
    OldBitmap: HBITMAP;
    BallXCoord: Integer;     // the current horizontal coordinates of the circle

implementation

{$R *.DFM}

procedure TForm1.Timer1Timer(Sender: TObject);
var
  ScreenDC,               // a handle to the screen device context
  WorkDC: HDC;            // a handle to a temporary device context
  OldBitmap: HBITMAP;     // holds the previous bitmap
begin
  {retrieve a handle to the device context for the screen}
  ScreenDC := GetDC(0);

  {create a memory device context}
  WorkDC := CreateCompatibleDC(Canvas.Handle);

  {restore the previous background to the screen}
  BitBlt(ScreenDC, BallXCoord, Form1.Top, 40, 40, OffscreenDC, 0, 0, SRCCOPY);

  {increment the horizontal coordinate of the circle}
  Inc(BallXCoord);

  {wrap the circle around the screen if it has gone beyond the edges}
  if BallXCoord>GetSystemMetrics(SM_CXSCREEN) then
    BallXCoord := -40;

  {save the background at the current location of the circle}
  BitBlt(OffscreenDC, 0, 0, 40, 40, ScreenDC, BallXCoord, Form1.Top, SRCCOPY);

  {select the AND mask of the circle into the memory device context, and
   copy it to the screen}
  OldBitmap := SelectObject(WorkDC, ANDMaskBitmap);
  BitBlt(ScreenDC, BallXCoord, Form1.Top, 40, 40, WorkDC, 0, 0, SRCAND);

  {select the OR mask of the circle into the memory device context, and
   copy it to the screen}
  SelectObject(WorkDC, ORMaskBitmap);
  BitBlt(ScreenDC, BallXCoord, Form1.Top, 40, 40, WorkDC, 0, 0, SRCPAINT);

  {select the old bitmap back into the memory device context, and delete or
   release all unneeded objects}
  SelectObject(WorkDC, OldBitmap);
  ReleaseDC(0, ScreenDC);
  DeleteDC(WorkDC);
end;

procedure TForm1.FormCreate(Sender: TObject);
var
  TempBrush: HBRUSH;     // a handle to a brush
begin
```

```
    {create a memory device context}
    OffscreenDC   := CreateCompatibleDC(Canvas.Handle);

    {a lot of attributes of the device context will change, so save its original
      state so we don't have to reselect the original objects back into the
      device context}
    SaveDC(OffscreenDC);

    {create the bitmap for the circle's AND mask}
    AndMaskBitmap := CreateCompatibleBitmap(Canvas.Handle, 40, 40);

    {select the bitmap into the memory device context and draw a black circle
      on a white background}
    SelectObject(OffscreenDC, AndMaskBitmap);
    SelectObject(OffscreenDC, GetStockObject(WHITE_BRUSH));
    SelectObject(OffscreenDC, GetStockObject(NULL_PEN));
    Rectangle(OffscreenDC, 0, 0, 41, 41);
    SelectObject(OffscreenDC, GetStockObject(BLACK_BRUSH));
    Ellipse(OffscreenDC, 0, 0, 40, 40);

    {create the bitmap for the circle's OR mask}
    ORMaskBitmap := CreateCompatibleBitmap(Canvas.Handle, 40, 40);

    {select the bitmap into the memory device context and draw a hatched circle
      on a black background}
    SelectObject(OffscreenDC, ORMaskBitmap);
    SelectObject(OffscreenDC, GetStockObject(BLACK_BRUSH));
    Rectangle(OffscreenDC, 0, 0, 41, 41);
    TempBrush := CreateHatchBrush(HS_DIAGCROSS, clRed);
    SelectObject(OffscreenDC, GetStockObject(BLACK_PEN));
    SelectObject(OffscreenDC, TempBrush);
    Ellipse(OffscreenDC, 0, 0, 40, 40);

    {restore the device context's original settings. this eliminates the need to
      reselect all of the original objects back into the device context when we
      are through}
    RestoreDC(OffscreenDC, -1);

    {delete the brush}
    DeleteObject(TempBrush);

    {finally create a bitmap to hold the background of the screen. this keeps
      the animated circle from leaving a trail behind it}
    BackgroundBitmap := CreateCompatibleBitmap(Canvas.Handle, 40, 40);

    {select the background bitmap into the memory device context}
    SelectObject(OffscreenDC, BackgroundBitmap);

    {initialize the coordinates of the circle so it will begin off screen
      to the left}
    BallXCoord := -40;
end;

procedure TForm1.FormDestroy(Sender: TObject);
begin
  {delete all unneeded bitmaps and device contexts}
  SelectObject(OffscreenDC, OldBitmap);
```

```
    DeleteObject(BackgroundBitmap);
    DeleteObject(ANDMaskBitmap);
    DeleteObject(ORMaskBitmap);
    DeleteDC(OffscreenDC);
end;
```

Figure 9-4: The animated circle

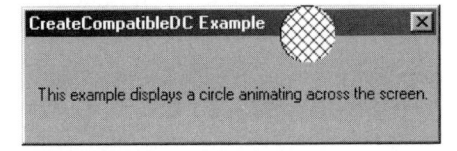

DeleteDC   Windows.pas

Syntax

```
DeleteDC(
  DC: HDC                    {the handle of a device context}
): BOOL;                     {returns TRUE or FALSE}
```

Description

The DeleteDC function deletes the specified device context. When an application uses CreateCompatibleDC, it should also call DeleteDC when finished with the handle.

Parameters

DC: The handle to the device context to be deleted.

Return Value

If the function succeeds, it returns TRUE; otherwise, it returns FALSE.

See Also

CreateCompatibleDC, GetDC, ReleaseDC

Example

See Listing 9-5 under CreateCompatibleDC.

DPtoLP   Windows.pas

Syntax

```
DPtoLP(
  DC: HDC;                   {the handle of a device context}
  var Points;                {a pointer to an array of TPoint structures}
  Count: Integer             {the number of entries in the array}
): BOOL;                     {returns TRUE or FALSE}
```

Description

The DPtoLP function converts points from device coordinates to logical coordinates. The Points parameter points to an array of TPoint structures containing the coordinates to be translated. These TPoint structures will receive the translated coordinates when the function returns. The coordinate transformation is performed based on the values set by the SetWindowOrgEx, SetViewportOrgEx, SetWindowExtEx, and SetViewportExtEx functions. The DPtoLP function will fail if any of the points in the TPoint structures specify a value greater in size than 27 bits. It will also fail if any of the transformed points are greater in size than 32 bits. In the event of failure, the values in the entire Points array are undefined.

Parameters

DC: A handle to the device context for which the coordinate transformations will be made.

Points: A pointer to an array of TPoint structures containing the coordinates to be converted.

Count: Specifies the number of entries in the array pointed to by the Points parameter.

Return Value

If the function succeeds, it returns TRUE; otherwise, it returns FALSE.

See Also

LPtoDP, SetViewportExtEx, SetViewportOrgEx, SetWindowExtEx, SetWindowOrgEx

Example

See Listing 9-12 under ScaleViewportExtEx.

EnumDisplaySettings   Windows.pas

Syntax

```
EnumDisplaySettings(
lpszDeviceName: PChar;          {the display device}
iModeNum: DWORD;                {the graphics mode}
var lpDevMode: TDeviceMode      {a pointer to a structure to receive device settings}
): BOOL;                        {returns TRUE or FALSE}
```

Description

The EnumDisplaySettings function retrieves information from the specified display device about the specified graphics mode. To retrieve all display modes available for the specified device, start by setting iModeNum to zero and incrementing it by one for each subsequent call to the function. This should continue until the function returns FALSE.

Parameters

lpszDeviceName: The name of the device for which information is to be retrieved. If this parameter is set to NIL, the function enumerates display modes for the current display device. The string pointed to by this parameter must be in the form of \\.\Display1, \\.\Display2, or \\.\Display3.

Windows 95: This parameter must always be set to NIL.

iModeNum: The index value for the graphics mode for which information is to be retrieved. This value must be less than the index of the display's last graphics mode. If the iModeNum parameter is out of range, the function will return an error.

var lpDevMode: A pointer to a TDeviceMode structure that receives information about the specified display mode. Of the members in the TDeviceMode structure, only the dmSize, dmBitsPerPel, dmPelsWidth, dmPelsHeight, dmDisplayFlags, and dmDisplayFrequency members are used by this function. The TDeviceMode structure is defined as:

```
TDeviceModeA = packed record
    dmDeviceName: array[0..CCHDEVICENAME - 1] of AnsiChar;   {not used}
    dmSpecVersion: Word;                                     {not used}
    dmDriverVersion: Word;                                   {not used}
    dmSize: Word;                                            {structure size}
    dmDriverExtra: Word;                                     {not used}
    dmFields: DWORD;                                         {not used}
    dmOrientation: SHORT;                                    {not used}
    dmPaperSize: SHORT;                                      {not used}
    dmPaperLength: SHORT;                                    {not used}
    dmPaperWidth: SHORT;                                     {not used}
    dmScale: SHORT;                                          {not used}
    dmCopies: SHORT;                                         {not used}
    dmDefaultSource: SHORT;                                  {not used}
    dmPrintQuality: SHORT;                                   {not used}
    dmColor: SHORT;                                          {not used}
    dmDuplex: SHORT;                                         {not used}
    dmYResolution: SHORT;                                    {not used}
    dmTTOption: SHORT;                                       {not used}
    dmCollate: SHORT;                                        {not used}
    dmFormName: array[0..CCHFORMNAME - 1] of AnsiChar;       {not used}
    dmLogPixels: Word;                                       {not used}
    dmBitsPerPel: DWORD;                                     {color depth}
    dmPelsWidth: DWORD;                                      {screen width}
    dmPelsHeight: DWORD;                                     {screen height}
    dmDisplayFlags: DWORD;                                   {display mode}
    dmDisplayFrequency: DWORD;                               {frequency}
    dmICMMethod: DWORD;                                      {not used}
    dmICMIntent: DWORD;                                      {not used}
    dmMediaType: DWORD;                                      {not used}
    dmDitherType: DWORD;                                     {not used}
    dmICCManufacturer: DWORD;                                {not used}
    dmICCModel: DWORD;                                       {not used}
    dmPanningWidth: DWORD;                                   {not used}
    dmPanningHeight: DWORD;                                  {not used}
end;
```

See the ChangeDisplaySettings function for a description of this data structure.

Return Value

If the function succeeds, it returns TRUE; otherwise, it returns FALSE.

See Also

ChangeDisplaySettings

Example

Listing 9-6: Enumerating all available display modes for the current display

```
procedure TForm1.Button1Click(Sender: TObject);
var
  DeviceInfo: TDevMode;         // holds device information
  DeviceCount: Integer;         // tracks the number of display modes
begin
  {initialize the tracking variable}
  DeviceCount := 0;

  {enumerate all display modes for the current display device}
  while EnumDisplaySettings(NIL, DeviceCount, DeviceInfo) do
  begin
    {display the relevant information for the display mode}
    ListBox1.Items.Add('Device '+IntToStr(DeviceCount)+' -');
    ListBox1.Items.Add('Pixels/Inch: '+IntToSTr(DeviceInfo.dmLogPixels));
    ListBox1.Items.Add('Bits/Pixel: '+IntToStr(DeviceInfo.dmBitsPerPel));
    ListBox1.Items.Add('Pixel Width: '+IntToStr(DeviceInfo.dmPelsWidth));
    ListBox1.Items.Add('Pixel Height: '+IntToStr(DeviceInfo.dmPelsHeight));

    {indicate the display mode type}
    case DeviceInfo.dmDisplayFlags of
      DM_GRAYSCALE:  ListBox1.Items.Add('Display Mode: Grayscale');
      DM_INTERLACED: ListBox1.Items.Add('Display Mode: Interlaced');
    end;

    {indicate the refresh rate}
    if (DeviceInfo.dmDisplayFrequency=0)or(DeviceInfo.dmDisplayFrequency=1) then
      ListBox1.Items.Add('Refresh Rate: Hardware Default')
    else
      ListBox1.Items.Add('Refresh Rate: '+IntToStr(DeviceInfo.dmDisplayFrequency)
              +' hrz');

    {add a blank line and increment the tracking variable}
    ListBox1.Items.Add('');
    Inc(DeviceCount);
  end;
end;
```

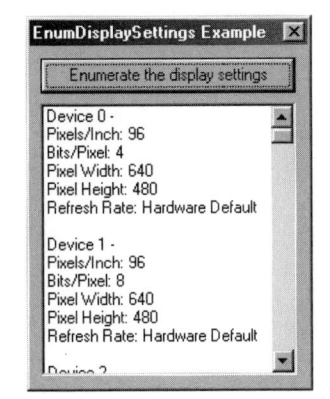

*Figure 9-5:
The available
display mode
information*

GetDC Windows.pas

Syntax

```
GetDC(
  hWnd: HWND           {the handle of a window}
): HDC;                {returns a device context}
```

Description

The GetDC function retrieves a device context for the client area of the window specified by the hWnd parameter. The device context retrieved will be a common, class, or private device context as determined by the class styles of the specified window. For common device contexts, the GetDC function initializes the device context with default attributes each time it is retrieved. Class and private device contexts retrieved by this function will retain their last settings. When the device context is no longer needed, it should be released by calling the ReleaseDC function.

Parameters

hWnd: A handle to the window for which a device context is retrieved. If this parameter is set to zero, the function retrieves a device context for the screen.

Return Value

If the function succeeds, it returns a device context for the client area of the specified window. If the function fails, it returns a zero.

See Also

GetWindowDC, ReleaseDC

Example

Listing 9-7: Retrieving a common device context for a window

```
procedure TForm1.FormPaint(Sender: TObject);
var
  FormDC: HDC;       // holds the device context
  OldFont: HFONT;    // holds the original font
```

```
begin
  {retrieve a common device context for the form}
  FormDC := GetDC(Form1.Handle);

  {select the form's font into the device context}
  OldFont := SelectObject(FormDC, Form1.Font.Handle);

  {output some text onto the device context}
  SetBkMode(FormDC, TRANSPARENT);
  TextOut(FormDC, 10, 10, 'Delphi Rocks!', Length('Delphi Rocks!'));

  {reselect the original font and release the device context}
  SelectObject(FormDC, OldFont);
  ReleaseDC(Form1.Handle, FormDC);
end;
```

Figure 9-6: Drawing on the device context

GetDCOrgEx   Windows.pas

Syntax

```
GetDCOrgEx(
  DC: HDC;                  {the handle of a device context}
  var Origin: TPoint        {a pointer to a TPoint structure}
): BOOL;                    {returns TRUE or FALSE}
```

Description

The GetDCOrgEx function retrieves the final translation origin from the specified device context. This location is the final offset that Windows will use when translating device coordinates into client coordinates.

Parameters

DC: A handle to the device context whose origin is being retrieved.

Origin: A pointer to a TPoint structure that will receive the origin coordinates. The coordinates are relative to the physical origin of the screen, and are given in device units.

Return Value

If the function succeeds, it returns TRUE; otherwise, it returns FALSE.

See Also

GetViewportOrgEx, GetWindowOrgEx

Example

See Listing 9-2 in the section titled "Mapping Modes."

GetDeviceCaps   Windows.pas

Syntax

```
GetDeviceCaps(
  DC: HDC;              {the handle of a device context}
  Index: Integer        {the capability index}
): Integer;             {returns the capability value}
```

Description

The GetDeviceCaps function gets device information about a particular capability from the specified device context. A wide variety of capabilities can be queried as shown in Table 9-7.

Parameters

DC: The handle of the device context for which the capability is being queried.

Index: A flag indicating the specific capability being queried. This parameter may be set to one value from Table 9-7.

Return Value

If the function succeeds, it returns a value specific to the queried capability. This function does not indicate an error condition.

See Also

CreateEnhMetaFile, GetDIBits, GetObjectType, GetSystemMetrics*, SetDIBits, SetDIBitsToDevice, StretchBlt, StretchDIBits

Example

Listing 9-8: Retrieving device capabilities

```
procedure TForm1.Button1Click(Sender: TObject);
begin
  with ListBox1.Items do
  begin
    {display the driver version}
    Add('Display Driver Version: '+IntToStr(GetDeviceCaps(Canvas.Handle,
      DRIVERVERSION)));

    {display the technology}
    case GetDeviceCaps(Canvas.Handle, TECHNOLOGY) of
      DT_PLOTTER:    Add('Driver Type: Vector Plotter');
      DT_RASDISPLAY: Add('Driver Type: Raster Display');
      DT_RASPRINTER: Add('Driver Type: Raster Printer');
      DT_RASCAMERA:  Add('Driver Type: Raster Camera');
      DT_CHARSTREAM: Add('Driver Type: Character Stream');
      DT_METAFILE:   Add('Driver Type: Metafile');
      DT_DISPFILE:   Add('Driver Type: Display File');
    end;

    {display the screen size}
```

```
    Add('Screen Size: '+IntToStr(GetDeviceCaps(Canvas.Handle, HORZSIZE))+' X '+
       IntToStr(GetDeviceCaps(Canvas.Handle, VERTSIZE))+' millimeters');
    Add('Screen Resolution: '+IntToStr(GetDeviceCaps(Canvas.Handle, HORZRES))+
       ' X '+IntToStr(GetDeviceCaps(Canvas.Handle, VERTRES))+' pixels');

    {display the pixels per logical inch}
    Add('Pixels/Logical Inch - Horizontal: '+IntToStr(GetDeviceCaps(
       Canvas.Handle, LOGPIXELSX)));
    Add('Pixels/Logical Inch - Vertical: '+IntToStr(GetDeviceCaps(
       Canvas.Handle, LOGPIXELSY)));

    {display the color depth and number of common graphical objects}
    Add('Bits/Pixel: '+IntToStr(GetDeviceCaps(Canvas.Handle, BITSPIXEL)));
    Add('Brushes: '+IntToStr(GetDeviceCaps(Canvas.Handle, NUMBRUSHES)));
    Add('Pens: '+IntToStr(GetDeviceCaps(Canvas.Handle, NUMPENS)));
    Add('Fonts: '+IntToStr(GetDeviceCaps(Canvas.Handle, NUMFONTS)));

    {display the number of entries in the color table}
    if GetDeviceCaps(Canvas.Handle, NUMCOLORS)>-1 then
      Add('Entries in color table: '+IntToStr(GetDeviceCaps(
         Canvas.Handle, NUMCOLORS)));

    {display pixel dimensions}
    Add('Pixel Width: '+IntToStr(GetDeviceCaps(Canvas.Handle, ASPECTX)));
    Add('Pixel Height: '+IntToStr(GetDeviceCaps(Canvas.Handle, ASPECTY)));
    Add('Pixel Diagonal: '+IntToStr(GetDeviceCaps(Canvas.Handle, ASPECTXY)));

    {indicate if the device can clip to a rectangle}
    if GetDeviceCaps(Canvas.Handle, CLIPCAPS)=1 then
      Add('Device can clip to a rectangle')
    else
      Add('Device can not clip to a rectangle');

    {display the palette size, reserved colors, and color depth}
    Add('Palette Size: '+IntToStr(GetDeviceCaps(Canvas.Handle, SIZEPALETTE)));
    Add('Number of Reserved Colors: '+IntToStr(GetDeviceCaps(
       Canvas.Handle, NUMRESERVED)));
    Add('Color Resolution: '+IntToStr(Trunc(IntPower(2, GetDeviceCaps(
       Canvas.Handle, COLORRES))))+' colors');

    {display the raster capabilities}
    Add('Raster Capabilities -');
    if (GetDeviceCaps(Canvas.Handle, RASTERCAPS) and
       RC_BANDING)=RC_BANDING then
         Add('     Requires Banding');
    if (GetDeviceCaps(Canvas.Handle, RASTERCAPS) and
       RC_BITBLT)=RC_BITBLT then
         Add('     Can Transfer Bitmaps');
    if (GetDeviceCaps(Canvas.Handle, RASTERCAPS) and
       RC_BITMAP64)=RC_BITMAP64 then
         Add('     Supports Bitmaps > 64K');
    if (GetDeviceCaps(Canvas.Handle, RASTERCAPS) and
       RC_DI_BITMAP)=RC_DI_BITMAP then
         Add('     Supports SetDIBits and GetDIBits');
    if (GetDeviceCaps(Canvas.Handle, RASTERCAPS) and
       RC_DIBTODEV)=RC_DIBTODEV then
         Add('     Supports SetDIBitsToDevice');
```

```
      if (GetDeviceCaps(Canvas.Handle, RASTERCAPS) and
          RC_FLOODFILL)=RC_FLOODFILL then
             Add('     Can Perform Floodfills');
      if (GetDeviceCaps(Canvas.Handle, RASTERCAPS) and
          RC_GDI20_OUTPUT)=RC_GDI20_OUTPUT then
             Add('     Supports Windows 2.0 Features');
      if (GetDeviceCaps(Canvas.Handle, RASTERCAPS) and
          RC_PALETTE)=RC_PALETTE then
             Add('     Palette Based');
      if (GetDeviceCaps(Canvas.Handle, RASTERCAPS) and
          RC_SCALING)=RC_SCALING then
             Add('     Supports Scaling');
      if (GetDeviceCaps(Canvas.Handle, RASTERCAPS) and
          RC_STRETCHBLT)=RC_STRETCHBLT then
             Add('     Supports StretchBlt');
      if (GetDeviceCaps(Canvas.Handle, RASTERCAPS) and
          RC_STRETCHDIB)=RC_STRETCHDIB then
             Add('     Supports StretchDIBits');

   {display curve capabilities}
   Add('Curve Capabilities -');
   if GetDeviceCaps(Canvas.Handle, CURVECAPS)=CC_NONE then
     Add('    Device Does Not Support Curves')
   else
   begin
      if (GetDeviceCaps(Canvas.Handle, CURVECAPS) and
          CC_CIRCLES)=CC_CIRCLES then
             Add('     Supports Circles');
      if (GetDeviceCaps(Canvas.Handle, CURVECAPS) and
          CC_PIE)=CC_PIE then
             Add('     Supports Pie Wedges');
      if (GetDeviceCaps(Canvas.Handle, CURVECAPS) and
          CC_CHORD)=CC_CHORD then
             Add('     Supports Chords');
      if (GetDeviceCaps(Canvas.Handle, CURVECAPS) and
          CC_ELLIPSES)=CC_ELLIPSES then
             Add('     Supports Ellipses');
      if (GetDeviceCaps(Canvas.Handle, CURVECAPS) and
          CC_WIDE)=CC_WIDE then
             Add('     Supports Wide Borders');
      if (GetDeviceCaps(Canvas.Handle, CURVECAPS) and
          CC_STYLED)=CC_STYLED then
             Add('     Supports Styled Borders');
      if (GetDeviceCaps(Canvas.Handle, CURVECAPS) and
          CC_WIDESTYLED)=CC_WIDESTYLED then
             Add('     Supports Wide And Styled Borders');
      if (GetDeviceCaps(Canvas.Handle, CURVECAPS) and
          CC_INTERIORS)=CC_INTERIORS then
             Add('     Supports Interiors');
      if (GetDeviceCaps(Canvas.Handle, CURVECAPS) and
          CC_ROUNDRECT)=CC_ROUNDRECT then
             Add('     Supports Rounded Rectangles');
   end;

   {display line capabilities}
   Add('Line Capabilities -');
   if GetDeviceCaps(Canvas.Handle, LINECAPS)=LC_NONE then
```

```
      Add('    Device Does Not Support Lines')
  else
  begin
    if (GetDeviceCaps(Canvas.Handle, LINECAPS) and
        LC_POLYLINE)=LC_POLYLINE then
          Add('      Supports Polylines');
    if (GetDeviceCaps(Canvas.Handle, LINECAPS) and
        LC_MARKER)=LC_MARKER then
          Add('      Supports Markers');
    if (GetDeviceCaps(Canvas.Handle, LINECAPS) and
        LC_POLYMARKER)=LC_POLYMARKER then
          Add('      Supports Multiple Markers');
    if (GetDeviceCaps(Canvas.Handle, LINECAPS) and
        LC_WIDE)=LC_WIDE then
          Add('      Supports Wide Lines');
    if (GetDeviceCaps(Canvas.Handle, LINECAPS) and
        LC_STYLED)=LC_STYLED then
          Add('      Supports Styled Lines');
    if (GetDeviceCaps(Canvas.Handle, LINECAPS) and
        LC_WIDESTYLED)=LC_WIDESTYLED then
          Add('      Supports Wide And Styled Lines');
    if (GetDeviceCaps(Canvas.Handle, LINECAPS) and
        LC_INTERIORS)=LC_INTERIORS then
          Add('      Supports Interiors');
  end;

  {display polygonal capabilities}
  Add('Polygonal Capabilities -');
  if GetDeviceCaps(Canvas.Handle, POLYGONALCAPS)=PC_NONE then
    Add('    Device Does Not Support Polygons')
  else
  begin
    if (GetDeviceCaps(Canvas.Handle, POLYGONALCAPS) and
        PC_POLYGON)=PC_POLYGON then
          Add('      Supports Alternate Fill Polygons');
    if (GetDeviceCaps(Canvas.Handle, POLYGONALCAPS) and
        PC_RECTANGLE)=PC_RECTANGLE then
          Add('      Supports Rectangles');
    if (GetDeviceCaps(Canvas.Handle, POLYGONALCAPS) and
        PC_WINDPOLYGON)=PC_WINDPOLYGON then
          Add('      Supports Winding Fill Polygons');
    if (GetDeviceCaps(Canvas.Handle, POLYGONALCAPS) and
        PC_SCANLINE)=PC_SCANLINE then
          Add('      Supports Single Scanlines');
    if (GetDeviceCaps(Canvas.Handle, POLYGONALCAPS) and
        PC_WIDE)=PC_WIDE then
          Add('      Supports Wide Borders');
    if (GetDeviceCaps(Canvas.Handle, POLYGONALCAPS) and
        PC_STYLED)=PC_STYLED then
          Add('      Supports Styled Borders');
    if (GetDeviceCaps(Canvas.Handle, POLYGONALCAPS) and
        PC_WIDESTYLED)=PC_WIDESTYLED then
          Add('      Supports Wide And Styled Borders');
    if (GetDeviceCaps(Canvas.Handle, POLYGONALCAPS) and
        PC_INTERIORS)=PC_INTERIORS then
```

```
            Add('     Supports Interiors');
    end;

    {display text capabilities}
    Add('Text Capabilities -');
    if (GetDeviceCaps(Canvas.Handle, TEXTCAPS) and
        TC_OP_CHARACTER)=TC_OP_CHARACTER then
          Add('     Capable of Character Output Precision');
    if (GetDeviceCaps(Canvas.Handle, TEXTCAPS) and
        TC_OP_STROKE)=TC_OP_STROKE then
          Add('     Capable of Stroke Output Precision');
    if (GetDeviceCaps(Canvas.Handle, TEXTCAPS) and
        TC_CP_STROKE)=TC_CP_STROKE then
          Add('     Capable of Stroke Clip Precision');
    if (GetDeviceCaps(Canvas.Handle, TEXTCAPS) and
        TC_CR_90)=TC_CR_90 then
          Add('     Supports 90 Degree Character Rotation');
    if (GetDeviceCaps(Canvas.Handle, TEXTCAPS) and
        TC_CR_ANY)=TC_CR_ANY then
          Add('     Supports Character Rotation to Any Angle');
    if (GetDeviceCaps(Canvas.Handle, TEXTCAPS) and
        TC_SF_X_YINDEP)=TC_SF_X_YINDEP then
          Add('     X And Y Scale Independent');
    if (GetDeviceCaps(Canvas.Handle, TEXTCAPS) and
        TC_SA_DOUBLE)=TC_SA_DOUBLE then
          Add('     Supports Doubled Character Scaling');
    if (GetDeviceCaps(Canvas.Handle, TEXTCAPS) and
        TC_SA_INTEGER)=TC_SA_INTEGER then
          Add('     Supports Integer Multiples Only When Scaling');
    if (GetDeviceCaps(Canvas.Handle, TEXTCAPS) and
        TC_SA_CONTIN)=TC_SA_CONTIN then
          Add('     Supports Any Multiples For Exact Character Scaling');
    if (GetDeviceCaps(Canvas.Handle, TEXTCAPS) and
        TC_EA_DOUBLE)=TC_EA_DOUBLE then
          Add('     Supports Double Weight Characters');
    if (GetDeviceCaps(Canvas.Handle, TEXTCAPS) and
        TC_IA_ABLE)=TC_IA_ABLE then
          Add('     Supports Italics');
    if (GetDeviceCaps(Canvas.Handle, TEXTCAPS) and
        TC_UA_ABLE)=TC_UA_ABLE then
          Add('     Supports Underlines');
    if (GetDeviceCaps(Canvas.Handle, TEXTCAPS) and
        TC_SO_ABLE)=TC_SO_ABLE then
          Add('     Supports Strikeouts');
    if (GetDeviceCaps(Canvas.Handle, TEXTCAPS) and
        TC_RA_ABLE)=TC_RA_ABLE then
          Add('     Supports Raster Fonts');
    if (GetDeviceCaps(Canvas.Handle, TEXTCAPS) and
        TC_VA_ABLE)=TC_VA_ABLE then
          Add('     Supports Vector Fonts');
    if (GetDeviceCaps(Canvas.Handle, TEXTCAPS) and
        TC_SCROLLBLT)=TC_SCROLLBLT then
          Add('     Cannot Scroll Using Blts');
  end;
end;
```

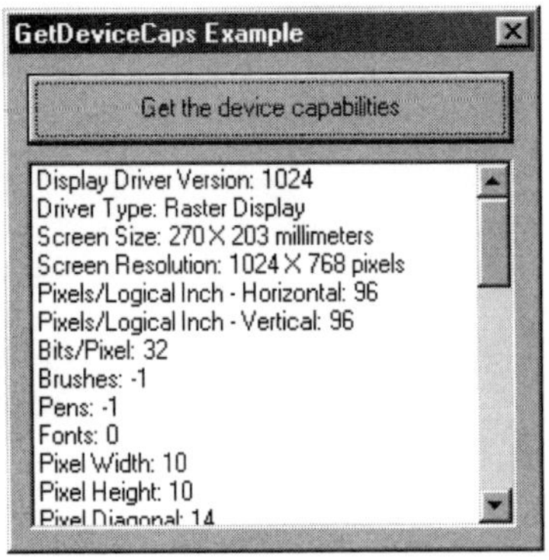

Figure 9-7:
The device capabilities

[GetDeviceCaps Example dialog showing:
Display Driver Version: 1024
Driver Type: Raster Display
Screen Size: 270 X 203 millimeters
Screen Resolution: 1024 X 768 pixels
Pixels/Logical Inch - Horizontal: 96
Pixels/Logical Inch - Vertical: 96
Bits/Pixel: 32
Brushes: -1
Pens: -1
Fonts: 0
Pixel Width: 10
Pixel Height: 10
Pixel Diagonal: 14]

Table 9-7: GetDeviceCaps Index values

Value	Description
DRIVERVERSION	The device driver version.
TECHNOLOGY	Device technology type. This flag returns one value from Table 9-8. The DC parameter can refer to an enhanced metafile, in which case the device technology returned is that of the device referenced in the metafile. Use the GetObjectType function to determine whether the device context refers to a device in an enhanced metafile.
HORZSIZE	Physical screen width in millimeters.
VERTSIZE	Physical screen height in millimeters.
HORZRES	Screen width in pixels.
VERTRES	Screen height in raster lines.
LOGPIXELSX	The number of horizontal pixels per logical inch.
LOGPIXELSY	The number of vertical pixels per logical inch.
BITSPIXEL	The number of adjacent color bits per pixel.
PLANES	The number of color planes.
NUMBRUSHES	The number of device-specific brushes.
NUMPENS	The number of device-specific pens.
NUMFONTS	The number of device-specific fonts.
NUMCOLORS	The number of entries in the device's color table, if the device has a color depth of 8 bits per pixel or less. It returns −1 for greater color depths.
ASPECTX	Relative width of a device pixel used for line drawing.
ASPECTY	Relative height of a device pixel used for line drawing.
ASPECTXY	Diagonal width of the device pixel used for line drawing.
CLIPCAPS	Clipping capability indicator of the device. If the device can clip to a rectangle, this value is 1; otherwise, it is 0.
SIZEPALETTE	The number of system palette entries. This result is valid only for Windows 3.0 or later drivers, and only if the device driver sets the RC_PALETTE bit in the RASTERCAPS index.
NUMRESERVED	Number of reserved entries in the system palette. This index is valid only for Windows 3.0 or later drivers, and only if the device driver sets the RC_PALETTE bit in the RASTERCAPS index.

Value	Description
COLORRES	Device color resolution in bits per pixel. This index is valid only for Windows 3.0 or later drivers, and only if the device driver sets the RC_PALETTE bit in the RASTERCAPS index.
PHYSICALWIDTH	Physical width of a printed page for printing devices, in device units. This is generally a larger number than the printable pixel width of the page because of non-printable margins.
PHYSICALHEIGHT	Physical height of a printed page for printing devices, in device units. This is generally a larger number than the printable pixel width of the page because of non-printable margins.
PHYSICALOFFSETX	Left printer margin. This is the distance from the left edge of the physical page to the left edge of the printable area in device units.
PHYSICALOFFSETY	Top printer margin. This is the distance from the top edge of the physical page to the top edge of the printable area in device units.
VREFRESH	**Windows NT/2000 and later:** The current vertical refresh rate for display devices in hertz. A value of 0 or 1 represents the display hardware's default refresh rate, generally settable by switches on a display card or computer motherboard, or by a configuration program that is not compatible with Win32 display functions such as ChangeDisplaySettings.
DESKTOPHORZRES	**Windows NT/2000 and later:** Virtual desktop width in pixels. This value may be larger than HORZRES if the device supports a virtual desktop or multiple displays.
DESKTOPVERTRES	**Windows NT/2000 and later:** Virtual desktop height in pixels. This value may be larger than VERTRES if the device supports a virtual desktop or multiple displays.
BLTALIGNMENT	**Windows NT/2000 and later:** Preferred horizontal drawing alignment, expressed as a multiple of pixels. For best drawing performance, windows should be horizontally aligned to a multiple of this value. A value of zero indicates that the device is accelerated, and any alignment may be used.
RASTERCAPS	Indicates the raster capabilities of the device. It returns one or more flags from Table 9-9.
CURVECAPS	Indicates the curve capabilities of the device. It returns one or more flags from Table 9-10.
LINECAPS	Indicates the line capabilities of the device. It returns one or more flags from Table 9-11.
POLYGONALCAPS	Indicates the polygon capabilities of the device. It returns one or more flags from Table 9-12.
TEXTCAPS	Indicates the text capabilities of the device. It returns one or more flags from Table 9-13.

Table 9-8: GetDeviceCaps Index TECHNOLOGY return values

Value	Description
DT_CHARSTREAM	A character stream.
DT_DISPFILE	A display file.
DT_METAFILE	A metafile.
DT_PLOTTER	A vector plotter.
DT_RASCAMERA	A raster camera.

Value	Description
DT_RASDISPLAY	A raster display.
DT_RASPRINTER	A raster printer.

Table 9-9: GetDeviceCaps Index RASTERCAPS return values

Value	Description
RC_BANDING	Device requires banding support.
RC_BITBLT	Device can transfer bitmaps.
RC_BITMAP64	Device can support bitmaps larger than 64KB.
RC_DI_BITMAP	Device can support the SetDIBits and GetDIBits functions.
RC_DIBTODEV	Device can support the SetDIBitsToDevice function.
RC_FLOODFILL	Device can perform flood fills.
RC_GDI20_OUTPUT	Device can support the features of Windows 2.0.
RC_PALETTE	Device is a palette-based device.
RC_SCALING	Device can scale.
RC_STRETCHBLT	Device can support the StretchBlt function.
RC_STRETCHDIB	Device can support the StretchDIBits function.

Table 9-10: GetDeviceCaps Index CURVECAPS return values

Value	Description
CC_NONE	Device is not capable of supporting curves.
CC_CIRCLES	Device is capable of drawing circles.
CC_PIE	Device is capable of drawing pie wedges.
CC_CHORD	Device is capable of drawing chord arcs.
CC_ELLIPSES	Device is capable of drawing ellipses.
CC_WIDE	Device is capable of drawing wide borders.
CC_STYLED	Device is capable of drawing styled borders.
CC_WIDESTYLED	Device is capable of drawing borders that are wide and styled.
CC_INTERIORS	Device is capable of drawing interiors.
CC_ROUNDRECT	Device is capable of drawing rounded rectangles.

Table 9-11: GetDeviceCaps Index LINECAPS return values

Value	Description
LC_NONE	Device is not capable of supporting lines.
LC_POLYLINE	Device is capable of drawing a polyline.
LC_MARKER	Device is capable of drawing a marker.
LC_POLYMARKER	Device is capable of drawing multiple markers.
LC_WIDE	Device is capable of drawing wide lines.
LC_STYLED	Device is capable of drawing styled lines.
LC_WIDESTYLED	Device is capable of drawing lines that are wide and styled.
LC_INTERIORS	Device is capable of drawing interiors.

Table 9-12: GetDeviceCaps Index POLYGONALCAPS return values

Value	Description
PC_NONE	Device is not capable of supporting polygons.
PC_POLYGON	Device is capable of drawing alternate-fill polygons.
PC_RECTANGLE	Device is capable of drawing rectangles.
PC_WINDPOLYGON	Device is capable of drawing winding-fill polygons.
PC_SCANLINE	Device is capable of drawing a single scanline.
PC_WIDE	Device is capable of drawing wide borders.
PC_STYLED	Device is capable of drawing styled borders.
PC_WIDESTYLED	Device is capable of drawing borders that are wide and styled.
PC_INTERIORS	Device is capable of drawing interiors.

Table 9-13: GetDeviceCaps Index TEXTCAPS return values

Value	Description
TC_OP_CHARACTER	Device has capability of character output precision.
TC_OP_STROKE	Device has capability of stroke output precision.
TC_CP_STROKE	Device has capability of stroke clip precision.
TC_CR_90	Device has capability of 90-degree character rotation.
TC_CR_ANY	Device has capability of any character rotation.
TC_SF_X_YINDEP	Device has capability to scale independently in the x and y directions.
TC_SA_DOUBLE	Device has capability of doubled character for scaling.
TC_SA_INTEGER	Device uses only integer multiples for character scaling.
TC_SA_CONTIN	Device uses any multiples for exact character scaling.
TC_EA_DOUBLE	Device is capable of drawing double-weight characters.
TC_IA_ABLE	Device is capable of italicizing.
TC_UA_ABLE	Device is capable of underlining.
TC_SO_ABLE	Device is capable of drawing strikeouts.
TC_RA_ABLE	Device is capable of drawing raster fonts.
TC_VA_ABLE	Device is capable of drawing vector fonts.
TC_SCROLLBLT	The device cannot scroll using a bit block transfer.

GetMapMode Windows.pas

Syntax

```
GetMapMode(
 DC: HDC              {the handle of a device context}
): Integer;           {returns the mapping mode}
```

Description

The GetMapMode function retrieves the current mapping mode of the specified device context.

Parameters

DC: The handle of the device context whose current mapping mode is retrieved.

Return Value

If the function succeeds, it returns a flag indicating the current mapping mode, and may be one value from Table 9-14. If the function fails, it returns a zero.

See Also

SetMapMode, SetViewportExtEx, SetWindowExtEx

Example

See Listing 9-2 in the section titled "Mapping Modes."

Table 9-14: GetMapMode return values

Value	Description
MM_ANISOTROPIC	The units, scaling, and orientation are set by SetWindowExtEx and SetViewportExtEx. The x and y axis scaling are set independently and are not required to be the same.
MM_HIENGLISH	High-resolution mapping in English units. Each unit is 0.001 inch with x being positive to the right and y being positive in the upward direction.
MM_HIMETRIC	High-resolution mapping in metric units. Each unit is 0.01 millimeter with x being positive to the right and y being positive in the upward direction.
MM_ISOTROPIC	The units, scaling, and orientation are set by SetWindowExtEx and SetViewportExtEx with the horizontal and vertical units set as equal. The units and orientation are settable, but the units for the x and y axes are forced to be the same by the GDI. This mode ensures a 1:1 aspect ratio.
MM_LOENGLISH	Low-resolution mapping in English units. Each unit is 0.01 inch with x being positive to the right and y being positive in the upward direction.
MM_LOMETRIC	Low-resolution mapping in metric units. Each unit is 0.1 millimeter with x being positive to the right and y being positive in the upward direction.
MM_TEXT	Each unit is mapped to one device pixel. This is not a device-independent setting. Devices with different resolutions or scalings will have different results from graphical functions, with x being positive to the right and y being positive in the downward direction. This is the default setting.
MM_TWIPS	Each unit is mapped to 1/1440 inch, which is 1/20 of a printer's point. Coordinates are oriented with x being positive to the right and y being positive in the upward direction.

GetSystemMetrics   Windows.pas

Syntax

```
GetSystemMetrics(
  nIndex: Integer         {the item index}
): Integer;               {returns the item measurement}
```

Description

The GetSystemMetrics function retrieves the dimensions, in pixels, of a specific Windows display element. A variety of items may be queried based on the value of the nIndex parameter. All measured results are provided in numerical values or pixels except for the SM_ARRANGE flag, which returns a combination of values from Table 9-16.

Parameters

nIndex: A flag indicating the Windows display element for which a measurement is to be retrieved. This parameter may be set to one value from Table 9-15.

Return Value

If the function succeeds, it returns the measurement of the queried item. If the function fails, it returns a zero.

See Also

GetDeviceCaps

Example

Listing 9-9: Retrieving specific item dimensions

```
procedure TForm1.Button1Click(Sender: TObject);
begin
  with ListBox1.Items do
  begin
    {display the minimized window arrangement}
    Add('Minimized Window Arrangement -');
    if (GetSystemMetrics(SM_ARRANGE) and ARW_BOTTOMLEFT)=ARW_BOTTOMLEFT then
       Add('     Starts in the lower left corner');
    if (GetSystemMetrics(SM_ARRANGE) and ARW_BOTTOMRIGHT)=ARW_BOTTOMRIGHT then
       Add('     Starts in the lower right corner');
    if (GetSystemMetrics(SM_ARRANGE) and ARW_HIDE)=ARW_HIDE then
       Add('     Minimized windows are hidden');
    if (GetSystemMetrics(SM_ARRANGE) and ARW_TOPLEFT)=ARW_TOPLEFT then
       Add('     Starts in the top left corner');
    if (GetSystemMetrics(SM_ARRANGE) and ARW_TOPRIGHT)=ARW_TOPRIGHT then
       Add('     Starts in the top right corner');

    if (GetSystemMetrics(SM_ARRANGE) and ARW_DOWN)=ARW_DOWN then
       Add('     Arranged vertically, top to bottom');
    if (GetSystemMetrics(SM_ARRANGE) and ARW_LEFT)=ARW_LEFT then
       Add('     Arranged horizontally, left to right');
    if (GetSystemMetrics(SM_ARRANGE) and ARW_RIGHT)=ARW_RIGHT then
       Add('     Arranged horizontally, right to left');
    if (GetSystemMetrics(SM_ARRANGE) and ARW_UP)=ARW_UP then
       Add('     Arrange vertically, bottom to top');

    {display window border dimensions}
    Add('Window border width: '+IntToStr(GetSystemMetrics(SM_CXEDGE)));
    Add('Window border height: '+IntToStr(GetSystemMetrics(SM_CYEDGE)));

    {display cursor dimensions}
    Add('Cursor width: '+IntToStr(GetSystemMetrics(SM_CXCURSOR)));
```

```
            Add('Cursor height: '+IntToStr(GetSystemMetrics(SM_CYCURSOR)));

            {display icon dimensions}
            Add('Icon width: '+IntToStr(GetSystemMetrics(SM_CXICON)));
            Add('Icon height: '+IntToStr(GetSystemMetrics(SM_CYICON)));

            {display maximized window dimensions}
            Add('Maximized window width: '+IntToStr(GetSystemMetrics(SM_CXMAXIMIZED)));
            Add('Maximized window height: '+IntToStr(GetSystemMetrics(SM_CYMAXIMIZED)));

            {display screen dimensions}
            Add('Screen width: '+IntToStr(GetSystemMetrics(SM_CXSCREEN)));
            Add('Screen height: '+IntToStr(GetSystemMetrics(SM_CYSCREEN)));

            {display the caption height}
            Add('Caption height: '+IntToStr(GetSystemMetrics(SM_CYCAPTION)));
     end;
end;
```

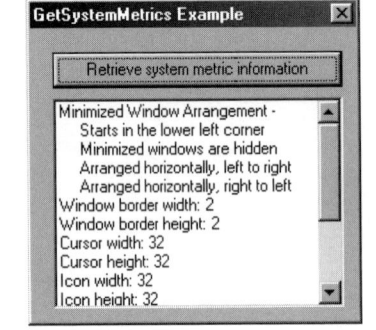

Figure 9-8: Specific system item dimensions

Table 9-15: GetSystemMetrics nIndex values

Value	Description
SM_ARRANGE	Returns a combination of values from Table 9-16 that specify how the system arranges minimized windows.
SM_CLEANBOOT	Returns a value that specifies how the system booted up: 0 = Normal boot 1 = Safe Mode boot 2 = Safe Mode boot with network support
SM_CMONITORS	**Windows 98/Me/2000 or later:** Returns the number of display monitors on the desktop.
SM_CMOUSEBUTTONS	Returns the number of buttons on the mouse, or zero if no mouse is installed.
SM_CXBORDER, SM_CYBORDER	The width and height of a window border. This is the same as the SM_CXEDGE value for windows with the 3-D look.
SM_CXCURSOR, SM_CYCURSOR	Width and height of a cursor. These are the dimensions supported by the current display driver. Because of the requirements of the display driver, the system cannot create cursors of other sizes.

Value	Description
SM_CXDOUBLECLK, SM_CYDOUBLECLK	Width and height of the rectangle around the location of a first click in a double-click operation. The second click must occur within this rectangle for the system to consider the two clicks a double-click. For a double-click to be generated, the second click must occur within a specified time frame, and within this specified rectangle.
SM_CXDRAG, SM_CYDRAG	Width and height of a rectangle centered on a drag point to allow for limited movement of the mouse pointer before a drag operation begins. This gives the user some allowance for mouse movement without inadvertently beginning a drag operation.
SM_CXEDGE, SM_CYEDGE	Dimensions of a 3-D border. These are the 3-D equivalents to SM_CXBORDER and SM_CYBORDER.
SM_CXFIXEDFRAME, SM_CYFIXEDFRAME	Thickness of the frame around a window that has a caption but is not sizable. SM_CXFIXEDFRAME is the horizontal border width and SM_CYFIXEDFRAME is the vertical border height.
SM_CXFULLSCREEN, SM_CYFULLSCREEN	Width and height of a full-screen window client area. The size of the window not obscured by the tray is available by calling the SystemParametersInfo function with the SPI_GETWORKAREA value.
SM_CXHSCROLL, SM_CYHSCROLL	Width of the arrow bitmap on a horizontal scroll bar; and height of a horizontal scroll bar.
SM_CXHTHUMB	Width of the thumb box in a horizontal scroll bar.
SM_CXICON, SM_CYICON	The default width and height of an icon. This is normally 32x32, but can depend on the installed display hardware. The LoadIcon function is restricted to loading only icons of these dimensions.
SM_CXICONSPACING, SM_CYICONSPACING	Dimensions of a grid cell for items in large icon view. The screen is mapped into rectangles of this size, with each item fitting into one of the rectangles when arranged. These values are always greater than or equal to SM_CXICON and SM_CYICON.
SM_CXMAXIMIZED, SM_CYMAXIMIZED	Default size of a maximized top-level window.
SM_CXMAXTRACK, SM_CYMAXTRACK	Default maximum size of a window that has a caption and sizing borders. The system will not allow the user to drag the window frame to a size larger. An application can override these values by processing the WM_GET-MINMAXINFO message.
SM_CXMENUCHECK, SM_CYMENUCHECK	Size of the default menu check mark bitmap.
SM_CXMENUSIZE, SM_CYMENUSIZE	Size of menu bar buttons.
SM_CXMIN, SM_CYMIN	Minimum width and height of a window.
SM_CXMINIMIZED, SM_CYMINIMIZED	Size of a normal minimized window.
SM_CXMINSPACING, SM_CYMINSPACING	Size of a grid cell for minimized windows. See SM_CXICONSPACING. Minimized windows are arranged into rectangles of this size. These values are always greater than or equal to SM_CXMINIMIZED and SM_CYMIN-IMIZED.
SM_CXMINTRACK, SM_CYMINTRACK	Minimum tracking width and height of a window. The system will not allow a user to drag the window frame to a size smaller than these dimensions. An application can override these values by processing the WM_GETMIN-MAXINFO message.

Value	Description
SM_CXSCREEN, SM_CYSCREEN	Width and height of the screen.
SM_CXSIZE, SM_CYSIZE	Width and height of a button in a window's caption or title bar.
SM_CXSIZEFRAME, SM_CYSIZEFRAME	Thickness of the sizing border around a window that can be resized. SM_CXSIZEFRAME is the horizontal border width and SM_CYSIZEFRAME is the vertical border height. Same as SM_CXFRAME and SM_CYFRAME.
SM_CXSMICON, SM_CYSMICON	Recommended size of a small icon. Small icons would normally appear in window captions and in small icon view.
SM_CXSMSIZE, SM_CYSMSIZE	Size of small caption buttons.
SM_CXVIRTUALSCREENSIZE, SM_CYVIRTUALSCREENSIZE	**Windows 98/Me/2000 or later:** Returns the width and height of the virtual screen, in pixels. The virtual screen is the bounding rectangle of all display monitors.
SM_CXVSCROLL, SM_CYVSCROLL	Width of a vertical scroll bar and height of the arrow bitmap on a vertical scroll bar.
SM_CYCAPTION	Height of normal caption area.
SM_CYKANJIWINDOW	For systems using double-byte character sets, the height of the Kanji window at the bottom of the screen.
SM_CYMENU	Height of a single-line menu bar.
SM_CYSMCAPTION	Height of a small caption.
SM_CYVTHUMB	Height of the thumb box in a vertical scroll bar.
SM_DBCSENABLED	Non-zero if the double-byte character set version of USER.EXE is installed; zero if DBCS is not installed.
SM_DEBUG	Non-zero if the debug USER.EXE is installed; zero if it is not.
SM_IMMENABLED	**Windows 2000 or later:** Returns a non-zero value if Input Method Manager/Input Method Editor features are enabled.
SM_MENUDROPALIGNMENT	Non-zero if drop-down menus are right aligned relative to the corresponding menu bar item; zero if they are left aligned.
SM_MIDEASTENABLED	Non-zero if the system is enabled for Hebrew/Arabic languages; zero if not.
SM_MOUSEPRESENT	Non-zero if a mouse is installed; zero if it is not.
SM_MOUSEWHEELPRESENT	**Windows NT/98/Me or later:** Returns a non-zero value if a mouse with a wheel is installed; zero if it is not.
SM_NETWORK	The least significant bit is set if a network is present; otherwise, it is cleared. The other bits are reserved.
SM_PENWINDOWS	Non-zero if the Microsoft Windows for Pen Computing extensions are installed; zero if it is not.
SM_REMOTESESSION	**Windows NT SP4 or later:** Returns a non-zero value if the calling process is associated with a terminal services client session.
SM_SECURE	Non-zero if security is present; zero if it is not present.
SM_SAMEDISPLAYFORMAT	**Windows 98/Me/2000 or later:** Returns a non-zero value if all display monitors have the same color format.
SM_SHOWSOUNDS	Non-zero if the user specifies that audible-only presentations also have a visual representation; zero if visual displays are not required for audible-only software.
SM_SLOWMACHINE	Non-zero if the computer has a low-end processor; zero otherwise.

Value	Description
SM_SWAPBUTTON	Non-zero if the left and right mouse buttons have been configured to be swapped; zero if they have not been so configured.
SM_XVIRTUALSCREEN, SM_YVIRTUALSCREEN	**Windows 98/Me/2000 or later:** Returns the coordinates of the origin of the virtual screen. The virtual screen is the bounding rectangle of all display monitors.

Table 9-16: GetSystemMetrics SM_ARRANGE values

Value	Description
ARW_BOTTOMLEFT	The default position for starting placement of minimized windows in the lower-left corner.
ARW_BOTTOMRIGHT	Begin minimized window placement in bottom right of the screen.
ARW_HIDE	Place minimized windows off the screen in a non-visible area.
ARW_TOPLEFT	Place minimized windows in the upper-left corner of the screen.
ARW_TOPRIGHT	Place minimized windows in the upper-right corner of the screen.
ARW_DOWN	Position minimized windows vertically, top to bottom.
ARW_LEFT	Position minimized windows horizontally, left to right.
ARW_RIGHT	Position minimized windows horizontally, right to left.
ARW_UP	Position minimized windows vertically, bottom to top.

GetViewportExtEx   *Windows.pas*

Syntax

```
GetViewportExtEx(
  DC: HDC;              {the handle of a device context}
  var Size: TSize       {the x and y extents of the viewport}
): BOOL;                {returns TRUE or FALSE}
```

Description

The GetViewportExtEx function retrieves the horizontal and vertical extents of the viewport associated with the device context handle.

Parameters

DC: The handle of the device context whose viewport extents are to be retrieved.

Size: A pointer to a TSize structure that receives the horizontal and vertical extents of the viewport associated with the specified device context.

Return Value

If the function succeeds, it returns TRUE; otherwise, it returns FALSE.

See Also

GetViewportOrgEx, GetWindowExtEx, GetWindowOrgEx, SetViewportExtEx, SetViewportOrgEx, SetWindowExtEx, SetWindowOrgEx

Example

See Listing 9-2 in the section titled "Mapping Modes."

GetViewportOrgEx   Windows.pas

Syntax

```
GetViewportOrgEx(
DC: HDC;                    {the handle of a device context}
var Point: TPoint           {the origin of the viewport coordinates}
): BOOL;                    {returns TRUE or FALSE}
```

Description

The GetViewportOrgEx function retrieves the origin of the coordinate system of the viewport associated with the specified device context.

Parameters

DC: The handle of the device context whose associated viewport's coordinate system origin is to be retrieved.

Point: A pointer to a TPoint structure that receives the x and y values of the origin of the viewport's coordinate system.

Return Value

If the function succeeds, it returns TRUE; otherwise, it returns FALSE.

See Also

GetViewportExtEx, GetWindowExtEx, GetWindowOrgEx, SetViewportExtEx, SetViewportOrgEx, SetWindowExtEx, SetWindowOrgEx

Example

See Listing 9-2 in the section titled "Mapping Modes."

GetWindowDC   Windows.pas

Syntax

```
GetWindowDC(
hWnd: HWND                  {the handle of a window}
): HDC;                     {returns the window's device context}
```

Description

The GetWindowDC function returns a device context for the window specified by the hWnd parameter. The retrieved device context refers to the entire specified window, including the non-client area such as the title bar, menu, scroll bars, and frame. This allows an application to implement custom graphics in the non-client areas, such as a custom title bar or border. When the device context is no longer needed, it should be released by calling the ReleaseDC function. Note that this function retrieves only a common device context, and any attributes modified in this device context will not be reflected in the window's private or class device context, if it has one.

Parameters

hWnd: The handle of the window for which a device context is retrieved.

Return Value

If the function succeeds, it returns a handle to the device context for the selected window. If the function fails, it returns zero.

See Also

BeginPaint, GetDC, GetSystemMetrics*, ReleaseDC

Example

Listing 9-10: Painting a custom caption bar

```
procedure TForm1.WMNCPaint(var Msg: TMessage);
var
  WinDC: HDC;        // holds the window device context
  OldFont: HFONT;    // holds the previous font
begin
  {call the inherited paint handler}
  inherited;

  {retrieve a handle to the window device context}
  WinDC := GetWindowDC(Form1.Handle);

  {initialize the font}
  Canvas.Font.Height := GetSystemMetrics(SM_CYCAPTION)-4;
  Canvas.Font.Name   := 'Times New Roman';
  Canvas.Font.Style  := [fsBold, fsItalic];

  {select the font into the window device context}
  OldFont := SelectObject(WinDC, Canvas.Font.Handle);

  {see if the window is active}
  if GetActiveWindow = 0 then
  begin
    {draw inactive colors}
    SetBkColor(WinDC, GetSysColor(COLOR_INACTIVECAPTION));
    SetTextColor(WinDC, GetSysColor(COLOR_INACTIVECAPTIONTEXT));
  end
  else
  begin
    {otherwise draw active colors}
    SetBkColor(WinDC, GetSysColor(COLOR_ACTIVECAPTION));
    SetTextColor(WinDC, GetSysColor(COLOR_CAPTIONTEXT));
  end;

  {draw the text of the caption in a bold, italic style}
  SetBkMode(WinDC, OPAQUE);

  TextOut(WinDC, GetSystemMetrics(SM_CXEDGE)+GetSystemMetrics(SM_CXSMICON)+6,
```

```
                GetSystemMetrics(SM_CYEDGE)+3, 'GetWindowDC Example',
                Length('GetWindowDC Example'));

  {replace the original font and release the window device context}
  SelectObject(WinDC, OldFont);
  ReleaseDC(Form1.Handle, WinDC);
end;

procedure TForm1.WMActivate(var Msg: TWMActivate);
begin
  {call the inherited message handle and repaint the caption bar}
  inherited;
  PostMessage(Form1.Handle, WM_NCPAINT, 0, 0);
end;
```

Figure 9-9:
The custom caption bar

GetWindowExtEx   Windows.pas

Syntax

GetWindowExtEx(
DC: HDC;   {the handle of a device context}
var Size: TSize;   {the x and y extents of the window}
): BOOL;   {returns TRUE or FALSE}

Description

The GetWindowExtEx function retrieves the horizontal and vertical extents of the window associated with the specified device context.

Parameters

DC: The handle of the device context for which the horizontal and vertical window extents are retrieved.

Size: A pointer to a TSize structure that receives the horizontal and vertical extents of the window associated with the specified device context.

Return Value

If the function succeeds, it returns TRUE; otherwise, it returns FALSE.

See Also

GetViewportExtEx, GetViewportOrgEx, GetWindowOrgEx, SetViewportExtEx, SetViewportOrgEx, SetWindowExtEx, SetWindowOrgEx

Example

See Listing 9-2 in the section titled "Mapping Modes."

GetWindowOrgEx   Windows.pas

Syntax

```
GetWindowOrgEx(
  DC: HDC;              {the handle of a device context}
  var Point: TPoint     {the origin of the window coordinates}
): BOOL;                {returns TRUE or FALSE}
```

Description

The GetWindowOrgEx function retrieves the origin of the window associated with the specified device context.

Parameters

DC: The handle of the device context whose associated window coordinate system origin is to be retrieved.

Point: A pointer to a TPoint structure that receives the x and y values of the origin of the window's coordinate system.

Return Value

If the function succeeds, it returns TRUE; otherwise, it returns FALSE.

See Also

GetViewportExtEx, GetViewportOrgEx, GetWindowExtEx, SetViewportExtEx, SetViewportOrgEx, SetWindowExtEx, SetWindowOrgEx

Example

See Listing 9-2 in the section titled "Mapping Modes."

LPtoDP   Windows.pas

Syntax

```
LPtoDP(
  DC: HDC;              {the handle of a device context}
  var Points;           {a pointer to an array of TPoint structures}
  Count: Integer        {the number of entries in the array}
): BOOL;                {returns TRUE or FALSE}
```

Description

The LPtoDP function converts points from logical coordinates to device coordinates. The Points parameter points to an array of TPoint structures containing the coordinates to be translated. These TPoint structures will receive the translated coordinates when the function returns. The coordinate transformation is performed based on the values set by the

SetWindowOrgEx, SetViewportOrgEx, SetWindowExtEx, and SetViewportExtEx functions. The LPtoDP function will fail if any of the points in the TPoint structures specify a value greater in size than 27 bits. It will also fail if any of the transformed points are greater in size than 32 bits. In the event of failure, the values in the entire Points array are undefined.

Parameters

DC: The device context for which the coordinate transformations will be made.

Points: A pointer to an array of TPoint structures containing the coordinates to be converted.

Count: Specifies the number of entries in the array pointed to by the Points parameter.

Return Value

If the function succeeds, it returns TRUE; otherwise, it returns FALSE.

See Also

DPtoLP, SetViewportExtEx, SetViewportOrgEx, SetWindowExtEx, SetWindowOrgEx

Example

See Listing 9-12 under ScaleViewportExtEx.

MapWindowPoints   Windows.pas

Syntax

```
MapWindowPoints(
hWndFrom: HWND;         {the handle of the source window}
hWndTo: HWND;           {the handle of the destination window}
var lpPoints:UINT;      {a pointer to an array of points}
cPoints: UINT           {the size of the array}
): Integer;             {returns pixel offsets}
```

Description

The MapWindowPoints function converts a set of points from a coordinate system relative to one window to the coordinate system of another window. Any number of points can be transformed with a single function call.

Parameters

hWndFrom: The handle of the window from which the points are to be translated. The points listed in the lpPoints parameter have dimensions relative to this window. If this parameter is set to NIL or HWND_DESKTOP, the points are relative to the screen.

hWndTo: The handle of the window to which the points are to be translated. If this parameter is set to NIL or HWND_DESKTOP, the points are relative to the screen.

lpPoints: A pointer to an array of TPoint structures containing the coordinates to be translated. These TPoint structures receive the translated coordinates when the function returns.

cPoints: Specifies the number of elements in the array pointed to by the lpPoints parameter.

Return Value

If the function succeeds, the lower order word of the return value specifies the number of pixels that are added to the horizontal dimension of the coordinates, and the high-order word of the return value specifies the number of pixels added to the vertical dimension of the coordinates. If the function fails, it returns a zero.

See Also

ClientToScreen, ScreenToClient

Example

Listing 9-II: Translating multiple coordinates from one coordinate system to another

```
var
  Form1: TForm1;
  DrawnRect: TRect;        // holds the rectangular coordinates
  Drawing: Boolean;        // indicates if a rectangle is being drawn

implementation

{$R *.DFM}

procedure TForm1.PaintBox1MouseDown(Sender: TObject; Button: TMouseButton;
  Shift: TShiftState; X, Y: Integer);
begin
  {indicate that a drawing operation has commenced, and initialize the
   rectangular coordinates}
  Drawing := TRUE;
  DrawnRect := Rect(X, Y, X, Y);
end;

procedure TForm1.PaintBox1MouseMove(Sender: TObject; Shift: TShiftState; X,
  Y: Integer);
begin
  {if we a redrawing...}
  if Drawing then
  with PaintBox1.Canvas do
  begin
    {initialize the canvas's pen and brush}
    Pen.Mode := pmNot;
    Pen.Width := 2;
    Brush.Style := bsClear;

    {draw a rectangle over the previous one to erase it}
    Rectangle(DrawnRect.Left, DrawnRect.Top, DrawnRect.Right, DrawnRect.Bottom);

    {set the rectangle to the current coordinates}
```

```
      DrawnRect := Rect(DrawnRect.Left, DrawnRect.Top, X, Y);

    {draw the new rectangle}
    Rectangle(DrawnRect.Left, DrawnRect.Top, DrawnRect.Right, DrawnRect.Bottom);
  end;
end;

procedure TForm1.PaintBox1MouseUp(Sender: TObject; Button: TMouseButton;
  Shift: TShiftState; X, Y: Integer);
begin
  {we are no longer drawing}
  Drawing := FALSE;

  {display the coordinates relative to the panel}
  Label2.Caption := 'Panel coordinates - L:'+IntToStr(DrawnRect.Left)+', T: '+
                    IntToStr(DrawnRect.Top)+', R: '+IntToStr(DrawnRect.Right)+
                    ', B: '+IntToStr(DrawnRect.Bottom);

  {translate the rectangular coordinates relative to the form}
  MapWindowPoints(Panel1.Handle, Form1.Handle, DrawnRect, 2);

  {display the coordinates relative to the form}
  Label3.Caption := 'Form coordinates - L:'+IntToStr(DrawnRect.Left)+', T: '+
                    IntToStr(DrawnRect.Top)+', R: '+IntToStr(DrawnRect.Right)+
                    ', B: '+IntToStr(DrawnRect.Bottom);
end;
```

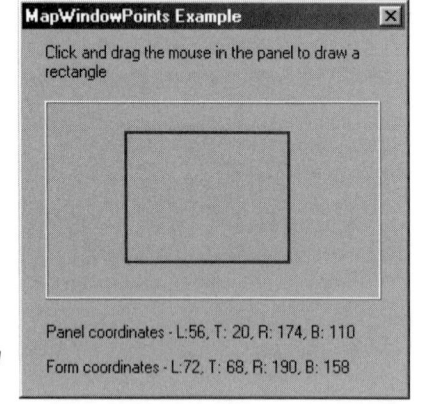

Figure 9-10:
The translated points

OffsetViewportOrgEx   Windows.pas

Syntax

```
OffsetViewportOrgEx(
  DC: HDC;              {the handle of a device context}
  X: Integer;           {the horizontal offset}
  Y: Integer;           {the vertical offset}
  Points: Pointer       {the previous origin}
): BOOL;                {returns TRUE or FALSE}
```

Description

The OffsetViewportOrgEx function modifies the existing origin of the viewport by adding a value to the current origin's location. The parameters can specify positive or negative offsets in the horizontal and vertical directions. The location of the previous origin is passed back in the Points parameter. OffsetViewportOrgEx moves the viewport origin to a new location relative to its existing coordinates. To place the origin at an absolute position regardless of the current position, use SetViewportOrgEx instead.

Parameters

DC: The handle of the device context whose viewport origin is to be modified.

X: The horizontal offset to add to or subtract from the current x value of the origin.

Y: The vertical offset to add to or subtract from the current y value of the origin.

Points: A pointer to a TPoint structure that receives the original location of the origin. This parameter can be set to NIL if the original coordinates are not needed.

Return Value

If the function succeeds, it returns TRUE; otherwise, it returns FALSE.

See Also

GetViewportOrgEx, OffsetWindowOrgEx, ScaleViewportExtEx, SetViewportOrgEx

Example

See Listing 9-12 under ScaleViewportExtEx.

OffsetWindowOrgEx Windows.pas

Syntax

```
OffsetWindowOrgEx(
DC: HDC;              {the handle of a device context}
X: Integer;           {the horizontal offset}
Y: Integer;           {the vertical offset}
Points: Pointer       {the previous origin}
): BOOL;              {returns TRUE or FALSE}
```

Description

The OffsetWindowOrgEx function modifies the existing origin of the window by adding a value to the current origin's location. The parameters can specify positive or negative offsets in the horizontal and vertical directions. The location of the previous origin is passed back in the Points parameter. OffsetWindowOrgEx moves the window origin to a new value relative to its existing coordinates. To place the origin at an absolute position regardless of the current position, use SetWindowOrgEx instead.

Parameters

DC: The handle of the device context whose associated window origin is to be modified.

X: The horizontal offset to add to or subtract from the current x value of the origin.

Y: The vertical offset to add to or subtract from the current y value of the origin.

Points: A pointer to a TPoint structure that receives the original location of the origin. This parameter can be set to NIL if the original coordinates are not needed.

Return Value

If the function succeeds, it returns TRUE; otherwise, it returns FALSE.

See Also

GetViewportOrgEx, OffsetViewportOrgEx, ScaleWindowExtEx, SetViewportOrgEx, SetWindowOrgEx

Example

See Listing 9-12 under ScaleViewportExtEx.

ReleaseDC   Windows.pas

Syntax

```
ReleaseDC(
hWnd: HWND;              {the handle of a window}
hDC: HDC                 {the device context}
): Integer;              {returns zero or one}
```

Description

The ReleaseDC function releases a device context retrieved by the GetDC or GetWindowDC functions, returning its resources to Windows. The ReleaseDC function affects only common device contexts. ReleaseDC has no effect on class or private device contexts.

Parameters

hWnd: The handle of the window whose associated device context is to be released.

hDC: The handle of the device context to be released.

Return Value

If the function succeeds, it returns a one; otherwise, it returns a zero.

See Also

CreateCompatibleDC, DeleteDC, GetDC, GetWindowDC

Example

See Listing 9-5 under CreateCompatibleDC and other functions throughout this chapter.

RestoreDC   Windows.pas

Syntax

```
RestoreDC(
DC: HDC;              {the handle of a device context}
SavedDC: Integer      {the state to be restored}
): BOOL;              {returns TRUE or FALSE}
```

Description

The RestoreDC function restores the state of a previously saved device context. Calling the SaveDC function can save the state of a device context. The SaveDC function returns a value identifying the saved device context, which should be used in the SavedDC parameter to restore an explicate state.

Parameters

DC: The handle of the device context whose state is to be restored. The device context should already exist and have states that were previously saved with the SaveDC function.

SavedDC: Specifies the instance number of the state to be restored. This value is returned by the SaveDC function when the state was originally saved. A negative value can be specified to restore a state relative to the current state (i.e., –1 restores the most recently saved state). If the restored state is not the most recently saved state, all other states between the most recently saved state and the specified state are disposed.

Return Value

If the function succeeds, it returns TRUE; otherwise, it returns FALSE.

See Also

CreateCompatibleDC, GetDC, GetWindowDC, SaveDC

Example

See Listing 9-5 under CreateCompatibleDC.

SaveDC   Windows.pas

Syntax

```
SaveDC(
DC: HDC              {the handle of a device context}
): Integer;          {returns a saved state index}
```

Description

This function saves the state of the specified device context into an internal stack maintained by Windows. This state includes the information and graphical objects associated with the device context such as bitmaps, brushes, palettes, fonts, the drawing mode, the mapping mode, etc. The state can be recalled with the RestoreDC function.

Parameters

DC: The handle of the device context for which state information is to be saved.

Return Value

If the function succeeds, it returns a value identifying the saved state, which can be used in subsequent calls to the RestoreDC function. If the function fails, it returns a zero.

See Also

CreateCompatibleDC, GetDC, GetWindowDC, RestoreDC

Example

See Listing 9-5 under CreateCompatibleDC.

ScaleViewportExtEx   Windows.pas

Syntax

```
ScaleViewportExtEx(
DC: HDC;               {the handle of a device context}
XM: Integer;           {the horizontal multiplier}
XD: Integer;           {the horizontal divisor}
YM: Integer;           {the vertical multiplier}
YD: Integer;           {the vertical divisor}
Size: PSize            {a pointer to the previous extents}
): BOOL;               {returns TRUE or FALSE}
```

Description

The ScaleViewportExtEx function modifies the existing extents of the viewport associated with the specified device context, according to the specified scaling factors. For horizontal and vertical extents, a multiplier and divisor parameter is available for making the extent in that direction larger or smaller. Parameters not used should be supplied with a value of 1. For example, making the horizontal extent half of the current value would require the XD parameter to be set to 2. All other parameters would be 1. Making the horizontal extent three-fourths of its current value could be accomplished by setting the XM parameter to 3 and the XD parameter to 4.

Parameters

DC: The handle of the device context whose viewport extents are to be scaled.

XM: The horizontal extent multiplier.

XD: The horizontal extent divisor.

YM: The vertical extent multiplier.

YD: The vertical extent divisor.

Size: A pointer to a TSize structure that receives the previous extent values.

Return Value

If the function succeeds, it returns TRUE; otherwise, it returns FALSE.

See Also

GetViewportExtEx, ScaleWindowExtEx

Example

Listing 9-12: Scaling viewports and windows

```
var
  Form1: TForm1;
  MyDisplayDC: HDC;           // a handle to the device context
  MyMapMode: Integer;         // holds the mapping mode
  PrevWindowSize: TSize;      // holds the previous window size
  PrevViewportSize: TSize;    // holds the previous viewport size
  PrevWindowPoint: TPoint;    // holds the previous window origin
  PrevViewportPoint: TPoint;  // holds the previous viewport origin

implementation

{$R *.DFM}

{re-import the corrected functions}
function OffsetViewportOrgEx; external gdi32 name 'OffsetViewportOrgEx';
function OffsetWindowOrgEx; external gdi32 name 'OffsetWindowOrgEx';

procedure TForm1.ReportPosition;
var
  ReturnValue: TPoint;       // holds the window and viewport origin
  ReturnSize: TSize;         // holds the window and viewport extents
begin
  {display the window origin}
  GetWindowOrgEx(MyDisplayDC,ReturnValue);
  Label9.Caption := IntToStr(ReturnValue.x)
       + ', ' + IntToStr(ReturnValue.y);

  {display the viewport origin}
  GetViewportOrgEx(MyDisplayDC,ReturnValue);
  Label10.Caption := IntToStr(ReturnValue.x)
       + ', ' + IntToStr(ReturnValue.y);

  {display the window extents}
  GetWindowExtEx(MyDisplayDC,ReturnSize);
  Label11.Caption := IntToStr(ReturnSize.cx)
       + ', ' + IntToStr(ReturnSize.cy);

  {display the viewport extents}
  GetViewportExtEx(MyDisplayDC,ReturnSize);
  Label12.Caption := IntToStr(ReturnSize.cx)
       + ', ' + IntToStr(ReturnSize.cy);
end;

procedure TForm1.ReadUserRequest;
begin
```

```
    {retrieve the selected mapping mode}
    case RadioGroup1.ItemIndex of
      0: MyMapMode := MM_TEXT;
      1: MyMapMode := MM_ANISOTROPIC;
      2: MyMapMode := MM_ISOTROPIC;
      3: MyMapMode := MM_HIENGLISH;
      4: MyMapMode := MM_HIMETRIC;
      5: MyMapMode := MM_LOENGLISH;
      6: MyMapMode := MM_LOMETRIC;
      7: MyMapMode := MM_TWIPS;
    end;
end;

procedure TForm1.PaintImage;
begin
  {erase the previous image}
  Panel1.Repaint;

  {get the values of the user controls}
  ReadUserRequest;

  {set the Map Mode according to the radio group}
  SetMapMode(MyDisplayDC,MyMapMode);

  {offset the window origin by the specified amount}
  OffsetWindowOrgEx(MyDisplayDC,
    StrToInt(EditOWX.text),StrToInt(EditOWY.text),
    @PrevWindowPoint);

  {offset the viewport origin by the specified amount}
  OffSetViewportOrgEx(MyDisplayDC,
    StrToInt(EditOVX.text),StrToInt(EditOVY.text),
    @PrevViewportPoint);

  {scale the window extents by the specified amount}
  ScaleWindowExtEx(MyDisplayDC,
    StrToInt(EditSWEXM.text),StrToInt(EditSWEXD.text),
    StrToInt(EditSWEYM.text),StrToInt(EditSWEYD.text),
    @PrevWindowSize);

  {scale the viewport extents by the specified amount}
  ScaleViewportExtEx(MyDisplayDC,
    StrToInt(EditSVEXM.text),StrToInt(EditSVEXD.text),
    StrToInt(EditSVEYM.text),StrToInt(EditSVEYD.text),
    @PrevViewportSize);

  {draw the image. note that the coordinates used are hard coded and do not
   change, demonstrating how the window origin and extents affect drawing
   operations}
  Windows.Rectangle(MyDisplayDC, 0, 0, 50, 50);
  Windows.Rectangle(MyDisplayDC, -25, 24, 75, 26);
  Windows.Rectangle(MyDisplayDC, 24, -25, 26, 75);

  {display the new origin and extent values}
  ReportPosition;
end;
```

```pascal
procedure TForm1.FormPaint(Sender: TObject);
begin
  {paint the image}
  PaintImage;
end;

procedure TForm1.FormCreate(Sender: TObject);
begin
  {retrieve a handle to the panel's device context}
  MyDisplayDC := GetDC(Panel1.handle);
end;

procedure TForm1.FormDestroy(Sender: TObject);
begin
  {release the device context}
  ReleaseDC(Panel1.handle,MyDisplayDC);
end;

procedure TForm1.BitBtn1Click(Sender: TObject);
var
  MyPoint: TPoint;    // holds converted points
begin
  {convert device units to logical units with DPtoLP}
  MyPoint.X := StrToInt(EditDevX.text);
  MyPoint.Y := StrToInt(EditDevY.text);

  {check for errors}
  if not DPtoLP(MyDisplayDC,MyPoint,1) then
    ShowMessage('Error in device coordinates')
  else
  begin
    {MyPoint now contains converted logical coordinates}
    EditLogX.text := IntToStr(MyPoint.X);
    EditLogY.text := IntToStr(MyPoint.Y);
  end;
end;

procedure TForm1.BitBtn2Click(Sender: TObject);
var
  MyPoint: TPoint;    // holds converted points
begin
  {convert device units to logical units with DPtoLP}
  MyPoint.X := StrToInt(EditLogX.Text);
  MyPoint.Y := StrToInt(EditLogY.Text);

  {check for errors}
  if not LPtoDP(MyDisplayDC,MyPoint,1) then
    ShowMessage('Error in logical coordinates')
  else
  begin
    {MyPoint now contains converted device coordinates}
    EditDevX.Text := IntToStr(MyPoint.X);
    EditDevY.Text := IntToStr(MyPoint.Y);
  end;
end;
```

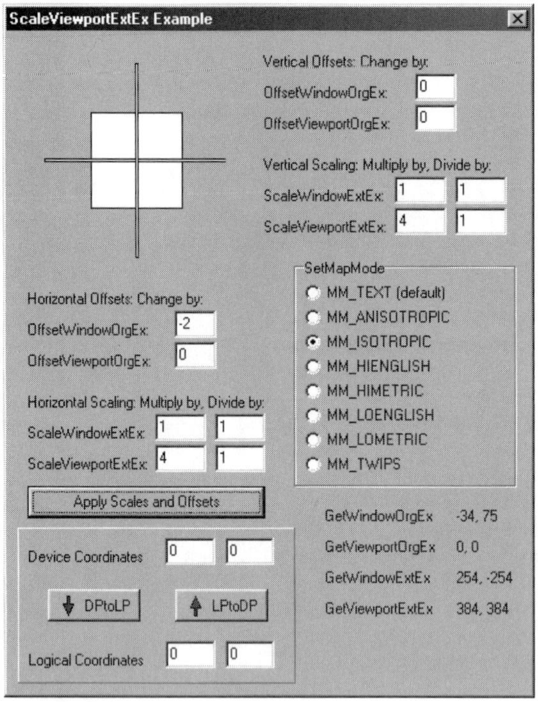

334 ■ Chapter 9

*Figure 9-11:
The scaled
image*

ScaleWindowExtEx   Windows.pas

Syntax

```
ScaleWindowExtEx(
DC: HDC;              {the handle of a device context}
XM: Integer;          {the horizontal multiplier}
XD: Integer;          {the horizontal divisor}
YM: Integer;          {the vertical multiplier}
YD: Integer;          {the vertical divisor}
Size: PSize           {a pointer to the previous extents}
): BOOL;              {returns TRUE or FALSE}
```

Description

The ScaleWindowExtEx function modifies the existing extents of the window associated with the specified device context, according to the specified scaling factors. For horizontal and vertical extents, a multiplier and divisor parameter is available for making the extent in that direction larger or smaller. Parameters not used should be supplied with a value of 1. For example, making the horizontal extent half of the current value would require the XD parameter to be set to 2. All other parameters would be 1. Making the horizontal extent three-fourths of its current value could be accomplished by setting the XM parameter to 3 and the XD parameter to 4.

Parameters

DC: The handle of the device context whose associated window extents are to be scaled.

XM: The horizontal extent multiplier.

XD: The horizontal extent divisor.

YM: The vertical extent multiplier.

YD: The vertical extent divisor.

Size: A pointer to a TSize structure that receives the previous extent values.

Return Value

If the function succeeds, it returns TRUE; otherwise, it returns FALSE.

See Also

GetWindowExtEx, ScaleViewportExtEx

Example

See Listing 9-12 under ScaleViewportExtEx.

ScreenToClient Windows.pas

Syntax

```
ScreenToClient(
hWnd: HWND;              {the handle of a window}
var lpPoint: TPoint      {a pointer to a TPoint structure}
): BOOL;                 {returns TRUE or FALSE}
```

Description

This function changes the coordinates of a point from screen coordinates to client coordinates. The point to be translated is in a TPoint structure pointed to by the lpPoint parameter. The function takes the coordinates pointed to by the lpPoint parameter and converts them into coordinates relative to the client area of the specified window. The results are placed back into this TPoint structure. The coordinates of the point being passed use the upper-left corner of the screen as the origin. The coordinates of the result use the upper-left corner of the client area of the specified window as the origin.

Parameters

hWnd: The handle to the window to which the point is converted. When the function returns, the point will be relative to the upper-left corner of the client area of this window.

lpPoint: A pointer to a TPoint structure that contains the point to be converted. This TPoint structure receives the converted point when the function returns.

Return Value

If the function succeeds, it returns TRUE; otherwise, it returns FALSE.

See Also

ClientToScreen, MapWindowPoints

Example

See Listing 9-4 under ClientToScreen.

ScrollDC   Windows.pas

Syntax

```
ScrollDC(
DC: HDC;                   {the handle of a device context}
DX: Integer;               {the horizontal scroll increment}
DY: Integer;               {the vertical scroll increment}
var Scroll: TRect;         {the scrolling rectangle}
Clip: TRect;               {the clipping rectangle}
Rgn: HRGN;                 {the exposed region}
Update: PRect              {the exposed rectangle}
): BOOL;                   {returns TRUE or FALSE}
```

Description

The ScrollDC function scrolls a rectangle of bits horizontally and vertically. The amount of scrolling is given in device units.

Parameters

DC: The handle to the device context that contains the rectangle where the bits are to be scrolled.

DX: The number of horizontal device units to scroll by. This value is positive for scrolling to the right, and negative for scrolling to the left.

DY: The number of vertical device units to scroll by. This value is positive for scrolling down, and negative for scrolling up.

Scroll: Specifies a TRect structure that contains the location of the rectangle to be scrolled.

Clip: Specifies a TRect structure that contains the location of the clipping rectangle.

Rgn: Specifies the handle of the region that the scrolling process uncovers. This region is not limited to being a rectangle. This parameter may be set to zero if the update region is not needed.

Update: A pointer to a TRect structure that receives the location of the rectangle uncovered by the scrolled area. The coordinates of this rectangle are given in client coordinates regardless of the current mapping mode of the specified device context. This parameter can be set to NIL if the update rectangle is not needed.

Return Value

If the function succeeds, it returns TRUE; otherwise, it returns FALSE.

See Also

BitBlt, InvalidateRect, InvalidateRgn

Example

Listing 9-13: Scrolling an image inside of a viewing area

```
var
  Form1: TForm1;
  PreviousX, PreviousY: Integer;       // tracks the previous scroll offset

implementation

{$R *.DFM}

procedure TForm1.FormCreate(Sender: TObject);
begin
  {initialize the scroll bars}
  ScrollBar1.Max := Image1.Picture.Bitmap.Width-Image1.Width;
  ScrollBar2.Max := Image1.Picture.Bitmap.Height-Image1.Height;

  {initialize the offset tracking variables}
  PreviousX := 0;
  PreviousY := 0;
end;

procedure TForm1.ScrollBar1Change(Sender: TObject);
var
  ScrollRect,               // the rectangular area to be scrolled
  ClipRect,                 // the clipping rectangle of the scrolled area
  UpdateRect: TRect;        // the area uncovered by scrolling
begin
  {initialize the scrolling and clipping rectangles to the entire area
   of the image}
  ScrollRect := Image1.BoundsRect;
  ClipRect := Image1.BoundsRect;

  {scroll the area horizontally by the specified amount}
  ScrollDC(Canvas.Handle, PreviousX-ScrollBar1.Position, 0, ScrollRect,
           ClipRect, 0, @UpdateRect);

  {copy the appropriate area of the original bitmap into the newly uncovered
   area}
  Canvas.CopyRect(UpdateRect, Image1.Picture.Bitmap.Canvas,
                  Rect((UpdateRect.Left-Image1.Left)+ScrollBar1.Position,
                       ScrollBar2.Position, (UpdateRect.Left-Image1.Left)+
                       ScrollBar1.Position+(UpdateRect.Right-UpdateRect.Left),
                       Image1.Height+ScrollBar2.Position));

  {record the current position}
  PreviousX := ScrollBar1.Position;
end;

procedure TForm1.ScrollBar2Change(Sender: TObject);
var
  ScrollRect,               // the rectangular area to be scrolled
  ClipRect,                 // the clipping rectangle of the scrolled area
  UpdateRect: TRect;        // the area uncovered by scrolling
begin
  {initialize the scrolling and clipping rectangles to the entire area
```

```
    of the image}
ScrollRect := Image1.BoundsRect;
ClipRect := Image1.BoundsRect;

{scroll the area vertically by the specified amount}
ScrollDC(Canvas.Handle, 0, PreviousY-ScrollBar2.Position, ScrollRect,
         ClipRect, 0, @UpdateRect);

{copy the appropriate area of the original bitmap into the newly uncovered
 area}
Canvas.CopyRect(UpdateRect, Image1.Picture.Bitmap.Canvas,
                Rect(ScrollBar1.Position, (UpdateRect.Top-Image1.Top)+
                ScrollBar2.Position, Image1.Width+ScrollBar1.Position,
                (UpdateRect.Top-Image1.Top)+ScrollBar2.Position+
                (UpdateRect.Bottom-UpdateRect.Top)));

{record the current position}
PreviousY := ScrollBar2.Position;
end;
```

Figure 9-12: The scrolled image

SetMapMode   Windows.pas

Syntax

SetMapMode(
DC: HDC;   {the handle of a device context}
p2: Integer   {the mapping mode}
): Integer;   {returns the previous mapping mode}

Description

This function sets a new method for mapping graphical units on the specified device context. The units may be measured in terms of pixels, inches, millimeters, or printer's points. The orientation of the x and y axes may also be set. This function is used to determine how software defined measurements are mapped to the physical graphical devices.

Parameters

DC: A handle to the device context whose mapping mode is to be set.

p2: A flag indicating the new mapping mode. This parameter can be set to one value from Table 9-17.

Graphical Device Interface Functions   339

Return Value

If the function succeeds, it returns the value of the previous mapping mode, and will be one value from the following table. If the function fails, it returns a zero.

See Also

GetMapMode, SetViewportExtEx, SetViewportOrgEx, SetWindowExtEx, SetWindowOrgEx

Example

See Listing 9-2 in the section titled "Mapping Modes."

Table 9-17: SetMapMode p2 values

Value	Description
MM_ANISOTROPIC	The units, scaling, and orientation are set by SetWindowExtEx and SetViewportExtEx. The x- and y-axis scaling are set independently and are not required to be the same.
MM_HIENGLISH	High-resolution mapping in English units. Each unit is 0.001 inch with x being positive to the right and y being positive in the upward direction.
MM_HIMETRIC	High-resolution mapping in metric units. Each unit is 0.01 millimeter with x being positive to the right and y being positive in the upward direction.
MM_ISOTROPIC	The units, scaling, and orientation are set by SetWindowExtEx and SetViewportExtEx with the horizontal and vertical units set as equal. The units and orientation are settable, but the units for the x- and y-axes are forced to be the same by the GDI. This mode ensures a 1:1 aspect ratio.
MM_LOENGLISH	Low-resolution mapping in English units. Each unit is 0.01 inch with x being positive to the right and y being positive in the upward direction.
MM_LOMETRIC	Low-resolution mapping in metric units. Each unit is 0.1 millimeter with x being positive to the right and y being positive in the upward direction.
MM_TEXT	Each unit is mapped to one device pixel. This is not a device-independent setting. Devices with different resolutions or scalings will have different results from graphical functions, with x being positive to the right and y being positive in the downward direction. This is the default setting.
MM_TWIPS	Each unit is mapped to 1/1440 inch, which is 1/20 of a printer's point. Coordinates are oriented with x being positive to the right and y being positive in the upward direction.

SetViewportExtEx   Windows.pas

Syntax

```
SetViewportExtEx(
  DC: HDC;           {the handle of a device context}
  XExt: Integer;     {the new horizontal extent}
  YExt: Integer;     {the new vertical extent}
  Size: PSize        {a pointer to the original extent}
): BOOL;             {returns TRUE or FALSE}
```

Description

This function establishes a new size for the viewport associated with the specified device context. Calls to this function are only valid when the SetMapMode function has set the mapping mode of the specified device context to MM_ANISOTROPIC or MM_ISOTROPIC. Calls to SetViewportExtEx are ignored for any other map modes. In the case of MM_ISOTROPIC, a call to the SetWindowExtEx function must be made before the SetViewportExtEx function is used.

Parameters

DC: A handle to the device context whose associated viewport's size is being modified.

XExt: The new horizontal size of the viewport in device units.

YExt: The new vertical size of the viewport in device units.

Size: A pointer to a TSize structure that receives the previous size of the viewport. If this parameter is set to NIL, the previous size is not returned.

Return Value

If the function succeeds, it returns TRUE; otherwise, it returns FALSE.

See Also

GetMapMode, GetViewportExtEx, SetMapMode, SetWindowExtEx

Example

See Listing 9-2 in the section titled "Mapping Modes."

SetViewportOrgEx   Windows.pas

Syntax

```
SetViewportOrgEx(
  DC: HDC;              {the handle of a device context}
  X: Integer;           {the new x value of origin}
  Y: Integer;           {the new y value of origin}
  Point: PPoint         {a pointer to the original origin values}
): BOOL;                {returns TRUE or FALSE}
```

Description

This function establishes a new coordinate system origin for the specified device context. Devices normally set their origin in the upper-left corner of their displayed or printed image. The SetViewportOrgEx function may be useful when plotting functions that will display negative values. By locating the origin of the device context where the origin of a graph is located (traditionally in the lower-left corner), an application can avoid performing a coordinate transform for every point that is plotted. Due to a small amount of overhead incurred by the GDI in accepting a new coordinate system origin, an application should be tested for speed when deciding to use this function. An application that already performs a calculation to plot points on a device context might run faster if the device origin is left at the default location while the application performs calculations that account for that location of the device origin.

Parameters

DC: The handle of the device context whose viewport origin is to be modified.

X: The horizontal location of the new origin in device units.

Y: The vertical location of the new origin in device units.

Point: A pointer to a TPoint structure that receives the location of the previous origin location in device units. If this parameter is set to NIL, the previous origin location is not returned.

Return Value

If the function succeeds, it returns TRUE; otherwise, it returns FALSE.

See Also

GetViewportOrgEx, SetWindowOrgEx

Example

See Listing 9-2 in the section titled "Mapping Modes."

SetWindowExtEx   Windows.pas

Syntax

```
SetWindowExtEx(
  DC: HDC;                {the handle of a device context}
  XExt: Integer;          {the new horizontal extent}
  YExt: Integer;          {the new vertical extent}
  Size: PSize             {a pointer to the original extent}
): BOOL;                  {returns TRUE or FALSE}
```

Description

This function establishes a new size for the window associated with the specified device context. Calls to this function are only valid when the SetMapMode function has set the mapping mode of the specified device context to MM_ANISOTROPIC or MM_ISOTROPIC. Calls to the SetWindowExtEx function are ignored with other mapping modes. In the case of MM_ISOTROPIC, a call to the SetWindowExtEx function must be made before the SetViewportExtEx function is used.

Parameters

DC: The handle of the device context whose associated window size is to be modified.

XExt: The new horizontal size of the window in device units.

YExt: The new vertical size of the window in device units.

Size: A pointer to a TSize structure that receives the previous size of the window. If this parameter is set to NIL, the previous size is not returned.

Return Value

If the function succeeds, it returns TRUE; otherwise, it returns FALSE.

See Also

GetMapMode, GetWindowExtEx, SetMapMode, SetViewportExtEx

Example

See Listing 9-2 in the section titled "Mapping Modes."

SetWindowOrgEx   Windows.pas

Syntax

```
SetWindowOrgEx(
 DC: HDC;              {the handle of a device context}
 X: Integer;           {the new horizontal location of the origin}
 Y: Integer;           {the new vertical location of the origin}
 Point: PPoint         {a pointer to the original origin values}
): BOOL;               {returns TRUE or FALSE}
```

Description

SetWindowOrgEx establishes a new coordinate system origin for the window associated with the specified device context. A window will normally have its origin in its upper-left corner. The SetWindowOrgEx function may be useful when plotting functions that will display negative values. By making the origin of the window and the origin of a graph coincide at the same point, an application can avoid performing a coordinate transform for every point that is plotted. Due to a small amount of overhead incurred by the GDI in accepting a new coordinate system origin, an application should be tested for speed when deciding to use this function. An application that already performs a calculation to plot points on a device context might run faster if the window origin is left at the default location while the application performs calculations that account for that location of the window origin.

Parameters

DC: The handle of the device context whose associated window's origin is to be modified.

X: The horizontal location of the new origin in device units.

Y: The vertical location of the new origin in device units.

Point: A pointer to a TPoint structure which receives the location of the previous origin, in device units. If this parameter is set to NIL, the previous origin location is not returned.

Return Value

If the function succeeds, it returns TRUE; otherwise, it returns FALSE.

See Also

GetWindowOrgEx, SetViewportOrgEx

Example

See Listing 9-2 in the section titled "Mapping Modes."

Chapter 10

Painting and Drawing Functions

Windows provides a plethora of functions for drawing simple graphics and graphics primitives. Windows is quite capable of performing high-end graphics manipulation, as is evident by the amount of digital image manipulation software on the market. However, drawing a simple graphic is sometimes the most efficient means of communicating with the user. For example, a simple rectangle can be drawn around a portion of an image to indicate it has been selected. Windows itself makes heavy use of the functions in this chapter for drawing standard user interface elements and common controls. Delphi encapsulates a large portion of the functions presented in this chapter as methods and properties of the TCanvas object. However, the complexity of the VCL sometimes gets in the way, and dropping down to the Windows API level is the only way to go. This chapter describes the most common functions used to draw simple graphics onto a device context.

Graphical Objects

In order to draw onto a device context, Windows needs some method of knowing exactly what it is supposed to draw—what color the objects should be, how wide it is, etc. These attributes are encapsulated in a graphical object. All of the CreateXXX functions, such as CreateBrush, CreateBitmap, or CreatePen, return a handle to a graphical object. Internally, this handle references data that contains all of the attributes defining the object.

In order to use most graphical objects, they need to be selected into a device context by using the SelectObject function. Once an object is selected into a device context it is automatically used by those functions that need the specific object. For example, a new pen can be created with the CreatePen object and selected into a device context. From then on, any drawing functions that require a pen will use the specific pen selected into the device context automatically. Only one object of a given type can be selected into a device context at any given time.

It is important to delete a graphical object when it is no longer needed. Each graphical object handle represents a certain amount of memory and resources, taking away from the overall resources available to the system. Although low resources are less of a problem in 32-bit Windows than with previous Windows versions, memory leaks can occur if graphical objects are not deleted properly. To delete a graphical object, it must first be unselected from its device context. This is done by saving a handle to the original object when the new object was selected, and then reselecting the original object when the new one is to be disposed. Once the object is no longer selected into any device context, it can be deleted by calling the DeleteObject function.

Pens and Brushes

Perhaps the most commonly used graphical objects in Windows drawing functions are the pen and the brush. A brush defines a color and pattern used to fill the interiors of closed figures, such as polygons, rectangles, paths, and regions. A pen defines a color and pattern used to outline figures, both closed and open. These two graphical objects are encapsulated by Delphi as the Pen and Brush properties of a TCanvas object. Delphi fully encompasses all functionality offered by the Windows brush functions. However, Windows offers two styles of pens, cosmetic and geometric, and Delphi currently does not encapsulate all of the functionality offered by these objects.

Cosmetic Pens A cosmetic pen is measured in device units and cannot be scaled. Currently, Windows supports a cosmetic pen of only 1 pixel in width. The pen style can be set to various patterns ranging from solid to a variety of different dash and dot combinations. Drawing with cosmetic pens is much faster than geometric pens.

Geometric Pens A geometric pen is measured in logical units, and will scale accordingly. They support the same pen styles available for cosmetic pens, but they also support user-defined styles and styles normally available only to brushes. Additionally, geometric pens can apply an end cap style to the end points of lines, and a join style where two lines meet. The end cap and join styles are illustrated in the following figures.

Windows 95: Geometric pens do not support user-defined pen styles, cannot use most of the cosmetic pen styles, and can only be used when drawing paths.

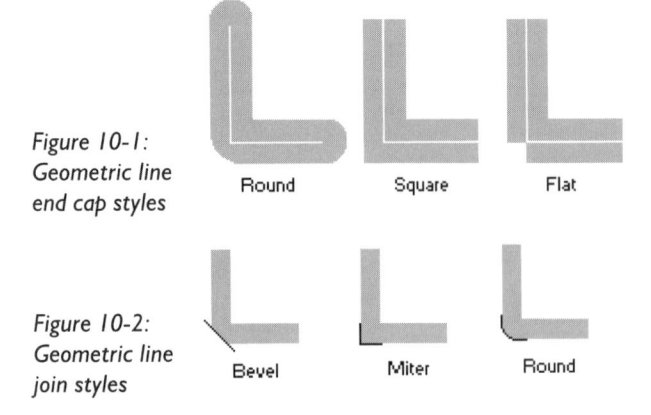

Figure 10-1: Geometric line end cap styles

Round   Square   Flat

Figure 10-2: Geometric line join styles

Bevel   Miter   Round

Delphi vs. the Windows API

The TCanvas, TBrush, and TPen objects do a wonderful job of encapsulating a majority of the painting and drawing functions that might be used for common purposes. However, Windows offers an extensive variety of functions above and beyond those encapsulated by these objects. Extended drawing capabilities offered by the API, including geometric and cosmetic pens and the myriad of region manipulation procedures, can add a wealth of functionality to your graphical Delphi applications without requiring vast amounts of custom coding.

Painting and Drawing Functions

The following painting and drawing functions are covered in this chapter:

Table 10-1: Painting and drawing functions

Function	Description
Arc	Draws an arc.
BeginPaint	Begins a painting operation.
Chord	Draws a chord.
CreateBrushIndirect	Creates a brush from a data structure.
CreateHatchBrush	Creates a hatch pattern brush.
CreatePatternBrush	Creates a pattern brush.
CreatePen	Creates a pen.
CreatePenIndirect	Creates a pen from a data structure.
CreateSolidBrush	Creates a brush of a solid color.
DeleteObject	Deletes a graphical object.
DrawCaption	Draws a window caption bar.
DrawEdge	Draws 3-D lines.
DrawFocusRect	Draws a focus rectangle.
DrawFrameControl	Draws standard user interface buttons.
DrawState	Draws disabled text or graphics.
Ellipse	Draws an ellipse.
EndPaint	Ends a painting operation.
EnumObjects	Enumerates graphical objects.
ExtCreatePen	Creates cosmetic or geometric pens.
ExtFloodFill	Fills an area with a color.
FillPath	Fills a path with a color.
FillRect	Fills a rectangle with a color.
FillRgn	Fills a region with a color.
FrameRect	Draws the perimeter of a rectangle.
FrameRgn	Draws the perimeter of a region.
GetBkColor	Retrieves the background color of a device context.
GetBkMode	Retrieves the background mode of a device context.
GetBoundsRect	Retrieves the accumulated bounding rectangle of a device context.
GetBrushOrgEx	Retrieves the origin of a brush pattern.
GetCurrentObject	Retrieves the currently selected object in a device context.
GetCurrentPositionEx	Retrieves the current position from a device context.
GetMiterLimit	Retrieves the miter limit of miter joined lines.
GetObject	Retrieves information about a graphical object.
GetObjectType	Determines the type of a graphical object.
GetPixel	Retrieves a pixel color.

Function	Description
GetPolyFillMode	Retrieves the current polygon fill mode.
GetROP2	Retrieves the foreground mix mode of a device context.
GetStockObject	Retrieves a handle to a predefined graphical object.
GetUpdateRect	Retrieves the bounding rectangle of the current update region.
GetUpdateRgn	Retrieves the update region.
GrayString	Draws a color-converted string.
InvalidateRect	Invalidates a rectangular area.
InvalidateRgn	Invalidates a region.
LineDDa	Draws a custom line.
LineTo	Draws a line.
LockWindowUpdate	Disables window painting.
MoveToEx	Moves the current position of a device context.
PaintDesktop	Paints the desktop wallpaper onto a device context.
PaintRgn	Fills a region with the current brush.
Pie	Draws a pie wedge.
PolyBezier	Draws a Bézier curve.
PolyBezierTo	Draws multiple Bézier curves.
Polygon	Draws a filled polygon.
Polyline	Draws a polygon outline.
PolylineTo	Draws a polygon outline, updating the current position.
PolyPolygon	Draws multiple filled polygons.
PolyPolyline	Draws multiple polygon outlines.
Rectangle	Draws a rectangle.
RoundRect	Draws a rounded rectangle.
SelectObject	Selects a graphical object into a device context.
SetBkColor	Sets the background color of a device context.
SetBkMode	Sets the background mode of a device context.
SetBoundsRect	Sets the bounding rectangle accumulation behavior.
SetBrushOrgEx	Sets the origin of a brush pattern.
SetMiterLimit	Sets the miter limit of miter joined lines.
SetPixel	Sets the color of a pixel in a device context.
SetPixelV	Sets the color of a pixel in a device context (generally faster than SetPixel).
SetPolyFillMode	Sets the polygon-filling mode.
SetROP2	Sets the foreground mix mode of the device context.
StrokeAndFillPath	Outlines and fills a path.
StrokePath	Outlines a path.

Arc   Windows.pas

Syntax

```
Arc(
  hDC: HDC;                {the handle of a device context}
  left: Integer;           {x coordinate of the upper-left corner}
```

top: Integer;	{y coordinate of the upper-left corner}
right: Integer;	{x coordinate of the lower-right corner}
bottom: Integer;	{y coordinate of the lower-right corner}
startX: Integer;	{x coordinate of the first radial ending point}
startY: Integer;	{y coordinate of the first radial ending point}
endX: Integer;	{x coordinate of the second radial ending point}
endY: Integer	{y coordinate of the second radial ending point}
): BOOL;	{returns TRUE or FALSE}

Description

This function draws an elliptical arc. The arc will be drawn with the current pen, and will not use or update the current position. The bounding rectangle defined by the left, top, right and bottom parameters defines the curve of the arc. The startX and startY parameters define the endpoints of a line starting from the center of the bounding rectangle and identify the starting location of the arc. The endX and endY parameters define the endpoints of a line starting from the center of the bounding rectangle and identify the ending location of the arc.

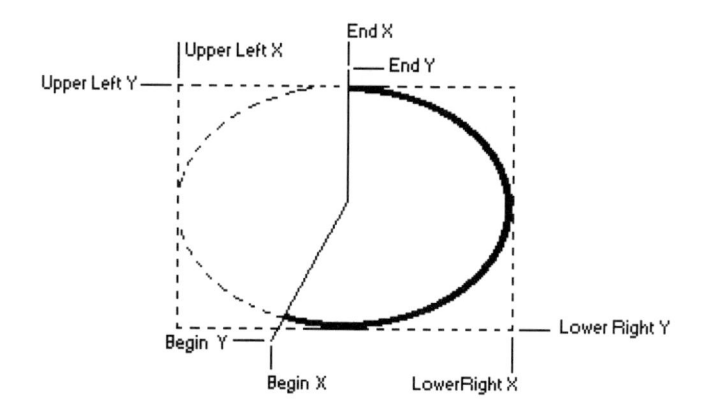

Figure 10-3:
Arc
coordinates

Parameters

hDC: Specifies the device context upon which the arc is drawn.

left: Specifies the horizontal coordinate of the upper-left corner of the bounding rectangle, in logical units.

Windows 95: The sum of the left and right parameters must be less than 32,767.

top: Specifies the vertical coordinate of the upper-left corner of the bounding rectangle, in logical units.

Windows 95: The sum of the top and bottom parameters must be less than 32,767.

right: Specifies the horizontal coordinate of the lower-right corner of the bounding rectangle, in logical units.

bottom: Specifies the vertical coordinate of the lower-right corner of the bounding rectangle, in logical units.

startX: Specifies the horizontal coordinate, in logical units, of the ending point of the radial line that defines the starting point of the arc.

startY: Specifies the vertical coordinate, in logical units, of the ending point of the radial line that defines the starting point of the arc.

endX: Specifies the horizontal coordinate, in logical units, of the ending point of the radial line that defines the ending point of the arc.

endY: Specifies the vertical coordinate, in logical units, of the ending point of the radial line that defines the ending point of the arc.

Return Value

If this function succeeds, it returns TRUE; otherwise, it returns FALSE.

See Also

Chord, Ellipse, Pie

Example

Listing 10-1: Drawing a rainbow

```
procedure TForm1.Button1Click(Sender: TObject);
var
  iCount: Integer;     // a general loop control variable
  ArcBounds: TRect;    // the bounding rectangle of the arc
begin
  {initialize the bounding rectangle}
  ArcBounds := PaintBox1.BoundsRect;

  {initialize the pen used to draw the arcs}
  PaintBox1.Canvas.Pen.Width := 2;

  {draw 5 arcs}
  for iCount := 1 to 5 do
  begin
    {Draw the arc}
    Arc(PaintBox1.Canvas.Handle, ArcBounds.Left, ArcBounds.Top, ArcBounds.Right,
        ArcBounds.Bottom,ArcBounds.Right, (ArcBounds.Bottom-ArcBounds.Top)div 2,
        ArcBounds.Left, (ArcBounds.Bottom-ArcBounds.Top)div 2);

    {reduce the size of the bounding rectangle for the next arc}
    InflateRect(ArcBounds, -2, -2);

    {change the color of the pen used to draw the next arc}
    PaintBox1.Canvas.Pen.Color := PaletteIndex(iCount+10);
  end;
end;
```

*Figure 10-4:
A rainbow
drawn with
arcs*

BeginPaint   Windows.pas

Syntax

```
BeginPaint(
    hWnd: HWND;                   {the handle of a window}
    var lpPaint: TPaintStruct     {a pointer to a TPaintStruct structure}
): HDC;                           {returns a device context handle}
```

Description

This function prepares the specified window for painting and fills the TPaintStruct structure pointed to by the lpPaint parameter with information concerning the painting operation. The BeginPaint function excludes any area outside of the update region by setting the clipping region of the device context. The update region is set by calling the InvalidateRect or InvalidateRgn functions, or by any action that affects the client area of the window, such as sizing, moving, scrolling, etc. BeginPaint sends a WM_ERASE-BKGND message to the window if the update region is marked for erasing. The BeginPaint function should be called in conjunction with EndPaint and only in response to a WM_PAINT message.

Parameters

hWnd: Specifies the handle of the window to be painted.

lpPaint: Specifies a pointer to a TPaintStruct structure that receives painting information. The TPaintStruct structure is defined as:

```
TPaintStruct = packed record
    hdc: HDC;                              {a handle to a device context}
    fErase: BOOL;                          {erase background flag}
    rcPaint: TRect;                        {painting rectangle coordinates}
    fRestore: BOOL;                        {reserved}
    fIncUpdate: BOOL;                      {reserved}
    rgbReserved: array[0..31] of Byte;     {reserved}
end;
```

hdc: Specifies the device context upon which painting operations should occur.

fErase: A flag indicating if the background should be erased. If this member is set to TRUE, the background of the device context should be erased before other drawing operations are performed. The application must handle erasing the background if the window class does not have a background brush.

rcPaint: A TRect structure defining the rectangular area within the device context where painting operations should occur.

fRestore: This member is reserved for internal use and should be ignored.

fIncUpdate: This member is reserved for internal use and should be ignored.

rgbReserved: This member is reserved for internal use and should be ignored.

Return Value

If this function succeeds, it returns a handle to the device context for the specified window; otherwise, it returns zero.

See Also

EndPaint, InvalidateRect, InvalidateRgn

Example

See Listing 10-29 under InvalidateRect and Listing 10-30 under InvalidateRgn.

Chord   Windows.pas

Syntax

```
Chord(
DC: HDC;                {the handle of a device context}
X1: Integer;            {x coordinate of the upper-left corner}
Y1: Integer;            {y coordinate of the upper-left corner}
X2: Integer;            {x coordinate of the lower-right corner}
Y2: Integer;            {y coordinate of the lower-right corner}
X3: Integer;            {x coordinate of the first radial ending point}
Y3: Integer;            {y coordinate of the first radial ending point}
X4: Integer;            {x coordinate of the second radial ending point}
Y4: Integer             {y coordinate of the second radial ending point}
): BOOL;                {returns TRUE or FALSE}
```

Description

This function draws a chord with the current pen and fills the chord with the current brush. A chord is a region bounded by an ellipse and a line segment. The extent of the chord is defined by the bounding rectangle. The curve is defined by a line identified by the X3, Y3, X4, and Y4 parameters. It will extend counterclockwise from the line's first intersection point on the bounding rectangle to the line's second intersection point on the bounding rectangle. If these two points are the same, a complete ellipse is drawn. This function will not affect the current position.

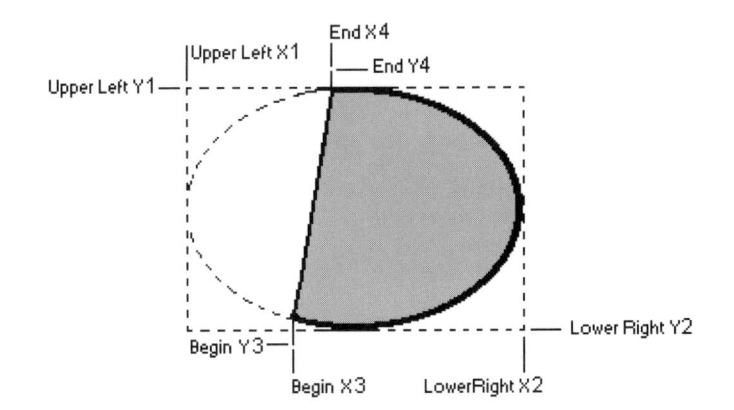

Figure 10-5: Chord coordinates

Parameters

DC: Specifies the device context upon which the chord is drawn.

X1: Specifies the horizontal coordinate of the upper-left corner of the bounding rectangle, in logical units.

Windows 95: The sum of the X1 and X2 parameters must be less than 32,767.

Y1: Specifies the vertical coordinate of the upper-left corner of the bounding rectangle, in logical units.

Windows 95: The sum of the Y1 and Y2 parameters must be less than 32,767.

X2: Specifies the horizontal coordinate of the lower-right corner of the bounding rectangle, in logical units.

Y2: Specifies the vertical coordinate of the lower-right corner of the bounding rectangle, in logical units.

X3: Specifies the horizontal coordinate, in logical units, of the ending point of the line that defines the starting point of the chord.

Y3: Specifies the vertical coordinate, in logical units, of the ending point of the line that defines the starting point of the chord.

X4: Specifies the horizontal coordinate, in logical units, of the ending point of the line that defines the ending point of the chord.

Y4: Specifies the vertical coordinate, in logical units, of the ending point of the line that defines the ending point of the chord.

Return Value

If this function succeeds, it returns TRUE; otherwise, it returns FALSE. To get extended error information, call the GetLastError function.

See Also

Arc, Ellipse, Pie

Example

Listing 10-2: Drawing a chord

```
procedure TForm1.Button1Click(Sender: TObject);
begin
  {initialize the brush and pen used to draw the chord}
  Canvas.Brush.Color := clLime;
  Canvas.Brush.Style := bsCross;
  Canvas.Pen.Color := clRed;

  {draw a chord}
  Chord(Canvas.Handle, 10, 10, 110, 110, 110, 85, 10, 85);
end;
```

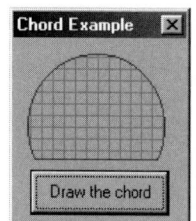

Figure 10-6: The chord

CreateBrushIndirect   Windows.pas

Syntax

CreateBrushIndirect(
const p1: TLogBrush   {a pointer to a TLogBrush structure}
): HBRUSH;   {returns a handle to a brush}

Description

This function creates a new brush based on the settings in the TLogBrush structure pointed to by the p1 parameter. If the brush's pattern is a monochrome bitmap, black pixels are drawn using the current text color and white pixels are drawn using the current background color. When the brush is no longer needed, it should be deleted by calling the DeleteObject function.

Parameters

p1: A pointer to a TLogBrush structure that defines the new brush. The TLogBrush structure is defined as:

TLogBrush = packed record
    lbStyle: UINT;   {brush style flag}
    lbColor: COLORREF;   {a color specifier}
    lbHatch: Longint;   {hatch style flag}
end;

    lbStyle: A flag indicating the brush style. This member can contain one value from Table 10-2.

lbColor: Specifies a color specifier defining the color of the brush. This member is ignored if the lbStyle member is set to BS_HOLLOW or BS_PATTERN. If the lbStyle member is set to BS_DIBPATTERN or BS_DIBPATTERNPT, the low-order word of this member will contain a flag indicating the type of color palette used by the DIB. This flag can be either DIB_PAL_COLORS, indicating that the DIB's palette is an array of indices into the currently realized logical palette, or DIB_RGB_COLORS, indicating that the DIB's palette is an array of literal RGB values.

lbHatch: Specifies a flag indicating the type of hatch style used by the brush. If the lbStyle member is set to BS_HATCHED, this member contains one flag from Table 10-3 specifying the orientation of the lines used to draw the hatch. If the lbStyle member is set to BS_DIBPATTERN, this member contains a handle to a packed DIB. If the lbStyle member is set to BS_DIBPATTERNPT, this member contains a pointer to a packed DIB. If the lbStyle member is set to BS_PATTERN, this member contains a handle to a bitmap. This bitmap handle cannot be a handle to a DIB. If the lbStyle member is set to BS_SOLID or BS_HOLLOW, this member is ignored.

Return Value

If the function succeeds, it returns the handle to a new brush; otherwise, it returns zero.

See Also

CreateDIBSection, CreateHatchBrush, CreatePatternBrush, CreateSolidBrush, DeleteObject, GetBrushOrgEx, SelectObject, SetBrushOrgEx

Example

Listing 10-3: Creating and using a new brush

```
procedure TForm1.Button1Click(Sender: TObject);
var
  Region: HRGN;             // a handle to a region
  LogBrush: TLogBrush;      // holds logical brush information
  NewBrush: HBrush;         // a handle to the new brush
begin
  {define the attributes of the new brush}
  with LogBrush do
  begin
    lbStyle := BS_HATCHED;
    lbColor := clBlue;
    lbHatch := HS_CROSS;
  end;

  {create the brush}
  NewBrush := CreateBrushIndirect(LogBrush);

  {create a region to fill}
  Region := CreateEllipticRgnIndirect(PaintBox1.BoundsRect);

  {fill the region with the new brush}
  FillRgn(PaintBox1.Canvas.Handle, Region, NewBrush);

  {delete the region and brush}
```

```
      DeleteObject(NewBrush);
      DeleteObject(Region);
   end;
```

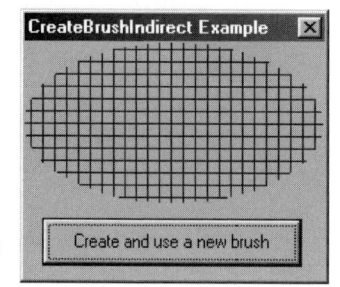

Figure 10-7:
The new brush pattern

Table 10-2: CreateBrushIndirect pl.lbStyle values

Value	Description
BS_DIBPATTERN	Indicates that the brush pattern is defined by a device-independent bitmap. The lbHatch member will contain a handle to the packed DIB used as the brush pattern.
	Windows 95: A DIB brush pattern can be no larger than 8 pixels square. If a DIB larger than this is specified as the pattern, only an 8-pixel square portion of the bitmap will be used.
BS_DIBPATTERNPT	Indicates that the brush pattern is defined by a device-independent bitmap. The lbHatch member will contain a pointer to the packed DIB used as the brush pattern.
	Windows 95: A DIB brush pattern can be no larger than 8 pixels square. If a DIB larger than this is specified as the pattern, only an 8-pixel square portion of the bitmap will be used.
BS_HATCHED	Indicates a hatched brush.
BS_HOLLOW	Indicates a hollow brush.
BS_PATTERN	Indicates that the brush pattern is defined by a device-dependent bitmap. The lbHatch member will contain a handle to the bitmap used as the brush pattern.
	Windows 95: A bitmap brush pattern can be no larger than 8 pixels square. If a bitmap larger than this is specified as the pattern, only an 8-pixel square portion of the bitmap will be used.
BS_SOLID	Indicates a solid brush.

Table 10-3: CreateBrushIndirect pl.lbHatch values

Value	Description
HS_BDIAGONAL	A hatch composed of 45-degree upward, left-to-right lines.
HS_CROSS	A hatch composed of horizontal and vertical lines.
HS_DIAGCROSS	Same as the HS_CROSS flag, rotated 45 degrees.
HS_FDIAGONAL	A hatch composed of 45-degree downward, left-to-right lines.
HS_HORIZONTAL	A hatch composed of horizontal lines.
HS_VERTICAL	A hatch composed of vertical lines.

CreateHatchBrush   Windows.pas

Syntax

```
CreateHatchBrush(
p1: Integer;              {the hatch style}
p2: COLORREF              {the color specifier}
): HBRUSH;                {returns a handle to a brush}
```

Description

This function creates a new brush with the specified color and hatch pattern. The patterns available for use by this function are illustrated in the following figure. If a hatch brush with the same pattern and color is used to paint the background of both a child window and its parent, it may be necessary to call the SetBrushOrgEx function to align the brush pattern before painting the background of the child window. When the brush is no longer needed, it should be deleted by calling the DeleteObject function.

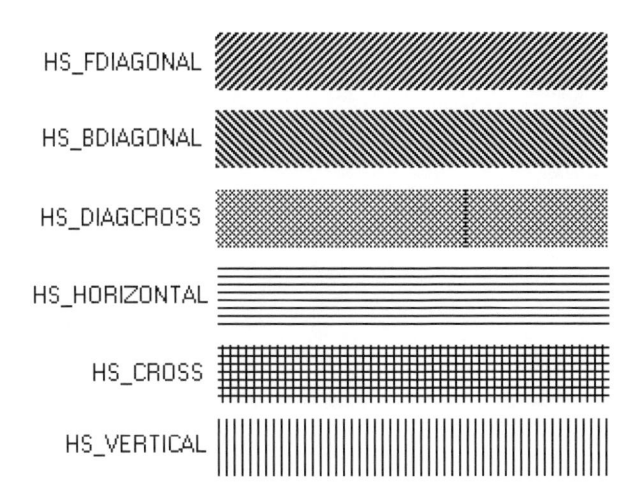

Figure 10-8: Hatch patterns

Parameters

p1: A flag specifying the hatch pattern of the brush. This parameter can be set to one value from Table 10-4.

p2: A color specifier indicating the foreground color used when drawing the hatch lines.

Return Value

If the function succeeds, it returns a handle to a new brush; otherwise, it returns zero.

See Also

CreateBrushIndirect, CreatePatternBrush, CreateSolidBrush, DeleteObject, GetBrushOrgEx, SelectObject, SetBrushOrgEx

Example

Listing 10-4: Creating a hatched brush

```
procedure TForm1.Button1Click(Sender: TObject);
var
   TheBrush: HBRUSH;     // holds the new brush
   HandleRgn: THandle;   // a region handle
begin
  {create the hatch brush}
  TheBrush := CreateHatchBrush(HS_DIAGCROSS, clRed);

  {create a region}
  HandleRgn := CreateEllipticRgnIndirect(ClientRect);

  {fill the region with the brush}
  FillRgn(Canvas.Handle, HandleRgn, TheBrush);

{delete the brush and region}
  DeleteObject(TheBrush);
  DeleteObject(HandleRgn);end;
```

Figure 10-9: The hatch brush

Table 10-4: CreateHatchBrush pl values

Value	Description
HS_BDIAGONAL	A hatch composed of 45-degree upward, left-to-right lines.
HS_CROSS	A hatch composed of horizontal and vertical lines.
HS_DIAGCROSS	Same as the HS_CROSS flag, rotated 45 degrees.
HS_FDIAGONAL	A hatch composed of 45-degree downward, left-to-right lines.
HS_HORIZONTAL	A hatch composed of horizontal lines.
HS_VERTICAL	A hatch composed of vertical lines.

CreatePatternBrush   Windows.pas

Syntax

```
CreatePatternBrush(
Bitmap: HBITMAP       {the handle of the bitmap}
): HBRUSH;            {returns a handle to the new brush}
```

Description

This function creates a new brush with the specified bitmap pattern. If the brush's pattern is a monochrome bitmap, black pixels are drawn using the current text color and white pixels are drawn using the current background color. When the brush is no longer needed, it should be deleted by calling the DeleteObject function. Note that deleting the brush does not delete the bitmap defining the brush's pattern.

Parameters

Bitmap: Specifies the handle of the bitmap used to define the brush pattern. This cannot be a handle to a DIB created by a call to the CreateDIBSection function.

> **Note:** Under Windows 95, a bitmap brush pattern can be no larger than 8 pixels square. If a bitmap larger than this is specified as the pattern, only an 8-pixel square portion of the bitmap will be used.

Return Value

If the function succeeds, it returns a handle to the new brush; otherwise, it returns zero.

See Also

CreateBitmap, CreateBitmapIndirect, CreateCompatibleBitmap, CreateDIBSection, CreateHatchBrush, DeleteObject, GetBrushOrgEx, LoadBitmap, SelectObject, SetBrushOrgEx

Example

Listing 10-5: Using a bitmap as a brush pattern

```
implementation

{$R *.DFM}
{$R BrushPatterns.Res}

procedure TForm1.Button1Click(Sender: TObject);
var
  NewBrush: HBrush;        // brush handle
  BitmapHandle: THandle;   // handle to a bitmap
begin
  {get a bitmap that is stored in the exe}
  BitmapHandle := LoadBitmap(Hinstance, 'BrushPattern');

  {Create the pattern brush with the bitmap as the pattern}
  NewBrush := CreatePatternBrush(BitmapHandle);

  {fill the region with the pattern using the brush}
  FillRect(Canvas.Handle, ClientRect, NewBrush);

  {clean up the memory}
```

```
DeleteObject(NewBrush);
DeleteObject(BitmapHandle);
end;
```

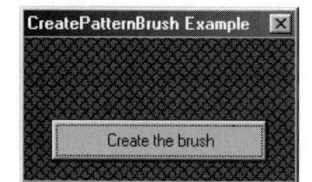

Figure 10-10:
The pattern brush

CreatePen   Windows.pas

Syntax

CreatePen(
Style: Integer;   {the pen style flag}
Width: Integer;   {the pen width}
Color: COLORREF   {the pen color}
): HPEN;   {returns the handle of a new pen}

Description

This function creates a new pen in the specified style, width, and color. When the pen is no longer needed, it should be deleted by calling the DeleteObject function.

Parameters

Style: A flag indicating the pen style. This parameter can be set to one value from Table 10-5.

Width: Specifies the width of the pen in logical units. A width of zero will create a pen exactly one pixel wide regardless of any current transformations. If this parameter is set to a value greater than one, the Style parameter must be set to the flags PS_NULL, PS_SOLID, or PS_INSIDEFRAME. If this parameter is greater than one and the Style parameter is set to PS_INSIDEFRAME, the line drawn with this pen will be inside the frame of all graphics primitives except those drawn with the polygon and polyline functions.

Color: A color specifier indicating the color of the pen.

Return Value

If the function succeeds, it returns a handle to the new pen; otherwise, it returns zero.

See Also

CreatePenIndirect, DeleteObject, ExtCreatePen, GetObject, SelectObject

Example

Listing 10-6: Creating a new pen

```
procedure TForm1.Button1Click(Sender: TObject);
var
  Style: Integer;      // holds the pen styles
  PenHandle: HPen;     // the handle of the pen
begin
  {erase any previous image}
  Canvas.Brush.Color := clBtnFace;
  Canvas.FillRect(Rect(10, 10, 111, 111));

  {determine the pen style}
  case RadioGroup1.ItemIndex of
    0: Style := PS_SOLID;
    1: Style := PS_DASH;
    2: Style := PS_DOT;
    3: Style := PS_DASHDOT;
    4: Style := PS_DASHDOTDOT;
    5: Style := PS_NULL;
    6: Style := PS_INSIDEFRAME;
  end;

  {create the pen}
  PenHandle := CreatePen(Style, 1, 0);

  {instruct the canvas to use the new pen}
  Canvas.Pen.Handle := PenHandle;

  {draw a square with the pen}
  Canvas.MoveTo(10, 10);
  Canvas.LineTo(110, 10);
  Canvas.LineTo(110, 110);
  Canvas.LineTo(10, 110);
  Canvas.LineTo(10, 10);

  {delete the pen}
  DeleteObject(PenHandle);
end;
```

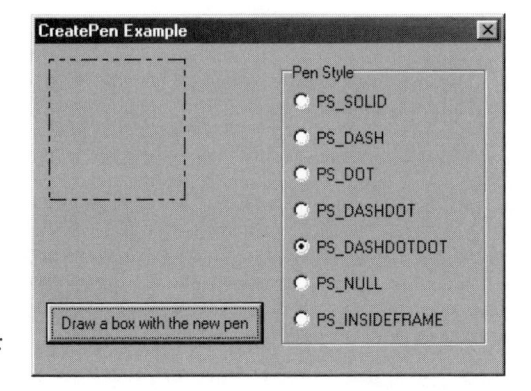

Figure 10-11:
The new pen

Table 10-5: CreatePen Style values

Value	Description
PS_SOLID	Specifies a solid pen.
PS_DASH	Specifies a dashed pen. This flag can be used only when the pen width is one or less.
PS_DOT	Specifies a dot pen. This flag can be used only when the pen width is one or less.
PS_DASHDOT	Specifies an alternating dash and dot pen. This flag can be used only when the pen width is one or less.
PS_DASHDOTDOT	Specifies an alternating dash dot dot pen. This flag can be used only when the pen width is one or less.
PS_NULL	Specifies an invisible pen.
PS_INSIDEFRAME	Specifies a solid pen. When this pen is used with drawing functions that require a bounding rectangle, the dimensions of the figure are shrunk to fit within the bounding rectangle with respect to the width of the pen.

CreatePenIndirect Windows.pas

Syntax

```
CreatePenIndirect(
const LogPen: TLogPen    {a pointer to a TLogPen structure}
): HPEN;                 {returns the handle of a new pen}
```

Description

This function creates a new pen in the style, width, and color specified by the TLogPen structure pointed to by the LogPen parameter. When the pen is no longer needed, it should be deleted by calling the DeleteObject function.

Parameters

LogPen: A pointer to a TLogPen structure defining the attributes of the new pen. The TLogPen structure is defined as:

```
TLogPen = packed record
     lopnStyle: UINT;         {the pen style}
     lopnWidth: TPoint;       {the pen width}
     lopnColor: COLORREF;     {the pen color}
end;
```

lopnStyle: A flag indicating the pen style. This member can be set to one value from Table 10-6.

lopnWidth: The x member of this TPoint structure specifies the width of the pen in logical units. The y member is not used. A width of zero will create a pen exactly one pixel wide regardless of any current transformations. If this member is set to a value greater than one, the lopnStyle member must be set to the flags PS_NULL, PS_SOLID, or PS_INSIDEFRAME. If this member is greater than one and the lopnStyle member is set to PS_INSIDEFRAME, the line drawn with this pen will be inside the frame of all graphics primitives except those drawn with the polygon and polyline functions.

lopnColor: A color specifier indicating the color of the pen.

Return Value

If the function succeeds, it returns a handle to the new pen; otherwise, it returns zero.

See Also

CreatePen, DeleteObject, ExtCreatePen, GetObject, SelectObject

Example

Listing 10-7: Creating a pen indirectly

```
procedure TForm1.Button1Click(Sender: TObject);
var
  Pen: TLogPen;      // the logical pen record
  PenHandle: HPen;   // the handle of a pen
begin
  {erase any previous image}
  Canvas.Brush.Color := clBtnFace;
  Canvas.FillRect(Rect(10, 10, 111, 111));

  {initialize the logical pen structure}
  with Pen do
  begin
    {determine the pen style}
    Case RadioGroup1.ItemIndex of
      0: lopnStyle := PS_SOLID;
      1: lopnStyle := PS_DASH;
      2: lopnStyle := PS_DOT;
      3: lopnStyle := PS_DASHDOT;
      4: lopnStyle := PS_DASHDOTDOT;
      5: lopnStyle := PS_NULL;
      6: lopnStyle := PS_INSIDEFRAME;
    end;

    {set the pen width and color}
    lopnWidth.X := 1;
    lopnColor   := clRed;
  end;

  {create the new pen}
  PenHandle := CreatePenIndirect(Pen);

  {draw a square with the new pen}
  Canvas.Pen.Handle := PenHandle;
  Canvas.MoveTo(10, 10);
  Canvas.LineTo(110, 10);
  Canvas.LineTo(110, 110);
  Canvas.LineTo(10, 110);
  Canvas.LineTo(10, 10);
```

Chapter 10

```
      {delete the new pen}
      DeleteObject(PenHandle);
   end;
```

Table 10-6: CreatePenIndirect LogPen.lopnStyle values

Value	Description
PS_SOLID	Specifies a solid pen.
PS_DASH	Specifies a dashed pen. This flag can be used only when the pen width is one or less.
PS_DOT	Specifies a dot pen. This flag can be used only when the pen width is one or less.
PS_DASHDOT	Specifies an alternating dash and dot pen. This flag can be used only when the pen width is one or less.
PS_DASHDOTDOT	Specifies an alternating dash dot dot pen. This flag can be used only when the pen width is one or less.
PS_NULL	Specifies an invisible pen.
PS_INSIDEFRAME	Specifies a solid pen. When this pen is used with drawing functions that require a bounding rectangle, the dimensions of the figure are shrunk to fit within the bounding rectangle with respect to the width of the pen.

CreateSolidBrush   Windows.pas

Syntax

```
CreateSolidBrush(
p1: COLORREF              {the brush color}
): HBRUSH;                {returns the handle of a new brush}
```

Description

This function creates a new solid brush in the specified color. Once the brush is no longer needed, it should be deleted by calling the DeleteObject function.

Parameters

p1: A color specifier indicating the color of the brush.

Return Value

If the function succeeds, it returns a handle to a new brush; otherwise, it returns zero.

See Also

CreateHatchBrush, CreatePatternBrush, DeleteObject, SelectObject

Example

Listing 10-8: Creating a solid brush

```
procedure TForm1.Button1Click(Sender: TObject);
var
  NewBrush: HBrush;    // the handle of the brush
  OldBrush: HBrush;    // the handle of the device context's original brush
```

```
      FormDC: HDC;          // the handle of the form device context
begin
  {create the brush}
  NewBrush := CreateSolidBrush(clGreen);

  {Get the form's device context}
  FormDC := GetDC(Form1.Handle);

  {Select the brush handle into the form's device context}
  SelectObject(FormDC, NewBrush);

  {fill a rectangle with the brush}
  FillRect(FormDC, Rect(10, 10, 170, 110), NewBrush);

  {clean up the memory}
  SelectObject(FormDC, OldBrush);
  DeleteObject(NewBrush);
end;
```

Figure 10-12: The solid brush

DeleteObject   Windows.pas

Syntax

```
DeleteObject(
  p1: HGDIOBJ              {a handle to a GDI object}
): BOOL;                   {returns TRUE or FALSE}
```

Description

This function will delete a logical pen, brush, font, bitmap, region, or palette, freeing its associated resources. The object's handle is invalidated when this function returns. This function will fail if it attempts to delete an object while it is selected into a device context.

Note: Deleting a pattern brush does not affect its bitmap. The brush's bitmap must be independently deleted.

Parameters

p1: Specifies the handle of the object to be deleted.

Chapter 10

Return Value

If the function succeeds, it returns TRUE. If the function fails, the specified handle is invalid, or the object is currently selected into a device context, it returns FALSE.

See Also

GetObject, SelectObject

Example

See Listing 10-3 under CreateBrushIndirect and other examples throughout the book.

DrawCaption   Windows.pas

Syntax

```
DrawCaption(
p1: HWND;                  {a handle to a window}
p2: HDC;                   {a handle to a device context}
const p3: TRect;           {the rectangular coordinates}
p4: UINT                   {drawing flags}
): BOOL;                   {returns TRUE or FALSE}
```

Description

This function draws a caption bar in the rectangular area identified by the p3 parameter. The caption bar retrieves its text and icon from the window identified by the p1 parameter.

Parameters

p1: A handle to the window containing the text and icon used in drawing the caption bar.

p2: A handle to the device context upon which the caption bar is drawn.

p3: Specifies the rectangular coordinates within which the caption bar is drawn.

p4: Specifies a series of flags defining drawing options. This parameter may be set to a combination of values from the following table.

Return Value

If the function succeeds, it returns TRUE; otherwise, it returns FALSE.

See Also

DrawEdge, DrawFocusRect, DrawFrameControl, DrawState, SetWindowRgn

Example

Listing 10-9: Programmatically drawing a caption bar

```
procedure TForm1.FormPaint(Sender: TObject);
begin
  DrawCaption(Handle, Canvas.Handle, Rect(16, 40, 288, 60),
           DC_ACTIVE or DC_ICON or DC_TEXT);
end;
```

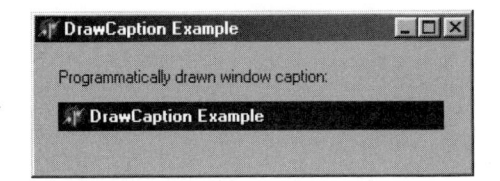

Figure 10-13:
The caption bar

Table 10-7: DrawCaption p4 values

Value	Description
DC_ACTIVE	The caption is drawn in the active caption color.
DC_GRADIENT	**Windows 98/Me/2000 or later:** Draws the caption as a color gradient.
DC_ICON	The window icon is drawn in the caption.
DC_INBUTTON	The caption is drawn in a pushed state.
DC_SMALLCAP	The text of the caption is drawn using the current small caption font.
DC_TEXT	The window text is drawn in the caption.

DrawEdge   Windows.pas

Syntax

```
DrawEdge(
hdc: HDC;                  {the device context}
var qrc: TRect;            {the rectangular coordinates}
edge: UINT;                {edge type flags}
grfFlags: UINT             {border type flags}
): BOOL;                   {returns TRUE or FALSE}
```

Description

This function draws a line or rectangle using the specified three-dimensional edge effect.

Parameters

hdc: Specifies the handle of the device context upon which the edge is drawn.

qrc: A pointer to a TRect structure containing the rectangular coordinates, in logical units, defining the edge.

edge: A series of flags specifying the type of edge to draw. This parameter must be set to a combination of one value from the inner border flags table (Table 10-8) and one value from the outer border flags table (Table 10-9). A single value from Table 10-10 can be used in place of the combined values.

grfFlags: A series of flags specifying the type of border to draw. This parameter can be set to a combination of flags from Table 10-11.

Return Value

If this function succeeds, it returns TRUE; otherwise, it returns FALSE. To get extended error information, call the GetLastError function.

Chapter 10

See Also

LineDDA, LineTo, MoveToEx, Rectangle

Example

Listing 10-10: Drawing 3-D edges

```
type
  TFlagsArray = array[0..18] of UINT;   // holds an array of border type flags

const
  {initialize the border flags array}
  BorderFlags: TFlagsArray = (BF_ADJUST, BF_BOTTOM, BF_BOTTOMLEFT,
                              BF_BOTTOMRIGHT, BF_DIAGONAL,
                              BF_DIAGONAL_ENDBOTTOMLEFT,
                              BF_DIAGONAL_ENDBOTTOMRIGHT,
                              BF_DIAGONAL_ENDTOPLEFT, BF_DIAGONAL_ENDTOPRIGHT,
                              BF_FLAT, BF_LEFT, BF_MIDDLE, BF_MONO, BF_RECT,
                              BF_RIGHT, BF_SOFT, BF_TOP, BF_TOPLEFT,
                              BF_TOPRIGHT);

procedure TForm1.Button1Click(Sender: TObject);
var
  TheRect: TRect;         // defines the edge rectangle
  Edge, Border: UINT;     // holds the edge flag values
  iCount: Integer;        // a general loop counter
begin
  {define the rectangle for the edge}
  TheRect := Rect(21, 200, 216, 300);

  {erase the last drawn edge}
  Canvas.Brush.Color := clBtnFace;
  Canvas.FillRect(TheRect);

  {define the kind of edge}
  case RadioGroup_Additional.ItemIndex of
   0: Edge := EDGE_BUMP;    //Combination BDR_RAISEDOUTER and BDR_SUNKENINNER
   1: Edge := EDGE_ETCHED;  //Combination BDR_SUNKENOUTER and BDR_RAISEDINNER
   2: Edge := EDGE_RAISED;  //Combination BDR_RAISEDOUTER and BDR_RAISEDINNER
   3: Edge := EDGE_SUNKEN;  //Combination BDR_SUNKENOUTER and BDR_SUNKENINNER
  end;

  {initialize the border flags}
  Border := 0;

  {determine the selected border type flags}
  for iCount := 0 to 18 do
    if CheckListBox2.Checked[iCount] then Border:=Border or BorderFlags[iCount];

  {draw the edge}
  DrawEdge(Canvas.Handle, TheRect, Edge, Border);
end;
```

Painting and Drawing Functions 369

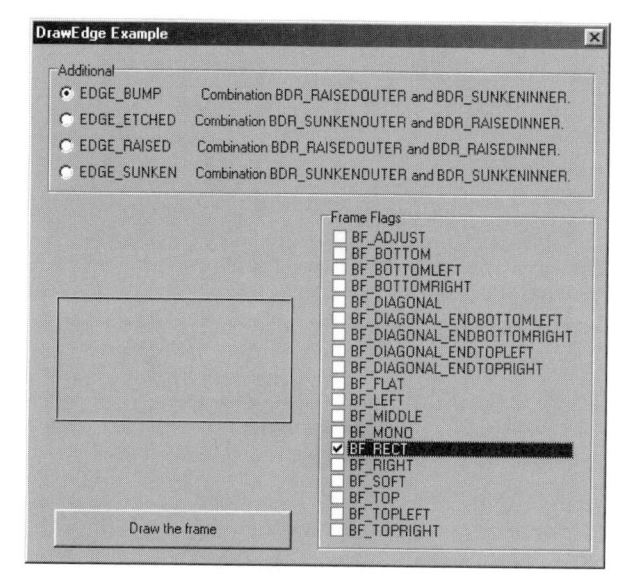

Figure 10-14:
An etched rectangle

Table 10-8: DrawEdge edge inner border flag values

Value	Description
BDR_RAISEDINNER	Indicates a raised inner edge.
BDR_SUNKENINNER	Indicates a sunken inner edge.

Table 10-9: DrawEdge edge outer border flag values

Value	Description
BDR_RAISEDOUTER	Indicates a raised outer edge.
BDR_SUNKENOUTER	Indicates a sunken outer edge.

Table 10-10: DrawEdge edge border combination flag values

Value	Description
EDGE_BUMP	Combination of BDR_RAISEDOUTER and BDR_SUNKENINNER.
EDGE_ETCHED	Combination of BDR_SUNKENOUTER and BDR_RAISEDINNER.
EDGE_RAISED	Combination of BDR_RAISEDOUTER and BDR_RAISEDINNER.
EDGE_SUNKEN	Combination of BDR_SUNKENOUTER and BDR_SUNKENINNER.

Table 10-11: DrawEdge grfFlags values

Value	Description
BF_ADJUST	The rectangular coordinates are decreased to account for the width of the edge lines.
BF_BOTTOM	Draws the bottom border of the rectangle.
BF_BOTTOMLEFT	Draws the bottom and left borders of the rectangle.

Value	Description
BF_BOTTOMRIGHT	Draws the bottom and right borders of the rectangle.
BF_DIAGONAL	Draws a diagonal border.
BF_DIAGONAL_ENDBOTTOMLEFT	Draws a diagonal border starting at the top-right corner and ending at the bottom left.
BF_DIAGONAL_ENDBOTTOMRIGHT	Draws a diagonal border starting at the top-left corner and ending at the bottom right.
BF_DIAGONAL_ENDTOPLEFT	Draws a diagonal border starting at the bottom-right corner and ending at the top left.
BF_DIAGONAL_ENDTOPRIGHT	Draws a diagonal border starting at the bottom-left corner and ending at the top right.
BF_FLAT	Draws a flat border.
BF_LEFT	Draws the left border of the rectangle.
BF_MIDDLE	Fills the interior of the rectangle.
BF_MONO	Draws a one-dimensional border.
BF_RECT	Draws a border around the entire rectangle.
BF_RIGHT	Draws the right border of the rectangle.
BF_SOFT	Draws the border in a soft style.
BF_TOP	Draws the top border of the rectangle.
BF_TOPLEFT	Draws the top and left borders of the rectangle.
BF_TOPRIGHT	Draws the top and right borders of the rectangle.

DrawFocusRect Windows.pas

Syntax

```
DrawFocusRect(
  hDC: HDC;              {the device context}
  const lprc: TRect      {the rectangular coordinates}
): BOOL;                 {returns TRUE or FALSE}
```

Description

This function draws a rectangle in a style that denotes focus. The rectangle is drawn using an XOR Boolean operation. Therefore, calling this function a second time with the same coordinates will erase the rectangle.

Parameters

hDC: A handle to the device context upon which the rectangle is drawn.

lprc: Specifies the rectangular coordinates defining the borders of the drawn rectangle.

Return Value

If the function succeeds, it returns TRUE; otherwise, it returns FALSE. To get extended error information, call the GetLastError function.

See Also

DrawCaption, DrawEdge, DrawFrameControl, FrameRect, Rectangle, RoundRect

Example

Listing 10-11: Drawing a focus rectangle

```
procedure TForm1.Button1Click(Sender: TObject);
var
  MyRect: TRect; // the focus rectangle coordinates
begin
  {set up the rectangle}
  MyRect := Rect(14, 10, 151, 90);

  {draw the focus rectangle}
  if not(DrawFocusRect(Canvas.Handle, MyRect)) then
    ShowMessage('DrawFocusRect not working');
end;
```

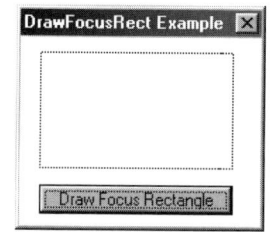

*Figure 10-15:
The focus
rectangle*

DrawFrameControl   Windows.pas

Syntax

```
DrawFrameControl(
DC: HDC;                    {a handle to a device context}
const Rect: TRect;          {the rectangular coordinates}
uType: UINT;                {frame control type flags}
uState: UINT                {frame control state flags}
): BOOL;                    {returns TRUE or FALSE}
```

Description

This function draws various system-defined buttons in the specified style and state.

Parameters

DC: The handle of the device context upon which the frame control is drawn.

Rect: Specifies the rectangular coordinates defining the size of the frame control.

uType: A series of flags indicating the type of frame control to be drawn. This parameter can be set to one value from Table 10-12.

uState: A series of flags indicating the state of the frame control to be drawn. This parameter can be a combination of flags from Tables 10-13 to 10-16, and is dependent upon the value of the uType parameter. For each uType parameter value, a separate table is given. One value may be taken from the table appropriate for the uType value, and can be combined with one or more values from the general state flags table (Table 10-17).

Return Value

If the function succeeds, it returns TRUE; otherwise, it returns FALSE. To get extended error information, call the GetLastError function.

See Also

DrawCaption, DrawEdge, DrawFocusRect, DrawState

Example

Listing 10-12: Drawing various frame controls

```
procedure TForm1.Button1Click(Sender: TObject);
var
  TheRect: TRect;      // the bounding rectangle for the control image
  TheType: UINT;       // holds the type of control
  TheState: UINT;      // holds the state of the control
begin
  {initialize the type and state flags}
  TheType := 0;
  TheState := 0;

  {define the bounding rectangle}
  TheRect := Rect(10, 10, 50, 50);

  {choose the type of frame control}
  case RadioGroup_ButtonType.ItemIndex of
    0:
    begin
      {indicate we are drawing a button}
      TheType := DFC_BUTTON;

      {choose the state of the control}
      case RadioGroup1.ItemIndex of
        0: TheState := DFCS_BUTTON3STATE;
        1: TheState := DFCS_BUTTONCHECK;
        2: TheState := DFCS_BUTTONPUSH;
        3: TheState := DFCS_BUTTONRADIO;
        4: TheState := DFCS_BUTTONRADIOIMAGE;
        5: TheState := DFCS_BUTTONRADIOMASK;
      end;
    end;
    1:
    begin
      {indicate we are drawing a caption bar button}
      TheType := DFC_CAPTION;

      {chose the state of the control}
      case RadioGroup2.ItemIndex of
        0: TheState := DFCS_CAPTIONCLOSE;
        1: TheState := DFCS_CAPTIONHELP;
        2: TheState := DFCS_CAPTIONMAX;
        3: TheState := DFCS_CAPTIONMIN;
        4: TheState := DFCS_CAPTIONRESTORE;
      end;
    end;
```

```
    2:
    begin
      {indicate we are drawing a menu item bitmap}
      TheType := DFC_MENU;

      {chose the state of the control}
      case RadioGroup3.ItemIndex of
        0: TheState := DFCS_MENUARROW;
        1: TheState := DFCS_MENUBULLET;
        2: TheState := DFCS_MENUCHECK;
      end;
    end;
    3:
    begin
      {indicate we are drawing a scroll bar button}
      TheType := DFC_SCROLL;

      {chose the TheState of the control}
      case RadioGroup4.ItemIndex of
        0: TheState := DFCS_SCROLLCOMBOBOX;
        1: TheState := DFCS_SCROLLDOWN;
        2: TheState := DFCS_SCROLLLEFT;
        3: TheState := DFCS_SCROLLRIGHT;
        4: TheState := DFCS_SCROLLSIZEGRIP;
        5: TheState := DFCS_SCROLLUP;
      end;
    end;
  end;

  {identify the state of the button}
  case RadioGroup5.ItemIndex of
    0:  TheState := TheState or DFCS_CHECKED;
    1:  TheState := TheState or DFCS_FLAT;
    2:  TheState := TheState or DFCS_INACTIVE;
    3:  TheState := TheState or DFCS_MONO;
    4:  TheState := TheState or DFCS_PUSHED;
  end;

  {erase any previous image}
  Canvas.Brush.Color := clBtnFace;
  Canvas.FillRect(TheRect);

  {draw the frame control}
  DrawFrameControl(Canvas.Handle, TheRect, TheType, TheState);
end;
```

Chapter 10

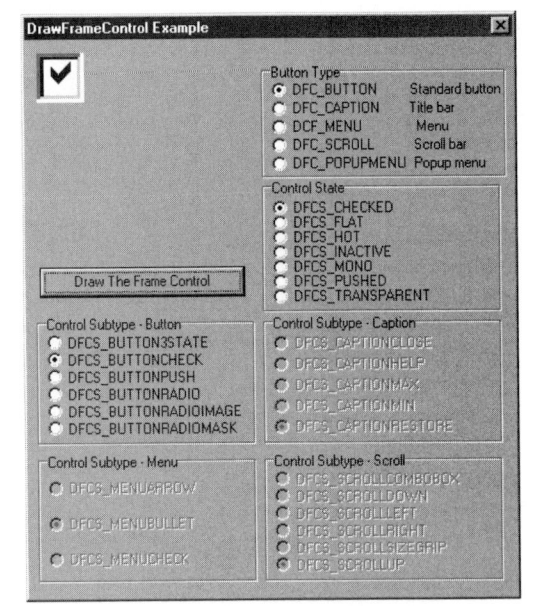

Figure 10-16: The frame control test bed

Table 10-12: DrawFrameControl uType values

Value	Description
DFC_BUTTON	Draws a standard button.
DFC_CAPTION	Draws caption bar buttons.
DFC_MENU	Draws images used in menus.
DFC_POPUPMENU	**Windows 98/Me/2000 or later:** Draws pop-up menu items.
DFC_SCROLL	Draws scroll bar buttons.

Table 10-13: DrawFrameControl uState values (for DFC_BUTTON)

Value	Description
DFCS_BUTTON3STATE	Draws a three-state button.
DFCS_BUTTONCHECK	Draws a check box.
DFCS_BUTTONPUSH	Draws a normal pushbutton.
DFCS_BUTTONRADIO	Draws a radio button.
DFCS_BUTTONRADIOIMAGE	Draws the radio button XOR mask.
DFCS_BUTTONRADIOMASK	Draws the radio button AND mask.

Table 10-14: DrawFrameControl uState values (for DFC_CAPTION)

Value	Description
DFCS_CAPTIONCLOSE	Draws a close button.
DFCS_CAPTIONHELP	Draws a help button.
DFCS_CAPTIONMAX	Draws a maximize button.

Value	Description
DFCS_CAPTIONMIN	Draws a minimize button.
DFCS_CAPTIONRESTORE	Draws a restore button.

Table 10-15: DrawFrameControl uState values (for DFC_MENU)

Value	Description
DFCS_MENUARROW	Draws a submenu arrow.
DFCS_MENUBULLET	Draws a bullet.
DFCS_MENUCHECK	Draws a check mark.

Table 10-16: DrawFrameControl uState values (for DFC_SCROLL)

Value	Description
DFCS_SCROLLCOMBOBOX	Draws a combo box drop-down button.
DFCS_SCROLLDOWN	Draws a scroll bar down button.
DFCS_SCROLLLEFT	Draws a scroll bar left button.
DFCS_SCROLLRIGHT	Draws a scroll bar right button.
DFCS_SCROLLSIZEGRIP	Draws a size grip.
DFCS_SCROLLUP	Draws a scroll bar up button.

Table 10-17: DrawFrameControl uState general state flags values

Value	Description
DFCS_ADJUSTRECT	The specified rectangle is reduced to exclude the surrounding edge of the control.
DFCS_CHECKED	Indicates that the button is pressed or checked.
DFCS_FLAT	Draws the button with a flat border.
DFCS_HOT	**Windows 98/Me/2000 or later:** Button is hot-tracked.
DFCS_INACTIVE	Draws the button as inactive (grayed).
DFCS_MONO	Draws the button with a monochrome border.
DFCS_PUSHED	Indicates that the button is pushed.
DFCS_TRANSPARENT	**Windows 98/Me/2000 or later:** Background is unaltered.

DrawState   Windows.pas

Syntax

```
DrawState(
  DC: HDC;                    {a handle to a device context}
  p2: HBRUSH;                 {the handle of a brush}
  p3: TFNDrawStateProc;       {the address of the callback function (optional)}
  p4: LPARAM;                 {bitmap or icon handle, or string pointer}
  p5: WPARAM;                 {string length}
  p6: Integer;                {the horizontal coordinate of the image location}
```

p7: Integer;   {the vertical coordinate of the image location}
p8: Integer;   {the image width}
p9: Integer;   {the image height}
p10: UINT   {image type and state flags}
): BOOL;   {returns TRUE or FALSE}

Description

This function displays an icon, bitmap, or text string, applying a visual effect to indicate its state. It can apply various state effects as determined by the flags specified in the p10 parameter, or it can call an application-defined callback function to draw complex, application-defined state effects.

Parameters

DC: A handle to the device context upon which the image is drawn.

p2: Specifies the handle of a brush. This brush will be used if the p10 parameter contains the DSS_MONO flag. If the p10 parameter does not contain this flag, this parameter is ignored.

p3: Specifies a pointer to an application-defined callback function. This function is called to draw the image in the specified state when the p10 parameter contains the DST_COMPLEX flag. If the p10 parameter does not contain this flag, this parameter is ignored.

p4: If the p10 parameter contains the DST_BITMAP flag, this parameter contains the handle to the bitmap to be drawn. If the p10 parameter contains the DST_ICON flag, this parameter contains the handle to the icon to be drawn. If the p10 parameter contains the DST_PREFIXTEXT or the DST_TEXT flags, this parameter contains a pointer to the string to be drawn. Otherwise, this parameter may be set to an application-defined value.

p5: Contains the length of the string to be drawn if the p10 parameter contains the DST_PREFIXTEXT or the DST_TEXT flags. This parameter may be set to zero if the strings are null-terminated. Otherwise, this parameter may be set to an application-defined value.

p6: Specifies the horizontal coordinate at which the image is drawn.

p7: Specifies the vertical coordinate at which the image is drawn.

p8: Specifies the width of the image, in device units. If the p10 parameter contains the DST_COMPLEX flag, this parameter is required. Otherwise, it can be set to zero, forcing the system to calculate the width of the image.

p9: Specifies the height of the image, in device units. If the p10 parameter contains the DST_COMPLEX flag, this parameter is required. Otherwise, it can be set to zero, forcing the system to calculate the height of the image.

p10: A series of flags indicating the image type and state. This parameter is set to a combination of one flag from the image type table (Table 10-18), and one flag from the image state table (Table 10-19).

Return Value

If the function succeeds, it returns TRUE; otherwise, it returns FALSE.

Callback Syntax

```
DrawStateProc(
  hDC: HDC;              {a handle to a device context}
  lData: LPARAM;         {application-defined data}
  wData: WPARAM;         {application-defined data}
  cx: Integer;           {the image width}
  cy: Integer            {the image height}
): BOOL;                 {returns TRUE or FALSE}
```

Description

This callback is used when the p10 parameter contains the DST_COMPLEX flag. Its purpose is to render the complex image in whatever manner desired. This callback function can perform any desired action.

Parameters

hDC: A handle to the device context upon which the image is drawn.

lData: Specifies application-specific data as passed to the DrawState function in the p4 parameter.

wData: Specifies application-specific data as passed to the DrawState function in the p5 parameter.

cx: Specifies the width of the image, in device units, as passed to the DrawState function in the p8 parameter.

cy: Specifies the width of the image, in device units, as passed to the DrawState function in the p9 parameter.

Return Value

The callback function should return TRUE to indicate that the function succeeded, or FALSE to indicate that it failed.

See Also

DrawFocusRect, DrawText, SetTextColor, TextOut

Example

Listing 10-13: Drawing images in a disabled state

```
procedure TForm1.FormPaint(Sender: TObject);
var
  Text: PChar;        // holds a string of text
begin
  {initialize the text string}
  Text := 'A DISABLED ICON';
```

```
         {draw the text to the screen in a disabled state}
         DrawState(Canvas.Handle, 0, nil, Integer(Text), 0, 20, 20, 0, 0,
                 DST_TEXT or DSS_DISABLED);

         {draw the application's icon in a disabled state}
         DrawState(Canvas.Handle, 0, nil, Application.Icon.Handle, 0, 50, 50, 0, 0,
                 DST_ICON or DSS_DISABLED);
    end;
```

Figure 10-17: The disabled images

Table 10-18: DrawState p10 image type values

Value	Description
DST_BITMAP	Indicates a bitmap image. The low-order word of the p4 parameter contains the bitmap handle.
DST_COMPLEX	Indicates an application-defined, complex image. The callback function identified by the p3 parameter is called to render the image.
DST_ICON	Indicates an icon image. The low-order word of p4 parameter contains the icon handle.
DST_PREFIXTEXT	Indicates that the image is text that may contain an accelerator mnemonic. Any ampersand (&) characters are translated into an underscore on the following character. The p4 parameter contains a pointer to the string, and the p5 parameter contains the string's length.
DST_TEXT	Indicates that the image is text. The p4 parameter contains a pointer to the string, and the p5 parameter contains the string's length.

Table 10-19: DrawState p10 image state values

Value	Description
DSS_DISABLED	Draws the image in an embossed form.
DSS_HIDEPREFIX	**Windows 2000 or later:** Ignores ampersand (&) characters in text, and will not underline the characters that follow. Must be used with DST_PREFIXTEXT.
DSS_MONO	Draws the image using the brush specified by the p2 parameter.
DSS_NORMAL	Draws the image in its original form.
DSS_PREFIXONLY	**Windows 2000 or later:** Draws only the underline at the position of the ampersand (&) character in the string (no actual string text is drawn). Must be used with DST_PREFIXTEXT.
DSS_RIGHT	Aligns text to the right.
DSS_UNION	Draws the image in a dithered form.

Ellipse   Windows.pas

Syntax

```
Ellipse(
  DC: HDC;          {the handle of the device context}
  X1: Integer;      {the horizontal coordinate of the upper-left corner}
  Y1: Integer;      {the vertical coordinate of the upper-left corner}
  X2: Integer;      {the horizontal coordinate of the lower-right corner}
  Y2: Integer       {the vertical coordinate of the lower-right corner}
): BOOL;            {returns TRUE or FALSE}
```

Description

This function draws an ellipse within the bounding rectangle defined by the X1, Y1, X2, and Y2 parameters. The center of the bounding rectangle defines the center of the ellipse. The ellipse is filled with the current brush and drawn with the current pen. The current position is neither used nor updated by this function.

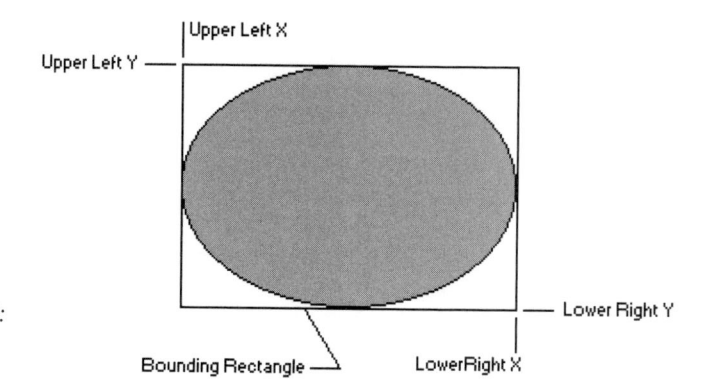

Figure 10-18:
Ellipse coordinates

Parameters

DC: A handle to the device context upon which the ellipse is drawn.

X1: Specifies the horizontal coordinate of the upper-left corner of the bounding rectangle defining the shape of the ellipse.

Windows 95: The sum of the X1 and X2 parameters must be less than 32,767.

Y1: Specifies the vertical coordinate of the upper-left corner of the bounding rectangle defining the shape of the ellipse.

Windows 95: The sum of the Y1 and Y2 parameters must be less than 32,767.

X2: Specifies the horizontal coordinate of the lower-right corner of the bounding rectangle defining the shape of the ellipse.

Y2: Specifies the vertical coordinate of the lower-right corner of the bounding rectangle defining the shape of the ellipse.

Return Value

If the function succeeds, it returns TRUE; otherwise, it returns FALSE. To get extended error information, call the GetLastError function.

See Also

Arc, Chord, CreateEllipticRgn, CreateEllipticRgnIndirect

Example

Listing 10-14: Drawing ellipses

```
procedure TForm1.Timer1Timer(Sender: TObject);
begin
  {set the canvas's brush to a random color}
  Canvas.Brush.Color := $01000000 or Random(10);

  {draw a random ellipse}
  Ellipse(Canvas.Handle, Random(ClientWidth), Random(ClientHeight),
          Random(ClientWidth), Random(ClientHeight))
end;
```

Figure 10-19: Random ellipses

EndPaint   Windows.pas

Syntax

```
EndPaint(
  hWnd: HWND;                    {the handle of a window}
  const lpPaint: TPaintStruct    {a pointer to a TPaintStruct structure}
): BOOL;                         {this function always returns TRUE}
```

Description

This function is used with the BeginPaint function to mark the end of painting operations in the specified window. Any caret hidden by the BeginPaint function will be restored.

Parameters

hWnd: Specifies the handle of the window being painted.

lpPaint: Specifies a pointer to a TPaintStruct structure containing painting information. The TPaintStruct structure is defined as:

```
TPaintStruct = packed record
     hdc: HDC;                          {a handle to a device context}
     fErase: BOOL;                      {erase background flag}
     rcPaint: TRect;                    {painting rectangle coordinates}
     fRestore: BOOL;                    {reserved}
     fIncUpdate: BOOL;                  {reserved}
     rgbReserved: array[0..31] of Byte; {reserved}
end;
```

See the BeginPaint function for a description of this data structure.

Return Value

This function always returns TRUE.

See Also

BeginPaint

Example

See Listing 10-29 under InvalidateRect and Listing 10-30 under InvalidateRgn.

EnumObjects   Windows.pas

Syntax

```
EnumObjects(
DC: HDC;                     {a handle to a device context}
p2: Integer;                 {object type flag}
p3: TFNGEnumObjProc;         {the application-defined callback function}
p4: LPARAM                   {application-defined data}
): Integer;                  {returns a success code}
```

Description

This function enumerates all pens or brushes available in the specified device context. Information for each brush or pen is passed to the application-defined callback pointed to by the p3 parameter. This continues until all objects have been enumerated or the callback function returns zero.

Parameters

DC: A handle to the device context containing the objects to be enumerated.

p2: A flag indicating what type of object to enumerate. If this parameter is set to OBJ_BRUSH, all brushes are enumerated. If this parameter is set to OBJ_PEN, all pens are enumerated.

p3: A pointer to the application-defined callback function.

p4: Specifies a 32-bit application-defined value that is passed to the callback function.

382 ■ Chapter 10

Return Value

This function returns the last value returned by the callback function. If there are too many objects to enumerate, the function returns –1. This function does not indicate an error condition.

Callback Syntax

```
EnumObjProc(
  lpLogObject: Pointer;     {a pointer to an object data structure}
  lpData: LPARAM            {application-defined data}
): Integer;                 {returns zero or one}
```

Description

This function is called once for each type of object enumerated in the specified device context. It may perform any desired action.

Parameters

lpLogObject: A pointer to a TLogPen structure if the p2 parameter of the EnumObjects function contains the OBJ_PEN flag, or a pointer to a TLogBrush structure if the p2 parameter contains the OBJ_BRUSH flag. See the CreatePenIndirect function for a description of the TLogPen structure, and the CreateBrushIndirect function for a description of the TLogBrush parameter.

lpData: Specifies the 32-bit application-defined value passed to the p4 parameter of the EnumObjects function. This value is intended for application-specific use.

Return Value

This function should return a one to continue enumeration, or zero to discontinue enumeration.

See Also

GetObject, GetObjectType

Example

Listing 10-15: Enumerating all pens in a device context

```
{the callback function prototype}
  function EnumObjProc(ObjType: PLogPen; lData: lParam): Integer; stdcall;

var
  Form1: TForm1;

implementation

{$R *.DFM}

function EnumObjProc(ObjType: PLogPen; lData: lParam): Integer;
var
  LocalObjType: TLogPen;        // holds logical pen information
  PenDescription: String;       // holds a pen description
```

```
begin
  {get the pen information}
  LocalObjType := ObjType^;

  {determine the type of pen being enumerated}
  case LocalObjType.lopnStyle of
    PS_SOLID:       PenDescription := 'PS_SOLID';
    PS_DASH:        PenDescription := 'PS_DASH';
    PS_DOT:         PenDescription := 'PS_DOT';
    PS_DASHDOT:     PenDescription := 'PS_DASHDOT';
    PS_DASHDOTDOT:  PenDescription := 'PS_DASHDOTDOT';
    PS_NULL:        PenDescription := 'PS_NULL';
    PS_INSIDEFRAME: PenDescription := 'PS_INSIDEFRAME';
  end;

  {determine the color of the pen being enumerated}
  case LocalObjType.lopnColor of
    clBlack:   PenDescription := PenDescription+' Color: clBlack';
    clMaroon:  PenDescription := PenDescription+' Color: clMaroon';
    clGreen:   PenDescription := PenDescription+' Color: clGreen';
    clOlive:   PenDescription := PenDescription+' Color: clOlive';
    clNavy:    PenDescription := PenDescription+' Color: clNavy';
    clPurple:  PenDescription := PenDescription+' Color: clPurple';
    clTeal:    PenDescription := PenDescription+' Color: clTeal';
    clGray:    PenDescription := PenDescription+' Color: clGray';
    clSilver:  PenDescription := PenDescription+' Color: clSilver';
    clRed:     PenDescription := PenDescription+' Color: clRed';
    clLime:    PenDescription := PenDescription+' Color: clLime';
    clYellow:  PenDescription := PenDescription+' Color: clYellow';
    clBlue:    PenDescription := PenDescription+' Color: clBlue';
    clFuchsia: PenDescription := PenDescription+' Color: clFuchsia';
    clAqua:    PenDescription := PenDescription+' Color: clAqua';
    clWhite:   PenDescription := PenDescription+' Color: clWhite';
  end;

  {indicate the pen's width}
  PenDescription:=PenDescription+' Width: '+IntToStr(LocalObjType.lopnWidth.X);

  {add the description to the list box}
  Form1.ListBox.Items.Add(PenDescription);

  {indicate that enumeration should continue}
  Result := 1;
end;

procedure TForm1.Button1Click(Sender: TObject);
begin
  {enumerate all pens in the form's device context}
  EnumObjects(Canvas.Handle, OBJ_PEN, @EnumObjProc, 0);
end;
```

ExtCreatePen   Windows.pas

Syntax

ExtCreatePen(
   PenStyle: DWORD;   {pen type, style, end cap, and join flags}

    Width: DWORD;   {the pen width}
    const Brush: TLogBrush;   {a pointer to a TLogBrush structure}
    StyleCount: DWORD;   {the number of entries in the custom style array}
    Style: Pointer   {a pointer to an array of dash and space length values}
    ): HPEN;   {returns the handle to a pen}

Description

This function creates a new cosmetic or geometric pen with the specified attributes. Geometric pens can be any width, and have the same attributes as a brush. Cosmetic pens must always be one pixel in size, but perform faster than geometric pens. Additionally, under Windows NT, this function can create a pen with a user-defined style pattern. When the application no longer needs the pen, it should be deleted by calling the DeleteObject function.

Parameters

PenStyle: A series of flags defining the pen's type, style, end caps, and joins. This parameter may contain a combination of one value from the pen type flags table and one value from the pen style flags table (Tables 10-20 and 10-21). If this parameter contains the PS_GEOMETRIC style flag, it can contain an additional combination of one value from the end cap flags table and one value from the join flags table (Tables 10-22 and 10-23).

Windows 95: The end cap and join styles are supported only for geometric pens when used to draw a path.

Width: Specifies the width of the pen, in logical units. If the PenStyle parameter contains the PS_COSMETIC flag, this parameter must be set to one.

Brush: A pointer to a TLogBrush structure defining additional pen attributes. If the PenStyle parameter contains the PS_COSMETIC flag, the lbColor member of this structure specifies the color of the pen, and the lbStyle member must be set to BS_SOLID. If the PenStyle parameter contains the PS_GEOMETRIC flag, all members of this structure are used to specify the pen attributes. The TLogBrush structure is defined as:

    TLogBrush = packed record
        lbStyle: UINT;   {brush style flag}
        lbColor: COLORREF;   {a color specifier}
        lbHatch: Longint;   {hatch style flag}
    end;

Note that if the lbHatch member points to a bitmap, it cannot be a bitmap created by the CreateDIBSection function. See the CreateBrushIndirect function for a description of this data structure.

StyleCount: Specifies the number of entries in the user-defined pen style array pointed to by the Style parameter. If the PenStyle parameter does not contain the PS_USERSTYLE flag, this parameter is ignored.

Style: A pointer to an array of DWORD values defining the pattern of dashes and spaces for a user-defined pen style. The first entry in the array specifies the length of the first dash, in logical units. The second entry specifies the length of the first space, in logical units. This continues until the line is fully defined. The pattern will be repeated as necessary when drawing a line created with the pen. If the PenStyle parameter does not contain the PS_USERSTYLE flag, this parameter is ignored.

Return Value

If the function succeeds, it returns the handle to a new pen; otherwise, it returns zero.

See Also

CreateBrushIndirect, CreatePen, CreatePenIndirect, DeleteObject, GetObject, SelectObject, SetMiterLimit

Example

Listing 10-16: Drawing paths with geometric pens

```
procedure TForm1.Button1Click(Sender: TObject);
var
  NewPen, OldPen: HPen;    // holds the old and new pens
  FormDC: HDC;             // holds a handle to the form's device context
  BrushInfo: TLogBrush;    // the logical brush structure
  MiterLimit: Single;      // the mite limit
begin
  {get the form's device context}
  FormDC := GetDC(Form1.Handle);

  {define the brush}
  with BrushInfo do
  begin
    lbStyle := BS_SOLID;
    lbColor := clBlue;
    lbHatch := 0;
  end;

  {create a geometric pen with square end caps and mitered joins, 20 units wide}
  NewPen := ExtCreatePen(PS_GEOMETRIC or PS_ENDCAP_SQUARE or PS_JOIN_MITER, 20,
                         BrushInfo, 0, nil);

  {select the pen into the form's device context}
  OldPen := SelectObject(FormDC, NewPen);

  {begin a path bracket}
  BeginPath(FormDC);

  {define a closed triangle path}
  MoveToEx(FormDC, ClientWidth div 2, 20, nil);
  LineTo(FormDC, ClientWidth-20, 90);
  LineTo(FormDC, 20, 90);
  CloseFigure(FormDC);

  {end the path bracket}
  EndPath(FormDC);

  {insure that the miter limit is 2 units}
  GetMiterLimit(FormDC, MiterLimit);
```

```
        if MiterLimit>2 then
          SetMiterLimit(FormDC, 2, NIL);

        {draw the path with the geometric pen}
        StrokePath(FormDC);

        {delete the pen and the device context}
        SelectObject(FormDC, OldPen);
        ReleaseDC(Form1.Handle, FormDC);
        DeleteObject(NewPen);
     end;
```

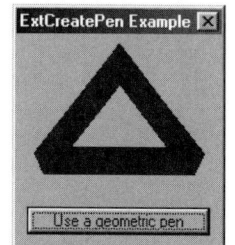

Figure 10-20: The geometric pen in action

Table 10-20: ExtCreatePen PenStyle pen type values

Value	Description
PS_GEOMETRIC	Indicates a geometric pen.
PS_COSMETIC	Indicates a cosmetic pen.

Table 10-21: ExtCreatePen PenStyle pen style values

Value	Description
PS_ALTERNATE	**Windows NT/2000 only:** Sets every other pixel when drawing a line (cosmetic pens only).
PS_SOLID	Creates a solid pen.
PS_DASH	**Windows 95 only:** Creates a dashed pen. This style is not supported for geometric pens.
PS_DOT	**Windows 95 only:** Creates a dotted pen. This style is not supported for geometric pens.
PS_DASHDOT	**Windows 95 only:** Creates an alternating dash and dot pen. This style is not supported for geometric pens.
PS_DASHDOTDOT	**Windows 95 only:** Creates an alternating dash and double dot pen. This style is not supported for geometric pens.
PS_NULL	Creates an invisible pen.
PS_USERSTYLE	**Windows NT only:** Creates a user-defined style pen. The Style parameter points to an array of DWORD values that specify the dashes and spaces of the pen.
PS_INSIDEFRAME	Creates a solid pen. When this pen is used in any function that specifies a bounding rectangle, the dimensions of the figure are reduced so that the entire figure, when drawn with the pen, will fit within the bounding rectangle (geometric pens only).

Table 10-22: ExtCreatePen PenStyle end cap values (geometric pens only)

Value	Description
PS_ENDCAP_FLAT	Line ends are flat.
PS_ENDCAP_ROUND	Line ends are round.
PS_ENDCAP_SQUARE	Line ends are square.

Table 10-23: ExtCreatePen PenStyle join values (geometric pens only)

Value	Description
PS_JOIN_BEVEL	Line joins are beveled.
PS_JOIN_MITER	Line joins are mitered when they are within the current limit set by the SetMiterLimit function. If it exceeds this limit, the join is beveled.
PS_JOIN_ROUND	Line joins are round.

ExtFloodFill   Windows.pas

Syntax

```
ExtFloodFill(
  DC: HDC;              {the handle of a device context}
  X: Integer;           {horizontal coordinate of fill origin}
  Y: Integer;           {vertical coordinate of fill origin}
  Color: COLORREF;      {the fill color}
  FillType: UINT        {fill type flags}
): BOOL;                {returns TRUE or FALSE}
```

Description

This function fills an area of the specified device context with the current brush.

Parameters

DC: A handle to the device context upon which the fill is drawn.

X: Specifies the horizontal coordinate, in logical units, of the origin of the fill.

Y: Specifies the vertical coordinate, in logical units, of the origin of the fill.

Color: A color specifier indicating the color of the border or area to be filled. The meaning of this parameter is dependent on the value of the FillType parameter.

FillType: A flag indicating the type of fill to perform. This parameter may be set to one value from the following table.

Return Value

If the function succeeds, it returns TRUE; otherwise, it returns FALSE. To get extended error information, call the GetLastError function.

See Also

FillPath, FillRect, FillRgn, GetDeviceCaps

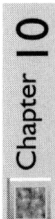

Example

Listing 10-17: Filling an area

```
procedure TForm1.Button1Click(Sender: TObject);
begin
  {set the color of the brush used for the flood fill}
  Canvas.Brush.Color := clLime;

  {fill the red square with the new brush color}
  ExtFloodFill(Canvas.Handle, 20, 20, clRed, FLOODFILLSURFACE);
end;
```

Table 10-24: ExtFloodFill FillType values

Value	Description
FLOODFILLBORDER	Indicates that the area to be filled is bounded by pixels of the color specified in the Color parameter. The function fills pixels in all directions from the origin with the color of the brush until the color specified by the Color parameter is encountered.
FLOODFILLSURFACE	Indicates that the area to be filled is defined by a solid color. The function fills pixels in all directions from the origin with the color of the brush while the color specified by the Color parameter is encountered.

FillPath   Windows.pas

Syntax

```
FillPath(
DC: HDC              {the handle of a device context}
): BOOL;             {returns TRUE or FALSE}
```

Description

This function closes any open paths in the device context, filling the path's interior with the current brush. The path is filled according to the current polygon filling mode. Note that after this function returns, the path is discarded from the device context.

Parameters

DC: A handle to a device context containing the valid path to be filled.

Return Value

If the function succeeds, it returns TRUE; otherwise, it returns FALSE. To get extended error information, call the GetLastError function.

See Also

BeginPath, ExtFloodFill, FillRgn, SetPolyFillMode, StrokeAndFillPath, StrokePath

Example

Listing 10-18: Filling a path

```
procedure TForm1.FormPaint(Sender: TObject);
begin
  {open a path bracket}
  BeginPath(Canvas.Handle);

  {draw text into the path, indicating that the path consists of the
   text interior}
  SetBkMode(Canvas.Handle, TRANSPARENT);
  Canvas.TextOut(10, 10, 'DELPHI ROCKS!');

  {end the path bracket}
  EndPath(Canvas.Handle);

  {initialize the canvas's brush}
  Canvas.Brush.Color := clBlue;
  Canvas.Brush.Style := bsDiagCross;

  {fill the path with the current brush}
  FillPath(Canvas.Handle);
end;
```

Figure 10-21:
The filled path

FillRect   Windows.pas

Syntax

```
FillRect(
  hDC: HDC;              {the handle of a device context}
  const lprc: TRect;     {the rectangular coordinates}
  hbr: HBRUSH            {the handle of the brush}
): Integer;              {returns zero or one}
```

Description

This function fills the specified rectangular area in the device context with the indicated brush. The top and left borders of the rectangle are included in the fill, but the bottom and right borders are excluded.

Parameters

hDC: The handle of the device context upon which the filled rectangle is drawn.

lprc: A pointer to a TRect structure defining the rectangular coordinates, in logical units, of the area to be filled.

hbr: Specifies the handle of the brush used to fill the rectangle. Optionally, a system color can be used to fill the rectangle by setting this parameter to one value from the following table. Note that when using a system color, a one must be added to the value (i.e., COLOR_ACTIVEBORDER+1).

Return Value

If the function succeeds, it returns one; otherwise, it returns zero. To get extended error information, call the GetLastError function.

See Also

CreateHatchBrush, CreatePatternBrush, CreateSolidBrush, ExtFloodFill, FillPath, FillRgn, FrameRect, GetStockObject

Example

See Listing 10-5 under CreatePatternBrush.

Table 10-25: FillRect hbr system color values

Value	Description
COLOR_3DDKSHADOW	The dark shadow color for three-dimensional display elements.
COLOR_3DLIGHT	The lighted edge color for three-dimensional display elements.
COLOR_ACTIVEBORDER	The active window border color.
COLOR_ACTIVECAPTION	The active window caption color.
COLOR_APPWORKSPACE	The background color used in multiple document interface applications.
COLOR_BACKGROUND	The desktop color.
COLOR_BTNFACE	The color of pushbutton faces.
COLOR_BTNHIGHLIGHT	The color of a highlighted pushbutton.
COLOR_BTNSHADOW	The shaded edge color on pushbuttons.
COLOR_BTNTEXT	The text color on pushbuttons.
COLOR_CAPTIONTEXT	The text color used in caption, size box, and scroll bar arrow box controls.
COLOR_GRAYTEXT	The color of disabled text. This will be set to zero if the display driver cannot support solid gray.
COLOR_HIGHLIGHT	The color used for selected items in a control.
COLOR_HIGHLIGHTTEXT	The color used for the text of selected items in a control.
COLOR_INACTIVEBORDER	The inactive window border color.
COLOR_INACTIVECAPTION	The inactive window caption color.
COLOR_INACTIVECAPTIONTEXT	The text color in an inactive caption bar.
COLOR_INFOBK	The background color for tooltip controls.
COLOR_INFOTEXT	The text color for tooltip controls.
COLOR_MENU	The menu background color.
COLOR_MENUTEXT	The text color used in menus.
COLOR_SCROLLBAR	The scroll bar gray area color.
COLOR_WINDOW	The window background color.
COLOR_WINDOWFRAME	The window frame color.
COLOR_WINDOWTEXT	The color of text used in a window.

FillRgn   Windows.pas

Syntax

```
FillRgn(
DC: HDC;              {the handle of a device context}
p2: HRGN;             {the handle of the region}
p3: HBRUSH            {the handle of the brush}
): BOOL;              {returns TRUE or FALSE}
```

Description

This function fills the specified region with the brush identified by the p3 parameter.

Parameters

DC: A handle to the device context upon which the filled region is drawn.

p2: Specifies a handle to the region to be filled.

p3: Specifies a handle to the brush used to fill the region.

Return Value

If the function succeeds, it returns TRUE; otherwise, it returns FALSE.

See Also

CreateBrushIndirect, CreateHatchBrush, CreatePatternBrush, CreateSolidBrush, FillPath, FillRect, FrameRgn, PaintRgn

Example

See Listing 10-3 under CreateBrushIndirect.

FrameRect   Windows.pas

Syntax

```
FrameRect(
hDC: HDC;              {the handle of a device context}
const lprc: TRect;     {the rectangular coordinates}
hbr: HBRUSH            {the handle of the brush}
): Integer;            {returns zero or one}
```

Description

This function draws a border around the specified rectangle on the device context using the brush identified by the hbr parameter. This border is always one logical unit in width.

Parameters

hDC: A handle to the device context upon which the rectangular frame is drawn.

lprc: A pointer to a TRect structure containing the rectangular coordinates defining the frame.

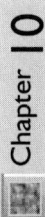

hbr: Specifies a handle to the brush used to draw the rectangular frame.

Return Value

If the function succeeds, it returns one; otherwise, it returns zero. To get extended error information, call the GetLastError function.

See Also

CreateHatchBrush, CreatePatternBrush, CreateSolidBrush, FillRect, FrameRgn, GetStockObject, Rectangle

Example

Listing 10-19: Drawing a rectangular frame

```
procedure TForm1.Button1Click(Sender: TObject);
var
  TheRect: TRect;      // the rectangular coordinates
begin
  {define the rectangle}
  TheRect := Rect(10, 10, 110, 110);

  {initialize the brush}
  Canvas.Brush.Color := clRed;
  Canvas.Brush.Style := bsCross;

  {frame the rectangle}
  FrameRect(Canvas.Handle, TheRect, Canvas.Brush.Handle);
end;
```

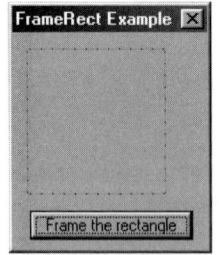

Figure 10-22: The framed rectangle

FrameRgn   Windows.pas

Syntax

```
FrameRgn(
  DC: HDC;            {the handle of a device context}
  p2: HRGN;           {the handle of the region}
  p3: HBRUSH;         {the handle of the brush}
  p4: Integer;        {the width of the frame}
  p5: Integer         {the height of the frame}
): BOOL;              {returns TRUE or FALSE}
```

Description

This function draws the perimeter of the specified region with the brush identified by the p3 parameter.

Parameters

DC: A handle to the device context upon which the framed region is drawn.

p2: A handle to the region whose perimeter is being drawn.

p3: Specifies the handle of the brush used to draw the frame.

p4: Specifies the width of vertical brush strokes when drawing the frame, in logical units.

p5: Specifies the height of horizontal brush strokes when drawing the frame, in logical units.

Return Value

If the function succeeds, it returns TRUE; otherwise, it returns FALSE.

See Also

CreateHatchBrush, CreatePatternBrush, CreateSolidBrush, FillRgn, FrameRect, PaintRgn

Example

Listing 10-20: Framing a region

```
procedure TForm1.Button1Click(Sender: TObject);
var
  RegionHandle: HRGN;                  // the region handle
  PointsArray: array[0..5] of TPoint;  // points defining the region
begin
  {define the region}
  PointsArray[0].X := 50;
  PointsArray[0].y := 50;
  PointsArray[1].x := 100;
  PointsArray[1].y := 50;
  PointsArray[2].x := 125;
  PointsArray[2].y := 75;
  PointsArray[3].x := 100;
  PointsArray[3].y := 100;
  PointsArray[4].x := 50;
  PointsArray[4].y := 100;
  PointsArray[5].x := 25;
  PointsArray[5].y := 75;

  {create the polygonal region}
  RegionHandle := CreatePolygonRgn(PointsArray, 6, ALTERNATE);

  {frame the region in black}
  Canvas.Brush.Color := clBlack;
  FrameRgn(Canvas.Handle, RegionHandle, Canvas.Brush.Handle, 2, 2);
end;
```

Figure 10-23:
The framed region

GetBkColor   Windows.pas

Syntax

```
GetBkColor(
  hDC: HDC              {the handle of a device context}
): COLORREF;            {returns the background color}
```

Description

This function retrieves the background color for the specified device context.

Parameters

hDC: A handle to the device context from which the background color is to be retrieved.

Return Value

If the function succeeds, it returns a color specifier describing the background color; otherwise, it returns CLR_INVALID.

See Also

GetBkMode, SetBkColor

Example

Listing 10-21: Drawing text with and without the background color

```
procedure TForm1.Button1Click(Sender: TObject);
begin
  {if the background color is not red, make it so}
  if GetBkColor(Canvas.Handle)<>clRed then
    SetBkColor(Canvas.Handle, clRed);

  {output some text. the background color will be used}
  Canvas.TextOut(20, 20, 'Text with a background color');

  {if the background mode is not transparent, make it so}
  if GetBkMode(Canvas.Handle)<>TRANSPARENT then
    SetBkMode(Canvas.Handle, TRANSPARENT);

  {draw some text. the background color will not be used}
  Canvas.TextOut(20, 40, 'Text drawn with a transparent background');
end;
```

Figure 10-24: Text with and without a background color

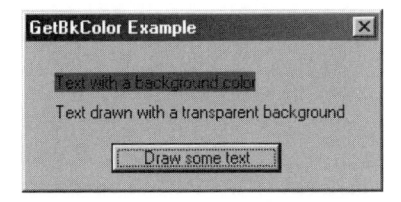

GetBkMode   Windows.pas

Syntax

```
GetBkMode(
hDC: HDC;            {the handle of a device context}
): Integer;          {returns the current background mode}
```

Description

This function retrieves the current background mix mode for the specified device context.

Parameters

hDC: A handle to the device context from which the background mix mode is to be retrieved.

Return Value

If the function succeeds, it returns a flag indicating the current background mix mode of the specified device context. This flag can be either OPAQUE or TRANSPARENT. See the SetBkMode function for a description of these flags. If the function fails, it returns zero.

See Also

GetBkColor, SetBkMode

Example

See Listing 10-21 under GetBkColor.

GetBoundsRect   Windows.pas

Syntax

```
GetBoundsRect(
DC: HDC;             {handle of the device context}
var p2: TRect;       {a pointer to a TRect structure}
p3: UINT             {operation flags}
): UINT;             {returns the accumulated bounding rectangle state}
```

Description

This function retrieves the current bounding rectangle for the specified device context. Windows maintains an accumulated bounding rectangle for each device context that identifies the extent of output from drawing functions. When a drawing function reaches beyond this boundary, the rectangle is extended. Thus, the bounding rectangle is the smallest rectangle that can be drawn around the area affected by all drawing operations in the device context.

Parameters

DC: A handle to the device context from which the accumulated bounding rectangle is to be retrieved.

p2: A pointer to a TRect structure that receives the coordinates of the device context's bounding rectangle.

p3: A flag indicating if the bounding rectangle will be cleared. If this parameter is set to zero, the bounding rectangle will not be modified. If this parameter is set to DCB_RESET, the bounding rectangle is cleared when the function returns.

Return Value

This function returns a code indicating the state of the bounding rectangle or an error condition, and will be one or more values from the following table.

See Also

GetUpdateRect, SetBoundsRect

Example

Listing 10-22: Setting and retrieving the device context's bounding rectangle

```
procedure TForm1.Button1Click(Sender: TObject);
var
  TheRect: TRect;         // receives the bounding rectangle
  FormDC: HDC;            // a handle to the form's device context
  BoundRectState: UINT;   // holds the bounding rectangle state
begin
  {get the device context of the form}
  FormDC := GetDC(Form1.Handle);

  {initialize and set the bounds rectangle}
  TheRect := Rect(10, 10, 110, 110);
  SetBoundsRect(FormDC, @TheRect, DCB_ENABLE);

  {retrieve the bounds rectangle}
  BoundRectState := GetBoundsRect(FormDC, TheRect, 0);

  {release the device context}
  ReleaseDC(Form1.Handle, FormDC);

  {display the bounds rectangle coordinates}
  with TheRect do
  begin
    Label1.Caption := 'Top: '+IntToStr(Top) +' Left: '+IntToStr(Left)+
                      ' Bottom: '+IntToStr(Bottom)+' Right: '+IntToStr(Right);
  end;

  {display the bounds rectangle state}
```

```
    case BoundRectState of
      DCB_DISABLE:  Label2.Caption := 'State: DCB_DISABLE';
      DCB_ENABLE:   Label2.Caption := 'State: DCB_ENABLE';
      DCB_RESET:    Label2.Caption := 'State: DCB_RESET';
      DCB_SET:      Label2.Caption := 'State: DCB_SET';
    end;
end;
```

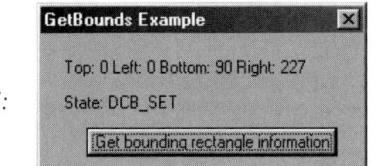

Figure 10-25:
The current bounds rect

Table 10-26: GetBoundsRect return values

Value	Description
0	Indicates that an error occurred.
DCB_DISABLE	Boundary accumulation is off.
DCB_ENABLE	Boundary accumulation is on.
DCB_RESET	The bounding rectangle is empty.
DCB_SET	The bounding rectangle is not empty.

GetBrushOrgEx   Windows.pas

Syntax

```
GetBrushOrgEx(
DC: HDC;                {the handle of a device context}
var p2: TPoint          {a pointer to a TPoint structure}
): BOOL;                {returns TRUE or FALSE}
```

Description

This function retrieves the origin of the brush for the specified device context. The brush origin is relative to the hatch or bitmap defining the brush's pattern. The default brush origin is at 0,0. A brush pattern can be no more than 8 pixels square. Thus, the origin can range from 0-7 vertically and horizontally. As the origin is moved, the brush pattern is offset by the specified amount. If an application is using a pattern brush to draw the backgrounds of child windows and parent windows, the brush origin may need to be moved to align the patterns. Note that under Windows NT, the system automatically tracks the brush origin so that patterns will be aligned.

Parameters

DC: A handle to the device context from which the brush origin is to be retrieved.

p2: A pointer to a TPoint structure that receives the coordinates of the brush origin, in device units.

Return Value

If the function succeeds, it returns TRUE; otherwise, it returns FALSE. To get extended error information, call the GetLastError function.

See Also

CreateBrushIndirect, CreateHatchBrush, CreatePatternBrush, FillRect, FillRgn, SelectObject, SetBrushOrgEx

Example

See Listing 10-42 under Rectangle.

GetCurrentObject   Windows.pas

Syntax

```
GetCurrentObject(
DC: HDC;                     {the handle of a device context}
p2: UINT                     {the object type flag}
): HGDIOBJ;                  {returns the handle to a GDI object}
```

Description

This function returns a handle to the specified object currently selected into the device context identified by the DC parameter.

Parameters

DC: A handle to the device context from which the currently selected object is to be retrieved.

p2: A flag specifying what type of object to retrieve. This parameter can be set to one value from the following table.

Return Value

If the function succeeds, it returns a handle to the currently selected object of the specified type. If the function fails, it returns zero.

See Also

DeleteObject, GetObject, GetObjectType, SelectObject

Example

See Listing 10-24 under GetObject.

Table 10-27: GetCurrentObject p2 values

Value	Description
OBJ_BITMAP	Retrieves the handle of the currently selected bitmap if the DC parameter identifies a memory device context.
OBJ_BRUSH	Retrieves the handle of the currently selected brush.
OBJ_COLORSPACE	Retrieves the handle of the currently selected color space.

Value	Description
OBJ_FONT	Retrieves the handle of the currently selected font.
OBJ_PAL	Retrieves the handle of the currently selected palette.
OBJ_PEN	Retrieves the handle of the currently selected pen.

GetCurrentPositionEx   Windows.pas

Syntax

```
GetCurrentPositionEx(
DC: HDC;                   {the handle of a device context}
Point: PPoint;             {a pointer to a TPoint structure}
): BOOL;                   {returns TRUE or FALSE}
```

Description

This function retrieves the coordinates of the current position in logical units.

Parameters

DC: A handle to the device context from which the current position is to be retrieved.

Point: A pointer to a TPoint structure that receives the coordinates of the current position, in logical units.

Return Value

If the function succeeds, it returns TRUE; otherwise, it returns FALSE.

See Also

LineTo, MoveToEx, PolyBezierTo, PolylineTo

Example

Listing 10-23: Displaying the current position

```
procedure TForm1.Button1Click(Sender: TObject);
var
  CurPosPt: TPoint;      // holds the current position
begin
  {set the background mode to transparent}
  SetBkMode(Canvas.Handle, TRANSPARENT);

  {display the first point}
  MoveToEx(Canvas.Handle, 60, 20, NIL);
  GetCurrentPositionEx(Canvas.Handle, @CurPosPt);
  TextOut(Canvas.Handle, CurPosPt.x-55, CurPosPt.y, PChar('X: '+IntToStr(CurPosPt.X)+
          ' Y: '+IntToStr(CurPosPt.Y)), Length('X: '+IntToStr(CurPosPt.X)+
          ' Y: '+IntToStr(CurPosPt.Y)));

  {display the second point}
  LineTo(Canvas.Handle, 160, 20);
  GetCurrentPositionEx(Canvas.Handle, @CurPosPt);
```

```
    TextOut(Canvas.Handle, CurPosPt.x+2, CurPosPt.y, PChar('X: '+IntToStr(CurPosPt.X)+
            ' Y: '+IntToStr(CurPosPt.Y)), Length('X: '+IntToStr(CurPosPt.X)+
            ' Y: '+IntToStr(CurPosPt.Y)));

    {display the third point}
    LineTo(Canvas.Handle, 160, 120);
    GetCurrentPositionEx(Canvas.Handle, @CurPosPt);
    TextOut(Canvas.Handle, CurPosPt.x+2, CurPosPt.y, PChar('X: '+IntToStr(CurPosPt.X)+
            ' Y: '+IntToStr(CurPosPt.Y)), Length('X: '+IntToStr(CurPosPt.X)+
            ' Y: '+IntToStr(CurPosPt.Y)));

    {display the fourth point}
    LineTo(Canvas.Handle, 60, 120);
    GetCurrentPositionEx(Canvas.Handle, @CurPosPt);
    TextOut(Canvas.Handle, CurPosPt.x-55, CurPosPt.y, PChar('X: '+IntToStr(CurPosPt.X)+
            ' Y: '+IntToStr(CurPosPt.Y)), Length('X: '+IntToStr(CurPosPt.X)+
            ' Y: '+IntToStr(CurPosPt.Y)));

    {close the figure}
    LineTo(Canvas.Handle, 60, 20);
end;
```

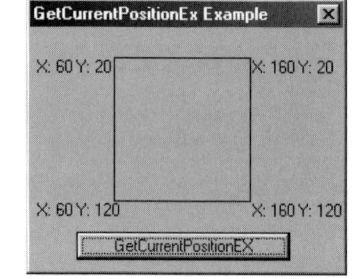

Figure 10-26: Tracking the current position

GetMiterLimit   Windows.pas

Syntax

```
GetMiterLimit(
 DC: HDC;                   {the handle of a device context}
 var Limit: Single          {a pointer to a variable receiving the miter limit}
): BOOL;                    {returns TRUE or FALSE}
```

Description

This function retrieves the miter limit for the specified device context. The miter limit is used for geometric lines that have miter joins, and is the maximum ratio of the miter length to the line width. The miter length is the distance from the intersection of the inner wall to the intersection of the outer wall.

Figure 10-27: Miter limit dimensions

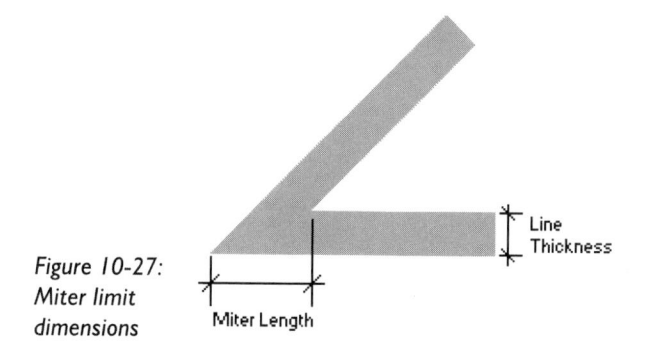

Parameters

DC: A handle to the device context from which the miter limit is to be retrieved.

Limit: A pointer to a variable of type Single that receives the device context's miter limit.

Return Value

If the function succeeds, it returns TRUE; otherwise, it returns FALSE. To get extended error information, call the GetLastError function.

See Also

ExtCreatePen, SetMiterLimit

Example

See Listing 10-16 under ExtCreatePen.

GetObject   Windows.pas

Syntax

```
GetObject(
  p1: HGDIOBJ;           {a handle to a graphics object}
  p2: Integer;           {the size of the buffer pointed to by the p3 parameter}
  p3: Pointer            {a pointer to a buffer receiving object information}
): Integer;              {returns the number of bytes written to the buffer}
```

Description

This function retrieves information about the graphical object identified by the p1 parameter. Depending on the object type, the p3 parameter should point to a buffer that receives a TBitmap, TDibSection, TExtLogPen, TLogBrush, TLogFont, or TLogPen structure containing information about the specified object.

> **Note:** If the p1 parameter contains a handle to a bitmap created with any function other than CreateDIBSection, the data structure returned in the buffer contains only the bitmap's width, height, and color format.

Parameters

p1: Specifies a handle to the graphical object whose information is to be retrieved. This can be a handle to a bitmap, DIB section, brush, font, pen, or palette.

p2: Specifies the size of the buffer pointed to by the p3 parameter.

p3: A pointer to a buffer that receives a data structure containing information about the specified graphical object. The type of data structure received is dependent on the type of object specified in the p1 parameter. If this parameter is set to NIL, the function returns the required size of the buffer to hold the retrieved information. If the p1 parameter contains a handle to a palette, the buffer pointed to by this parameter receives a 16-bit value indicating the number of entries in the palette. If the p1 parameter contains a handle to a bitmap, pen, brush, or font, the buffer pointed to by this parameter receives a TBitmap, TLogPen, TLogBrush, or TLogFont data structure, respectively. See the CreateBitmapIndirect, CreatePenIndirect, CreateBrushIndirect, or CreateFontIndirect functions for descriptions of these data structures. If the p1 parameter contains a handle to a bitmap returned by the CreateDIBSection function, the buffer pointed to by this parameter receives a TDibSection structure. If the p1 parameter contains a handle to a pen returned by the ExtCreatePen function, the buffer pointed to by this parameter receives a TExtLogPen structure.

The TDibSection data structure is defined as:

```
TDIBSection = packed record
     dsBm: TBitmap;                       {a TBitmap structure}
     dsBmih: TBitmapInfoHeader;           {a TBitmapInfoHeader structure}
     dsBitfields: array[0..2] of DWORD;   {color masks}
     dshSection: THandle;                 {a handle to a file mapping object}
     dsOffset: DWORD;                     {bit values offset}
end;
```

dsBm: Specifies a TBitmap structure containing information about the bitmap's type, dimensions, and a pointer to its bits. See the CreateBitmapIndirect function for a description of this data structure.

dsBmih: Specifies a TBitmapInfoHeader structure containing information about the bitmap's color format. See the CreateDIBSection function for a description of this data structure.

dsBitfields: An array containing the three color masks, if the bitmap has a color depth greater than 8 bits per pixel.

dshSection: Specifies a handle to the file mapping object passed to the CreateDIBSection when the bitmap was created. If a file mapping object was not used to create the bitmap, this member will contain zero.

dsOffset: Specifies the offset within the file mapping object to the start of the bitmap bits. If a file mapping object was not used to create the bitmap, this member will contain zero.

The TExtLogPen data structure is defined as:

```
TExtLogPen = packed record
    elpPenStyle: DWORD;                     {type, style, end cap, and join flags}
    elpWidth: DWORD;                        {the pen width}
    elpBrushStyle: UINT;                    {the brush style}
    elpColor: COLORREF;                     {the pen color}
    elpHatch: Longint;                      {the hatch style}
    elpNumEntries: DWORD;                   {the number of entries in the array}
    elpStyleEntry: array[0..0] of DWORD;    {specifies a user-defined style}
end;
```

elpPenStyle: A series of flags defining the pen's type, style, end caps, and joins. See the ExtCreatePen function for a list of available flags.

elpWidth: Specifies the width of the pen in logical units. If the PenStyle parameter contains the PS_COSMETIC flag, this parameter must be set to one.

elpBrushStyle: A flag indicating the brush style of the pen. See the CreateBrushIndirect function for a list of available styles.

elpColor: Specifies the color of the pen.

elpHatch: Specifies the hatch pattern of the pen. See the CreateHatchBrush function for a list of available flags.

elpNumEntries: Specifies the number of entries in the user-defined pen style array pointed to by the elpStyleEntry member. If the elpPenStyle member does not contain the PS_USERSTYLE flag, this member is ignored.

elpStyleEntry: A pointer to an array of DWORD values defining the pattern of dashes and spaces for a user-defined pen style. The first entry in the array specifies the length of the first dash, in logical units. The second entry specifies the length of the first space, in logical units. This continues until the line is fully defined. The pattern will be repeated as necessary when drawing a line created with the pen. If the elpPenStyle member does not contain the PS_USERSTYLE flag, this member is ignored.

Return Value

If the function succeeds, it returns the number of bytes written to the buffer pointed to by the p3 parameter; otherwise, it returns zero. To get extended error information, call the GetLastError function.

See Also

CreateBitmapIndirect, CreateBrushIndirect, CreateDIBSection, CreateFontIndirect, CreatePenIndirect, ExtCreatePen, GetBitmapBits, GetDIBits, GetCurrentObject, GetObjectType, GetRegionData, GetStockObject

Chapter 10

Example

Listing 10-24: Retrieving information about an object

```
function GetStyle(Style: Integer): string;
begin
  {display the brush style}
  case Style of
    BS_DIBPATTERN:    Result := 'BS_DIBPATTERN';
    BS_DIBPATTERN8X8: Result := 'BS_DIBPATTERN8X8';
    BS_DIBPATTERNPT:  Result := 'BS_DIBPATTERNPT';
    BS_HATCHED:       Result := 'BS_HATCHED';
    BS_HOLLOW:        Result := 'BS_HOLLOW';
    BS_PATTERN:       Result := 'BS_PATTERN';
    BS_PATTERN8X8:    Result := 'BS_PATTERN8X8';
    BS_SOLID:         Result := 'BS_SOLID';
  end;
end;

function GetHatch(Hatch: Integer): string;
begin
  {display the hatch style}
  case Hatch of
    HS_BDIAGONAL:  Result := 'HS_BDIAGONAL';
    HS_CROSS:      Result := 'HS_CROSS';
    HS_DIAGCROSS:  Result := 'HS_DIAGCROSS';
    HS_FDIAGONAL:  Result := 'HS_FDIAGONAL';
    HS_HORIZONTAL: Result := 'HS_HORIZONTAL';
    HS_VERTICAL:   Result := 'HS_VERTICAL';
  end;
end;

procedure TForm1.Button1Click(Sender: TObject);
var
  hObject: HGDIOBJ;      // holds the handle to a brush object
  LogBrush: TLogBrush;   // holds brush information
  FormDC: HDC;           // a handle to the form's device context
begin
  {retrieve the form's device context}
  FormDC := GetDC(Form1.Handle);

  {initialize the form's brush, and then retrieve a handle to it}
  Canvas.Brush.Color := clRed;
  Canvas.Brush.Style := bsDiagCross;
  hObject := GetCurrentObject(Canvas.Handle, OBJ_BRUSH);

  {retrieve information about the object}
  GetObject(hObject, SizeOf(TLogBrush), @LogBrush);

  {indicate the type of object retrieved}
  case GetObjectType(hObject) of
    OBJ_BITMAP:   Edit4.Text := 'Bitmap';
    OBJ_BRUSH:    Edit4.Text := 'Brush';
    OBJ_FONT:     Edit4.Text := 'Font';
    OBJ_PAL:      Edit4.Text := 'Palette';
    OBJ_PEN:      Edit4.Text := 'Pen';
    OBJ_EXTPEN:   Edit4.Text := 'Extended Pen';
```

```
      OBJ_REGION:        Edit4.Text := 'Region';
      OBJ_DC:            Edit4.Text := 'Device Context';
      OBJ_MEMDC:         Edit4.Text := 'Memory Device Context';
      OBJ_METAFILE:      Edit4.Text := 'Metafile';
      OBJ_METADC:        Edit4.Text := 'Metafile Device Context';
      OBJ_ENHMETAFILE:   Edit4.Text := 'Enhanced Metafile';
      OBJ_ENHMETADC:     Edit4.Text := 'Enhanced Metafile Device Context';
    end;

    {display the object's information}
    with LogBrush do
    begin
      Edit1.Text := GetStyle(lbStyle);
      Edit2.Text := IntToHex(lbColor, 8);
      Edit3.Text := GetHatch(lbHatch);
    end;

    {select the brush into the form's device context}
    SelectObject(FormDC, hObject);

    {draw an ellipse with the brush}
    Ellipse(FormDC, 50, 10, 150, 110);

    {delete the device context}
    ReleaseDC(Form1.Handle, FormDC);
  end;
```

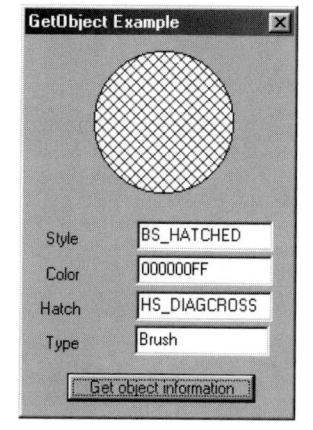

Figure 10-28: The object information

GetObjectType   Windows.pas

Syntax

GetObjectType(
  h: HGDIOBJ   {a handle to a graphic object}
): DWORD;   {returns an object type flag}

Description

This function returns a flag indicating what type of object is referenced by the h parameter.

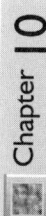

Chapter 10

Parameters

h: A handle to a graphical object whose type is to be retrieved.

Return Value

If the function succeeds, it returns a flag indicating the object type, and it can be one value from the following table. If the function fails, it returns zero.

See Also

DeleteObject, GetCurrentObject, GetObject, GetStockObject, SelectObject

Example

See Listing 10-24 under GetObject.

Table 10-28: GetObjectType return values

Value	Description
OBJ_BITMAP	Bitmap
OBJ_BRUSH	Brush
OBJ_FONT	Font
OBJ_PAL	Palette
OBJ_PEN	Pen
OBJ_EXTPEN	Extended pen
OBJ_REGION	Region
OBJ_DC	Device context
OBJ_MEMDC	Memory device context
OBJ_METAFILE	Metafile
OBJ_METADC	Metafile device context
OBJ_ENHMETAFILE	Enhanced metafile
OBJ_ENHMETADC	Enhanced metafile device context

GetPixel   Windows.pas

Syntax

```
GetPixel(
DC: HDC;           {the handle of a device context}
X: Integer;        {the horizontal pixel coordinate}
Y: Integer         {the vertical pixel coordinate}
): COLORREF;       {returns a color specifier}
```

Description

This function retrieves the color of the pixel at the specified coordinates in the indicated device context. The coordinates must be within the boundaries of the current clipping region.

Painting and Drawing Functions — 407

Parameters

DC: A handle to the device context from which the pixel color is retrieved.

X: The horizontal coordinate of the pixel within the device context in logical units.

Y: The vertical coordinate of the pixel within the device context in logical units.

Return Value

If the function succeeds, it returns the color specifier of the pixel at the indicated coordinates. If the function fails, it returns CLR_INVALID.

See Also

SetPixel, SetPixelV

Example

See Listing 10-44 under SetPixel.

GetPolyFillMode   Windows.pas

Syntax

```
GetPolyFillMode(
  DC: HDC              {the handle of a device context}
): Integer;            {returns the polygon fill mode}
```

Description

This function retrieves the current polygon fill mode for the given device context.

Parameters

DC: A handle to the device context from which the current polygon fill mode is to be retrieved.

Return Value

If the function succeeds, it returns a flag indicating the polygon fill mode of the specified device context, and may be one value from Table 10-29. If the function fails, it returns zero. See Figure 10-45 under SetPolyFillMode for an illustration of these flags.

See Also

FillPath, Polygon, PolyPolygon, SetPolyFillMode

Example

Listing 10-25: Setting and retrieving the polygon fill mode

```
procedure TForm1.FormPaint(Sender: TObject);
var
  PointsArray: Array[0..10] of TPoint;  // holds the polygon definition
  FillMode: Integer;                     // holds the fill mode
begin
  {define the polygon}
```

```
      PointsArray[0].X := 145;
      PointsArray[0].Y := 220;
      PointsArray[1].X := 145;
      PointsArray[1].Y := 20;
      PointsArray[2].X := 310;
      PointsArray[2].Y := 20;
      PointsArray[3].X := 310;
      PointsArray[3].Y := 135;
      PointsArray[4].X := 105;
      PointsArray[4].Y := 135;
      PointsArray[5].X := 105;
      PointsArray[5].Y := 105;
      PointsArray[6].X := 280;
      PointsArray[6].Y := 105;
      PointsArray[7].X := 280;
      PointsArray[7].Y := 50;
      PointsArray[8].X := 175;
      PointsArray[8].Y := 50;
      PointsArray[9].X := 175;
      PointsArray[9].Y := 220;

      {set the polygon fill mode to the selected value}
      if RadioGroup1.ItemIndex = 0 then
        SetPolyFillMode(Canvas.Handle, ALTERNATE)
      else
        SetPolyFillMode(Canvas.Handle, WINDING);

      {display the device context's polygon fill mode}
      FillMode := GetPolyFillMode(Canvas.Handle);
      if FillMode = Alternate then
        Caption := 'GetPolyFillMode Example - Alternate'
      else
        Caption := 'GetPolyFillMode Example - Winding';

      {set the brush to red and draw a filled polygon}
      Canvas.Brush.Color := clRed;
      Polygon(Canvas.Handle, PointsArray, 10);
    end;
```

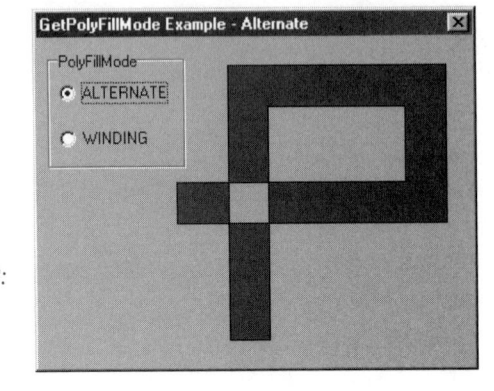

*Figure 10-29:
A specific
polygon fill
mode*

Table 10-29: GetPolyFillMode return values

Value	Description
ALTERNATE	Fills the polygon using the Alternate method.
WINDING	Fills the polygon using the Winding method.

GetROP2   Windows.pas

Syntax

```
GetROP2(
  DC: HDC              {the handle of a device context}
): Integer;            {returns the foreground mix mode}
```

Description

This function retrieves the foreground mix mode for the specified device context. The foreground mix mode determines how the color of the pen used in drawing operations is combined with the color of pixels on the specified device context.

Parameters

DC: A handle to the device context from which the foreground mix mode is to be retrieved.

Return Value

If the function succeeds, it returns a flag indicating the device context's foreground mix mode, and can be one flag from the following table. If the function fails, it returns zero.

See Also

LineTo, PolyBezier, Polyline, Rectangle, SetROP2

Example

Listing 10-26: Using the foreground mix mode to draw a dragable rectangle

```
var
  Form1: TForm1;
  RectDragging: Boolean;    // indicates if a dragging operation has begun
  OldRect: TRect;           // holds the old rectangular coordinates

implementation

{$R *.DFM}

procedure TForm1.FormMouseDown(Sender: TObject; Button: TMouseButton;
  Shift: TShiftState; X, Y: Integer);
begin
  {indicate that a dragging operation has begun}
  RectDragging := TRUE;
end;

procedure TForm1.FormMouseMove(Sender: TObject; Shift: TShiftState; X,
```

```
              Y: Integer);
        begin
          {if we are dragging a rectangle...}
          if RectDragging then
          begin
            {initialize the canvas's pen}
            Canvas.Pen.Width := 5;

            {if the foreground mix mode is not R2_NOT, make it so}
            if GetRop2(Canvas.Handle)<>R2_NOT then
              SetRop2(Canvas.Handle, R2_NOT);

            {set the brush to be clear so only the lines show}
            Canvas.Brush.Style := bsClear;

            {draw a rectangle over the previous one to erase it}
            Canvas.Rectangle(OldRect.Left, OldRect.Top, OldRect.Right, OldRect.Bottom);

            {draw a rectangle at the new position}
            Canvas.Rectangle(X-20, Y-20, X+20, Y+20);

            {store the current rectangle coordinates for next time}
            OldRect := Rect(X-20, Y-20, X+20, Y+20);
          end;
        end;

        procedure TForm1.FormMouseUp(Sender: TObject; Button: TMouseButton;
          Shift: TShiftState; X, Y: Integer);
        begin
          {dragging has stopped}
          RectDragging := FALSE;
        end;
```

Figure 10-30: Drawing the dragable rectangle

Table 10-30: GetROP2 return values

Value	Description
R2_BLACK	The destination pixel is always black.
R2_COPYPEN	The destination pixel is set to the pen color.
R2_MASKNOTPEN	The destination pixel is a combination of the colors common to the screen and the inverse of the pen.

Value	Description
R2_MASKPEN	The destination pixel is a combination of the colors common to the screen and the pen.
R2_MASKPENNOT	The destination pixel is a combination of the colors common to the pen and the inverse of the screen.
R2_MERGENOTPEN	The destination pixel is a combination of the screen and the inverse of the pen.
R2_MERGEPEN	The destination pixel is a combination of the pen and the screen.
R2_MERGEPENNOT	The destination pixel is a combination of the pen and the inverse of the screen.
R2_NOP	The destination pixel is not modified.
R2_NOT	The destination pixel is the inverse of the screen.
R2_NOTCOPYPEN	The destination pixel is the inverse of the pen.
R2_NOTMASKPEN	The destination pixel is the inverse of the R2_MASKPEN flag.
R2_NOTMERGEPEN	The destination pixel is the inverse of the R2_MERGEPEN flag.
R2_NOTXORPEN	The destination pixel is the inverse of the R2_XORPEN flag.
R2_WHITE	The destination pixel is always white.
R2_XORPEN	The destination pixel is a combination of the colors in the pen and in the screen, but not in both.

GetStockObject   Windows.pas

Syntax

GetStockObject(
Index: Integer   {the stock object type flag}
): HGDIOBJ;   {returns a handle to the graphical object}

Description

This function retrieves a handle to a predefined pen, brush, font, or palette. When the application no longer needs the object, it is not necessary to delete it by calling the DeleteObject function.

> **Note:** Use the DKGRAY_BRUSH, GRAY_BRUSH, and LTGRAY_BRUSH stock brushes only in windows with the CS_HREDRAW and CS_VREDRAW class styles, or misalignment of brush patterns may occur if the window is moved or sized. The origin of stock brushes cannot be modified.

Parameters

Index: A flag indicating the type of stock object to retrieve. This parameter may be set to one value from Table 10-31.

Return Value

If the function succeeds, it returns a handle to the predefined graphical object; otherwise, it returns zero.

See Also

DeleteObject, GetObject, GetObjectType, SelectObject

Example

Listing 10-27: Using a stock object

```
procedure TForm1.Button1Click(Sender: TObject);
var
  ARegion: HRGN;      // holds a region
begin
  {create a region to be filled}
  ARegion := CreateRectRgn(20, 20, 190, 110);

  {fill the region with a stock brush}
  FillRgn(Canvas.Handle, ARegion, GetStockObject(BLACK_BRUSH));
end;
```

Table 10-31: GetStockObject Index values

Value	Description
BLACK_BRUSH	Retrieves a handle to a black brush.
DKGRAY_BRUSH	Retrieves a handle to a dark gray brush.
GRAY_BRUSH	Retrieves a handle to a gray brush.
HOLLOW_BRUSH	Retrieves a handle to a hollow brush.
LTGRAY_BRUSH	Retrieves a handle to a light gray brush.
WHITE_BRUSH	Retrieves a handle to a white brush.
BLACK_PEN	Retrieves a handle to a black pen.
NULL_PEN	Retrieves a handle to a null pen.
WHITE_PEN	Retrieves a handle to a white pen.
ANSI_FIXED_FONT	Retrieves a handle to a Windows fixed-pitch (monospace) system font.
ANSI_VAR_FONT	Retrieves a handle to a Windows variable-pitch (proportional space) system font.
DEVICE_DEFAULT_FONT	**Windows NT only:** Retrieves a handle to a device-dependent font.
DEFAULT_GUI_FONT	**Windows 95 only:** Retrieves a handle to the default font used in user interface objects.
OEM_FIXED_FONT	Retrieves a handle to an original equipment manufacturer dependent fixed-pitch (monospace) font.
SYSTEM_FONT	Retrieves a handle to the system font.
SYSTEM_FIXED_FONT	Retrieves a handle to the fixed-pitch (monospace) system font used in Windows versions earlier than 3.0.
DEFAULT_PALETTE	Retrieves a handle to the default palette containing the static colors in the system palette.

GetUpdateRect   Windows.pas

Syntax

```
GetUpdateRect(
  hWnd: HWND;              {the handle to a window}
  var lpRect: TRect;       {a pointer to a TRect structure}
  bErase: BOOL             {background erasure flag}
): BOOL;                   {returns TRUE or FALSE}
```

Description

This function retrieves the coordinates of the smallest rectangle that can be drawn around the invalid region in the specified window. The rectangle will be in terms of client coordinates unless the window was created with the CS_OWNDC class style and the mapping mode is not MM_TEXT. In this case, the rectangle will be in terms of logical coordinates. Note that this function must be used before the BeginPaint function is called, as BeginPaint validates the update region, causing this function to return an empty rectangle.

Parameters

hWnd: A handle to the window whose update region's bounding rectangle is to be retrieved.

lpRect: A pointer to a TRect structure that receives the coordinates of the bounding rectangle.

bErase: A flag indicating if the background in the invalid region should be erased. If this parameter is set to TRUE and the region is not empty, the WM_ERASEBKGND message is sent to the specified window.

Return Value

If the function succeeds, it returns TRUE; otherwise, it returns FALSE.

See Also

BeginPaint, GetUpdateRgn, InvalidateRect

Example

See Listing 10-29 under InvalidateRect.

GetUpdateRgn   Windows.pas

Syntax

```
GetUpdateRgn(
  hWnd: HWND;              {the handle to a window}
  hRgn: HRGN;              {a region handle}
  bErase: BOOL             {background erasure flag}
): Integer;                {returns the type of invalid region}
```

Description

This function retrieves the handle of the invalid region in the specified window. The region is relative to the window's client area. Note that this function must be used before the BeginPaint function is called, as BeginPaint validates the update region, causing this function to return an empty region.

Parameters

hWnd: A handle to the window from which the update region is to be retrieved.

hRgn: A handle to a pre-existing region. This handle will be reset to point to the invalid region when the function returns.

bErase: A flag indicating if the background in the invalid region should be erased and the non-client areas of child windows are redrawn. If this parameter is set to TRUE and the region is not empty, the WM_ERASEBKGND message is sent to the specified window and non-client areas of child windows are redrawn.

Return Value

This function returns a result indicating the type of region retrieved or an error condition, and may be one value from Table 10-32.

See Also

GetUpdateRect, InvalidateRgn

Example

See Listing 10-30 under InvalidateRgn.

Table 10-32: GetUpdateRgn return values

Value	Description
NULLREGION	Indicates an empty region.
SIMPLEREGION	Indicates a single rectangular region.
COMPLEXREGION	Indicates a region consisting of more than one rectangle.
ERROR	Indicates an error occurred.

GrayString   Windows.pas

Syntax

```
GrayString(
hDC: HDC;                           {the handle of a device context}
hBrush: HBRUSH;                     {the brush handle}
lpOutputFunc: TFNGrayStringProc;    {a pointer to the callback function}
lpData: LPARAM;                     {a pointer to the string}
nCount: Integer;                    {the length of the string}
X: Integer;                         {the horizontal output coordinate}
Y: Integer;                         {the vertical output coordinate}
```

nWidth: Integer;	{the width of the offscreen bitmap}
nHeight: Integer	{the height of the offscreen bitmap}
): BOOL;	{returns TRUE or FALSE}

Description

This function draws text at the specified location on the indicated device context. The text is drawn by creating an offscreen bitmap, drawing the text into the bitmap, converting the color of the text using the specified brush or a default brush, and finally copying the bitmap onto the specified canvas at the indicated coordinates. The font currently selected in the specified device context is used to draw the text. If the lpOutputFunc parameter is set to NIL, the lpData parameter must contain a pointer to a string and the TextOut function is used to draw the string into the offscreen bitmap. Otherwise, the lpData parameter can point to any type of user-defined data, such as a bitmap, and the callback function pointed to by the lpOutputFunc parameter must draw the data into the offscreen bitmap.

Parameters:

hDC: A handle to the device context upon which the string is drawn.

hBrush: A handle to a brush used to convert the color of the text. If this parameter is set to zero, this function uses the default brush used to draw window text.

lpOutputFunc: A pointer to a callback function that will handle the output of the text. If this parameter is set to NIL, the function uses the TextOut function to draw the text onto the offscreen bitmap.

lpData: If the lpOutputFunc parameter contains NIL, this parameter specifies a pointer to the string to be drawn. This must be a null-terminated string if the nCount parameter is set to zero. Otherwise, this parameter contains a pointer to data that will be passed to the callback function.

nCount: Specifies the length of the string pointed to by the lpData parameter, in characters. If this parameter is set to 0, the function will calculate the length of the string if it is null-terminated. If this parameter is set to –1 and the callback function pointed to by the lpOutputFunc parameter returns FALSE, the string will be displayed in its original form.

X: Specifies the horizontal coordinate at which to display the string, in device units.

Y: Specifies the vertical coordinate at which to display the string, in device units.

nWidth: Specifies the width, in device units, of the offscreen bitmap into which the string is drawn. If this parameter is set to zero, the function will calculate the width of the offscreen bitmap if the lpData parameter contains a pointer to a string.

nHeight: Specifies the height, in device units, of the offscreen bitmap into which the string is drawn. If this parameter is set to zero, the function will calculate the height of the offscreen bitmap if the lpData parameter contains a pointer to a string.

Return Value

If the function succeeds, it returns TRUE; otherwise, it returns FALSE.

Callback Syntax

GrayStringOutputProc(
hdc: HDC;   {the handle of the offscreen bitmap device context}
lpData: LPARAM;   {a pointer to the data to be drawn}
cchData: Integer   {the length of the string}
): BOOL;   {returns TRUE or FALSE}

Description

This callback function is used to draw the specified string or user-defined data in an application-specific manner. The hdc parameter specifies a handle to a device context representing the offscreen bitmap created by the GrayString function. The callback function must draw the data in whatever manner desired onto this device context, which will be copied onto the device context specified by the hDC parameter of the GrayString function when the callback function returns. This callback function can perform any desired action.

Parameters

hdc: A handle to the device context of the offscreen bitmap upon which the data or string must be drawn. The device context will have the same width and height as specified by the nWidth and nHeight parameters of the GrayString function.

lpData: A pointer to the data to be drawn, as specified by the lpData parameter of the GrayString function.

cchData: Specifies the length of the string, in characters, as passed to the GrayString function in the nCount parameter.

Return Value

The callback function should return TRUE to indicate it was successful; it should return FALSE otherwise.

See Also

DrawText, GetSysColor*, SetTextColor, TabbedTextOut, TextOut

Example

Listing 10-28: Drawing grayed text

```
procedure TForm1.FormPaint(Sender: TObject);
var
  Str: PChar;       // points to the string to be drawn
begin
  {initialize the string pointer}
  Str := 'Delphi Rocks!';

  {initialize the brush used to draw the string}
  Canvas.Brush.Color := clRed;
```

```
        {draw the string}
        GrayString(Canvas.Handle, Canvas.Brush.Handle, NIL, LPARAM(Str), Length(Str),
               10, 10, 0, 0);
end;
```

Figure 10-31: The grayed text

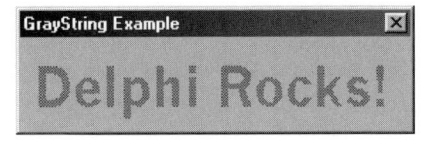

InvalidateRect   Windows.pas

Syntax

InvalidateRect(
hWnd: HWND;   {the handle of a window}
lpRect: PRect;   {a pointer to the rectangular coordinates}
bErase: BOOL   {background erasure flag}
): BOOL;   {returns TRUE or FALSE}

Description

This function adds the specified rectangle to the invalid region of the indicated window, causing it to receive a WM_PAINT message.

Parameters

hWnd: A handle to the window containing the invalid region to which the specified rectangle is added. If this parameter is set to zero, all windows are invalidated and will receive the WM_ERASEBKGND and WM_NCPAINT messages before the function returns.

lpRect: A pointer to a TRect structure containing the rectangular coordinates of the area to be added to the invalid region. If this parameter is set to NIL, the entire client area is added to the invalid region.

bErase: A flag indicating if the background in the invalid region should be erased. If this parameter is set to TRUE and the region is not empty, the background of the entire invalid region is erased when the BeginPaint function is called.

Return Value

If the function succeeds, it returns TRUE; otherwise, it returns FALSE.

See Also

BeginPaint, GetUpdateRect, InvalidateRgn

Example

Listing 10-29: Drawing only the invalid rectangle of a canvas

```
procedure TForm1.Button2Click(Sender: TObject);
var
```

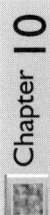

```
    InvalidRectangle: TRect; //rectangle to invalidate
begin
  {define the rectangle}
  InvalidRectangle := Rect(10, 10, 110, 110);

  {erase only the rectangular area}
  InvalidateRect(Form1.Handle, @InvalidRectangle, TRUE);
end;

procedure TForm1.WMPaint(var Msg: TWMPaint);
var
  InvalidRect: TRect;            // holds the invalid rectangular area
  PaintStruct: TPaintStruct;     // holds painting information
begin
  {retrieve the invalid rectangle}
  GetUpdateRect(Handle, InvalidRect, TRUE);

  {begin the painting process. this validates the invalid region}
  BeginPaint(Handle, PaintStruct);

  {if the entire client area is invalid...}
  if EqualRect(InvalidRect, ClientRect) then
    {...redraw the bitmap in Image1 to the canvas}
    Canvas.Draw(0, 0, Image1.Picture.Bitmap)
  else
  begin
    {...otherwise, draw a red rectangle in the entire invalid rectangular
     area, and label it as a previously invalid area}
    Canvas.Brush.Color := clRed;
    Canvas.Rectangle(InvalidRect.Left, InvalidRect.Top, InvalidRect.Right,
                     InvalidRect.Bottom);
    Canvas.TextOut(InvalidRect.Left+10, InvalidRect.Top+10, 'Invalid Rect');
  end;

  {end the painting operation}
  EndPaint(Handle, PaintStruct);
end;
```

Figure 10-32:
The invalid rectangle

InvalidateRgn   Windows.pas

Syntax

```
InvalidateRgn(
hWnd: HWND;              {the handle of a window}
hRgn: HRGN;              {the handle of a region}
bErase: BOOL             {background erasure flag}
): BOOL;                 {always returns TRUE}
```

Description

This function adds the given region to the invalid region of the specified window, causing it to receive a WM_PAINT message.

Parameters

hWnd: A handle to the window containing the invalid region to which the specified region is added.

hRgn: A handle to the region defining the area to be added to the invalid region. The region is assumed to be in client coordinates. If this parameter is set to zero, the entire client area is added to the invalid region.

bErase: A flag indicating if the background in the invalid region should be erased. If this parameter is set to TRUE and the region is not empty, the background of the entire invalid region is erased when the BeginPaint function is called.

Return Value

This function always returns TRUE.

See Also

BeginPaint, GetUpdateRgn, InvalidateRect

Example

Listing 10-30: Drawing only the invalid region of a canvas

```
procedure TForm1.Button2Click(Sender: TObject);
var
  PointsArray: array[0..2] of TPoint; // an array of points defining the region
  RegionHandle: HRGN;                 // a handle to the region
begin
  {define the region}
  PointsArray[0].X := 20;
  PointsArray[0].y := 20;
  PointsArray[1].x := 100;
  PointsArray[1].y := 65;
  PointsArray[2].x := 20;
  PointsArray[2].y := 120;

  {create the region}
  RegionHandle := CreatePolygonRgn(PointsArray, 3, ALTERNATE);
```

```
  {invalidate the region}
  InvalidateRgn(Form1.Handle, RegionHandle, TRUE);

  {the region is no longer needed, so delete it}
  DeleteObject(RegionHandle);
end;

procedure TForm1.WMPaint(var Msg: TWMPaint);
var
  InvalidRgn: HRGN;           // a handle to the invalid region
  PaintStruct: TPaintStruct;  // holds painting information
begin
  {GetUpdateRgn requires a handle to a pre-existing region, so create one}
  InvalidRgn := CreateRectRgn(0, 0, 1, 1);

  {retrieve the handle to the update region}
  GetUpdateRgn(Handle, InvalidRgn, FALSE);

  {begin the painting operation}
  BeginPaint(Handle, PaintStruct);

  {if the region is equal to the entire client area...}
  if EqualRgn(InvalidRgn, CreateRectRgnIndirect(ClientRect)) then
    {...draw the bitmap in Image1 to the form's canvas}
    Canvas.Draw(0, 0, Image1.Picture.Bitmap)
  else
  begin
    {...otherwise draw the invalid region in red}
    Canvas.Brush.Color := clRed;
    FillRgn(Canvas.Handle, InvalidRgn, Canvas.Brush.Handle);
  end;

  {end the painting operation}
  EndPaint(Handle, PaintStruct);

  {delete the region object, as it is no longer needed}
  DeleteObject(InvalidRgn);
end;
```

Figure 10-33:
The invalid region

LineDDA   Windows.pas

Syntax

```
LineDDA(
  p1: Integer;              {the horizontal coordinate of the starting point}
  p2: Integer;              {the vertical coordinate of the starting point}
  p3: Integer;              {the horizontal coordinate of the ending point}
  p4: Integer;              {the vertical coordinate of the ending point}
  p5: TFNLineDDAProc;       {a pointer to the callback function}
  p6: LPARAM                {application-defined data}
): BOOL;                    {returns TRUE or FALSE}
```

Description

This function draws a line by passing the coordinates for each point on the line, except the endpoint, to the application-defined callback function. The callback function determines how the line will actually be drawn. If the default mapping modes and transformations are in effect, the coordinates passed to the callback function match the pixels on the video display.

Parameters

p1: Specifies the horizontal coordinate of the line's starting point.

p2: Specifies the vertical coordinate of the line's starting point.

p3: Specifies the horizontal coordinate of the line's ending point.

p4: Specifies the vertical coordinate of the line's ending point.

p5: A pointer to the application-defined callback function.

p6: Specifies an application-defined value.

Return Value

If the function succeeds, it returns TRUE; otherwise, it returns FALSE.

Callback Syntax

```
LineDDAProc(
  X: Integer;               {the horizontal line coordinate}
  Y: Integer;               {the vertical line coordinate}
  lpData: LPARAM            {application-defined data}
);                          {this procedure does not return a value}
```

Description

This procedure is called for each pixel in the line defined by the LineDDA function. The callback function can perform any desired drawing action based on these coordinates, such as placing a pixel, copying a bitmap, etc.

Parameters

X: The current horizontal coordinate along the line.

Y: The current vertical coordinate along the line.

lpData: Specifies a 32-bit application-defined data as passed to the LineDDA function in the p6 parameter. This value is intended for application-specific purposes.

Return Value

This procedure does not return a value.

See Also

ExtCreatePen, LineTo

Example

Listing 10-31: Drawing an animated selection rectangle

```
{the callback function prototype}
  procedure AnimLines(X, Y: Integer; lpData: lParam); stdcall;

var
  Form1: TForm1;
  Offset: Integer;

const
  AL_HORIZONTAL = 1;    // indicates if the line to be drawn is
  AL_VERTICAL = 2;      // horizontal or vertical

implementation

{$R *.DFM}

procedure AnimLines(X, Y: Integer; lpData: lParam);
var
  Coord: Integer;       // holds the coordinate used in the calculation
begin
  {if the line is horizontal, use the X coordinate, otherwise use Y}
  if lpData=AL_HORIZONTAL then
    Coord := X
  else
    Coord := Y;

  {determine if the pixel at this point should be black or white}
  if (Coord mod 5=Offset) then
    SetPixelV(Form1.Canvas.Handle, X, Y, clBlack)
  else
    SetPixelV(Form1.Canvas.Handle, X, Y, clWhite);
end;

procedure TForm1.Timer1Timer(Sender: TObject);
begin
  {increment the offset}
  Inc(Offset);
```

```
      {if the offset has gone too far, reset it}
      if Offset>4 then Offset := 0;

      {draw a rectangle with animated lines}
      LineDDA(20, 20, 120, 20, @AnimLines, AL_HORIZONTAL);
      LineDDA(120, 20, 120, 120, @AnimLines, AL_VERTICAL);
      LineDDA(20, 20, 20, 120, @AnimLines, AL_VERTICAL);
      LineDDA(20, 120, 120, 120, @AnimLines, AL_HORIZONTAL);
   end;
```

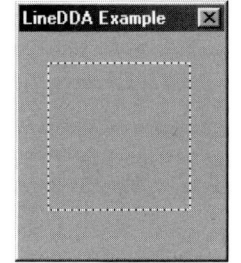

Figure 10-34: The animated rectangle

LineTo Windows.pas

Syntax

```
LineTo(
 DC: HDC;              {the handle of a device context}
 X: Integer;           {the horizontal coordinate of the line destination}
 Y: Integer;           {the vertical coordinate of the line destination}
): BOOL;               {returns TRUE or FALSE}
```

Description

This function draws a line using the current pen selected into the specified device context. The line is drawn from the current position to the specified coordinates. The point at the specified coordinates is excluded from the actual drawn pixels of the line. The current position will be updated to the specified coordinates when the function returns.

Parameters

DC: A handle to the device context upon which the line is drawn.

X: Specifies the horizontal coordinate of the endpoint of the line, in logical units.

Y: Specifies the vertical coordinate of the endpoint of the line, in logical units.

Return Value

If the function succeeds, it returns TRUE; otherwise, it returns FALSE.

See Also

LineDDA, MoveToEx, PolyBezier, PolyBezierTo, Polyline, PolylineTo, PolyPolyline

Example

See Listing 10-23 under GetCurrentPositionEx.

LockWindowUpdate   Windows.pas

Syntax

```
LockWindowUpdate(
hWndLock: HWND          {the handle of a window}
): BOOL;                {returns TRUE or FALSE}
```

Description

This function disables or enables all painting and drawing operations within the specified window. A locked window cannot be moved, and only one window may be locked at a time. Windows records the areas in which any painting or drawing operations are attempted in the locked window. When the window is unlocked, the area affected by these drawing operations is invalidated, causing a WM_PAINT message to be sent to the window. If the GetDC or BeginPaint functions are used on a locked window, the returned device context will contain an empty visible region.

Parameters

hWndLock: A handle to the window for which drawing operations are to be disabled. If this parameter is set to zero, the currently locked window is enabled.

Return Value

If the function succeeds, it returns TRUE; otherwise, it returns FALSE.

See Also

BeginPaint, GetDC

Example

Listing 10-32: Enabling and disabling window updating

```
procedure TForm1.Button1Click(Sender: TObject);
begin
 {disable window painting}
 LockWindowUpdate(Form1.Handle);
end;

procedure TForm1.Button2Click(Sender: TObject);
begin
  {enable window painting}
  LockWindowUpdate(0);
end;
```

MoveToEx Windows.pas

Syntax

```
MoveToEx(
DC: HDC;              {the handle of a device context}
p2: Integer;          {the horizontal coordinate}
p3: Integer;          {the vertical coordinate}
p4: PPoint            {a pointer to a TPoint structure}
): BOOL;              {TRUE if successful}
```

Description

This function moves the current position of the indicated device context to the specified coordinates, returning the old position. This affects all drawing functions that use the current position as a starting point.

Parameters

DC: A handle to the device context whose current position is to be set.

p2: Specifies the horizontal coordinate of the new current position in logical units.

p3: Specifies the vertical coordinate of the new current position in logical units.

p4: A pointer to a TPoint structure that receives the coordinates of the old current position. This parameter may be set to NIL if the old current position coordinates are not needed.

Return Value

If the function succeeds, it returns TRUE; otherwise, it returns FALSE.

See Also

LineTo, PolyBezierTo, PolylineTo

Example

See Listing 10-23 under GetCurrentPositionEx.

PaintDesktop Windows.pas

Syntax

```
PaintDesktop(
hDC: HDC              {the handle of a device context}
): BOOL;              {returns TRUE or FALSE}
```

Description

This function paints the clipping region in the given device context with the desktop wallpaper bitmap or pattern.

Parameters

hDC: A handle to the device context upon which the desktop wallpaper or pattern is drawn.

Return Value

If the function succeeds, it returns TRUE; otherwise, it returns FALSE.

See Also

BitBlt, GetDC, SystemParametersInfo*

Example

Listing 10-33: Drawing the desktop onto a form

```
procedure TForm1.FormPaint(Sender: TObject);
begin
  {display the desktop wallpaper}
  PaintDesktop(Canvas.Handle);
end;

procedure TForm1.WMMoving(var Msg: TMessage);
begin
  {display the desktop wallpaper when moving}
  PaintDesktop(Canvas.Handle);
end;
```

PaintRgn   Windows.pas

Syntax

```
PaintRgn(
  DC: HDC;           {the handle of a device context}
  RGN: HRGN          {the handle of a region}
): BOOL;             {returns TRUE or FALSE}
```

Description

This function paints the specified region onto the device context using its currently selected brush.

Parameters

DC: A handle to the device context upon which the region is drawn.

RGN: A handle to the region to be drawn.

Return Value

If the function succeeds, it returns TRUE; otherwise, it returns FALSE.

See Also

ExtFloodFill, FillPath, FillRect, FillRgn, FrameRect, FrameRgn

Example

Listing 10-34: Filling a region with the current brush

```
procedure TForm1.FormPaint(Sender: TObject);
var
  PointsArray: Array[0..5] of TPoint;    // points defining a region
  RegionHandle: HRgn;                    // the handle of the region
begin
  {define the region}
  PointsArray[0].X := 50;
  PointsArray[0].y := 50;
  PointsArray[1].x := 100;
  PointsArray[1].y := 50;
  PointsArray[2].x := 125;
  PointsArray[2].y := 75;
  PointsArray[3].x := 100;
  PointsArray[3].y := 100;
  PointsArray[4].x := 50;
  PointsArray[4].y := 100;
  PointsArray[5].x := 25;
  PointsArray[5].y := 75;

  {create the region}
  RegionHandle := CreatePolygonRgn(PointsArray, 6, ALTERNATE);

  {paint the region using the canvas's brush}
  Canvas.Brush.Color := clGreen;
  Canvas.Brush.Style := bsBDiagonal;
  PaintRgn(Canvas.Handle, RegionHandle);
end;
```

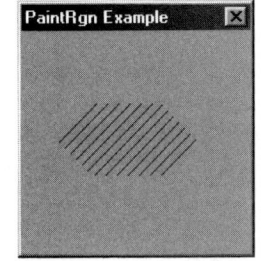

Figure 10-35:
The painted region

Pie   Windows.pas

Syntax

```
Pie(
  DC: HDC;              {the handle of a device context}
  X1: Integer;          {x coordinate of the upper-left corner}
  Y1: Integer;          {y coordinate of the upper-left corner}
  X2: Integer;          {x coordinate of the lower-right corner}
  Y2: Integer;          {y coordinate of the lower-right corner}
  X3: Integer;          {x coordinate of the first radial ending point}
```

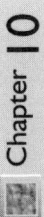

Y3: Integer;   {y coordinate of the first radial ending point}
X4: Integer;   {x coordinate of the second radial ending point}
Y4: Integer   {y coordinate of the second radial ending point}
): BOOL;   {returns TRUE or FALSE}

Description

This function draws a pie-shaped wedge with the current pen and fills the wedge with the current brush. A pie is a region bounded by an ellipse and two radial line segments. The extent of the pie-shaped wedge is defined by the bounding rectangle. The X3 and Y3 parameters define the endpoints of a radial line starting from the center of the bounding rectangle and identify the starting location of the wedge area. The X4 and Y4 parameters define the endpoints of a radial line starting from the center of the bounding rectangle and identify the ending location of the wedge area. The wedge is drawn in a counterclockwise direction, and will not affect the current position.

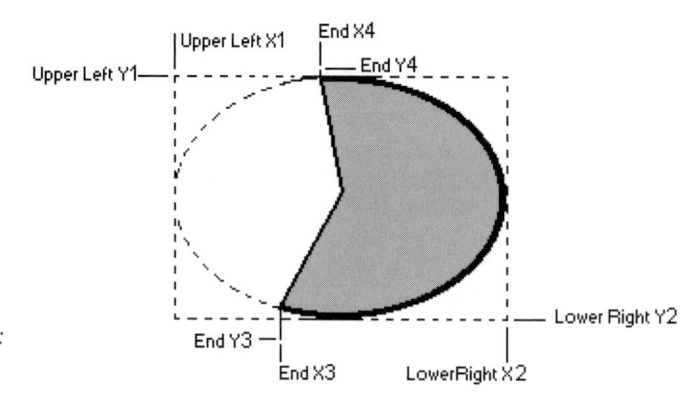

Figure 10-36: Pie coordinates

Parameters

DC: Specifies the device context upon which the pie is drawn.

X1: Specifies the horizontal coordinate of the upper-left corner of the bounding rectangle, in logical units.

Windows 95: The sum of the X1 and X2 parameters must be less than 32,767.

Y1: Specifies the vertical coordinate of the upper-left corner of the bounding rectangle, in logical units.

Windows 95: The sum of the Y1 and Y2 parameters must be less than 32,767.

X2: Specifies the horizontal coordinate of the lower-right corner of the bounding rectangle, in logical units.

Y2: Specifies the vertical coordinate of the lower-right corner of the bounding rectangle, in logical units.

X3: Specifies the horizontal coordinate, in logical units, of the ending point of the radial line that defines the starting point of the pie.

Y3: Specifies the vertical coordinate, in logical units, of the ending point of the radial line that defines the starting point of the pie.

X4: Specifies the horizontal coordinate, in logical units, of the ending point of the radial line that defines the ending point of the pie.

Y4: Specifies the vertical coordinate, in logical units, of the ending point of the radial line that defines the ending point of the pie.

Return Value

If this function succeeds, it returns TRUE; otherwise, it returns FALSE. To get extended error information, call the GetLastError function.

See Also

Arc, Chord, Ellipse

Example

Listing 10-35: Drawing a pie wedge

```
procedure TForm1.FormPaint(Sender: TObject);
begin
  {draw a pie shaped wedge}
  Canvas.Brush.Color := clRed;
  Canvas.Brush.Style := bsDiagCross;
  Pie(Canvas.Handle, 10, 10, 110, 110, 10, 60, 60, 10);
end;
```

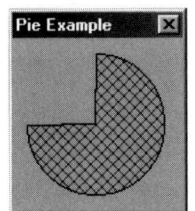

Figure 10-37:
The pie wedge

PolyBezier   Windows.pas

Syntax

```
PolyBezier(
 DC: HDC;              {the handle of a device context}
 const Points;         {a pointer to an array of coordinates}
 Count: DWORD          {the number of entries in the array}
): BOOL;               {returns TRUE or FALSE}
```

Description

This function draws one or more cubic Bézier curves on the specified device context using its current pen. The Points parameter points to an array of TPoint structures containing the start point, control points, and endpoint of the Bézier curves. The first point in the array defines the starting point of the curve. The next two points are used as the control points, and the fourth point defines the ending point. Every three points after that define the two control points and the endpoint of another Bézier curve, using the endpoint of the previous curve as its starting point. This function does not affect the current position.

Parameters

DC: A handle to the device context upon which the bézier curve is drawn.

Points: A pointer to an array of TPoint structures containing the control points and endpoints of the Bézier curves.

Count: Specifies the number of entries in the array pointed to by the Points parameter.

Return Value

If the function succeeds, it returns TRUE; otherwise, it returns FALSE.

See Also

MoveToEx, PolyBezierTo

Example

Listing 10-36: Drawing a Bézier curve

```
procedure TForm1.FormPaint(Sender: TObject);
var
  Points: array[0..6] of TPoint; // points defining the bezier curve
begin
  {define the bezier curve}
  Points[0].X := 10;
  Points[0].Y := 50;
  Points[1].X := 40;
  Points[1].Y := 90;
  Points[2].X := 80;
  Points[2].Y := 10;
  Points[3].X := 110;
  Points[3].Y := 50;
  Points[4].X := 140;
  Points[4].Y := 10;
  Points[5].X := 180;
  Points[5].Y := 90;
  Points[6].X := 210;
  Points[6].Y := 50;

  {draw the bezier curve}
  PolyBezier(Canvas.Handle, Points, 7);
end;
```

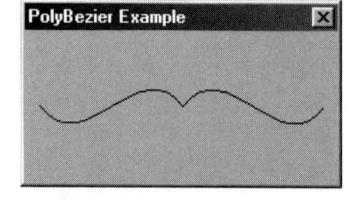

Figure 10-38:
The Bézier curve

PolyBezierTo   Windows.pas

Syntax

```
PolyBezierTo(
DC: HDC;                    {the handle of a device context}
const Points;               {a pointer to an array of coordinates}
Count: DWORD                {the number of entries in the array}
): BOOL;                    {returns TRUE or FALSE}
```

Description

This function draws one or more cubic Bézier curves on the specified device context using its current pen. The Points parameter points to an array of TPoint structures containing the start point, control points, and endpoint of the Bézier curves. The first point in the array defines the starting point of the curve. The next two points are used as the control points, and the fourth point defines the ending point. Every three points after that define the two control points and the endpoint of another Bézier curve, using the endpoint of the previous curve as its starting point. The current position will be updated to the last point in the Points array.

Parameters

DC: A handle to the device context upon which the Bézier curve is drawn.

Points: A pointer to an array of TPoint structures containing the control points and endpoints of the Bézier curves.

Count: Specifies the number of entries in the array pointed to by the Points parameter.

Return Value

If the function succeeds, it returns TRUE; otherwise, it returns FALSE.

See Also

MoveToEx, PolyBezier

Example

Listing 10-37: Drawing a Bézier curve and updating the current position

```
procedure TForm1.FormPaint(Sender: TObject);
var
  Points: array[0..2] of TPoint;  // the points defining the bezier curve
begin
  {define the bezier curve}
  Points[0].X := 40;
  Points[0].Y := 110;
  Points[1].X := 80;
  Points[1].Y := 30;
  Points[2].X := 110;
  Points[2].Y := 70;
```

```
  {move the current position to the correct starting point}
  MoveToEx(Canvas.Handle, 10, 70, NIL);

  {draw the bezier curve}
  PolyBezierTo(Canvas.Handle, Points, 3);

  {the current position was updated, so we can use this to continue
   drawing an image}
  LineTo(Canvas.Handle, 110, 10);
  LineTo(Canvas.Handle, 10, 10);
  LineTo(Canvas.Handle, 10, 70);
end;
```

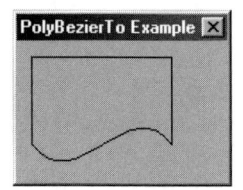

Figure 10-39: The Bézier curve

Polygon   Windows.pas

Syntax

```
Polygon(
DC: HDC;                     {the handle of a device context}
const Points;                {a pointer to an array of coordinates}
Count: DWORD                 {the number of entries in the array}
): BOOL;                     {returns TRUE or FALSE}
```

Description

This function draws a polygon on the specified device context using its current pen, and fills the polygon using the device context's current brush and polygon fill mode. The Points parameter points to an array of TPoint structures defining the vertices of the polygon. The polygon will automatically be closed by drawing a line from the last vertex in the array to the first vertex in the array. This function does not affect the current position.

Parameters

DC: A handle to the device context upon which the polygon is drawn.

Points: A pointer to an array of TPoint structures containing the vertices of the polygon. This array must contain at least two vertices or the function will fail.

Count: Specifies the number of entries in the array pointed to by the Points parameter.

Return Value

If the function succeeds, it returns TRUE; otherwise, it returns FALSE. To get extended error information, call the GetLastError function.

See Also

GetPolyFillMode, Polyline, PolylineTo, PolyPolygon, PolyPolyline, SetPolyFillMode

Example

See Listing 10-25 under GetPolyFillMode.

Polyline   Windows.pas

Syntax

```
Polyline(
  DC: HDC;                {the handle of a device context}
  const Points;           {a pointer to an array of coordinates}
  Count: DWORD            {the number of entries in the array}
): BOOL;                  {returns TRUE or FALSE}
```

Description

This function draws a polygon on the specified device context using its current pen. The Points parameter points to an array of TPoint structures defining the vertices of the polygon. The polygon is drawn by connecting the points in the array with line segments. This function does not affect the current position.

Parameters

DC: A handle to the device context upon which the polygon is drawn.

Points: A pointer to an array of TPoint structures containing the vertices of the polygon.

Count: Specifies the number of entries in the array pointed to by the Points parameter.

Return Value

If the function succeeds, it returns TRUE; otherwise, it returns FALSE.

See Also

LineTo, MoveToEx, PolylineTo, PolyPolyline

Example

Listing 10-38: Drawing a polygon outline

```
procedure TForm1.FormPaint(Sender: TObject);
var
  PointsArray: array[0..6] of TPoint;    // points defining the polygon
begin
  {define the vertices of the polygon}
  PointsArray[0].X := 50;
  PointsArray[0].y := 50;
  PointsArray[1].x := 100;
  PointsArray[1].y := 50;
  PointsArray[2].x := 125;
  PointsArray[2].y := 75;
  PointsArray[3].x := 100;
  PointsArray[3].y := 100;
  PointsArray[4].x := 50;
  PointsArray[4].y := 100;
  PointsArray[5].x := 25;
```

```
      PointsArray[5].y := 75;
      PointsArray[6].X := 50;
      PointsArray[6].Y := 50;

   {draw the polygon}
   Polyline(Canvas.Handle, PointsArray, 7);
end;
```

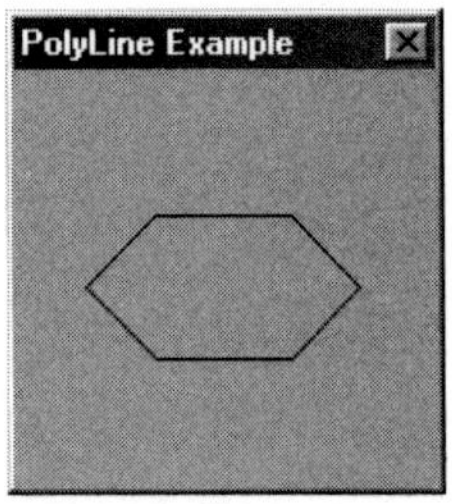

Figure 10-40: The unfilled polygon

PolylineTo   Windows.pas

Syntax

```
PolylineTo(
DC: HDC;                   {the handle of a device context}
const Points;              {a pointer to an array of coordinates}
Count: DWORD               {the number of entries in the array}
): BOOL;                   {returns TRUE or FALSE}
```

Description

This function draws a polygon on the specified device context using its current pen. The Points parameter points to an array of TPoint structures defining the vertices of the polygon. The polygon is drawn by connecting the points in the array with line segments, starting from the current position. The current position is updated to the last coordinate in the array of vertices when the function returns.

Parameters

DC: A handle to the device context upon which the polygon is drawn.

Points: A pointer to an array of TPoint structures containing the vertices of the polygon.

Count: Specifies the number of entries in the array pointed to by the Points parameter.

Return Value

If the function succeeds, it returns TRUE; otherwise, it returns FALSE.

See Also

LineTo, MoveToEx, Polyline, PolyPolyline

Example

Listing 10-39: Drawing an unfilled polygon starting from the current position

```
procedure TForm1.FormPaint(Sender: TObject);
var
  PointsArray: array[0..5] of TPoint; // the points defining the polygon
begin
  {move the current position to where the polygon will start}
  MoveToEx(Canvas.Handle, 50, 50, nil);

  {define the polygon}
  PointsArray[0].x := 100;
  PointsArray[0].y := 50;
  PointsArray[1].x := 125;
  PointsArray[1].y := 75;
  PointsArray[2].x := 100;
  PointsArray[2].y := 100;
  PointsArray[3].x := 50;
  PointsArray[3].y := 100;
  PointsArray[4].x := 25;
  PointsArray[4].y := 75;
  PointsArray[5].X := 50;
  PointsArray[5].Y := 50;

  {draw the polygon, starting at the current position}
  PolylineTo(Canvas.Handle, PointsArray, 6);
end;
```

PolyPolygon   Windows.pas

Syntax

```
PolyPolygon(
  DC: HDC;              {the handle of a device context}
  var Points;           {a pointer to an array of coordinates}
  var nPoints;          {a pointer to an array of vertex counts}
  p4: Integer           {the number of polygons}
): BOOL;                {returns TRUE or FALSE}
```

Description

This function draws a series of closed polygons on the specified device context using its current pen, and fills the polygons using the device context's current brush and polygon fill mode. The Points parameter points to an array of TPoint structures defining the vertices of each polygon. The nPoints parameter points to an array of integers, where each integer specifies the number of entries in the Points array that define one polygon. The polygon will automatically be closed by drawing a line from the last vertex defining the polygon to the first vertex defining the polygon. This function does not affect the current position.

Parameters

DC: A handle to the device context upon which the polygons are drawn.

Points: A pointer to an array of TPoint structures containing the vertices of each polygon. The vertices are arranged in consecutive order, and should only be specified once. The polygons defined by this array can overlap.

nPoints: A pointer to an array of integers, where each integer specifies the number of entries in the array pointed to by the Points parameter that define an individual polygon.

p4: Indicates the total number of polygons that will be drawn.

Return Value

If the function succeeds, it returns TRUE; otherwise, it returns FALSE. To get extended error information, call the GetLastError function.

See Also

GetPolyFillMode, Polygon, Polyline, PolylineTo, PolyPolyline, SetPolyFillMode

Example

Listing 10-40: Drawing multiple polygons

```
procedure TForm1.FormPaint(Sender: TObject);
var
  PointsArray: array[0..9] of TPoint;   // holds the vertices of the polygons
  NPoints: array[0..1] of Integer;      // the number of vertices in each polygon
begin
  {define the polygons -}
  {first polygon}
  PointsArray[0].X := 50;
  PointsArray[0].y := 50;
  PointsArray[1].x := 100;
  PointsArray[1].y := 50;
  PointsArray[2].x := 125;
  PointsArray[2].y := 75;
  PointsArray[3].x := 100;
  PointsArray[3].y := 100;
  PointsArray[4].x := 50;
  PointsArray[4].y := 100;
  PointsArray[5].x := 25;
  PointsArray[5].y := 75;
  {second polygon}
  PointsArray[6].X := 200;
  PointsArray[6].y := 25;
  PointsArray[7].X := 300;
  PointsArray[7].Y := 25;
  PointsArray[8].X := 300;
  PointsArray[8].Y := 125;
  PointsArray[9].X := 200;
  PointsArray[9].Y := 125;

  {indicate how many vertices are in each polygon}
  NPoints[0] := 6;
```

```
      NPoints[1] := 4;

      {draw the polygons}
      PolyPolygon(Canvas.Handle, PointsArray, NPoints, 2);
    end;
```

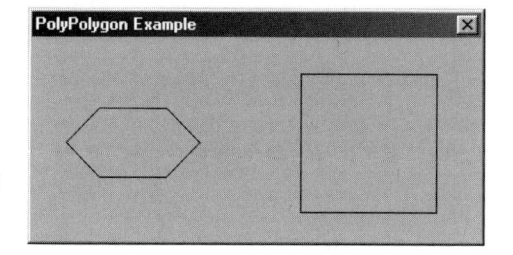

Figure 10-41:
Multiple
polygons

PolyPolyline   Windows.pas

Syntax

```
PolyPolyline(
DC: HDC;                  {the handle of a device context}
const PointStructs;       {a pointer to an array of coordinates}
const Points;             {a pointer to an array of vertex counts}
p4: DWORD                 {the number of polygons}
): BOOL;                  {returns TRUE or FALSE}
```

Description

This function draws a series of polygons on the specified device context using its current pen. The PointStructs parameter points to an array of TPoint structures defining the vertices of each polygon. The Points parameter points to an array of integers, where each integer specifies the number of entries in the PointStructs array that define one polygon. The polygon is drawn by connecting the points in the array with line segments. This function does not affect the current position.

Parameters

DC: A handle to the device context upon which the polygons are drawn.

PointStructs: A pointer to an array of TPoint structures containing the vertices of each polygon. The vertices are arranged in consecutive order, and should only be specified once.

Points: A pointer to an array of integers, where each integer specifies the number of entries in the array pointed to by the PointStructs parameter that define an individual polygon.

p4: Indicates the total number of polygons that will be drawn.

Return Value

If the function succeeds, it returns TRUE; otherwise, it returns FALSE.

See Also

Polygon, Polyline, PolylineTo, PolyPolygon

Example

Listing 10-41: Drawing multiple unfilled polygons

```
procedure TForm1.FormPaint(Sender: TObject);
var
  PointsArray: array[0..11] of TPoint; // the vertices defining the polygons
  NPoints: array[0..1] of Integer;     // the number of vertices in each polygon
begin
  {define the polygons -}
  {first polygon}
  PointsArray[0].X := 50;
  PointsArray[0].y := 50;
  PointsArray[1].x := 100;
  PointsArray[1].y := 50;
  PointsArray[2].x := 125;
  PointsArray[2].y := 75;
  PointsArray[3].x := 100;
  PointsArray[3].y := 100;
  PointsArray[4].x := 50;
  PointsArray[4].y := 100;
  PointsArray[5].x := 25;
  PointsArray[5].y := 75;
  PointsArray[6].X := 50;
  PointsArray[6].Y := 50;
  {second polygon}
  PointsArray[7].X := 200;
  PointsArray[7].y := 25;
  PointsArray[8].X := 300;
  PointsArray[8].Y := 25;
  PointsArray[9].X := 300;
  PointsArray[9].Y := 125;
  PointsArray[10].X := 200;
  PointsArray[10].Y := 125;
  PointsArray[11].X := 200;
  PointsArray[11].Y := 25;

  {indicate how many vertices are in each polygon}
  NPoints[0] := 7;
  NPoints[1] := 5;

  {draw the unfilled polygons}
  PolyPolyline(Canvas.Handle, PointsArray, NPoints, 2);
end;
```

Rectangle   Windows.pas

Syntax

```
Rectangle(
  DC: HDC;              {the handle of a device context}
  X1: Integer;          {the horizontal coordinate of the upper-left corner}
```

Y1: Integer;   {the vertical coordinate of the upper-left corner}
X2: Integer;   {the horizontal coordinate of the lower-right corner}
Y2: Integer   {the vertical coordinate of the lower-right corner}
): BOOL;   {returns TRUE or FALSE}
```

*Description*

This function draws a rectangle on the specified device context at the indicated coordinates using the current pen and fills it with the current brush. This function does not affect the current position.

*Parameters*

DC: A handle to the device context upon which the rectangle is drawn.

X1: Specifies the horizontal coordinate of the upper-left corner of the rectangle, in logical units.

Y1: Specifies the vertical coordinate of the upper-left corner of the rectangle, in logical units.

X2: Specifies the horizontal coordinate of the lower-right corner of the rectangle, in logical units.

Y2: Specifies the vertical coordinate of the lower-right corner of the rectangle, in logical units.

*Return Value*

If the function succeeds, it returns TRUE; otherwise, it returns FALSE. To get extended error information, call the GetLastError function.

*See Also*

CreateRectRgn, CreateRectRgnIndirect, FillRect, FrameRect, Polygon, Polyline, RoundRect

*Example*

**Listing 10-42: Drawing a rectangle with an animated fill**

```
var
  Form1: TForm1;
  BrushOffset: Integer;   // holds the current brush offset

implementation

{$R *.DFM}

procedure TForm1.Timer1Timer(Sender: TObject);
var
  BrushPt: TPoint;   // holds the current brush origin
  BrushHndl, OldBrush: HBRUSH;   // handles to brushes
  FormDC: HDC;   // the form's device context
begin
  {retrieve the form's device context}
```
```

```
    FormDC := GetDC(Form1.Handle);

    {increment the brush offset}
    Inc(BrushOffset);

    {create a hatched brush}
    BrushHndl := CreateHatchBrush(HS_DIAGCROSS, clRed);

    {set the brushes origin}
    SetBrushOrgEx(FormDC, BrushOffset, BrushOffset, nil);

    {select the brush into the device context}
    OldBrush := SelectObject(FormDC, BrushHndl);

    {retrieve the current brush origin}
    GetBrushOrgEx(FormDC, BrushPt);

    {if the brush origin is beyond the limit, reset it}
    if BrushPt.X>7 then
    begin
      BrushOffset := 0;
      SetBrushOrgEx(FormDC, BrushOffset, BrushOffset, nil);
    end;

    {draw the rectangle}
    Rectangle(FormDC, 10, 10, 110, 110);

    {delete the new brush}
    SelectObject(FormDC, OldBrush);
    DeleteObject(BrushHndl);

    {release the form's device context}
    ReleaseDC(Form1.Handle, FormDC);
end;
```

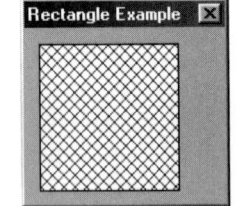

Figure 10-42: The animated rectangle

RoundRect   Windows.pas

Syntax

```
RoundRect(
DC: HDC;                 {the handle of a device context}
X1: Integer;             {the horizontal coordinate of the upper-left corner}
Y1: Integer;             {the vertical coordinate of the upper-left corner}
X2: Integer;             {the horizontal coordinate of the lower-right corner}
Y2: Integer;             {the vertical coordinate of the lower-right corner}
```

X3: Integer;	{the width of the corner ellipse}
Y3: Integer	{the height of the corner ellipse}
): BOOL;	{returns TRUE or FALSE}

Description

This function draws a rectangle on the specified device context at the indicated coordinates using the current pen and fills it with the current brush. The corners of the rectangle will be rounded according to the ellipse formed by the X3 and Y3 parameters. This function does not affect the current position.

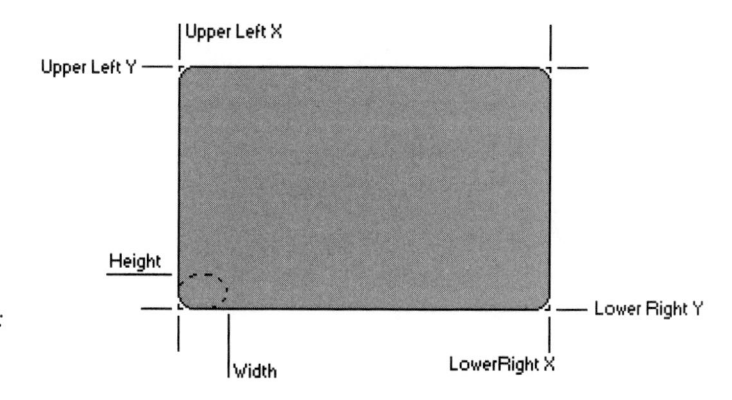

Figure 10-43: RoundRect coordinates

Parameters

DC: A handle to the device context upon which the rounded rectangle is drawn.

X1: Specifies the horizontal coordinate of the upper-left corner of the rounded rectangle, in logical units.

Y1: Specifies the vertical coordinate of the upper-left corner of the rounded rectangle, in logical units.

X2: Specifies the horizontal coordinate of the lower-right corner of the rounded rectangle, in logical units.

Y2: Specifies the vertical coordinate of the lower-right corner of the rounded rectangle, in logical units.

X3: Indicates the width of the ellipse used to draw the corners.

Y3: Indicates the height of the ellipse used to draw the corners.

Return Value

If the function succeeds, it returns TRUE; otherwise, it returns FALSE. To get extended error information, call the GetLastError function.

See Also

CreateRoundRectRgn, FillRect, FrameRect, Polygon, Polyline, Rectangle

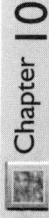

Example

Listing 10-43: Drawing a rounded rectangle

```
procedure TForm1.FormPaint(Sender: TObject);
begin
  {create a rounded rectangle}
  RoundRect(Canvas.Handle, 10, 10, 110, 110, 20, 20);
end;
```

Figure 10-44:
The rounded
rectangle

SelectObject   Windows.pas

Syntax

```
SelectObject(
  DC: HDC;              {the handle to a device context}
  p2: HGDIOBJ          {the handle to a graphical object}
): HGDIOBJ;            {returns a handle to the previously selected object}
```

Description

This function selects the specified graphical object into the indicated device context for use. Most graphical objects must be selected into a device context before they can be used in drawing functions. The newly selected object replaces the previously selected object of the same type. The application should reselect the previously selected object back into the device context when the new object is no longer needed. A graphical object must not be destroyed while it is selected into a device context.

Parameters

DC: A handle to the device context into which the object is selected.

p2: Specifies a handle to the graphical object to be selected into the device context, such as a brush, pen, bitmap, region, or font. Note that bitmaps can only be selected into one device context at a time.

Return Value

If the selected object is not a region and the function succeeds, it returns a handle to the previously selected object of the same type. If the function succeeds and the selected object is a region, it returns one value from the following table. If the function fails and the selected object is not a region, it returns zero; otherwise, it returns GDI_ERROR.

See Also

CombineRgn, CreateBitmap, CreateBitmapIndirect, CreateBrushIndirect, CreateCompatibleBitmap, CreateDIBitmap, CreateEllipticRgn, CreateEllipticRgnIndirect, CreateFont, CreateFontIndirect, CreateHatchBrush, CreatePatternBrush, CreatePen, CreatePenIndirect, CreatePolygonRgn, CreateRectRgn, CreateRectRgnIndirect, CreateSolidBrush, DeleteObject, SelectClipRgn

Example

See Listing 10-8 under CreateSolidBrush and other examples throughout this book.

Table 10-33: SelectObject return values

Value	Description
COMPLEXREGION	The region consists of multiple rectangles.
NULLREGION	The region is empty.
SIMPLEREGION	The region is a single rectangle.

SetBkColor   Windows.pas

Syntax

```
SetBkColor(
  DC: HDC;              {the handle of a device context}
  Color: COLORREF       {the new background color}
): COLORREF;            {returns the previous background color}
```

Description

This function sets the background color for the specified device context. If the device cannot represent the specified color, the nearest physical color is used.

Parameters

DC: A handle to the device context whose background color is being set.

Color: A color specifier identifying the new color.

Return Value

If the function succeeds, it returns the previous background color; otherwise, it returns CLR_INVALID.

See Also

CreatePen, ExtCreatePen, GetBkColor, GetBkMode, SetBkMode

Example

See Listing 10-21 under GetBkColor.

SetBkMode   Windows.pas

Syntax

```
SetBkMode(
  DC: HDC;              {the handle of a device context}
  BkMode: Integer       {a background mode flag}
): Integer;             {returns the previous background mode}
```

Description

This function sets the background mix mode of the given device context.

Parameters

DC: A handle to the device context whose background mix mode is to be set.

BkMode: A flag indicating the new background mix mode. This parameter can be set to one value from the following table.

Return Value

If the function succeeds, it returns the previous background mix mode; otherwise, it returns zero.

See Also

CreatePen, ExtCreatePen, GetBkColor, GetBkMode, SetBkColor

Example

See Listing 10-21 under GetBkColor.

Table 10-34: SetBkMode BkMode values

Value	Description
OPAQUE	The background color is used to fill the gaps in text, hatched brushes, and pen patterns.
TRANSPARENT	The color of the device context shows through the gaps in text, hatched brushes, and pen patterns.

SetBoundsRect   Windows.pas

Syntax

```
SetBoundsRect(
  DC: HDC;              {handle of the device context}
  p2: TRect;            {a pointer to a TRect structure}
  p3: UINT              {operation flags}
): UINT;                {returns the previous bounding rectangle state}
```

Description

This function modifies the bounding rectangle accumulation behavior of the given device context. Windows maintains an accumulated bounding rectangle for each device context that identifies the extent of output from drawing functions. When a drawing function reaches beyond this boundary, the rectangle is extended. Thus, the bounding rectangle is the smallest rectangle that can be drawn around the area affected by all drawing operations in the device context.

Parameters

DC: A handle to the device context whose bounding rectangle accumulation behavior is to be modified.

p2: A pointer to a TRect structure containing the rectangular coordinates, in logical units, of the new bounding rectangle. This parameter can be set to NIL if the bounding rectangle does not need to be set.

p3: A series of flags indicating how the specified rectangle is to be combined with the current bounding rectangle, and whether bounding rectangle accumulation is enabled. This parameter may be set to a combination of values from Table 10-35.

Return Value

This function returns a code indicating the state of the bounding rectangle or an error condition, and will be one or more values from Table 10-36.

See Also

GetBoundsRect, GetUpdateRect

Example

See Listing 10-22 under GetBoundsRect.

Table 10-35: SetBoundsRect p3 values

Value	Description
DCB_ACCUMULATE	Adds the rectangle specified by the p2 parameter to the current bounding rectangle by performing a union. If both the DCB_RESET and DCB_ACCUMULATE flags are specified, the bounding rectangle is set to the exact rectangle specified by the p2 parameter.
DCB_DISABLE	Turns bounding rectangle accumulation off. This is the default state.
DCB_ENABLE	Turns bounding rectangle accumulation on.
DCB_RESET	Clears the bounding rectangle.

Table 10-36: SetBoundsRect Return values

Value	Description
0	Indicates that an error occurred.
DCB_DISABLE	Boundary accumulation is off.
DCB_ENABLE	Boundary accumulation is on.
DCB_RESET	The bounding rectangle is empty.
DCB_SET	The bounding rectangle is not empty.

SetBrushOrgEx   Windows.pas

Syntax

SetBrushOrgEx(
DC: HDC;   {the handle of a device context}
X: Integer;   {the horizontal coordinate of the origin}
Y: Integer;   {the vertical coordinate of the origin}
PrevPt: PPoint   {a pointer to a TPoint structure}
): BOOL;   {returns TRUE or FALSE}

Description

This function sets the origin of the next brush selected into the specified device context. The brush origin is relative to the hatch or bitmap defining the brush's pattern. The default brush origin is at 0,0. A brush pattern can be no more than 8 pixels square. Thus, the origin can range from 0-7 vertically and horizontally. As the origin is moved, the brush pattern is offset by the specified amount. If an application is using a pattern brush to draw the backgrounds of child windows and parent windows, the brush origin may need to be moved to align the patterns. Note that under Windows NT, the system automatically tracks the brush origin so that patterns will be aligned.

Parameters

DC: A handle to the device context whose brush origin is to be set.

X: Specifies the horizontal coordinate of the brush origin in device units.

Y: Specifies the vertical coordinate of the brush origin in device units.

PrevPt: A pointer to a TPoint structure that receives the coordinates of the previous brush origin. This parameter can be set to NIL if the previous coordinates are not needed.

Return Value

If the function succeeds, it returns TRUE; otherwise, it returns FALSE. To get extended error information, call the GetLastError function.

See Also

CreateBrushIndirect, CreateHatchBrush, CreatePatternBrush, FillRect, FillRgn, GetBrushOrgEx, SelectObject

Example

See Listing 10-42 under Rectangle.

SetMiterLimit   Windows.pas

Syntax

SetMiterLimit(
DC: HDC;   {the handle of a device context}
NewLimit: Single;   {the new miter limit}

```
      OldLimit: PSingle        {receives the old miter limit}
      ): BOOL;                 {returns TRUE or FALSE}
```

Description

This function sets the miter limit for the specified device context. The miter limit is used for geometric lines that have miter joins and is the maximum ratio of the miter length to the line width. The miter length is the distance from the intersection of the inner wall to the intersection of the outer wall. The default miter limit is 10.0.

Parameters

DC: A handle to the device context whose miter limit is to be set.

NewLimit: Specifies the new miter limit for the given device context.

OldLimit: A pointer to a variable that receives the old miter limit. This parameter can be set to NIL if the old miter limit is not needed.

Return Value

If the function succeeds, it returns TRUE; otherwise, it returns FALSE. To get extended error information, call the GetLastError function.

See Also

ExtCreatePen, GetMiterLimit

Example

See Listing 10-16 under ExtCreatePen.

SetPixel   Windows.pas

Syntax

```
      SetPixel(
      DC: HDC;                 {the handle of a device context}
      X: Integer;              {the horizontal pixel coordinate}
      Y: Integer;              {the vertical pixel coordinate}
      Color: COLORREF          {the new pixel color}
      ): COLORREF;             {returns a color specifier}
```

Description

This function sets the color of the pixel at the specified coordinates in the indicated device context. The coordinates must be within the boundaries of the current clipping region.

Parameters

DC: A handle to the device context in which the new pixel color is set.

X: The horizontal coordinate of the pixel within the device context, in logical units.

Y: The vertical coordinate of the pixel within the device context, in logical units.

Color: Specifies the color of the pixel.

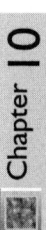

Return

If the function succeeds, it returns the color to which the pixel was set. This may be different from the specified color if an exact color match could not be found. If the function fails, it returns CLR_INVALID.

See Also

GetPixel, SetPixelV

Example

Listing 10-44: Implementing a cheap bitmap fade-in effect

```
procedure TForm1.Button1Click(Sender: TObject);
begin
  {erase the current image}
  Canvas.Brush.Color := Color;
  Canvas.FillRect(ClientRect);

  {begin the effect}
  Timer1.Enabled := TRUE;
end;

procedure TForm1.Timer1Timer(Sender: TObject);
var
  X, Y: Integer;      // tracks pixel coordinates
  iCount: Integer;    // a general loop counter
begin
  {begin the cheap fade effect}
  for iCount := 0 to 20000 do
  begin
    {retrieve a random coordinate}
    X := Random(Image1.Width-1);
    Y := Random(Image1.Height-1);

    {in a 4x4 pixel square at this coordinate, retrieve the pixels in the
     source image, and set them in the form's canvas}
    SetPixel(Canvas.Handle, X+Image1.Left, Y+Image1.Top,
             GetPixel(Image1.Picture.Bitmap.Canvas.Handle, X, Y));
    SetPixel(Canvas.Handle, X+1+Image1.Left, Y+Image1.Top,
             GetPixel(Image1.Picture.Bitmap.Canvas.Handle, X+1, Y));
    SetPixel(Canvas.Handle, X+Image1.Left, Y+1+Image1.Top,
             GetPixel(Image1.Picture.Bitmap.Canvas.Handle, X, Y+1));
    SetPixel(Canvas.Handle, X+1+Image1.Left, Y+1+Image1.Top,
             GetPixel(Image1.Picture.Bitmap.Canvas.Handle, X+1, Y+1));
  end;

  {draw the finished image so that there are no holes left}
  Canvas.Draw(Image1.Left, Image1.Top, Image1.Picture.Bitmap);

  {disable the timer}
  Timer1.Enabled := FALSE;
end;
```

SetPixelV   Windows.pas

Syntax

```
SetPixelV(
  DC: HDC;              {the handle of a device context}
  X: Integer;           {the horizontal pixel coordinate}
  Y: Integer;           {the vertical pixel coordinate}
  Color: COLORREF       {the new pixel color}
): BOOL;                {returns TRUE or FALSE}
```

Description

This function sets the color of the pixel at the specified coordinates in the indicated device context. It is generally faster than SetPixel because it does not have to return a color. The coordinates must be within the boundaries of the current clipping region.

Parameters

DC: A handle to the device context in which the new pixel color is set.

X: The horizontal coordinate of the pixel within the device context, in logical units.

Y: The vertical coordinate of the pixel within the device context, in logical units.

Color: Specifies the color of the pixel.

Return Value

If the function succeeds, it returns TRUE; otherwise, it returns FALSE. To get extended error information, call the GetLastError function.

See Also

GetPixel, SetPixel

Example

See Listing 10-31 under LineDDA.

SetPolyFillMode   Windows.pas

Syntax

```
SetPolyFillMode(
  DC: HDC;                  {the handle of a device context}
  PolyFillMode: Integer     {the polygon fill mode flag}
): Integer;                 {returns the previous polygon fill mode}
```

Description

This function sets the polygon fill mode of the specified device context. The polygon fill mode determines how complex polygons and regions are to be filled. To determine what pixels will be filled when using the Alternate mode, select any pixel within the polygon's interior and draw an imaginary line in the positive X direction out to infinity. For each line in the polygon crossed by the imaginary line, a value is incremented. The pixel will be highlighted if this value is an odd number. To determine what pixels will be filled when using the Winding mode, select any pixel within the polygon's interior and draw an imaginary line in the positive X direction out to infinity. For each line in the polygon crossed by the imaginary line, if the polygon line was drawn in a positive Y direction, a value is incremented; if the polygon line was drawn in a negative Y direction, a value is decremented. The pixel will be highlighted if this value is non-zero.

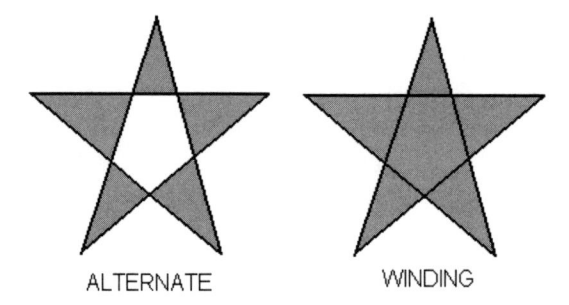

Figure 10-45: Polygon fill mode results

ALTERNATE   WINDING

Parameters

DC: A handle to the device context whose current polygon fill mode is to be set.

PolyFillMode: A flag indicating the new polygon fill mode. This parameter may be set to one value from Table 10-37.

Return Value

If the function succeeds, it returns a value from the following table indicating the previous polygon fill mode. If the function fails, it returns zero.

See Also

FillPath, GetPolyFillMode, Polygon, PolyPolygon

Example

See Listing 10-25 under GetPolyFillMode.

Table 10-37: SetPolyFillMode return values

Value	Description
ALTERNATE	Fills the polygon using the Alternate method.
WINDING	Fills the polygon using the Winding method.

SetROP2   Windows.pas

Syntax

```
SetROP2(
   DC: HDC;              {the handle of a device context}
   p2: Integer           {the foreground mix mode flag}
): Integer;              {returns the previous foreground mix mode}
```

Description

This function sets the foreground mix mode for the specified device context. The foreground mix mode determines how the color of the pen used in drawing operations is combined with the color of pixels on the specified device context.

Parameters

DC: A handle to the device context whose foreground mix mode is to be set.

p2: A flag specifying the new foreground mix mode. This parameter can be set to one value from Table 10-38.

Return Value

If the function succeeds, it returns a value from the following table indicating the previous foreground mix mode. If the function fails, it returns zero.

See Also

GetROP2, LineTo, PolyBezier, Polyline, Rectangle

Example

See Listing 10-26 under GetROP2.

Table 10-38: SetROP2 p2 return values

Value	Description
R2_BLACK	The destination pixel is always black.
R2_COPYPEN	The destination pixel is set to the pen color.
R2_MASKNOTPEN	The destination pixel is a combination of the colors common to the screen and the inverse of the pen.
R2_MASKPEN	The destination pixel is a combination of the colors common to the screen and the pen.
R2_MASKPENNOT	The destination pixel is a combination of the colors common to the pen and the inverse of the screen.
R2_MERGENOTPEN	The destination pixel is a combination of the screen and the inverse of the pen.
R2_MERGEPEN	The destination pixel is a combination of the pen and the screen.
R2_MERGEPENNOT	The destination pixel is a combination of the pen and the inverse of the screen.
R2_NOP	The destination pixel is not modified.
R2_NOT	The destination pixel is the inverse of the screen.
R2_NOTCOPYPEN	The destination pixel is the inverse of the pen.
R2_NOTMASKPEN	The destination pixel is the inverse of the R2_MASKPEN flag.
R2_NOTMERGEPEN	The destination pixel is the inverse of the R2_MERGEPEN flag.
R2_NOTXORPEN	The destination pixel is the inverse of the R2_XORPEN flag.
R2_WHITE	The destination pixel is always white.
R2_XORPEN	The destination pixel is a combination of the colors in the pen and in the screen, but not in both.

StrokeAndFillPath   Windows.pas

Syntax

```
StrokeAndFillPath(
  DC: HDC                         {the handle of a device context}
): BOOL;                          {returns TRUE or FALSE}
```

Description

This function closes any open figures in the path in the specified device context, and outlines and fills the path with the device context's currently selected pen and brush, respectively. The path is filled according to the current polygon filling mode. Note that after this function returns, the path is discarded from the device context.

Parameters

DC: A handle to the device context containing the path to be outlined and filled.

Return Value

If the function succeeds, it returns TRUE; otherwise, it returns FALSE. To get extended error information, call the GetLastError function.

See Also

BeginPath, FillPath, SetPolyFillMode, StrokePath

Example

Listing 10-45: Outlining and filling a path simultaneously

```
procedure TForm1.FormPaint(Sender: TObject);
begin
  {begin a path bracket}
  BeginPath(Canvas.Handle);

  {draw some cool text}
  SetBkMode(Canvas.Handle, TRANSPARENT);
  Canvas.TextOut(10, 10, 'DELPHI ROCKS!');

  {end the path bracket}
  EndPath(Canvas.Handle);

  {initialize the pen and brush to be used in filling and outlining the path}
  Canvas.Pen.Color := clRed;
  Canvas.Pen.Style := psSolid;
  Canvas.Brush.Color := clBlue;
  Canvas.Brush.Style := bsDiagCross;

  {fill and outline the path}
  StrokeAndFillPath(Canvas.Handle);
end;
```

Figure 10-46:
The outlined and filled path

StrokePath   Windows.pas

Syntax

```
StrokePath(
  DC: HDC              {the handle of a device context}
): BOOL;               {returns TRUE or FALSE}
```

Description

This function outlines the path contained in the specified device context with the currently selected pen. Note that after this function returns, the path is discarded from the device context.

Parameters

DC: A handle to the device context containing the path to be outlined.

Return Value

If the function succeeds, it returns TRUE; otherwise, it returns FALSE. To get extended error information, call the GetLastError function.

See Also

BeginPath, EndPath, ExtCreatePen, FillPath, StrokeAndFillPath

Example

Listing 10-46: Outlining a path

```
procedure TForm1.FormPaint(Sender: TObject);
begin
  {begin a path bracket}
  BeginPath(Canvas.Handle);

  {draw some cool text}
  SetBkMode(Canvas.Handle, TRANSPARENT);
  Canvas.TextOut(10, 10, 'DELPHI ROCKS!');

  {end the path bracket}
  EndPath(Canvas.Handle);

  {initialize the pen to be used in outlining the path}
  Canvas.Pen.Color := clRed;
  Canvas.Pen.Style := psSolid;
```

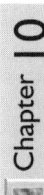

```
   {outline the path}
   StrokePath(Canvas.Handle);
end;
```

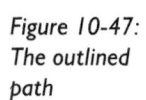

*Figure 10-47:
The outlined
path*

Chapter 11

Region and Path Functions

When producing graphical output on a device context, it is often necessary to confine the output to an area smaller than the client area, or to a non-rectangular area. Monochrome masks, offscreen buffers, and raster operations could be combined to produce the desired effect, resulting in a rather complicated method of graphical output. Alternatively, the developer can take advantage of a special Windows feature known as regions and paths. The region and path functions are not encapsulated by the Delphi VCL, and are therefore almost undocumented in most Delphi literature. These functions can be used to create startling effects, and can provide elegant solutions that might otherwise involve the complicated series of steps suggested above. This chapter discusses the region and path functions available in the Win32 API.

Regions and Paths

At first, a region and a path may appear to be very similar. They both define a shape. They can be filled or outlined with user-defined brushes and pens as desired. Upon further inspection, however, the differences between regions and paths become apparent.

Regions

A region is a closed, polygonal shape. It is not a shape in the visual sense; it acts as a shape definition that can be rendered with various techniques. Generally, a region is constructed with specific functions that create a shape definition in the form of a polygonal primitive, such as a rectangle or ellipse. As such, regions tend to be simpler in shape than paths. However, regions can be combined with other regions in various ways to produce more complex shapes. The CombineRgn function performs this service, using various flags representing Boolean operations to combine regions in different ways, as illustrated in the following figure.

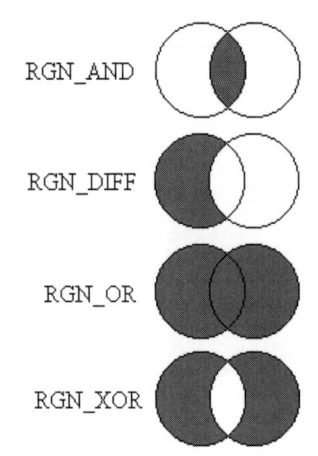

*Figure 11-1:
CombineRgn
region
combination
methods*

Unlike a path, a region can be used for hit testing. Hit testing is the act of determining where the mouse cursor is relative to a given area, usually in response to a mouse click. By using the PtInRect or PtInRegion functions combined with rectangles or regions, the developer can create hot spots of very complex shapes. For example, an application could define 50 different regions in the form of the 50 states. Using these regions as hot spots on a map of the United States, a particular state could be highlighted when the mouse cursor enters its perimeter, or information could be displayed when it is clicked upon. This could easily be accomplished in the OnMouseDown event of a TImage or the form itself, using the PtInRegion function to compare the clicked coordinates with each region until the correct region is found. Also different from paths, a region can be moved relative to its original coordinates, and can be compared to other regions for equality.

If more detailed information on a region is required, an application can use the GetRegionData function to retrieve the various attributes of a region. In particular, a region is internally defined as a series of rectangles, sorted in top to bottom, left to right order. The GetRegionData function can be used to retrieve the individual rectangles that define a region, as illustrated in the following example.

Listing 11-1: Retrieving region information

```
procedure TForm1.Button1Click(Sender: TObject);
var
  TheRegion: HRGN;              // holds the region
  RegionDataSize: DWORD;        // holds the size of region information
  RegionData: Pointer;          // a pointer to the region information
  iCount: Integer;              // general loop control variable
  RectPointer: ^TRect;          // a pointer used to extract rectangle coordinates
begin
  {create a round rectangular region}
  TheRegion := CreateRoundRectRgn(10, 10, 110, 110, 30, 30);

  {initialize the canvas's brush and draw the region}
  Canvas.Brush.Color := clRed;
  FillRgn(Canvas.Handle, TheRegion, Canvas.Brush.Handle);

  {retrieve the size of the buffer required to hold the region data,
```

```
      and allocate the specified memory}
  RegionDataSize := GetRegionData(TheRegion, 0, NIL);
  GetMem(RegionData, RegionDataSize);

  {retrieve the information about the round rectangular region}
  GetRegionData(TheRegion, RegionDataSize, RegionData);

  {display the information}
  with ListBox1.Items do
  begin
    {display the number of rectangles in the region, and the size of
     the region's bounding rectangle}
    Add('Number of rectangles: '+IntToStr(TRgnData(RegionData^).rdh.nCount));
    Add('Region bounding rectangle -');
    Add('Left: '+IntToStr(TRgnData(RegionData^).rdh.rcBound.Left)+
        ' Top: '+IntToStr(TRgnData(RegionData^).rdh.rcBound.Top)+
        ' Right: '+IntToStr(TRgnData(RegionData^).rdh.rcBound.Right)+
        ' Bottom: '+IntToStr(TRgnData(RegionData^).rdh.rcBound.Bottom));
    Add('');

    {initialize a pointer to the address of the buffer containing the
     coordinates of the rectangles defining the region}
    RectPointer := @TRgnData(RegionData^).Buffer;

    {set the canvas's pen to a different color so the rectangles will show}
    Canvas.Pen.Color := clBlack;

    {loop through the indicated number of rectangles}
    for iCount := 0 to TRgnData(RegionData^).rdh.nCount-1 do
    begin
      {the RectPointer pointer by definition will typecast the values in the
       Buffer array as a TRect, thereby allowing the application to extract
       the necessary members}
      Add('Rect: '+IntToStr(iCount)+
          ' - L: '+IntToStr(RectPointer^.Left)+
          ', T: '+IntToStr(RectPointer^.Top)+
          ', R: '+IntToStr(RectPointer^.Right)+
          ', B: '+IntToStr(RectPointer^.Bottom));

      {draw this specific rectangle over the region}
      Canvas.Rectangle(RectPointer^.Left, RectPointer^.Top, RectPointer^.Right,
                  RectPointer^.Bottom);
      {since the pointer is a pointer to a TRect, incrementing its value will
       move it forward by the size of a TRect structure. thus, it will be
       pointing to the next rectangle in the series}
      Inc(RectPointer);
    end;
  end;

  {delete the region and free the allocated memory}
  FreeMem(RegionData);
  DeleteObject(TheRegion);
end;
```

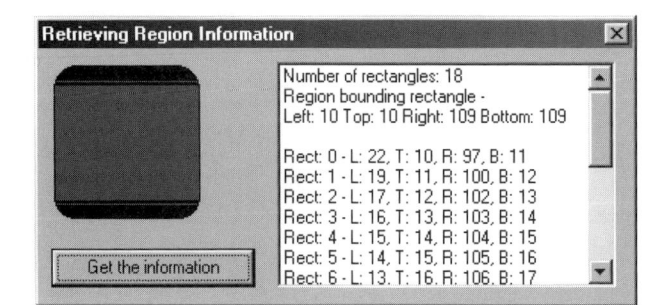

Figure 11-2:
The region information

[Screenshot: "Retrieving Region Information" dialog showing rounded rectangle region with listing — Number of rectangles: 18; Region bounding rectangle - Left: 10 Top: 10 Right: 109 Bottom: 109; Rect: 0 - L: 22, T: 10, R: 97, B: 11; Rect: 1 - L: 19, T: 11, R: 100, B: 12; Rect: 2 - L: 17, T: 12, R: 102, B: 13; Rect: 3 - L: 16, T: 13, R: 103, B: 14; Rect: 4 - L: 15, T: 14, R: 104, B: 15; Rect: 5 - L: 14, T: 15, R: 105, B: 16; Rect: 6 - L: 13, T: 16, R: 106, B: 17; with "Get the information" button.]

Paths

Like a region, a path is a shape definition. However, paths do not need to form a closed polygonal shape. A path can be anything from a rectangle to a complex series of lines and Bézier curves. A path is created by using a series of GDI drawing functions in what is known as a path bracket. A path bracket is a section of code that starts with the BeginPath function and ends with the EndPath function. Specific drawing functions used between these two functions will not produce output to the screen. They will instead define the shape of a path. As such, paths are generally much more complex in shape than regions. See the BeginPath function for a list of drawing functions that can be used in a path bracket.

Unlike regions, where any number of which can be created, a path is associated with the device context in which it was defined. Only one path can exist in a device context at a time, and when another path bracket is started or the device context is destroyed, the current path is destroyed. However, a path can be converted into a region by using the PathToRegion function. This allows the developer to create incredibly complex region shapes. The points defining the path can be retrieved by calling the GetPath function. This function returns an array of TPoint structures containing the coordinates of the points defining the region, in logical units. A common use for this function is in algorithms that fit text to a path or shape, such as a curve.

Special Effects

Perhaps the most common use of a region or path is to define a clipping region. When a clipping region is defined and selected into a device context, any graphical output to the device context is confined within the boundaries of the region. Any output that would appear outside of the region is discarded, or clipped. Combining the functionality of regions with paths and using the result as a clipping region can produce some astonishing special effects. For example, a path can be created by using the TextOut function to define a word or sentence. This path can then be converted into a region, and used in conjunction with bitmap functions and some animation techniques to produce a truly unique splash screen. The following example demonstrates this technique. Note that the bitmap used inside of the text is moving from right to left.

Listing II-2: Cool special effects produced with regions and paths

```
var
  Form1: TForm1;
  Offset: Integer;              // bitmap offset counter
  Buffer, TileBitmap: TBitmap;  // offscreen and texture bitmaps

implementation

{$R *.DFM}

procedure TForm1.FormPaint(Sender: TObject);
begin
  {draw a frame of the effect}
  DrawEffect;
end;

procedure TForm1.FormCreate(Sender: TObject);
begin
  {initialize the offset counter}
  Offset := 0;

  {create an offscreen buffer the size of the form's client area}
  Buffer := TBitmap.Create;
  Buffer.Width  := ClientWidth;
  Buffer.Height := ClientHeight;

  {create and load the texture bitmap used in the letters}
  TileBitmap := TBitmap.Create;
  TileBitmap.LoadFromFile(ExtractFilePath(ParamStr(0))+'Tile.bmp');
end;

procedure TForm1.FormDestroy(Sender: TObject);
begin
  {free the offscreen and texture bitmaps}
  Buffer.Free;
  TileBitmap.Free;
end;

procedure TForm1.Timer1Timer(Sender: TObject);
begin
  {increment the offset counter}
  Inc(Offset);

  {if the offset is larger than the texture bitmap (64 pixels), reset it}
  if Offset>63 then
    Offset := 0;

  {draw a frame of the effect}
  DrawEffect;
end;

procedure TForm1.DrawEffect;
var
  iCount: Integer;      // a general loop counter
  ClipRgn: HRGN;        // holds the region
begin
```

```
{begin a path bracket}
BeginPath(Canvas.Handle);

{output some text, defining the path as the interior of the text}
SetBkMode(Canvas.Handle, TRANSPARENT);
TextOut(Canvas.Handle, 10, 60, 'DELPHI', 6);

{end the path bracket}
EndPath(Canvas.Handle);

{convert the path into a region, and select this region as the offscreen
 buffer's clipping region}
ClipRgn := PathToRegion(Canvas.Handle);
SelectClipRgn(Buffer.Canvas.Handle, ClipRgn);

{draw the texture bitmap into the area defined by the region.  it will get
 clipped to the interior of the letters}
for iCount := 0 to 4 do
  Buffer.Canvas.Draw(iCount*64-Offset, 60, TileBitmap);

{delete the clipping region of the offscreen buffer}
SelectClipRgn(Buffer.Canvas.Handle, 0);

{reset the clipping region of the offscreen buffer, this time defining the
 clipping region as the area outside of the letters}
ExtSelectClipRgn(Buffer.Canvas.Handle, ClipRgn, RGN_DIFF);

{draw the image of the Earth onto the offscreen buffer. the previously drawn
 letters will not be obscured by the bitmap, as they are protected by the
 current clipping region}
Buffer.Canvas.Draw(0, 0, Image1.Picture.Bitmap);

{draw the offscreen buffer to the form. this eliminates flicker and is an
 animation technique known as double buffering}
Canvas.Draw(0, 0, Buffer);
end;
```

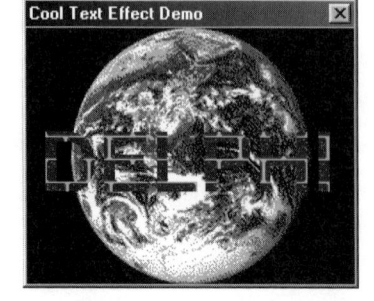

Figure 11-3:
A cool new
splash screen

Delphi vs. the Windows API

Simply put, if you want to use regions and paths, you must use the Windows API, as there is no direct support for it under Delphi. These functions are simply not encapsulated by any object in the current version. This chapter will demonstrate some simple, yet powerful, techniques that allow you to harness the power of regions and paths to perform interesting special effects and special drawing functionality. Indeed, many commercially available components and applications make heavy use of these functions, especially those that provide shaped forms and controls. Without using the API, many of these techniques would be very difficult and time consuming to code.

Region and Path Functions

The following region and path functions are covered in this chapter:

Table 11-1: Region and path functions

Function	Description
AbortPath	Discards a path and closes an open path bracket.
BeginPath	Starts a path bracket.
CloseFigure	Closes an open figure in a path bracket.
CombineRgn	Combines two regions using a Boolean operation.
CopyRect	Copies one rectangle's coordinates into another.
CreateEllipticRgn	Creates an elliptical region.
CreateEllipticRgnIndirect	Creates an elliptical region based on properties defined in a data structure.
CreatePolygonRgn	Creates a polygonal region.
CreatePolyPolygonRgn	Creates a region consisting of multiple polygons.
CreateRectRgn	Creates a rectangular region.
CreateRectRgnIndirect	Creates a rectangular region based on properties defined in a data structure.
CreateRoundRectRgn	Creates a rounded rectangular region.
EndPath	Ends an open path bracket.
EqualRect	Determines if the coordinates of two rectangles are equal.
EqualRgn	Determines if the size and shape of two regions are equal.
ExcludeClipRect	Creates a new clipping region minus the specified region.
ExtCreateRegion	Transforms an existing region.
ExtSelectClipRgn	Selects a clipping region, combining it with the existing clipping region using Boolean operations.
FlattenPath	Converts curves in a path into flat line segments.
GetClipBox	Retrieves the bounding box of the clipping region.
GetClipRgn	Retrieves a handle to the current clipping region.
GetPath	Retrieves the points that define a path.
GetRegionData	Retrieves information about a region.
GetRgnBox	Retrieves the bounding box of a region.
InflateRect	Modifies the size of a rectangle.
IntersectRect	Creates a rectangle from the intersection of two rectangles.
InvertRect	Inverts the colors of the pixels within the area defined by a rectangle.
InvertRgn	Inverts the colors of the pixels within the area defined by a region.
IsRectEmpty	Determines if a rectangle is empty.
OffsetClipRgn	Moves a clipping region.
OffsetRect	Moves a rectangle.
OffsetRgn	Moves a region.

Function	Description
PathToRegion	Converts a path into a region.
PtInRect	Determines if a specific coordinate falls within a rectangle.
PtInRegion	Determines if a specific coordinate falls within a region.
PtVisible	Determines if a specific coordinate falls within the clipping region.
RectInRegion	Determines if a rectangle falls within a region.
RectVisible	Determines if a rectangle falls within the clipping region.
SelectClipPath	Selects the current path as the clipping region.
SelectClipRgn	Selects a region as the clipping region.
SetRect	Initializes a rectangle.
SetRectEmpty	Empties a rectangle.
SetRectRgn	Converts a region into a rectangular region.
SetWindowRgn	Sets the window region to the specific region.
SubtractRect	Subtracts one rectangle from another.
UnionRect	Creates a rectangle from the sum of two rectangles.
WidenPath	Redefines a path shape with respect to the current pen.

AbortPath Windows.pas

Syntax

```
AbortPath(
DC: HDC                  {a handle to a device context}
): BOOL;                 {returns TRUE or FALSE}
```

Description

This function discards any path in the device context identified by the DC parameter. If the function is called inside an open path bracket, the path bracket is closed and the path is discarded.

Parameters

DC: A handle to a device context containing the path to be eliminated.

Return Value

If the function succeeds, it returns TRUE; otherwise, it returns FALSE. To get extended error information, call the GetLastError function.

See Also

BeginPath, CloseFigure, EndPath

Example

See Listing 11-3 under CloseFigure.

BeginPath   Windows.pas

Syntax

```
BeginPath(
 DC: HDC                  {a handle to a device context}
 ): BOOL;                 {returns TRUE or FALSE}
```

Description

This function opens a path bracket for the specified device context. Any previously existing paths in the specified device context are discarded. Use the EndPath function to close a path bracket. Once a path bracket has been started, certain drawing functions used with the specified device context will be translated into path information, and will not display any visible output. Once the path bracket is closed, the path is associated with the specified device context. It can be converted into a region by calling the PathToRegion function.

Windows NT/2000/XP: The following functions can be used inside a path bracket: AngleArc, Arc, ArcTo, Chord, CloseFigure, Ellipse, LineTo, MoveToEx, Pie, PolyBezier, PolyBezierTo, PolyDraw, Polygon, Polyline, PolylineTo, PolyPolygon, PolyPolyline, Rectangle, RoundRect, and TextOut.

Windows 95/98/Me: The following functions can be used inside a path bracket: CloseFigure, ExtTextOut, LineTo, MoveToEx, PolyBezier, PolyBezierTo, Polygon, Polyline, PolylineTo, PolyPolygon, PolyPolyline, and TextOut.

Parameters

DC: A handle to the device context in which certain drawing functions will be translated into path information.

Return Value

If the function succeeds, it returns TRUE; otherwise, it returns FALSE. To get extended error information, call the GetLastError function.

See Also

CloseFigure, EndPath, FillPath, LineTo, MoveToEx, PathToRegion, PolyBezier, PolyBezierTo, Polygon, Polyline, PolylineTo, PolyPolygon, PolyPolyline, SelectClipPath, StrokeAndFillPath, StrokePath, WidenPath, TextOut

Example

See Listing 11-19 under SelectClipPath, and other examples throughout this chapter.

CloseFigure   Windows.pas

Syntax

```
CloseFigure(
 DC: HDC                  {a handle to a device context}
 ): BOOL;                 {returns TRUE or FALSE}
```

Description

This function closes the figure created in a path bracket in the specified device context. Performing a LineTo operation from the current point to the point specified in the most recent call to the MoveToEx function closes the figure. Using the line join style identified by the currently selected geometric pen will connect the lines. If the LineTo function is called to close the figure before calling the CloseFigure function, the end cap style of the currently selected geometric pen is used to draw the ends of the lines. This function is useful only when called within an open path bracket. A figure in a path bracket is open unless explicitly closed by calling this function. After this function is called, any other drawing functions used in the path will start a new figure.

Parameters

DC: Specifies the device context containing the path whose current figure will be closed.

Return Value

If the function succeeds, it returns TRUE; otherwise, it returns FALSE. To get extended error information, call the GetLastError function.

See Also

BeginPath, EndPath, ExtCreatePen, LineTo, MoveToEx

Example

Listing 11-3: Closing an open figure in a path bracket

```
procedure TForm1.Button1Click(Sender: TObject);
begin
  {start a path bracket.  all subsequent drawing functions will define a
   path and will not produce visible output}
  BeginPath(Canvas.Handle);

  {start drawing a path}
  Canvas.MoveTo(65, 15);
  Canvas.LineTo(25, 234);
  Canvas.MoveTo(78, 111);
  Canvas.LineTo(98, 79);

  {if the path is incorrect, there was a mistake, or for any reason desired,
   the current path can be abandoned}
  AbortPath(Canvas.Handle);

  {the path was closed and abandoned, so we must start a new path bracket}
  BeginPath(Canvas.Handle);

  {draw three lines into the path}
  Canvas.MoveTo(25, 10);
  Canvas.LineTo(125, 10);
  Canvas.LineTo(125, 110);
  Canvas.LineTo(25, 110);

  {close the current figure. this should create a square path}
  CloseFigure(Canvas.Handle);
```

```
    {end the path bracket.  the path will now be associated with
     the device context}
    EndPath(Canvas.Handle);

    {initialize the device context's pen and brush as desired}
    Canvas.Pen.Width :=3;
    Canvas.Pen.Color := clRed;
    Canvas.Brush.Color := clLime;

    {render the path onto the device context}
    StrokeAndFillPath(Canvas.Handle);
end;
```

*Figure 11-4:
The closed
figure*

CombineRgn   Windows.pas

Syntax

CombineRgn(
p1: HRGN;   {a handle to the combined region}
p2: HRGN;   {a handle to the first region}
p3: HRGN;   {a handle to the second region}
p4: Integer   {region combination flag}
): Integer;   {returns the type of the combined region}

Description

This function combines the regions identified by the p2 and p3 parameters according to the flag indicated in the p4 parameter. The region identified by the p1 parameter is reset to point to the resulting region. The regions identified by the p1, p2, and p3 parameters do not need to be unique (i.e., the result region identified by the p1 parameter can be the same region identified by the p2 or p3 parameters). When the combined region is no longer needed, it should be deleted by calling the DeleteObject function.

Parameters

p1: A handle to a region that will receive a handle to the combined region. This parameter must specify a handle to an existing region.

p2: A handle to the first region to be combined.

p3: A handle to the second region to be combined.

p4: A flag indicating how the regions identified by the p2 and p3 parameters are to be combined. This parameter can contain one value from Table 11-2.

Return Value

This function returns a result indicating the type of region created or an error condition, and may be one value from Table 11-3.

See Also

CreateEllipticRgn, CreateEllipticRgnIndirect, CreatePolygonRgn, CreatePolyPolygonRgn, CreateRectRgn, CreateRectRgnIndirect, CreateRoundRectRgn, DeleteObject

Example

Listing 11-4: Combining two regions to create a special effect

```
var
  Form1: TForm1;
  BinocularRgn: HRGN;    // a handle to the combined region
implementation

{$R *.DFM}

procedure TForm1.FormCreate(Sender: TObject);
var
  Circle1, Circle2: HRGN;   // holds two circular regions
begin
  {the handle to the combined region must identify a pre-existing region, so
   create a bogus region}
  BinocularRgn := CreateEllipticRgnIndirect(BoundsRect);

  {create two circular regions, the first taking up 3/4 of the left side
   of the area covered by Image1, and the second taking up 3/4 of the right
   side of the area covered by Image1}
  Circle1 := CreateEllipticRgn(Image1.Left, Image1.Top,
                               Image1.Left+MulDiv(Image1.Width,3,4),
                               Image1.Top+Image1.Height);
  Circle2 := CreateEllipticRgn(Image1.Left +(Image1.Width div 4),
                               Image1.Top, Image1.Left+Image1.Width,
                               Image1.Top+Image1.Height);

  {combine the two regions, creating a region reminiscent of a view through
   a pair of binoculars}
  CombineRgn(BinocularRgn, Circle1, Circle2, RGN_OR);

  {delete the two circular regions as they are no longer needed}
  DeleteObject(Circle1);
  DeleteObject(Circle2);
end;

procedure TForm1.FormPaint(Sender: TObject);
var
  ClipRect: TRect;      // holds the current clipping region coordinates
```

```
begin
  {select the combined region into the device context as a clipping region}
  SelectClipRgn(Canvas.Handle, BinocularRgn);

  {draw the contents of the image (which is invisible) onto the surface of the
   form. it will be clipped to the current clipping region, resulting in what
   looks like the view of a ship through a pair of binoculars}
  Canvas.Draw(Image1.Left, Image1.Top, Image1.Picture.Bitmap);

  {draw the perimeter of the region in red to make it stand out}
  Canvas.Brush.Color := clRed;
  FrameRgn(Canvas.Handle, BinocularRgn, Canvas.Brush.Handle, 2, 2);

  {retrieve the smallest rectangle that will fit around the currently visible
   portion of the device context}
  GetClipBox(Canvas.Handle, ClipRect);

  {delete the clipping region so that drawing can be performed on the entire
   device context surface}
  SelectClipRgn(Canvas.Handle, 0);

  {draw the extents of the previously selected clipping region}
  Canvas.Brush.Style := bsClear;
  Canvas.Pen.Color := clBlack;
  Rectangle(Canvas.Handle, ClipRect.Left, ClipRect.Top, ClipRect.Right,
            ClipRect.Bottom);
end;

procedure TForm1.FormDestroy(Sender: TObject);
begin
  {delete the combined region}
  DeleteObject(BinocularRgn);
end;
```

Figure 11-5:
The combined region used as a clipping region

Table 11-2: CombineRgn p4 values

Value	Description
RGN_AND	The resulting region is the intersection of the two specified regions.
RGN_COPY	The resulting region is a copy of the region identified by the p2 parameter.
RGN_DIFF	The resulting region is the area of the region identified by the p2 parameter that is not in the area of the region identified by the p3 parameter.

Value	Description
RGN_OR	The resulting region is the union of the two specified regions.
RGN_XOR	The resulting region is the union of the two specified regions excluding any overlapping areas.

Table 11-3: CombineRgn return values

Value	Description
NULLREGION	Indicates an empty region.
SIMPLEREGION	Indicates a single rectangular region.
COMPLEXREGION	Indicates a region consisting of more than one rectangle.
ERROR	Indicates an error occurred and no region was created.

CopyRect   Windows.pas

Syntax

```
CopyRect(
  var lprcDst: TRect;        {a pointer to the destination rectangle}
  const lprcSrc: TRect       {a pointer to the source rectangle}
): BOOL;                     {returns TRUE or FALSE}
```

Description

This function copies the coordinates in the rectangle pointed to by the lprcSrc parameter into the coordinates of the rectangle pointed to by the lprcDst parameter.

Parameters

lprcDst: A pointer to a TRect structure that receives the coordinates of the rectangle pointed to by the lprcSrc parameter.

lprcSrc: A pointer to a TRect structure containing the coordinates to be copied to the rectangle pointed to by the lprcDst parameter.

Return Value

If the function succeeds, it returns TRUE; otherwise, it returns FALSE. To get extended error information, call the GetLastError function.

See Also

IsRectEmpty, SetRect, SetRectEmpty, SetRectRgn

Example

See Listing 11-16 under OffsetRect.

CreateEllipticRgn   Windows.pas

Syntax

CreateEllipticRgn(
p1: Integer;   {the upper-left bounding box horizontal coordinate}
p2: Integer;   {the upper-left bounding box vertical coordinate}
p3: Integer;   {the lower-right bounding box horizontal coordinate}
p4: Integer   {the lower-right bounding box vertical coordinate}
): HRGN;   {returns a handle to a region}

Description

This function creates an elliptical region. The specified coordinates represent the smallest rectangle that can be drawn around the resulting ellipse. When the region is no longer needed, it should be deleted by calling the DeleteObject function.

Parameters

p1: Specifies the horizontal coordinate of the upper-left corner of the rectangle bounding the ellipse in logical units.

p2: Specifies the vertical coordinate of the upper-left corner of the rectangle bounding the ellipse in logical units.

p3: Specifies the horizontal coordinate of the lower-right corner of the rectangle bounding the ellipse in logical units.

p4: Specifies the vertical coordinate of the lower-right corner of the rectangle bounding the ellipse in logical units.

Return Value

If the function succeeds, it returns a handle to an elliptical region; otherwise, it returns zero.

See Also

CreateEllipticRgnIndirect, DeleteObject

Example

See Listing 11-4 under CombineRgn.

CreateEllipticRgnIndirect   Windows.pas

Syntax

CreateEllipticRgnIndirect(
const p1: TRect   {a pointer to rectangular coordinates}
): HRGN;   {returns a handle to a region}

Description

This function creates an elliptical region based on the rectangular coordinates pointed to by the p1 parameter. The specified coordinates represent the smallest rectangle that can be drawn around the resulting ellipse. When the region is no longer needed, it should be deleted by calling the DeleteObject function.

Parameters

p1: A pointer to a TRect structure containing coordinates, in logical units, that define the smallest rectangle that can be drawn around the resulting ellipse.

Return Value

If the function succeeds, it returns a handle to an elliptical region; otherwise, returns zero.

See Also

CreateEllipticRgn, DeleteObject

Example

Listing 11-5: Dynamically creating an elliptical region based on the form size

```
var
  Form1: TForm1;
  TheRegion: HRGN;          // holds the elliptical region

implementation

{$R *.DFM}

procedure TForm1.FormPaint(Sender: TObject);
begin
  {erase the current image on the form}
  Canvas.Brush.Color := clBtnFace;
  Canvas.FillRect(BoundsRect);

  {outline the elliptical region in red}
  Canvas.Brush.Color := clRed;
  FrameRgn(Canvas.Handle, TheRegion, Canvas.Brush.Handle, 2, 2);
end;

procedure TForm1.FormResize(Sender: TObject);
begin
  {delete the current region, if it exists}
  if TheRegion<>0 then
    DeleteObject(TheRegion);

  {create a new elliptical region based on the boundaries of the client area}
  TheRegion := CreateEllipticRgnIndirect(ClientRect);

  {repaint the form}
  Repaint;
end;

procedure TForm1.FormDestroy(Sender: TObject);
begin
  {delete the elliptical region}
  DeleteObject(TheRegion);
end;
```

Figure 11-6: The dynamically created region

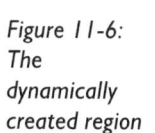

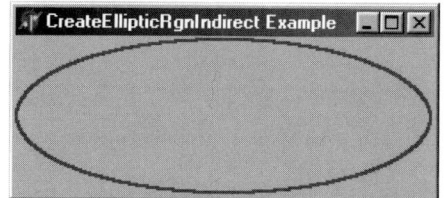

CreatePolygonRgn   Windows.pas

Syntax

```
CreatePolygonRgn(
const Points;              {the array of points}
Count: Integer;            {the number of points in the array}
FillMode: Integer          {the fill mode flag}
): HRGN;                   {returns a handle to a region}
```

Description

This function creates a polygonal region in the shape described by the array of vertices pointed to by the Points parameter. When the region is no longer needed, it should be deleted by calling the DeleteObject function.

Parameters

Points: A pointer to an array of TPoint structures describing the vertices of the polygon, in device units. The polygon is assumed to be closed, and each vertex can be specified only once.

Count: Specifies the number of TPoint entries in the array pointed to by the Points parameter.

FillMode: A flag specifying the fill mode used when determining which pixels are included in the region. If this parameter is set to Alternate, the region is filled between odd-numbered and even-numbered sides of the specified polygon. If this parameter is set to Winding, any part of the region with a non-zero winding value is filled. See the SetPolyFillMode function for more information on these flags.

Return Value

If the function succeeds, it returns a handle to the polygonal region; otherwise, it returns zero.

See Also

CreatePolyPolygonRgn, DeleteObject, SetPolyFillMode

Example

Listing 11-6: Creating a star shaped region

```
var
  Form1: TForm1;
```

```
    PolygonRgn, ScaledRgn: HRGN;   // holds the original and scaled regions

implementation

{$R *.DFM}

procedure TForm1.FormCreate(Sender: TObject);
var
  Vertices: array[0..9] of TPoint;  // holds the vertices of the polygon region
  RegionData: Pointer;              // a pointer to region data
  RgnDataSize: DWORD;               // the size of the region data
  Transform: TXForm;                // the scaling transformation matrix
begin
  {specify a polygon in the shape of a star}
  Vertices[0] := Point(120, 5);
  Vertices[1] := Point(140, 70);
  Vertices[2] := Point(210, 70);
  Vertices[3] := Point(150, 100);
  Vertices[4] := Point(180, 175);
  Vertices[5] := Point(120, 120);
  Vertices[6] := Point(60, 175);
  Vertices[7] := Point(90, 100);
  Vertices[8] := Point(30, 70);
  Vertices[9] := Point(100, 70);

  {create a star shaped polygonal region}
  PolygonRgn := CreatePolygonRgn(Vertices, 10, WINDING);

  {retrieve the size of the region's data}
  RgnDataSize := GetRegionData(PolygonRgn, 0, NIL);

  {allocate enough memory to hold the region data}
  GetMem(RegionData, RgnDataSize);

  {retrieve the region data for the star shaped region}
  GetRegionData(PolygonRgn, RgnDataSize, RegionData);

  {initialize a transformation matrix to indicate a slight increase in size
   and a translation in position}
  with Transform do
  begin
    eM11 := 1.35;
    eM12 := 0;
    eM21 := 0;
    eM22 := 1.35;
    eDx  := -42;
    eDy  := -35;
  end;

  {create a new, scaled region based on the original star shaped region}
  ScaledRgn := ExtCreateRegion(@Transform, RgnDataSize, TRgnData(RegionData^));

  {free the region data as it is no longer needed}
  FreeMem(RegionData, RgnDataSize);
end;

procedure TForm1.FormPaint(Sender: TObject);
```

```pascal
var
  TempRgn: HRGN;     // holds a retrieved region handle
begin
  {select the scaled star shaped region as a clipping region}
  SelectClipRgn(Canvas.Handle, ScaledRgn);

  {draw the cityscape image onto the form. it will be clipped to the boundaries
   of the star shaped region}
  Canvas.Draw(0, 0, Image1.Picture.Bitmap);

  {even though we explicitly know what the clipping region is, we can retrieve
   it from the device context, using the retrieved region in any region
   functions. the GetClipRgn function requires the specified region handle
   to identify an existing region, so set it to the original star shaped
   region.  this will retrieve the current clipping region, which is the
   scaled region}
  TempRgn := PolygonRgn;
  GetClipRgn(Canvas.Handle, TempRgn);

  {draw the edges of the region to make it stand out}
  Canvas.Brush.Color := clRed;
  FrameRgn(Canvas.Handle, TempRgn, Canvas.Brush.Handle, 2, 2);
end;

procedure TForm1.FormMouseDown(Sender: TObject; Button: TMouseButton;
  Shift: TShiftState; X, Y: Integer);
begin
  {select the scaled star shaped region as a clipping region}
  SelectClipRgn(Canvas.Handle, ScaledRgn);

  {indicate if the clicked area of the canvas is visible within
   the current clipping region (the scaled star shaped region)}
  if PtVisible(Canvas.Handle, X, Y) then
    Caption := 'CreatePolygonRgn Example - Visible'
  else
    Caption := 'CreatePolygonRgn Example - Invisible';
end;

procedure TForm1.FormDestroy(Sender: TObject);
begin
  {free all resources associated with both regions}
  DeleteObject(PolygonRgn);
  DeleteObject(ScaledRgn);
end;
```

Figure 11-7:
The star
shaped region

CreatePolyPolygonRgn   Windows.pas

Syntax

CreatePolyPolygonRgn(
const pPtStructs;   {the array of points}
const pIntArray;   {the array of vertex counts}
p3: Integer;   {the number of entries in the vertex count array}
p4: Integer   {the fill mode flag}
): HRGN;   {returns a handle to a region}

Description

This function creates a region defined from multiple polygons. The vertices of each polygon are specified consecutively in the array of TPoint structures pointed to by the pPtStructs parameter. Each entry in the array pointed to by the pIntArray parameter indicates the number of points in the array of TPoint structures that define the vertices of each polygon. The polygons defined by this array are allowed to overlap. When the region is no longer needed, it should be deleted by calling the DeleteObject function.

Parameters

pPtStructs: A pointer to an array of TPoint structures describing the vertices of each polygon, in device units. Each polygon is described consecutively and is assumed to be closed, and each vertex can be specified only once.

pIntArray: A pointer to an array of integers. Each integer specifies the number of points in the array pointed to by the pPtStructs parameter that defines one polygon.

p3: Specifies the number of entries in the array pointed to by the pIntArray parameter.

p4: A flag specifying the fill mode used when determining which pixels are included in the region. If this parameter is set to Alternate, the region is filled between odd-numbered and even-numbered sides of the specified polygon. If this parameter is set to Winding, any part of the region with a non-zero winding value is filled. See the SetPolyFillMode function for more information on these flags.

Return Value

If the function succeeds, it returns a handle to the polygonal region; otherwise, it returns zero.

See Also

CreatePolygonRgn, DeleteObject, SetPolyFillMode

Example

Listing 11-7: Creating a multiple polygon region

```
var
  Form1: TForm1;
  HotSpotRgn: HRGN;      // holds the multiple polygon region
```

Region and Path Functions   475

```
implementation

{$R *.DFM}

procedure TForm1.FormCreate(Sender: TObject);
var
  PolyPoints: array[0..11] of TPoint;      // holds the points of the polygons
  VertexCounts: array[0..1] of Integer;    // holds the vertex counts
begin
  {define one polygon in the region}
  PolyPoints[0] := Point(68, 80);
  PolyPoints[1] := Point(76, 72);
  PolyPoints[2] := Point(87, 80);
  PolyPoints[3] := Point(86, 96);
  PolyPoints[4] := Point(100, 96);
  PolyPoints[5] := Point(100, 160);
  PolyPoints[6] := Point(68, 160);

  {define another polygon in the region}
  PolyPoints[7] := Point(173, 53);
  PolyPoints[8] := Point(184, 66);
  PolyPoints[9] := Point(184, 146);
  PolyPoints[10] := Point(160, 146);
  PolyPoints[11] := Point(160, 66);

  {indicate that the firs polygon consists of 7 points, and the second
   consists of 5 points}
  VertexCounts[0] := 7;
  VertexCounts[1] := 5;

  {create the multiple polygon region}
  HotSpotRgn := CreatePolyPolygonRgn(PolyPoints, VertexCounts, 2, WINDING);
end;

procedure TForm1.Button1Click(Sender: TObject);
begin
  {invert the area defined by the multiple polygon region}
  InvertRgn(Canvas.Handle, HotSpotRgn);
end;

procedure TForm1.Image1MouseDown(Sender: TObject; Button: TMouseButton;
  Shift: TShiftState; X, Y: Integer);
var
  TranslatedPt: TPoint;     // holds a form specific coordinate
begin
  {since the region is defined in logical coordinates relative to the form,
   the indicated location of the mouse click must be translated appropriately}
  TranslatedPt := Image1.ClientToScreen(Point(X,Y));
  TranslatedPt := Form1.ScreenToClient(TranslatedPt);

  {indicate if the point is within the 'hotspot' area defined by the
   multiple polygon region}
  if PtInRegion(HotSpotRgn, TranslatedPt.X, TranslatedPt.Y) then
    Caption := 'Clicked on a hotspot'
  else
    Caption := 'No hot spot clicked';
end;
```

```
procedure TForm1.FormDestroy(Sender: TObject);
begin
  {delete the region}
  DeleteObject(HotSpotRgn);
end;
```

Figure 11-8: Using the multiple polygon region as a hot spot

CreateRectRgn   Windows.pas

Syntax

CreateRectRgn(
p1: Integer;   {the upper-left horizontal coordinate}
p2: Integer;   {the upper-left vertical coordinate}
p3: Integer;   {the lower-right horizontal coordinate}
p4: Integer   {the lower-right vertical coordinate}
): HRGN;   {returns a handle to a region}

Description

This function creates a rectangular region based on the specified coordinates. When the region is no longer needed, it should be deleted by calling the DeleteObject function.

Parameters

p1: Specifies the horizontal coordinate of the upper-left corner of the rectangle, in device units.

p2: Specifies the vertical coordinate of the upper-left corner of the rectangle, in device units.

p3: Specifies the horizontal coordinate of the lower-right corner of the rectangle, in device units.

p4: Specifies the vertical coordinate of the lower-right corner of the rectangle, in device units.

Return Value

If the function succeeds, it returns a handle to the region; otherwise, it returns zero.

See Also

CreateRectRgnIndirect, CreateRoundRectRgn, DeleteObject

Example

Listing 11-8: Creating a rectangular region

```
procedure TForm1.Button1Click(Sender: TObject);
var
  RegionHandle: HRGN;     // holds the rectangular region
begin
  {initialize the canvas's brush}
  Canvas.Brush.Style := bsCross;
  Canvas.Brush.Color := clRed;

  {create a rectangular region}
  RegionHandle := CreateRectRgn(10, 40, 175, 175);

  {paint the region}
  FillRgn(Canvas.Handle, RegionHandle, Canvas.Brush.Handle);

  {delete the region}
  DeleteObject(RegionHandle);
end;
```

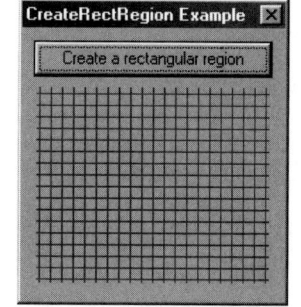

Figure 11-9: The rectangular region

CreateRectRgnIndirect   Windows.pas

Syntax

CreateRectRgnIndirect(
  const p1: TRect   {the rectangular region coordinates}
): HRGN;   {returns a handle to a region}

Description

This function creates a rectangular region based on the coordinates in the rectangle identified by the p1 parameter. When the region is no longer needed, it should be deleted by calling the DeleteObject function.

Chapter 11

Parameters

p1: A TRect structure containing the rectangular coordinates defining the region in device units.

Return Value

If the function succeeds, it returns a handle to the region; otherwise, it returns zero.

See Also

CreateRectRgn, CreateRoundRectRgn, DeleteObject

Example

Listing 11-9: Indirectly creating a rectangular region

```
procedure TForm1.Button1Click(Sender: TObject);
var
  RegionHandle: HRGN;     // a handle to the region
begin
  {create a rectangular region the size of the form's client area}
  RegionHandle := CreateRectRgnIndirect(Form1.ClientRect);

  {initialize the brush}
  Canvas.Brush.Style := bsDiagCross;
  Canvas.Brush.Color := clRed;

  {fill the rectangular region}
  FillRgn(Canvas.Handle, RegionHandle, Canvas.Brush.Handle);

  {we no longer need the region, so delete it}
  DeleteObject(RegionHandle);
end;
```

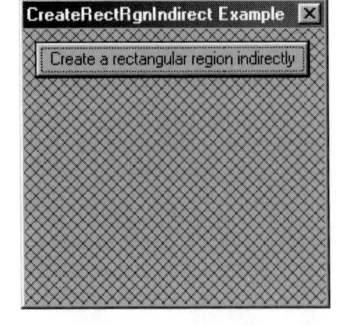

Figure 11-10: The rectangular region

CreateRoundRectRgn   Windows.pas

Syntax

CreateRoundRectRgn(
p1: Integer;   {the upper-left horizontal coordinate}
p2: Integer;   {the upper-left vertical coordinate}
p3: Integer;   {the lower-right horizontal coordinate}

p4: Integer;	{the lower-right vertical coordinate}
p5: Integer;	{the width of the rounded corner ellipse}
p6: Integer	{the height of the rounded corner ellipse}
): HRGN;	{returns a handle to a region}

Description

This function creates a rectangular region with rounded corners, based on the specified coordinates. When the region is no longer needed, it should be deleted by calling the DeleteObject function.

Parameters

p1: Specifies the horizontal coordinate of the upper-left corner of the rectangle in device units.

p2: Specifies the vertical coordinate of the upper-left corner of the rectangle in device units.

p3: Specifies the horizontal coordinate of the lower-right corner of the rectangle in device units.

p4: Specifies the vertical coordinate of the lower-right corner of the rectangle in device units.

p5: Specifies the width of the ellipse used to define the rounded corners of the rectangle in device units.

p6: Specifies the height of the ellipse used to define the rounded corners of the rectangle in device units.

Return Value

If the function succeeds, it returns a handle to the region; otherwise, it returns zero.

See Also

CreateRectRgn, CreateRectRgnIndirect, DeleteObject

Example

Listing 11-10: Creating a rounded rectangular region

```
procedure TForm1.Button1Click(Sender: TObject);
var
  RegionHandle: HRGN;    // holds the region
begin
  {create a rounded rectangular region}
  RegionHandle := CreateRoundRectRgn(10, 40, 217, 175, 80, 80);

  {initialize the brush}
  Canvas.Brush.Style := bsDiagCross;
  Canvas.Brush.Color := clBlue;

  {draw the perimeter of the region}
  FrameRgn(Canvas.Handle, RegionHandle, Canvas.Brush.Handle, 8, 8);
```

```
    {delete the region}
    DeleteObject(RegionHandle);
end;
```

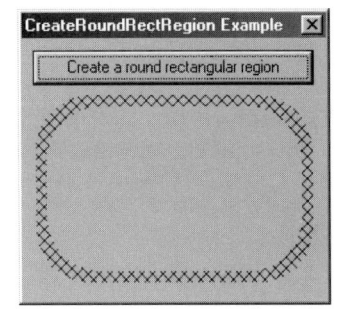

Figure 11-11: The rounded rectangular region

EndPath   Windows.pas

Syntax

```
EndPath(
  DC: HDC                    {a handle to a device context}
): BOOL;                     {returns TRUE or FALSE}
```

Description

This function closes an open path bracket. The resulting path is associated with the device context identified by the DC parameter.

Parameters

DC: Specifies the device context that will contain the resulting path.

Return Value

If the function succeeds, it returns TRUE; otherwise, it returns FALSE. To get extended error information, call the GetLastError function.

See Also

BeginPath

Example

See Listing 11-19 under SelectClipPath, and other examples throughout this chapter.

EqualRect   Windows.pas

Syntax

```
EqualRect(
  const lprc1: TRect;        {the first rectangle to compare}
  const lprc2: TRect         {the second rectangle to compare}
): BOOL;                     {returns TRUE or FALSE}
```

Description

This function determines if the coordinates identified by the two rectangles are identical.

Parameters

lprc1: A pointer to a TRect structure containing coordinates to be compared.

lprc2: A pointer to a TRect structure containing coordinates to be compared.

Return Value

If the function succeeds and the coordinates of the rectangle identified by the lprc1 parameter are identical to the coordinates of the rectangle identified by the lprc2 parameter, it returns TRUE. If the function fails, or the coordinates are not identical, it returns FALSE. To get extended error information, call the GetLastError function.

See Also

EqualRgn, IsRectEmpty, PtInRect

Example

See Listing 11-16 under OffsetRect.

EqualRgn   Windows.pas

Syntax

```
EqualRgn(
p1: HRGN;              {a handle to the first region to compare}
p2: HRGN               {a handle to the second region to compare}
): BOOL;               {returns TRUE or FALSE}
```

Description

This function determines if the two regions are identical in size and shape and occupy the same coordinates.

Parameters

p1: A handle to a region to be compared.

p2: A handle to a region to be compared.

Return Value

If the two regions are identical in size and shape and reside at the same coordinates, the function returns TRUE; otherwise, it returns FALSE. A return value of ERROR indicates that at least one of the specified region handles is invalid.

See Also

CreateEllipticRgn, CreateEllipticRgnIndirect, CreatePolygonRgn, CreatePolyPolygonRgn, CreateRectRgn, CreateRectRgnIndirect, CreateRoundRectRgn

Example

Listing 11-11: Comparing two regions

```
procedure TForm1.FormPaint(Sender: TObject);
var
  Region1, Region2: HRGN;  // holds the regions to be compared
begin
  {create an elliptical region}
  Region1 := CreateEllipticRgn(50, 50, 150, 150);

  {transform the region into a rectangular region. this function can be
   performed on any pre-existing region}
  SetRectRgn(Region1, 50, 50, 150, 150);

  {create a rectangular region identical to Region1}
  Region2 := CreateRectRgn(50, 50, 150, 150);

  {paint both regions red}
  Canvas.Brush.Color := clRed;
  PaintRgn(Canvas.Handle, Region1);
  PaintRgn(Canvas.Handle, Region2);

  {indicate if the regions are identical}
  if EqualRgn(Region1, Region2) then
    Label1.Caption := 'Regions Equal'
  else
    Label1.Caption := 'Regions Not Equal';

  {delete both regions as they are no longer needed}
  DeleteObject(Region1);
  DeleteObject(Region2);
end;
```

ExcludeClipRect   Windows.pas

Syntax

ExcludeClipRect(
DC: HDC;   {a handle to a device context}
p2: Integer;   {the upper-left horizontal coordinate}
p3: Integer;   {the upper-left vertical coordinate}
p4: Integer;   {the lower-right horizontal coordinate}
p5: Integer   {the lower-right vertical coordinate}
): Integer;   {returns the type of clipping region}

Description

This function excludes the rectangle defined by the given coordinates from the clipping region of the specified device context. The upper and left edges of the defined rectangle are excluded from the clipping region, but not the lower and right edges.

Parameters

DC: A handle to the device context containing the clipping region to be modified.

p2: Specifies the horizontal coordinate of the upper-left corner of the rectangle in logical units.

p3: Specifies the vertical coordinate of the upper-left corner of the rectangle in logical units.

p4: Specifies the horizontal coordinate of the lower-right corner of the rectangle in logical units.

p5: Specifies the vertical coordinate of the lower-right corner of the rectangle in logical units.

Return Value

This function returns a result indicating the type of region created or an error condition, and may be one value from Table 11-4.

See Also

OffsetClipRgn, SetRect, SetRectRgn

Example

Listing 11-12: Drawing a foreground image only once

```
    {the record structure defining a moving dot}
    TDot = record
      Pos: TPoint;
      Vel: TPoint;
    end;

var
  Form1: TForm1;
  Dots: array[0..9] of TDot;    // the array of moving dots
  Offscreen: TBitmap;           // the offscreen double buffer

implementation

{$R *.DFM}

procedure TForm1.FormPaint(Sender: TObject);
begin
  {draw the foreground image.  this will be drawn only once}
  Canvas.Draw(Image2.Left, Image2.Top, Image2.Picture.Bitmap);
end;

procedure TForm1.FormCreate(Sender: TObject);
var
  iCount: Integer;    // a general loop control variable
begin
  {create and initialize the offscreen bitmap}
  OffScreen := TBitmap.Create;
  OffScreen.Width  := Form1.ClientWidth;
  OffScreen.Height := Form1.ClientHeight;

  {create and initialize the array of moving dots}
  for iCount := 0 to 9 do
```

```
    begin
      Dots[iCount].Pos.X := Random(ClientWidth);
      Dots[iCount].Pos.Y := Random(ClientHeight);
      if Random(2)=0 then Dots[iCount].Vel.X := -1 else Dots[iCount].Vel.X := 1;
      if Random(2)=0 then Dots[iCount].Vel.Y := -1 else Dots[iCount].Vel.Y := 1;
    end;
end;

procedure TForm1.FormDestroy(Sender: TObject);
begin
  {the offscreen bitmap is no longer needed, so free it}
  Offscreen.Free;
end;

procedure TForm1.Timer1Timer(Sender: TObject);
var
  iCount: Integer;      // a general loop counter
begin
  {erase the last frame of animation in the offscreen bitmap}
  Offscreen.Canvas.Brush.Color := clBlack;
  Offscreen.Canvas.FillRect(Offscreen.Canvas.ClipRect);

  {loop through all 10 moving dots}
  for iCount := 0 to 9 do
  begin
    {change the dot's position according to velocity}
    Dots[iCount].Pos.X := Dots[iCount].Pos.X+Dots[iCount].Vel.X;
    Dots[iCount].Pos.Y := Dots[iCount].Pos.Y+Dots[iCount].Vel.Y;

    {reverse the dot's velocity if it has reached the edge of the screen}
    if (Dots[iCount].Pos.X<0) or (Dots[iCount].Pos.X>ClientWidth) then
      Dots[iCount].Vel.X := 0-Dots[iCount].Vel.X;
    if (Dots[iCount].Pos.Y<0) or (Dots[iCount].Pos.Y>ClientHeight) then
      Dots[iCount].Vel.Y := 0-Dots[iCount].Vel.Y;

    {draw a red dot on the offscreen bitmap (2X2 pixels)}
    Offscreen.Canvas.Pixels[Dots[iCount].Pos.X,Dots[iCount].Pos.Y] := clRed;
    Offscreen.Canvas.Pixels[Dots[iCount].Pos.X+1,Dots[iCount].Pos.Y] := clRed;
    Offscreen.Canvas.Pixels[Dots[iCount].Pos.X,Dots[iCount].Pos.Y+1] := clRed;
    Offscreen.Canvas.Pixels[Dots[iCount].Pos.X+1,Dots[iCount].Pos.Y+1] := clRed;
  end;

  {the bitmap stored in Image1 has already been drawn to the form.  this happens
   only once, when the Paint event fires, which happens only when the form is
   displayed the first time or after it has been uncovered by a top level
   window. since we don't want to destroy this foreground image, we exclude
   its rectangular area from the clipping region. this will effectively cut a
   hole in the clipping region, and any drawing attempted in this area will be
   denied}
  ExcludeClipRect(Canvas.Handle, Image2.Left, Image2.Top,
                  Image2.Left+Image2.Width, Image2.Top+Image2.Height);

  {draw the offscreen bitmap to the screen. the hole in the clipping region
   prevents the bitmap from being drawn over the foreground bitmap}
  Canvas.Draw(0, 0, Offscreen);
end;
```

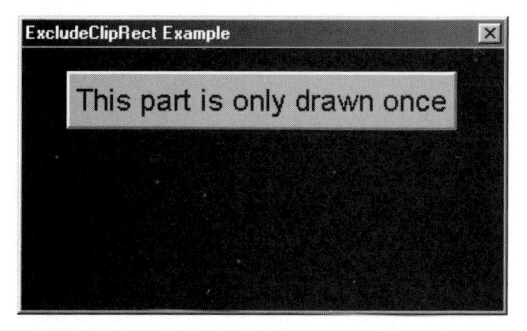

Figure 11-12:
The foreground image is unaffected during continuous animation

Table 11-4: ExcludeClipRect return values

Value	Description
NULLREGION	Indicates an empty region.
SIMPLEREGION	Indicates a single rectangular region.
COMPLEXREGION	Indicates a region consisting of more than one rectangle.
ERROR	Indicates an error occurred.

ExtCreateRegion   Windows.pas

Syntax

ExtCreateRegion(
p1: PXForm;   {a pointer to a TXForm structure}
p2: DWORD;   {the size of the region data structure}
const p3: TRgnData   {a pointer to a TRgnData structure}
): HRGN;   {returns a handle to a region}

Description

This function creates a new region by applying the transformation matrix identified by the p1 parameter to the region data specified by the p3 parameter.

Note: Under Windows 95, shearing and rotation transformations are not supported and the function will fail if the structure identified by the p1 parameter contains anything other than scaling or translation values.

Parameters

p1: A pointer to a TXForm structure containing a transformation matrix that is applied to the region identified by the p3 parameter. If this parameter is NIL, the region is not transformed in any way. See Table 11-5 describing how the members of this structure are used for various transformations. The TXForm data structure is defined as:

TXForm = packed record
    eM11: Single;   {rotation, scaling, or reflection value}
    eM12: Single;   {rotation or shearing value}

```
    eM21: Single;         {rotation or shearing value}
    eM22: Single;         {rotation, scaling, or reflection value}
    eDx: Single;          {the horizontal translation}
    eDy: Single;          {the vertical translation}
end;
```

eM11: Specifies the horizontal scaling value, the cosine of the rotation angle, or the horizontal reflection value.

eM12: Specifies the horizontal proportionality constant for shearing or the sine of the rotation angle.

eM21: Specifies the vertical proportionality constant for shearing or the negative sine of the rotation angle.

eM22: Specifies the vertical scaling value, the cosine of the rotation angle, or the vertical reflection value.

eDx: Specifies the horizontal translation value.

eDy: Specifies the vertical translation value.

p2: Specifies the size of the region data pointed to by the p3 parameter, in bytes.

p3: A pointer to a TRgnData structure containing information on the region to be transformed. This is a variable length data structure that must be initialized by a previous call to the GetRegionData function. The TRgnData structure is defined as:

```
TRgnData = record
    rdh: TRgnDataHeader;           {region data information}
    Buffer: array[0..0] of CHAR;   {an array of rectangles}
end;
```

rdh: Specifies a TRgnDataHeader structure containing information about the definition of the region. The TRgnDataHeader structure is defined as:

```
TRgnDataHeader = packed record
    dwSize: DWORD;        {the size of the structure}
    iType: DWORD;         {a region type flag}
    nCount: DWORD;        {the number of rectangles}
    nRgnSize: DWORD;      {the size of the rectangular coordinate buffer}
    rcBound: TRect;       {the bounding rectangle coordinates}
end;
```

dwSize: Specifies the size of the TRgnDataHeader structure, in bytes. This member should be set to SizeOf(TRgnDataHeader).

iType: Specifies a flag indicating the type of region. Currently, this member can only contain the value RDH_RECTANGLES.

nCount: Specifies the number of rectangles defining the region.

nRgnSize: Specifies the size of buffer required to receive the coordinates of the rectangles defining the region. This is the size of the buffer identified by the Buffer member of the TRgnData structure.

rcBound: Specifies a TRect structure containing the coordinates of the bounding rectangle for the region, in logical units.

Buffer: Specifies a variable length buffer containing the coordinates that make up the rectangles defining the region.

Return Value

If the function succeeds, it returns a handle to the new, transformed region; otherwise, it returns zero.

See Also

CreateEllipticRgn, CreateEllipticRgnIndirect, CreatePolygonRgn, CreatePolyPolygonRgn, CreateRectRgn, CreateRectRgnIndirect, CreateRoundRectRgn, GetRegionData

Example

See Listing 11-6 under CreatePolygonRgn.

Table 11-5: ExtCreateRegion pl transformation values

Transformation	eM11 Value	eM12 Value	eM21 Value	eM22 Value
Rotation	Cosine of the rotation angle	Sine of the rotation angle	Negative sine of the rotation angle	Cosine of the rotation angle
Scaling	Horizontal scaling value	Zero	Zero	Vertical scaling value
Shearing	Zero	Horizontal proportionality value	Vertical proportionality value	Zero
Reflection	Horizontal reflection value	Zero	Zero	Vertical reflection value

ExtSelectClipRgn   Windows.pas

Syntax

```
ExtSelectClipRgn(
DC: HDC;                 {a handle to a device context}
p2: HRGN;                {a handle to a region}
p3: Integer              {region combination flags}
): Integer;              {returns the type of the combined region}
```

Description

This function combines the clipping region of the device context identified by the DC parameter with the region identified by the p2 parameter according to the flag specified in the p3 parameter. The coordinates of the region identified by the p2 parameter are assumed to be in device units. This function uses a copy of the region identified by the p2 parameter; the original region is unaffected and can be used in other functions.

Parameters

DC: A handle to the device context containing the clipping region to be combined with the specified region.

p2: A handle to the region to be combined with the specified device context's clipping region.

p3: A flag indicating how the device context's clipping region and the specified region are to be combined. This parameter can contain one value from Table 11-6.

Return Value

This function returns a result indicating the type of region created or an error condition, and may be one value from Table 11-7. If an error occurs, the clipping region of the specified device context is unaffected.

See Also

GetClipBox, GetClipRgn, OffsetClipRgn, SelectClipPath, SelectClipRgn

Example

See Listing 11-15 under OffsetClipRgn.

Table 11-6: ExtSelectClipRgn p3 values

Value	Description
RGN_AND	The resulting region is the intersection of the two specified regions.
RGN_COPY	The resulting region is a copy of the region identified by the p2 parameter. This functionality is identical to the SelectClipRgn function. If this flag is specified and the p2 parameter contains zero, the current clipping region is reset to the default clipping region for the specified device context.
RGN_DIFF	The resulting region is the area of the region identified by the p2 parameter that is not in the area of the current clipping region.
RGN_OR	The resulting region is the union of the two specified regions.
RGN_XOR	The resulting region is the union of the two specified regions excluding any overlapping areas.

Table 11-7: ExtSelectClipRgn return values

Value	Description
NULLREGION	Indicates an empty region.
SIMPLEREGION	Indicates a single rectangular region.
COMPLEXREGION	Indicates a region consisting of more than one rectangle.
ERROR	Indicates an error occurred.

FlattenPath   Windows.pas

Syntax

```
FlattenPath(
DC: HDC                  {a handle to a device context}
): BOOL;                 {returns TRUE or FALSE}
```

Description

This function converts any curves located in the path selected into the specified device context into a series of straight line segments.

Parameters

DC: A handle to the device context containing the path to be converted into line segments.

Return Value

If the function succeeds, it returns TRUE; otherwise, it returns FALSE. To get extended error information, call the GetLastError function.

See Also

GetPath, PathToRegion, WidenPath

Example

See Listing 11-13 under GetPath.

GetClipBox   Windows.pas

Syntax

```
GetClipBox(
DC: HDC;                 {a handle to a device context}
var Rect: TRect          {a pointer to a TRect structure}
): Integer;              {returns the type of clipping region}
```

Description

This function retrieves the coordinates of the smallest rectangle that can be drawn around the currently visible area in the device context identified by the DC parameter.

Parameters

DC: A handle to the device context from which the visible area bounding rectangle is to be retrieved.

Rect: A pointer to a TRect structure that receives the coordinates of the smallest rectangle encompassing the visible area of the specified device context, in logical units.

Return Value

This function returns a result indicating the type of region created or an error condition, and may be one value from the following table.

See Also

ExtSelectClipRgn, GetClipRgn, GetRgnBox, OffsetClipRgn, SelectClipPath, SelectClipRgn

Example

See Listing 11-4 under CombineRgn.

Table 11-8: GetClipBox return values

Value	Description
NULLREGION	Indicates an empty region.
SIMPLEREGION	Indicates a single rectangular region.
COMPLEXREGION	Indicates a region consisting of more than one rectangle.
ERROR	Indicates an error occurred.

GetClipRgn   Windows.pas

Syntax

```
GetClipRgn(
DC: HDC;                {a handle to a device context}
rgn: HRGN               {a handle to a pre-existing region}
): Integer;             {returns an error code}
```

Description

This function retrieves a handle to the application-defined clipping region set by the last call to the SelectClipRgn function. The region identified by the rgn parameter must be a pre-existing region.

Parameters

DC: Specifies a handle to the device context containing the application-defined clipping region to be retrieved.

rgn: Specifies a handle to a pre-existing region. This handle will identify a copy of the application-defined clipping region when the function returns. Any changes to this copied region will not affect the actual clipping region.

Return Value

If the function succeeds and the device context does not contain a clipping region, it returns 0. If the function succeeds and the device context does contain a clipping region, it returns 1. If the function fails, it returns –1.

See Also

GetClipBox, GetRgnBox, SelectClipRgn

Example

See Listing 11-6 under CreatePolygonRgn.

GetPath   Windows.pas

Syntax

```
GetPath(
  DC: HDC;              {a handle to a device context}
  var Points;           {a pointer to an array of TPoint structures}
  var Types;            {a pointer to an array of bytes}
  nSize: Integer        {the number of entries in the arrays}
): Integer;             {returns the number of points retrieved}
```

Description

This function retrieves the coordinates and vertex types of the line segment endpoints and Bézier curve control points defining the path in the specified device context. The endpoints and control points of the path are stored in the array of TPoint structures pointed to by the Points parameter, and the vertex types are stored in the array of bytes pointed to by the Types parameter.

Parameters

DC: A handle to the device context containing the path from which points and vertex types are to be retrieved.

Points: A pointer to an application-allocated array of TPoint structures that receives the endpoints of lines and control points of curves in the path. These coordinates are specified in logical units.

Types: A pointer to an application-allocated array of bytes, where each entry receives a flag indicating the type of vertex retrieved. There will be one entry in this array corresponding to each entry in the array pointed to by the Points parameter. The value of entries in this array may be one value from Table 11-9.

nSize: Specifies the total number of entries in the arrays pointed to by the Points and Types parameters. If this parameter is set to zero, the function returns the total number of entries required to hold all points defining the path.

Return Value

If the function succeeds, it returns the total number of points retrieved from the path. If the function fails, the nSize parameter specifies an amount less than the actual number of points in the path, or there are not enough entries in the arrays pointed to by the Points and Types parameters, the function returns –1. To get extended error information, call the GetLastError function.

See Also

BeginPath, EndPath, FlattenPath, PathToRegion, WidenPath

Example

Listing 11-13: Retrieving the points defining a flattened curve

```
procedure TForm1.Button1Click(Sender: TObject);
type
  TPointsArray = array[0..0] of TPoint;   // array of TPoints storing vertices
  TTypesArray = array[0..0] of Byte;      // array of bytes storing vertex types
var
  CurvePts: array[0..3] of TPoint;        // array of points defining the curve
  Points: ^TPointsArray;                  // pointer to array of points
  Types: ^TTypesArray;                    // pointer to array of bytes
  PtCount: Integer;                       // the number of points in the path
  iCount: Integer;                        // general loop control variable
  FormDC: HDC;                            // a handle to the form's DC
  ThePen, OldPen: HPEN;                   // pen handles
  InfoString: String;                     // a string describing a point
begin
  {define points used to draw a bézier curve}
  CurvePts[0] := Point(30, 80);
  CurvePts[1] := Point(55, 30);
  CurvePts[2] := Point(105, 30);
  CurvePts[3] := Point(130, 80);

  {retrieve a handle to the form's device context}
  FormDC := GetDC(Form1.Handle);

  {begin a path bracket}
  BeginPath(FormDC);

  {draw a bézier curve}
  PolyBezier(FormDC, CurvePts, 4);

  {end the path bracket}
  EndPath(FormDC);

  {convert the path into a series of line segments}
  FlattenPath(FormDC);

  {retrieve the number of points defining the path}
  PtCount := GetPath(FormDC, Points^, Types^, 0);

  {allocate enough memory to store the points and their type flags}
  GetMem(Points, SizeOf(TPoint)*PtCount);
  GetMem(Types, PtCount);

  {retrieve the points and vertex types of the path}
  GetPath(FormDC, Points^, Types^, PtCount);

  {for each point in the path...}
  for iCount := 0 to PtCount-1 do
  begin
    {record the point's coordinates}
    InfoString := 'X: '+IntToStr(Points[iCount].X)+
                  'Y: '+IntToStr(Points[iCount].Y);

    {record the type of point}
```

```
       case (Types[iCount] and not PT_CLOSEFIGURE) of
         PT_MOVETO:   InfoString := InfoString+' Type: MoveTo';
         PT_LINETO:   InfoString := InfoString+' Type: LineTo';
         PT_BEZIERTO: InfoString := InfoString+' Type: BezierTo';
       end;

       {since the PT_CLOSEFIGURE flag can be combined with the other flags, check
        it separately and record if the figure in the path is closed}
       if (Types[iCount] and PT_CLOSEFIGURE)=PT_CLOSEFIGURE then
         InfoString := InfoString+', Close Figure';

       {display the information about this point in the path}
       ListBox1.Items.Add(InfoString);
     end;

     {create and select a pen into the device context}
     ThePen := CreatePen(PS_SOLID, 1, clBlack);
     OldPen := SelectObject(FormDC, ThePen);

     {draw the path}
     StrokePath(FormDC);

     {the pen is no longer needed, so delete it}
     SelectObject(FormDC, OldPen);
     DeleteObject(ThePen);

     {free the memory used to store the points and vertex types}
     FreeMem(Points);
     FreeMem(Types);
   end;
```

Figure 11-13: The line segment endpoints of a flattened curve

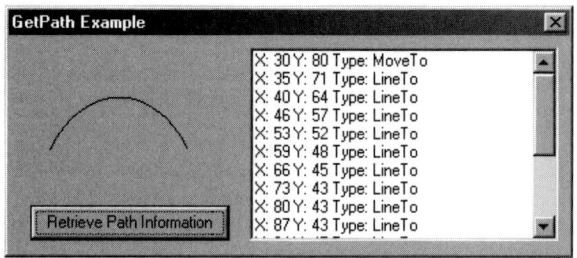

Table 11-9: GetPath Types values

Value	Description
PT_MOVETO	The associated point begins a new figure.
PT_LINETO	The associated point and the previous point form a line segment.
PT_BEZIERTO	The associated point is a control point or endpoint for a Bézier curve. The point preceding the first PT_BEZIERTO point is the starting point for the Bézier curve. The following two PT_BEZIERTO points are the control points for the curve. These will be followed by another PT_BEZIERTO point identifying the endpoint of the Bézier curve if one was specified.
PT_CLOSEFIGURE	This value may be combined with the PT_LINETO or PT_BEZIERTO flags using the Boolean OR operator, and signifies the last point in a closed figure.

GetRegionData Windows.pas

Syntax

```
GetRegionData(
  RGN: HRGN;            {a handle of a region}
  p2: DWORD;            {the size of the region data buffer}
  p3: PRgnData          {a pointer to a TRgnData structure}
): DWORD;               {returns a 1 if successful}
```

Description

This function retrieves information about the region identified by the RGN parameter, primarily information concerning the rectangles that define the region. This information is stored in the variable length data structure pointed to by the p3 parameter.

Parameters

RGN: A handle to the region for which information is to be retrieved.

p2: Specifies the size of the data structure pointed to by the p3 parameter, in bytes. If this value is not large enough to hold the region data, the function returns the required size of the buffer, in bytes.

p3: A pointer to a TRgnData structure that receives information about the specified region. The TRgnData structure is a variable length structure, memory for which must be allocated by the application. If this parameter is set to NIL, the function returns the required size of the buffer, in bytes, to hold the region data. The TRgnData structure is defined as:

```
TRgnData = record
    rdh: TRgnDataHeader;           {region data information}
    Buffer: array[0..0] of CHAR;   {an array of rectangles}
end;
```

See the ExtCreateRegion function for a description of this data structure.

Return Value

If the function succeeds, it returns one; otherwise, it returns zero.

See Also

ExtCreateRegion, GetClipRgn

Example

See Listing 11-6 under CreatePolygonRgn.

GetRgnBox Windows.pas

Syntax

```
GetRgnBox(
  RGN: HRGN;            {a handle to a region}
```

```
    var p2: TRect                {a pointer to a TRect structure}
    ): Integer;                  {returns the type of region}
```

Description

This function retrieves the coordinates of the smallest rectangle that can be drawn around the specified region.

Parameters

RGN: A handle to the region for which a bounding rectangle is to be retrieved.

p2: A pointer to a TRect structure that receives the coordinates of the smallest rectangle encompassing the specified region, in logical units.

Return Value

This function returns a result indicating the type of region for which the bounding box was retrieved or an error condition, and may be one value from the following table.

See Also

GetClipBox, GetClipRgn, GetRegionData

Example

See Listing 11-17 under OffsetRgn and Listing 11-18 under PathToRegion.

Table 11-10: GetRgnBox return values

Value	Description
NULLREGION	Indicates an empty region.
SIMPLEREGION	Indicates a single rectangular region.
COMPLEXREGION	Indicates a region consisting of more than one rectangle.
ERROR	Indicates an error occurred.

InflateRect   Windows.pas

Syntax

```
InflateRect(
    var lprc: TRect;             {a pointer to a TRect structure}
    dx: Integer;                 {the horizontal increase or decrease value}
    dy: Integer                  {the vertical increase or decrease value}
    ): BOOL;                     {returns TRUE or FALSE}
```

Description

This function modifies the size of the rectangle identified by the lprc parameter by adding the value in the dx parameter to the rectangle's left and right sides and the value in the dy parameter to the rectangle's top and bottom sides.

Parameters

lprc: A pointer to a TRect structure containing the rectangle to be increased or decreased in size.

dx: Specifies the amount by which to increase or decrease the width of the rectangle. A positive value increases the width, a negative value decreases it.

dy: Specifies the amount by which to increase or decrease the height of the rectangle. A positive value increases the height, a negative value decreases it.

Return Value

If the function succeeds, it returns TRUE; otherwise, it returns FALSE. To get extended error information, call the GetLastError function.

See Also

CopyRect, IntersectRect, OffsetRect, PtInRect, SetRect, UnionRect

Example

See Listing 11-16 under OffsetRect.

IntersectRect   Windows.pas

Syntax

```
IntersectRect(
  var lprcDst: TRect;        {the rectangle receiving the intersection coordinates}
  const lprcSrc1: TRect;     {the first rectangle}
  const lprcSrc2: TRect      {the second rectangle}
): BOOL;                     {returns TRUE or FALSE}
```

Description

This function determines the intersection between the rectangles identified by the lprcSrc1 and lprcSrc2 parameters. The coordinates of the intersection rectangle are stored in the TRect structure pointed to by the lprcDst parameter. If there is no intersection, the coordinates of the lprcDst rectangle will all be set to zero.

Parameters

lprcDst: A pointer to a TRect structure that receives the coordinates of the intersection between the rectangles identified by the lprcSrc1 and lprcSrc2 parameters.

lprcSrc1: A pointer to a TRect structure containing the coordinates of the first rectangle.

lprcSrc2: A pointer to a TRect structure containing the coordinates of the second rectangle.

Return Value

If the function succeeds and the rectangles intersect, it returns TRUE. If the function fails, or the rectangles do not intersect, it returns FALSE. To get extended error information, call the GetLastError function.

Region and Path Functions 497

See Also

InflateRect, OffsetRect, PtInRect, SetRect, UnionRect

Example

See Listing 11-16 under OffsetRect.

InvertRect   Windows.pas

Syntax

```
InvertRect(
hDC: HDC;              {a handle to a device context}
const lprc: TRect      {a pointer to a TRect structure}
): BOOL;               {returns TRUE or FALSE}
```

Description

This function performs a Boolean NOT operation on the color value of every pixel in the specified device context that falls within the rectangular area defined by the rectangle pointed to by the lprc parameter.

Parameters

hDC: A handle to the device context containing the color pixels to be inverted.

lprc: A pointer to a TRect structure containing the coordinates of the rectangular area to invert, in logical units.

Return Value

If the function succeeds, it returns TRUE; otherwise, it returns FALSE. To get extended error information, call the GetLastError function.

See Also

FillRect, InvertRgn, SetRect

Example

Listing 11-14: Inverting a rectangular portion of an image

```
procedure TForm1.Button1Click(Sender: TObject);
var
  TheRect: TRect;     // holds the rectangular coordinates
begin
  {create a rectangle}
  SetRect(TheRect, 46, 40, 106, 100);

  {invert the pixels inside the rectangle}
  InvertRect(Image1.Canvas.Handle, TheRect);

  {repaint the new image}
  Image1.Refresh;
end;
```

*Figure 11-14:
The inverted rectangular area*

InvertRgn   Windows.pas

Syntax

```
InvertRgn(
DC: HDC;              {a handle to a device context}
p2: HRGN              {a handle to a region}
): BOOL;              {returns TRUE or FALSE}
```

Description

This function performs a Boolean NOT operation on the color value of every pixel in the specified device context that falls within the region identified by the p2 parameter.

Parameters

DC: A handle to the device context containing the color pixels to be inverted.

p2: A handle to the region defining the area to invert. The coordinates of this region are assumed to be in logical units.

Return Value

If the function succeeds, it returns TRUE; otherwise, it returns FALSE.

See Also

FillRgn, InvertRect, PaintRgn

Example

See Listing 11-7 under CreatePolyPolygonRgn.

IsRectEmpty   Windows.pas

Syntax

```
IsRectEmpty(
const lprc: TRect     {a pointer to a TRect structure}
): BOOL;              {returns TRUE or FALSE}
```

Description

This function determines if the specified rectangle is empty. A rectangle is considered empty if its bottom side is less than or equal to its top side or its right side is less than or equal to its left side.

Parameters

lprc: A pointer to the TRect structure to be tested. The coordinates of this rectangle are in logical units.

Return Value

If the function succeeds and the rectangle is empty, it returns TRUE. If the function fails, or the rectangle is not empty, it returns FALSE. To get extended error information, call the GetLastError function.

See Also

EqualRect, PtInRect, SetRect, SetRectEmpty, SetRectRgn

Example

See Listing 11-21 under SetRectEmpty.

OffsetClipRgn   Windows.pas

Syntax

```
OffsetClipRgn(
DC: HDC;                {a handle to a device context}
p2: Integer;            {the horizontal offset}
p3: Integer             {the vertical offset}
): Integer;             {returns the type of region}
```

Description

This function moves the clipping region of the specified device context by the horizontal and vertical amounts identified by the p2 and p3 parameters.

Parameters

DC: A handle to the device context containing the clipping region to move.

p2: Specifies the horizontal offset by which to move the clipping region in logical units.

p3: Specifies the vertical offset by which to move the clipping region in logical units.

Return Value

This function returns a result indicating the type of clipping region resulting from the movement, or an error condition, and may be one value from Table 11-11.

See Also

OffsetRgn, SelectClipRgn

Example

Listing 11-15: Performing special animation effects by moving the clipping region

```
var
  Form1: TForm1;
  MovingRgn: HRGN;                    // holds a region
  XPos, YPos, XVel, YVel: Integer;    // holds the region's velocity and position

implementation

{$R *.DFM}

procedure TForm1.FormCreate(Sender: TObject);
begin
  {create a small circular region to be used as the clipping region}
  MovingRgn := CreateEllipticRgn(0, 0, 75, 75);

  {initialize the region's position and velocity}
  XPos := 1;
  YPos := 1;
  XVel := 1;
  YVel := 1;
end;

procedure TForm1.Timer1Timer(Sender: TObject);
var
  TempBitmap: TBitmap;    // holds an offscreen bitmap
begin
  {create the offscreen bitmap and initialize its size to that of the
   invisible TImage. this offscreen bitmap is used to eliminate flicker}
  TempBitmap := TBitmap.Create;
  TempBitmap.Width := Image1.Width;
  TempBitmap.Height := Image1.Height;

  {increase the region's position by its velocity}
  Inc(XPos, XVel);
  Inc(YPos, YVel);

  {if the region has reached the edge of the screen, reverse its velocity}
  if (XPos<0) or (XPos>ClientRect.Right-75) then
    XVel := 0-XVel;
  if (YPos<0) or (YPos>ClientRect.Bottom-75) then
    YVel := 0-YVel;

  {select the circular region into the device context of the offscreen bitmap,
   indicating that it should be logically ANDed with the bitmap's current
   clipping region}
  ExtSelectClipRgn(TempBitmap.Canvas.Handle, MovingRgn, RGN_AND);

  {move the clipping region to the position being tracked}
  OffsetClipRgn(TempBitmap.Canvas.Handle, XPos, YPos);

  {draw the picture stored in Image1 into the bitmap. the clipping region will
   only allow the bitmap to be drawn within the small circular area of the
   region}
  TempBitmap.Canvas.Draw(0, 0, Image1.Picture.Bitmap);
```

```
   {draw the offscreen bitmap to the form. this will result in an animation of
    a small, bouncing circle}
   Canvas.Draw(Image1.Left, Image1.Top, TempBitmap);

   {free the offscreen bitmap}
   TempBitmap.Free;
end;

procedure TForm1.FormDestroy(Sender: TObject);
begin
   {we no longer need the region, so delete it}
   DeleteObject(MovingRgn);
end;
```

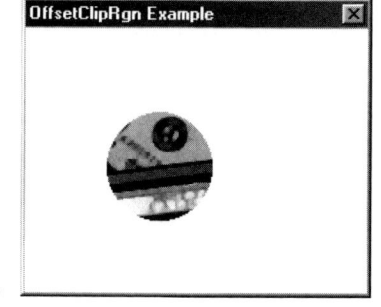

Figure 11-15: The offset clipping region

Table 11-11: OffsetClipRgn return values

Value	Description
NULLREGION	Indicates an empty region.
SIMPLEREGION	Indicates a single rectangular region.
COMPLEXREGION	Indicates a region consisting of more than one rectangle.
ERROR	Indicates an error occurred.

OffsetRect   Windows.pas

Syntax

```
OffsetRect(
var lprc: TRect;         {a pointer to a TRect structure}
dx: Integer;             {the horizontal offset}
dy: Integer              {the vertical offset}
): BOOL;                 {returns TRUE or FALSE}
```

Description

This function moves the specified rectangle by the horizontal and vertical amounts specified by the dx and dy parameters.

Parameters

lprc: A pointer to a TRect structure containing the rectangular coordinates to be moved, in logical units.

dx: Specifies the horizontal offset by which to move the rectangle, in logical units.

dy: Specifies the vertical offset by which to move the rectangle, in logical units.

Return Value

If the function succeeds, it returns TRUE; otherwise, it returns FALSE. To get extended error information, call the GetLastError function.

See Also

CopyRect, InflateRect, IntersectRect, OffsetRgn, SubtractRect, UnionRect

Example

Listing 11-16: A demonstration of various rectangle manipulation functions

```
var
  Form1: TForm1;
  Rect1, Rect2: TRect;                   // the two test rectangles
  DragRect: PRect;                       // points to the rectangle being dragged
  DraggingRect: Boolean;                 // indicates if a drag is occurring
  MouseOffsetX, MouseOffsetY: Integer;   // used to offset the dragged rectangle

implementation

{$R *.DFM}

procedure TForm1.FormCreate(Sender: TObject);
begin
  {initialize the two test rectangles}
  SetRect(Rect1, 10, 30, 110, 130);
  SetRect(Rect2, 60, 80, 160, 180);

  {initialize the drag flag to indicate that dragging is not occurring}
  DraggingRect := FALSE;
end;

procedure TForm1.FormPaint(Sender: TObject);
var
  Intersection, Union: TRect;   // shows the union and intersection
begin
  {retrieve the union of the two test rectangles}
  UnionRect(Union, Rect1, Rect2);

  {draw this union rectangle in green}
  Form1.Canvas.Brush.Color := clGreen;
  Form1.Canvas.FillRect(Union);

  {draw the two test rectangles in red}
  Form1.Canvas.Brush.Color := clRed;
  Form1.Canvas.FillRect(Rect1);
  Form1.Canvas.FillRect(Rect2);

  {retrieve the intersection of the two test rectangles}
  IntersectRect(Intersection, Rect1, Rect2);
```

```
    {draw this intersection in blue}
    Form1.Canvas.Brush.Color := clBlue;
    Form1.Canvas.FillRect(Intersection);

    {indicate if the two rectangles are at exactly the same coordinates}
    if EqualRect(Rect1, Rect2) then
      Form1.Caption := 'OffsetRectExample - Rectangles are equal'
    else
      Form1.Caption := 'OffsetRectExample - Rectangles are not equal';
end;

procedure TForm1.FormMouseDown(Sender: TObject; Button: TMouseButton;
  Shift: TShiftState; X, Y: Integer);
begin
  {if the mouse was clicked inside of the first rectangle...}
  if PtInRect(Rect1, Point(X, Y)) then
  begin
    {indicate that dragging has commenced}
    DraggingRect := TRUE;

    {indicate that we are dragging rectangle 1}
    DragRect := @Rect1;
  end;

  {if the mouse was clicked inside of the second rectangle...}
  if PtInRect(Rect2, Point(X, Y)) then
  begin
    {indicate that dragging has commenced}
    DraggingRect := TRUE;

    {indicate that we are dragging rectangle 2}
    DragRect := @Rect2;
  end;

  {if a dragging operation has started...}
  if DraggingRect then
  begin
    {retrieve the offset of the current mouse coordinate within the
     dragged rectangle.  this is used when moving the rectangle so that the
     original spot where the mouse was clicked inside of the rectangle is
     preserved.  otherwise, when the rectangle is moved the upper left hand
     corner of the rectangle will be positioned at the mouse cursor position.}
    MouseOffsetX := X-DragRect^.Left;
    MouseOffsetY := Y-DragRect^.Top;
  end;
end;

procedure TForm1.FormMouseMove(Sender: TObject; Shift: TShiftState; X,
  Y: Integer);
begin
  {if a dragging operation is occurring...}
  if DraggingRect then
  begin
    {erase the form}
    Form1.Canvas.Brush.Color := clBtnFace;
    Form1.Canvas.FillRect(DragRect^);
```

```
      {move the dragged rectangle, offsetting it from the current mouse position
       so that the original clicked location within the rectangle is preserved}
      OffsetRect(DragRect^, X-DragRect^.Left-MouseOffsetX,
                 Y-DragRect^.Top-MouseOffsetY);

      {repaint the form}
      Form1.Repaint;
    end;
end;

procedure TForm1.FormMouseUp(Sender: TObject; Button: TMouseButton;
  Shift: TShiftState; X, Y: Integer);
begin
  {indicate that dragging has stopped}
  DraggingRect := FALSE;
end;

procedure TForm1.SpeedButton1Click(Sender: TObject);
begin
  {increase or decrease the size of the last dragged rectangle. the amount by
   which to increase or decrease the size is stored in the Tag property of
   the speed buttons on the toolbar}
  if DragRect<>NIL then
    InflateRect(DragRect^, TSpeedButton(Sender).Tag, TSpeedButton(Sender).Tag);

  {repaint the form to show the results}
  Form1.Repaint;
end;

procedure TForm1.Button1Click(Sender: TObject);
begin
  {force rectangle 2 to become an exact duplicate of rectangle 1}
  CopyRect(Rect2, Rect1);

  {repaint the form to show the results}
  Form1.Repaint;
end;
```

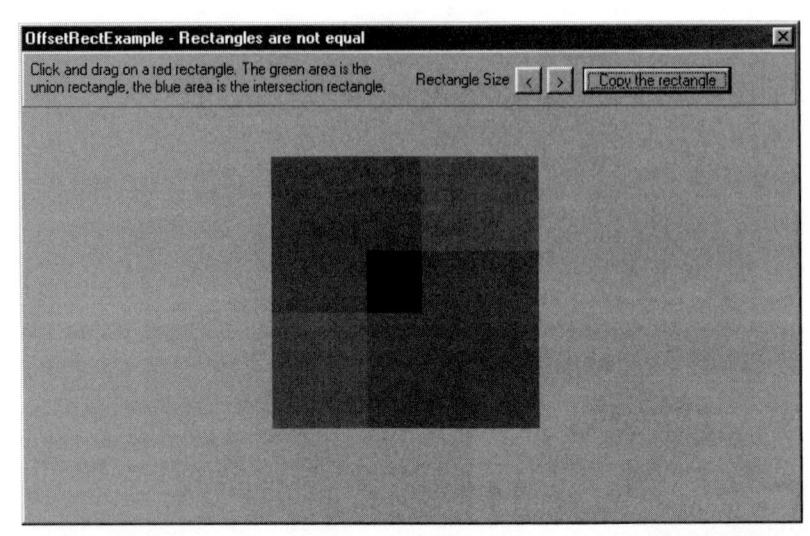

Figure 11-16:
The rectangle function test bed

OffsetRgn   Windows.pas

Syntax

OffsetRgn(
RGN: HRGN;   {a handle to a region}
p2: Integer;   {the horizontal offset}
p3: Integer   {the vertical offset}
): Integer;   {returns the type of region}

Description

This function moves the specified region by the horizontal and vertical amounts specified by the p2 and p3 parameters.

Parameters

RGN: A handle to the region to be moved.

p2: Specifies the horizontal offset by which to move the region, in logical units.

p3: Specifies the vertical offset by which to move the region, in logical units.

Return Value

This function returns a result indicating the type of region resulting from the movement, or an error condition, and may be one value from the following table.

See Also

EqualRgn, OffsetClipRgn, OffsetRect

Example

Listing 11-17: Moving a region to produce special animation effects

```
var
  Form1: TForm1;
  MovingRgn: HRGN;      // a handle to the moving region
  XVel, YVel: Integer;  // the region's velocity

implementation

{$R *.DFM}

procedure TForm1.FormCreate(Sender: TObject);
begin
  {create an elliptical region}
  MovingRgn := CreateEllipticRgn(0, 0, 75, 75);

  {initialize its velocity}
  XVel := 1;
  YVel := 1;
end;

procedure TForm1.FormPaint(Sender: TObject);
begin
```

```
    {select the circular region as a clipping region for the form}
    SelectClipRgn(Canvas.Handle, MovingRgn);

    {draw the image in the invisible TImage onto the form. the circular
     clipping region prevents any drawing outside of the circular region}
    Canvas.Draw(Image1.Left, Image1.Top, Image1.Picture.Bitmap);
end;

procedure TForm1.Timer1Timer(Sender: TObject);
var
  RegionBounds: TRect;  // holds the bounding rectangle of the region
begin
  {retrieve the smallest rectangle that can be drawn around the circular region}
  GetRgnBox(MovingRgn, RegionBounds);

  {the bounding rectangle is used to determine if the circular region has
   reached the edges of the screen. if so, reverse the velocity}
  if (RegionBounds.Left<0) or (RegionBounds.Left>ClientRect.Right-75) then
    XVel := 0-XVel;
  if (RegionBounds.Top<0) or (RegionBounds.Top>ClientRect.Bottom-75) then
    YVel := 0-YVel;

  {move the region by its current velocity}
  OffsetRgn(MovingRgn, XVel, YVel);

  {repaint the form to show the results}
  Repaint;
end;

procedure TForm1.FormDestroy(Sender: TObject);
begin
  {the region is no longer needed, so destroy it}
  DeleteObject(MovingRgn);
end;
```

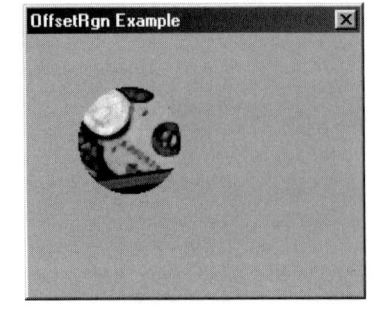

Figure 11-17:
The moving region

Table 11-12: OffsetRgn return values

Value	Description
NULLREGION	Indicates an empty region.
SIMPLEREGION	Indicates a single rectangular region.
COMPLEXREGION	Indicates a region consisting of more than one rectangle.
ERROR	Indicates an error occurred.

PathToRegion   Windows.pas

Syntax

```
PathToRegion(
  DC: HDC                  {a handle to a device context}
): HRGN;                   {returns a handle to a region}
```

Description

This function converts the path in the specified device context into a region. The path must be closed, and it is discarded from the device context when the function returns. When the region is no longer needed, it should be deleted by calling the DeleteObject function.

Parameters

DC: A handle to the device context containing the closed path to be converted into a region.

Return Value

If the function succeeds, it returns a handle to a new region; otherwise, it returns zero. To get extended error information, call the GetLastError function.

See Also

BeginPath, EndPath, GetPath

Example

Listing 11-18: Converting a path into a region

```
var
  Form1: TForm1;
  TextRgn: HRGN;         // holds the text region
  YVel: Integer;         // the region's vertical velocity
  TempBitmap: TBitmap;   // an offscreen bitmap used to eliminate flicker

implementation

{$R *.DFM}

procedure TForm1.FormCreate(Sender: TObject);
begin
  {begin the a path bracket for the form's device context}
  BeginPath(Canvas.Handle);

  {set the background mode to transparent. this is necessary so that the path
   will consist of the area inside of the text. without this, the path is
   defined as the area outside of the text}
  SetBkMode(Canvas.Handle, TRANSPARENT);

  {Output a word to the form. this is captured as part of the path. note that
   the form's font is set to size 48 Arial}
  TextOut(Canvas.Handle, 1, 1, 'DELPHI', Length('DELPHI'));
```

```
    {end the path bracket}
    EndPath(Canvas.Handle);

    {convert the path into a region. note that this discards the path in the
     device context}
    TextRgn := PathToRegion(Canvas.Handle);

    {create the offscreen bitmap and initialize it to the size of the
     invisible TImage}
    TempBitmap := TBitmap.Create;
    TempBitmap.Width := Image1.Width;
    TempBitmap.Height := Image1.Height;

    {initialize the vertical velocity}
    YVel := 1;
end;

procedure TForm1.Timer1Timer(Sender: TObject);
var
  RegionBounds: TRect;    // holds the bounding rectangle of the region
begin
    {retrieve the bounding rectangle of the region}
    GetRgnBox(TextRgn, RegionBounds);

    {if the region is at the top or bottom edge of the form, reverse its velocity}
    if (RegionBounds.Top<0) or (RegionBounds.Top>ClientRect.Bottom-
                              (RegionBounds.Bottom-RegionBounds.Top)) then
      YVel := 0-YVel;

    {offset the region vertically by its velocity}
    OffsetRgn(TextRgn, 0, YVel);

    {draw the graphic in the invisible TImage to the offscreen bitmap}
    TempBitmap.Canvas.Draw(0, 0, Image1.Picture.Bitmap);

    {invert the area inside of the text region}
    InvertRgn(TempBitmap.Canvas.Handle, TextRgn);

    {copy the offscreen bitmap to the form, eliminating flicker}
    Canvas.Draw(0, 0, TempBitmap);
end;

procedure TForm1.FormDestroy(Sender: TObject);
begin
    {the region is no longer needed, so destroy it}
    DeleteObject(TextRgn);
end;
```

*Figure 11-18:
The converted
path*

PtInRect   Windows.pas

Syntax

```
PtInRect(
const lprc: TRect;        {a pointer to a TRect structure}
pt: TPoint                {a pointer to a TPoint structure}
): BOOL;                  {returns TRUE or FALSE}
```

Description

This function determines if the point identified by the pt parameter lies inside of the rectangle pointed to by the lprc parameter. The point is considered to be outside of the rectangle if it lies exactly on the bottom or right edges of the rectangle.

Parameters

lprc: A pointer to a TRect structure containing the coordinates within which the point is to be tested.

pt: A pointer to a TPoint structure containing the point to be tested.

Return Value

If the function succeeds and the point lies within the rectangle, it returns TRUE. If the function fails, or the point is not located within the rectangle, it returns FALSE. To get extended error information, call the GetLastError function.

See Also

EqualRect, IsRectEmpty, PtInRegion, PtVisible, RectInRegion, SetRect

Example

See Listing 11-16 under OffsetRect.

PtInRegion   Windows.pas

Syntax

```
PtInRegion(
RGN: HGRN;                {a handle to a region}
p2: Integer;              {a horizontal coordinate}
```

```
p3: Integer              {a vertical coordinate}
): BOOL;                 {returns TRUE or FALSE}
```

Description

This function determines if the point identified by the p2 and p3 parameters lies inside of the region specified by the RGN parameter.

Parameters

RGN: A handle to the region within which the point is to be tested.

p2: Specifies the horizontal coordinate of the point to test.

p3: Specifies the vertical coordinate of the point to test.

Return Value

If the function succeeds and the point lies within the region, it returns TRUE. If the function fails, or the point is not located within the region, it returns FALSE.

See Also

PtInRect, PtVisible, RectInRegion

Example

See Listing 11-7 under CreatePolyPolygonRgn.

PtVisible   Windows.pas

Syntax

```
PtVisible(
DC: HDC;                 {a handle to a device context}
p2: Integer;             {a horizontal coordinate}
p3: Integer              {a vertical coordinate}
): BOOL;                 {returns TRUE or FALSE}
```

Description

This function determines if the point identified by the p2 and p3 parameters lies inside of the clipping region of the specified device context.

Parameters

DC: A handle to the device context containing the clipping region within which the point is to be tested.

p2: Specifies the horizontal coordinate of the point to test.

p3: Specifies the vertical coordinate of the point to test.

Return Value

If the function succeeds and the point lies within the clipping region, it returns TRUE. If the function fails, or the point is not located within the clipping region, it returns FALSE.

See Also

PtInRect, PtInRegion, RectInRegion, RectVisible

Example

See Listing 11-6 under CreatePolygonRgn.

RectInRegion   Windows.pas

Syntax

```
RectInRegion(
RGN: HRGN;              {a handle to a region}
const p2: TRect         {a pointer to a TRect structure}
): BOOL;                {returns TRUE or FALSE}
```

Description

This function determines if any portion of the rectangle pointed to by the p2 parameter lies within the region identified by the RGN parameter. Note that the bottom and right sides of the rectangle are excluded from the comparison.

Parameters

RGN: A handle to the region within which the rectangle is tested.

p2: A pointer to a TRect structure containing the rectangular coordinates to test.

Return Value

If the function succeeds and some portion of the rectangle lies within the region, it returns TRUE. If the function fails, or no part of the rectangle lies within the region, it returns FALSE.

See Also

PtInRect, PtInRegion, PtVisible, RectVisible, SelectClipRegion

Example

See Listing 11-20 under SelectClipRgn.

RectVisible   Windows.pas

Syntax

```
RectVisible(
DC: HDC;                {a handle to a device context}
const Rect: TRect       {a pointer to a TRect structure}
): BOOL;                {returns TRUE or FALSE}
```

Description

This function determines if any portion of the rectangle pointed to by the Rect parameter lies within the clipping region of the device context identified by the DC parameter.

Chapter 11

Parameters

DC: A handle to the device context containing the clipping region within which the rectangle is tested.

Rect: A pointer to a TRect structure containing the rectangular coordinates to test.

Return Value

If the function succeeds and some portion of the rectangle lies within the clipping region, it returns TRUE. If the function fails, or no part of the rectangle lies within the clipping region, it returns FALSE.

See Also

GetClipRgn, PtInRegion, PtVisible, RectInRegion, SelectClipRgn

Example

See Listing 11-20 under SelectClipRgn.

SelectClipPath   Windows.pas

Syntax

```
SelectClipPath(
DC: HDC;              {a handle to a device context}
Mode: Integer         {region combination flag}
): BOOL;              {returns TRUE or FALSE}
```

Description

This function selects the current path in the specified device context as the device context's clipping region, combining it with the current clipping region according to the flag specified in the Mode parameter.

Parameters

DC: A handle to the device context containing the path to be used as a clipping region. This must be a closed path.

Mode: A flag indicating how the clipping region formed from the path is to be combined with the device context's current clipping region. This parameter can contain one value from Table 11-13.

Return Value

If the function succeeds, it returns TRUE; otherwise, it returns FALSE. To get extended error information, call the GetLastError function.

See Also

BeginPath, EndPath, PathToRegion, SelectClipRgn

Example

Listing II-19: Creating special text effects

```
var
  Form1: TForm1;
  ThePalette: HPalette;    // a handle to the application-defined palette

implementation

{$R *.DFM}

procedure TForm1.FormCreate(Sender: TObject);
var
  NewPalette: PLogPalette;    // a pointer to logical palette information
  iCount: Integer;            // a general loop counter
begin
  {initialize the form's font}
  Font.Name := 'Arial';
  Font.Size := 48;

  {retrieve enough memory to create a 75 entry palette}
  GetMem(NewPalette, SizeOf(TLogPalette)+75*SizeOf(TPaletteEntry));

  {initialize specific palette information}
  NewPalette^.palVersion := $300;
  NewPalette^.palNumEntries := 75;

  {retrieve the first 10 system palette entries}
  GetSystemPaletteEntries(Form1.Canvas.Handle, 0, 10, NewPalette^.palPalEntry);

  {create a gradient palette for the remaining entries}
  for iCount := 10 to 74 do
  begin
    NewPalette^.palPalEntry[iCount].peRed   := 255;
    NewPalette^.palPalEntry[iCount].peGreen := ((256 div 64)*(iCount-10));
    NewPalette^.palPalEntry[iCount].peBlue  := 0;
    NewPalette^.palPalEntry[iCount].peFlags := PC_NOCOLLAPSE;
  end;

  {create a new palette}
  ThePalette := CreatePalette(NewPalette^);

  {free the memory allocated for the logical palette information}
  FreeMem(NewPalette);
end;

{this draws gradient, radial lines originating from the center of the text}
procedure TForm1.DrawRadial;
var
  iCount: Integer;         // a general loop counter variable
  RayOrigin: TPoint;       // the origin of the radial lines
  Radius: Integer;         // the radius within which to draw the lines
  NewPen, OldPen: HPen;    // holds a new and old pen
begin
  {begin a path bracket within the form's device context}
  BeginPath(Canvas.Handle);
```

```
{set the background mode to transparent. this is necessary so that the path
 will consist of the area inside of the text. without this, the path is
 defined as the area outside of the text}
SetBkMode(Canvas.Handle, TRANSPARENT);

{output a word onto the form. this is captured as part of the path}
TextOut(Canvas.Handle, 50, 50, 'Delphi Rocks!', Length('Delphi Rocks!'));

{end the path bracket}
EndPath(Canvas.Handle);

{select this path as a clipping region for the form's device context}
SelectClipPath(Canvas.Handle, RGN_COPY);

{the radial lines should originate from the center of the text}
RayOrigin.X := (Canvas.TextWidth('Delphi Rocks!') div 2)+50;
RayOrigin.Y := (Canvas.TextHeight('Delphi Rocks!') div 2)+50;

{the radius of the circle within which the lines are drawn will be
 equal to the length of the text}
Radius := Canvas.TextWidth('Delphi Rocks!');

{draw lines in a 90 degree arc}
for iCount := 0 to 89 do
begin
  {create a new pen, specifying a color from the new palette}
  NewPen := CreatePen(PS_SOLID, 1, PaletteIndex(75-Trunc(iCount*(64/90)+10)));

  {select this pen into the device context}
  OldPen := SelectObject(Canvas.Handle, NewPen);

  {draw a line starting at the center of the text. these lines will radiate
   outwards in a circular fashion. the following code draws a line in the
   first quadrant of a circular area within the text, and then reflects that
   line to the other 3 quadrants}
  MoveToEx(Canvas.Handle, RayOrigin.X, RayOrigin.Y, NIL);
  LineTo(Canvas.Handle, RayOrigin.X+Trunc(Radius*cos(iCount/(180/PI))),
         RayOrigin.Y+Trunc(Radius*sin(iCount/(180/PI))));
  MoveToEx(Canvas.Handle, RayOrigin.X, RayOrigin.Y, NIL);
  LineTo(Canvas.Handle, RayOrigin.X+Trunc(Radius*cos(iCount/(180/PI))),
         RayOrigin.Y-Trunc(Radius*sin(iCount/(180/PI))));
  MoveToEx(Canvas.Handle, RayOrigin.X, RayOrigin.Y, NIL);
  LineTo(Canvas.Handle, RayOrigin.X-Trunc(Radius*cos(iCount/(180/PI))),
         RayOrigin.Y-Trunc(Radius*sin(iCount/(180/PI))));
  MoveToEx(Canvas.Handle, RayOrigin.X, RayOrigin.Y, NIL);
  LineTo(Canvas.Handle, RayOrigin.X-Trunc(Radius*cos(iCount/(180/PI))),
         RayOrigin.Y+Trunc(Radius*sin(iCount/(180/PI))));

  {delete the new pen}
  SelectObject(Canvas.Handle, OldPen);
  DeleteObject(NewPen);
 end;
end;

{this function draws gradient filled text}
procedure TForm1.DrawGradient;
var
```

Region and Path Functions 515

```
    iCount: Integer;          // a general loop counter
    TempRect: TRect;          // holds a temporary rectangle
    NewBrush, OldBrush: HBrush;  // holds an old and new brush
begin
  {begin a path bracket within the form's device context}
  BeginPath(Canvas.Handle);

  {set the background mode to transparent. this is necessary so that the path
   will consist of the area inside of the text. without this, the path is
   defined as the area outside of the text}
  SetBkMode(Canvas.Handle, TRANSPARENT);

  {output a word onto the form. this is captured as part of the path}
  TextOut(Canvas.Handle, 50, 150, 'Delphi Rocks!', Length('Delphi Rocks!'));

  {end the path bracket}
  EndPath(Canvas.Handle);

  {select this path as a clipping region for the form's device context}
  SelectClipPath(Canvas.Handle, RGN_COPY);

  {draw a series of rectangles within the text, resulting in a gradient fill}
  for iCount := 0 to 64 do
  begin
    {create a new brush, specifying a color from the new palette}
    NewBrush := CreateSolidBrush(PaletteIndex(iCount+10));

    {select the brush into the device context}
    OldBrush := SelectObject(Form1.Canvas.Handle, NewBrush);

    {create a rectangle, incremented from the left side of the text}
    TempRect := Rect(Trunc(50+iCount*Canvas.TextWidth('Delphi Rocks!')/64), 150,
                     Trunc(50+(iCount*Canvas.TextWidth('Delphi Rocks!')/64)+
                     (Canvas.TextWidth('Delphi Rocks!')/64)),
                     150+Canvas.TextHeight('Delphi Rocks!'));

    {fill the rectangle with the brush. the final product will be the illusion
     of gradient filled text}
    FillRect(Canvas.Handle, TempRect, NewBrush);

    {delete the new brush}
    SelectObject(Form1.Canvas.Handle, OldBrush);
    DeleteObject(NewBrush);
  end;
end;

procedure TForm1.FormPaint(Sender: TObject);
begin
  {select and realize the new palette into the form's device context}
  SelectPalette(Form1.Canvas.Handle, ThePalette, FALSE);
  RealizePalette(Form1.Canvas.Handle);

  {draw radially filled text}
  DrawRadial;

  {draw gradient filled text}
  DrawGradient;
```

```
end;

procedure TForm1.FormDestroy(Sender: TObject);
begin
  {the palette is no longer needed, so delete it}
  DeleteObject(ThePalette);
end;
```

Figure 11-19:
Using paths to
create special
text effects

Table 11-13: SelectClipPath Mode values

Value	Description
RGN_AND	The resulting region is the intersection of the current clipping region and the path.
RGN_COPY	The resulting region is the path.
RGN_DIFF	The resulting region is the area of the current clipping region that is not in the area of the path.
RGN_OR	The resulting region is the union of the current clipping region and the path.
RGN_XOR	The resulting region is the union of the current clipping region and the path excluding any overlapping areas.

SelectClipRgn   Windows.pas

Syntax

```
SelectClipRgn(
  DC: HDC;              {a handle to a device context}
  p2: HRGN              {a handle to a region}
): Integer;             {returns the type of region}
```

Description

This function selects the region identified by the p2 parameter as the clipping region for the specified device context.

Parameters

DC: A handle to the device context whose clipping region is to be set.

p2: A handle to the region to be selected as the specified device context's clipping region. This function uses a copy of the region; the original region is unaffected and can be used in other functions. The coordinates of the region are assumed to be in device units. If this parameter is set to zero, the device context's current clipping region is removed.

Return Value

This function returns a result indicating the type of clipping region set, or an error condition, and may be one value from Table 11-14.

See Also

ExtSelectClipRgn, GetClipRgn, OffsetClipRgn, SelectClipPath

Example

Listing 11-20: Clipping drawing to a defined region

```
var
  Form1: TForm1;
  ClippingRegion: HRGN;       // a handle to the clipping region
  DraggingRect: Boolean;      // indicates that a drag operation is occurring
  TheRect: TRect;             // the dragged rectangle
  MouseOffsetX,               // used to offset the dragged rectangle
  MouseOffsetY: Integer;

implementation

{$R *.DFM}

procedure TForm1.FormCreate(Sender: TObject);
begin
  {create an elliptical region to be used for clipping}
  ClippingRegion := CreateEllipticRgn(40, 40, ClientWidth-50, ClientHeight-50);

  {create a rectangle}
  SetRect(TheRect, (ClientWidth div 2)-30, (ClientHeight div 2)-30,
          (ClientWidth div 2)+30, (ClientHeight div 2)+30);

  {initialize the dragging flag}
  DraggingRect := FALSE;
end;

procedure TForm1.FormPaint(Sender: TObject);
begin
  {select the elliptical region as the clipping region}
  SelectClipRgn(Canvas.Handle, ClippingRegion);

  {indicate if the dragged rectangle is visible within the clipping region}
  if RectVisible(Canvas.Handle, TheRect) then
    Caption := Caption+'Rect Visible'
  else
    Caption := Caption+'Rect Not Visible';

  {draw the perimeter of the clipping region in red}
  Canvas.Brush.Color := clRed;
```

```
      FrameRgn(Canvas.Handle, ClippingRegion, Canvas.Brush.Handle, 4, 4);

      {draw the draggable rectangle in blue}
      Canvas.Brush.Color := clBlue;
      Canvas.FillRect(TheRect);
    end;

    procedure TForm1.FormMouseDown(Sender: TObject; Button: TMouseButton;
      Shift: TShiftState; X, Y: Integer);
    begin
      {if the mouse was clicked within the draggable rectangle}
      if PtInRect(TheRect, Point(X, Y)) then
      begin
        {indicate that a drag operation has commenced}
        DraggingRect := TRUE;

        {retrieve the offset of the current mouse coordinate within the
         dragged rectangle.  this is used when moving the rectangle so that the
         original spot where the mouse was clicked inside of the rectangle is
         preserved.  otherwise, when the rectangle is moved the upper left hand
         corner of the rectangle will be positioned at the mouse cursor position}
        MouseOffsetX := X-TheRect.Left;
        MouseOffsetY := Y-TheRect.Top;
      end;
    end;

    procedure TForm1.FormMouseMove(Sender: TObject; Shift: TShiftState; X,
      Y: Integer);
    begin
      {if a drag operation is occurring...}
      if DraggingRect then
      begin
        {erase the form's canvas}
        Form1.Canvas.Brush.Color := clBtnFace;
        Form1.Canvas.FillRect(TheRect);

        {move the dragged rectangle, offsetting it from the current mouse position
         so that the original clicked location within the rectangle is preserved}
        OffsetRect(TheRect, X-TheRect.Left-MouseOffsetX,
                   Y-TheRect.Top-MouseOffsetY);

        {initialize the form's caption}
        Caption := 'SelectClipRgn Example - ';

        {indicate if the rectangle is within the elliptical region}
        if RectInRegion(ClippingRegion, TheRect) then
          Caption := Caption+'Rect In Region - '
        else
          Caption := Caption+'Rect Not In Region - ';

        {repaint the form to display the changes}
        Form1.Repaint;
      end;
    end;

    procedure TForm1.FormMouseUp(Sender: TObject; Button: TMouseButton;
      Shift: TShiftState; X, Y: Integer);
```

```
begin
  {indicate that the drag operation has stopped}
  DraggingRect := FALSE;
end;

procedure TForm1.FormDestroy(Sender: TObject);
begin
  {the region is no longer needed, so delete it}
  DeleteObject(ClippingRegion);
end;
```

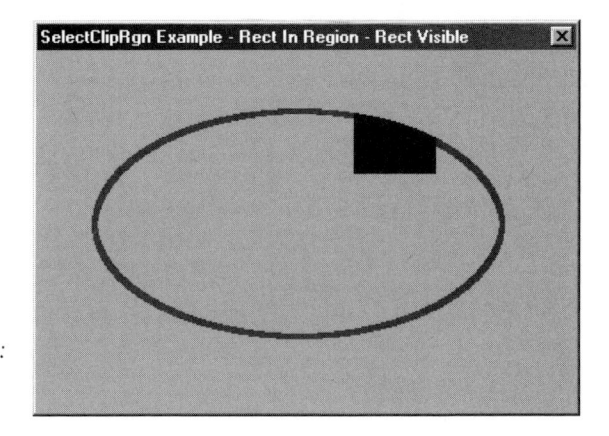

Figure 11-20:
The clipping region

Table 11-14: SelectClipRgn return values

Value	Description
NULLREGION	Indicates an empty region.
SIMPLEREGION	Indicates a single rectangular region.
COMPLEXREGION	Indicates a region consisting of more than one rectangle.
ERROR	Indicates an error occurred.

SetRect   Windows.pas

Syntax

```
SetRect(
var lprc: TRect;             {a pointer to a TRect structure}
xLeft: Integer;              {the upper-left horizontal coordinate}
yTop: Integer;               {the upper-left vertical coordinate}
xRight: Integer;             {the lower-right horizontal coordinate}
yBottom: Integer             {the lower-right vertical coordinate}
): BOOL;                     {returns TRUE or FALSE}
```

Description

This function sets the coordinates of the rectangle pointed to by the lprc parameter to the specified coordinates.

Parameters

lprc: A pointer to a TRect structure whose coordinates are to be set.

xLeft: Specifies the upper-left horizontal coordinate of the rectangle.

yTop: Specifies the upper-left vertical coordinate of the rectangle.

xRight: Specifies the lower-right horizontal coordinate of the rectangle.

yBottom: Specifies the lower-right vertical coordinate of the rectangle.

Return Value

If the function succeeds, it returns TRUE; otherwise, it returns FALSE. To get extended error information, call the GetLastError function.

See Also

CopyRect, IntersectRect, SetRectEmpty, SetRectRgn, SubtractRect, UnionRect

Example

See Listing 11-20 under SelectClipRgn, and other examples throughout this chapter.

SetRectEmpty   Windows.pas

Syntax

```
SetRectEmpty(
var lprc: TRect            {a pointer to a TRect structure}
): BOOL;                   {returns TRUE or FALSE}
```

Description

This function sets all coordinates of the specified rectangle to zero.

Parameters

lprc: A pointer to a TRect structure whose coordinates are to be set to zero.

Return Value

If the function succeeds, it returns TRUE; otherwise, it returns FALSE. To get extended error information, call the GetLastError function.

See Also

CopyRect, IntersectRect, SetRect, SetRectRgn, SubtractRect, UnionRect

Example

Listing 11-21: Emptying out a rectangle

```
var
  Form1: TForm1;
  TheRect: TRect;      // holds the rectangle

implementation
```

```
{$R *.DFM}

procedure TForm1.FormActivate(Sender: TObject);
begin
  {create a new rectangle}
  SetRect(TheRect, 8, 40, 169, 160);
end;

procedure TForm1.FormPaint(Sender: TObject);
begin
  {display the rectangle}
  Form1.Canvas.Brush.Color := clRed;
  Form1.Canvas.FillRect(TheRect);
end;

procedure TForm1.Button1Click(Sender: TObject);
begin
  {empty the rectangle}
  SetRectEmpty(TheRect);

  {indicate if the rectangle is empty}
  if IsRectEmpty(TheRect) then
    Button1.Caption := 'Rectangle is empty'
  else
    Button1.Caption := 'Rectangle is not empty';

  {repaint the form to show the changes}
  Form1.Repaint;
end;
```

SetRectRgn   Windows.pas

Syntax

```
SetRectRgn(
Rgn: HRgn;              {a handle to a pre-existing region}
X1: Integer;            {the upper-left horizontal coordinate}
Y1: Integer;            {the upper-left vertical coordinate}
X2: Integer;            {the lower-right horizontal coordinate}
Y2: Integer             {the lower-right vertical coordinate}
): BOOL;                {returns TRUE or FALSE}
```

Description

This function converts the region identified by the Rgn parameter into a rectangular region at the specified coordinates. Note that the bottom and right edges of the rectangle are excluded from the region.

Parameters

Rgn: Specifies a handle to the region to be converted into a rectangular region.

X1: Specifies the upper-left horizontal coordinate of the rectangular region in logical units.

Y1: Specifies the upper-left vertical coordinate of the rectangular region in logical units.

X2: Specifies the lower-right horizontal coordinate of the rectangular region in logical units.

Y2: Specifies the lower-right vertical coordinate of the rectangular region in logical units.

Return Value

If the function succeeds, it returns TRUE; otherwise, it returns FALSE.

See Also

CreateRectRgn, CreateRectRgnIndirect, CreateRoundRectRgn, SetRect

Example

See Listing 11-11 under EqualRgn.

SetWindowRgn   Windows.pas

Syntax

```
SetWindowRgn(
hWnd: HWND;              {a handle to a window}
hRgn: HRGN;              {a handle to a region}
bRedraw: BOOL            {window redraw flag}
): BOOL;                 {returns TRUE or FALSE}
```

Description

This function sets the specified window's region to the region identified by the hRgn parameter. The window region determines the area within the window where drawing is permitted, and Windows will not allow any drawing to succeed outside of the window region. When this function returns, the operating system is responsible for the specified region, and it should not be used in any subsequent functions. This function is typically used to create windows with a non-rectangular shape.

Parameters

hWnd: A handle to the window whose region is to be set.

hRgn: A handle to the region to be used as the window region. The coordinates of this region are relative to the window, not the client area. If this parameter is set to zero, the window region is reset to the default region.

bRedraw: Indicates if the window should be redrawn when the region is set. If this value is set to TRUE, the window is redrawn and the WM_WINDOWPOSCHANGING and WM_WINDOWPOSCHANGED messages are sent to the window. If this value is set to FALSE, the window is not redrawn.

Return Value

If the function succeeds, it returns TRUE; otherwise, it returns FALSE.

See Also

CreateEllipticRgn, CreateEllipticRgnIndirect, CreatePolygonRgn, CreatePolyPolygonRgn, CreateRectRgn, CreateRectRgnIndirect, CreateRoundRectRgn, ExtCreateRegion, ExtSelectClipRgn, SelectClipRgn

Example

Listing II-22: Creating a round window for an analog clock application

```
var
  Form1: TForm1;
  OriginX, OriginY: Integer;      // holds the center coordinates of the window

implementation

uses Math;

{$R *.DFM}

procedure TForm1.FormCreate(Sender: TObject);
var
  NewShape: HRGN;    // holds the region
begin
  {create a circular region}
  NewShape := CreateEllipticRgn(GetSystemMetrics(SM_CXBORDER)+3,
                                GetSystemMetrics(SM_CYCAPTION)+3,
                                GetSystemMetrics(SM_CXBORDER)+103,
                                GetSystemMetrics(SM_CYCAPTION)+103);

  {determine the center of the circle. this is used when drawing the numbers
   of the clock}
  OriginX := (GetSystemMetrics(SM_CXBORDER)+90) div 2;
  OriginY := ((GetSystemMetrics(SM_CXBORDER)+90) div 2)-3;

  {set the window region to the circular region. this will create
   a round window}
  SetWindowRgn(Handle, NewShape, TRUE);
end;

procedure TForm1.FormPaint(Sender: TObject);
var
  iCount: Integer;                       // a general loop control variable
  Hour, Minute, Second, MilSec: Word;    // used to decode the time
begin
  {set the background mode to transparent for drawing text}
  SetBkMode(Canvas.Handle, TRANSPARENT);

  {draw a highlighted bevel}
  Canvas.Pen.Color := clWhite;
  Canvas.Pen.Width := 2;
  Arc(Canvas.Handle, 1, 1, 98, 98, 98, 1, 1, 98);

  {draw a shadowed bevel}
  Canvas.Pen.Color := clBtnShadow;
  Arc(Canvas.Handle, 1, 1, 98, 98, 1, 98, 98, 1);
```

```pascal
  {for every hour of the day...}
  for iCount := 1 to 12 do
  begin
    {...draw an hour measurement in a circular form around the window}
    Canvas.TextOut(Trunc(Sin(((360/12)*iCount)*(PI/180))*40)+OriginX,
                   Trunc(-Cos(-((360/12)*iCount)*(PI/180))*40)+OriginY,
                   IntToStr(iCount));
  end;

  {retrieve the current time in a useable format}
  DecodeTime(Now, Hour, Minute, Second, MilSec);

  {translate military hours to civilian hours}
  if Hour>12 then Hour := Hour-12;

  {draw the hour hand}
  Canvas.Pen.Color := clBlack;
  Canvas.MoveTo(50, 50);
  Canvas.LineTo(Trunc(Sin(((360/12)*Hour)*(PI/180))*30)+50,
                Trunc(-Cos(-((360/12)*Hour)*(PI/180))*30)+50);

  {draw the minutes hand}
  Canvas.MoveTo(50, 50);
  Canvas.LineTo(Trunc(Sin(((360/60)*Minute)*(PI/180))*40)+50,
                Trunc(-Cos(-((360/60)*Minute)*(PI/180))*40)+50);

  {draw the seconds hand}
  Canvas.Pen.Color := clRed;
  Canvas.MoveTo(50, 50);
  Canvas.LineTo(Trunc(Sin(((360/60)*Second)*(PI/180))*40)+50,
                Trunc(-Cos(-((360/60)*Second)*(PI/180))*40)+50);
end;

procedure TForm1.Timer1Timer(Sender: TObject);
begin
  {repaint the form once per second}
  Repaint;
end;

procedure TForm1.WMNCHitTest(var Msg: TWMNCHitTest);
begin
  {this allows the user to drag the window by clicking anywhere on the form}
  inherited;
  Msg.Result := HTCAPTION;
end;
```

Figure 11-21:
The analog clock

SubtractRect   Windows.pas

Syntax

SubtractRect(
var lprcDst: TRect;   {a pointer to the destination TRect structure}
const lprcSrc1: TRect;   {a pointer to the first rectangle}
const lprcSrc2: TRect;   {a pointer to the second rectangle}
): BOOL;   {returns TRUE or FALSE}

Description

This function subtracts the rectangular coordinates pointed to by the lprcSrc2 parameter from the rectangular coordinates pointed to by the lprcSrc1 parameter. Note that this function succeeds only when the two rectangles intersect completely in either the horizontal or vertical axis.

Parameters

lprcDst: A pointer to a TRect structure that receives the resulting coordinates from subtracting the rectangle pointed to by the lprcSrc2 parameter from the rectangle pointed to by the lprcSrc1 parameter.

lprcSrc1: A pointer to a TRect structure from which the rectangle pointed to by the lprcSrc2 parameter is subtracted.

lprcSrc2: A pointer to a TRect structure containing the rectangle to be subtracted from the rectangle pointed to by the lprcSrc1 parameter.

Return Value

If the function succeeds, it returns TRUE; otherwise, it returns FALSE.

See Also

EqualRect, IntersectRect, SetRect, UnionRect

Example

Listing 11-23: Subtracting one rectangle from another

```
procedure TForm1.FormPaint(Sender: TObject);
var
  Rect1, Rect2, Subtract: TRect;     // holds the rectangles
begin
  {set the coordinates of the two test rectangles}
  SetRect(Rect1, 10, 10, 110, 110);
  SetRect(Rect2, 60, 10, 160, 160);

  {subtract rectangle 2 from rectangle 1}
  SubtractRect(Subtract, Rect1, Rect2);

  with Form1.Canvas do
  begin
    {initialize canvas objects to draw outlines}
    Brush.Style := bsClear;
```

```
      Pen.Style := psSolid;

      {draw the outlines of rectangle 1 and 2}
      Rectangle(Rect1.Left, Rect1.Top, Rect1.Right, Rect1.Bottom);
      Rectangle(Rect2.Left, Rect2.Top, Rect2.Right, Rect2.Bottom);

      {initialize canvas objects to draw the result}
      Brush.Style := bsSolid;
      Brush.Color := clRed;

      {fill the resulting rectangle with red}
      FillRect(Subtract);
   end;
end;
```

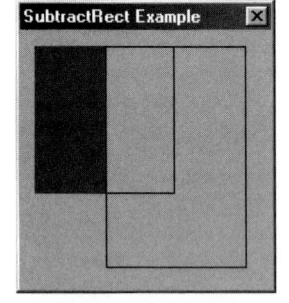

Figure 11-22: The resulting rectangle

UnionRect   Windows.pas

Syntax

```
UnionRect(
var lprcDst: TRect;          {a pointer to the destination TRect structure}
const lprcSrc1: TRect;       {a pointer to the first rectangle}
const lprcSrc2: TRect        {a pointer to the second rectangle}
): BOOL;                     {returns TRUE or FALSE}
```

Description

This function creates a rectangle that is the union of the rectangles pointed to by the lprcSrc1 and lprcSrc2 parameters.

Parameters

lprcDst: A pointer to a TRect structure that receives the resulting coordinates from the union of the rectangles pointed to by the lprcSrc1 and lprcSrc2 parameters.

lprcSrc1: A pointer to a TRect structure containing a rectangle to be joined.

lprcSrc2: A pointer to a TRect structure containing a rectangle to be joined.

Return Value

If the function succeeds and the rectangle pointed to by the lprcDst parameter is not empty, it returns TRUE. If the function fails, or the rectangle pointed to by the lprcDst parameter is empty, it returns FALSE. To get extended error information, call the GetLastError function.

See Also

EqualRect, InflateRect, IntersectRect, IsRectEmpty, SetRect, SetRectEmpty, SubtractRect

Example

See Listing 11-16 under OffsetRect.

WidenPath   Windows.pas

Syntax

```
WidenPath(
  DC: HDC              {a handle to a device context}
): BOOL;               {returns TRUE or FALSE}
```

Description

This function widens the path contained in the specified device context. The new path is defined as the area that would be painted if the StrokePath function were called using the currently selected pen. Any Bézier curves defining a part of the path are converted into line segments.

Parameters

DC: A handle to the device context containing the path to be widened.

Return Value

If the function succeeds, it returns TRUE; otherwise, it returns FALSE. To get extended error information, call the GetLastError function.

See Also

BeginPath, CreatePen, EndPath, ExtCreatePen, FlattenPath, GetPath, PathToRegion, SetMiterLimit

Example

Listing 11-24: Drawing the outline of text

```
procedure TForm1.FormPaint(Sender: TObject);
begin
  {begin a path bracket}
  BeginPath(Canvas.Handle);

  {set the background mode to TRANSPARENT so that the path will be defined as
   the area inside of the text}
  SetBkMode(Canvas.Handle, TRANSPARENT);

  {draw some text. note that the form's font is set to size 48 Arial, bold}
  TextOut(Canvas.Handle, 20, 20, 'Delphi Rocks!', Length('Delphi Rocks!'));
```

```
{end the path bracket}
EndPath(Canvas.Handle);;

{modify the pen so that it is 4 pixels wide}
Canvas.Pen.Width := 4;

{widen the path defined by the text. due to the pen width, above, the new
 path is a 4 pixel wide outline of the letters}
WidenPath(Canvas.Handle);

{reset the pen width and brush color for drawing the path}
Canvas.Pen.Width := 1;
Canvas.Brush.Color := clRed;

{set the fill mode so that the path will be drawn correctly}
SetPolyFillMode(Canvas.Handle, WINDING);

{fill the path with the red brush}
FillPath(Canvas.Handle);
end;
```

Figure 11-23: The text outline

Chapter 12

Bitmap and Metafile Functions

It's hard to imagine writing a Windows application without performing some sort of image manipulation. Graphical images can be classified in two categories: bitmapped and vector based. The Win32 API provides the developer with a wide variety of functions with which to manipulate these types of graphical images. Windows natively supports bitmap images and a vector-based image format known as a metafile. This chapter describes the Win32 API functions available for handling these types of graphics.

Note that the example programs in this chapter assume that the video driver has been set to 256 colors. Some examples may not work properly if the color depth is different.

Bitmaps

A bitmap is an array of bytes that store the color information of image elements known as pixels. A pixel is a small square of color that, when viewed together as a whole, form the bitmapped image, as illustrated in Figure 12-1.

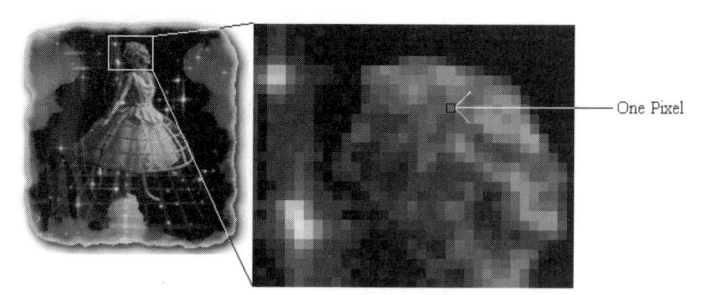

Figure 12-1: A pixel is the smallest element of an image

The number of bits that are used to describe one individual pixel varies widely according to the color depth of the image. The pixels of a 16-color image can be described with 4 bits per pixel; thus, 1 single byte can contain 2 pixels of the image. A 256-color image uses 1 byte for each pixel, whereas a true color (16.7 million-color) image uses 3 bytes for an individual pixel. See Table 12-6 under CreateDIBSection for a thorough description of bitmap color depths.

Device-dependent Bitmaps

Device-dependent bitmaps are so named because they are very dependent on the device upon which they are displayed for certain information. DDBs only store information on their width and height, their color format, and the array of pixels describing the image. They do not contain any information concerning the color palette of the image they contain or their original resolution. This bitmap type was the only one available to early Windows programmers, and still exists only for backward compatibility. Win32 developers should use device-independent bitmaps.

Device-independent Bitmaps

Device-independent bitmaps contain more information about their image than device-dependent bitmaps. For example, device-independent bitmaps contain the color palette for the image, the resolution of the device upon which the bitmap was originally created, and a data compression flag. Perhaps the biggest advantage of device-independent bitmaps is that the developer has direct access to the bytes making up the pixels of the bitmap. This allows a developer to modify the image directly, as opposed to device-dependent bitmaps that require the developer to use GDI functions to manipulate the bitmap image.

By default, device-independent bitmaps are oriented in a "bottom-up" fashion, meaning that the origin of the bitmap pixels starts in the lower left-hand corner of the image. However, a device-independent bitmap can be oriented in a top-down fashion like device-dependent bitmaps by providing a negative value for their height.

Bitmap Operations

Numerous functions exist for displaying bitmap images on the screen. The action of copying the pixels of a bitmap to the screen is known as a Blt (pronounced "blit"), meaning Bit bLock Transfer. Some functions, such as the BitBlt and StretchBlt functions, are intended for use with device-dependent bitmaps, and require device contexts as the source and destination of the pixel transfer action. Device-independent bitmaps use the SetDIBitsToDevice and StretchDIBits functions to copy the DIB directly to a device context.

Some functions, such as StretchBlt and StretchDIBits, allow the bitmap to be drawn at a size different from its original dimensions. Windows will add pixels to or remove pixels from the bitmap as needed according to the stretching mode of the destination device context. Calling the SetStretchBltMode function sets the stretching mode of the destination device context.

Scaling A bitmap can be stretched and still retain its original aspect ratio by finding the smallest side of the rectangular area defining the new bitmap size and determining the ratio of this new dimension versus the original size of the same side of the bitmap. For example, if a 5 X 10 pixel bitmap where to be stretched into a 10 X 20 pixel area, the smallest side of this new area is 10 (the height). The height of the original bitmap is 5, and $10 \div 5$ is 2, for a 200% increase in size. Multiplying all sides of the original bitmap's dimensions by 2 results in a new bitmap size of 10 X 20 pixels, thus retaining its original aspect ratio. The following example demonstrates using this formula to allow the user to scale a bitmap to any size while retaining the bitmap's original aspect ratio.

Listing 12-1: Scaling a bitmap and retaining the original aspect ratio

```
var
  Form1: TForm1;
  ScaleRect: TRect;       // holds the user drawn rectangle coordinates
  IsDragging: Boolean;    // indicates if the user is drawing a rectangle
  ScaledImage: TBitmap;   // holds the image to be scaled

implementation

{$R *.DFM}

procedure TForm1.FormMouseDown(Sender: TObject; Button: TMouseButton;
  Shift: TShiftState; X, Y: Integer);
begin
  {indicate that the user is dragging a rectangle}
  IsDragging := TRUE;

  {initialize the rectangle}
  ScaleRect := Rect(X, Y, X, Y);
end;

procedure TForm1.FormMouseMove(Sender: TObject; Shift: TShiftState; X,
  Y: Integer);
begin
  {if we are dragging a rectangle}
  if IsDragging then
  begin
    {draw over the current rectangle to erase it}
    Canvas.Pen.Style := psSolid;
    Canvas.Pen.Color := clBlack;
    Canvas.Pen.Mode := pmNot;
    Canvas.Brush.Style := bsClear;
    Canvas.Rectangle(ScaleRect.Left, ScaleRect.Top, ScaleRect.Right,
                     ScaleRect.Bottom);

    {modify the user drawn rectangle coordinates to the new coordinates}
    ScaleRect := Rect(ScaleRect.Left, ScaleRect.Top, X, Y);

    {draw a new rectangle}
    Canvas.Rectangle(ScaleRect.Left, ScaleRect.Top, ScaleRect.Right,
                     ScaleRect.Bottom);
  end;
end;

procedure TForm1.FormMouseUp(Sender: TObject; Button: TMouseButton;
  Shift: TShiftState; X, Y: Integer);
var
  Ratio: Real;       // holds the scaling ratio
begin
  {indicate that the user is no longer dragging a rectangle}
  IsDragging := FALSE;

  {clear the entire window}
  Canvas.Brush.Color := clBtnFace;
```

```
  Canvas.Brush.Style := bsSolid;
  Canvas.FillRect(Form1.ClientRect);

  {redraw a new, empty rectangle at the current rectangle coordinates}
  Canvas.Brush.Style := bsClear;
  Canvas.Rectangle(ScaleRect.Left, ScaleRect.Top, ScaleRect.Right,
                   ScaleRect.Bottom);

  {select the images palette into the form's canvas and realize it}
  SelectPalette(Canvas.Handle, ScaledImage.Palette, FALSE);
  RealizePalette(Canvas.Handle);

  {determine the appropriate scaling ratio}
  if ScaleRect.Right-ScaleRect.Left<ScaleRect.Bottom-ScaleRect.Top then
    Ratio := (ScaleRect.Right-ScaleRect.Left)/ScaledImage.Width
  else
    Ratio := (ScaleRect.Bottom-ScaleRect.Top)/ScaledImage.Height;

  {copy the image to the canvas, centered in the rectangle and scaled so that
   the aspect ratio of the original image is retained}
  StretchBlt(Canvas.Handle, ScaleRect.Left+(((ScaleRect.Right-ScaleRect.Left)
             div 2)-(Trunc(ScaledImage.Width*Ratio) div 2)), ScaleRect.Top+
             (((ScaleRect.Bottom-ScaleRect.Top) div 2)-(Trunc(ScaledImage.Height
             *Ratio) div 2)), Trunc(ScaledImage.Width*Ratio),
             Trunc(ScaledImage.Height*Ratio), ScaledImage.Canvas.Handle, 0, 0,
             ScaledImage.Width, ScaledImage.Height, SRCCOPY);
end;

procedure TForm1.FormCreate(Sender: TObject);
begin
  {create and load the image to be scaled}
  ScaledImage := TBitmap.Create;
  ScaledImage.LoadFromFile('Image9.bmp');
end;

procedure TForm1.FormDestroy(Sender: TObject);
begin
  {free the image bitmap}
  ScaledImage.Free;
end;
```

Figure 12-2: The scaled, aspect ratio corrected bitmap

Raster Operations In addition to simply copying the pixels from a bitmap to the screen, certain functions can perform raster operations on the pixels. A raster operation determines how the pixels from the source, the destination, and the destination device context's selected brush are combined. The most commonly used raster operations are listed in the functions throughout this chapter. However, there are 256 total raster operations, although some may not be applicable to all functions. See Appendix C for a full description of all available raster operations.

Certain raster operations can be used to produce special effects, such as the illusion of transparency. To copy a bitmap to a destination using raster operations to simulate the effect of transparent pixels, the application must have two versions of the bitmap to be copied, known as an AND mask and an OR mask. The AND mask image is a monochrome silhouette of the original bitmap. The white pixels indicate where the background will show through (the transparent pixels), and the black pixels indicate where the actual image of the bitmap will appear. The OR mask contains the real image of the bitmap to be copied, where the black pixels of the image indicate transparency. First, the application copies the AND mask to the destination using the SRCAND raster operation. This combines the pixels of the source and destination using a Boolean AND operation. The white pixels of the AND mask will preserve the original pixels of the background image, where the black pixels will turn the pixels in the background image black, resulting in a carved-out area for the final bitmap image. Once this is complete, the application copies the OR mask to the destination using the SRCPAINT raster operation. This combines the pixels of the source and destination using a Boolean OR operation. The black pixels of the OR mask will preserve the original pixels of the bitmap, where the actual pixels of the image should fall into the black pixels in the background produced by the first step. The result is the illusion of a transparent copy operation. The following example demonstrates the technique of using masks to produce transparency with bitmaps.

Listing 12-2: Displaying a bitmap with transparent pixels

```
procedure TForm1.FormCreate(Sender: TObject);
begin
  {copy the background image to the destination}
  Image3.Canvas.Draw(0, 0, Image1.Picture.Bitmap);

  {combine the AND mask image with the background image in the destination
   using a Boolean AND operation. this carves out an area for the final
   foreground image}
  BitBlt(Image3.Canvas.Handle, (Image3.Width div 2)-(Image2.Width div 2),
         (Image3.Height div 2)-(Image2.Height div 2), Image2.Width,
         Image2.Height, Image2.Canvas.Handle, 0, 0, SRCAND);

  {copy the result of step one into the 'background' image used for step 2}
  Image4.Canvas.Draw(0, 0, Image3.Picture.Bitmap);

  {copy the 'background' image resulting from step 1 into the destination}
  Image6.Canvas.Draw(0, 0, Image4.Picture.Bitmap);

  {combine the OR mask image with the result from step 1 in the destination
   using a Boolean OR operation.  this copies the foreground image into the
   area carved out by step 1 while preserving the pixels around it, thereby
   creating the illusion of transparency.}
  BitBlt(Image6.Canvas.Handle, (Image6.Width div 2)-(Image5.Width div 2),
         (Image6.Height div 2)-(Image5.Height div 2), Image5.Width,
         Image5.Height, Image5.Canvas.Handle, 0, 0, SRCPAINT);
end;
```

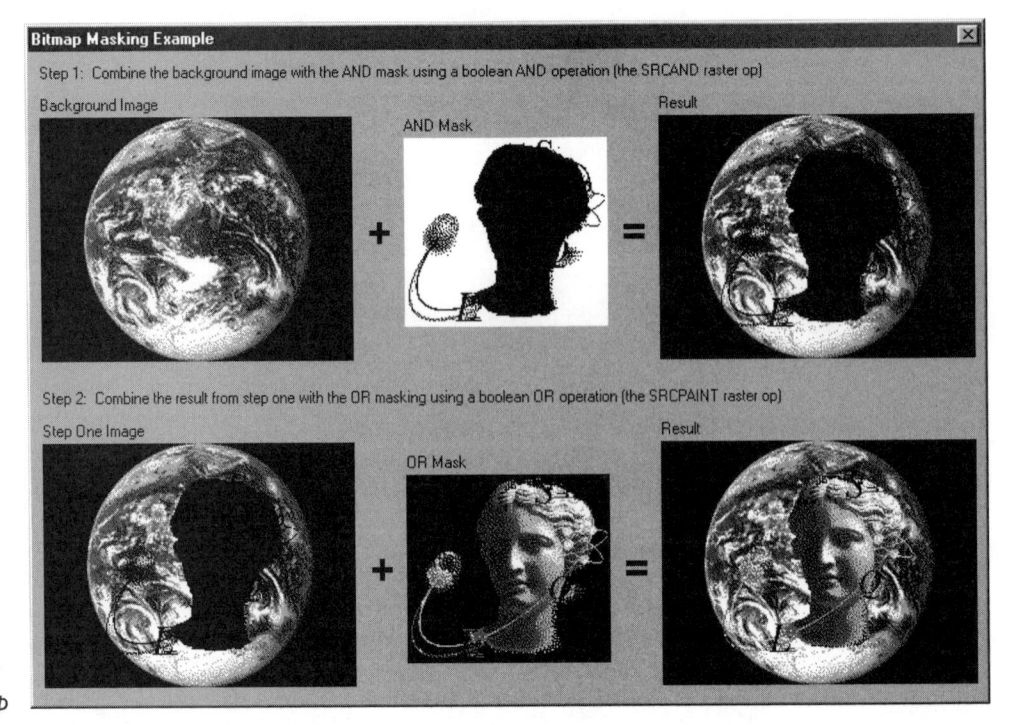

Figure 12-3: The transparently copied bitmap

DIBs and the GDI Although a device-independent bitmap differs from a device-dependent bitmap in many ways, a DIB can still be selected into a device context and modified using GDI functions like a regular device-dependent bitmap. This gives the developer a tremendous amount of flexibility when dealing with bitmaps, as custom drawing functions can be utilized alongside regular GDI drawing functions to manipulate the bitmap image. The following example demonstrates selecting a DIB into a device context and drawing on the bitmap using GDI drawing functions.

Listing 12-3: Manipulating a DIB using GDI drawing functions

```
procedure TForm1.Button1Click(Sender: TObject);
var
  Dib: HBITMAP;              // holds a handle to the DIB
  DibInfo: PBitmapInfo;      // a pointer to the bitmap information data structure
  BitsPtr: PByte;            // holds a pointer to the bitmap bits
  ReferenceDC: HDC;          // a handle to the reference device context
  iCount: Integer;           // general loop counter
  OldBitmap: HBITMAP;        // holds a handle to the old DC bitmap
  ScratchCanvas: TCanvas;    // holds a temporary canvas for drawing

  APolygon: array[0..2] of TPoint;          // holds a polygon

  SystemPalette: array[0..255] of TPaletteEntry;  // required for converting the
                                                  // system palette into a DIB
                                                  // compatible palette
begin
  {get the memory needed for the bitmap information data structure}
  GetMem(DibInfo, SizeOf(TBitmapInfo)+256*SizeOf(TRGBQuad));

  {initialize the bitmap information}
  DibInfo^.bmiHeader.biWidth         := 64;      // create a 64 X 64 pixel DIB,
  DibInfo^.bmiHeader.biHeight        := -64;     // oriented top-down
  DibInfo^.bmiHeader.biPlanes        := 1;
  DibInfo^.bmiHeader.biBitCount      := 8;       // 256 colors
  DibInfo^.bmiHeader.biCompression   := BI_RGB;  // no compression
  DibInfo^.bmiHeader.biSizeImage     := 0;       // let Windows determine size
  DibInfo^.bmiHeader.biXPelsPerMeter := 0;
  DibInfo^.bmiHeader.biYPelsPerMeter := 0;
  DibInfo^.bmiHeader.biClrUsed       := 0;
  DibInfo^.bmiHeader.biClrImportant  := 0;
  DibInfo^.bmiHeader.biSize          := SizeOf(TBitmapInfoHeader);

  {retrieve the current system palette}
  GetSystemPaletteEntries(Form1.Canvas.Handle, 0, 256, SystemPalette);

  {the system palette is returned as an array of TPaletteEntry structures,
   which store the palette colors in the form of Red, Green, and Blue. however,
   the TBitmapInfo structure's bmiColors member takes an array of TRGBQuad
   structures, which store the palette colors in the form of Blue, Green, and
   Red.  therefore, we must translate the TPaletteEntry structures into the
   appropriate TRGBQuad structures to get the correct color entries.}
  for iCount := 0 to 255 do
  begin
    DibInfo^.bmiColors[iCount].rgbBlue    := SystemPalette[iCount].peBlue;
    DibInfo^.bmiColors[iCount].rgbRed     := SystemPalette[iCount].peRed;
```

```
    DibInfo^.bmiColors[iCount].rgbGreen    := SystemPalette[iCount].peGreen;
    DibInfo^.bmiColors[iCount].rgbReserved := 0;
  end;

  {create a memory based device context}
  ReferenceDC := CreateCompatibleDC(0);

  {create the dib based on the memory device context and the
   initialized bitmap information}
  Dib := CreateDIBSection(ReferenceDC, DibInfo^, DIB_RGB_COLORS,
                          Pointer(BitsPtr), 0, 0);

  {select the Dib into the device context}
  OldBitmap := SelectObject(ReferenceDC, Dib);

  {create a canvas and set its handle to the created device context}
  ScratchCanvas := TCanvas.Create;
  ScratchCanvas.Handle := ReferenceDC;

  {fill the canvas with red}
  ScratchCanvas.Brush.Color := clRed;
  ScratchCanvas.FillRect(ScratchCanvas.ClipRect);

  {draw a green circle}
  ScratchCanvas.Brush.Color := clLime;
  ScratchCanvas.Ellipse(0, 0, 32, 32);

  {draw a triangle}
  ScratchCanvas.Brush.Color := clBlue;
  APolygon[0] := Point(63, 63);
  APolygon[1] := Point(32, 63);
  APolygon[2] := Point(48, 32);
  ScratchCanvas.Polygon(APolygon);

  {the above functions have drawn directly into the Dib. now we can draw the
   Dib onto the form surface using Dib functions}
  SetDIBitsToDevice(Form1.Canvas.Handle, 30, 5, 64, 64, 0, 0, 0, 64, BitsPtr,
                    DibInfo^, DIB_RGB_COLORS);

  {draw the DIB again, but this time let's stretch it to twice its size}
  StretchDIBits(Form1.Canvas.Handle, 105, 5, 128, 128, 0, 0, 64, 64, BitsPtr,
                DibInfo^, DIB_RGB_COLORS, SRCCOPY);

  {we no longer need the DIB, so delete it, the canvas, and the
   allocated memory for the information data structure}
  SelectObject(ReferenceDC, OldBitmap);
  ScratchCanvas.Free;
  DeleteObject(Dib);
  DeleteDC(ReferenceDC);
  FreeMem(DibInfo, SizeOf(TBitmapInfo)+256*SizeOf(TRGBQuad));
end;
```

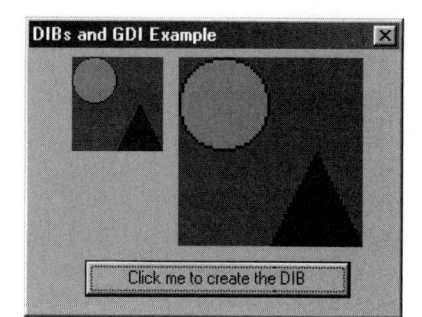

*Figure 12-4:
The modified device-independent bitmap*

Metafiles

A metafile is a vector-based graphics format for storing images. The image is stored as a series of instructions that describe how to draw the image, rather than an array of pixels that explicitly describe the image like a bitmap. This affords metafiles a certain amount of device independence in that a metafile can be displayed in its original size and resolution on a printing device or on the screen.

Specifically, a metafile is a collection of metafile records that correspond to GDI function calls for drawing lines and shapes, and filling regions, etc. When a metafile is displayed, it replays these GDI functions in sequence upon a specified device context, drawing the image as if the specific GDI drawing functions had been called programmatically.

The method by which a metafile stores its image allows it to be scaled to almost any size with little to no loss of resolution. Thus, metafile graphics are commonly used for clipart or to store technical drawings such as CAD designs or architectural plans. In addition, since metafile records only describe the image and do not store each individual pixel, metafiles are usually much smaller than a bitmap would be for the same image. However, since the GDI functions used to describe the image are replayed each time the metafile is drawn to the screen, metafiles are drawn much slower than bitmaps.

Enhanced Metafiles

Win32 applications should use the enhanced metafile format instead of the Win16 metafile format. The enhanced metafile format contains a header describing the original resolution and dimensions for which the metafile was created. It also stores a palette for the metafile image. The Win16 metafile format contains neither. Note that enhanced metafiles are subject to the limitations of the Windows 95 GDI. Delphi's TMetafile object encapsulates both the Win16 and the enhanced metafile formats.

Delphi vs. the Windows API

The TBitmap and TMetafile objects encapsulate almost all of the API functionality you would ever need to work with these graphics formats. These objects publish many properties that provide information about the graphic that you could otherwise only access through API calls. Even loading and saving to and from files on disk is supported. So, given the extreme versatility of these objects, why would one ever need to resort to API function calls? Cross language portability would be the reason. There is no equivalent TBitmap or TMetafile object in C++, for example. Thus, if you're dealing with applications that could be sending bitmap information between two languages (for example, a C++ DLL is handing back the handle to a bitmap), you may need to make use of some API functions to access the image. Performance is another reason. While the TBitmap object does provide properties to access the individual bits of an image, the responsiveness is rather slow. High-speed graphics programming often requires working directly with the pixels of an image, and the API functions that deal with DIBs are perfectly suited for such an application.

Bitmap and Metafile Functions

The following bitmap and metafile functions are covered in this chapter:

Table 12-1: Bitmap and metafile functions

Function	Description
BitBlt	Copies bits from one device context to another.
CloseEnhMetaFile	Closes an enhanced metafile device context and returns a handle to the metafile.
CopyEnhMetaFile	Creates a duplicate of an enhanced metafile.
CopyImage	Creates a duplicate of an icon, bitmap, or cursor.
CreateBitmap	Creates a device-dependent bitmap.
CreateBitmapIndirect	Creates a device-dependent bitmap from information in a data structure.
CreateCompatibleBitmap	Creates a device-dependent bitmap compatible with a specified device context.
CreateDIBitmap	Creates a device-dependent bitmap from a device-independent bitmap.
CreateDIBSection	Creates a device-independent bitmap.
CreateEnhMetaFile	Creates an enhanced metafile.
DeleteEnhMetaFile	Deletes an enhanced metafile.
EnumEnhMetaFile	Enumerates the metafile records in an enhanced metafile.
GetBitmapBits	Retrieves pixels from a bitmap into an array.
GetBitmapDimensionEx	Retrieves the preferred bitmap dimensions.
GetDIBits	Creates a device-independent bitmap from a device-dependent bitmap.
GetEnhMetaFile	Opens an enhanced metafile.
GetEnhMetaFileDescription	Retrieves the enhanced metafile description string.
GetEnhMetaFileHeader	Retrieves the enhanced metafile header.
GetStretchBltMode	Retrieves the current bitmap stretching mode.
LoadBitmap	Loads a bitmap resource.
LoadImage	Loads an icon, cursor, or bitmap from a resource or a file.
PatBlt	Fills a specified rectangle with the brush of the destination DC, and can perform certain raster operations.
PlayEnhMetaFile	Draws a metafile onto a device context.
PlayEnhMetaFileRecord	Draws a single metafile record onto a device context.
SetBitmapBits	Sets the pixels of a device-dependent bitmap.
SetBitmapDimensionEx	Sets the preferred bitmap dimensions.

Function	Description
SetDIBits	Sets the pixels in a device-dependent bitmap to the pixel values of a device-independent bitmap.
SetDIBitsToDevice	Draws a device-independent bitmap to a device context.
SetStretchBltMode	Sets the bitmap stretching mode.
StretchBlt	Draws and scales pixels from one device context to another.
StretchDIBits	Draws and scales a device-independent bitmap onto a device context.

BitBlt Windows.pas

Syntax

```
BitBlt(
  DestDC: HDC;          {a handle to the destination device context}
  X: Integer;           {the horizontal coordinate of the destination rectangle}
  Y: Integer;           {the vertical coordinate of the destination rectangle}
  Width: Integer;       {the width of the source and destination rectangle}
  Height: Integer;      {the height of the source and destination rectangle}
  SrcDC: HDC;           {a handle to the source device context}
  XSrc: Integer;        {the horizontal coordinate of the source rectangle}
  YSrc: Integer;        {the vertical coordinate of the source rectangle}
  Rop: DWORD            {the raster operation code}
): BOOL;                {returns TRUE or FALSE}
```

Description

This function copies a rectangle of pixels from the bitmap in the specified source device context into the bitmap in the specified destination device context. The width and height of the destination rectangle determine the width and height of the source rectangle. If the color formats of the source and destination device contexts differ, this function converts the color format of the source into the color format of the destination.

Parameters

DestDC: A handle to the device context to which the pixels are copied.

X: The horizontal coordinate of the upper-left corner of the destination rectangle in the destination device context, measured in logical units.

Y: The vertical coordinate of the upper-left corner of the destination rectangle in the destination device context, measured in logical units.

Width: The width of the source and destination rectangles measured in logical units.

Height: The height of the source and destination rectangles measured in logical units.

SrcDC: A handle to the device context from which the pixels are copied. This cannot be the handle to a metafile device context.

XSrc: The horizontal coordinate of the upper-left corner of the source rectangle in the source device context, measured in logical units.

YSrc: The vertical coordinate of the upper-left corner of the source rectangle in the source device context, measured in logical units.

Rop: A raster operation code that determines how the colors of the pixels in the source are combined with the colors of the pixels in the destination. This parameter can be one value from Table 12-2.

Return Value

If the function succeeds, it returns TRUE; otherwise, it returns FALSE. To get extended error information, call the GetLastError function.

See Also

GetDC, CreateCompatibleDC, CreateBitmap, LoadBitmap, StretchBlt

Example

See Listing 12-16 under LoadImage and other examples throughout this chapter.

Table 12-2: BitBlt Rop values

Value	Description
BLACKNESS	Fills the pixels in the specified rectangle in the destination with the color in index 0 of the physical palette. By default, this color is black.
CAPTUREBLT	**Windows 98/Me/2000 or later:** Includes any portion of windows layered on top of the source window (useful for screen capture).
DSTINVERT	Inverts the colors of the pixels in the specified rectangle in the destination.
MERGECOPY	Combines the pixel colors of the source rectangle with the pixel colors of the pattern contained in the brush selected into the destination device context using the Boolean AND operator.
MERGEPAINT	Inverts the pixel colors of the source rectangle and combines them with the pixel colors of the destination rectangle using the Boolean OR operator.
NOMIRRORBITMAP	**Windows 98/Me/2000 or later:** Prevents the image from being mirrored.
NOTSRCCOPY	Inverts the pixel colors of the source rectangle and copies them into the destination rectangle.
NOTSRCERASE	Combines the pixel colors of the source and destination rectangles using the Boolean OR operator, then inverts the resulting color.
PATCOPY	Copies the pattern contained in the brush selected into the destination device context directly into the destination.
PATINVERT	Combines the pixel colors of the pattern contained in the brush selected into the destination device context with the colors of the pixels in the destination using the Boolean XOR operator.
PATPAINT	Combines the colors of the pattern contained in the brush selected into the destination device context with the inverted pixel colors of the source rectangle using the Boolean OR operator, then combines the result with the pixel colors of the destination rectangle using the Boolean OR operator.
SRCAND	Combines the pixel colors of the source and destination rectangles using the Boolean AND operator.
SRCCOPY	Copies the pixel colors of the source rectangle directly into the destination rectangle.

Value	Description
SRCERASE	Combines the pixel colors of the source rectangle with the inverted colors of the destination rectangle using the Boolean AND operator.
SRCINVERT	Combines the pixel colors of the source and destination rectangles using the Boolean XOR operator.
SRCPAINT	Combines the pixel colors of the source and destination rectangles using the Boolean OR operator.
WHITENESS	Fills the pixels in the specified rectangle in the destination with the color in index 255 of the physical palette. By default, this color is white.

CloseEnhMetaFile Windows.pas

Syntax

```
CloseEnhMetaFile(
  DC: HDC              {a handle to a metafile device context}
): HENHMETAFILE;       {returns a handle to an enhanced metafile}
```

Description

This function closes the specified enhanced metafile device context and returns a handle to the new enhanced metafile. This handle can be used in all functions requiring a handle to an enhanced metafile. When the metafile is no longer needed, it should be removed by calling DeleteEnhMetaFile.

Parameters

DC: A handle to an enhanced metafile device context.

Return Value

If the function succeeds, it returns a handle to an enhanced metafile; otherwise, it returns zero.

See Also

CopyEnhMetaFile, CreateEnhMetaFile, DeleteEnhMetaFile, GetEnhMetaFileDescription, GetEnhMetaFileHeader, PlayEnhMetaFile

Example

See Listing 12-10 under CreateEnhMetaFile.

CopyEnhMetaFile Windows.pas

Syntax

```
CopyEnhMetaFile(
  p1: HENHMETAFILE;    {a handle to an enhanced metafile}
  p2: PChar            {a string specifying a filename}
): HENHMETAFILE;       {returns a handle to an enhanced metafile}
```

Chapter 12

Description

This function copies the specified enhanced metafile to a file or memory, returning a handle to the copied enhanced metafile. When the metafile is no longer needed, it should be removed by calling DeleteEnhMetaFile.

Parameters

p1: A handle to the enhanced metafile to be copied.

p2: A null-terminated string specifying the destination filename. If this parameter is NIL, the function simply copies the enhanced metafile to memory.

Return Value

If the function succeeds, it returns a handle to the copied enhanced metafile; otherwise, it returns zero. To get extended error information, call the GetLastError function.

See Also

CreateEnhMetaFile, DeleteEnhMetaFile, GetEnhMetaFileDescription, GetEnhMetaFileHeader, PlayEnhMetaFile

Example

See Listing 12-14 under GetEnhMetaFile.

CopyImage   Windows.pas

Syntax

```
CopyImage(
    hImage: THandle;           {a handle to an image}
    ImageType: UINT;           {the image type flag}
    X: Integer;                {width of new image}
    Y: Integer;                {height of new image}
    Flags: UINT                {the copy operation flags}
): THandle;                    {returns a handle to the copied image}
```

Description

This function makes a duplicate of the specified image (bitmap, icon, or cursor). The new image can be expanded or compressed as desired, and can be converted to a monochrome color format.

Parameters

hImage: A handle to the image being copied.

ImageType: A flag indicating the type of image to be copied. This parameter can be one value from Table 12-3.

X: Indicates the desired width of the copied image in pixels.

Y: Indicates the desired height of the copied image in pixels.

Flags: A value indicating how the image should be copied. This parameter can be one or more values from Table 12-4.

Return Value

If the function succeeds, it returns a handle to the copied image; otherwise, it returns zero. To get extended error information, call the GetLastError function.

See Also

LoadBitmap, LoadCursor*, LoadCursorFromFile*, LoadIcon*, LoadImage

Example

Listing 12-4: Creating a monochrome image to perform a transparent copy

```
var
  ForegroundImage: TBitmap;     // holds the foreground image

implementation

procedure TForm1.FormCreate(Sender: TObject);
begin
  {create the foreground bitmap and load it}
  ForegroundImage := TBitmap.Create;
  ForegroundImage.LoadFromFile('Foreground.bmp');
end;

procedure TForm1.FormDestroy(Sender: TObject);
begin
  {free the foreground bitmap}
  ForegroundImage.Free;
end;

procedure TForm1.FormPaint(Sender: TObject);
var
  TempBitmap: HBITMAP;      // a handle to the copied image
  OldBitmap: HBITMAP;       // holds the old bitmap from the DC
  OffscreenDC: HDC;         // a handle to an offscreen device context
begin
  {make a monochrome mask of the foreground image}
  TempBitmap := CopyImage(ForegroundImage.Handle, IMAGE_BITMAP,
                          ForegroundImage.Width, ForegroundImage.Height,
                          LR_MONOCHROME);

  {create an memory device context}
  OffscreenDC := CreateCompatibleDC(0);

  {select the monochrome mask image into the memory device context}
  OldBitmap := SelectObject(OffscreenDC, TempBitmap);

  {blit the monochrome mask onto the background image. $00220326 is a raster
   operation that inverts the pixels of the source rectangle and then combines
   these pixels with those of the destination bitmap using the Boolean AND
   operator. this carves out an area for the regular foreground bitmap}
```

```
        BitBlt(Image1.Picture.Bitmap.Canvas.Handle, 150, 50, 100, 100, OffscreenDC,
            0, 0, $00220326);

        {blit the foreground bitmap onto the background by combining the foreground
         and background pixels with the Boolean OR operator.  the result is the
         foreground orb being copied onto the background while the edges of the
         orb image appear transparent}
        BitBlt(Image1.Picture.Bitmap.Canvas.Handle, 150, 50, 100, 100,
            ForegroundImage.Canvas.Handle, 0, 0, SRCPAINT);

        {select the previous bitmap back into the memory device context}
        SelectObject(OffscreenDC, OldBitmap);

        {delete the mask bitmap and the memory device context}
        DeleteObject(TempBitmap);
        DeleteDC(OffscreenDC);
     end;
```

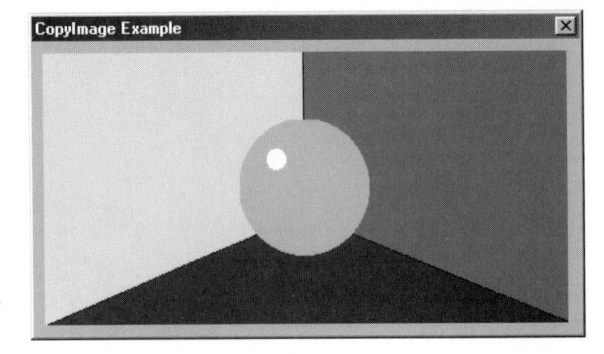

Figure 12-5: The transparently copied image

Table 12-3: CopyImage ImageType values

Value	Description
IMAGE_BITMAP	The image is a bitmap.
IMAGE_CURSOR	The image is a cursor.
IMAGE_ENHMETAFILE	The image is an enhanced metafile.
IMAGE_ICON	The image is an icon.

Table 12-4: CopyImage Flags values

Value	Description
LR_COPYDELETEORG	The original image is deleted after the copy is made.
LR_COPYFROMRESOURCE	The function tries to reload an icon or cursor resource from the resource file instead of making a copy. The image retrieved from the resource file is the image closest to the desired size; it does not stretch the image to the indicated width and height. If the image was not loaded with the LoadIcon or LoadCursor functions or by the LoadImage function with the LR_SHARED flag set, this function fails.
LR_COPYRETURNORG	Creates an exact duplicate of the original image. The X and Y parameters are ignored.

Value	Description
LR_CREATEDIBSECTION	If a new bitmap is created, it is created as a DIB section; otherwise, it is created as a device-dependent bitmap. This flag is valid only in conjunction with IMAGE_BITMAP.
LR_MONOCHROME	Creates a black and white version of the original image.

CreateBitmap   Windows.pas

Syntax

```
CreateBitmap(
  Width: Integer;           {width of bitmap in pixels}
  Height: Integer;          {height of bitmap in pixels}
  Planes: Longint;          {number of color planes}
  BitCount: Longint;        {number of bits required to identify a color}
  Bits: Pointer             {a pointer to an array of color data}
): HBITMAP;                 {returns a handle to a bitmap}
```

Description

This function creates a new bitmap with the specified width, height, and color depth. An array of pixel information can be specified to create a bitmap with an initial image. If the Width and Height parameters are set to zero, this function returns a handle to a 1 pixel by 1 pixel monochrome bitmap. Once the bitmap is created, it can be selected into a device context with the SelectObject function. When the bitmap is no longer needed, it should be deleted with the DeleteObject function.

Although this function can be used to create color bitmaps, for performance reasons applications should use CreateBitmap to create monochrome bitmaps and CreateCompatibleBitmap to create color bitmaps. CreateCompatibleBitmap requires a device context, returning a bitmap that has the same color format as the given device. For this reason, SelectObject calls are faster with a color bitmap returned from CreateCompatibleBitmap.

Parameters

Width: The width of the bitmap in pixels.

Height: The height of the bitmap in pixels.

Planes: The number of color planes used by the device.

BitCount: The number of bits required to describe the color of one pixel (i.e., 8 bits for 256-color images, 24 bits for 16.7 million-color images, etc.).

Bits: A pointer to an array of bytes that contains the color data describing the image of the bitmap. This array specifies the color of the pixels in a rectangular area. Each horizontal row of pixels in the rectangle is known as a scan line. Each scan line must be word aligned, meaning that its width must be a multiple of 2. A scan line can be padded with zeros to facilitate the word alignment. If this parameter is NIL, the new bitmap is not defined and does not contain an image.

Chapter 12

Return Value

If the function succeeds, it returns a handle to a bitmap; otherwise, it returns zero.

See Also

CreateBitmapIndirect, CreateCompatibleBitmap, CreateDIBitmap, DeleteObject, GetBitmapBits, GetBitmapDimensionEx, SelectObject, SetBitmapBits, SetBitmapDimensionEx

Example

Listing 12-5: Creating a bitmap

```
{Note: This example works correctly only under a 256 color video driver}

procedure TForm1.Button1Click(Sender: TObject);
var
   TheBitmap: HBitmap;                   // a handle for the new bitmap
   TheBits: array[0..4095] of Byte;      // an array of original bitmap bits
   GotBits: array[0..4095] of Byte;      // an array to retrieve the bitmap bits
   LoopX,                                // general loop counter variables
   LoopY: Integer;
   OffScreen: HDC;                       // an offscreen device context
   TheSize: TSize;                       // holds the bitmap size dimensions
begin
   {set every bit in the new bitmap to the color stored
    in the system palette slot 3}
   FillMemory(@TheBits, 4096, 3);

   {set a 10 X 10 pixel square in the middle of the
    image to the color in system palette slot 1}
   for LoopX:=27 to 37 do
   begin
      TheBits[LoopX*64+27]:=1;
      TheBits[LoopX*64+28]:=1;
      TheBits[LoopX*64+29]:=1;
      TheBits[LoopX*64+30]:=1;
      TheBits[LoopX*64+31]:=1;
      TheBits[LoopX*64+32]:=1;
      TheBits[LoopX*64+33]:=1;
      TheBits[LoopX*64+34]:=1;
      TheBits[LoopX*64+35]:=1;
      TheBits[LoopX*64+36]:=1;
   end;

   {create a 64 X 64 pixel bitmap, using the information
    in the array TheBits}
   TheBitmap:=CreateBitmap(64,64,1,8,@thebits);

   {set the preferred bitmap dimensions. this is not used
    by Windows, it simply sets some user-defined information}
   SetBitmapDimensionEx(TheBitmap,100,100,nil);
```

Bitmap and Metafile Functions ■ 547

```
   {create an offscreen device context that is
    compatible with the screen}
   OffScreen:=CreateCompatibleDC(0);

   {select the new bitmap into the offscreen device context}
   SelectObject(OffScreen, TheBitmap);

   {copy the bitmap from the offscreen device context
    onto the canvas of the form. this will display the bitmap}
   BitBlt(Form1.Canvas.Handle,162,16,64,64,OffScreen,0,0,SRCCOPY);

   {retrieve the bits that make up the bitmap image}
   GetBitmapBits(TheBitmap, 4096,@GotBits);

   {display the bits in the string grid}
   for LoopX:=0 to 63 do
     for LoopY:=0 to 63 do
       StringGrid1.Cells[LoopX,LoopY]:=IntToStr(GotBits[LoopX*64+LoopY]);

   {retrieve the user-defined, preferred bitmap dimensions}
   GetBitmapDimensionEx(TheBitmap,TheSize);

   {Display these dimensions}
   Label1.Caption:='Preferred bitmap dimensions - Width: '+IntToStr(TheSize.CX)+
                   ' Height: '+IntToStr(TheSize.CY);

   {delete the offscreen device context}
   DeleteDC(OffScreen);

   {delete the new bitmap}
   DeleteObject(TheBitmap);
end;
```

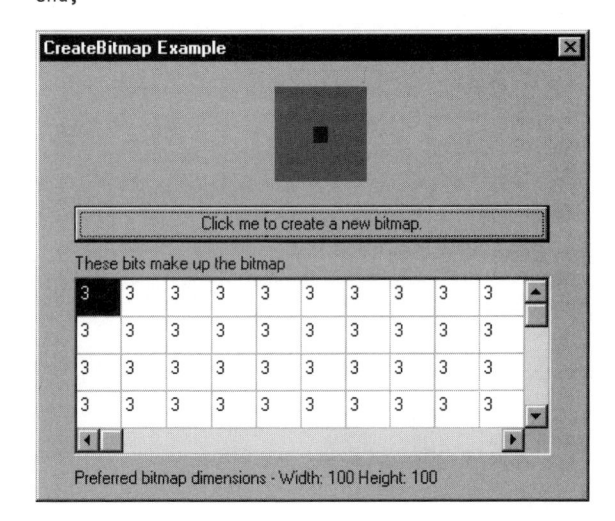

*Figure 12-6:
The new
bitmap*

CreateBitmapIndirect   Windows.pas

Syntax

CreateBitmapIndirect(
const p1: TBitmap   {a pointer to a bitmap information structure}
): HBITMAP;   {returns a handle to a bitmap}

Description

This function creates a new bitmap with the specified width, height, and color depth. An array of pixel information can be specified to create a bitmap with an initial image. If the bmWidth and bmHeight parameters are set to zero, this function returns a handle to a 1 pixel by 1 pixel monochrome bitmap. Once the bitmap is created, it can be selected into a device context with the SelectObject function. When the bitmap is no longer needed, it should be deleted with the DeleteObject function.

Although this function can be used to create color bitmaps, for performance reasons applications should use CreateBitmapIndirect to create monochrome bitmaps and CreateCompatibleBitmap to create color bitmaps. CreateCompatibleBitmap requires a device context, returning a bitmap that has the same color format as the given device. For this reason, SelectObject calls are faster with a color bitmap returned from CreateCompatibleBitmap.

Parameters

p1: Identifies a TBitmap data structure containing information about the bitmap image being created. The TBitmap data structure is defined as:

TBitmap = packed record
    bmType: Longint;   {the bitmap type}
    bmWidth: Longint;   {the width of the bitmap in pixels}
    bmHeight: Longint;   {the height of the bitmap in pixels}
    bmWidthBytes: Longint;   {the number of bytes in a scan line}
    bmPlanes: Word;   {the number of color planes}
    bmBitsPixel: Word;   {the number of bits describing one pixel}
    bmBits: Pointer;   {a pointer to a bitmap image}
end;

bmType: Indicates the type of bitmap. As of this writing, this member must be set to zero.

bmWidth: The width of the bitmap in pixels.

bmHeight: The height of the bitmap in pixels.

bmWidthBytes: The number of bytes in each scan line of the array pointed to by the bmBits parameter. The scan lines formed by this array must be word aligned, so the value of this member must be a multiple of 2.

bmPlanes: The number of color planes used by the device.

bmBitsPixel: The number of bits required to describe the color of one pixel (i.e., 8 bits for 256-color images, 24 bits for 16.7 million-color images, etc.).

bmBits: A pointer to an array of bytes that contains the color data describing the image of the bitmap. This array specifies the color of the pixels in a rectangular area. Each horizontal row of pixels in the rectangle is known as a scan line. Each scan line must be word aligned, meaning that its width must be a multiple of 2. A scan line can be padded with zeros to facilitate the word alignment. If this parameter is NIL, the new bitmap is not defined and does not contain an image.

Return Value

If the function succeeds, it returns a handle to the new bitmap; otherwise, it returns zero.

See Also

BitBlt, CreateBitmap, CreateCompatibleBitmap, CreateDIBitmap, DeleteObject, SelectObject

Example

Listing 12-6: Indirectly creating a bitmap

```
{Note: This example works correctly only under a 256 color video driver}

procedure TForm1.Button1Click(Sender: TObject);
var
  TheBitmap: HBITMAP;                  // a handle to the new bitmap
  BitmapInfo: Windows.TBitmap;         // the bitmap information structure
  OffscreenDC: HDC;                    // a handle to a memory device context
  BitmapBits: array[0..4095] of byte;  // holds the bitmap image
begin
  {initialize the bitmap image to the color in palette slot 5}
  FillMemory(@BitmapBits, 4096, 5);

  {define the new bitmap}
  BitmapInfo.bmType       := 0;
  BitmapInfo.bmWidth      := 64;
  BitmapInfo.bmHeight     := 64;
  BitmapInfo.bmWidthBytes := 64;
  BitmapInfo.bmPlanes     := 1;
  BitmapInfo.bmBitsPixel  := 8;           // 8 bits/pixel, a 256 color bitmap
  BitmapInfo.bmBits       := @BitmapBits;

  {create the bitmap based on the bitmap information}
  TheBitmap := CreateBitmapIndirect(BitmapInfo);

  {create a memory device context compatible with the screen}
  OffscreenDC := CreateCompatibleDC(0);

  {select the new bitmap and a stock pen into the memory device context}
  SelectObject(OffscreenDC, TheBitmap);
  SelectObject(OffscreenDC, GetStockObject(WHITE_PEN));

  {draw a single line on the bitmap}
  MoveToEx(OffscreenDC, 0, 0, nil);
  LineTo(OffscreenDC, 64, 64);

  {display the bitmap}
```

```
BitBlt(PaintBox1.Canvas.Handle, (PaintBox1.Width div 2)-32,
       (PaintBox1.Height div 2)-32, 64, 64, OffscreenDC, 0, 0, SRCCOPY);

{we are done with the memory device context and bitmap, so delete them}
DeleteDC(OffscreenDC);
DeleteObject(TheBitmap);
end;
```

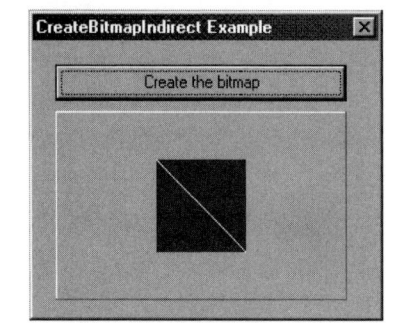

Figure 12-7: The new bitmap created indirectly

CreateCompatibleBitmap   Windows.pas

Syntax

```
CreateCompatibleBitmap(
DC: HDC;                  {a handle to a device context}
Width: Integer;           {the width of the bitmap in pixels}
Height: Integer           {the height of the bitmap in pixels}
): HBITMAP;               {returns a handle to the bitmap}
```

Description

This function creates a bitmap whose color format (i.e., 8 bits per pixel, 24 bits per pixel, etc.) and palette matches the color format and palette of the display device associated with the specified device context. If a DIB section bitmap created with the CreateDibSection function is selected into the specified device context, this function creates a DIB bitmap. Use the DeleteObject function to delete the bitmap when it is no longer needed. If the Width and Height parameters are set to zero, this function returns a handle to a 1 pixel by 1 pixel monochrome bitmap.

Parameters

DC: A handle to the device context from which the bitmap retrieves its color format.

Width: The width of the bitmap in pixels.

Height: The height of the bitmap in pixels.

Return Value

If the function succeeds, it returns a handle to the new bitmap; otherwise, it returns zero.

See Also

CreateBitmap, CreateBitmapIndirect, CreateDIBSection, DeleteObject, SelectObject

Example

Listing 12-7: Creating a bitmap compatible with the current display device

```
{Note: This example works correctly only under a 256 color video driver}

procedure TForm1.Button1Click(Sender: TObject);
var
   TheBitmap: HBitmap;                 // a handle for the new bitmap
   TheBits: array[0..4095] of Byte;    // an array of original bitmap bits
   LoopX: Integer;                     // general loop counter variables
   OffScreen: HDC;                     // an offscreen device context
   ScreenDC: HDC;                      // a handle to a temporary device context
begin
   {set every bit in the new bitmap to the color stored
    in the system palette slot 3}
   FillMemory(@TheBits, 4095, 3);

   {set a 10 X 10 pixel square in the middle of the
    image to the color in system palette slot 1}
   for LoopX:=27 to 37 do
   begin
      TheBits[LoopX*64+27]:=1;
      TheBits[LoopX*64+28]:=1;
      TheBits[LoopX*64+29]:=1;
      TheBits[LoopX*64+30]:=1;
      TheBits[LoopX*64+31]:=1;
      TheBits[LoopX*64+32]:=1;
      TheBits[LoopX*64+33]:=1;
      TheBits[LoopX*64+34]:=1;
      TheBits[LoopX*64+35]:=1;
      TheBits[LoopX*64+36]:=1;
   end;

   {retrieve a device context for the desktop}
   ScreenDC := GetDC(0);

   {create a 64 X 64 pixel bitmap that is
    color compatible with the current display device}
   TheBitmap := CreateCompatibleBitmap(ScreenDC, 64, 64);

   {release the desktop device context}
   ReleaseDC(0,ScreenDC);

   {set the bitmap image}
   SetBitmapBits(TheBitmap, 64*64, @TheBits);

   {create an offscreen device context that is
    compatible with the screen}
   OffScreen := CreateCompatibleDC(0);
```

```
      {select the new bitmap into the offscreen device context}
      SelectObject(OffScreen, TheBitmap);

      {copy the bitmap from the offscreen device context
       onto the canvas of the form. this will display the bitmap}
      BitBlt(Form1.Canvas.Handle,(Width div 2)-32,16,64,64,OffScreen,0,0,SRCCOPY);

      {delete the offscreen device context}
      DeleteDC(OffScreen);

      {delete the new bitmap}
      DeleteObject(TheBitmap);
end;
```

Figure 12-8: The compatible bitmap

CreateDIBitmap   Windows.pas

Syntax

```
CreateDIBitmap(
DC: HDC;                            {a handle to a reference device context}
var InfoHeader: TBitmapInfoHeader;  {a pointer to a TBitmapInfoHeader data
                                       structure}
dwUsage: DWORD;                     {bitmap initialization flags}
InitBits: PChar;                    {a pointer to the DIB bitmap bit values}
var InitInfo: TBitmapInfo;          {a pointer to a TBitmapInfo data structure}
wUsage: UINT                        {color type flags}
): HBITMAP;                         {returns a handle to a device-dependent bitmap}
```

Description

This function creates a device-dependent bitmap based on the attributes and image of the specified device-independent bitmap. When the new bitmap is no longer needed, it should be deleted using the DeleteObject function.

Parameters

DC: A handle to a device context. The format of the new device-dependent bitmap is based on this device context. Therefore, it must not be a memory device context. This parameter can be set to the value returned from either GetDC or CreateDC.

InfoHeader: A handle to a TBitmapInfoHeader data structure. CreateDIBitmap uses the information in this structure to set the attributes of the new device-dependent bitmap, such as its width and height. The TBitmapInfoHeader data structure is defined as:

```
TBitmapInfoHeader = packed record
     biSize: DWORD;              {the size of the structure in bytes}
     biWidth: Longint;           {the width of the bitmap in pixels}
     biHeight: Longint;          {the height of the bitmap in pixels}
     biPlanes: Word;             {the number of color planes}
     biBitCount: Word;           {the bits per pixel required to describe a color}
     biCompression: DWORD;       {compression flags}
     biSizeImage: DWORD;         {the size of the image in bytes}
     biXPelsPerMeter: Longint;   {horizontal pixels per meter of the target device}
     biYPelsPerMeter: Longint;   {vertical pixels per meter of the target device}
     biClrUsed: DWORD;           {the number of color indices used}
     biClrImportant: DWORD;      {the number of important color indices}
end;
```

See the CreateDIBSection function for a description of this data structure.

dwUsage: A flag specifying how the new device-dependent bitmap is to be initialized. If this parameter is set to zero, the bits of the new bitmap's image will not be initialized. If this parameter is set to CBM_INIT, Windows uses the information pointed to by the InitBits and InitInfo parameters to set the bits of the new device-dependent bitmap to match those in the device-independent bitmap.

InitBits: A pointer to the image representing the DIB, in the form of an array of bytes. If the dwUsage parameter is set to zero, this parameter is ignored.

InitInfo: A pointer to a TBitmapInfo data structure describing the dimensions and color format of the DIB image pointed to by the InitBits parameter. If the dwUsage parameter is set to zero, this parameter is ignored. The TBitmapInfo data structure is defined as:

```
TBitmapInfo = packed record
    bmiHeader: TBitmapInfoHeader;            {bitmap header information}
    bmiColors: array[0..0] of TRGBQuad;      {the color table used by the bitmap}
end;
```

See the CreateDIBSection function for a description of this data structure.

wUsage: A flag indicating the type of color information stored in the bmiColors member of the TBitmapInfo data structure pointed to by the InitInfo parameter. This parameter can be one value from Table 12-5.

Return Value

If the function succeeds, it returns a handle to a device-dependent bitmap; otherwise, it returns zero.

See Also

CreateBitmap, CreateBitmapIndirect, CreateDIBSection, DeleteObject

Example

Listing 12-8: Creating a device-dependent bitmap from a device-independent bitmap

```
procedure TForm1.Button1Click(Sender: TObject);
var
  Dib: HBITMAP;            // holds a handle to a new device-independent bitmap
  DDB: HBITMAP;            // holds a handle to a new device-dependent bitmap
  DibInfo: PBitmapInfo;    // a pointer to a bitmap information structure
  BitsPtr: PByte;          // a pointer to the DIB bitmap bits
  ReferenceDC: HDC;        // holds a handle to a reference device context
  ScreenDC: HDC;           // holds a handle to a screen device context
  iCount: Integer;         // general loop counter

  SystemPalette: array[0..255] of TPaletteEntry;  // required for converting the
                                                  // system palette into a DIB
                                                  // compatible palette
begin
  {allocate memory for the DIB}
  GetMem(DibInfo, SizeOf(TBitmapInfo)+256*SizeOf(TRGBQuad));

  {initialize the DIB information}
  DibInfo^.bmiHeader.biWidth         := 64;      // create a 64 X 64 pixel DIB,
  DibInfo^.bmiHeader.biHeight        := -64;     // oriented top-down
  DibInfo^.bmiHeader.biPlanes        := 1;
  DibInfo^.bmiHeader.biBitCount      := 8;       // 256 colors
  DibInfo^.bmiHeader.biCompression   := BI_RGB;  // no compression
  DibInfo^.bmiHeader.biSizeImage     := 0;       // let Windows determine size
  DibInfo^.bmiHeader.biXPelsPerMeter := 0;
  DibInfo^.bmiHeader.biYPelsPerMeter := 0;
  DibInfo^.bmiHeader.biClrUsed       := 0;
  DibInfo^.bmiHeader.biClrImportant  := 0;
  DibInfo^.bmiHeader.biSize          := SizeOf(TBitmapInfoHeader);

  {retrieve the current system palette}
  GetSystemPaletteEntries(Form1.Canvas.Handle, 0, 256, SystemPalette);

  {the system palette is returned as an array of TPaletteEntry structures,
   which store the palette colors in the form of Red, Green, and Blue. however,
   the TBitmapInfo structure's bmiColors member takes an array of TRGBQuad
   structures, which store the palette colors in the form of Blue, Green, and
   Red.  therefore, we must translate the TPaletteEntry structures into the
   appropriate TRGBQuad structures to get the correct color entries.}
  for iCount := 0 to 255 do
  begin
    DibInfo^.bmiColors[iCount].rgbBlue     := SystemPalette[iCount].peBlue;
    DibInfo^.bmiColors[iCount].rgbRed      := SystemPalette[iCount].peRed;
    DibInfo^.bmiColors[iCount].rgbGreen    := SystemPalette[iCount].peGreen;
    DibInfo^.bmiColors[iCount].rgbReserved := 0;
  end;

  {create a memory based device context}
  ReferenceDC := CreateCompatibleDC(0);
```

```
{create the dib based on the memory device context and the
 initialized bitmap information}
Dib := CreateDIBSection(ReferenceDC, DibInfo^, DIB_RGB_COLORS,
                        Pointer(BitsPtr), 0, 0);

{draw bands of color into the DIB}
FillMemory(BitsPtr, 8*64, $03);
FillMemory(Pointer(LongInt(BitsPtr)+8*64), 8*64, $05);
FillMemory(Pointer(LongInt(BitsPtr)+2*(8*64)), 8*64, $03);
FillMemory(Pointer(LongInt(BitsPtr)+3*(8*64)), 8*64, $05);
FillMemory(Pointer(LongInt(BitsPtr)+4*(8*64)), 8*64, $03);
FillMemory(Pointer(LongInt(BitsPtr)+5*(8*64)), 8*64, $05);
FillMemory(Pointer(LongInt(BitsPtr)+6*(8*64)), 8*64, $03);
FillMemory(Pointer(LongInt(BitsPtr)+7*(8*64)), 8*64, $05);

{get a screen based DC which is used as a reference point
 when creating the device-dependent bitmap}
ScreenDC := GetDC(0);

{create a device-dependent bitmap from the DIB}
DDB := CreateDIBitmap(ScreenDC, DibInfo^.bmiHeader, CBM_INIT, PChar(BitsPtr),
                      DibInfo^, DIB_RGB_COLORS);

{delete the screen based device context}
ReleaseDC(0, ScreenDC);

{select the device-dependent bitmap into the offscreen DC}
SelectObject(ReferenceDC, DDB);

{copy the device-independent bitmap to the form}
SetDIBitsToDevice(Form1.Canvas.Handle, 50, 5, 64, 64, 0, 0, 0, 64, BitsPtr,
                  DibInfo^, DIB_RGB_COLORS);

{copy the device-dependent bitmap to the form}
BitBlt(Form1.Canvas.Handle, 166, 5, 64, 64, ReferenceDC, 0, 0, SRCCOPY);

{we no longer need the bitmaps or the device context, so free everything}
DeleteDC(ReferenceDC);
DeleteObject(Dib);
DeleteObject(DDB);
FreeMem(DibInfo, SizeOf(TBitmapInfo)+256*SizeOf(TRGBQuad));
end;
```

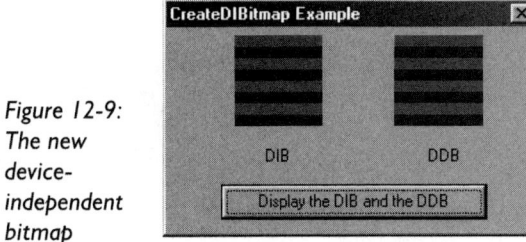

*Figure 12-9:
The new device-independent bitmap*

Table 12-5: CreateDIBitmap wUsage values

Value	Description
DIB_PAL_COLORS	The bmiColors member of the TBitmapInfo structure is an array of 16-bit indices into the currently realized logical palette of the specified device context. This value should not be used if the bitmap will be saved to disk.
DIB_RGB_COLORS	The bmiColors member of the TBitmapInfo structure is an array of literal RGB color values.

CreateDIBSection   Windows.pas

Syntax

```
CreateDIBSection(
DC: HDC;                       {a handle to a device context}
const p2: TBitmapInfo;         {a pointer to a TBitmapInfo data structure}
p3: UINT;                      {color type flags}
var p4: Pointer;               {a variable that receives a pointer to the bitmap bits}
p5: THandle;                   {a handle to a file mapping object}
p6: DWORD                      {an offset to the bitmap bit values}
): HBITMAP;                    {returns a handle to a DIB}
```

Description

This function creates a device-independent bitmap based on the specified bitmap attributes. It returns a handle to this new bitmap, and a pointer to the bit values that make up the bitmap image. The developer can specify a file mapping object to store the bitmap image bits, or let Windows automatically allocate the memory. When the bitmap is no longer needed, it should be deleted with a call to DeleteObject.

Parameters

DC: A handle to a device context. If the p3 parameter contains the DIB_PAL_COLORS flag, the new DIB's color palette will match the logical palette of the device context identified by this parameter.

p2: A pointer to a TBitmapInfo data structure. This data structure contains information describing the type of DIB to create, such as its dimensions, color format, and compression. The TBitmapInfo data structure is defined as:

```
TBitmapInfo = packed record
    bmiHeader: TBitmapInfoHeader;         {bitmap header information}
    bmiColors: array[0..0] of TRGBQuad;   {the color table used by the bitmap}
end;
```

bmiHeader: A TBitmapInfoHeader data structure containing information about the dimensions and color format of the DIB. The TBitmapInfoHeader data structure is defined as:

```
TBitmapInfoHeader = packed record
    biSize: DWORD;              {the size of the structure in bytes}
```

```
        biWidth: Longint;            {the width of the bitmap in pixels}
        biHeight: Longint;           {the height of the bitmap in pixels}
        biPlanes: Word;              {the number of color planes}
        biBitCount: Word;            {the bits per pixel required to describe a color}
        biCompression: DWORD;        {compression flags}
        biSizeImage: DWORD;          {the size of the image in bytes}
        biXPelsPerMeter: Longint;    {horizontal pixels per meter of the target device}
        biYPelsPerMeter: Longint;    {vertical pixels per meter of the target device}
        biClrUsed: DWORD;            {the number of color indices used}
        biClrImportant: DWORD;       {the number of important color indices}
end;
```

biSize: The size of the TBitmapInfoHeader in bytes. This member should be set to SizeOf(TBitmapInfoHeader).

biWidth: Specifies the width of the bitmap in pixels.

biHeight: Specifies the height of the bitmap in pixels. If this value is positive, the DIB is oriented in a bottom-up fashion, with its origin in the lower-left corner. If this value is negative, the DIB is oriented in a top-down fashion, with its origin in the upper-left corner like a regular bitmap.

biPlanes: Specifies the number of color planes in use.

biBitCount: The number of bits required to describe the color of one pixel (i.e., 8 bits for 256-color images, 24 bits for 16.7 million-color images, etc.). This member can be one value from Table 12-6.

biCompression: A flag indicating the type of compression used for bottom-up oriented DIBs (top-down oriented DIBs cannot use compression). This member can be one value from Table 12-7.

biSizeImage: Specifies the size of the image in bytes. This member may be set to 0 for DIBs using the BI_RGB flag in the biCompression member. Although the biWidth member can be set to any value, each scan line of a DIB must be double-word aligned. To find the correct value for this member that will cause the scan lines of the DIB to be double-word aligned, use the following formula:

```
  (((((biBitCount * biWidth) + 31) div 32) * 4) * ABS(biHeight))
```

Any extra bits will be padded with zeros and will not be used.

biXPelsPerMeter: Specifies the horizontal pixels per meter resolution of the target display device indicated by the DC parameter. This value may be used to select a bitmap from the application resources that best matches the characteristics of the current display device.

biYPelsPerMeter: Specifies the vertical pixels per meter resolution of the target display device indicated by the DC parameter.

biClrUsed: Specifies the number of color indices from the color table that are in use by the bitmap. If this member is zero, the bitmap uses the maximum number of colors indicated by the biBitCount member for the compression mode indicated by the biCompression member. If the DIB is a packed bitmap, meaning that the array of bits describing the image directly follows the TBitmapInfo structure and one pointer references the entire contiguous chunk of data, then this member must be set to either zero or the actual size of the color table. If the p3 parameter is set to DIB_PAL_COLORS and the DIB is a packed bitmap, this member must be set to an even number so that the DIB bitmap values will start on a double-word boundary.

biClrImportant: Specifies the number of slots in the color table that are considered important for displaying the bitmap correctly. The colors in the bmiColors array should be arranged in the order of importance, with the most important colors going into the first entries of the array. This member may be set to zero, in which case all colors are considered important.

bmiColors: An array of either TRGBQuad records or double-word values that define the color table of the bitmap. The TRGBQuad data structure is defined as:

```
TRGBQuad = packed record
     rgbBlue: Byte;              {blue color intensity}
     rgbGreen: Byte;             {green color intensity}
     rgbRed: Byte;               {red color intensity}
     rgbReserved: Byte;          {reserved value}
end;
```

rgbBlue: Specifies the blue color intensity.

rgbGreen: Specifies the green color intensity.

rgbRed: Specifies the red color intensity.

rgbReserved: This member is reserved and must be set to zero.

p3: A flag indicating the type of color information stored in the bmiColors member of the TBitmapInfo data structure pointed to by the p2 parameter. This parameter can be one value from Table 12-8.

p4: A pointer to a variable that receives a pointer to the DIB's bitmap bit values.

p5: An optional handle to a file mapping object created from a call to the CreateFileMapping function. This file mapping object is used to create the DIB bitmap. The DIB's bit values will be located at the offset indicated by the p6 parameter into the file mapping object. This file mapping object can be retrieved at a later time by a call to the GetObject function using the HBITMAP handle returned by CreateDIBSection. The developer must manually close the file mapping object once the bitmap is deleted. If this parameter is zero, Windows allocates the memory for the DIB, the p6 parameter is ignored, and the file mapping handle returned from GetObject will be zero.

p6: Specifies the offset from the beginning of the file mapping object referred to by the p5 parameter to the DIB's bitmap bit values. The bitmap bit values are double-word aligned, so this parameter must be a multiple of 4. If the p5 parameter is zero, this parameter is ignored.

Return Value

If the function succeeds, it returns a handle to a new device-independent bitmap, and the variable indicated by the p4 parameter contains a pointer to the bitmap's bit values. If the function fails, it returns zero, and the variable indicated by the p4 parameter contains NIL. To get extended error information, call the GetLastError function.

See Also

CreateFileMapping*, DeleteObject, GetObject, SetDIBits, SetDIBitsToDevice, StretchDIBits

Example

Listing 12-9: Creating a device-independent bitmap

```
procedure TForm1.Button1Click(Sender: TObject);
var
  Dib: HBITMAP;            // holds a handle to the DIB
  DibInfo: PBitmapInfo;    // a pointer to the bitmap information data structure
  BitsPtr: PByte;          // holds a pointer to the bitmap bits
  ReferenceDC: HDC;        // a handle to the reference device context
  iCount: Integer;         // general loop counter

  SystemPalette: array[0..255] of TPaletteEntry;  // required for converting the
                                                  // system palette into a DIB
                                                  // compatible palette
begin
  {get the memory needed for the bitmap information data structure}
  GetMem(DibInfo, SizeOf(TBitmapInfo)+256*SizeOf(TRGBQuad));

  {initialize the bitmap information}
  DibInfo^.bmiHeader.biWidth         := 64;    // create a 64 X 64 pixel DIB,
  DibInfo^.bmiHeader.biHeight        := -64;   // oriented top-down
  DibInfo^.bmiHeader.biPlanes        := 1;
  DibInfo^.bmiHeader.biBitCount      := 8;     // 256 colors
  DibInfo^.bmiHeader.biCompression   := BI_RGB; // no compression
  DibInfo^.bmiHeader.biSizeImage     := 0;     // let Windows determine size
  DibInfo^.bmiHeader.biXPelsPerMeter := 0;
  DibInfo^.bmiHeader.biYPelsPerMeter := 0;
  DibInfo^.bmiHeader.biClrUsed       := 0;
  DibInfo^.bmiHeader.biClrImportant  := 0;
  DibInfo^.bmiHeader.biSize          := SizeOf(TBitmapInfoHeader);

  {retrieve the current system palette}
  GetSystemPaletteEntries(Form1.Canvas.Handle, 0, 256, SystemPalette);

  {the system palette is returned as an array of TPaletteEntry structures,
   which store the palette colors in the form of Red, Green, and Blue. however,
   the TBitmapInfo structure's bmiColors member takes an array of TRGBQuad
   structures, which store the palette colors in the form of Blue, Green, and
```

Red. therefore, we must translate the TPaletteEntry structures into the
appropriate TRGBQuad structures to get the correct color entries.}
```
for iCount := 0 to 255 do
begin
  DibInfo^.bmiColors[iCount].rgbBlue     := SystemPalette[iCount].peBlue;
  DibInfo^.bmiColors[iCount].rgbRed      := SystemPalette[iCount].peRed;
  DibInfo^.bmiColors[iCount].rgbGreen    := SystemPalette[iCount].peGreen;
  DibInfo^.bmiColors[iCount].rgbReserved := 0;
end;

{create a memory based device context}
ReferenceDC := CreateCompatibleDC(0);

{create the dib based on the memory device context and the
 initialized bitmap information}
Dib := CreateDIBSection(ReferenceDC, DibInfo^, DIB_RGB_COLORS,
                       Pointer(BitsPtr), 0, 0);

{delete the reference device context}
DeleteDC(ReferenceDC);

{fill the DIB image bits with alternating bands of color}
FillMemory(BitsPtr, 8*64, $03);
FillMemory(Pointer(LongInt(BitsPtr)+8*64), 8*64, $05);
FillMemory(Pointer(LongInt(BitsPtr)+2*(8*64)), 8*64, $03);
FillMemory(Pointer(LongInt(BitsPtr)+3*(8*64)), 8*64, $05);
FillMemory(Pointer(LongInt(BitsPtr)+4*(8*64)), 8*64, $03);
FillMemory(Pointer(LongInt(BitsPtr)+5*(8*64)), 8*64, $05);
FillMemory(Pointer(LongInt(BitsPtr)+6*(8*64)), 8*64, $03);
FillMemory(Pointer(LongInt(BitsPtr)+7*(8*64)), 8*64, $05);

{draw the DIB onto the form surface}
SetDIBitsToDevice(Form1.Canvas.Handle, 30, 5, 64, 64, 0, 0, 0, 64, BitsPtr,
                  DibInfo^, DIB_RGB_COLORS);

{draw the DIB again, but this time let's stretch it to twice its size}
StretchDIBits(Form1.Canvas.Handle, 105, 5, 128, 128, 0, 0, 64, 64, BitsPtr,
              DibInfo^, DIB_RGB_COLORS, SRCCOPY);

{we no longer need the DIB, so delete it and the
 allocated memory for the information data structure}
DeleteObject(Dib);
FreeMem(DibInfo, SizeOf(TBitmapInfo)+256*SizeOf(TRGBQuad));
end;
```

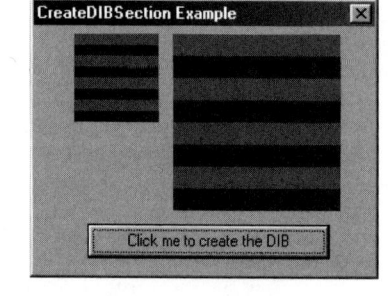

*Figure 12-10:
The DIB,
original size
and double
in size*

Table 12-6: CreateDIBSection p2.bmiHeader.biBitCount values

Value	Description
1	This bitmap has a maximum of two colors, and the bmiColors array contains only two entries. A single bit represents each pixel in the bitmap image. If the bit is off, that pixel is drawn using the color in the first slot of the bmiColors array. If the bit is on, that pixel is drawn using the color in the second slot of the bmiColors array.
4	This bitmap has a maximum of 16 colors, and the bmiColors array can contain up to 16 entries. Each byte in the bitmap bit values represents two pixels. The first 4 bits in the byte represent the index into the color palette for the first pixel, and the last 4 bits represent the index for the second pixel.
8	This bitmap has a maximum of 256 colors, and the bmiColors array can contain up to 256 entries. Each byte in the bitmap bit values represents one pixel, specifying that pixel's index into the 256-entry bmiColors array.
16	This bitmap has a maximum of 65,536 colors. If the biCompression member of the TBitmapInfoHeader structure is set to BI_RGB, the bmiColors member is set to NIL. In this case, each word in the bitmap bit values represents one pixel. Moving from the least significant bit to the most significant, the last 5 bits of the word specify the pixel's blue intensity, the next 5 bits specify the green intensity, and the next 5 bits specify the red intensity. The most significant bit of the word is not used. If the biCompression member of the TBitmapInfoHeader structure is set to BI_BITFIELDS, the bmiColors member contains three double-word values that represent a bitmask. These bitmasks are applied to the word value for each pixel using the Boolean AND operator to retrieve the red, green, and blue color intensities, respectively, for that pixel. **Windows NT/2000 or later:** The bits set in each double-word mask must be contiguous and should not overlap the bits of another mask. In this case, the developer does not have to use all of the bits describing the pixel. **Windows 95/98/Me:** Only the following double-word bitmask values are allowed: a 5-5-5 format, where the blue mask is $0000001F, green is $000003E0, and red is $00007C00, or a 5-6-5 format, where the blue mask is $0000001F, green is $000007E0, and red is $0000F800.
24	This bitmap has a maximum of 16.7 million colors, and the bmiColors member is set to NIL. Each pixel in the bitmap image is represented by 3 bytes. These 3 bytes indicate the relative intensities of the blue, green, and red colors, respectively, of the pixel.
32	This bitmap has a maximum of approximately 4.3 billion colors. If the biCompression member of the TBitmapInfoHeader structure is set to BI_RGB, the bmiColors member is set to NIL. In this case, each double word in the bitmap bit values represents one pixel. Moving from the least significant bit to the most significant, the last byte of the double word specifies the pixel's blue intensity, the next byte specifies the green intensity, and the next byte specifies the red intensity. The most significant byte of the double word is not used. If the biCompression member of the TBitmapInfoHeader structure is set to BI_BITFIELDS, the bmiColors member contains three double-word values that represent a bitmask. These bitmasks are applied to the double-word value for each pixel using the Boolean AND operator to retrieve the red, green, and blue color intensities, respectively, for that pixel. **Windows NT/2000 or later:** The bits set in each double-word mask must be contiguous and should not overlap the bits of another mask. In this case, the developer does not have to use all of the bits describing the pixel. **Windows 95/98/Me:** Only a blue mask of $000000FF, green mask of $0000FF00, and red mask of $00FF0000 are allowed.

Table 12-7: CreateDIBSection p2.bmiHeader.biCompression values

Value	Description
BI_RGB	No compression.
BI_RLE8	A run-length encoded format for 256-color bitmaps (color format is 8 bits per pixel). This compression format consists of two-byte pairs. The first byte in a pair is a count byte, specifying how many times to repeat the following byte when drawing the image. The second byte is an index into the color table.
BI_RLE4	A run-length encoded format for 16-color bitmaps (color format is 4 bits per pixel). This compression format consists of two-byte pairs. The first byte in a pair is a count byte, specifying how many times to repeat the following byte when drawing the image. The second byte specifies two indices into the color table, the first index in the high-order 4 bits, and the second in the low-order 4 bits.
BI_BITFIELDS	This format is valid only for 16 and 32 bits per pixel color bitmaps. The bitmap is not compressed, and the color table consists of three double-word color masks, one each for the red, blue, and green intensities. These color masks, when combined with the bits describing each individual pixel using the Boolean AND operator, specify the red, green, and blue intensities, respectively, of each pixel.

Table 12-8: CreateDIBSection p3 values

Value	Description
DIB_PAL_COLORS	The bmiColors member of the TBitmapInfo structure is an array of 16-bit indices into the currently realized logical palette of the specified device context. This value should not be used if the bitmap will be saved to disk.
DIB_RGB_COLORS	The bmiColors member of the TBitmapInfo structure is an array of literal RGB color values.

CreateEnhMetaFile   Windows.pas

Syntax

```
CreateEnhMetaFile(
    DC: HDC;          {a handle to a reference device context}
    p2: PChar;        {a pointer to a filename}
    p3: PRect;        {a pointer to a bounding rectangle}
    p4: PChar         {a pointer to a description string}
    ): HDC;           {returns a handle to a metafile device context}
```

Description

This function creates an enhanced metafile device context. This device context can be used with any GDI function to draw into the enhanced metafile. A handle to the metafile is obtained by calling the CloseEnhMetaFile function, and using the PlayEnhMetaFile function draws the metafile.

Parameters

DC: A handle to a device context used as a reference for the new enhanced metafile device context. This reference device context is used to record the resolution and units of the device on which the metafile originally appeared. If this parameter is zero, the current display device is used as the reference. This information is used to scale the metafile when it is drawn.

p2: A pointer to a null-terminated string describing a filename in which to store the enhanced metafile. The extension of this filename is typically .EMF. If this parameter is NIL, the enhanced metafile will only exist in memory, and is deleted upon the call to the DeleteEnhMetaFile function.

p3: A pointer to a rectangle describing the dimensions of the picture stored in the enhanced metafile. These dimensions are in terms of .01 millimeter units (i.e., a value of 3 equals .03 millimeters). If this parameter is NIL, the dimensions of the smallest rectangle surrounding the metafile picture will automatically be calculated. This information is used to scale the metafile when it is drawn.

p4: A pointer to a null-terminated string containing a description of the metafile and its contents. Typically, this consists of the application name followed by a null character, followed by the title of the metafile, terminating with two null characters (i.e., 'CreateEnhMetaFile Example Program'+Chr(0)+'Example Metafile'+Chr(0)+Chr(0)). This parameter can be NIL, in which case there will be no description string stored in the metafile.

Windows 95: The maximum length for the enhanced metafile description is 16,384 bytes.

Return Value

If the function succeeds, it returns a handle to an enhanced metafile device context, which can be used in any GDI function call. Otherwise, it returns zero.

See Also

CloseEnhMetaFile, CopyEnhMetaFile, DeleteEnhMetaFile, GetEnhMetaFileDescription, GetEnhMetaFileHeader, PlayEnhMetaFile

Example

Listing 12-10: Creating an enhanced metafile

```
procedure TForm1.Button1Click(Sender: TObject);
var
   {these hold important screen dimension information used when creating
    the reference rectangle}
   WidthInMM,
   HeightInMM,
   WidthInPixels,
   HeightInPixels: Integer;

   {holds millimeter per pixel ratios}
   MMPerPixelHorz,
   MMPerPixelVer: Integer;

   {the reference rectangle}
   ReferenceRect: TRect;

   {a handle to the metafile device context}
   MetafileDC: HDC;
```

```
    {the handle to a metafile}
    TheMetafile: HENHMETAFILE;

    {a handle to a brush used in drawing on the metafile}
    TheBrush: HBRUSH;
    OldBrush: HBRUSH;
begin
    {the CreateEnhMetaFile function assumes that the dimensions in the reference
     rectangle are in terms of .01 millimeter units (i.e., a 1 equals .01
     millimeters, 2 equals .02 millimeters, etc.). therefore, the following
     lines are required to obtain a millimeters per pixel ratio. this can then
     be used to create a reference rectangle with the appropriate dimensions.}

    {retrieve the size of the screen in millimeters}
    WidthInMM:=GetDeviceCaps(Form1.Canvas.Handle, HORZSIZE);
    HeightInMM:=GetDeviceCaps(Form1.Canvas.Handle, VERTSIZE);

    {retrieve the size of the screen in pixels}
    WidthInPixels:=GetDeviceCaps(Form1.Canvas.Handle, HORZRES);
    HeightInPixels:=GetDeviceCaps(Form1.Canvas.Handle, VERTRES);

    {compute a millimeter per pixel ratio. the millimeter measurements must be
     multiplied by 100 to get the appropriate unit measurement that the
     CreateEnhMetaFile is expecting (where a 1 equals .01 millimeters)}
    MMPerPixelHorz:=(WidthInMM * 100) div WidthInPixels;
    MMPerPixelVer:=(HeightInMM * 100) div HeightInPixels;

    {create our reference rectangle for the metafile}
    ReferenceRect.Top:=0;
    ReferenceRect.Left:=0;
    ReferenceRect.Right:=Image1.Width * MMPerPixelHorz;
    ReferenceRect.Bottom:=Image1.Height * MMPerPixelVer;

    {create a metafile that will be saved to disk}
    MetafileDC:=CreateEnhMetaFile(Form1.Canvas.Handle, 'Example.emf',
                                  @ReferenceRect,
                                  'CreateEnhMetaFile Example Program'+Chr(0)+
                                  'Example Metafile'+Chr(0)+Chr(0));

    {display some text in the metafile}
    TextOut(MetafileDC,15,15,'This is an enhanced metafile.',29);

    {create a diagonal hatched brush and select it into the metafile}
    TheBrush:=CreateHatchBrush(HS_DIAGCROSS, clRed);
    OldBrush:=SelectObject(MetafileDC, TheBrush);

    {draw a filled rectangle}
    Rectangle(MetafileDC, 15, 50, 250, 250);

    {delete the current brush}
    SelectObject(MetafileDC, OldBrush);
    DeleteObject(TheBrush);

    {create a horizontal hatched brush and select it into the metafile}
    TheBrush:=CreateHatchBrush(HS_CROSS, clBlue);
    OldBrush:=SelectObject(MetafileDC, TheBrush);
```

```
    {draw a filled ellipse}
    Ellipse(MetafileDC, 15, 50, 250, 250);

    {delete the current brush}
    SelectObject(MetafileDC, OldBrush);
    DeleteObject(TheBrush);

    {close the metafile, saving it to disk and retrieving a handle}
    TheMetafile:=CloseEnhMetaFile(MetafileDC);

    {draw the metafile into the Image1 canvas}
    PlayEnhMetaFile(Image1.Canvas.Handle, TheMetafile, Image1.Canvas.Cliprect);

    {we are done with the metafile, so delete its handle}
    DeleteEnhMetaFile(TheMetafile);
end;
```

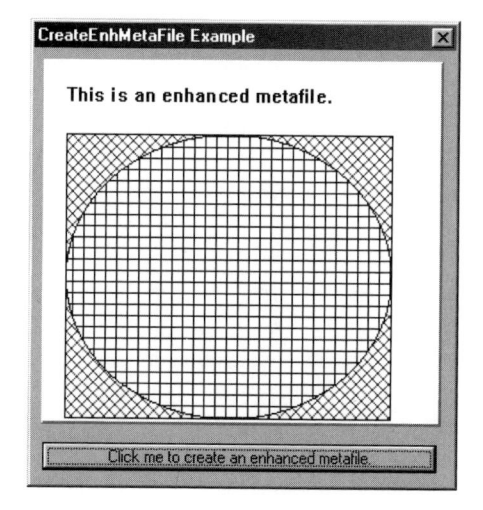

Figure 12-11: The new metafile

DeleteEnhMetaFile   Windows.pas

Syntax

DeleteEnhMetaFile(
p1: HENHMETAFILE   {a handle to an enhanced metafile}
): BOOL;   {returns TRUE or FALSE}

Description

This function deletes the metafile associated with the given handle. If this metafile is stored in memory, it deletes the metafile and frees the associated memory. If this handle identifies a metafile stored in a file on disk, the handle and associated memory is freed but the file is not destroyed.

Parameters

p1: A handle to the enhanced metafile to be deleted.

Return Value

If the function succeeds, it returns TRUE; otherwise, it returns FALSE.

See Also

CopyEnhMetaFile, CreateEnhMetaFile, GetEnhMetaFile

Example

See Listing 12-10 under CreateEnhMetaFile.

EnumEnhMetaFile   Windows.pas

Syntax

```
EnumEnhMetaFile(
  DC: HDC;                     {a handle to a device context}
  p2: HENHMETAFILE;            {a handle to the enhanced metafile being enumerated}
  p3: TFNEnhMFEnumProc;        {a pointer to an application-defined callback function}
  p4: Pointer;                 {a pointer to application-defined data}
  const p5: TRect              {a pointer to a TRect structure}
): BOOL;                       {returns TRUE or FALSE}
```

Description

This function iterates through all of the metafile records stored in the specified enhanced metafile, passing each one to an application-defined callback function. This callback function processes the record as needed, and enumeration continues until all records have been processed or the callback function returns zero.

Parameters

DC: A handle to the device context into which the metafile can be played. This parameter is passed directly to the callback function, and can be set to zero if the callback will not play the metafile records.

p2: A handle to the enhanced metafile whose records are to be enumerated.

p3: The address of the application-defined callback function.

p4: A pointer to application-defined data. This data is intended for application-specific purposes only, and is passed directly to the application-defined callback function.

p5: A pointer to a TRect data structure containing the upper-left and lower-right coordinates of the rectangle containing the metafile picture, measured in logical units. Points along the edge of this rectangle are included in the picture. If the DC parameter contains zero, this parameter is ignored.

Return Value

If the function succeeds and the callback function enumerated all enhanced metafile records, it returns TRUE. If the function fails, or the callback function did not enumerate all enhanced metafile records, it returns FALSE.

Callback Syntax

```
EnumerateEnhMetafile(
    DisplaySurface: HDC;                      {a handle to a device context}
    var MetafileTable: THandleTable;          {a pointer to a metafile handle table}
    var MetafileRecord: TEnhMetaRecord;       {a pointer to a metafile record}
    ObjectCount: Integer;                     {the number of objects with handles}
    var Data: Longint                         {a pointer to application-defined data}
): Integer;                                   {returns an integer value}
```

Description

This function receives a pointer to a metafile record for every record stored in the enhanced metafile being enumerated. It can perform any desired task.

Parameters

DisplaySurface: A handle to the device context into which the metafile record can be played. If metafile records are not going to be played by the callback function, this parameter can be zero.

MetafileTable: A pointer to an array of type HGDIOBJ. This array contains handles to graphics objects, such as pens and brushes, in the metafile. The first entry in this array is a handle to the enhanced metafile itself.

MetafileRecord: A pointer to a TEnhMetaRecord structure. This data structure defines the current metafile record being enumerated. The TEnhMetaRecord structure is defined as:

```
TEnhMetaRecord = packed record
    iType: DWORD;                    {the record type}
    nSize: DWORD;                    {the record size}
    dParm: array[0..0] of DWORD;     {an array of parameters}
end;
```

iType: Indicates the record type and indirectly the GDI function that created the record. This is a constant of the form EMR_XXX. All record types are listed in the Windows.pas file.

nSize: The size of the record in bytes.

dParm: An array of parameters used by the GDI function identified by the iType member.

ObjectCount: An integer indicating the number of GDI graphics objects with handles in the handle table pointed to by the MetafileTable parameter.

Data: A pointer to application-defined data. This data is intended for application-specific purposes only.

Return Value

The callback function should return a non-zero value to continue enumeration; otherwise, it should return zero.

See Also

GetEnhMetaFile, PlayEnhMetaFile, PlayEnhMetaFileRecord

Example

Listing 12-11: Changing the brushes in an enhanced metafile

```
{the callback function for enumerating enhanced metafile records}
function EnumerateEnhMetafile(DisplaySurface: HDC;
                              var MetafileTable: THandleTable;
                              var MetafileRecord: TEnhMetaRecord;
                              ObjectCount: Integer;
                              var Data: Longint): Integer; stdcall;

implementation

procedure TForm1.FileListBox1Click(Sender: TObject);
var
  TheMetafile: HENHMETAFILE;    // holds an enhanced metafile
begin
  {open and retrieve a handle to the selected metafile}
  TheMetafile:=GetEnhMetaFile(PChar(FileListBox1.FileName));

  {erase the last image}
  Image1.Canvas.FillRect(Image1.Canvas.ClipRect);

  {enumerate the records in the metafile}
  EnumEnhMetaFile(Image1.Canvas.Handle, TheMetafile, @EnumerateEnhMetafile,
                  nil, Image1.BoundsRect);
end;

{this function will fire for every record stored in the metafile}
function EnumerateEnhMetafile(DisplaySurface: HDC;
                              var MetafileTable: THandleTable;
                              var MetafileRecord: TEnhMetaRecord;
                              ObjectCount: Integer;
                              var Data: Longint): Integer;
var
  NewBrush: HBRUSH;         // holds a new brush
  BrushInfo: TLogBrush;     // defines a new brush
begin
  {if the metafile is trying to create a brush...}
  if MetafileRecord.iType=EMR_CREATEBRUSHINDIRECT then
  begin
    {...intercept it and create our own brush}
    BrushInfo.lbStyle := BS_SOLID;
    BrushInfo.lbColor := clRed;
    BrushInfo.lbHatch := 0;
    NewBrush := CreateBrushIndirect(BrushInfo);

    {select this brush into the device context where the
     metafile is being played. this will replace all brushes
     in the metafile with a red, solid brush}
    SelectObject(DisplaySurface,NewBrush);
  end
  else
```

```
     {if it's not a create brush record, play it}
     PlayEnhMetaFileRecord(DisplaySurface, MetafileTable, MetafileRecord,
                           ObjectCount);

  Result:=1;  // continue enumeration
end;
```

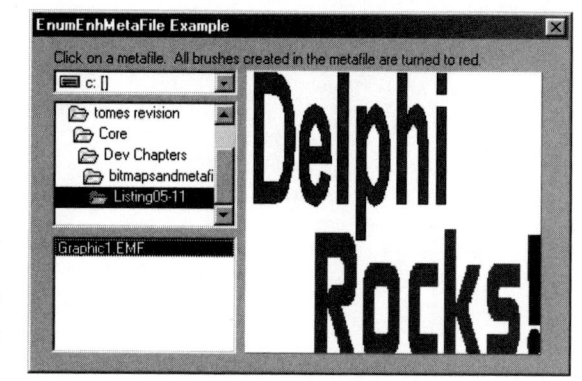

*Figure 12-12:
All brushes in
the enhanced
metafile were
changed*

GetBitmapBits   Windows.pas

Syntax

```
GetBitmapBits(
Bitmap: HBITMAP;          {a handle to a bitmap}
Count: Longint;           {the number of bytes in the Bits array}
Bits: Pointer             {a pointer to an array of bytes}
): Longint;               {returns the number of bytes retrieved from the bitmap}
```

Description

This function copies the color information from the specified bitmap into a buffer. The GetBitmapBits function is included for compatibility purposes. Win32-based applications should use the GetDIBits function.

Parameters

Bitmap: A handle to the bitmap from which color information is retrieved.

Count: Indicates the number of bytes pointed to by the Bits parameter.

Bits: A pointer to an array of bytes that receives the color information from the bitmap.

Return Value

If the function succeeds, it returns the number of bytes retrieved from the bitmap; otherwise, it returns zero.

See Also

CreateBitmap, GetDIBits, SetBitmapBits, SetDIBits

Example

Listing 12-12: Retrieving bitmap color data

```
procedure TForm1.Button1Click(Sender: TObject);
type
  TBitmapBits = array[0..0] of Byte;
var
  BitmapBits: ^TBitmapBits;         // holds the bytes from the bitmap
  LoopRow, LoopCol: Integer;        // loop control variables
begin
  {set the string grid to the dimensions of the bitmap}
  StringGrid1.ColCount:=Image1.Picture.Bitmap.Width;
  StringGrid1.RowCount:=Image1.Picture.Bitmap.Height;

  {dynamically allocate the needed space for the bitmap color data}
  GetMem(BitmapBits,StringGrid1.RowCount*StringGrid1.ColCount);

  {retrieve the color data from the bitmap}
  GetBitmapBits(Image1.Picture.Bitmap.Handle, StringGrid1.RowCount*
                StringGrid1.ColCount, BitmapBits);

  {display the values that define the bitmap in the string grid. since this
   is a 256 color bitmap, these values represent indexes into the bitmap's
   color palette.}
  for LoopRow:=0 to Image1.Height-1 do
    for LoopCol:=0 to Image1.Width-1 do
      StringGrid1.Cells[LoopCol, LoopRow]:=IntToStr(BitmapBits[LoopRow*
                Image1.Width+LoopCol]);

  {free the allocated memory}
  FreeMem(BitmapBits);
end;
```

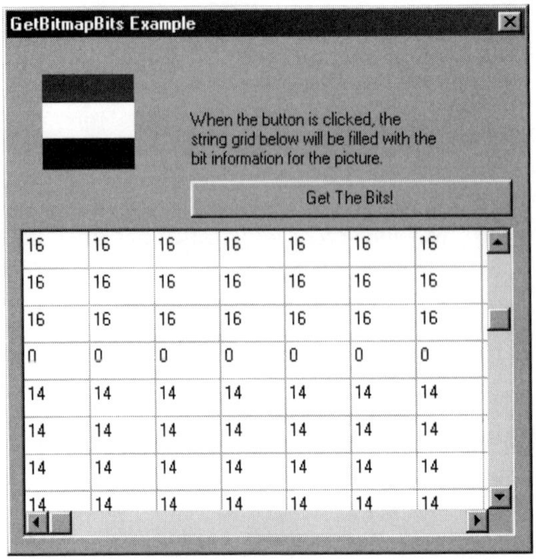

Figure 12-13: The bitmap bits

GetBitmapDimensionEx   Windows.pas

Syntax

GetBitmapDimensionEx(
p1: HBITMAP;   {a handle to a bitmap}
var p2: TSize   {the address of a TSize structure}
): BOOL;   {returns TRUE or FALSE}

Description

This function retrieves the preferred bitmap dimensions set by the call to SetBitmapDimensionEx. If this function has not been called, the TSize structure returned by GetBitmapDimensionEx will contain zero in every field.

Parameters

p1: A handle to the bitmap whose preferred dimensions are to be retrieved.

p2: A pointer to a TSize structure. The TSize structure describes the width and height of a rectangle, and is defined as:

TSize = record
    cx: Longint;   {the preferred width}
    cy: Longint;   {the preferred height}
end;

cx: The bitmap's preferred width. Each unit represents 0.1 millimeters.

cy: The bitmap's preferred height. Each unit represents 0.1 millimeters.

Return Value

If the function succeeds, it returns TRUE; otherwise, it returns FALSE. To get extended error information, call the GetLastError function.

See Also

SetBitmapDimensionEx

Example

See Listing 12-5 under CreateBitmap.

GetDIBits   Windows.pas

Syntax

GetDIBits(
DC: HDC;   {a handle to a device context}
Bitmap: HBITMAP;   {a handle to a regular bitmap}
StartScan: UINT;   {the starting scan line}
NumScans: UINT;   {the total number of scan lines}
Bits: Pointer;   {a pointer to the DIB bitmap bit values}
var BitsInfo: TBitmapInfo;   {a pointer to the DIB bitmap information structure}

        Usage: UINT   {color type flags}
        ): Integer;   {returns the number of scan lines copied}

Description

This function creates a device-independent bitmap from the image stored in a device-dependent bitmap by retrieving the bit values from the specified device-dependent bitmap and storing them in a buffer in the format defined by the TBitmapInfo structure pointed to by the BitsInfo parameter. The Bitmap parameter can also specify the handle to a device-independent bitmap, in which case this function can be used to create a copy of the DIB in the desired format specified by the TBitmapInfo structure. If the color format of the requested DIB does not match the color format of the specified bitmap, a color palette will be generated for the DIB using default colors for the requested color format. If the BitsInfo parameter indicates a color format of 16 bits per pixel or higher for the DIB, no color table is generated.

Parameters

DC: A handle to a device context. The device-dependent bitmap specified by the Bitmap parameter uses the currently realized palette of this device context for its color information.

Bitmap: A handle to the device-dependent bitmap from which the bit values are copied.

StartScan: Specifies the starting scan line to retrieve from the device-dependent bitmap.

NumScans: Specifies the total number of scan lines to retrieve from the device-dependent bitmap.

Bits: A pointer to a buffer that receives the bitmap bit values. The application is responsible for allocating enough memory for this pointer to store the bitmap image, and for freeing this memory when it is no longer needed. The first six members of the TBitmapInfoHeader structure contained in the TBitmapInfo structure pointed to by the BitsInfo parameter must be initialized to indicate the dimensions and color format of the requested DIB bit values. If this parameter is NIL, the function fills the TBitmapInfo structure pointed to by the BitsInfo parameter with the dimensions and color format of the device-dependent bitmap specified by the Bitmap parameter. In this case, the biSize member of the TBitmapInfoHeader structure must be set to SizeOf(TBitmapInfoHeader) or the function will fail. In addition, if the biBitCount member is set to zero, the TBitmapInfo structure is filled in without the bitmap's color table. This is useful for querying bitmap attributes.

BitsInfo: A pointer to a TBitmapInfo data structure describing desired format for the DIB, including information about its dimensions and color table. The TBitmapInfo data structure is defined as:

TBitmapInfo = packed record
      bmiHeader: TBitmapInfoHeader;   {bitmap header information}
      bmiColors: array[0..0] of TRGBQuad; {the color table used by the bitmap}
   end;

The TBitmapInfoHeader data structure is defined as:

```
TBitmapInfoHeader = packed record
     biSize: DWORD;              {the size of the structure in bytes}
     biWidth: Longint;           {the width of the bitmap in pixels}
     biHeight: Longint;          {the height of the bitmap in pixels}
     biPlanes: Word;             {the number of color planes}
     biBitCount: Word;           {the bits per pixel required to describe a color}
     biCompression: DWORD;       {compression flags}
     biSizeImage: DWORD;         {the size of the image in bytes}
     biXPelsPerMeter: Longint;   {horizontal pixels per meter of the target device}
     biYPelsPerMeter: Longint;   {vertical pixels per meter of the target device}
     biClrUsed: DWORD;           {the number of color indices used}
     biClrImportant: DWORD;      {the number of important color indices}
end;
```

The TRGBQuad data structure is defined as:

```
TRGBQuad = packed record
     rgbBlue: Byte;       {blue color intensity}
     rgbGreen: Byte;      {green color intensity}
     rgbRed: Byte;        {red color intensity}
     rgbReserved: Byte;   {reserved value}
end;
```

For an explanation of these data structures, see the CreateDIBSection function.

Usage: A flag indicating the type of color information stored in the bmiColors member of the TBitmapInfo structure pointed to by the BitsInfo parameter. This parameter can be one value from Table 12-9.

Return Value

If the function succeeds and the Bits parameter is not NIL, it returns the number of scan lines copied from the device-dependent bitmap. If the function succeeds and the Bits parameter is NIL, the TBitmapInfo structure pointed to by the BitsInfo parameter is initialized with the dimensions and format of the device-dependent bitmap, and the function returns the total number of scan lines in the device-dependent bitmap. If the function fails, it returns zero.

See Also

CreateDIBitmap, CreateDIBSection, GetBitmapBits, SetDIBits

Example

Listing 12-13: Creating a DIB from a device-dependent bitmap

```
procedure TForm1.Button1Click(Sender: TObject);
var
  TheBitmap: HBITMAP;                   // a handle to a regular bitmap
  RegularBitmapInfo: Windows.TBitmap;   // a Windows bitmap information structure
```

```
      BitmapInfo: PBitmapInfo;              // a pointer to a DIB info structure
      BitmapBits: Pointer;                  // a pointer to DIB bit values
    begin
      {get a handle to a system bitmap}
      TheBitmap:=LoadBitmap(0, MakeIntResource(OBM_CHECKBOXES));

      {fill in a Windows TBITMAP information structure}
      GetObject(TheBitmap, SizeOf(Windows.TBitmap), @RegularBitmapInfo);

      {get the memory for the DIB bitmap header}
      GetMem(BitmapInfo, SizeOf(TBitmapInfo)+256*SizeOf(TRGBQuad));

      {initialize the bitmap information}
      BitmapInfo^.bmiHeader.biWidth         := RegularBitmapInfo.bmWidth;
      BitmapInfo^.bmiHeader.biHeight        := RegularBitmapInfo.bmHeight;
      BitmapInfo^.bmiHeader.biPlanes        := 1;
      BitmapInfo^.bmiHeader.biBitCount      := 8;       // 256 colors
      BitmapInfo^.bmiHeader.biCompression   := BI_RGB;  // no compression
      BitmapInfo^.bmiHeader.biSizeImage     := 0;       // let Windows determine size
      BitmapInfo^.bmiHeader.biXPelsPerMeter := 0;
      BitmapInfo^.bmiHeader.biYPelsPerMeter := 0;
      BitmapInfo^.bmiHeader.biClrUsed       := 0;
      BitmapInfo^.bmiHeader.biClrImportant  := 0;
      BitmapInfo^.bmiHeader.biSize          := SizeOf(TBitmapInfoHeader);

      {allocate enough memory to hold the bitmap bit values}
      GetMem(BitmapBits,RegularBitmapInfo.bmWidth*RegularBitmapInfo.bmHeight);

      {retrieve the bit values from the regular bitmap in a DIB format}
      GetDIBits(Form1.Canvas.Handle, TheBitmap, 0, RegularBitmapInfo.bmHeight,
                BitmapBits, BitmapInfo^, 0);

      {display this new DIB bitmap}
      SetDIBitsToDevice(Form1.Canvas.Handle, (Form1.Width div 2)-
                        (BitmapInfo^.bmiHeader.biWidth div 2), 25,
                         BitmapInfo^.bmiHeader.biWidth,
                         BitmapInfo^.bmiHeader.biHeight, 0, 0, 0,
                         BitmapInfo^.bmiHeader.biHeight, BitmapBits, BitmapInfo^,
                         DIB_RGB_COLORS);

      {delete the regular bitmap}
      DeleteObject(TheBitmap);

      {cleanup allocated memory}
      FreeMem(BitmapInfo, SizeOf(TBitmapInfo)+256*SizeOf(TRGBQuad));
      FreeMem(BitmapBits,RegularBitmapInfo.bmWidth*RegularBitmapInfo.bmHeight);
    end;
```

Figure 12-14:
The DIB image created from a device-dependent bitmap

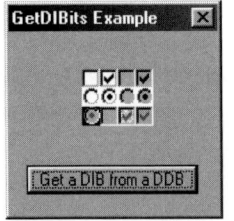

Table 12-9: GetDIBits Usage values

Value	Description
DIB_PAL_COLORS	The bmiColors member of the TBitmapInfo structure is an array of 16-bit indices into the currently realized logical palette of the specified device context. This value should not be used if the bitmap will be saved to disk.
DIB_RGB_COLORS	The bmiColors member of the TBitmapInfo structure is an array of literal RGB color values.

GetEnhMetaFile   Windows.pas

Syntax

```
GetEnhMetaFile(
  p1: PChar            {an enhanced metafile filename}
): HENHMETAFILE;       {returns a handle to an enhanced metafile}
```

Description

This function creates an enhanced metafile and returns its handle, based on the enhanced metafile information stored in the specified file. When the application no longer needs the enhanced metafile, it should be deleted by using the DeleteObject function. This function will only open metafiles in the enhanced format.

Parameters

p1: A null-terminated string containing the filename of the enhanced metafile to open.

Return Value

If the function succeeds, it returns a handle to an enhanced metafile; otherwise, it returns zero.

See Also

CreateEnhMetaFile, DeleteEnhMetaFile, GetEnhMetaFileHeader, GetEnhMetaFileDescription

Example

Listing 12-14: Opening enhanced metafiles

```
procedure TForm1.FileListBox1DblClick(Sender: TObject);
var
  TheMetafile: HENHMETAFILE;         // a handle to the original metafile
  CopyMetafile: HENHMETAFILE;        // a handle to the copied metafile
  MetafileInfo: TEnhMetaHeader;      // the metafile header structure
  MetafileDescription: PChar;        // holds the metafile description
  DescriptionSize: UINT;             // holds the size of the description
  CorrectedRect: TRect;              // an aspect ratio corrected rectangle
  ScaleVert,                         // these are used to compute the
  ScaleHorz,                         // corrected aspect ratio
  ScaleLeast: Real;
begin
  {open and retrieve a handle to the selected metafile}
```

```
TheMetafile:=GetEnhMetaFile(PChar(FileListBox1.FileName));

{retrieve the size of the description string}
DescriptionSize:=GetEnhMetaFileDescription(TheMetaFile, 0, nil);

{dynamically allocate a buffer large enough to hold the description}
MetafileDescription:=StrAlloc(DescriptionSize+1);

{retrieve the metafile description string, if one exists}
GetEnhMetaFileDescription(TheMetaFile, DescriptionSize, MetafileDescription);

{retrieve the metafile header info}
GetEnhMetaFileHeader(TheMetafile, SizeOf(MetafileInfo), @MetafileInfo);

{find the smallest ratio between the size of the metafile bounding rectangle
 and the TImage rectangle}
ScaleVert:=Image1.Height / (MetafileInfo.rclBounds.Bottom-
                            MetafileInfo.rclBounds.Top);
ScaleHorz:=Image1.Width  / (MetafileInfo.rclBounds.Right-
                            MetafileInfo.rclBounds.Left);

{find the smallest ratio}
if ScaleVert<ScaleHorz then
   ScaleLeast:=ScaleVert
else
   ScaleLeast:=ScaleHorz;

{determine the new bounding rectangle using this scaling factor}
CorrectedRect.Left   :=Trunc(MetafileInfo.rclBounds.Left*ScaleLeast);
CorrectedRect.Top    :=Trunc(MetafileInfo.rclBounds.Top*ScaleLeast);
CorrectedRect.Right  :=Trunc(MetafileInfo.rclBounds.Right*ScaleLeast);
CorrectedRect.Bottom:=Trunc(MetafileInfo.rclBounds.Bottom*ScaleLeast);

{adjust the new bounding rectangle so it starts in the
 upper-left hand corner}
CorrectedRect.Left:=0;
CorrectedRect.Top:=0;
CorrectedRect.Right:=CorrectedRect.Right-CorrectedRect.Left;
CorrectedRect.Bottom:=CorrectedRect.Bottom-CorrectedRect.Top;

{start displaying the metafile information}
with ListBox1.Items do
begin
   Clear;
   Add('Description -');
   if DescriptionSize>0 then
   begin
      {the description is a string in the form of the program name used
       to create the metafile followed by a null terminator, followed
       by the name of the metafile followed by two null terminators. this
       line will display the first part of the description (the name of the
       program used to create the metafile)}
      Add(string(MetafileDescription));

      {by advancing the address of the string one past the first null
       terminator, we gain access the second half containing the
       name of the metafile}
```

```
        Add(string(PChar(MetafileDescription+StrLen(MetafileDescription)+1))));
    end
    else
        Add('No description found.');
    Add('Type: '+IntToStr(MetafileInfo.iType));
    Add('Size: '+IntToStr(MetafileInfo.nSize));
    Add('Bounding Rectangle -');
    Add('        Left: '+IntToStr(MetafileInfo.rclBounds.Left));
    Add('         Top: '+IntToStr(MetafileInfo.rclBounds.Top));
    Add('       Right: '+IntToStr(MetafileInfo.rclBounds.Right));
    Add('      Bottom: '+IntToStr(MetafileInfo.rclBounds.Bottom));
    Add('Frame Rectangle - (1 = .01 millimeters)');
    Add('        Left: '+IntToStr(MetafileInfo.rclFrame.Left));
    Add('         Top: '+IntToStr(MetafileInfo.rclFrame.Top));
    Add('       Right: '+IntToStr(MetafileInfo.rclFrame.Right));
    Add('      Bottom: '+IntToStr(MetafileInfo.rclFrame.Bottom));
    Add('Signature: '+IntToStr(MetafileInfo.dSignature));
    Add('Version: '+IntToStr(MetafileInfo.nVersion));
    Add('Bytes: '+IntToStr(MetafileInfo.nBytes));
    Add('Records: '+IntToStr(MetafileInfo.nRecords));
    Add('Handles: '+IntToStr(MetafileInfo.nHandles));
    Add('Reserved: '+IntToStr(MetafileInfo.sReserved));
    Add('Description Size: '+IntToStr(MetafileInfo.nDescription));
    Add('Description Offset: '+IntToStr(MetafileInfo.offDescription));
    Add('Palette Entries: '+IntToStr(MetafileInfo.nPalEntries));
    Add('Reference Resolution, Pixels - ');
    Add('          Horizontal: '+IntToStr(MetafileInfo.szlDevice.cx));
    Add('            Vertical: '+IntToStr(MetafileInfo.szlDevice.cy));
end;

{erase any previous images}
Image1.Canvas.Fillrect(Image1.Canvas.Cliprect);
Image2.Canvas.Fillrect(Image2.Canvas.Cliprect);

{display the metafile as it originally appears}
PlayEnhMetaFile(Image1.Canvas.Handle, TheMetafile, CorrectedRect);

{make a copy of the original metafile in memory}
CopyMetafile:=CopyEnhMetaFile(TheMetafile, nil);

{display this copied metafile}
PlayEnhMetaFile(Image2.Canvas.Handle, CopyMetafile, Image1.Canvas.Cliprect);

{delete the handles to both metafiles, as they are no longer needed}
DeleteEnhMetaFile(TheMetafile);
DeleteEnhMetaFile(CopyMetafile);

{return the memory allocated for the description string}
StrDispose(MetafileDescription);
end;
```

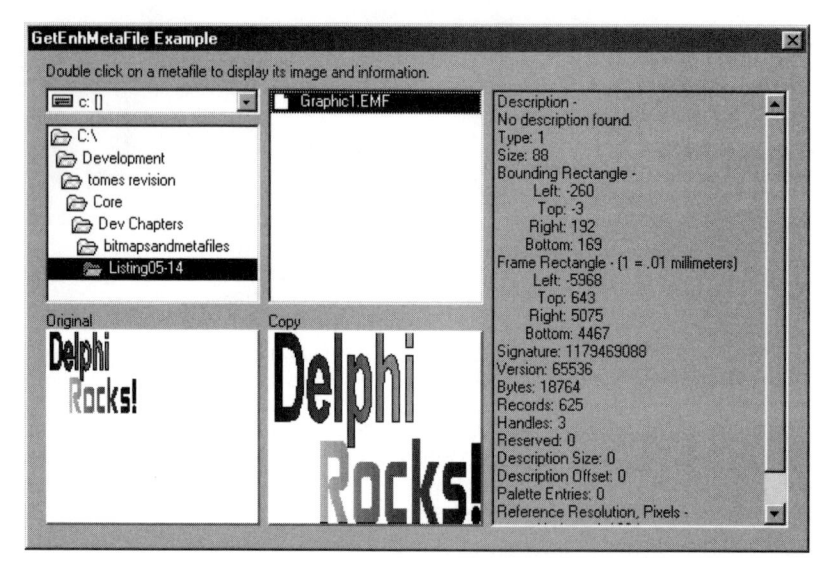

Figure 12-15: An enhanced metafile

GetEnhMetaFileDescription   Windows.pas

Syntax

```
GetEnhMetaFileDescription(
  p1: HENHMETAFILE;       {a handle to a metafile}
  p2: UINT;               {the size of the buffer pointed to by the p3 parameter}
  p3: PChar               {a pointer to a buffer}
): UINT;                  {returns the length of the description}
```

Description

This function extracts a description string from an enhanced metafile, copying it to the specified buffer. This description is optional, so some enhanced metafiles may not contain one. The description string contains two individual strings, separated by a null character and terminated by two null characters (i.e., 'CreateEnhMetaFile Example Program'+Chr(0)+'Example Metafile'+Chr(0)+Chr(0)). Typically, the first string contains the name of the graphics package that created the enhanced metafile, and the second string contains the title of the enhanced metafile picture. See the CreateEnhMetaFile function for information on including a description in an enhanced metafile.

Windows 95: The maximum length for the description string is 16,384 bytes.

Parameters

p1: A handle to the metafile whose description string is to be retrieved.

p2: Specifies the size of the text buffer pointed to by the p3 parameter, in characters. If the description string is longer than this value, it will be truncated.

p3: A pointer to a text buffer that receives the description string. This parameter can be NIL.

Return Value

If the function succeeds, it returns the number of characters copied into the buffer. If the function succeeds and the p3 parameter contains a value of NIL, it returns the length of the description string in characters. If the description string does not exist, it returns zero. If the function fails, it returns GDI_ERROR.

See Also

CreateEnhMetaFile

Example

See Listing 12-14 under GetEnhMetaFile.

GetEnhMetaFileHeader   Windows.pas

Syntax

```
GetEnhMetaFileHeader(
p1: HENHMETAFILE;         {a handle to an enhanced metafile}
p2: UINT;                 {the size of the buffer pointed to by the p3 parameter}
p3: PEnhMetaHeader        {a pointer to a TEnhMetaHeader record}
): UINT;                  {returns the number of bytes copied}
```

Description

This function retrieves the record containing header information for the specified enhanced metafile. The header information completely describes the enhanced metafile, including such things as its color palette, its dimensions, and its size.

Parameters

p1: A handle to the enhanced metafile whose header information is to be retrieved.

p2: Specifies the size of the buffer pointed to by the p3 parameter in bytes. This should be set to SizeOf(TEnhMetaHeader).

p3: A pointer to a TEnhMetaHeader structure that receives the information about the specified enhanced metafile. This parameter can be NIL. The TEnhMetaHeader structure is defined as:

```
TEnhMetaHeader = packed record
    iType: DWORD;              {the record type identifier}
    nSize: DWORD;              {the enhanced metafile record size, in bytes}
    rclBounds: TRect;          {the bounding rectangle dimensions}
    rclFrame: TRect;           {the rectangular picture dimensions}
    dSignature: DWORD;         {the enhanced metafile signature}
    nVersion: DWORD;           {the enhanced metafile version}
    nBytes: DWORD;             {the size of the enhanced metafile in bytes}
    nRecords: DWORD;           {the number of records in the enhanced metafile}
    nHandles: Word;            {the number of handles in the handle table}
    sReserved: Word;           {a reserved value}
```

```
            nDescription: DWORD;        {the number of characters in the description string}
            offDescription: DWORD;      {the offset to the description string}
            nPalEntries: DWORD;         {the number of entries in the color palette}
            szlDevice: TSize;           {the reference device resolution in pixels}
            szlMillimeters: TSize;      { the reference device resolution in millimeters}
    end;
```

iType: This is set to the enhanced metafile record identifier EMR_HEADER.

nSize: Specifies the size of the TEnhMetaHeader record structure in bytes.

rclBounds: A TRect structure containing the coordinates in device units of the smallest rectangle that completely contains the picture stored in the enhanced metafile. These dimensions are provided by the GDI.

rclFrame: A TRect structure containing the coordinates, in .01 millimeter units, of the rectangle surrounding the picture stored in the enhanced metafile. These coordinates are provided by the function that originally created the enhanced metafile.

dSignature: This is set to the metafile signature constant ENHMETA_SIGNATURE.

nVersion: The metafile version. The most current version at the time of this writing is $10000.

nBytes: The size of the enhanced metafile in bytes.

nRecords: The number of records stored in the metafile.

nHandles: The number of handles stored in the enhanced metafile handle table. Note that index 0 of this table is reserved.

sReserved: This member is reserved and is set to zero.

nDescription: The number of characters in the optional enhanced metafile description string. If the enhanced metafile does not contain a description string, this member is set to zero.

offDescription: The offset from the beginning of the TEnhMetaHeader record to the array containing the characters of the optional enhanced metafile description string. If the enhanced metafile does not contain a description string, this member is set to zero.

nPalEntries: The number of entries in the enhanced metafile's color palette. If the enhanced metafile does not contain a color palette, this member is set to zero.

szlDevice: A TSize structure containing the horizontal and vertical resolution of the reference device for the enhanced metafile, in pixels.

szlMillimeters: A TSize structure containing the horizontal and vertical resolution of the reference device for the enhanced metafile, in millimeters.

Return Value

If the function succeeds, it returns the number of bytes that were copied to the TEnhMetaHeader record structure pointed to by the p3 parameter. If the function succeeds and the p3 parameter is set to NIL, it returns the size of the buffer needed to hold the header information. If the function fails, it returns zero.

GetStretchBltMode   Windows.pas

Syntax

```
GetStretchBltMode(
  DC: HDC            {a handle to a device context}
): Integer;          {returns the bitmap stretch mode}
```

Description

This function retrieves the current bitmap stretch mode. This mode defines how rows and columns of a bitmap are added or removed when the StretchBlt function is called.

Parameters

DC: A handle to the device context whose stretch mode is to be retrieved.

Return Value

If the function succeeds, it returns the current bitmap stretch mode. This can be one value from the following table. If the function fails, it returns zero.

See Also

SetStretchBltMode, StretchBlt

Example

See Listing 12-15 under LoadBitmap.

Table 12-10: GetStretchBltMode return values

Value	Description
BLACKONWHITE	Performs a Boolean AND operation using the color values for eliminated and existing pixels. If the bitmap is a monochrome bitmap, this mode preserves black pixels at the expense of white pixels.
COLORONCOLOR	Deletes pixels without making any attempt to preserve pixel information.
HALFTONE	Maps pixels from the source bitmap into blocks of pixels on the destination bitmap. The destination pixel color is the average of the colors from the source pixels. This mode requires more processing time than the other flags, but produces higher quality images. If this flag is used, the application must call the SetBrushOrgEx function to reset the brush origin or brush misalignment will occur.
STRETCH_ANDSCANS	The same as BLACKONWHITE.
STRETCH_DELETESCANS	The same as COLORONCOLOR.
STRETCH_HALFTONE	The same as HALFTONE.
STRETCH_ORSCANS	The same as WHITEONBLACK.

Value	Description
WHITEONBLACK	Performs a Boolean OR operation using the color values for eliminated and existing pixels. If the bitmap is a monochrome bitmap, this mode preserves white pixels at the expense of black pixels.

LoadBitmap   Windows.pas

Syntax

```
LoadBitmap(
hInstance: HINST;             {an instance handle}
lpBitmapName: PAnsiChar;      {a bitmap resource name}
): HBITMAP;                   {returns a handle to a bitmap}
```

Description

This function loads a bitmap from the executable file's resources, returning its handle. When the application is finished with the bitmap, it should be deleted by calling the DeleteObject function. This function assumes the bitmap will contain only 16 colors. Use the LoadResource function to load bitmaps with a higher color resolution.

Parameters

hInstance: A handle to a module instance whose executable file contains the bitmap resource to load.

lpBitmapName: A pointer to a null-terminated string containing the resource name of the bitmap to load. The MakeIntResource function can be used with a resource identifier to provide a value for this parameter. To load one of the predefined bitmap resources used by the Win32 API, set the hInstance parameter to zero and use the MakeIntResource function with one of the values from Table 12-11 for this parameter.

Return Value

If the function succeeds, it returns a handle to the bitmap loaded from the executable file's resources; otherwise, it returns zero.

See Also

BitBlt, CreateBitmap, CreateBitmapIndirect, CreateCompatibleBitmap, CreateDIBitmap, CreateDIBSection, DeleteObject, LoadResource*, StretchBlt

Example

Listing 12-15: Loading a predefined bitmap

```
procedure TForm1.ComboBox1Change(Sender: TObject);
var
   TheBitmap: HBITMAP;             // holds the bitmap
   BitmapInfo: Windows.TBitmap;    // holds the bitmap information
   OffscreenDC: HDC;               // a handle to an offscreen device context
```

```
{this defines all of the system bitmaps available in Windows}
type
   TBitmapTypes = array[0..25] of Integer;
const
   BitmapTypes: TBitmapTypes = (OBM_CLOSE,OBM_UPARROW,OBM_DNARROW,OBM_RGARROW,
                                OBM_LFARROW,OBM_REDUCE,OBM_ZOOM,OBM_RESTORE,
                                OBM_REDUCED,OBM_ZOOMD,OBM_RESTORED,OBM_UPARROWD,
                                OBM_DNARROWD,OBM_RGARROWD,OBM_LFARROWD,
                                OBM_MNARROW,OBM_COMBO,OBM_UPARROWI,OBM_DNARROWI,
                                OBM_RGARROWI,OBM_LFARROWI,OBM_BTSIZE,
                                OBM_CHECK,OBM_CHECKBOXES,OBM_BTNCORNERS,
                                OBM_SIZE);
begin
   {erase the last images}
   Image1.Canvas.Brush.Color:=clBtnFace;
   Image2.Canvas.Brush.Color:=clBtnFace;
   Image1.Canvas.Fillrect(Image1.Canvas.Cliprect);
   Image2.Canvas.Fillrect(Image2.Canvas.Cliprect);

   {load the selected bitmap}
   TheBitmap:=LoadBitmap(0, MakeIntResource(BitmapTypes[ComboBox1.ItemIndex]));

   {create an offscreen device context and select the bitmap into it}
   OffscreenDC:=CreateCompatibleDC(0);
   SelectObject(OffscreenDC, TheBitmap);

   {fill in a BITMAP information structure}
   GetObject(TheBitmap, SizeOf(Windows.TBitmap), @BitmapInfo);

   {draw the bitmap into Image1}
   BitBlt(Image1.Canvas.Handle, 45,45,Image1.Width, Image1.Height,OffscreenDC,
          0,0,SRCCOPY);

   {verify the stretch mode in Image2 is what we want}
   if GetStretchBltMode(Image2.Canvas.Handle)<>COLORONCOLOR then
      SetStretchBltMode(Image2.Canvas.Handle, COLORONCOLOR);

   {draw the bitmap into Image2, stretching it to fill the image}
   StretchBlt(Image2.Canvas.Handle, 0, 0, Image2.Width, Image2.Height,
              OffscreenDC, 0, 0, BitmapInfo.bmWidth, BitmapInfo.bmHeight,
              SRCCOPY);

   {delete the bitmap}
   DeleteObject(TheBitmap);

   {delete the offscreen device context}
   DeleteDC(OffscreenDC);
end;
```

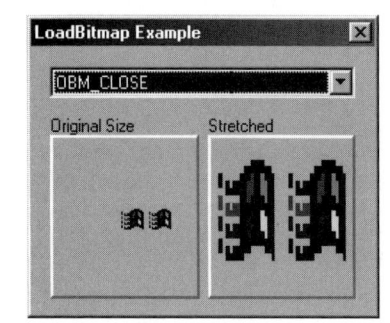

Figure 12-16:
A predefined bitmap resource

Table 12-11: LoadBitmap lpBitmapName values

Value	Description
OBM_BTNCORNERS	Loads the bitmap resource for the system corner marker.
OBM_BTSIZE	Loads the bitmap resource for the sizing button.
OBM_CHECK	Loads the bitmap resource for the default check mark.
OBM_CHECKBOXES	Loads the collection of system check box symbols.
OBM_CLOSE	Loads the default system menu icon resource.
OBM_COMBO	Loads the bitmap resource for the combo box drop-down arrow.
OBM_DNARROW	Loads the bitmap resource for a scroll bar down arrow in an up state.
OBM_DNARROWD	Loads the bitmap resource for a scroll bar down arrow in a down state.
OBM_DNARROWI	Loads the bitmap resource for a scroll bar down arrow in a disabled state.
OBM_LFARROW	Loads the bitmap resource for a scroll bar left arrow in an up state.
OBM_LFARROWD	Loads the bitmap resource for a scroll bar left arrow in a down state.
OBM_LFARROWI	Loads the bitmap resource for a scroll bar left arrow in a disabled state.
OBM_MNARROW	Loads the bitmap resource used to indicate a menu item that contains a submenu.
OBM_REDUCE	Loads the bitmap resource for a minimize button in an up state.
OBM_REDUCED	Loads the bitmap resource for a minimize button in a down state.
OBM_RESTORE	Loads the bitmap resource for a restore button in an up state.
OBM_RESTORED	Loads the bitmap resource for a restore button in a down state.
OBM_RGARROW	Loads the bitmap resource for a scroll bar right arrow in an up state.
OBM_RGARROWD	Loads the bitmap resource for a scroll bar right arrow in a down state.
OBM_RGARROWI	Loads the bitmap resource for a scroll bar right arrow in a disabled state.
OBM_SIZE	Loads the bitmap resource for the sizing corner.
OBM_UPARROW	Loads the bitmap resource for a scroll bar up arrow in an up state.
OBM_UPARROWD	Loads the bitmap resource for a scroll bar up arrow in a down state.
OBM_UPARROWI	Loads the bitmap resource for a scroll bar up arrow in a disabled state.
OBM_ZOOM	Loads the bitmap resource for a maximize button in an up state.
OBM_ZOOMD	Loads the bitmap resource for a maximize button in a down state.

LoadImage   Windows.pas

Syntax

```
LoadImage(
hInst: HINST;            {a handle of the instance containing the image}
ImageName: PChar;        {the image name}
ImageType: UINT;         {the image type flag}
X: Integer;              {width of new image}
Y: Integer;              {height of new image}
Flags: UINT              {the load operation flags}
): THandle;              {returns a handle to the loaded image}
```

Description

This function loads an icon, cursor, enhanced metafile, or bitmap from either a file or the executable resources. The image can be sized as desired, and numerous options affect the final loaded image.

Parameters

hInst: A handle to the module instance containing the image to be loaded.

ImageName: A pointer to a null-terminated string containing the name of the image resource to be loaded. If the Flags parameter contains the LR_LOADFROMFILE flag, this parameter contains a pointer to a null-terminated string specifying the filename of the image to load.

ImageType: A flag indicating the type of image to be loaded. This parameter can be one value from Table 12-12.

X: Indicates the desired width of the image in pixels. If this parameter is set to zero and the Flags parameter does not contain the LR_DEFAULTSIZE flag, the loaded image width is set to the width of the original resource. If this parameter is set to zero and the Flags parameter contains the LR_DEFAULTSIZE flag, the width is set to the value returned from GetSystemMetrics(SM_CXICON) or GetSystemMetrics(SM_CXCURSOR), depending on whether the loaded image is an icon or cursor.

Y: Indicates the desired height of the image in pixels. If this parameter is set to zero and the Flags parameter does not contain the LR_DEFAULTSIZE flag, the loaded image height is set to the height of the original resource. If this parameter is zero and the Flags parameter contains the LR_DEFAULTSIZE flag, the height is set to the value returned from GetSystemMetrics(SM_CYICON) or GetSystemMetrics(SM_CYCURSOR), depending on whether the loaded image is an icon or cursor.

Flags: A value indicating additional actions performed when the image is loaded. This parameter can be one or more values from Table 12-13.

Return Value

If the function succeeds, it returns a handle to the loaded image; otherwise, it returns zero.

See Also

CopyImage, GetSystemMetrics*, LoadBitmap, LoadCursor*, LoadIcon*

Example

Listing 12-16: Loading bitmap images from files

```
procedure TForm1.FileListBox1Click(Sender: TObject);
var
  TheBitmap: THandle;            // holds a newly loaded bitmap image
  BitmapInfo: Windows.TBitmap;   // holds the bitmap information
  TheOffscreenDC: HDC;           // holds a handle to a memory device context
begin
  {create a memory device context}
  TheOffscreenDC := CreateCompatibleDC(0);

  {load the specified bitmap file}
  TheBitmap := LoadImage(0,PChar(FileListBox1.FileName),IMAGE_BITMAP,0,0,
                         LR_LOADFROMFILE);

  {retrieve information about the bitmap (width and height will be used)}
  GetObject(TheBitmap, SizeOf(Windows.TBitmap), @BitmapInfo);

  {select the bitmap into the memory device context}
  SelectObject(TheOffscreenDC, TheBitmap);

  {copy the image to Image1 at its original size}
  BitBlt(Image1.Canvas.Handle,0,0,Image1.Width,Image1.Height,TheOffscreenDC,
         0,0,SRCCOPY);

  {copy the image to Image2, and compress it to fit}
  StretchBlt(Image2.Canvas.Handle,0,0,Image2.Width,Image2.Height,TheOffscreenDC,
             0,0,BitmapInfo.bmWidth,BitmapInfo.bmHeight,SRCCOPY);

  {update the images on screen}
  Image1.Refresh;
  Image2.Refresh;

  {delete the loaded image and the offscreen device context}
  DeleteDC(TheOffscreenDC);
  DeleteObject(TheBitmap);
end;
```

Bitmap and Metafile Functions 587

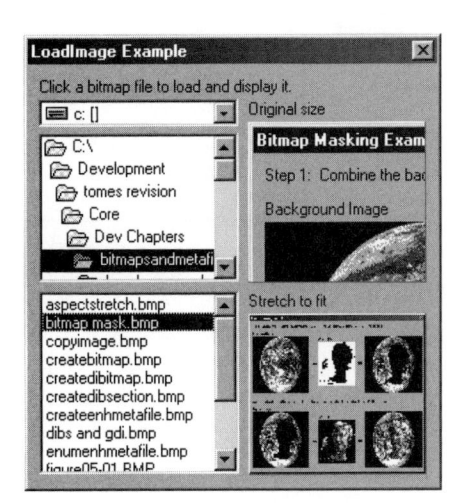

*Figure 12-17:
The loaded
bitmap image*

Table 12-12: LoadImage ImageType values

Value	Description
IMAGE_BITMAP	The image is a bitmap.
IMAGE_CURSOR	The image is a cursor.
IMAGE_ENHMETAFILE	The image is an enhanced metafile.
IMAGE_ICON	The image is an icon.

Table 12-13: LoadImage Flags values

Value	Description
LR_CREATEDIBSECTION	If the ImageType parameter contains the value IMAGE_BITMAP, this function returns a handle to a DIB section bitmap.
LR_DEFAULTCOLOR	Loads the image in its defined color format. This is the default flag.
LR_DEFAULTSIZE	For icon or cursor images only, this flag causes the function to load the image using the default width and height as reported by the GetSystem-Metrics function.
LR_LOADFROMFILE	Indicates that the null-terminated string pointed to by the ImageName parameter contains a filename, and the image is loaded from disk.
LR_LOADMAP3DCOLORS	Searches the pixels of the loaded image, and replaces dark gray pixels (RGB(128,128,128)) with the COLOR_3DSHADOW system color, replaces gray pixels (RGB(192,192,192)) with the COLOR_3DFACE system color, and replaces light gray pixels (RGB(223,223,223)) with the COLOR_3DLIGHT system color.
LR_LOADTRANSPARENT	Retrieves the color value of the first pixel in the image, replacing all pixels in the image of the same color with the COLOR_WINDOW system color. This has the same effect as blitting the image to the canvas using the BrushCopy function. If the LR_LOADMAP3DCOLORS flag is included, LR_LOAD-TRANSPARENT takes precedence, but replaces the indicated pixel color with the COLOR_3DFACE system color.
LR_MONOCHROME	Creates a black and white version of the original image.

Value	Description
LR_SHARED	For resources, this flag causes the function to return the same handle for identical resources loaded multiple times. Without this flag, LoadImage returns a different handle when the same resource is loaded. Do not specify this flag for images loaded from files, or for images that will change after loading.

PatBlt   Windows.pas

Syntax

```
PatBlt(
DC: HDC;              {a handle to a device context}
X: Integer;           {the horizontal start coordinate of rectangle to be filled}
Y: Integer;           {the vertical start coordinate of rectangle to be filled}
Width: Integer;       {the width of the rectangle to be filled}
Height: Integer;      {the height of the rectangle to be filled}
Rop: DWORD            {the raster operation flag}
): BOOL;              {returns TRUE or FALSE}
```

Description

This function fills a rectangle using the brush currently selected into the specified device context, combining the colors of the brush and the destination using the specified raster operation. Some devices may not support the PatBlt function; use the GetDeviceCaps function to determine if the target device supports bit block transfers.

Parameters

DC: A handle to the device context upon which the filled rectangle is drawn.

X: The horizontal coordinate of the upper-left corner of the rectangle to be filled in logical units.

Y: The vertical coordinate of the upper-left corner of the rectangle to be filled in logical units.

Width: The width of the rectangle to be filled in logical units.

Height: The height of the rectangle to be filled in logical units.

Rop: A raster operation code. This determines how the pixels of the brush used to paint the rectangle are combined with the pixels on the device context, and can be one value from the following table.

Return Value

If the function succeeds, it returns TRUE; otherwise, it returns FALSE. To get extended error information, call the GetLastError function.

See Also

GetDeviceCaps, CreateBrush, CreatePatternBrush

Example

Listing 12-17: Filling a background

```
procedure TForm1.Button1Click(Sender: TObject);
var
  BitmapPattern: HBITMAP;      // holds the bitmap brush pattern
  PatternBrush: HBRUSH;        // holds the handle to the patterned brush
  OldBrush: HBRUSH;            // tracks the original brush
begin
  {load a bitmap from the resource file}
  BitmapPattern := LoadBitmap(hInstance, 'BRUSHPATTERN');

  {use it to create a patterned brush}
  PatternBrush := CreatePatternBrush(BitmapPattern);

  {select this new brush into the main form's device context}
  OldBrush := SelectObject(Canvas.Handle, PatternBrush);

  {paint a pattern filled rectangle}
  PatBlt(Canvas.Handle, 0, 0, Width, Height, PATINVERT);

  {replace the original brush handle}
  SelectObject(Canvas.Handle, OldBrush);

  {we no longer need the patterned brush or the bitmap, so delete them}
  DeleteObject(PatternBrush);
  DeleteObject(BitmapPattern);
end;
```

*Figure 12-18:
The pattern
brush result*

Table 12-14: PatBlt Rop values

Value	Description
BLACKNESS	Fills the pixels in the specified rectangle in the destination with the color in index 0 of the physical palette. By default, this color is black.
DSTINVERT	Inverts the colors of the pixels in the specified rectangle in the destination.
PATCOPY	Copies the pattern contained in the brush selected into the destination device context directly into the destination.
PATINVERT	Combines the pixel colors of the pattern contained in the brush selected into the destination device context with the colors of the pixels in the destination using the Boolean XOR operator.
WHITENESS	Fills the pixels in the specified rectangle in the destination with the color in index 255 of the physical palette. By default, this color is white.

PlayEnhMetaFile   Windows.pas

Syntax

```
PlayEnhMetaFile(
DC: HDC;                  {a handle to a device context}
p2: HENHMETAFILE;         {a handle to an enhanced metafile}
const p3: TRect           {a pointer to a rectangle structure}
): BOOL;                  {returns TRUE or FALSE}
```

Description

This function displays the enhanced metafile identified by the p2 parameter on the specified device context. The metafile can be clipped by defining a clipping region in the device context before playing the metafile. If the enhanced metafile contains a color palette, the application can maintain color consistency by creating and realizing a color palette into the device context before playing the metafile. Use the GetEnhMetaFilePaletteEntries function to retrieve the color palette of the enhanced metafile. An enhanced metafile can be embedding into a newly created enhanced metafile by using this function to play the metafile into the device context for the new metafile. The state of the specified device context is preserved by this function. If an object was created but not deleted when the original metafile was created, this function deletes the errant object after the metafile is played.

Parameters

DC: A handle to the device context upon which the enhanced metafile will be drawn.

p2: A handle to the enhanced metafile to draw.

p3: A pointer to a TRect structure. The enhanced metafile will be drawn within the coordinates specified by this structure. These coordinates are specified in logical units. The rclFrame member of the enhanced metafile header is used to map the metafile into the specified rectangular coordinates.

Return Value

If the function succeeds, it returns TRUE; otherwise, it returns FALSE. To get extended error information, call the GetLastError function.

See Also

CreateEnhMetaFile, GetEnhMetaFile, GetEnhMetaFileHeader, PlayEnhMetaFileRecord

Example

See Listing 12-10 under CreateEnhMetaFile.

PlayEnhMetaFileRecord   Windows.pas

Syntax

```
PlayEnhMetaFileRecord(
DC: HDC;                     {a handle to a device context}
var p2: THandleTable;        {a pointer to a metafile handle table}
const p3: TEnhMetaRecord;    {a pointer to a metafile record}
p4: UINT                     {the number of handles in the metafile handle table}
): BOOL;                     {returns TRUE or FALSE}
```

Description

This function executes the GDI functions identified by the enhanced metafile record. PlayEnhMetaRecord is intended to be used with the EnumEnhMetaFile function to process and play an enhanced metafile one record at a time. The DC, p2, and p3 parameters must exactly match the device context, handle table, and handle table count passed to the callback function used by the EnumEnhMetaFile function. If the record passed in the p3 parameter is not recognized, it is ignored and the function returns a value of TRUE.

Parameters

DC: A handle to the device context upon which the enhanced metafile is being played.

p2: A pointer to a table of GDI object handles. These objects define the enhanced metafile picture.

p3: A pointer to the TEnhMetaRecord structure defining the enhanced metafile record to be played. The TEnhMetaRecord is defined as:

```
TEnhMetaRecord = packed record
     iType: DWORD;                  {the enhanced metafile record identifier}
     nSize: DWORD;                  {the size of the record in bytes}
     dParm: array[0..0] of DWORD;   {an array of parameters}
end;
```

See the EnumEnhMetaFile callback function for an explanation of this structure.

p4: A count of the number of handles stored in the enhanced metafile handle table.

Return Value

If the function succeeds, it returns TRUE; otherwise, it returns FALSE.

See Also

EnumEnhMetaFile, PlayEnhMetaFile

Example

See Listing 12-11 under EnumEnhMetaFile.

SetBitmapBits   Windows.pas

Syntax

```
SetBitmapBits(
  p1: HBITMAP;            {a handle to a bitmap}
  p2: DWORD;              {the number of bytes in the bits array}
  bits: Pointer           {a pointer to an array of bytes}
): Longint;               {returns the number of bytes used to set the bitmap}
```

Description

This function sets the image for the specified bitmap from the values stored in the bits array. The SetBitmapBits function is included for compatibility purposes. Win32-based applications should use the SetDIBits function.

Parameters

p1: A handle to the bitmap whose image will be set from the values in the array pointed to by the bits parameter.

p2: Specifies the number of bytes pointed to by the bits parameter.

bits: A pointer to an array of bytes containing the image data for the bitmap.

Return Value

If the function succeeds, it returns the number of bytes used to set the bitmap bits; otherwise, it returns zero.

See Also

CreateBitmap, GetBitmapBits, SetDIBits

Example

Listing 12-18: Setting the bitmap bits

```
{This example will run properly only with a 256 color video driver.}
var
   Started: Boolean = FALSE;           // controls the overall loop

procedure TForm1.Button1Click(Sender: TObject);
var
   BitmapBits: array[0..9999] of byte;   // holds the new bitmap bit information
   BitmapImage: TBitmap;                 // the bitmap image
   Loop: Integer;                        // a general loop counter
begin
   {toggle the loop control variable}
   Started:=not Started;

   {change the button caption to reflect the new state}
   if Started then
     Button1.Caption := 'Stop'
   else
     Button1.Caption := 'Start';
```

```
{create a 100X100 pixel bitmap}
BitmapImage := TBitmap.Create;
BitmapImage.Height := 100;
BitmapImage.Width := 100;

{force this to be a device-dependent bitmap}
BitmapImage.HandleType := bmDDB;

{this loop continues until the button is pressed again}
while Started do
begin
  {fill the bitmap bit information with white}
  FillChar(BitmapBits, SizeOf(BitmapBits), 255);

  {set 10000 random pixels to black}
  for Loop := 0 to 1000 do
  begin
    BitmapBits[Random(100)*100+Random(100)]:=0;
    BitmapBits[Random(100)*100+Random(100)]:=0;
    BitmapBits[Random(100)*100+Random(100)]:=0;
    BitmapBits[Random(100)*100+Random(100)]:=0;
    BitmapBits[Random(100)*100+Random(100)]:=0;
    BitmapBits[Random(100)*100+Random(100)]:=0;
    BitmapBits[Random(100)*100+Random(100)]:=0;
    BitmapBits[Random(100)*100+Random(100)]:=0;
    BitmapBits[Random(100)*100+Random(100)]:=0;
    BitmapBits[Random(100)*100+Random(100)]:=0;
  end;

  {blast the new bits into the bitmap}
  SetBitmapBits(BitmapImage.Handle, 10000, @BitmapBits);

  {copy the bitmap to the canvas of the form}
  BitBlt(Form1.Canvas.Handle, 84, 8, 100, 100, BitmapImage.Canvas.Handle, 0,
         0, SRCCOPY);

  {this is required for proper Windows operation}
  Application.ProcessMessages;
end;

{free our bitmap}
BitmapImage.Free
end;
```

Figure 12-19: Using SetBitmapBits to produce a TV snow effect

SetBitmapDimensionEx   Windows.pas

Syntax

```
SetBitmapDimensionEx(
  hBitmap: HBITMAP;        {a handle to a bitmap}
  Width: Integer;          {the preferred width of the bitmap}
  Height: Integer;         {the preferred height of the bitmap}
  Size: PSize              {a pointer to a TSize structure}
): BOOL;                   {returns TRUE or FALSE}
```

Description

This function sets the preferred width and height of the specified bitmap, in terms of 0.1 millimeter units. These dimensions are for application-specific use, do not affect the appearance of the bitmap image, and are not used by Windows. Once set, these dimensions can be retrieved using the GetBitmapDimensionEx function.

Parameters

hBitmap: A handle to a bitmap whose preferred dimensions are to be set. This cannot be a handle to a bitmap returned by the CreateDIBSection function.

Width: An integer specifying the bitmap's preferred width in terms of 0.1 millimeter units.

Height: An integer specifying the bitmap's preferred height in terms of 0.1 millimeter units.

Size: A pointer to a TSize structure that will receive the previously set dimensions. This parameter can be NIL.

Return Value

If the function succeeds, it returns TRUE; otherwise, it returns FALSE. To get extended error information, call the GetLastError function.

See Also

GetBitmapDimensionEx

Example

See Listing 12-5 under CreateBitmap.

SetDIBits   Windows.pas

Syntax

```
SetDIBits(
  DC: HDC;                      {a handle to a device context}
  Bitmap: HBITMAP;              {a handle to a regular bitmap}
  StartScan: UINT;              {the starting scan line}
  NumScans: UINT;               {the total number of scan lines}
  Bits: Pointer;                {a pointer to the DIB bitmap bit values}
  var BitsInfo: TBitmapInfo;    {a pointer to the DIB bitmap information structure}
```

Usage: UINT	{color type flags}	
): Integer;	{returns the number of scan lines copied}	

Description

This function copies the bit values from the specified area in the DIB bit values pointed to by the Bits parameter directly into the device-dependent bitmap indicated by the Bitmap parameter. Note that optimal bitmap copy speed is obtained when the DIB bitmap bits specify indices into the system palette.

Parameters

DC: A handle to a device context. If the DIB_PAL_COLORS flag is specified in the Usage parameter, the bit values copied from the DIB use the colors in the currently realized palette of this device context. If the DIB_PAL_COLORS flag is not specified, this parameter is ignored.

Bitmap: A handle to the bitmap whose bit values are being set.

StartScan: Specifies the scan line to start the copy operation from in the DIB image pointed to by the Bits parameter.

NumScans: Specifies the number of scan lines to copy to the device-dependent bitmap from the image pointed to by the Bits parameter.

Bits: A pointer to the image representing the DIB, in the form of an array of bytes.

BitsInfo: A pointer to a TBitmapInfo data structure describing the DIB, including information about its dimensions and color table. The TBitmapInfo data structure is defined as:

```
TBitmapInfo = packed record
    bmiHeader: TBitmapInfoHeader;       {bitmap header information}
    bmiColors: array[0..0] of TRGBQuad; {the color table used by the bitmap}
end;
```

The TBitmapInfoHeader data structure is defined as:

```
TBitmapInfoHeader = packed record
    biSize: DWORD;              {the size of the structure in bytes}
    biWidth: Longint;           {the width of the bitmap in pixels}
    biHeight: Longint;          {the height of the bitmap in pixels}
    biPlanes: Word;             {the number of color planes}
    biBitCount: Word;           {the bits per pixel required to describe a color}
    biCompression: DWORD;       {compression flags}
    biSizeImage: DWORD;         {the size of the image in bytes}
    biXPelsPerMeter: Longint;   {horizontal pixels per meter of the target device}
    biYPelsPerMeter: Longint;   {vertical pixels per meter of the target device}
    biClrUsed: DWORD;           {the number of color indices used}
    biClrImportant: DWORD;      {the number of important color indices}
end;
```

Chapter 12

The TRGBQuad data structure is defined as:

```
TRGBQuad = packed record
    rgbBlue: Byte;              {blue color intensity}
    rgbGreen: Byte;             {green color intensity}
    rgbRed: Byte;               {red color intensity}
    rgbReserved: Byte;          {reserved value}
end;
```

For an explanation of these data structures, see the CreateDIBSection function.

Usage: A flag indicating the type of color information stored in the bmiColors member of the TBitmapInfo structure pointed to by the BitsInfo parameter. This parameter can be one value from Table 12-15.

Return Value

If the function succeeds, it returns the number of scan lines that were copied to the device-dependent bitmap; otherwise, it returns zero. To get extended error information, call the GetLastError function.

See Also

BitBlt, CreateBitmap, GetDIBits, SetBitmapBits

Example

Listing 12-19: Setting the image of a DDB from a DIB

```
{This example will run properly only with a 256 color video driver.}
var
    Started: Boolean = FALSE;           // controls the overall loop

procedure TForm1.Button1Click(Sender: TObject);
var
    TheBitmap: HBitmap;         // a handle for a regular bitmap
    OffScreen: HDC;             // an offscreen device context
    Dib: HBITMAP;               // holds a handle to the device-independent bitmap
    DibInfo: PBitmapInfo;       // a pointer to the bitmap information data structure
    BitsPtr: PByte;             // holds a pointer to the bitmap bits
    ReferenceDC: HDC;           // a handle to the reference device context
    Loop: Integer;              // a general loop counter

    SystemPalette: array[0..255] of TPaletteEntry;  // required for converting the
                                                    // system palette into a DIB
                                                    // compatible palette
begin
    {toggle the loop control variable}
    Started := not Started;

    {change the button caption to reflect the new state}
    if Started then
        Button1.Caption := 'Stop'
    else
        Button1.Caption := 'Start';
```

```
{create a 128 X 128 pixel bitmap}
TheBitmap := CreateBitmap(128, 128, 1, 8, nil);

{create an offscreen device context that is
 compatible with the screen}
OffScreen := CreateCompatibleDC(0);

{select the new bitmap into the offscreen device context}
SelectObject(OffScreen, TheBitmap);

{get the memory needed for the bitmap information data structure}
GetMem(DibInfo, SizeOf(TBitmapInfo)+256*SizeOf(TRGBQuad));

{initialize the bitmap information}
DibInfo^.bmiHeader.biWidth         := 128;     // create a 128 X 128 pixel
DibInfo^.bmiHeader.biHeight        := -128;    // oriented top-down
DibInfo^.bmiHeader.biPlanes        := 1;
DibInfo^.bmiHeader.biBitCount      := 8;       // 256 colors
DibInfo^.bmiHeader.biCompression   := BI_RGB;  // no compression
DibInfo^.bmiHeader.biSizeImage     := 0;       // let Windows determine size
DibInfo^.bmiHeader.biXPelsPerMeter := 0;
DibInfo^.bmiHeader.biYPelsPerMeter := 0;
DibInfo^.bmiHeader.biClrUsed       := 0;
DibInfo^.bmiHeader.biClrImportant  := 0;
DibInfo^.bmiHeader.biSize          := SizeOf(TBitmapInfoHeader);

{retrieve the current system palette}
GetSystemPaletteEntries(Form1.Canvas.Handle, 0, 256, SystemPalette);

{the system palette is returned as an array of TPaletteEntry structures,
 which store the palette colors in the form of Red, Green, and Blue. however,
 the TBitmapInfo structure's bmiColors member takes an array of TRGBQuad
 structures, which store the palette colors in the form of Blue, Green, and
 Red.  therefore, we must translate the TPaletteEntry structures into the
 appropriate TRGBQuad structures to get the correct color entries.}
for Loop := 0 to 255 do
begin
  DibInfo^.bmiColors[Loop].rgbBlue     := SystemPalette[Loop].peBlue;
  DibInfo^.bmiColors[Loop].rgbRed      := SystemPalette[Loop].peRed;
  DibInfo^.bmiColors[Loop].rgbGreen    := SystemPalette[Loop].peGreen;
  DibInfo^.bmiColors[Loop].rgbReserved := 0;
end;

{create a memory based device context}
ReferenceDC := CreateCompatibleDC(0);

{create the dib based on the memory device context and the
 initialized bitmap information}
Dib := CreateDIBSection(ReferenceDC, DibInfo^, DIB_RGB_COLORS,
                        Pointer(BitsPtr), 0, 0);

{delete the reference device context}
DeleteDC(ReferenceDC);

{this loop continues until the button is pressed again}
while Started do
begin
```

```
   {fill the bitmap bit information with white}
   FillMemory(BitsPtr, 128*128, $FF);

   {set 10000 random pixels to black. this loop has been 'unrolled' somewhat
    for optimization}
   for Loop := 0 to 1000 do
   begin
      PByte(Longint(BitsPtr)+Random(128)*128+Random(128))^ := 0;
      PByte(Longint(BitsPtr)+Random(128)*128+Random(128))^ := 0;
      PByte(Longint(BitsPtr)+Random(128)*128+Random(128))^ := 0;
      PByte(Longint(BitsPtr)+Random(128)*128+Random(128))^ := 0;
      PByte(Longint(BitsPtr)+Random(128)*128+Random(128))^ := 0;
      PByte(Longint(BitsPtr)+Random(128)*128+Random(128))^ := 0;
      PByte(Longint(BitsPtr)+Random(128)*128+Random(128))^ := 0;
      PByte(Longint(BitsPtr)+Random(128)*128+Random(128))^ := 0;
      PByte(Longint(BitsPtr)+Random(128)*128+Random(128))^ := 0;
      PByte(Longint(BitsPtr)+Random(128)*128+Random(128))^ := 0;
      PByte(Longint(BitsPtr)+Random(128)*128+Random(128))^ := 0;
   end;

   {copy the bit values from the DIB directly into the DDB bitmap}
   SetDIBits(Form1.Canvas.Handle, TheBitmap, 0, 128, BitsPtr, DibInfo^,
             DIB_RGB_COLORS);

   {copy the bitmap to the canvas of the form}
   BitBlt(Form1.Canvas.Handle, (Form1.Width div 2)-64, 8, 128, 128,
          Offscreen, 0, 0, SRCCOPY);

   {this is required for proper Windows operation}
   Application.ProcessMessages;
   end;

   {destroy the offscreen device context}
   DeleteDC(Offscreen);

   {free our bitmaps}
   DeleteObject(TheBitmap);
   DeleteObject(Dib);
   FreeMem(DibInfo, SizeOf(TBitmapInfo)+256*SizeOf(TRGBQuad));
end;
```

Figure 12-20: The DDB image was set from bits stored in a DIB

Table 12-15: SetDIBits Usage values

Value	Description
DIB_PAL_COLORS	The bmiColors member of the TBitmapInfo structure is an array of 16-bit indices into the currently realized logical palette of the specified device context. This value should not be used if the bitmap will be saved to disk.
DIB_RGB_COLORS	The bmiColors member of the TBitmapInfo structure is an array of literal RGB color values.

SetDIBitsToDevice *Windows.pas*

Syntax

```
SetDIBitsToDevice(
  DC: HDC;                    {a handle to a device context}
  DestX: Integer;             {the horizontal coordinate of the destination rectangle}
  DestY: Integer;             {the vertical coordinate of the destination rectangle}
  Width: DWORD;               {the width of the DIB}
  Height: DWORD;              {the height of the DIB}
  SrcX: Integer;              {the horizontal coordinate of the source rectangle}
  SrcY: Integer;              {the vertical coordinate of the source rectangle}
  nStartScan: UINT;           {the starting scan line}
  NumScans: UINT;             {the total number of scan lines}
  Bits: Pointer;              {a pointer to the bitmap bit values}
  var BitsInfo: TBitmapInfo;  {a pointer to the DIB bitmap information data structure}
  Usage: UINT                 {color type flags}
): Integer;                   {returns the number of scan lines copied}
```

Description

This function copies pixels from the specified section of the DIB image onto the destination device context. This copy operation can be banded for large device-independent bitmaps by repeatedly calling SetDIBitsToDevice and passing a different portion of the DIB in the nStartScan and NumScans parameters. Note that optimal bitmap copy speed is obtained when the DIB bitmap bits specify indices into the system palette. This function will fail when called by a process running in the background while an MS-DOS process runs full screen in the foreground.

Parameters

DC: The device context upon which the DIB image is copied and displayed.

DestX: The horizontal coordinate of the upper-left corner of the destination rectangle in the destination device context, measured in logical units.

DestY: The vertical coordinate of the upper-left corner of the destination rectangle in the destination device context, measured in logical units.

Width: The width of the DIB image, measured in logical units.

Height: The height of the DIB image, measured in logical units.

SrcX: The horizontal coordinate of the lower-left corner of the DIB, measured in logical units.

SrcY: The vertical coordinate of the lower-left corner of the DIB, measured in logical units.

nStartScan: Specifies the scan line to start the copy operation from in the DIB image pointed to by the Bits parameter.

NumScans: Specifies the number of scan lines to copy to the destination from the image pointed to by the Bits parameter.

Bits: A pointer to the image representing the DIB in the form of an array of bytes.

BitsInfo: A pointer to a TBitmapInfo data structure describing the DIB, including information about its dimensions and color table. The TBitmapInfo data structure is defined as:

```
TBitmapInfo = packed record
    bmiHeader: TBitmapInfoHeader;        {bitmap header information}
    bmiColors: array[0..0] of TRGBQuad;  {the color table used by the bitmap}
end;
```

The TBitmapInfoHeader data structure is defined as:

```
TBitmapInfoHeader = packed record
    biSize: DWORD;                {the size of the structure in bytes}
    biWidth: Longint;             {the width of the bitmap in pixels}
    biHeight: Longint;            {the height of the bitmap in pixels}
    biPlanes: Word;               {the number of color planes}
    biBitCount: Word;             {the bits per pixel required to describe a color}
    biCompression: DWORD;         {compression flags}
    biSizeImage: DWORD;           {the size of the image in bytes}
    biXPelsPerMeter: Longint;     {horizontal pixels per meter of the target device}
    biYPelsPerMeter: Longint;     {vertical pixels per meter of the target device}
    biClrUsed: DWORD;             {the number of color indices used}
    biClrImportant: DWORD;        {the number of important color indices}
end;
```

The TRGBQuad data structure is defined as:

```
TRGBQuad = packed record
    rgbBlue: Byte;        {blue color intensity}
    rgbGreen: Byte;       {green color intensity}
    rgbRed: Byte;         {red color intensity}
    rgbReserved: Byte;    {reserved value}
end;
```

For an explanation of these data structures, see the CreateDIBSection function.

Usage: A flag indicating the type of color information stored in the bmiColors member of the TBitmapInfo structure pointed to by the BitsInfo parameter. This parameter can be one value from the following table.

Return Value

If the function succeeds, it returns the number of scan lines that were copied to the destination device context; otherwise, it returns zero. To get extended error information, call the GetLastError function.

See Also

SetDIBits, StretchDIBits

Example

See Listing 12-9 under CreateDIBSection.

Table 12-16: SetDIBitsToDevice Usage values

Value	Description
DIB_PAL_COLORS	The bmiColors member of the TBitmapInfo structure is an array of 16-bit indices into the currently realized logical palette of the specified device context. This value should not be used if the bitmap will be saved to disk.
DIB_RGB_COLORS	The bmiColors member of the TBitmapInfo structure is an array of literal RGB color values.

SetStretchBltMode   Windows.pas

Syntax

```
SetStretchBltMode(
  DC: HDC;              {a handle to a device context}
  p2: Integer           {the bitmap stretch mode flag}
): Integer;             {returns the previous stretch mode}
```

Description

This function sets the bitmap stretching mode on the specified device context. This mode defines how rows and columns of a bitmap are added or removed when the StretchBlt function is called.

Parameters

DC: A handle to the device context whose bitmap stretch mode is to be modified.

p2: The bitmap stretch mode identifier. This parameter can be one value from the following table. The display device driver may support additional stretching modes.

Return Value

If the function succeeds, it returns the previous stretch mode flag; otherwise, it returns zero.

See Also

GetStretchBltMode, SetBrushOrgEx, StretchBlt

Example

See Listing 12-15 under LoadBitmap.

Table 12-17: SetStretchBltMode p2 values

Value	Description
BLACKONWHITE	Performs a Boolean AND operation using the color values for eliminated and existing pixels. If the bitmap is a monochrome bitmap, this mode preserves black pixels at the expense of white pixels.
COLORONCOLOR	Deletes pixels without making any attempt to preserve pixel information.
HALFTONE	Maps pixels from the source bitmap into blocks of pixels on the destination bitmap. The destination pixel color is the average of the colors from the source pixels. This mode requires more processing time than the other flags, but produces higher quality images. If this flag is used, the application must call the SetBrushOrgEx function to reset the brush origin or brush misalignment will occur.
STRETCH_ANDSCANS	The same as BLACKONWHITE.
STRETCH_DELETESCANS	The same as COLORONCOLOR.
STRETCH_HALFTONE	The same as HALFTONE.
STRETCH_ORSCANS	The same as WHITEONBLACK.
WHITEONBLACK	Performs a Boolean OR operation using the color values for eliminated and existing pixels. If the bitmap is a monochrome bitmap, this mode preserves white pixels at the expense of black pixels.

StretchBlt   Windows.pas

Syntax

```
StretchBlt(
  DestDC: HDC;              {a handle to the destination device context}
  X: Integer;               {the horizontal coordinate of the destination rectangle}
  Y: Integer;               {the vertical coordinate of the destination rectangle}
  Width: Integer;           {the width of the destination rectangle}
  Height: Integer;          {the height of the destination rectangle}
  SrcDC: HDC;               {a handle to the source device context}
  XSrc: Integer;            {the horizontal coordinate of the source rectangle}
  YSrc: Integer;            {the vertical coordinate of the source rectangle}
  SrcWidth: Integer;        {the width of the source rectangle}
  SrcHeight: Integer;       {the height of the source rectangle}
  Rop: DWORD                {the raster operation code}
): BOOL;                    {returns TRUE or FALSE}
```

Description

This function copies a rectangle of pixels from the bitmap in the specified source device context into the bitmap in the specified destination device context. The copied bitmap area can be stretched or compressed as desired. The stretch mode set by the SetStretchBltMode function determines how the bitmap is stretched or compressed. If the color formats of the source and destination device contexts differ, this function converts the color format of the source into the color format of the destination. If the specified raster operation indicates that colors from the source and destination are merged, the merge takes place after the source bitmap is stretched or compressed. Note that if the sign of the source and destination width and height differ, StretchBlt creates a mirror image of the copied bitmap area.

Parameters

DestDC: A handle to the device context to which the pixels are copied.

X: The horizontal coordinate of the upper-left corner of the destination rectangle in the destination device context, measured in logical units.

Y: The vertical coordinate of the upper-left corner of the destination rectangle in the destination device context, measured in logical units.

Width: The width of the destination rectangle measured in logical units.

Height: The height of the destination rectangle measured in logical units.

SrcDC: A handle to the device context from which the pixels are copied. This cannot be the handle to a metafile device context.

XSrc: The horizontal coordinate of the upper-left corner of the source rectangle in the source device context, measured in logical units.

YSrc: The vertical coordinate of the upper-left corner of the source rectangle in the source device context, measured in logical units.

SrcWidth: The width of the source rectangle measured in logical units.

SrcHeight: The height of the source rectangle measured in logical units.

Rop: A raster operation code that determines how the colors of the pixels in the source are combined with the colors of the pixels in the destination. This parameter can be one value from the following table.

Return Value

If the function succeeds, it returns TRUE; otherwise, it returns FALSE. To get extended error information, call the GetLastError function.

See Also

BitBlt, GetDC, CreateCompatibleDC, CreateBitmap, LoadBitmap, SetStretchBltMode

Example

See Listing 12-16 under LoadImage, and other examples throughout this chapter.

Table 12-18: StretchBlt Rop values

Value	Description
BLACKNESS	Fills the pixels in the specified rectangle in the destination with the color in index 0 of the physical palette. By default, this color is black.
DSTINVERT	Inverts the colors of the pixels in the specified rectangle in the destination.

Value	Description
MERGECOPY	Combines the pixel colors of the source rectangle with the pixel colors of the pattern contained in the brush selected into the destination device context using the Boolean AND operator.
MERGEPAINT	Inverts the pixel colors of the source rectangle and combines them with the pixel colors of the destination rectangle using the Boolean OR operator.
NOTSRCCOPY	Inverts the pixel colors of the source rectangle and copies them into the destination rectangle.
NOTSRCERASE	Combines the pixel colors of the source and destination rectangles using the Boolean OR operator, then inverts the resulting color.
PATCOPY	Copies the pattern contained in the brush selected into the destination device context directly into the destination.
PATINVERT	Combines the pixel colors of the pattern contained in the brush selected into the destination device context with the colors of the pixels in the destination using the Boolean XOR operator.
PATPAINT	Combines the colors of the pattern contained in the brush selected into the destination device context with the inverted pixel colors of the source rectangle using the Boolean OR operator, then combines the result with the pixel colors of the destination rectangle using the Boolean OR operator.
SRCAND	Combines the pixel colors of the source and destination rectangles using the Boolean AND operator.
SRCCOPY	Copies the pixel colors of the source rectangle directly into the destination rectangle.
SRCERASE	Combines the pixel colors of the source rectangle with the inverted colors of the destination rectangle using the Boolean AND operator.
SRCINVERT	Combines the pixel colors of the source and destination rectangles using the Boolean XOR operator.
SRCPAINT	Combines the pixel colors of the source and destination rectangles using the Boolean OR operator.
WHITENESS	Fills the pixels in the specified rectangle in the destination with the color in index 255 of the physical palette. By default, this color is white.

StretchDIBits   Windows.pas

Syntax

```
StretchDIBits(
  DC: HDC;                        {a handle to a device context}
  DestX: Integer;                 {the horizontal coordinate of the destination rectangle}
  DestY: Integer;                 {the vertical coordinate of the destination rectangle}
  DestWidth: Integer;             {the width of the destination rectangle}
  DestHeight: Integer;            {the height of the destination rectangle}
  SrcX: Integer;                  {the horizontal coordinate of the source rectangle}
  SrcY: Integer;                  {the vertical coordinate of the source rectangle}
  SrcWidth: Integer;              {the width of the source rectangle}
  SrcHeight: Integer;             {the height of the source rectangle}
  Bits: Pointer;                  {a pointer to the bitmap bit values}
  var BitsInfo: TBitmapInfo;      {a pointer to the DIB bitmap information data structure}
```

Usage: UINT   {color type flag}
Rop: DWORD   {the raster operation code}
): Integer;   {returns the number of scan lines copied}

Description

This function copies pixels from the specified rectangular area of the DIB image into the specified rectangular area of the destination device context. The copied bitmap area can be stretched or compressed as desired. The stretch mode set by the SetStretchBltMode function determines how the bitmap is stretched or compressed. Optimal bitmap copy speed is obtained when the DIB bitmap bits specify indices into the system palette. Note that if the signs of the source and destination width and height differ, StretchDIBits creates a mirror image of the copied bitmap area. This function will reliably copy a bitmap image onto a printer device context.

Parameters

DC: The device context upon which the DIB image is copied and displayed.

DestX: The horizontal coordinate of the upper-left corner of the destination rectangle in the destination device context, measured in logical units.

DestY: The vertical coordinate of the upper-left corner of the destination rectangle in the destination device context, measured in logical units.

DestWidth: The width of the destination rectangle measured in logical units.

DestHeight: The height of the destination rectangle measured in logical units.

SrcX: The horizontal coordinate of the upper-left corner of the source rectangle in the source device context measured in logical units.

SrcY: The vertical coordinate of the upper-left corner of the source rectangle in the source device context measured in logical units.

SrcWidth: The width of the source rectangle measured in logical units.

SrcHeight: The height of the source rectangle measured in logical units.

Bits: A pointer to the image representing the DIB in the form of an array of bytes.

BitsInfo: A pointer to a TBitmapInfo data structure describing the DIB, including information about its dimensions and color table. The TBitmapInfo data structure is defined as:

TBitmapInfo = packed record
    bmiHeader: TBitmapInfoHeader;   {bitmap header information}
    bmiColors: array[0..0] of TRGBQuad;   {the color table used by the bitmap}
end;

The TBitmapInfoHeader data structure is defined as:

TBitmapInfoHeader = packed record
    biSize: DWORD;   {the size of the structure in bytes}
    biWidth: Longint;   {the width of the bitmap in pixels}
    biHeight: Longint;   {the height of the bitmap in pixels}

606 ■ Chapter 12

```
        biPlanes: Word;              {the number of color planes}
        biBitCount: Word;            {the bits per pixel required to describe a color}
        biCompression: DWORD;        {compression flags}
        biSizeImage: DWORD;          {the size of the image in bytes}
        biXPelsPerMeter: Longint;    {horizontal pixels per meter of the target device}
        biYPelsPerMeter: Longint;    {vertical pixels per meter of the target device}
        biClrUsed: DWORD;            {the number of color indices used}
        biClrImportant: DWORD;       {the number of important color indices}
    end;
```

The TRGBQuad data structure is defined as:

```
    TRGBQuad = packed record
        rgbBlue: Byte;               {blue color intensity}
        rgbGreen: Byte;              {green color intensity}
        rgbRed: Byte;                {red color intensity}
        rgbReserved: Byte;           {reserved value}
    end;
```

For an explanation of these data structures, see the CreateDIBSection function.

Usage: A flag indicating the type of color information stored in the bmiColors member of the TBitmapInfo structure pointed to by the BitsInfo parameter. This parameter can be one value from Table 12-19.

Rop: A raster operation code that determines how the colors of the pixels in the source are combined with the colors of the pixels in the destination. This parameter can be one value from Table 12-20.

Return Value

If the function succeeds, it returns the number of scan lines that were copied to the destination device context; otherwise, it returns GDI_ERROR. To get extended error information, call the GetLastError function.

See Also

SetDIBits, SetDIBitsToDevice, SetStretchBltMode

Example

See Listing 12-9 under CreateDIBSection.

Table 12-19: StretchDIBits Usage values

Value	Description
DIB_PAL_COLORS	The bmiColors member of the TBitmapInfo structure is an array of 16-bit indices into the currently realized logical palette of the specified device context. This value should not be used if the bitmap will be saved to disk.
DIB_RGB_COLORS	The bmiColors member of the TBitmapInfo structure is an array of literal RGB color values.

Table 12-20: StretchDIBits Rop values

Value	Description
BLACKNESS	Fills the pixels in the specified rectangle in the destination with the color in index 0 of the physical palette. By default, this color is black.
DSTINVERT	Inverts the colors of the pixels in the specified rectangle in the destination.
MERGECOPY	Combines the pixel colors of the source rectangle with the pixel colors of the pattern contained in the brush selected into the destination device context using the Boolean AND operator.
MERGEPAINT	Inverts the pixel colors of the source rectangle and combines them with the pixel colors of the destination rectangle using the Boolean OR operator.
NOTSRCCOPY	Inverts the pixel colors of the source rectangle and copies them into the destination rectangle.
NOTSRCERASE	Combines the pixel colors of the source and destination rectangles using the Boolean OR operator, then inverts the resulting color.
PATCOPY	Copies the pattern contained in the brush selected into the destination device context directly into the destination.
PATINVERT	Combines the pixel colors of the pattern contained in the brush selected into the destination device context with the colors of the pixels in the destination using the Boolean XOR operator.
PATPAINT	Combines the colors of the pattern contained in the brush selected into the destination device context with the inverted pixel colors of the source rectangle using the Boolean OR operator, then combines the result with the pixel colors of the destination rectangle using the Boolean OR operator.
SRCAND	Combines the pixel colors of the source and destination rectangles using the Boolean AND operator.
SRCCOPY	Copies the pixel colors of the source rectangle directly into the destination rectangle.
SRCERASE	Combines the pixel colors of the source rectangle with the inverted colors of the destination rectangle using the Boolean AND operator.
SRCINVERT	Combines the pixel colors of the source and destination rectangles using the Boolean XOR operator.
SRCPAINT	Combines the pixel colors of the source and destination rectangles using the Boolean OR operator.
WHITENESS	Fills the pixels in the specified rectangle in the destination with the color in index 255 of the physical palette. By default, this color is white.

Chapter 13

Text Output Functions

Drawing text to the screen is the most common graphical function performed by Windows in almost any application. As such, the API functions for manipulating and displaying text are very numerous and robust. Although Delphi encapsulates some of the text output API functions, the Delphi developer can dramatically extend the textual drawing capabilities of an application by utilizing the functions described in this chapter.

It is easy enough to simply draw some text on a surface. However, some applications may need tight control on the placement of text, or may need some specified text formatting capabilities, such as drawing text within the confines of a bounding box. Advanced font information may be required, or the application may need to manipulate the fonts that are available in the system. The text output functions discussed here give the developer access to this type of advanced functionality.

Fonts

Currently, Windows supports three types of fonts: raster, vector, and TrueType. The differences between font types lie in the method by which the font's glyphs define the shape of a character. A glyph for a raster font is a bitmap of a specific size containing an image for each individual character. Vector fonts store their glyphs as a series of endpoints used to create line segments defining the outline of the character. TrueType font glyphs are stored as a series of lines, curves, and hints that are used to draw the character outline. Due to the fact that raster fonts store their glyphs as bitmaps, raster fonts generally lose a lot of resolution when scaled. Vector fonts can generally be scaled up or down, but will start losing resolution when scaled to a certain degree past their original size, and are slow to draw. However, TrueType fonts can be drawn relatively fast because the GDI subsystem is optimized for drawing them. In addition, the hints stored in TrueType font glyph definitions provide scaling correction for the curves and lines of the character outline, allowing TrueType fonts to be scaled to any size with no loss of resolution.

Font Families

Windows categorizes all fonts into five families. A font family is a collection of fonts sharing similar stroke widths and serif attributes. When considering a choice of font, font families allow the developer to indicate the general style desired, leaving the actual font selection to Windows. For example, using the appropriate functions and specifying only a font family, the developer can enumerate all symbol fonts installed on the system. Font families also allow the developer to create a logical font based off only specific characteristics, allowing Windows to select the most appropriate font from the specified font family based on those characteristics.

The five font family categories defined by Windows are:

Table 13-1: Font families

Family Name	Constant	Description
Decorative	FF_DECORATIVE	Indicates a novelty or decorative font, such as Old English.
Modern	FF_MODERN	Indicates a monospaced font with consistent stroke widths, with or without serifs, such as Courier New.
Roman	FF_ROMAN	Indicates a proportional font with variable stroke widths, containing serifs, such as Times New Roman.
Script	FF_SCRIPT	Indicates a font resembling handwriting, such as Brush Script.
Swiss	FF_SWISS	Indicates a proportional font with variable stroke widths, without serifs, such as Arial.

Character Sets

By definition, a font defines the image for each individual character within a collection of characters. This collection of characters is called a character set. Each character set contains the symbols, numbers, punctuation marks, letters, and other printable or displayable images of a written language, with each character identified by a number.

There are five major character sets: Windows, Unicode, OEM, symbol, and vendor specific. The Windows character set is equivalent to the ANSI character set. The Unicode character set is used for Eastern languages that contain thousands of symbols in their alphabet, and currently is the only character set that uses two bytes to identify a single character. The OEM character set is generally equivalent to the Windows character set except that it usually contains characters at the upper and lower ranges of the available character space that can only be displayed in a full screen DOS session. The Symbol character set contains characters useful in representing mathematical or scientific equations, or graphical characters used for illustration. Vendor-specific character sets usually provide characters that are not available under the other character sets, and are most likely to be implemented at the printer or output device level.

In many cases, a font will define a default character. When a string contains a character that is not defined in the character set of a device context's selected font, the default character is substituted for the offending character when the text is displayed. Most TrueType fonts define the default character as an unfilled rectangle (☐).

For purposes of line breaks and justification, most fonts define a break character. The break character identifies the character that is most commonly used to separate words in a line of text. Most fonts using the Windows character set define the break character as the space (" ") character.

Character Dimensions

Font sizes are typically measured in units called points. One point equals .013837 of an inch, commonly approximated to 1/72 of an inch. Note that a logical inch in Windows is approximately 30 to 40 percent larger than a physical inch in order to facilitate more legible fonts on the screen.

Specific dimensions as illustrated by Figure 13-1 define a character glyph image. The baseline of a glyph is an imaginary line that defines the base upon which a character stands. The descent is the space below the baseline containing the descenders of certain characters such as "g" and "y." Internal leading defines space above the character where accent and diacritical marks reside. External leading actually lies outside of the glyph image; it will never contain glyph image data and is used solely for extra vertical spacing between lines. The ascent is defined as the distance from the baseline to the top of the internal leading space. The height is the sum of the ascent and the descent, and defines the total vertical space that can be occupied by glyph image data. Calling the GetOutlineTextMetrics or GetTextMetrics functions can retrieve these character dimensions. The measurements retrieved by these functions will be in logical units, so their actual value is dependent upon the current mapping mode of the device context specified in the called function.

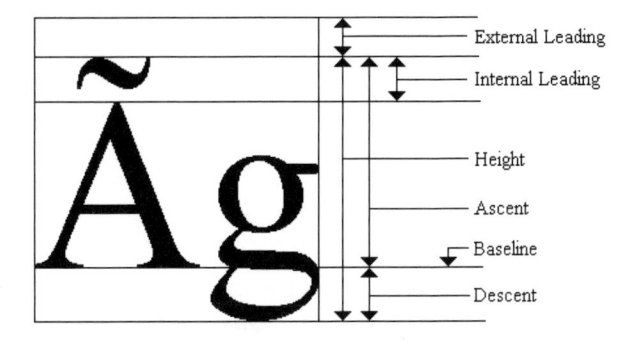

Figure 13-1: The dimensions of a glyph

The Windows Font Table

Windows stores a reference to all non-device fonts in an internal array known as the font table. Any font in this internal table is available for use by any Windows application. An application can programmatically add a font resource to this internal table by calling the AddFontResource function. Once this function has completed successfully, the application installing the font should inform all other applications of the change to the font table by sending the WM_FONTCHANGE message with the SendMessage function, specifying HWND_BROADCAST as the value of the hWnd parameter. When the application has terminated, or the font is no longer needed, it should be removed by a call to the RemoveFontResource function. Note that the font will not actually be removed from the internal font tables until all device contexts have unselected the font, if the font had been selected into the device context prior to the call to RemoveFontResource.

The AddFontResource function only installs the font to the internal font table for the duration of the installing application, or until the font is completely released as described above. In previous versions of Windows, permanently installing a font required an application to modify the Fonts section of the Win.ini file. Under Windows 95 or later, an application can permanently install a font by simply copying the font file into the Fonts directory under the Windows directory.

When an application calls the CreateFont or CreateFontIndirect functions, a new font is not actually created. These functions return a handle to a logical font definition that is used by the Windows font mapper to select an appropriate physical font from the Windows font table. The Windows font mapper takes the desired font characteristics defined by the logical font and uses an internal algorithm to compare them with the characteristics of physical fonts currently installed on the system. This font mapping algorithm takes place when the logical font is selected into a device context by a call to the SelectObject function, and results in a selection of the font that most closely matches the desired characteristics. Subsequently, the selected font returned by the font mapper may not exactly match the requested font.

Font Embedding

Most advanced word processors offer the ability to embed TrueType fonts into a document. Embedding a TrueType font into a document allows the document to be viewed or edited by the word processing application on another system in its original appearance if the destination system does not have the specific font installed. However, as fonts are owned and copyrighted by their original developer, there are certain caveats that must be followed when embedding a font.

The developer of the font may not allow the font to be embedded. A font may allow embedding, but in a read-only context. If a document contains any embedded read-only fonts, the document may be viewed or printed, but the document itself must be read-only and may not be modified, nor can the font be unembedded and installed permanently into the system. Some fonts may be licensed as read-write, indicating that the font can be embedded into a document and permanently installed on the destination system. An application can determine the embedding status of a font by using the GetOutlineTextMetrics function. In any event, unless specific permission is granted from the font developer, fonts can only be embedded in a document and may not be embedded within an application, nor can an application be distributed with documents containing embedded fonts.

To embed a font within a document, the application must retrieve the data for the entire font file by calling the GetFontData function, setting the p2 and p3 parameters to zero. The font data is then written to the output file along with the text of the document in the file format determined by the application. Typically, applications use a file format that contains the name of each font embedded within the document and an indication of read-only or read-write licensing. Note that if a read-only font is embedded in a document, it must be encrypted, although the encryption algorithm does not need to be very complex.

When the application opens a document that contains an embedded font, it must first determine if the font allows read-only embedding or read-write embedding. The font data is then extracted from the document file and written to disk using file manipulation functions such as CreateFile and WriteFile. If the font is a read-write font, it can be directly written out to a file with a TTF extension in the Fonts subdirectory under the Windows directory to permanently install the font to the system. If the font is read-only, it must be unencrypted and written out to a hidden file. This hidden file should not have a TTF extension. Once the read-only font is extracted and written to disk, it can be installed to the internal Windows font table using the CreateScalableFontResource and AddFontResource functions, specifying a value of 1 for the p1 parameter of the CreateScalableFontResource function to indicate a read-only font. Note that read-only fonts will not be identified by the EnumFontFamilies or EnumFontFamiliesEx functions. When the document containing the read-only embedded font is closed, the FOT file created by the CreateScalableFontResource function and the file created when extracting the read-only font must be deleted, and the font must be removed from the Windows font table by calling the RemoveFontResource function.

The following example demonstrates embedding a TrueType font into a text document. The document is written to disk in a proprietary format. Note that checks for read-only licensing have been omitted for code clarity.

Listing 13-1: Embedding TrueType fonts into a document

```
{================================================================================
    The Ventilate font used in this example was generously donated by and is
    copyright © 1997 by Brian J. Bonislawsky - Astigmatic One Eye.  Used with
    permission.

    Astigmatic One Eye is a great source for shareware and freeware fonts of
    all types.  Check them out at http://www.comptechdev.com/cavop/aoe/

    Note that this example makes use of a document that already contains an
    embedded TrueType font.
 =================================================================================}
procedure TForm1.Button1Click(Sender: TObject);
var
  SavedFile: THandle;      // holds a handle to the open file
  TextSize: LongInt;       // holds the size of the text in the memo
  TheText: PChar;          // holds the text in the memo
  BytesWritten: DWORD;     // holds the number of bytes written to the file
  FontData: Pointer;       // points to retrieved font data
  FontDataSize: Integer;   // holds the size of the font data
  MemoDC: HDC;             // a handle to a common device context
  OldFont: THandle;        // holds the previously selected font in the DC
begin
  {create the file that will contain the saved document and embedded font}
  SavedFile := CreateFile('ProprietaryFileFormat.PFF', GENERIC_WRITE, 0, NIL,
                          CREATE_ALWAYS, FILE_ATTRIBUTE_NORMAL or
                          FILE_FLAG_SEQUENTIAL_SCAN, 0);

  {retrieve the size of the text in the memo, adding one
   for the null terminator}
  TextSize := Length(Memo1.Text)+1;
```

```
{retrieve enough memory to hold all of the text}
GetMem(TheText, TextSize);

{copy the text to a null-terminated text buffer}
StrPCopy(TheText, Memo1.Text);

{explicitly set the end of the text}
TheText[TextSize] := #0;

{our proprietary file format is such that the first four bytes of the file
 contain the number of bytes following that contain the text of the
 document.  After these text bytes, the next four bytes indicate how many
 bytes following contain the embedded TrueType font information.  therefore,
 we write out the first four bytes of the document as an integer containing
 the size of the document's text, and then write out that many indicated bytes
 containing the text of the document}
WriteFile(SavedFile, TextSize, SizeOf(TextSize), BytesWritten, NIL);
WriteFile(SavedFile, TheText^, TextSize, BytesWritten, NIL);

{in order to get the font file data for embedding, the font must be selected
 into a device context.  we retrieve a device context for the memo, but since
 this returns a common DC with default settings, we must select the memo's
 font into the retrieved device context.}
MemoDC := GetDC(Memo1.Handle);
OldFont := SelectObject(MemoDC, Memo1.Font.Handle);

{at this point, the selected font should be checked to see if it allows
 embedding.  if the font does not allow embedding, the document should
 simply be saved and the following code should be skipped.  if the font
 allows embedding in a read-only format, once the font data is retrieved,
 it should be encrypted before being written out to the document file}

{retrieve the size of buffer required to hold the entire font file data}
FontDataSize := GetFontData(MemoDC, 0, 0, NIL, 0);

{allocate the required memory}
GetMem(FontData, FontDataSize);

{retrieve the entire font file data}
GetFontData(MemoDC, 0, 0, FontData, FontDataSize);

{now, write out an integer indicating how many bytes following contain the
 font data, and then write out that many bytes containing the actual font
 data}
WriteFile(SavedFile, FontDataSize, SizeOf(FontDataSize), BytesWritten, NIL);
WriteFile(SavedFile, FontData^, FontDataSize, BytesWritten, NIL);

{select the original font back into the device context, and delete the DC}
SelectObject(MemoDC, OldFont);
ReleaseDC(Memo1.Handle, MemoDC);

{flush the file buffers to force the file to be written to disk}
FlushFileBuffers(SavedFile);

{close the file handle}
CloseHandle(SavedFile);
```

```
  {the file has been saved, so free all allocated memory that
   is no longer needed}
  FreeMem(TheText, TextSize);
  FreeMem(FontData, FontDataSize);
end;

procedure TForm1.Button2Click(Sender: TObject);
var
  SavedFile: THandle;              // holds a handle to the open file
  TextSize: LongInt;               // holds the size of the text in the memo
  TheText: PChar;                  // holds the text in the memo
  BytesRead: DWORD;                // the number of bytes read from the file
  BytesWritten: DWORD;             // the number of bytes written to the file
  FontData: Pointer;               // points to retrieved font data
  FontDataSize: Integer;           // holds the size of the font data
  NewFontFile: THandle;            // holds the font file handle
  CurDir: array[0..MAX_PATH] of char; // holds the current directory path
begin
  {open the document containing the embedded font}
  SavedFile := CreateFile('ProprietaryFileFormat.PFF', GENERIC_READ, 0, NIL,
                          OPEN_EXISTING, FILE_ATTRIBUTE_NORMAL or
                          FILE_FLAG_SEQUENTIAL_SCAN, 0);

  {read in the number of bytes occupied by the text of the document}
  ReadFile(SavedFile, TextSize, SizeOf(TextSize), BytesRead, NIL);

  {allocate the required buffer size to hold the text of the document}
  GetMem(TheText, TextSize);

  {initialize the buffer to null characters}
  FillMemory(TheText, TextSize, 0);

  {explicitly set the file pointer to point past the first four bytes, so that
   reading begins at the start of the document text}
  SetFilePointer(SavedFile, SizeOf(TextSize), nil, FILE_BEGIN);

  {read in the indicated number of 'document text' bytes from the file}
  ReadFile(SavedFile, TheText^, TextSize, BytesRead, NIL);

  {explicitly set the file pointer past the document text. it should now be
   pointing the integer indicating the size of the embedded font data}
  SetFilePointer(SavedFile, SizeOf(TextSize)+TextSize, nil, FILE_BEGIN);

  {read in the embedded font data size}
  ReadFile(SavedFile, FontDataSize, SizeOf(FontData), BytesRead, NIL);

  {retrieve enough memory to hold the font data}
  GetMem(FontData, FontDataSize);

  {explicitly set the file pointer to point past the four bytes containing the
   size of the font data. it should now be pointing to the start of the font
   data}
  SetFilePointer(SavedFile, SizeOf(TextSize)+TextSize+SizeOf(FontData),
                 nil, FILE_BEGIN);
```

```
{read the font data into the font data buffer}
ReadFile(SavedFile, FontData^, FontDataSize, BytesRead, NIL);

{we are done with the document file, so close it}
CloseHandle(SavedFile);

{at this point, the application should determine, based on the information
 stored in the document file, if the font is read-only or read-write. if it
 is read-write, it can be written directly to the Fonts directory under the
 Windows directory.  if it is read-only, it should be written to a hidden
 file. in this example, we will write the font out as a regular TTF file
 in the application's directory.}

{create the file that will contain the font information}
NewFontFile := CreateFile('TempFont.TTF', GENERIC_WRITE, 0, NIL,
                          CREATE_ALWAYS, FILE_ATTRIBUTE_NORMAL or
                          FILE_FLAG_SEQUENTIAL_SCAN, 0);

{write the font data into the font file}
WriteFile(NewFontFile, FontData^, FontDataSize, BytesWritten, NIL);

{flush the file buffers to insure that the file is written to disk}
FlushFileBuffers(NewFontFile);

{close the font file}
CloseHandle(NewFontFile);

{retrieve the current directory}
GetCurrentDirectory(MAX_PATH, @CurDir[0]);

{since the font was written out as a regular TTF file, create font resource
 file, indicating that it is a read-write file}
CreateScalableFontResource(0, PChar(CurDir+'\TempFont.fot'),
                           PChar(CurDir+'\TempFont.ttf'),
                           nil);

{add the font to the internal font table}
AddFontResource(PChar(CurDir+'\TempFont.fot'));

{inform other applications that the font table has changed}
SendMessage(HWND_BROADCAST, WM_FONTCHANGE, 0, 0);

{assign the retrieved document text to the memo}
Memo1.Text := Copy(string(TheText), 0, StrLen(TheText));

{free the allocated text buffer}
FreeMem(TheText, TextSize);

{the installed font was the Ventilate font, so set the memo's
 font accordingly}
Memo1.Font.Name := 'Ventilate';
Memo1.Font.Size := 16;

{free the buffer allocated to hold the font data}
FreeMem(FontData, FontDataSize);

{now that the font has been installed, enable the document save button}
```

```
    Button1.Enabled := TRUE;
end;

procedure TForm1.FormDestroy(Sender: TObject);
var
  CurDir: array[0..MAX_PATH] of char;   // holds the current directory
begin
  {retrieve the current directory}
  GetCurrentDirectory(MAX_PATH, @CurDir[0]);

  {remove the font from the internal font table}
  RemoveFontResource(PChar(CurDir+'\TempFont.fot'));

  {inform all applications of the change to the font table}
  SendMessage(HWND_BROADCAST, WM_FONTCHANGE, 0, 0);

  {the application (and the document) are being closed, so delete the font
   resource file and the font file from the hard disk as if this were a
   read-only font}
  DeleteFile(CurDir+'\TempFont.fot');
  DeleteFile(CurDir+'\TempFont.ttf');
end;
```

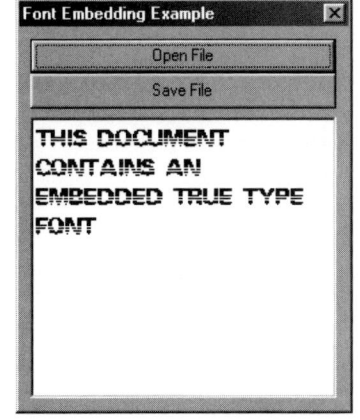

Figure 13-2:
This document
uses an
embedded
TrueType font

Delphi vs. the Windows API

While the TCanvas object encapsulates a minor amount of text output functionality, it in no way offers the breadth of functionality achieved by using the API functions. With the API, an application can display text aligned in a variety of ways (vertical in addition to horizontal), wrapped within a bounding box, constrained within specified margins, etc. Additionally, if the application is manipulating font resources, including installing new fonts or modifying the orientation of output text, you have to use the API functions. Most of these functions are relatively simple, and their power provides an extreme amount of flexibility when it comes to outputting text in your Delphi applications.

Text Output Functions

The following text output functions are covered in this chapter:

Table 13-2: Text output functions

Function	Description
AddFontResource	Adds the font resource contained in the specified file to the internal Windows font table.
CreateFont	Creates a logical font.
CreateFontIndirect	Creates a logical font based on information specified in a data structure.
CreateScalableFontResource	Creates a font resource file from a TrueType font file.
DrawText	Draws formatted text onto a device context within a specified rectangle.
DrawTextEx	Draws formatted text onto a device context within a specified rectangle according to specified margin widths.
EnumFontFamilies	Enumerates installed fonts.
EnumFontFamiliesEx	Enumerates installed fonts matching specified font characteristics.
GetCharABCWidths	Retrieves character widths and spacing for TrueType fonts.
GetCharWidth	Retrieves character widths.
GetFontData	Retrieves TrueType font file information.
GetGlyphOutline	Retrieves a bitmap or outline of a TrueType character.
GetKerningPairs	Retrieves character kerning pairs.
GetOutlineTextMetrics	Retrieves text metrics for TrueType fonts.
GetRasterizerCaps	Retrieves information concerning TrueType font availability.
GetTabbedTextExtent	Retrieves the width and height of a character string containing tabs.
GetTextAlign	Retrieves text alignment.
GetTextCharacterExtra	Retrieves intercharacter spacing.
GetTextColor	Retrieves the color used when drawing text.
GetTextExtentExPoint	Retrieves the number of characters in a specified string that will fit within a specified space.
GetTextExtentPoint32	Retrieves the width and height of a specified string.
GetTextFace	Retrieves the name of a font selected into a device context.
GetTextMetrics	Retrieves text metrics for a font.
RemoveFontResource	Deletes a font resource from the internal Windows font table.
SetTextAlign	Sets text alignment.
SetTextCharacterExtra	Sets intercharacter spacing.
SetTextColor	Sets the color used when drawing text.
SetTextJustification	Sets text justification.
TabbedTextOut	Draws a string onto a device context, expanding tab characters.
TextOut	Draws text onto a device context.

AddFontResource   Windows.pas

Syntax

```
AddFontResource(
p1: PChar                    {the font resource filename}
): Integer;                  {returns the number of fonts added}
```

Description

This function adds the font resource contained in the specified font resource file to the internal system font tables, making the font available to all applications. If the font is successfully added to the internal tables, the application that added the font should inform all other applications of the change. This is accomplished by sending the WM_FONTCHANGE message with the SendMessage function, specifying HWND_BROADCAST as the value of the hWnd parameter. When the font is no longer needed, it must be removed from the internal system font tables by a call to the RemoveFontResource function.

Parameters

p1: A pointer to a null-terminated string containing the name of the font resource to add. The specified file can contain font resources (*.FON), a raw bitmapped font (*.FNT), raw TrueType font information (*.TTF), or a TrueType font resource (*.FOT).

Return Value

If the function succeeds, it returns the number of fonts that were added to the internal system font tables; otherwise, it returns zero. To get extended error information, call the GetLastError function.

See Also

CreateScalableFontResource, GetFontData, RemoveFontResource

Example

See Listing 13-4 under CreateScalableFontResource.

CreateFont   Windows.pas

Syntax

```
CreateFont(
nHeight: Integer;            {the font height in logical units}
nWidth: Integer;             {the average character width in logical units}
nEscapement: Integer;        {the escapement vector angle}
nOrientation: Integer;       {the character baseline angle}
fnWeight: Integer;           {the bolding weight}
fdwItalic: DWORD;            {the italics flag}
fdwUnderline: DWORD;         {the underline flag}
fdwStrikeOut: DWORD;         {the strikeout flag}
fdwCharSet: DWORD;           {the character set}
fdwOutputPrecision: DWORD;   {the output precision flag}
```

fdwClipPrecision: DWORD;   {the clipping precision flags}
fdwQuality: DWORD;   {the output quality flag}
fdwPitchAndFamily: DWORD;   {the pitch and font family flags}
lpszFace: PChar   {the font typeface name}
): HFONT;   {returns a handle to the new font}

Description

This function creates a logical font matching the specified font attributes. This font can be selected into any device context that supports text output functions. When the font is no longer needed, it should be deleted by using the DeleteObject function.

Parameters

nHeight: Specifies the height of the character or character cells within the font. Character height is a measurement of the character cell height value minus the internal leading value. This value is expressed in logical units, and will be dependent on the current mapping mode. The Windows font mapper interprets the value of the nHeight parameter as described in Table 13-3, and will retrieve the largest font available up to the specified size. For the MM_TEXT mapping mode, use the following formula to express a font height for any specific point size:

```
nHeight := -MulDiv(PointSize, GetDeviceCaps(hDeviceContext, LOGPIXELSY), 72);
```

nWidth: Specifies the average width of characters within the font. This value is expressed in logical units, and will be dependent on the current mapping mode. If this parameter is set to zero, the Windows font mapper will choose an appropriate font based on the absolute values of the difference between the current device's aspect ratio and the digitized aspect ratio of all appropriate fonts.

nEscapement: Specifies the angle between the baseline of a line of text and the X axis, in tenths of a degree.

Windows NT/2000 and later: If the graphics mode is set to GM_ADVANCED, the angle of a line of text and the angle of each character within that line of text can be set independently. If the graphics mode is set to GM_COMPATIBLE, the nEscapement parameter specifies the angle for both the line of text and the characters within that line of text, and the nEscapement and nOrientation parameters should be set to the same value.

Windows 95/98/Me: The nEscapement parameter always specifies the angle for both the line of text and the characters within that line of text, and the nEscapement and nOrientation parameters should be set to the same value.

nOrientation: Specifies the angle between the baseline of each individual character and the x-axis, in tenths of a degree.

Windows 95/98/Me: The nEscapement parameter always specifies the angle for both the line of text and the characters within that line of text, and the nEscapement and nOrientation parameters should be set to the same value.

fnWeight: Specifies the boldness of the font. The value of this parameter can be in the range of 0-1000, or can be set to one value from Table 13-4. A weight of zero indicates the default boldness value for the specified font.

fdwItalic: Specifies the italics attribute for the font. If this parameter is set to TRUE, the font will be italicized.

fdwUnderline: Specifies the underlining attribute for the font. If this parameter is set to TRUE, the font will be underlined.

fdwStrikeOut: Specifies the strikeout attribute for the font. If this parameter is set to TRUE, the font will be struck out.

fdwCharSet: Specifies the character set that the Windows font mapper uses to choose an appropriate font, and can be set to one value from Table 13-5. The font typeface name specified in the lpszFace parameter must be a font that defines characters for the specified character set. If this parameter is set to DEFAULT_CHARSET, the font size and typeface name will be used to find an appropriate font. However, if the specified typeface name is not found, any font from any character set matching the specified values can be used, and can lead to unexpected results.

fdwOutputPrecision: Specifies how closely the resulting font must match the given height, width, character orientation, escapement, pitch, and font type values. This parameter can be set to one value from Table 13-6. Note that the OUT_DEVICE_PRECIS, OUT_RASTER_PRECIS, and OUT_TT_PRECIS flags control the Windows font mapper behavior when more then one font exists with the name specified by the lpszFace parameter.

fdwClipPrecision: Specifies how characters partially outside of the clipping region are drawn. This parameter can be set to one or more values from Table 13-7.

fdwQuality: Specifies how closely the Windows font mapper matches the specified font attributes with an actual font. This parameter can be set to one value from Table 13-8.

fdwPitchAndFamily: The font pitch and font family flags. This parameter can contain a combination of one value from the pitch flags table (Table 13-9), and one value from the font family flags table (Table 13-10). The values from these tables are combined by using the Boolean OR operator. The pitch describes how the widths of individual character glyphs vary, and the family describes the general look and feel of the font. If the specified typeface name is unavailable, the function returns the closest matching font from the specified font family.

lpszFace: A pointer to a null-terminated string containing the typeface name of the font. The font typeface name cannot exceed 32 characters in length, including the null terminator. Use the EnumFontFamilies function to retrieve a list of all installed font typeface names. If this parameter is NIL, the Windows font mapper will choose the first font from the specified font family matching the specified attributes.

Return Value

If the function succeeds, it returns a handle to the newly created logical font; otherwise, it returns zero. To get extended error information, call the GetLastError function.

See Also

CreateFontIndirect, DeleteObject, EnumFontFamilies, EnumFontFamiliesEx, SelectObject

Example

Listing 13-2: Creating various fonts

```
procedure TForm1.FormPaint(Sender: TObject);
var
  NewFont, OldFont: HFont;      // holds the old and new fonts
begin
  {set the background mode for transparency}
  SetBkMode(Form1.Canvas.Handle, TRANSPARENT);

  {create a bold font}
  NewFont := CreateFont(-MulDiv(16, GetDeviceCaps(Form1.Canvas.Handle,
                        LOGPIXELSY), 72), 0, 0, 0, FW_BOLD, 0, 0, 0,
                        DEFAULT_CHARSET, OUT_TT_ONLY_PRECIS,
                        CLIP_DEFAULT_PRECIS, DEFAULT_QUALITY, DEFAULT_PITCH or
                        FF_DONTCARE, 'Arial');

  {select the font into the form's device context}
  OldFont := SelectObject(Form1.Canvas.Handle, NewFont);

  {output a line of text}
  TextOut(Form1.Canvas.Handle, 8, Label1.Top+Label1.Height, 'Delphi Rocks!',
          Length('Delphi Rocks!'));

  {select the old font back into the device context and delete the new font}
  SelectObject(Form1.Canvas.Handle, OldFont);
  DeleteObject(NewFont);

  {create a strikeout font}
  NewFont := CreateFont(-MulDiv(16, GetDeviceCaps(Form1.Canvas.Handle,
                        LOGPIXELSY), 72), 0, 0, 0, FW_DONTCARE, 0, 0, 1,
                        DEFAULT_CHARSET, OUT_TT_ONLY_PRECIS,
                        CLIP_DEFAULT_PRECIS, DEFAULT_QUALITY, DEFAULT_PITCH or
                        FF_ROMAN, '');

  {select the font into the form's device context}
  OldFont := SelectObject(Form1.Canvas.Handle, NewFont);

  {output a line of text}
  TextOut(Form1.Canvas.Handle, 8, Label2.Top+Label2.Height, 'Delphi Rocks!',
          Length('Delphi Rocks!'));

  {select the old font back into the device context and delete the new font}
  SelectObject(Form1.Canvas.Handle, OldFont);
  DeleteObject(NewFont);

  {create an underlined font}
  NewFont := CreateFont(-MulDiv(16, GetDeviceCaps(Form1.Canvas.Handle,
                        LOGPIXELSY), 72), 0, 0, 0, FW_DONTCARE, 0, 1, 0,
                        DEFAULT_CHARSET, OUT_TT_ONLY_PRECIS,
                        CLIP_DEFAULT_PRECIS, DEFAULT_QUALITY, DEFAULT_PITCH or
                        FF_DECORATIVE, '');

  {select the font into the form's device context}
  OldFont := SelectObject(Form1.Canvas.Handle, NewFont);
```

```
{output a line of text}
TextOut(Form1.Canvas.Handle, 8, Label3.Top+Label3.Height, 'Delphi Rocks!',
        Length('Delphi Rocks!'));

{select the old font back into the device context and delete the new font}
SelectObject(Form1.Canvas.Handle, OldFont);
DeleteObject(NewFont);

{create an italicized font}
NewFont := CreateFont(-MulDiv(16, GetDeviceCaps(Form1.Canvas.Handle,
                      LOGPIXELSY), 72), 0, 0, 0, FW_DONTCARE, 1, 0, 0,
                      DEFAULT_CHARSET, OUT_TT_ONLY_PRECIS,
                      CLIP_DEFAULT_PRECIS, DEFAULT_QUALITY, DEFAULT_PITCH or
                      FF_SCRIPT, '');

{select the font into the form's device context}
OldFont := SelectObject(Form1.Canvas.Handle, NewFont);

{output a line of text}
TextOut(Form1.Canvas.Handle, 8, Label4.Top+Label4.Height, 'Delphi Rocks!',
        Length('Delphi Rocks!'));

{select the old font back into the device context and delete the new font}
SelectObject(Form1.Canvas.Handle, OldFont);
DeleteObject(NewFont);
end;
```

Figure 13-3: Various fonts created with the CreateFont function

Table 13-3: CreateFont nHeight font mapper interpretation values

Value	Description
nHeight>0	The font mapper converts the value of nHeight into device units, matching the result against the cell height of available fonts.
nHeight=0	The font mapper uses a default font height when searching for a matching font.
nHeight<0	The font mapper converts the value of nHeight into device units, matching the absolute value of the result against the character height of available fonts.

Table 13-4: CreateFont fnWeight values

Value	Description
FW_DONTCARE	Uses the default bolding value (0).
FW_THIN	Extra thin font weight (100).
FW_EXTRALIGHT	Thin font weight (200).
FW_LIGHT	Below average bolding (300).
FW_NORMAL	Normal bolding (400).
FW_MEDIUM	Above average bolding (500).
FW_SEMIBOLD	Light bolding (600).
FW_BOLD	Bolded font (700).
FW_EXTRABOLD	Extra bolding (800).
FW_HEAVY	Very heaving bolding (900).

Table 13-5: CreateFont fdwCharSet values

Value	Description
ANSI_CHARSET	The ANSI character set.
DEFAULT_CHARSET	The default character set.
SYMBOL_CHARSET	The symbol character set.
SHIFTJIS_CHARSET	The shiftjis character set.
GB2312_CHARSET	The GB2312 character set.
HANGEUL_CHARSET	The Korean character set.
CHINESEBIG5_CHARSET	The Chinese character set.
OEM_CHARSET	The original equipment manufacturer character set.
JOHAB_CHARSET	**Windows 95 or later:** The Johab character set.
HEBREW_CHARSET	**Windows 95 or later:** The Hebrew character set.
ARABIC_CHARSET	**Windows 95 or later:** The Arabic character set.
GREEK_CHARSET	**Windows 95 or later:** The Grecian character set.
TURKISH_CHARSET	**Windows 95 or later:** The Turkish character set.
VIETNAMESE_CHARSET	**Windows 95 or later:** The Vietnamese character set.
THAI_CHARSET	**Windows 95 or later:** The Thai character set.
EASTEUROPE_CHARSET	**Windows 95 or later:** The eastern Europe character set.
RUSSIAN_CHARSET	**Windows 95 or later:** The Russian character set.
MAC_CHARSET	**Windows 95 or later:** The Macintosh character set.
BALTIC_CHARSET	**Windows 95 or later:** The Baltic character set.

Table 13-6: CreateFont fdwOutputPrecision values

Value	Description
OUT_DEFAULT_PRECIS	The default font mapper behavior.
OUT_DEVICE_PRECIS	Chooses a device font when more than one font of the specified name exists.
OUT_OUTLINE_PRECIS	**Windows NT/2000 or later:** Chooses a font from TrueType and other vector-based fonts.

Value	Description
OUT_RASTER_PRECIS	Chooses a raster font when more than one font of the specified name exists.
OUT_STROKE_PRECIS	**Windows 98/NT/2000 or later:** Not used by the font mapper. However, this flag is returned when TrueType and other vector fonts are enumerated.
	Windows 95 only: Chooses a font from vector-based fonts.
OUT_TT_ONLY_PRECIS	Chooses a font only from TrueType fonts. If no TrueType fonts exist, the font mapper reverts to default behavior.
OUT_TT_PRECIS	Chooses a TrueType font when more than one font of the specified name exists.

Table 13-7: CreateFont fdwClipPrecision values

Value	Description
CLIP_DEFAULT_PRECIS	The default clipping behavior.
CLIP_STROKE_PRECIS	This flag is used only when enumerating fonts.
CLIP_EMBEDDED	This flag must be included when using a read-only embedded font.
CLIP_LH_ANGLES	Specifies that font rotation is dependent upon the coordinate system. If this flag is not specified, device fonts always rotate counterclockwise.

Table 13-8: CreateFont fdwQuality values

Value	Description
DEFAULT_QUALITY	Uses the default font quality.
DRAFT_QUALITY	Raster font scaling is enabled, and bold, italic, underline, and strikeout fonts are fabricated as needed. Exact attribute matching is a higher priority than font quality.
PROOF_QUALITY	Raster font scaling is disabled, and the physical font closest to the specified size is chosen. Bold, italic, underline, and strikeout fonts are fabricated as needed. Font quality is a higher priority than exact attribute matching.

Table 13-9: CreateFont fdwPitchAndFamily pitch flag values

Value	Description
DEFAULT_PITCH	The default font pitch is used.
FIXED_PITCH	The width of all character glyphs is equal.
VARIABLE_PITCH	The width of all character glyphs is dependent upon the individual glyph image.

Table 13-10: CreateFont fdwPitchAndFamily font family flag values

Value	Description
FF_DECORATIVE	Indicates a novelty or decorative font, such as Old English.
FF_DONTCARE	The general font style is unknown or unimportant.
FF_MODERN	Indicates a monospaced font with consistent stroke widths, with or without serifs, such as Courier New.
FF_ROMAN	Indicates a proportional font with variable stroke widths, containing serifs, such as Times New Roman.
FF_SCRIPT	Indicates a font resembling handwriting, such as Brush Script.
FF_SWISS	Indicates a proportional font with variable stroke widths, without serifs, such as Arial.

CreateFontIndirect   Windows.pas

Syntax

```
CreateFontIndirect(
  const p1: TLogFont        {a pointer to a logical font structure}
): HFONT;                   {returns a handle to the new font}
```

Description

This function creates a logical font matching the font attributes specified by the TLogFont structure pointed to by the p1 parameter. This font can be selected into any device context that supports text output functions. When the font is no longer needed, it should be deleted by using the DeleteObject function.

Parameters

p1: A pointer to a TLogFont data structure describing the attributes of the desired font. The TLogFont structure is defined as:

```
TLogFont = packed record
    lfHeight: Longint;            {font height in logical units}
    lfWidth: Longint;             {the average character width}
    lfEscapement: Longint;        {the escapement vector angle}
    lfOrientation: Longint;       {the character baseline angle}
    lfWeight: Longint;            {the bolding weight}
    lfItalic: Byte;               {the italics flag}
    lfUnderline: Byte;            {the underline flag}
    lfStrikeOut: Byte;            {the strikeout flag}
    lfCharSet: Byte;              {the character set}
    lfOutPrecision: Byte;         {the output precision flag}
    lfClipPrecision: Byte;        {the clipping precision flags}
    lfQuality: Byte;              {the output quality flag}
    lfPitchAndFamily: Byte;       {the pitch and family flags}
    lfFaceName: array[0..LF_FACESIZE – 1] of AnsiChar;    {the font typeface name}
end;
```

lfHeight: Specifies the height of the character or character cells within the font. Character height is a measurement of the character cell height value minus the internal leading value. This value is expressed in logical units, and will be dependent on the current mapping mode. The Windows font mapper interprets the value of the lfHeight member as described in Table 13-11, and will retrieve the largest font available up to the specified size. For the MM_TEXT mapping mode, use the following formula to express a font height for any specific point size:

```
lfHeight := -MulDiv(PointSize, GetDeviceCaps(hDeviceContext, LOGPIXELSY), 72);
```

lfWidth: Specifies the average width of characters within the font. This value is expressed in logical units, and will be dependent on the current mapping mode. If this member is set to zero, the Windows font mapper will choose an appropriate font based on the absolute values of the difference between the current device's aspect ratio and the digitized aspect ratio of all appropriate fonts.

lfEscapement: Specifies the angle between the baseline of a line of text and the x-axis in tenths of a degree.

Windows NT/2000 or later: If the graphics mode is set to GM_ADVANCED, the angle of a line of text and the angle of each character within that line of text can be set independently. If the graphics mode is set to GM_COMPATIBLE, the lfEscapement member specifies the angle for both the line of text and the characters within that line of text, and the lfEscapement and lfOrientation members should be set to the same value.

Windows 95/98/Me: The lfEscapement member always specifies the angle for both the line of text and the characters within that line of text, and the lfEscapement and lfOrientation members should be set to the same value.

lfOrientation: Specifies the angle between the baseline of each individual character and the x-axis in tenths of a degree.

Windows 95/98/Me: The lfEscapement member always specifies the angle for both the line of text and the characters within that line of text, and the lfEscapement and lfOrientation members should be set to the same value.

lfWeight: Specifies the boldness of the font. The value of this member can be in the range of 0-1000, or can be set to one value from Table 13-12. A weight of zero indicates the default boldness value for the specified font.

lfItalic: Specifies the italics attribute for the font. If this member is set to TRUE, the font will be italicized.

lfUnderline: Specifies the underlining attribute for the font. If this member is set to TRUE, the font will be underlined.

lfStrikeOut: Specifies the strikeout attribute for the font. If this member is set to TRUE, the font will be struck out.

lfCharSet: Specifies the character set which the Windows font mapper uses to choose an appropriate font, and can be set to one value from Table 13-13. The font typeface name specified in the lfFaceName member must be a font that defines characters for the specified character set. If this member is set to DEFAULT_CHARSET, the font size and typeface name will be used to find an appropriate font. However, if the specified typeface name is not found, any font from any character set matching the specified values can be used, and can lead to unexpected results.

lfOutPrecision: Specifies how closely the resulting font must match the given height, width, character orientation, escapement, pitch, and font type values. This member can be set to one value from Table 13-14. Note that the OUT_DEVICE_PRECIS, OUT_RASTER_PRECIS, and OUT_TT_PRECIS flags control the Windows font mapper behavior when more then one font exists with the name specified by the lfFaceName member.

lfClipPrecision: Specifies how characters partially outside of the clipping region are drawn. This member can be set to one or more values from Table 13-15.

lfQuality: Specifies how closely the Windows font mapper matches the specified font attributes with an actual font. This member can be set to one value from Table 13-16.

lfPitchAndFamily: The font pitch and font family flags. This member can contain a combination of one value from the pitch flags table (Table 13-17), and one value from the font family flags table (Table 13-18). The values from these tables are combined by using the Boolean OR operator. The pitch describes how the widths of individual character glyphs vary, and the family describes the general look and feel of the font. If the specified typeface name is unavailable, the function returns the closest matching font from the specified font family.

lfFaceName: A pointer to a null-terminated string containing the typeface name of the font. The font typeface name cannot exceed 32 characters in length, including the null terminator. Use the EnumFontFamilies function to retrieve a list of all installed font typeface names. If this member is NIL, the Windows font mapper will choose the first font from the specified font family matching the specified attributes.

Return Value

If the function succeeds, it returns a handle to the newly created logical font; otherwise, it returns zero.

See Also

CreateFont, DeleteObject, EnumFontFamilies, EnumFontFamiliesEx, SelectObject

Example

Listing 13-3: Creating a font indirectly

```
procedure TForm1.FormPaint(Sender: TObject);
var
  FontInfo: TLogFont;       // the logical font information
  NewFont, OldFont: HFont;  // holds the old and new fonts
begin
  {set the background mode for transparency}
  SetBkMode(Form1.Canvas.Handle, TRANSPARENT);

  {initialize the logical font information, setting the weight and escapement
   values to those specified by the trackbars.}
  with FontInfo do
  begin
```

```
    lfHeight := 24;
    lfWidth := 0;
    lfEscapement := TrackBar1.Position*10;
    lfOrientation := TrackBar1.Position*10;
    lfWeight := TrackBar2.Position;
    lfItalic := 0;
    lfUnderline := 0;
    lfStrikeOut := 0;
    lfFaceName := 'Arial';
  end;

  {create the new font}
  NewFont := CreateFontIndirect(FontInfo);

  {select the new font into the form's device context}
  OldFont := SelectObject(Form1.Canvas.Handle, NewFont);

  {output a string of rotated text}
  TextOut(Form1.Canvas.Handle, Form1.Width div 2, 140, 'Delphi Rocks!',
    Length('Delphi Rocks!'));

  {select the original font back into the device context,
   and delete the new one}
  SelectObject(Form1.Canvas.Handle, OldFont);
  DeleteObject(NewFont);
end;
```

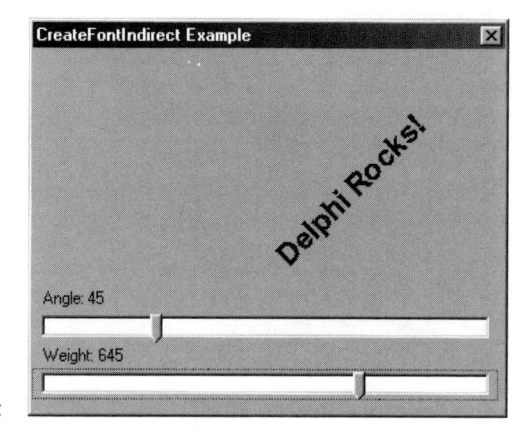

Figure 13-4: A rotated font

Table 13-II: CreateFontIndirect pl.lfHeight font mapper interpretation values

Value	Description
lfHeight>0	The font mapper converts the value of lfHeight into device units, matching the result against the cell height of available fonts.
lfHeight=0	The font mapper uses a default font height when searching for a matching font.
lfHeight<0	The font mapper converts the value of lfHeight into device units, matching the absolute value of the result against the character height of available fonts.

Table 13-12: CreateFontIndirect pl.lfWeight values

Value	Description
FW_DONTCARE	Uses the default bolding value (0).
FW_THIN	Extra thin font weight (100).
FW_EXTRALIGHT	Thin font weight (200).
FW_LIGHT	Below average bolding (300).
FW_NORMAL	Normal bolding (400).
FW_MEDIUM	Above average bolding (500).
FW_SEMIBOLD	Light bolding (600).
FW_BOLD	Bolded font (700).
FW_EXTRABOLD	Extra bolding (800).
FW_HEAVY	Very heaving bolding (900).

Table 13-13: CreateFontIndirect pl.lfCharSet values

Value	Description
ANSI_CHARSET	The ANSI character set.
DEFAULT_CHARSET	The default character set.
SYMBOL_CHARSET	The symbol character set.
SHIFTJIS_CHARSET	The shiftjis character set.
GB2312_CHARSET	The GB2312 character set.
HANGEUL_CHARSET	The Korean character set.
CHINESEBIG5_CHARSET	The Chinese character set.
OEM_CHARSET	The original equipment manufacturer character set.
JOHAB_CHARSET	**Windows 95 or later:** The Johab character set.
HEBREW_CHARSET	**Windows 95 or later:** The Hebrew character set.
ARABIC_CHARSET	**Windows 95 or later:** The Arabic character set.
GREEK_CHARSET	**Windows 95 or later:** The Grecian character set.
TURKISH_CHARSET	**Windows 95 or later:** The Turkish character set.
VIETNAMESE_CHARSET	**Windows 95 or later:** The Vietnamese character set.
THAI_CHARSET	**Windows 95 or later:** The Thai character set.
EASTEUROPE_CHARSET	**Windows 95 or later:** The eastern Europe character set.
RUSSIAN_CHARSET	**Windows 95 or later:** The Russian character set.
MAC_CHARSET	**Windows 95 or later:** The Macintosh character set.
BALTIC_CHARSET	**Windows 95 or later:** The Baltic character set.

Table 13-14: CreateFontIndirect pl.lfOutputPrecision values

Value	Description
OUT_DEFAULT_PRECIS	The default font mapper behavior.
OUT_DEVICE_PRECIS	Chooses a device font when more than one font of the specified name exists.
OUT_OUTLINE_PRECIS	**Windows NT/2000 or later:** Chooses a font from TrueType and other vector-based fonts.

Value	Description
OUT_RASTER_PRECIS	Chooses a raster font when more than one font of the specified name exists.
OUT_STROKE_PRECIS	**Windows 98/NT/2000 or later:** Not used by the font mapper. However, this flag is returned when TrueType and other vector fonts are enumerated. **Windows 95 only:** Chooses a font from vector-based fonts.
OUT_TT_ONLY_PRECIS	Chooses a font only from TrueType fonts. If no TrueType fonts exist, the font mapper reverts to default behavior.
OUT_TT_PRECIS	Chooses a TrueType font when more than one font of the specified name exists.

Table 13-15: CreateFontIndirect pl.lfClipPrecision values

Value	Description
CLIP_DEFAULT_PRECIS	The default clipping behavior.
CLIP_STROKE_PRECIS	This flag is used only when enumerating fonts.
CLIP_EMBEDDED	This flag must be included when using a read-only embedded font.
CLIP_LH_ANGLES	Specifies that font rotation is dependent upon the coordinate system. If this flag is not specified, device fonts always rotate counterclockwise.

Table 13-16: CreateFontIndirect pl.lfQuality values

Value	Description
DEFAULT_QUALITY	Uses the default font quality.
DRAFT_QUALITY	Raster font scaling is enabled, and bold, italic, underline, and strikeout fonts are fabricated as needed. Exact attribute matching is a higher priority than font quality.
PROOF_QUALITY	Raster font scaling is disabled, and the physical font closest to the specified size is chosen. Bold, italic, underline, and strikeout fonts are fabricated as needed. Font quality is a higher priority than exact attribute matching.

Table 13-17: CreateFontIndirect pl.lfPitchAndFamily pitch flag values

Value	Description
DEFAULT_PITCH	The default font pitch is used.
FIXED_PITCH	The width of all character glyphs is equal.
VARIABLE_PITCH	The width of all character glyphs is dependent upon the individual glyph image.

Table 13-18: CreateFontIndirect pl.lfPitchAndFamily font family flag values

Value	Description
FF_DECORATIVE	Indicates a novelty or decorative font, such as Old English.
FF_DONTCARE	The general font style is unknown or unimportant.
FF_MODERN	Indicates a monospaced font with consistent stroke widths, with or without serifs, such as Courier New.

Value	Description
FF_ROMAN	Indicates a proportional font with variable stroke widths, containing serifs, such as Times New Roman.
FF_SCRIPT	Indicates a font resembling handwriting, such as Brush Script.
FF_SWISS	Indicates a proportional font with variable stroke widths, without serifs, such as Arial.

CreateScalableFontResource   Windows.pas

Syntax

```
CreateScalableFontResource(
p1: DWORD;             {read-only flag}
p2: PChar;             {the font resource filename}
p3: PChar;             {the scaleable font filename}
p4: PChar              {the scaleable font file path}
): BOOL;               {returns TRUE or FALSE}
```

Description

This function is used to create a font resource file that is subsequently used by the AddFontResource function to add a TrueType font to the internal Windows font tables. This makes the TrueType font available to all applications. When an application is finished using the TrueType font, it should remove it from the system by calling the RemoveFontResource function.

If only a filename is specified in the p3 parameter with a path in the p4 parameter, the font resource file will not contain any absolute path information, but the system will expect the .TTF file to be located in the System directory. If p3 contains a full path and filename and p4 is set to NIL, the .TTF file must be located in the exact path specified for Windows to install the font.

Parameters

p1: Indicates if the font is a read-only embedded font. If this parameter is set to zero, the font has read and write permission. A value of one indicates that this is a read-only font, and the font will be hidden from other applications and will not appear when the EnumFontFamilies or EnumFontFamiliesEx functions are called.

p2: A pointer to a null-terminated string containing the filename and extension (usually .FOT) of the font resource file that will be created by this function.

p3: A pointer to a null-terminated string containing the name of the TrueType font file used to create the scaleable font resource file. If this string contains only a TrueType font filename and extension, the p4 parameter must point to a string containing the path to the specified file.

p4: A pointer to a null-terminated string containing the path to the scaleable font file. If the p3 parameter contains a full path and filename to the TrueType font, this parameter must be set to NIL.

Return Value

If the function succeeds, it returns TRUE; otherwise, it returns FALSE. To get extended error information, call the GetLastError function.

See Also

AddFontResource, EnumFontFamilies, EnumFontFamiliesEx, RemoveFontResource

Example

Listing 13-4: Installing a new TrueType font

```
{==============================================================================
    The Ventilate font used in this example was generously donated by and is
    copyright © 1997 by Brian J. Bonislawsky - Astigmatic One Eye.  Used with
    permission.

    Astigmatic One Eye is a great source for shareware and freeware fonts of
    all types.  Check them out at http://www.comptechdev.com/cavop/aoe/
==============================================================================}

procedure TForm1.FormCreate(Sender: TObject);
var
  CurDir: array[0..MAX_PATH] of char;     // holds the current directory
begin
  {retrieve the current directory}
  GetCurrentDirectory(MAX_PATH, @CurDir[0]);

  {create a font resource file}
  CreateScalableFontResource(0, PChar(CurDir+'\Ventilat.fot'),
                             PChar(CurDir+'\Ventilat.ttf'),
                             nil);

  {add the font to the internal Windows font tables, making it available
   to any application}
  AddFontResource(PChar(CurDir+'\ventilat.fot'));

  {inform all applications of the change to the font tables}
  SendMessage(HWND_BROADCAST, WM_FONTCHANGE, 0, 0);
end;

procedure TForm1.FormDestroy(Sender: TObject);
var
  CurDir: array[0..MAX_PATH] of char;     // holds the current directory
begin
  {retrieve the current directory}
  GetCurrentDirectory(MAX_PATH, @CurDir[0]);

  {remove the font resource from the internal Windows font tables}
  RemoveFontResource(PChar(CurDir+'\ventilat.fot'));

  {inform all applications of the change to the font tables}
  SendMessage(HWND_BROADCAST, WM_FONTCHANGE, 0, 0);
end;

procedure TForm1.FormPaint(Sender: TObject);
```

```
var
  NewFont, OldFont: HFont;     // holds the old and new fonts
begin
  {set the background mode for transparency}
  SetBkMode(Form1.Canvas.Handle, TRANSPARENT);

  {create a font from the newly installed font resource}
  NewFont := CreateFont(-MulDiv(48, GetDeviceCaps(Form1.Canvas.Handle,
                        LOGPIXELSY), 72), 0, 0, 0, FW_DONTCARE, 0, 0, 0,
                        DEFAULT_CHARSET, OUT_TT_ONLY_PRECIS,
                        CLIP_DEFAULT_PRECIS, DEFAULT_QUALITY, DEFAULT_PITCH or
                        FF_DONTCARE, 'Ventilate');

  {select the font into the form's device context}
  OldFont := SelectObject(Form1.Canvas.Handle, NewFont);

  {output a line of text}
  TextOut(Form1.Canvas.Handle, 8, 8, 'Delphi Rocks!', Length('Delphi Rocks!'));

  {select the old font back into the device context and delete the new font}
  SelectObject(Form1.Canvas.Handle, OldFont);
  DeleteObject(NewFont);
end;
```

Figure 13-5: Using the new font

DrawText   Windows.pas

Syntax

DrawText(
hDC: HDC;   {a handle to a device context}
lpString: PChar;   {the output string}
nCount: Integer;   {the length of the output string}
var lpRect: TRect;   {the formatting rectangle}
uFormat: UINT   {the text formatting flags}
): Integer;   {returns the height of the output text}

Description

This function draws the specified string of text onto the device context specified by the hDC parameter. The text is drawn within the specified rectangle, and is formatted according to the formatting flags identified by the uFormat parameter. The device context's selected font, text color, background color, and background mode are used when drawing the text. Unless otherwise specified by a specific formatting flag, the text is assumed to have multiple lines and will be clipped by the boundaries of the specified rectangle.

Note that strings containing the mnemonic prefix character (&) will underline the character that follows it, and two mnemonic prefix characters will be interpreted as a literal ampersand (&) character.

Parameters

hDC: A handle to the device context upon which the text is to be drawn.

lpString: A pointer to a null-terminated string containing the text to be drawn.

nCount: Specifies the length of the string pointed to by the lpString parameter in characters. If this parameter is set to –1, the string pointed to by the lpString parameter is assumed to be a null-terminated string, and the function will automatically calculate the string length.

lpRect: Specifies the rectangular coordinates, in logical units, within which the text will be drawn and formatted.

uFormat: A series of flags specifying how the text will be output and formatted within the specified rectangle. This parameter can contain one or more values from the following table.

Return Value

If the function succeeds, it returns the height of the text in logical units; otherwise, it returns zero.

See Also

DrawTextEx, GrayString, TabbedTextOut, TextOut

Example

Listing 13-5: Drawing formatted text

```
procedure TForm1.FormPaint(Sender: TObject);
var
  BoundingRect: TRect;                       // the text formatting rectangle
  CurDirectory: array[0..MAX_PATH] of char;  // the directory string
begin
  {create the text formatting bounding rectangle}
  BoundingRect := Rect(Label1.Left, Label1.Top+Label1.Height+3,
                       Form1.Width-(Label1.Left*2), Label1.Top+Label1.Height+83);

  {draw this rectangle visually on the form}
  Form1.Canvas.Rectangle(BoundingRect.Left, BoundingRect.Top,
                         BoundingRect.Right, BoundingRect.Bottom);

  {set the form's background mode for transparency}
  SetBkMode(Form1.Canvas.Handle, TRANSPARENT);

  {draw text at the bottom left of the rectangle}
  DrawText(Form1.Canvas.Handle, 'Delphi Rocks!', -1, BoundingRect,
           DT_BOTTOM or DT_SINGLELINE);

  {draw text in the very center of the rectangle}
```

```
        DrawText(Form1.Canvas.Handle, 'Delphi Rocks!', -1, BoundingRect,
                DT_CENTER or DT_VCENTER or DT_SINGLELINE);

        {draw text at the top right of the rectangle}
        DrawText(Form1.Canvas.Handle, 'Delphi Rocks!', -1, BoundingRect,
                DT_TOP or DT_RIGHT);

        {create a new text formatting bounding rectangle}
        BoundingRect := Rect(Label2.Left, Label2.Top+Label2.Height+3,
                             Label2.Width+Label2.Left, Label2.Top+Label2.Height+73);

        {draw the rectangle visually}
        Form1.Canvas.Rectangle(BoundingRect.Left, BoundingRect.Top,
                               BoundingRect.Right, BoundingRect.Bottom);

        {draw word wrapped text within the rectangle}
        DrawText(Form1.Canvas.Handle, 'Delphi is the most awesome Windows '+
                'development environment on the market.', -1, BoundingRect,
                DT_WORDBREAK);

        {create a new text formatting bounding rectangle}
        BoundingRect := Rect(Label3.Left, Label3.Top+Label3.Height+3,
                             Label3.Width+Label3.Left, Label3.Top+Label3.Height+25);

        {retrieve the current directory}
        GetCurrentDirectory(MAX_PATH, CurDirectory);

        {draw the directory string within the rectangle, reducing it as necessary}
        DrawText(Form1.Canvas.Handle, CurDirectory, -1, BoundingRect,
                DT_PATH_ELLIPSIS);
end;
```

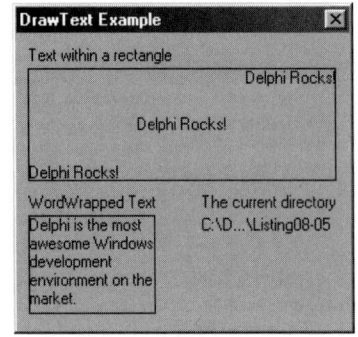

Figure 13-6: Formatted text output

Table 13-19: DrawText uFormat values

Value	Description
DT_BOTTOM	The output text is justified to the bottom of the rectangle. This flag must be combined with the DT_SINGLELINE flag.
DT_CALCRECT	Automatically determines the width and height of the rectangle. For multiline text, the bottom of the rectangle is extended to include the last line of text. For single line text, the right side of the rectangle is extended to include the last character. The function returns the height of the text, but the text is not drawn.

Text Output Functions

Value	Description
DT_CENTER	Centers the text horizontally within the rectangle.
DT_EDITCONTROL	Duplicates the text display behavior of an edit control. Specifically, the function will not draw the last line of text if it is only partially visible.
DT_END_ELLIPSIS	If the string is too large to fit within the specified rectangle, this flag causes the function to replace characters at the end of the string with ellipses (…) such that the resulting string will fit within the rectangle.
DT_EXPANDTABS	Tab characters are expanded when the text is drawn. By default, a tab character expands to eight characters.
DT_EXTERNALLEADING	The returned font height will include the external leading value for the selected font.
DT_HIDEPREFIX	**Windows 2000 or later:** Ampersand (&) characters are ignored, and do not cause the very next character to be underlined. Unlike DT_NOPREFIX, these ampersand characters will not appear in the output text (unless two are found side by side, "&&").
DT_LEFT	The output text is justified to the left of the rectangle.
DT_MODIFYSTRING	Modifies the specified string to match the displayed text. This flag is only useful when combined with the DT_END_ELLIPSES or DT_PATH_ELLIPSIS flags.
DT_NOCLIP	Causes the text to be drawn without clipping it to the boundaries of the specified rectangle. This has a side effect of increased performance.
DT_NOFULLWIDTHCHARBREAK	**Windows 98/Me/2000 or later:** Used with Unicode strings to cause line breaks like ASCII strings. Ignored unless DT_WORDBREAK is also specified.
DT_NOPREFIX	Turns off mnemonic prefix character processing. Specifically, mnemonic prefix characters in the string will be interpreted as literal & characters, and will not cause the following character to be underlined.
DT_PATH_ELLIPSIS	If the string is too large to fit within the specified rectangle, this flag causes the function to replace characters in the middle of the string with ellipses (…) such that the resulting string will fit within the rectangle. If the string contains backslashes (\), as in the case of a path, the function will attempt to preserve as much text as possible following the last backslash in the string.
DT_PREFIXONLY	**Windows 2000 or later:** Draws only an underline character at the position in the string of the ampersand character.
DT_RIGHT	The output text is justified to the right of the rectangle.
DT_RTLREADING	Draws the text in a right-to-left reading order. This flag can only be used when the font selected into the specified device context is a Hebrew or Arabic font; otherwise, it is ignored.
DT_SINGLELINE	The specified text is interpreted as a single line, and carriage returns and line feed characters are ignored.
DT_TABSTOP	Specifies the number of characters that result from expanding a tab. The high-order byte of the low-order word of the uFormat parameter (bits 8-15) should be set to the number of characters to which tabs are expanded.
DT_TOP	The output text is justified to the top of the rectangle. This flag must be combined with the DT_SINGLELINE flag.
DT_VCENTER	Centers the text vertically within the window.
DT_WORDBREAK	Implements a word wrapping algorithm such that any word that would extend past the edge of the rectangle causes a line break to be inserted, with the breaking word drawn on the following line.

DrawTextEx   Windows.pas

Syntax

```
DrawTextEx(
 DC: HDC;                       {a handle to a device context}
 lpchText: PChar;               {the output string}
 cchText: Integer;              {the length of the output string}
 var p4: TRect;                 {the formatting rectangle}
 dwDTFormat: UINT;              {the text formatting flags}
 DTParams: PDrawTextParams      {additional formatting options}
): Integer;                     {returns the height of the output text}
```

Description

This function draws the specified string of text onto the device context specified by the DC parameter. The text is drawn within the specified rectangle, and is formatted according to the formatting flags identified by the dwDTFormat parameter and the additional formatting options identified by the DTParams parameter. The device context's selected font, text color, background color, and background mode are used when drawing the text. Unless otherwise specified by a specific formatting flag, the text is assumed to have multiple lines, and will be clipped by the boundaries of the specified rectangle.

Note that strings containing the mnemonic prefix character (&) will underline the character that follows it, and two mnemonic prefix characters will be interpreted as a literal & character.

Parameters

DC: A handle to the device context upon which the text is to be drawn.

lpchText: A pointer to a null-terminated string containing the text to be drawn.

cchText: Specifies the length of the string pointed to by the lpchText parameter, in characters. If this parameter is set to –1, the string pointed to by the lpchText parameter is assumed to be a null-terminated string, and the function will automatically calculate the string length.

p4: Specifies the rectangular coordinates, in logical units, within which the text will be drawn and formatted.

dwDTFormat: A series of flags specifying how the text will be output and formatted within the specified rectangle. This parameter can contain one or more values from Table 13-20.

DTParams: A pointer to a TDrawTextParams structure that contains additional text formatting options. If this parameter is set to NIL, DrawTextEx behaves exactly like the DrawText function. The TDrawTextParams structure is defined as:

```
TDrawTextParams = packed record
  cbSize: UINT;              {the size of the TDrawTextParams structure}
  iTabLength: Integer;       {the tab stop size}
  iLeftMargin: Integer;      {the left margin}
```

```
        iRightMargin: Integer;      {the right margin}
        uiLengthDrawn: UINT;        {receives the number of characters drawn}
end;
```

cbSize: Specifies the size of the TDrawTextParams structure. This member should be set to SizeOf(TDrawTextParams).

iTabLength: Specifies the width of each tab stop, in units equal to the average character width.

iLeftMargin: Specifies the left margin within the formatting rectangle in logical units.

iRightMargin: Specifies the right margin within the formatting rectangle in logical units.

uiLengthDrawn: Receives the number of characters drawn by the DrawTextEx function, including white space.

Return Value

If the function succeeds, it returns the height of the text in logical units; otherwise, it returns zero.

See Also

DrawText, GrayString, TabbedTextOut, TextOut

Example

Listing 13-6: Drawing text with margins

```
{the large string to be drawn}
const
TheString = 'This function draws the specified string of text onto the '+
            'device context specified by the DC parameter. The text is '+
            'drawn within the specified rectangle, and is formatted '+
            'according to the formatting flags identified by the dwDTFormat '+
            'parameter and the additional formatting options identified by '+
            'the DTParams parameter. The device context''s selected font, '+
            'text color, background color, and background mode are used '+
            'when drawing the text. Unless otherwise specified by a '+
            'specific formatting flag, the text is assumed to have multiple '+
            'lines, and will be clipped by the boundaries of the specified '+
            'rectangle.';

var
  Form1: TForm1;
  ResizingMargins: Boolean;    // indicates if margins are being resized

implementation

{$R *.DFM}

procedure TForm1.PaintBox1Paint(Sender: TObject);
var
  BoundingRect: TRect;             // the text formatting bounding rectangle
  DrawingParams: TDrawTextParams;  // additional text formatting options
```

```
begin
  with PaintBox1.Canvas do
  begin
    {erase the last image}
    Brush.Color := clWhite;
    FillRect(ClipRect);

    {the text formatting rectangle is the size of the paintbox}
    BoundingRect := ClipRect;

    with DrawingParams do
    begin
      {set the size of the optional formatting parameters structure}
      cbSize := SizeOf(TDrawTextParams);

      {initialize the tab length and margins to those specified
       by the panels}
      iTabLength := 0;
      iLeftMargin := (Panel1.Left-PaintBox1.Left);
      iRightMargin := 200-Panel2.Width;
    end;

    {draw the text, with margins}
    DrawTextEx(PaintBox1.Canvas.Handle, TheString, Length(TheString),
               BoundingRect, DT_WORDBREAK, @DrawingParams);
  end;
end;

procedure TForm1.FormCreate(Sender: TObject);
begin
  {we are not initially resizing margins}
  ResizingMargins := FALSE;
end;

procedure TForm1.Panel1MouseDown(Sender: TObject; Button: TMouseButton;
  Shift: TShiftState; X, Y: Integer);
begin
  {the user is dragging a panel and resizing margins}
  ResizingMargins := TRUE;
end;

procedure TForm1.Panel1MouseUp(Sender: TObject; Button: TMouseButton;
  Shift: TShiftState; X, Y: Integer);
begin
  {margins have been resized, so update the screen}
  ResizingMargins := FALSE;
  PaintBox1.Refresh;
end;

procedure TForm1.Panel1MouseMove(Sender: TObject; Shift: TShiftState; X,
  Y: Integer);
begin
  {resize the panel if the user has started to resize margins}
  if ResizingMargins then
  begin
    Panel1.Left  := Panel1.Left+X;
    Panel1.Width := Panel2.Left - Panel1.Left;
```

```
      end;

      {confine the panel to a maximum size}
      if Panel1.Left<PaintBox1.Left then
      begin
        Panel1.Left  := PaintBox1.Left;
        Panel1.Width := 200;
      end;
    end;

    procedure TForm1.Panel2MouseMove(Sender: TObject; Shift: TShiftState; X,
      Y: Integer);
    begin
      {resize the panel if the user has started to resize margins}
      if ResizingMargins then
        Panel2.Width := X;

      {confine the panel to a maximum size}
      if Panel2.Width>200 then
        Panel2.Width := 200;
    end;
```

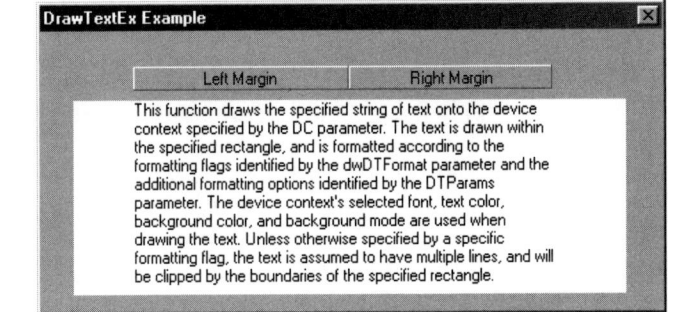

Figure 13-7: Formatted text with margins

Table 13-20: DrawTextEx dwDTFormat values

Value	Description
DT_BOTTOM	The output text is justified to the bottom of the rectangle. This flag must be combined with the DT_SINGLELINE flag.
DT_CALCRECT	Automatically determines the width and height of the rectangle. For multi-line text, the bottom of the rectangle is extended to include the last line of text. For single line text, the right side of the rectangle is extended to include the last character. The function returns the height of the text, but the text is not drawn.
DT_CENTER	Centers the text horizontally within the rectangle.
DT_EDITCONTROL	Duplicates the text display behavior of an edit control. Specifically, the function will not draw the last line of text if it is only partially visible.
DT_END_ELLIPSIS	If the string is too large to fit within the specified rectangle, this flag causes the function to replace characters at the end of the string with ellipses (...) such that the resulting string will fit within the rectangle.
DT_EXPANDTABS	Tab characters are expanded when the text is drawn. By default, a tab character expands to eight characters.

Value	Description
DT_EXTERNALLEADING	The returned font height will include the external leading value for the selected font.
DT_HIDEPREFIX	**Windows 2000 or later:** Ampersand (&) characters are ignored and do not cause the very next character to be underlined. Unlike DT_NOPREFIX, these ampersand characters will not appear in the output text (unless two are found side by side, "&&").
DT_LEFT	The output text is justified to the left of the rectangle.
DT_MODIFYSTRING	Modifies the specified string to match the displayed text. This flag is only useful when combined with DT_END_ELLIPSES or DT_PATH_ELLIPSIS.
DT_NOCLIP	Causes the text to be drawn without clipping it to the boundaries of the specified rectangle. This has a side effect of increased performance.
DT_NOFULLWIDTHCHARBREAK	**Windows 98/Me/2000 or later:** Used with Unicode strings to cause line breaks like ASCII strings. Ignored unless DT_WORDBREAK is also specified.
DT_NOPREFIX	Turns off mnemonic prefix character processing. Specifically, mnemonic prefix characters in the string will be interpreted as a literal & character and will not cause the following character to be underlined.
DT_PATH_ELLIPSIS	If the string is too large to fit within the specified rectangle, this flag causes the function to replace characters in the middle of the string with ellipses (…) such that the resulting string will fit within the rectangle. If the string contains backslashes (\), as in the case of a path, the function will attempt to preserve as much text as possible following the last backslash in the string.
DT_PREFIXONLY	**Windows 2000 or later:** Draws only an underline character at the position in the string of the ampersand character.
DT_RIGHT	The output text is justified to the right of the rectangle.
DT_RTLREADING	Draws the text in a right-to-left reading order. This flag can only be used when the font selected into the specified device context is a Hebrew or Arabic font; otherwise, it is ignored.
DT_SINGLELINE	The specified text is interpreted as a single line, and carriage returns and line feed characters are ignored.
DT_TABSTOP	Specifies the number of characters that result from expanding a tab. The high-order byte of the low-order word of the uFormat parameter (bits 8-15) should be set to the number of characters to which tabs are expanded.
DT_TOP	The output text is justified to the top of the rectangle. This flag must be combined with the DT_SINGLELINE flag.
DT_VCENTER	Centers the text vertically within the window.
DT_WORDBREAK	Implements a word wrapping algorithm such that any word that would extend past the edge of the rectangle causes a line break to be inserted, with the breaking word drawn on the following line.

EnumFontFamilies Windows.pas

Syntax

```
EnumFontFamilies(
  DC: HDC;                  {a handle to a device context}
  p2: PChar;                {the font typeface name}
  p3: TFNFontEnumProc;      {a pointer to the callback function}
```

p4: LPARAM	{32-bit application-defined data}
): BOOL;	{returns TRUE or FALSE}

Description

This function passes font information for every font available in the specified device context with the specified typeface to an application-defined callback function. This includes TrueType, raster, and vector fonts, but excludes any read-only TrueType fonts. The enumeration will continue until all fonts have been enumerated or the callback function returns zero.

Parameters

DC: A handle to the device context whose fonts are to be enumerated. The function enumerates all fonts available on the specified device context.

p2: A pointer to a null-terminated string containing the typeface name whose associated fonts are to be enumerated. If this parameter is set to NIL, the function enumerates one randomly selected font from each typeface.

p3: The address of the application-defined callback function.

p4: Contains a 32-bit application-defined value that is passed to the enumeration function.

Return Value

If the last value returned by the callback function is a non-zero value, the function returns TRUE. If the last value returned by the callback function is zero, the function returns FALSE. This function does not indicate an error upon failure.

Callback Syntax

EnumFontFamProc(	
LogFont: PEnumLogFont;	{a pointer to logical font attributes}
TextMetrics: PNewTextMetric;	{a pointer to physical font attributes}
FontType: Integer;	{the font type flags}
lParam: LPARAM	{the 32-bit application-defined data}
): Integer;	{returns a non-zero value to continue enumeration}

Description

This function receives a pointer to a TEnumLogFont structure and a TNewTextMetric structure for each font enumerated, and may perform any desired task.

Parameters

LogFont: A pointer to a TEnumLogFont structure containing logical font attributes for the currently enumerated font. The TEnumLogFont structure is defined as:

```
TEnumLogFont = packed record
    elfLogFont: TLogFont;                                        {the logical font info}
    elfFullName: array[0..LF_FULLFACESIZE – 1] of AnsiChar; {the full font name}
    elfStyle: array[0..LF_FACESIZE – 1] of AnsiChar;      {the font style}
end;
```

elfLogFont: Specifies a TLogFont structure describing the logical attributes of the font. The TLogFont structure is defined as:

```
TLogFont = packed record
    lfHeight: Longint;              {the font height}
    lfWidth: Longint;               {character width}
    lfEscapement: Longint;          {escapement angle}
    lfOrientation: Longint;         {baseline angle}
    lfWeight: Longint;              {the bolding weight}
    lfItalic: Byte;                 {the italics flag}
    lfUnderline: Byte;              {the underline flag}
    lfStrikeOut: Byte;              {the strikeout flag}
    lfCharSet: Byte;                {the character set}
    lfOutPrecision: Byte;           {output precision flag}
    lfClipPrecision: Byte;          {clipping precision}
    lfQuality: Byte;                {output quality flag}
    lfPitchAndFamily: Byte;         {pitch and family flags}
    lfFaceName: array[0..LF_FACESIZE – 1] of AnsiChar;  {font typeface name}
end;
```

See the CreateFontIndirect function for a description of this data structure.

elfFullName: A null-terminated string containing the full, unique name for the enumerated font.

elfStyle: A null-terminated string containing the style of the font.

TextMetrics: A pointer to a TNewTextMetric structure containing physical font attributes for the currently enumerated font. Note that if the currently enumerated font is not a TrueType font, this parameter will point to a TTextMetric structure. All measurements returned by this structure are in logical units and depend on the current mapping mode of the specified device context. The TNewTextMetric structure is defined as:

```
TNewTextMetric = record
    tmHeight: Longint;              {the height of a character}
    tmAscent: Longint;              {the ascent of a character}
    tmDescent: Longint;             {the descent of a character}
    tmInternalLeading: Longint;     {the internal leading}
    tmExternalLeading: Longint;     {the external leading}
    tmAveCharWidth: Longint;        {the average character width}
    tmMaxCharWidth: Longint;        {the maximum character width}
    tmWeight: Longint;              {the boldness value}
    tmOverhang: Longint;            {the overhang width}
    tmDigitizedAspectX: Longint;    {the horizontal aspect}
    tmDigitizedAspectY: Longint;    {the vertical aspect}
    tmFirstChar: AnsiChar;          {the first character}
    tmLastChar: AnsiChar;           {the last character}
    tmDefaultChar: AnsiChar;        {the default character}
    tmBreakChar: AnsiChar;          {the word break character}
```

tmItalic: Byte;	{the italics flag}
tmUnderlined: Byte;	{the underlined flag}
tmStruckOut: Byte;	{the strikeout flag}
tmPitchAndFamily: Byte;	{the pitch and family flags}
tmCharSet: Byte;	{the character set}
ntmFlags: DWORD;	{attribute bitmask}
ntmSizeEM: UINT;	{the em square size in notional units}
ntmCellHeight: UINT;	{the cell height in notional units}
ntmAvgWidth: UINT;	{the average character width in notional units}

end;

Except for the last four members, this data structure is identical to the TTextMetric data structure. See the GetTextMetrics function for a description of the TTextMetric structure containing the other members.

ntmFlags: A bitmask specifying various attributes of the font. Each bit in the mask identifies a different font attribute as described in Table 13-21. If a specific bit is set, that attribute is present in the currently enumerated font.

ntmSizeEM: Specifies the size of the em square for the font in notional units. A notional unit is the unit for which the font was originally designed.

ntmCellHeight: Specifies the height of a character cell for the font in notional units.

ntmAvgWidth: Specifies the average character width for the font in notional units.

FontType: Specifies a series of flags indicating the type of font being enumerated. This parameter may contain one or more values from Table 13-22. Note that if neither the RASTER_FONTTYPE nor the TRUETYPE_FONTTYPE flag is present, the enumerated font is a vector font.

lParam: Specifies the 32-bit application-defined value passed to the EnumFontFamilies function in the p4 parameter.

Return Value

The callback function should return a non-zero value to continue enumeration, or a zero to terminate enumeration.

See Also

CreateFontIndirect, EnumFontFamiliesEx, GetTextMetrics

Example

Listing 13-7: Enumerating available fonts

```
{the callback function prototype}
function FontEnumProc(LogFont: PEnumLogFont; TextMetrics: PNewTextMetric;
                      FontType: Integer; lParam: LPARAM): Integer; stdcall;

var
  Form1: TForm1;

implementation
```

```
{$R *.DFM}

procedure TForm1.FormActivate(Sender: TObject);
var
  RasterStatus: TRasterizerStatus;    // holds raster capabilities
begin
  {set the size of the raster status structure}
  RasterStatus.nSize := SizeOf(TRasterizerStatus);

  {retrieve the rasterizer status}
  GetRasterizerCaps(RasterStatus, SizeOf(TRasterizerStatus));

  {indicate if TrueType fonts are enabled and available}
  if (RasterStatus.wFlags and TT_ENABLED) = TT_ENABLED then
    CheckBox1.Checked := TRUE;
  if (RasterStatus.wFlags and TT_AVAILABLE) = TT_AVAILABLE then
    CheckBox2.Checked := TRUE;

  {enumerate all installed fonts}
  EnumFontFamilies(Form1.Canvas.Handle, NIL, @FontEnumProc, 0);
end;

function FontEnumProc(LogFont: PEnumLogFont; TextMetrics: PNewTextMetric;
                      FontType: Integer; lParam: LPARAM): Integer; stdcall;
begin
  {add the font name and it's font type to the list box}
  Form1.ListBox1.Items.AddObject(TEnumLogFont(LogFont^).elfLogFont.lfFaceName,
                                TObject(FontType));

  {continue enumeration}
  Result := 1;
end;

procedure TForm1.ListBox1DrawItem(Control: TWinControl; Index: Integer;
  Rect: TRect; State: TOwnerDrawState);
begin
  {indicate if the font is a TrueType or other type of font}
  if Integer(ListBox1.Items.Objects[Index]) = TRUETYPE_FONTTYPE then
    ListBox1.Canvas.Draw(Rect.Left, Rect.Top, Image2.Picture.Bitmap)
  else
    ListBox1.Canvas.Draw(Rect.Left, Rect.Top, Image1.Picture.Bitmap);

  {draw the font name}
  Rect.Left := Rect.Left + 18;
  Rect.Top  := Rect.Top + 2;
  TextOut(ListBox1.Canvas.Handle, Rect.Left, Rect.Top,
          PChar(ListBox1.Items[Index]), Length(ListBox1.Items[Index]));
end;
```

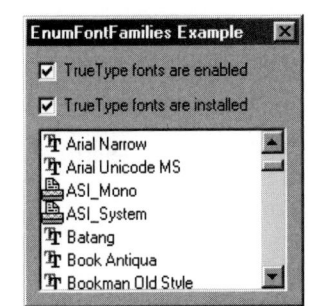

Figure 13-8: The available font names

Table 13-21: EnumFontFamilies EnumFontFamProc TextMetrics.ntmFlags bit values

Bit Position	Description
0	Indicates an italic font.
1	Indicates an underscored font.
2	Indicates a negative image font.
3	Indicates an outline font.
4	Indicates a strikeout font.
5	Indicates a bold font.

Table 13-22: EnumFontFamilies EnumFontFamProc FontType values

Value	Description
DEVICE_FONTTYPE	Indicates a device resident font, or that the specified device supports download TrueType fonts.
RASTER_FONTTYPE	Indicates a raster, or bitmap, font.
TRUETYPE_FONTTYPE	Indicates a TrueType font.

EnumFontFamiliesEx   Windows.pas

Syntax

```
EnumFontFamiliesEx(
DC: HDC;                  {a handle to a device context}
var p2: TLogFont;         {a TLogFont structure}
p3: TFNFontEnumProc;      {a pointer to the callback function}
p4: LPARAM;               {32-bit application-defined data}
p5: DWORD                 {this parameter is reserved}
): BOOL;                  {returns TRUE or FALSE}
```

Description

This function passes font information for every font available in the specified device context that matches the attributes defined by the TLogFont structure to an application-defined callback function. This includes TrueType, raster, and vector fonts, but excludes any read-only TrueType fonts. The enumeration will continue until all fonts have been enumerated or the callback function returns zero.

Parameters

DC: A handle to the device context whose fonts are to be enumerated. The function enumerates all fonts available on the specified device context.

p2: A pointer to a TLogFont structure containing information that determines which fonts to enumerate. The TLogFont structure is defined as:

```
TLogFont = packed record
    lfHeight: Longint;                {the font height in logical units}
    lfWidth: Longint;                 {the average character width}
    lfEscapement: Longint;            {the escapement vector angle}
    lfOrientation: Longint;           {the character baseline angle}
    lfWeight: Longint;                {the bolding weight}
    lfItalic: Byte;                   {the italics flag}
    lfUnderline: Byte;                {the underline flag}
    lfStrikeOut: Byte;                {the strikeout flag}
    lfCharSet: Byte;                  {the character set}
    lfOutPrecision: Byte;             {the output precision flag}
    lfClipPrecision: Byte;            {the clipping precision flags}
    lfQuality: Byte;                  {the output quality flag}
    lfPitchAndFamily: Byte;           {the pitch and family flags}
    lfFaceName: array[0..LF_FACESIZE – 1] of AnsiChar;    {the font typeface name}
end;
```

See the CreateFontIndirect function for a description of this data structure. Only the lfCharSet, lfFaceName, and lfPitchAndFamily members determine the behavior of the EnumFontFamiliesEx function.

lfCharSet: If this member is set to DEFAULT_CHARSET, the function enumerates every font in every character set. If this member is set to a specific character set, only fonts that define characters for the indicated character set will be enumerated.

lfFaceName: If this member is set to an empty string, one randomly selected font from each typeface is enumerated. If this member is set to a valid typeface name, only fonts with the specified typeface name will be enumerated.

lfPitchAndFamily: This member is only used with Hebrew or Arabic fonts, and must be set to zero for any other font type. For Hebrew and Arabic fonts, this member can be set to MONO_FONT to enumerate only fonts containing all codepage characters.

p3: The address of the application-defined callback function.

p4: Contains a 32-bit application-defined value that is passed to the enumeration function.

p5: This parameter is reserved for future use, and must be set to zero.

Return Value

If the last value returned by the callback function is a non-zero value, the function returns TRUE. If the last value returned by the callback function is zero, the function returns FALSE. This function does not indicate an error upon failure.

Callback Syntax

```
EnumFontFamExProc(
    LogFont: PEnumLogFontEx;        {a pointer to logical font attributes}
    TextMetrics: PNewTextMetric;    {a pointer to physical font attributes}
    FontType: Integer;              {the font type flags}
    lParam: LPARAM                  {the 32-bit application-defined data}
): Integer;                         {returns a non-zero value to continue enumeration}
```

Description

This function receives a pointer to a TEnumLogFontEx structure and a TNewTextMetricEx structure for each font enumerated, and may perform any desired task.

Parameters

LogFont: A pointer to a TEnumLogFontEx structure containing logical font attributes for the currently enumerated font. The TEnumLogFontEx structure is defined as:

```
TEnumLogFontEx = packed record
    elfLogFont: TLogFont;                              {the logical font info}
    elfFullName: array[0..LF_FULLFACESIZE – 1] of Char; {the full font name}
    elfStyle: array[0..LF_FACESIZE – 1] of Char;       {the font style}
    elfScript: array[0..LF_FACESIZE – 1] of Char;      {the font script}
end;
```

elfLogFont: Specifies a TLogFont structure describing the logical attributes of the font. See the CreateFontIndirect function for a description of this data structure.

elfFullName: A null-terminated string containing the full, unique name for the enumerated font.

elfStyle: A null-terminated string containing the style of the font.

elfScript: A null-terminated string containing the script of the font.

TextMetrics: A pointer to a TNewTextMetricEx structure containing physical font attributes for the currently enumerated font. Note that if the currently enumerated font is not a TrueType font, this parameter will point to a TTextMetric structure.

Windows 95/98/Me: The TNewTextMetricEx structure is not implemented, and this parameter will instead point to a TNewTextMetric structure. The TNewTextMetricEx structure is defined as:

```
TNewTextMetricEx = packed record
    ntmTm: TNewTextMetric;          {a TNewTextMetric structure}
    ntmFontSig: TFontSignature;     {a TFontSignature structure}
end;
```

ntmTm: A TNewTextMetric structure containing physical font attributes for the currently enumerated font. The TNewTextMetric structure is defined as:

```
TNewTextMetric = record
    tmHeight: Longint;              {the height of a character}
    tmAscent: Longint;              {the ascent of a character}
```

```
    tmDescent: Longint;              {the descent of a character}
    tmInternalLeading: Longint;      {the internal leading}
    tmExternalLeading: Longint;      {the external leading}
    tmAveCharWidth: Longint;         {the average character width}
    tmMaxCharWidth: Longint;         {the maximum character width}
    tmWeight: Longint;               {the boldness value}
    tmOverhang: Longint;             {the overhang width}
    tmDigitizedAspectX: Longint;     {the horizontal aspect}
    tmDigitizedAspectY: Longint;     {the vertical aspect}
    tmFirstChar: AnsiChar;           {the first character}
    tmLastChar: AnsiChar;            {the last character}
    tmDefaultChar: AnsiChar;         {the default character}
    tmBreakChar: AnsiChar;           {the word break character}
    tmItalic: Byte;                  {the italics flag}
    tmUnderlined: Byte;              {the underlined flag}
    tmStruckOut: Byte;               {the strikeout flag}
    tmPitchAndFamily: Byte;          {the pitch and family flags}
    tmCharSet: Byte;                 {the character set}
    ntmFlags: DWORD;                 {attribute bitmask}
    ntmSizeEM: UINT;                 {the em square size in notional units}
    ntmCellHeight: UINT;             {the cell height in notional units}
    ntmAvgWidth: UINT;               {the average character width}
end;
```

See the EnumFontFamilies function for a description of this data structure.

ntmFontSig: A TFontSignature structure identifying the code pages and Unicode subranges for which the currently enumerated font provides glyph images. The TFontSignature structure is defined as:

```
TFontSignature = packed record
    fsUsb: array[0..3] of DWORD;     {the Unicode subset bitmask}
    fsCsb: array[0..1] of DWORD;     {the code page bitmask}
end;
```

fsUsb: A 128-bit Unicode subset bitmask that identifies 126 Unicode subranges, where each bit except the two most significant bits identifies a single subrange. The most significant bit is always set, and the second most significant bit is currently reserved and will not be set.

fsCsb: A 64-bit code page bitmask identifying a specific character set or code page, where each bit identifies a single code page. The low-order double word specifies Windows code pages, and the high-order double word specifies non-Windows code pages. The code page for each individual bit is listed in Table 13-23.

FontType: Specifies a series of flags indicating the type of font being enumerated. This parameter may contain one or more values from Table 13-24. Note that if neither the

RASTER_FONTTYPE nor the TRUETYPE_FONTTYPE flag is present, the enumerated font is a vector font.

lParam: Specifies the 32-bit application-defined value passed to the EnumFontFamiliesEx function in the p4 parameter.

Return Value

The callback function should return a non-zero value to continue enumeration, or a zero to terminate enumeration.

See Also

CreateFontIndirect, EnumFontFamilies, GetTextMetrics

Example

Listing 13-8: Enumerating only symbol fonts

```
{the callback function prototype}
function FontEnumExProc(LogFont: PEnumLogFontEx; TextMetrics: PNewTextMetric;
                       FontType: Integer; lParam: LPARAM): Integer; stdcall;

var
  Form1: TForm1;

implementation

{$R *.DFM}

procedure TForm1.FormActivate(Sender: TObject);
var
  FontInfo: TLogFont;    // holds the font enumeration information
begin
  {initialize the font information to enumerate all fonts belonging
   to the symbol character set}
  FontInfo.lfCharSet       := SYMBOL_CHARSET;
  FontInfo.lfFaceName      := '';
  FontInfo.lfPitchAndFamily := 0;

  {enumerate the fonts}
  EnumFontFamiliesEx(Form1.Canvas.Handle, FontInfo, @FontEnumExProc, 0, 0);
end;

function FontEnumExProc(LogFont: PEnumLogFontEx; TextMetrics: PNewTextMetric;
                       FontType: Integer; lParam: LPARAM): Integer; stdcall;
begin
  {add the font typeface name and its type to the list box}
  Form1.ListBox1.Items.AddObject(TEnumLogFontEx(LogFont^).elfLogFont.lfFaceName,
                                 TObject(FontType));

  {continue enumeration}
  Result := 1;
end;

procedure TForm1.ListBox1DrawItem(Control: TWinControl; Index: Integer;
  Rect: TRect; State: TOwnerDrawState);
```

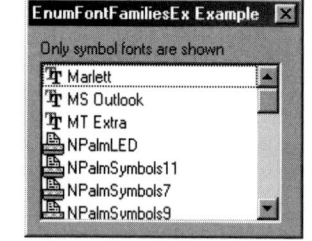

```
begin
  {indicate if the font is a TrueType or other type of font}
  if Integer(ListBox1.Items.Objects[Index]) = TRUETYPE_FONTTYPE then
    ListBox1.Canvas.Draw(Rect.Left, Rect.Top, Image2.Picture.Bitmap)
  else
    ListBox1.Canvas.Draw(Rect.Left, Rect.Top, Image1.Picture.Bitmap);

  {draw the font name}
  Rect.Left := Rect.Left + 18;
  Rect.Top  := Rect.Top + 2;
  TextOut(ListBox1.Canvas.Handle, Rect.Left, Rect.Top,
          PChar(ListBox1.Items[Index]), Length(ListBox1.Items[Index]));
end;
```

Figure 13-9:
All available
symbol fonts

Table 13-23: EnumFontFamiliesEx EnumFontFamExProc TextMetrics.ntmFontSig.fsCsb values

Bit	Code Page	Description
0	1252	Latin 1
1	1250	Latin 2 (Eastern Europe)
2	1251	Cyrillic
3	1253	Greek
4	1254	Turkish
5	1255	Hebrew
6	1256	Arabic
7	1257	Baltic
8-16		Reserved for ANSI
17	874	Thai
18	932	JIS/Japan
19	936	Chinese simplified characters
20	949	Korean Unified Hangeul Code
21	950	Chinese traditional characters
22-29		Reserved for alternate ANSI and OEM use
30-21		Reserved by the system
32-47		Reserved for OEM use
48	869	IBM Greek
49	866	MS-DOS Russian
50	865	MS-DOS Nordic
51	864	Arabic
52	863	MS-DOS Canadian French

Bit	Code Page	Description
53	862	Hebrew
54	861	MS-DOS Icelandic
55	860	MS-DOS Portuguese
56	857	IBM Turkish
57	855	IBM Cyrillic
58	852	Latin 2
59	776	Baltic
60	737	Greek
61	708	Arabic (ASMO 708)
62	850	WE/Latin 1
63	437	United States

Table 13-24: EnumFontFamiliesEx EnumFontFamExProc FontType values

Value	Description
DEVICE_FONTTYPE	Indicates a device resident font, or that the specified device supports download TrueType fonts.
RASTER_FONTTYPE	Indicates a raster, or bitmap, font.
TRUETYPE_FONTTYPE	Indicates a TrueType font.

GetCharABCWidths   Windows.pas

Syntax

```
GetCharABCWidths(
  DC: HDC;              {a handle to a device context}
  p2: UINT;             {the first character in the range}
  p3: UINT;             {the last character in the range}
  const ABCStructs      {points to an array of TABC structures}
  ): BOOL;              {returns TRUE or FALSE}
```

Description

This function retrieves various spacing width values for the currently selected TrueType font in the device context identified by the DC parameter. These values are retrieved from a range of consecutive characters within the font. For each character in the range, a matching TABC structure in the array of TABC structures pointed to by the ABCStructs parameter receives three width values. The A spacing value is the distance added to the current position before placing the next character glyph when outputting a line of text. The B spacing value is the actual width of the character glyph. The C spacing value is the distance added to the right of the glyph to provide white space for separating characters. A negative value for the A or C spacing values indicates a font with an underhang or overhang. Note that this function succeeds only for TrueType fonts. To retrieve the width for non-TrueType font characters, use the GetCharWidth function.

Parameters

DC: A handle to the device context whose character widths for the currently selected font are to be retrieved.

p2: Specifies the value of the first character in the range of characters.

p3: Specifies the value of the last character in the range of characters.

ABCStructs: A pointer to an array of TABC structures that receive the ABC spacing widths of each character in the defined range. There must be at least as many TABC structures in the array as there are characters in the range defined by the p2 and p3 parameters. The TABC structure is defined as:

```
TABC = packed record
     abcA: Integer;         {the next character offset}
     abcB: UINT;            {the width of the glyph}
     abcC: Integer;         {the white space}
end;
```

abcA: Specifies the distance added to the current position before placing the next character glyph when outputting a line of text in logical units.

abcB: Specifies the actual width of the character glyph in logical units.

abcC: Specifies the distance added to the right of the glyph to provide white space for separating characters in logical units.

Return Value

If the function succeeds, it returns TRUE; otherwise, it returns FALSE. To get extended error information, call the GetLastError function.

See Also

GetCharWidth, GetOutlineTextMetrics, GetTextMetrics

Example

Listing 13-9: Retrieving ABC widths for all uppercase letters

```
procedure TForm1.FormActivate(Sender: TObject);
var
  CharWidths: array[0..25]of TABC;    // holds character ABC widths
  Count: Integer;                      // general loop control variable
begin
  {initialize the string grid}
  StringGrid1.Cells[0,0] := 'Character';
  StringGrid1.Cells[1,0] := '''A'' Width';
  StringGrid1.Cells[2,0] := '''B'' Width';
  StringGrid1.Cells[3,0] := '''C'' Width';

  {retrieve ABC widths for all upper case letters}
  GetCharABCWidths(Form1.Canvas.Handle, Ord('A'), Ord('Z'), CharWidths);

  {display the ABC widths for all uppercase letters}
  for Count := 0 to 26 do
```

```
  begin
    StringGrid1.Cells[0, Count+1] := Char(Ord('A')+Count);
    StringGrid1.Cells[1, Count+1] := IntToStr(CharWidths[Count].abcA);
    StringGrid1.Cells[2, Count+1] := IntToStr(CharWidths[Count].abcB);
    StringGrid1.Cells[3, Count+1] := IntToStr(CharWidths[Count].abcC);
  end;
end;
```

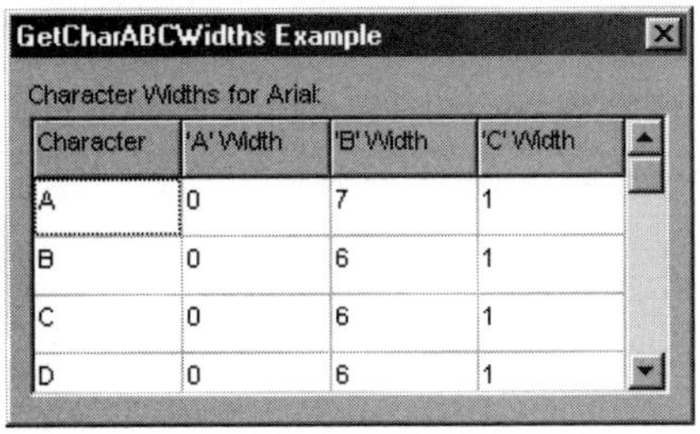

Figure 13-10: The uppercase letter ABC widths

GetCharWidth   Windows.pas

Syntax

GetCharWidth(
DC: HDC;   {a handle to a device context}
p2: UINT;   {the first character in the range}
p3: UINT;   {the last character in the range}
const Widths   {a pointer to an array of integers}
): BOOL;   {returns TRUE or FALSE}

Description

This function retrieves the width of each character in a range of characters for the currently selected TrueType font in the device context identified by the DC parameter. For each character in the range, a matching integer in the array of integers pointed to by the Widths parameter receives the character width. This function is useful for both TrueType and non-TrueType fonts. However, TrueType fonts should use the GetCharABCWidths function to retrieve more accurate values.

Parameters

DC: A handle to the device context whose character widths for the currently selected font are to be retrieved.

p2: Specifies the value of the first character in the range of characters.

p3: Specifies the value of the last character in the range of characters.

Widths: A pointer to an array of integers that receive the character widths of each character in the defined range. There must be at least as many integers in the array as there are characters in the range defined by the p2 and p3 parameters.

Return Value

If this function succeeds, it returns TRUE; otherwise, it returns FALSE. To get extended error information, call the GetLastError function.

See Also

GetCharABCWidths, GetTextExtentExPoint, GetTextExtentPoint32

Example

Listing 13-10: Retrieving character widths for all uppercase letters

```
procedure TForm1.FormActivate(Sender: TObject);
var
  CharWidths: array[0..25] of Integer;    // holds the character widths
  Count: Integer;                         // general loop control variable
begin
  {initialize the string grid}
  StringGrid1.Cells[0,0] := 'Character';
  StringGrid1.Cells[1,0] := 'Width';

  {retrieve the widths of all uppercase letters}
  GetCharWidth(Form1.Canvas.Handle, Ord('A'), Ord('Z'), CharWidths);

  {display the character widths}
  for Count := 0 to 26 do
  begin
    StringGrid1.Cells[0, Count+1] := Char(Ord('A')+Count);
    StringGrid1.Cells[1, Count+1] := IntToStr(CharWidths[Count]);
  end;
end;
```

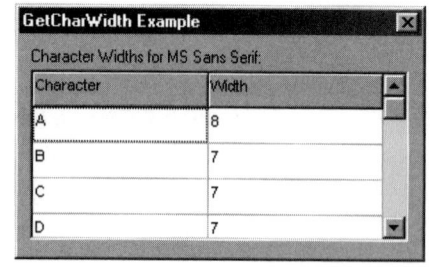

Figure 13-11: The uppercase letter character widths

GetFontData   Windows.pas

Syntax

```
GetFontData(
  DC: HDC;           {a handle to a device context}
  p2: DWORD;         {the font metric table}
  p3: DWORD;         {the offset into the font metric table}
  p4: Pointer;       {a pointer to a buffer receiving the information}
  p5: DWORD          {the amount of data to retrieve}
): DWORD;            {returns the number of bytes retrieved}
```

Description

This function retrieves information from the font metric table specified by the p2 parameter for the TrueType font currently selected into the device context identified by the DC parameter. GetFontData can be used to retrieve an entire TrueType font file for purposes of embedding a font into a document.

Parameters

DC: Specifies a handle to the device context whose currently selected font's information is to be retrieved.

p2: Specifies the font metric table from which data is to be retrieved. The TrueType font metric tables are described in the TrueType font file specification published by Microsoft. If this parameter is set to zero, the function retrieves information starting at the beginning of the font file.

p3: Specifies the offset from the beginning of the specified metric table where the function begins retrieving information. If this parameter is set to zero, the function retrieves information starting at the beginning of the specified metric table.

p4: A pointer to a buffer that receives the retrieved information. If this parameter is set to NIL, the function returns the size of buffer required to hold the requested information.

p5: Specifies the amount of information to retrieve, in bytes. If this parameter is set to zero, the function returns the size of the metric table specified by the p2 parameter.

Return Value

If the function succeeds, it returns the number of bytes of font data retrieved; otherwise, it returns GDI_ERROR.

See Also

AddFontResource, CreateScalableFontResource, GetTextMetrics, RemoveFontResource

Example

See Listing 13-1 demonstrating font embedding in the introduction.

GetGlyphOutline   Windows.pas

Syntax

```
GetGlyphOutline(
  DC: HDC;                          {a handle to a device context}
  p2: UINT;                         {the character}
  p3: UINT;                         {data format flags}
  const p4: TGlyphMetrics;          {a pointer to a TGlyphMetrics structure}
  p5: DWORD;                        {the size of the data buffer}
  p6: Pointer;                      {a pointer to the data buffer}
  const p7: TMat2                   {the rotation matrix}
): DWORD;                           {returns an error code}
```

Description

This function retrieves outline information for the specified character in the TrueType (only) font currently selected into the device context identified by the DC parameter. The outline information retrieved is in the form of either a monochrome bitmap or a series of lines and curves describing the glyph shape in its native format. This information is stored in the buffer pointed to by the p6 parameter.

Parameters

DC: A handle to the device context whose currently selected TrueType font is used when retrieving the outline information.

p2: Identifies the code of the character whose outline is to be retrieved.

p3: Specifies the format of the retrieved outline information. This parameter can contain one value from Table 13-25.

p4: A pointer to a TGlyphMetrics structure which receives information concerning the physical attributes of the character glyph. The TGlyphMetrics structure is defined as:

```
TGlyphMetrics = packed record
    gmBlackBoxX: UINT;         {the smallest rectangle width}
    gmBlackBoxY: UINT;         {the smallest rectangle height}
    gmptGlyphOrigin: TPoint;   {the smallest rectangle origin}
    gmCellIncX: SHORT;         {the next character cell horizontal offset}
    gmCellIncY: SHORT;         {the next character cell vertical offset}
end;
```

gmBlackBoxX: Indicates the width of the smallest rectangle that the glyph image would completely fit inside, in device units.

gmBlackBoxY: Indicates the height of the smallest rectangle that the glyph image would completely fit inside, in device units.

gmptGlyphOrigin: Indicates the horizontal and vertical coordinates within the character cell of the origin of the smallest rectangle that the glyph image would completely fit inside, in device units.

gmCellIncX: Indicates the horizontal offset from the beginning of the current character cell to the beginning of the next character cell in device units.

gmCellIncY: Indicates the vertical offset from the beginning of the current character cell to the beginning of the next character cell in device units.

p5: Specifies the size of the data buffer pointed to by the p6 parameter. If this parameter is set to zero, the function returns the required size of the buffer.

p6: A pointer to a buffer that receives the glyph outline information. If this parameter is set to NIL, the function returns the required size of the buffer.

p7: A pointer to a TMat2 structure defining a 3 X 3 transformation matrix, used to rotate the font to any angle. The TMat2 structure is defined as:

```
TMat2 = packed record
    eM11: TFixed;              {a fixed-point angle}
```

```
        eM12: TFixed;            {a fixed-point angle}
        eM21: TFixed;            {a fixed-point angle}
        eM22: TFixed;            {a fixed-point angle}
end;
```

eM11: Identifies the angle of font rotation, in the form of a TFixed structure, for the M11 value of a 3 X 3 transformation matrix.

eM12: Identifies the angle of font rotation, in the form of a TFixed structure, for the M12 value of a 3 X 3 transformation matrix.

eM21: Identifies the angle of font rotation, in the form of a TFixed structure, for the M21 value of a 3 X 3 transformation matrix.

eM22: Identifies the angle of font rotation, in the form of a TFixed structure, for the M22 value of a 3 X 3 transformation matrix.

The TFixed structure defines a real number in a fixed-point format. The TFixed structure is defined as:

```
TFixed = packed record
        fract: Word;             {the fractional portion}
        value: SHORT;            {the integer portion}
end;
```

fract: Identifies the fractional portion of the real number.

value: Identifies the integer portion of the real number.

Return Value

If the function succeeds, it returns a non-zero value, and the buffer pointed to by the p6 parameter will contain the glyph outline information. If the function fails, it returns GDI_ERROR.

See Also

GetOutlineTextMetrics

Example

Listing 13-11: Retrieving glyph bitmaps

```
var
  Form1: TForm1;
  SelectedChar: Byte;  // holds the selected character
  Angle: Integer;      // holds the rotation angle

implementation

{$R *.DFM}

function MakeFixed(Value: Double): TFixed;
var
  TheValue: longint;  // intermediate storage variable
begin
  {convert the indicated number into a TFixed record}
```

```
      TheValue := Trunc(Value*65536);
      Result := TFixed(Longint(TheValue));
    end;

procedure DrawGlyph;
var
  BitmapSize: Longint;              // holds the required size of the bitmap
  BitmapBits: Pointer;              // a pointer to the bitmap
  BitmapInfo: Windows.TBitmap;      // Windows bitmap information
  GlyphBitmap: HBITMAP;             // a handle to the final bitmap
  GlyphMetrics: TGlyphMetrics;      // holds glyph metric information
  Matrix: TMat2;                    // holds the rotation matrix
begin
  {initialize the rotation matrix. note that all angle values
   must be converted to radians}
  Matrix.eM11 := MakeFixed(Cos(Angle*(PI/180)));
  Matrix.eM12 := MakeFixed(Sin(Angle*(PI/180)));
  Matrix.eM21 := MakeFixed(-Sin(Angle*(PI/180)));
  Matrix.eM22 := MakeFixed(Cos(Angle*(PI/180)));

  {retrieve the required size of the bitmap}
  BitmapSize := GetGlyphOutline(Form1.Canvas.Handle, SelectedChar, GGO_BITMAP,
                                GlyphMetrics, 0, NIL, Matrix);

  {allocate enough memory to hold the bitmap}
  GetMem(BitmapBits, BitmapSize);

  {retrieve the glyph bitmap}
  GetGlyphOutline(Form1.Canvas.Handle, SelectedChar, GGO_BITMAP, GlyphMetrics,
                  BitmapSize, BitmapBits, Matrix);

  {initialize the bitmap information structure to create
   an actual Windows bitmap}
  with BitmapInfo do
  begin
    bmType := 0;
    bmWidth := (GlyphMetrics.gmBlackBoxX+31) and not 31;
    bmHeight := GlyphMetrics.gmBlackBoxY;
    bmWidthBytes := bmWidth shr 3;
    bmPlanes := 1;
    bmBitsPixel := 1;
    bmBits := BitmapBits;
  end;

  {create the Windows bitmap}
  GlyphBitmap := CreateBitmapIndirect(BitmapInfo);

  {assign the final bitmap to the image for display}
  Form1.Image1.Picture.Bitmap.Handle := GlyphBitmap;
  Form1.Image1.Picture.Bitmap.Width := GlyphMetrics.gmBlackBoxX;

  {free the allocated bitmap memory}
  FreeMem(BitmapBits, BitmapSize);
end;
```

Text Output Functions 661

```
procedure TForm1.FormCreate(Sender: TObject);
begin
  {create the image's bitmap and initialize variables}
  Image1.Picture.Bitmap := TBitmap.Create;
  SelectedChar := Ord('A');
  Angle := 0;
end;

procedure TForm1.FormActivate(Sender: TObject);
begin
  {draw the bitmap upon activation}
  DrawGlyph;
end;

procedure TForm1.SpeedButton1Click(Sender: TObject);
begin
  {select the indicated character and draw its bitmap}
  SelectedChar := Ord(PChar(TSpeedButton(Sender).Caption)[0]);
  DrawGlyph;
end;

procedure TForm1.ScrollBar1Change(Sender: TObject);
begin
  {change the rotation angle and update the screen}
  Angle := ScrollBar1.Position;
  Label2.Caption := IntToStr(Angle);
  DrawGlyph;
end;
```

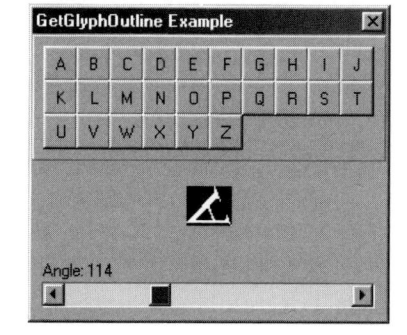

Figure 13-12:
The rotated
glyph

Table 13-25: GetGlyphOutline p3 values

Value	Description
GGO_BITMAP	Retrieves the glyph outline in the form of a double-word aligned, row-oriented monochrome bitmap.
GGO_NATIVE	Retrieves the glyph outline in its native format (a series of lines and curves), measured in the font's design units. The p7 parameter is ignored.
GGO_METRICS	Retrieves only the TGlyphMetrics information for the p4 parameter.

GetKerningPairs   Windows.pas

Syntax

```
GetKerningPairs(
    DC: HDC;                {a handle to a device context}
    Count: DWORD;           {the number of TKerningPair structures in the array}
    var KerningPairs        {a pointer to an array of TKerningPair structures}
): DWORD;                   {returns the number of kerning pairs retrieved}
```

Description

This function retrieves the character kerning pairs for the currently selected font in the device context identified by the DC parameter.

Parameters

DC: A handle to the device context whose currently selected font's kerning pairs are to be retrieved.

Count: Specifies the number of TKerningPair structures in the array pointed to by the KerningPairs parameter. If the selected font contains more kerning pairs than this parameter indicates, the function fails.

KerningPairs: A pointer to an array of TKerningPair structures that receives the character kerning pairs of the currently selected font. This array must contain at least as many TKerningPair structures as indicated by the Count parameter. If this parameter is set to NIL, the function returns the total number of kerning pairs in the font. The TKerningPair structure is defined as:

```
TKerningPair = packed record
    wFirst: Word;               {the first kerning pair character}
    wSecond: Word;              {the second kerning pair character}
    iKernAmount: Integer;       {the kerning amount}
end;
```

wFirst: Specifies the value of the first character in the kerning pair.

wSecond: Specifies the value of the second character in the kerning pair.

iKernAmount: Specifies the intercharacter space adjustment, in logical units, if the two characters appear side by side in the same typeface and size. Typically, this value is negative, causing the characters to be spaced closer together.

Return Value

If the function succeeds, it returns the number of kerning pairs retrieved; otherwise, it returns zero.

See Also

GetTextCharacterExtra, SetTextCharacterExtra

Example

Listing 13-12: Retrieving kerning pairs for the currently selected font

```
{Whoops! Delphi incorrectly imports this function, so we must reimport it
 manually to obtain the full functionality of this function}
function GetKerningPairs(DC: HDC; Count: DWORD;
                        KerningPairs: Pointer): DWORD; stdcall;

var
  Form1: TForm1;

implementation

{$R *.DFM}

{reimport the function}
function GetKerningPairs; external gdi32 name 'GetKerningPairs';

procedure TForm1.FormActivate(Sender: TObject);
type
  TKerningPairs = array[0..0] of TKerningPair;   // holds the kerning pairs
var
  FaceName: array[0..255] of char;  // holds the selected font typeface name
  KerningPairs: ^TKerningPairs;     // a pointer to the kerning pair array
  NumPairs: DWORD;                  // holds the number of pairs
  Count: Integer;                   // general loop control variable
begin
  {retrieve the name of the currently selected font and display it}
  GetTextFace(Form1.Canvas.Handle, 255, @FaceName[0]);
  Label2.Caption := FaceName;

  {retrieve the total number of kerning pairs in the selected font}
  NumPairs := GetKerningPairs(Form1.Canvas.Handle, 0, nil);

  {allocate enough memory to hold all of the kerning pairs}
  GetMem(KerningPairs, SizeOf(TKerningPair)*NumPairs);

  {retrieve the kerning pairs for the font}
  GetKerningPairs(Form1.Canvas.Handle, NumPairs, KerningPairs);

  {display every kerning pair and its kerning amount}
  Memo1.Lines.Clear;
  Memo1.Lines.Add('Pair'+#9+'Kern Amount');
  for Count := 0 to NumPairs-1 do
    Memo1.Lines.Add(Char(KerningPairs^[Count].wFirst)+
                    Char(KerningPairs^[Count].wSecond)+#9+
                    IntToStr(KerningPairs^[Count].iKernAmount));

  {free the kerning pairs array memory}
  FreeMem(KerningPairs,SizeOf(TKerningPair)*NumPairs);
end;
```

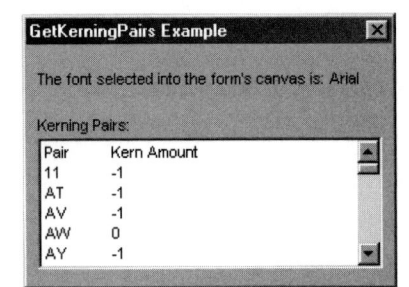

Figure 13-13: The kerning pairs

GetOutlineTextMetrics   Windows.pas

Syntax

```
GetOutlineTextMetrics(
   DC: HDC;                      {a handle to a device context}
   p2: UINT;                     {the size of the TOutlineTextMetric buffer}
   OTMetricStructs: Pointer      {a pointer to the TOutlineTextMetric buffer}
): UINT;                         {returns an error code}
```

Description

This function retrieves metric information, such as height, ascent, descent, and other physical measurements, for the currently selected TrueType (only) font in the device context identified by the DC parameter. This function provides TrueType-specific information in addition to the information retrieved by the GetTextMetrics function.

Parameters

DC: A handle to the device context whose currently selected TrueType font's text metrics are retrieved.

p2: Specifies the size of the buffer pointed to by the OTMetricStructs parameter in bytes.

OTMetricStructs: A pointer to a buffer that receives a TOutlineTextMetric structure describing the text metrics of the TrueType font. If this parameter is set to NIL, the function returns the required size for the TOutlineTextMetric buffer. Due to the strings located at the end of this structure, the structure can vary in size. The developer should first query the function for the appropriate size, and then dynamically allocate the buffer. Note that the sizes returned by the members of this structure are in logical units and depend on the mapping mode of the specified device context. The TOutlineTextMetric structure is defined as:

```
TOutlineTextMetric = record
     otmSize: UINT;                    {the size of the structure}
     otmTextMetrics: TTextMetric;      {contains additional font information}
     otmFiller: Byte;                  {a byte aligning value}
     otmPanoseNumber: TPanose;         {specifies PANOSE information}
     otmfsSelection: UINT;             {inherent font attributes}
     otmfsType: UINT;                  {licensing and embedding flags}
     otmsCharSlopeRise: Integer;       {italic cursor slope enumerator}
```

```
    otmsCharSlopeRun: Integer;          {italic cursor slope denominator}
    otmItalicAngle: Integer;            {the italics angle}
    otmEMSquare: UINT;                  {em square dimensions}
    otmAscent: Integer;                 {the typographic ascent}
    otmDescent: Integer;                {the typographic descent}
    otmLineGap: UINT;                   {the typographic line spacing}
    otmsCapEmHeight: UINT;              {unused}
    otmsXHeight: UINT;                  {unused}
    otmrcFontBox: TRect;                {the bounding box}
    otmMacAscent: Integer;              {the Macintosh ascent}
    otmMacDescent: Integer;             {the Macintosh descent}
    otmMacLineGap: UINT;                {the Macintosh line spacing}
    otmusMinimumPPEM: UINT;             {the smallest recommended size}
    otmptSubscriptSize: TPoint;         {the recommended subscript size}
    otmptSubscriptOffset: TPoint;       {the recommended subscript offset}
    otmptSuperscriptSize: TPoint;       {the recommended superscript size}
    otmptSuperscriptOffset: TPoint;     {the recommended superscript offset}
    otmsStrikeoutSize: UINT;            {the strikeout line width}
    otmsStrikeoutPosition: Integer;     {the strikeout offset}
    otmsUnderscoreSize: Integer;        {the underscore line width}
    otmsUnderscorePosition: Integer;    {the underscore position}
    otmpFamilyName: PAnsiChar;          {the font family name offset}
    otmpFaceName: PAnsiChar;            {the font face name offset}
    otmpStyleName: PAnsiChar;           {the font style name offset}
    otmpFullName: PAnsiChar;            {the full font name offset}
end;
```

otmSize: Specifies the size of the allocated TOutlineTextMetric structure in bytes.

otmTextMetrics: Specifies a TTextMetric structure containing additional physical information for the font. The TTextMetric structure is defined as:

```
TTextMetric = record
    tmHeight: Longint;                  {the height of a character}
    tmAscent: Longint;                  {the ascent of a character}
    tmDescent: Longint;                 {the descent of a character}
    tmInternalLeading: Longint;         {the internal leading}
    tmExternalLeading: Longint;         {the external leading}
    tmAveCharWidth: Longint;            {the average character width}
    tmMaxCharWidth: Longint;            {the maximum character width}
    tmWeight: Longint;                  {the boldness value}
    tmOverhang: Longint;                {the overhang width}
    tmDigitizedAspectX: Longint;        {the horizontal aspect}
    tmDigitizedAspectY: Longint;        {the vertical aspect}
    tmFirstChar: AnsiChar;              {the first character}
    tmLastChar: AnsiChar;               {the last character}
    tmDefaultChar: AnsiChar;            {the default character}
    tmBreakChar: AnsiChar;              {the word break character}
```

```
       tmItalic: Byte;                {the italics flag}
       tmUnderlined: Byte;            {the underlined flag}
       tmStruckOut: Byte;             {the strikeout flag}
       tmPitchAndFamily: Byte;        {the pitch and family flags}
       tmCharSet: Byte;               {the character set}
end;
```

See the GetTextMetrics function for a description of this data structure.

otmFiller: Specifies a value used solely for byte aligning the structure.

otmPanoseNumber: A TPanose structure containing the PANOSE font classification information for the TrueType font. This is used to associate the font with other fonts having similar appearance but varying names. The TPanose structure is defined as:

```
TPanose = packed record
       bFamilyType: Byte;             {the family type}
       bSerifStyle: Byte;             {the serif style}
       bWeight: Byte;                 {the boldness}
       bProportion: Byte;             {the proportionality}
       bContrast: Byte;               {the contrast}
       bStrokeVariation: Byte;        {the stroke variation}
       bArmStyle: Byte;               {the arm style}
       bLetterform: Byte;             {the letter form}
       bMidline: Byte;                {the midline position}
       bXHeight: Byte;                {the xheight}
end;
```

    bFamilyType: Specifies the family type and can contain one value from Table 13-26.

    bSerifStyle: Specifies the serif style and can contain one value from Table 13-27.

    bWeight: Specifies the font weight (boldness) and can contain one value from Table 13-28.

    bProportion: Specifies the font proportionality and can contain one value from Table 13-29.

    bContrast: Specifies font contrast and can contain one value from Table 13-30.

    bStrokeVariation: Specifies the stroke variation within the font and can contain one value from Table 13-31.

    bArmStyle: Specifies glyph arm style and can contain one value from Table 13-32.

    bLetterform: Specifies the glyph letter form and can contain one value from Table 13-33.

    bMidline: Specifies the midline and can contain one value from Table 13-34.

bXHeight: Specifies the xheight and can contain one value from Table 13-35.

otmfsSelection: Specifies a bitmask indicating certain attributes inherently built into the font pattern, such as bold or italics. The bits of this member indicate the various attributes, as shown in Table 13-36.

otmfsType: Specifies a bitmask indicating the licensing attributes of the font. If bit 1 is set, the font may not be embedded in a document; if it is not set, embedding is allowed. If bit 2 is set, the font may be embedded only as a read-only font.

otmsCharSlopeRise: Used with the otmsCharSlopeRun member, this value specifies the enumerator of the ratio used to create an italic cursor that has the same slope as the italicized font, as indicated by the otmItalicAngle member.

otmsCharSlopeRun: Used with the otmsCharSlopeRise member, this value specifies the denominator of the ratio used to create an italic cursor that has the same slope as the italicized font, as indicated by the otmItalicAngle member.

otmItalicAngle: Specifies the italics angle for the font, in tenths of a degree rotating counterclockwise from vertical. Most fonts have a negative value, indicating a font leaning to the right. This member will be set to zero for non-italicized fonts.

otmEMSquare: Specifies the horizontal and vertical dimensions, in logical units, of the font's em square.

otmAscent: The typographic value that specifies the maximum extent to which characters in this font rise above the baseline.

otmDescent: The typographic value that specifies the maximum extent to which characters in this font descend below the baseline.

otmLineGap: Specifies the typographic line spacing.

otmsCapEmHeight: This member is no longer used.

otmsXHeight: This member is no longer used.

otmrcFontBox: Specifies the font's bounding box.

otmMacAscent: The maximum extent to which characters in this font rise above the baseline on the Macintosh computer.

otmMacDescent: The maximum extent to which characters in this font descend below the baseline on the Macintosh computer.

otmMacLineGap: The line spacing used by this font on the Macintosh computer.

otmusMinimumPPEM: Specifies the smallest recommended font size in pixels per em square.

otmptSubscriptSize: A TPoint structure that specifies the recommended subscript width and height.

otmptSubscriptOffset: A TPoint structure that specifies the recommended horizontal and vertical subscript offset from the origin of the character to the origin of the subscript.

otmptSuperscriptSize: A TPoint structure that specifies the recommended superscript width and height.

otmptSuperscriptOffset: A TPoint structure that specifies the recommended horizontal and vertical superscript offset from the baseline of the character to the baseline of the superscript.

otmsStrikeoutSize: Specifies the width of the strikeout line.

otmsStrikeoutPosition: Specifies the offset of the strikeout line from the baseline.

otmsUnderscoreSize: Specifies the width of the underscore line.

otmsUnderscorePosition: Specifies the offset of the underscore line from the baseline.

otmpFamilyName: Specifies the offset from the beginning of the TOutlineTextMetric structure to the beginning of the string containing the font family name.

otmpFaceName: Specifies the offset from the beginning of the TOutlineTextMetric structure to the beginning of the string containing the font face name.

otmpStyleName: Specifies the offset from the beginning of the TOutlineTextMetric structure to the beginning of the string containing the font style name.

otmpFullName: Specifies the offset from the beginning of the TOutlineTextMetric structure to the beginning of the string containing the full, unique font name.

Return Value

If the function succeeds, it returns a non-zero value; otherwise, it returns zero. To get extended error information, call the GetLastError function.

See Also

GetGlyphOutline, GetTextMetrics

Example

Listing 13-13: Retrieving TrueType font text metrics

```
{note: the form must have a TrueType font set as its selected font before
 this example will work properly}

procedure TForm1.FormActivate(Sender: TObject);
var
  FontInfo: POutlineTextMetric;     // a pointer to the text metric info
  FaceName: array[0..255] of char;  // holds the font face name
  TheSize: LongInt;                 // holds the required buffer size
begin
  {retrieve and display the selected font's face name}
  GetTextFace(Form1.Canvas.Handle, 256, FaceName);
  Label2.Caption := FaceName;

  {retrieve the required buffer size}
  TheSize := GetOutlineTextMetrics(Form1.Canvas.Handle, 0, nil);

  {allocate the buffer}
  GetMem(FontInfo, TheSize);

  {set the size member}
  FontInfo^.otmSize := TheSize;
```

```
{retrieve the TrueType font attributes}
GetOutlineTextMetrics(Form1.Canvas.Handle, TheSize,
                      FontInfo);

{clear the list box and begin displaying the physical font attributes}
ListBox1.Items.Clear;
with FontInfo^.otmTextMetrics, ListBox1.Items do
begin
  {display the various font measurements}
  Label15.Caption := IntToStr(tmHeight);
  Label14.Caption := IntToStr(tmAscent);
  Label13.Caption := IntToStr(tmDescent);
  Label12.Caption := IntToStr(tmInternalLeading);
  Label11.Caption := IntToStr(tmExternalLeading);

  {display the average and maximum character width}
  Add('Average Char Width: '+IntToStr(tmAveCharWidth));
  Add('Max Char Width: '+IntToStr(tmMaxCharWidth));

  {display the boldness setting}
  case tmWeight of
    FW_DONTCARE:   Add('Weight: Don''t care');
    FW_THIN:       Add('Weight: Thin');
    FW_EXTRALIGHT: Add('Weight: Extra light');
    FW_LIGHT:      Add('Weight: Light');
    FW_NORMAL:     Add('Weight: Normal');
    FW_MEDIUM:     Add('Weight: Medium');
    FW_SEMIBOLD:   Add('Weight: Semibold');
    FW_BOLD:       Add('Weight: Bold');
    FW_EXTRABOLD:  Add('Weight: Extra bold');
    FW_HEAVY:      Add('Weight: Heavy');
  end;

  {display the overhang measurement}
  Add('Overhang: '+IntToStr(tmOverhang));

  {display the horizontal and vertical aspect}
  Add('Digitized Aspect X: '+IntToStr(tmDigitizedAspectX));
  Add('Digitized Aspect Y: '+IntToStr(tmDigitizedAspectY));

  {display the important font characters}
  Add('First Character: '+Char(tmFirstChar));
  Add('Last Char: '+Char(tmLastChar));
  Add('Default Char: '+Char(tmDefaultChar));
  Add('Break Char: '+Char(tmBreakChar));

  {indicate italic, underlined, or strikeout attributes}
  CheckBox1.Checked := (tmItalic>0);
  CheckBox2.Checked := (tmUnderlined>0);
  CheckBox3.Checked := (tmStruckOut>0);

  {display the font pitch}
  Add('Pitch: ');
  if ((tmPitchAndFamily and $0F) and TMPF_FIXED_PITCH)= TMPF_FIXED_PITCH then
    Add('     Fixed pitch');
  if ((tmPitchAndFamily and $0F) and TMPF_VECTOR) = TMPF_VECTOR then
    Add('     Vector');
```

```
        if ((tmPitchAndFamily and $0F) and TMPF_TRUETYPE) = TMPF_TRUETYPE then
          Add('     TrueType');
        if ((tmPitchAndFamily and $0F) and TMPF_DEVICE) = TMPF_DEVICE then
          Add('     Device');
        if (tmPitchAndFamily and $0F) = 0 then
          Add('     Monospaced bitmap font');

        {display the font family}
        case (tmPitchAndFamily and $F0) of
          FF_DECORATIVE: Add('Family: Decorative');
          FF_DONTCARE:   Add('Family: Don''t care');
          FF_MODERN:     Add('Family: Modern');
          FF_ROMAN:      Add('Family: Roman');
          FF_SCRIPT:     Add('Family: Script');
          FF_SWISS:      Add('Family: Swiss');
        end;

        {display the character set}
        case tmCharSet of
          ANSI_CHARSET:         Add('Character set: ANSI');
          DEFAULT_CHARSET:      Add('Character set: Default');
          SYMBOL_CHARSET:       Add('Character set: Symbol');
          SHIFTJIS_CHARSET:     Add('Character set: ShiftJis');
          GB2312_CHARSET:       Add('Character set: GB2312');
          HANGEUL_CHARSET:      Add('Character set: Hangeul');
          CHINESEBIG5_CHARSET:  Add('Character set: Chinese Big5');
          OEM_CHARSET:          Add('Character set: OEM');
        else
          Add('Windows 95 only character set');
        end;
      end;

      {display TrueType specific information}
      with FontInfo^, ListBox1.Items do
      begin
        Add('');
        Add('');
        Add('TrueType specific information');
        Add('-------------------------------');
        Add('');
        Add('Panose Information: ');

        {display the Panose family type}
        case otmPanoseNumber.bFamilyType of
          PAN_ANY:                Add('     Family Type: Any');
          PAN_NO_FIT:             Add('     Family Type: No fit');
          PAN_FAMILY_TEXT_DISPLAY: Add('    Family Type: Text and display');
          PAN_FAMILY_SCRIPT:      Add('     Family Type: Script');
          PAN_FAMILY_DECORATIVE:  Add('     Family Type: Decorative');
          PAN_FAMILY_PICTORIAL:   Add('     Family Type: Pictorial');
        end;

        {display the Panose serif style}
        case otmPanoseNumber.bSerifStyle of
          PAN_ANY:                Add('     Serif Style: Any');
          PAN_NO_FIT:             Add('     Serif Style: No fit');
          PAN_SERIF_COVE:         Add('     Serif Style: Cove');
```

```
      PAN_SERIF_OBTUSE_COVE:           Add('     Serif Style: Obtuse cove');
      PAN_SERIF_SQUARE_COVE:            Add('     Serif Style: Square cove');
      PAN_SERIF_OBTUSE_SQUARE_COVE: Add('     Serif Style: Obtuse square cove');
      PAN_SERIF_SQUARE:                 Add('     Serif Style: Square');
      PAN_SERIF_THIN:                   Add('     Serif Style: Thin');
      PAN_SERIF_BONE:                   Add('     Serif Style: Bone');
      PAN_SERIF_EXAGGERATED:            Add('     Serif Style: Exaggerated');
      PAN_SERIF_TRIANGLE:               Add('     Serif Style: Triangle');
      PAN_SERIF_NORMAL_SANS:            Add('     Serif Style: Normal sans serif');
      PAN_SERIF_OBTUSE_SANS:            Add('     Serif Style: Obtuse sans serif');
      PAN_SERIF_PERP_SANS:              Add('     Serif Style: Perp sans serif');
      PAN_SERIF_FLARED:                 Add('     Serif Style: Flared');
      PAN_SERIF_ROUNDED:                Add('     Serif Style: Rounded');
    end;

    {display the Panose weight}
    case otmPanoseNumber.bWeight of
      PAN_ANY:               Add('     Weight: Any');
      PAN_NO_FIT:            Add('     Weight: No fit');
      PAN_WEIGHT_VERY_LIGHT: Add('     Weight: Very light');
      PAN_WEIGHT_LIGHT:      Add('     Weight: Light');
      PAN_WEIGHT_THIN:       Add('     Weight: Thin');
      PAN_WEIGHT_BOOK:       Add('     Weight: Book');
      PAN_WEIGHT_MEDIUM:     Add('     Weight: Medium');
      PAN_WEIGHT_DEMI:       Add('     Weight: Demi');
      PAN_WEIGHT_BOLD:       Add('     Weight: Bold');
      PAN_WEIGHT_HEAVY:      Add('     Weight: Heavy');
      PAN_WEIGHT_BLACK:      Add('     Weight: Black');
      PAN_WEIGHT_NORD:       Add('     Weight: Nord');
    end;

    {display the Panose proportion}
    case otmPanoseNumber.bProportion of
      PAN_ANY:                   Add('     Proportion: Any');
      PAN_NO_FIT:                Add('     Proportion: No fit');
      PAN_PROP_OLD_STYLE:        Add('     Proportion: Old style');
      PAN_PROP_MODERN:           Add('     Proportion: Modern');
      PAN_PROP_EVEN_WIDTH:       Add('     Proportion: Even width');
      PAN_PROP_EXPANDED:         Add('     Proportion: Expanded');
      PAN_PROP_CONDENSED:        Add('     Proportion: Condensed');
      PAN_PROP_VERY_EXPANDED:    Add('     Proportion: Very expanded');
      PAN_PROP_VERY_CONDENSED:   Add('     Proportion: Very condensed');
      PAN_PROP_MONOSPACED:       Add('     Proportion: Monospaced');
    end;

    {display the Panose contrast}
    case otmPanoseNumber.bContrast of
      PAN_ANY:                    Add('     Contrast: Any');
      PAN_NO_FIT:                 Add('     Contrast: No fit');
      PAN_CONTRAST_NONE:          Add('     Contrast: None');
      PAN_CONTRAST_VERY_LOW:      Add('     Contrast: Very low');
      PAN_CONTRAST_LOW:           Add('     Contrast: Low');
      PAN_CONTRAST_MEDIUM_LOW:    Add('     Contrast: Medium low');
      PAN_CONTRAST_MEDIUM:        Add('     Contrast: Medium');
      PAN_CONTRAST_MEDIUM_HIGH:   Add('     Contrast: Medium high');
      PAN_CONTRAST_HIGH:          Add('     Contrast: High');
      PAN_CONTRAST_VERY_HIGH:     Add('     Contrast: Very high');
```

```
        end;

        {display the Panose stroke variation}
        case otmPanoseNumber.bStrokeVariation of
          PAN_ANY:                 Add('    Stroke variation: Any');
          PAN_NO_FIT:              Add('    Stroke variation: No fit');
          PAN_STROKE_GRADUAL_DIAG: Add('    Stroke variation: Gradual diagonal');
          PAN_STROKE_GRADUAL_TRAN: Add('    Stroke variation: Gradual transition');
          PAN_STROKE_GRADUAL_VERT: Add('    Stroke variation: Gradual vertical');
          PAN_STROKE_GRADUAL_HORZ: Add('    Stroke variation: Gradual horizontal');
          PAN_STROKE_RAPID_VERT:   Add('    Stroke variation: Rapid vertical');
          PAN_STROKE_RAPID_HORZ:   Add('    Stroke variation: Rapid horizontal');
          PAN_STROKE_INSTANT_VERT: Add('    Stroke variation: Instant vertical');
        end;

        {display the Panose arm style}
        case otmPanoseNumber.bArmStyle of
          PAN_ANY:                         Add('    Arm style: Any');
          PAN_NO_FIT:                      Add('    Arm style: No fit');
          PAN_STRAIGHT_ARMS_HORZ:          Add('    Arm style: Straight '+
                                               'horizontal');
          PAN_STRAIGHT_ARMS_WEDGE:         Add('    Arm style: Straight wedge');
          PAN_STRAIGHT_ARMS_VERT:          Add('    Arm style: Straight vertical');
          PAN_STRAIGHT_ARMS_SINGLE_SERIF:  Add('    Arm style: Straight '+
                                               'single_serif');
          PAN_STRAIGHT_ARMS_DOUBLE_SERIF:  Add('    Arm style: Straight '+
                                               'double-serif');
          PAN_BENT_ARMS_HORZ:              Add('    Arm style: Nonstraight '+
                                               'horizontal');
          PAN_BENT_ARMS_WEDGE:             Add('    Arm style: Nonstraight wedge');
          PAN_BENT_ARMS_VERT:              Add('    Arm style: Nonstraight '+
                                               'vertical');
          PAN_BENT_ARMS_SINGLE_SERIF:      Add('    Arm style: Nonstraight '+
                                               'single-serif');
          PAN_BENT_ARMS_DOUBLE_SERIF:      Add('    Arm style: Nonstraight '+
                                               'double-serif');
        end;

        {display the Panose letter form}
        case otmPanoseNumber.bLetterform of
          PAN_ANY:                    Add('    Letter form: Any');
          PAN_NO_FIT:                 Add('    Letter form: No fit');
          PAN_LETT_NORMAL_CONTACT:    Add('    Letter form: Normal contact');
          PAN_LETT_NORMAL_WEIGHTED:   Add('    Letter form: Normal weighted');
          PAN_LETT_NORMAL_BOXED:      Add('    Letter form: Normal boxed');
          PAN_LETT_NORMAL_FLATTENED:  Add('    Letter form: Normal flattened');
          PAN_LETT_NORMAL_ROUNDED:    Add('    Letter form: Normal rounded');
          PAN_LETT_NORMAL_OFF_CENTER: Add('    Letter form: Normal off center');
          PAN_LETT_NORMAL_SQUARE:     Add('    Letter form: Normal square');
          PAN_LETT_OBLIQUE_CONTACT:   Add('    Letter form: Oblique contact');
          PAN_LETT_OBLIQUE_WEIGHTED:  Add('    Letter form: Oblique weighted');
          PAN_LETT_OBLIQUE_BOXED:     Add('    Letter form: Oblique boxed');
          PAN_LETT_OBLIQUE_FLATTENED: Add('    Letter form: Oblique flattened');
          PAN_LETT_OBLIQUE_ROUNDED:   Add('    Letter form: Oblique rounded');
          PAN_LETT_OBLIQUE_OFF_CENTER:Add('    Letter form: Oblique off center');
          PAN_LETT_OBLIQUE_SQUARE:    Add('    Letter form: Oblique square');
        end;
```

```
{display the Panose midline}
case otmPanoseNumber.bMidline of
  PAN_ANY:                         Add('    Midline: Any');
  PAN_NO_FIT:                      Add('    Midline: No fit');
  PAN_MIDLINE_STANDARD_TRIMMED:    Add('    Midline: Standard trimmed');
  PAN_MIDLINE_STANDARD_POINTED:    Add('    Midline: Standard pointed');
  PAN_MIDLINE_STANDARD_SERIFED:    Add('    Midline: Standard serifed');
  PAN_MIDLINE_HIGH_TRIMMED:        Add('    Midline: High trimmed');
  PAN_MIDLINE_HIGH_POINTED:        Add('    Midline: High pointed');
  PAN_MIDLINE_HIGH_SERIFED:        Add('    Midline: High serifed');
  PAN_MIDLINE_CONSTANT_TRIMMED:    Add('    Midline: Constant trimmed');
  PAN_MIDLINE_CONSTANT_POINTED:    Add('    Midline: Constant pointed');
  PAN_MIDLINE_CONSTANT_SERIFED:    Add('    Midline: Constant serifed');
  PAN_MIDLINE_LOW_TRIMMED:         Add('    Midline: Low trimmed');
  PAN_MIDLINE_LOW_POINTED:         Add('    Midline: Low pointed');
  PAN_MIDLINE_LOW_SERIFED:         Add('    Midline: Low serifed');
end;

{display the Panose xheight}
case otmPanoseNumber.bXHeight of
  PAN_ANY:                         Add('    XHeight: Any');
  PAN_NO_FIT:                      Add('    XHeight: No fit');
  PAN_XHEIGHT_CONSTANT_SMALL:      Add('    XHeight: Constant small');
  PAN_XHEIGHT_CONSTANT_STD:        Add('    XHeight: Constant standard');
  PAN_XHEIGHT_CONSTANT_LARGE:      Add('    XHeight: Constant large');
  PAN_XHEIGHT_DUCKING_SMALL:       Add('    XHeight: Ducking small');
  PAN_XHEIGHT_DUCKING_STD:         Add('    XHeight: Ducking standard');
  PAN_XHEIGHT_DUCKING_LARGE:       Add('    XHeight: Ducking large');
end;

{display the inherent font attributes}
Add('Selection: ');
if (otmfsSelection and $01)>0 then
  Add('    Italic');
if (otmfsSelection and $02)>0 then
  Add('    Underscore');
if (otmfsSelection and $04)>0 then
  Add('    Negative');
if (otmfsSelection and $08)>0 then
  Add('    Outline');
if (otmfsSelection and $10)>0 then
  Add('    Strikeout');
if (otmfsSelection and $20)>0 then
  Add('    Bold');

{display font embedding information}
Add('Type:');
if (otmfsType and $02)>0 then
  Add('    Embedding Forbidden');
if (otmfsType and $02)<1 then
  Add('    Embedding Allowed');
if (otmfsType and $04)>0 then
  Add('    Embedding Read-Only');

{display italics attributes}
Add('Slope Rise: '+IntToStr(otmsCharSlopeRise));
Add('Slope Run: '+IntToStr(otmsCharSlopeRun));
```

```
      Add('Italic Angle: '+IntToStr(otmItalicAngle));

      {display important physical attributes}
      Add('EM Square: '+IntToStr(otmEMSquare));
      Add('Typographic Ascent: '+IntToStr(otmAscent));
      Add('Typographic Descent: '+IntToStr(otmDescent));
      Add('Typographic Line Gap: '+IntToStr(otmLineGap));

      {display the bounding box coordinates}
      Add('Font Bounding Box: ');
      Add('     Left: '+IntToStr(otmrcFontBox.Left));
      Add('     Top: '+IntToStr(otmrcFontBox.Top));
      Add('     Right: '+IntToStr(otmrcFontBox.Right));
      Add('     Bottom: '+IntToStr(otmrcFontBox.Bottom));

      {display the Macintosh attributes}
      Add('Mac Ascent: '+IntToStr(otmMacAscent));
      Add('MacDescent: '+IntToStr(otmMacDescent));
      Add('Mac Line Gap: '+IntToStr(otmMacLineGap));

      {display the minimum size}
      Add('Minimum Size: '+IntToStr(otmusMinimumPPEM));

      {display subscript suggestions}
      Add('Subscript Size: ');
      Add('     Horizontal: '+IntToStr(otmptSubscriptSize.X));
      Add('     Vertical: '+IntToStr(otmptSubscriptSize.Y));
      Add('Subscript Offset: ');
      Add('     Horizontal: '+IntToStr(otmptSubscriptOffset.X));
      Add('     Vertical: '+IntToStr(otmptSubscriptOffset.Y));

      {display superscript suggestions}
      Add('Superscript Size: ');
      Add('     Horizontal: '+IntToStr(otmptSuperscriptSize.X));
      Add('     Vertical: '+IntToStr(otmptSuperscriptSize.Y));
      Add('Superscript Offset: ');
      Add('     Horizontal: '+IntToStr(otmptSuperscriptOffset.X));
      Add('     Vertical: '+IntToStr(otmptSuperscriptOffset.Y));

      {display line sizes and positions}
      Add('Strikeout Size: '+IntToStr(otmsStrikeoutSize));
      Add('Strikeout Position: '+IntToStr(otmsStrikeoutPosition));
      Add('Underscore Size: '+IntToStr(otmsUnderscoreSize));
      Add('Underscore Position: '+IntToStr(otmsUnderscorePosition));

      {display font family, face, and name strings}
      Add('Family Name: '+PChar(Longint(FontInfo)+FontInfo^.otmpFamilyName));
      Add('Face Name: '+PChar(Longint(FontInfo)+FontInfo^.otmpFaceName));
      Add('Style Name: '+PChar(Longint(FontInfo)+FontInfo^.otmpStyleName));
    end;

    {display the full font name}
    Label17.Caption := PChar(Longint(FontInfo)+FontInfo^.otmpFullName);

    {free the allocated text metric buffer}
    FreeMem(FontInfo, TheSize);
  end;
```

Text Output Functions ■ 675

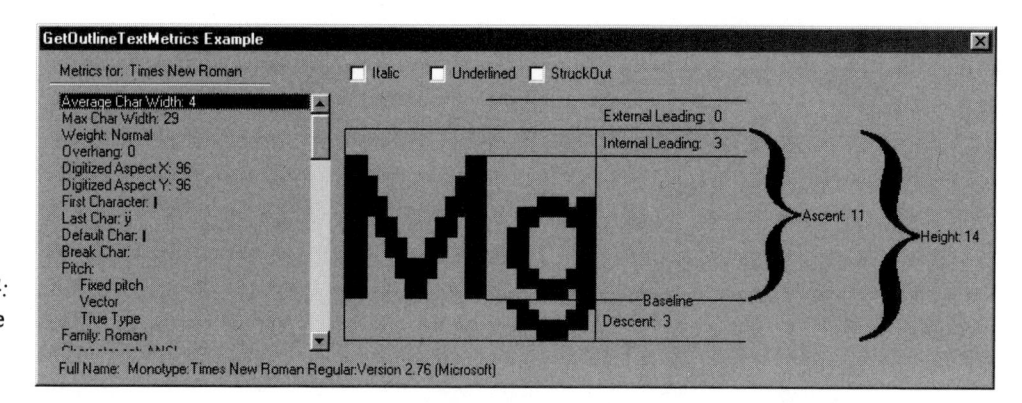

*Figure 13-14:
The TrueType
font
information*

Table 13-26: GetOutlineTextMetrics OTMetricStructs.otmPanoseNumber.bFamilyType values

Value	Description
PAN_ANY	Any family.
PAN_NO_FIT	No fit.
PAN_FAMILY_TEXT_DISPLAY	Text and display family.
PAN_FAMILY_SCRIPT	Script family.
PAN_FAMILY_DECORATIVE	Decorative family.
PAN_FAMILY_PICTORIAL	Pictorial family.

Table 13-27: GetOutlineTextMetrics OTMetricStructs.otmPanoseNumber.bSerifStyle values

Value	Description
PAN_ANY	Any serif style.
PAN_NO_FIT	No fit.
PAN_SERIF_COVE	Cove serifs.
PAN_SERIF_OBTUSE_COVE	Obtuse cove serifs.
PAN_SERIF_SQUARE_COVE	Square cove serifs.
PAN_SERIF_OBTUSE_SQUARE_COVE	Obtuse square cove serifs.
PAN_SERIF_SQUARE	Square serifs.
PAN_SERIF_THIN	Thin serifs.
PAN_SERIF_BONE	Bone serifs.
PAN_SERIF_EXAGGERATED	Exaggerated serifs.
PAN_SERIF_TRIANGLE	Triangle serifs.
PAN_SERIF_NORMAL_SANS	Normal sans serif.
PAN_SERIF_OBTUSE_SANS	Obtuse sans serif.
PAN_SERIF_PERP_SANS	Perp sans serif.
PAN_SERIF_FLARED	Flared serifs.
PAN_SERIF_ROUNDED	Rounded serifs.

Table 13-28: GetOutlineTextMetrics OTMetricStructs.otmPanoseNumber.bWeight values

Value	Description
PAN_ANY	Any boldness.
PAN_NO_FIT	No fit.
PAN_WEIGHT_VERY_LIGHT	Very light boldness.
PAN_WEIGHT_LIGHT	Light boldness.
PAN_WEIGHT_THIN	Thin boldness.
PAN_WEIGHT_BOOK	Book boldness.
PAN_WEIGHT_MEDIUM	Medium boldness.
PAN_WEIGHT_DEMI	Demibold.
PAN_WEIGHT_BOLD	Bold.
PAN_WEIGHT_HEAVY	Heavy boldness.
PAN_WEIGHT_BLACK	Black boldness.
PAN_WEIGHT_NORD	Nord boldness.

Table 13-29: GetOutlineTextMetrics OTMetricStructs.otmPanoseNumber.bProportion values

Value	Description
PAN_ANY	Any proportion.
PAN_NO_FIT	No fit.
PAN_PROP_OLD_STYLE	Old style proportion.
PAN_PROP_MODERN	Modern proportion.
PAN_PROP_EVEN_WIDTH	Even width proportion.
PAN_PROP_EXPANDED	Expanded proportion.
PAN_PROP_CONDENSED	Condensed proportion.
PAN_PROP_VERY_EXPANDED	Very expanded proportion.
PAN_PROP_VERY_CONDENSED	Very condensed proportion.
PAN_PROP_MONOSPACED	Monospaced proportion.

Table 13-30: GetOutlineTextMetrics OTMetricStructs.otmPanoseNumber.bContrast values

Value	Description
PAN_ANY	Any contrast.
PAN_NO_FIT	No fit.
PAN_CONTRAST_NONE	No contrast.
PAN_CONTRAST_VERY_LOW	Very low contrast.
PAN_CONTRAST_LOW	Low contrast.
PAN_CONTRAST_MEDIUM_LOW	Medium low contrast.
PAN_CONTRAST_MEDIUM	Medium contrast.
PAN_CONTRAST_MEDIUM_HIGH	Medium high contrast.
PAN_CONTRAST_HIGH	High contrast.
PAN_CONTRAST_VERY_HIGH	Very high contrast.

Table 13-31: GetOutlineTextMetrics OTMetricStructs.otmPanoseNumber.bStrokeVariation values

Value	Description
PAN_ANY	Any stroke variation.
PAN_NO_FIT	No fit.
PAN_STROKE_GRADUAL_DIAG	Gradual, diagonal stroke variation.
PAN_STROKE_GRADUAL_TRAN	Gradual, transitional stroke variation.
PAN_STROKE_GRADUAL_VERT	Gradual, vertical stroke variation.
PAN_STROKE_GRADUAL_HORZ	Gradual, horizontal stroke variation.
PAN_STROKE_RAPID_VERT	Rapid, vertical stroke variation.
PAN_STROKE_RAPID_HORZ	Rapid, horizontal stroke variation.
PAN_STROKE_INSTANT_VERT	Instant, vertical stroke variation.

Table 13-32: GetOutlineTextMetrics OTMetricStructs.otmPanoseNumber.bArmStyle values

Value	Description
PAN_ANY	Any arm style.
PAN_NO_FIT	No fit.
PAN_STRAIGHT_ARMS_HORZ	Straight arms, horizontal arm style.
PAN_STRAIGHT_ARMS_WEDGE	Straight arms, wedge arm style.
PAN_STRAIGHT_ARMS_VERT	Straight arms, vertical arm style.
PAN_STRAIGHT_ARMS_SINGLE_SERIF	Straight arms, single serif arm style.
PAN_STRAIGHT_ARMS_DOUBLE_SERIF	Straight arms, double serif arm style.
PAN_BENT_ARMS_HORZ	Bent arms, horizontal arm style.
PAN_BENT_ARMS_WEDGE	Bent arms, wedge arm style.
PAN_BENT_ARMS_VERT	Bent arms, vertical arm style.
PAN_BENT_ARMS_SINGLE_SERIF	Bent arms, single serif arm style.
PAN_BENT_ARMS_DOUBLE_SERIF	Bent arms, double serif arm style.

Table 13-33: GetOutlineTextMetrics OTMetricStructs.otmPanoseNumber.bLetterform values

Value	Description
PAN_ANY	Any letter form.
PAN_NO_FIT	No fit.
PAN_LETT_NORMAL_CONTACT	Normal, contact letter form.
PAN_LETT_NORMAL_WEIGHTED	Normal, weighted letter form.
PAN_LETT_NORMAL_BOXED	Normal, boxed letter form.
PAN_LETT_NORMAL_FLATTENED	Normal, flattened letter form.
PAN_LETT_NORMAL_ROUNDED	Normal, rounded letter form.
PAN_LETT_NORMAL_OFF_CENTER	Normal, off-center letter form.
PAN_LETT_NORMAL_SQUARE	Normal, square letter form.
PAN_LETT_OBLIQUE_CONTACT	Oblique, contact letter form.
PAN_LETT_OBLIQUE_WEIGHTED	Oblique, weighted letter form.
PAN_LETT_OBLIQUE_BOXED	Oblique, boxed letter form.

Value	Description
PAN_LETT_OBLIQUE_FLATTENED	Oblique, flattened letter form.
PAN_LETT_OBLIQUE_ROUNDED	Oblique, rounded letter form.
PAN_LETT_OBLIQUE_OFF_CENTER	Oblique, off-center letter form.
PAN_LETT_OBLIQUE_SQUARE	Oblique, square letter form.

Table 13-34: GetOutlineTextMetrics OTMetricStructs.otmPanoseNumber.bMidline values

Value	Description
PAN_ANY	Any midline.
PAN_NO_FIT	No fit.
PAN_MIDLINE_STANDARD_TRIMMED	Standard, trimmed midline.
PAN_MIDLINE_STANDARD_POINTED	Standard, pointed midline.
PAN_MIDLINE_STANDARD_SERIFED	Standard, serifed midline.
PAN_MIDLINE_HIGH_TRIMMED	High, trimmed midline.
PAN_MIDLINE_HIGH_POINTED	High, pointed midline.
PAN_MIDLINE_HIGH_SERIFED	High, serifed midline.
PAN_MIDLINE_CONSTANT_TRIMMED	Constant, trimmed midline.
PAN_MIDLINE_CONSTANT_POINTED	Constant, pointed midline.
PAN_MIDLINE_CONSTANT_SERIFED	Constant, serifed midline.
PAN_MIDLINE_LOW_TRIMMED	Low, trimmed midline.
PAN_MIDLINE_LOW_POINTED	Low, pointed midline.
PAN_MIDLINE_LOW_SERIFED	Low, serifed midline.

Table 13-35: GetOutlineTextMetrics OTMetricStructs.otmPanoseNumber.bXHeight values

Value	Description
PAN_ANY	Any xheight.
PAN_NO_FIT	No fit.
PAN_XHEIGHT_CONSTANT_SMALL	Constant, small xheight.
PAN_XHEIGHT_CONSTANT_STD	Constant, standard xheight.
PAN_XHEIGHT_CONSTANT_LARGE	Constant, large xheight.
PAN_XHEIGHT_DUCKING_SMALL	Ducking, small xheight.
PAN_XHEIGHT_DUCKING_STD	Ducking, standard xheight.
PAN_XHEIGHT_DUCKING_LARGE	Ducking, large xheight.

Table 13-36: GetOutlineTextMetrics OTMetricStructs.otmfsSelection values

Bit	Description
0	Indicates an italic font.
1	Indicates an underscored font.
2	Indicates a negative font.
3	Indicates an outline font.

Bit	Description
4	Indicates a strikeout font.
5	Indicates a bold font.

GetRasterizerCaps   Windows.pas

Syntax

```
GetRasterizerCaps(
var p1: TRasterizerStatus;    {a pointer to a TRasterizerStatus structure}
p2: UINT                      {the size of the TRasterizerStatus structure}
): BOOL;                      {returns TRUE or FALSE}
```

Description

This function returns information in the TRasterizerStatus structure pointed to by the p1 parameter that indicates if TrueType fonts are installed or enabled on the system.

Parameters

p1: A pointer to a TRasterizerStatus structure that receives information concerning availability of TrueType fonts on the system. The TRasterizerStatus structure is defined as:

```
TRasterizerStatus = packed record
    nSize: SHORT;          {the size of the TRasterizerStatus structure}
    wFlags: SHORT;         {TrueType availability flags}
    nLanguageID: SHORT;    {the language identifier}
end;
```

nSize: Specifies the size of the TRasterizerStatus structure in bytes. This member should be set to SizeOf(TRasterizerStatus).

wFlags: A series of flags specifying TrueType font availability. This member can contain one or more values from Table 13-37.

nLanguageID: Specifies the language identifier, as indicated by the system's Setup.inf file.

p2: Specifies the number of bytes to copy into the TRasterizerStatus structure. The actual number of bytes copied is the value of this parameter or the size of the TRasterizerStatus structure, whichever is less.

Return Value

If the function succeeds, it returns TRUE; otherwise, it returns FALSE. To get extended error information, call the GetLastError function.

See Also

GetOutlineTextMetrics, GetTextMetrics

Example

See Listing 13-7 under EnumFontFamilies.

Table 13-37: GetRasterizerCaps pl.wFlags values

Value	Description
TT_AVAILABLE	At least one TrueType font is installed and available on the system.
TT_ENABLED	TrueType fonts are supported by the system.

GetTabbedTextExtent   Windows.pas

Syntax

```
GetTabbedTextExtent(
hDC: HDC;                        {a handle to a device context}
lpString: PChar;                 {the string whose dimensions are to be determined}
nCount: Integer;                 {the number of characters in the string}
nTabPositions: Integer;          {the number of tab stops}
lpnTabStopPositions: Pointer     {a pointer to an array of tab stop positions}
): DWORD;                        {returns the width and height of the string}
```

Description

This function returns the width and height of a string containing tab characters. The font currently selected into the specified device context is used as the basis for the string dimensions, and any tab characters in the string are expanded to the tab stop positions as indicated by the array pointed to by the lpnTabStopPositions parameter. The current clipping region of the specified device context does not affect the computed dimensions. In instances where a string containing kerning pairs is output to a device supporting character kerning, the dimensions returned by this function may not match the sum of the individual character dimensions in the string.

Parameters

hDC: A handle to a device context whose currently selected font is used to determine the length of the string.

lpString: A pointer to a null-terminated string containing the text with tab characters.

nCount: Specifies the length of the string pointed to by the lpString parameter in characters.

nTabPositions: Specifies the number of entries in the array of tab stops pointed to by the lpnTabStopPositions parameter.

lpnTabStopPositions: A pointer to an array of integers. Each integer entry in the array indicates a tab stop position, in device units. The tab stops must be arranged in an increasing order, with the smallest tab stop position as the first entry in the array and each tab stop position increasing thereafter. If this parameter is set to NIL and the nTabPositions parameter is set to zero, tab characters are expanded to eight times the average character width of the selected font.

Return Value

If the function succeeds, it returns the width and height of the string, where the height is in the high-order word of the return value and the width is in the low-order word. If the function fails, it returns zero.

See Also

GetTextExtentPoint32, TabbedTextOut

Example

See Listing 13-17 under TabbedTextOut.

GetTextAlign   Windows.pas

Syntax

GetTextAlign(
DC: HDC   {a handle to a device context}
): UINT;   {returns the text alignment flags}

Description

This function retrieves a set of flags indicating the current text alignment defined for the specified device context. The alignment is based on a bounding rectangle surrounding all characters within the string. Calling the GetTextExtentPoint32 function can retrieve the string's bounding rectangle dimensions. Text alignment is based on the starting point of the string, as defined by text output functions such as TextOut.

Parameters

DC: A handle to the device context whose text alignment is to be retrieved.

Return Value

If the function succeeds, it returns one or more text alignment flags from the following table; otherwise, it returns GDI_ERROR. To get extended error information, call the GetLastError function. Unlike most functions, the returned flags do not represent individual bits, and cannot simply be combined with the return value to determine if a particular flag is present. Instead, the flags must be inspected in the following groups of related flags:

TA_LEFT, TA_RIGHT, and TA_CENTER
TA_BOTTOM, TA_TOP, and TA_BASELINE
TA_NOUPDATECP and TA_UPDATECP

For vertical baseline fonts, the related flags are:

TA_LEFT, TA_RIGHT, and VTA_BASELINE
TA_BOTTOM, TA_TOP, and VTA_CENTER
TA_NOUPDATECP and TA_UPDATECP

To determine if any particular flag is present in the return value, the related group of flags must be combined using the Boolean OR operator, and the result combined with the return value using the Boolean AND operator. For example, to determine if the text is right aligned, assume that TextAlignment contains the return value from a call to the GetTextAlign function and use the formula:

```
if (TextAlignment and (TA_LEFT or TA_CENTER or TA_RIGHT)) = TA_RIGHT then
    Label2.Caption := 'Right';
```

See Also

DrawText, DrawTextEx, GetTextExtentPoint32, SetTextAlign, TextOut

Example

See Listing 13-16 under SetTextAlign.

Table 13-38: GetTextAlign return values

Value	Description
TA_BASELINE	The starting point is on the text baseline.
TA_BOTTOM	The starting point is on the bottom of the bounding rectangle for the text.
TA_TOP	The starting point is on the top of the bounding rectangle for the text.
TA_CENTER	The starting point is the horizontal center of the bounding rectangle for the text.
TA_LEFT	The starting point is on the left of the bounding rectangle for the text.
TA_RIGHT	The starting point is on the right of the bounding rectangle for the text.
TA_RTLREADING	Indicates that the text is in a right-to-left reading order. This value is meaningful only when the selected font is either Hebrew or Arabic.
TA_NOUPDATECP	Does not update the current position after drawing text.
TA_UPDATECP	Updates the current position after drawing text.
VTA_BASELINE	Vertical baseline fonts only: The starting point is on the text baseline.
VTA_CENTER	Vertical baseline fonts only: The starting point is the vertical center of the bounding rectangle for the text.

GetTextCharacterExtra Windows.pas

Syntax

```
GetTextCharacterExtra(
    DC: HDC              {a handle to a device context}
): Integer;              {returns the intercharacter spacing amount}
```

Description

This function retrieves the amount of extra space, in logical units, added between characters when drawing a line of text on the specified device context.

Parameters

DC: A handle to the device context whose extra character spacing value is to be retrieved.

Return Value

If the function succeeds, it returns the amount of extra space added between characters; otherwise, it returns $80000000.

See Also

DrawText, DrawTextEx, SetTextCharacterExtra, TextOut

Example

See Listing 13-16 under SetTextAlign.

GetTextColor   Windows.pas

Syntax

```
GetTextColor(
  DC: HDC            {a handle to a device context}
): COLORREF;         {returns a 32-bit color specifier}
```

Description

This function retrieves the current color used when drawing text on the device context identified by the DC parameter.

Parameters

DC: A handle to the device context whose text color is to be retrieved.

Return Value

If the function succeeds, it returns the 32-bit color specifier identifying the color used when drawing text. If the function fails, it returns CLR_INVALID.

See Also

SetTextColor, TextOut

Example

See Listing 13-16 under SetTextAlign.

GetTextExtentExPoint   Windows.pas

Syntax

```
GetTextExtentExPoint(
  DC: HDC;           {a handle to a device context}
  p2: PChar;         {the string from which to retrieve character extents}
  p3: Integer;       {the number of characters in the string}
  p4: Integer;       {the maximum string width}
  p5: PInteger;      {an integer receiving the maximum character count}
  p6: PInteger;      {points to an array of integers receiving the extents}
  var p7: TSize      {a TSize structure receiving the string dimensions}
): BOOL;             {returns TRUE or FALSE}
```

Description

This function retrieves the maximum number of characters from the string pointed to by the p2 parameter that will fit within the maximum allowed width specified by the p4 parameter. In addition, it fills an array of integers corresponding to each character in the string with the offset from the beginning of the string to the beginning of the character when it is drawn on the specified device context. The font currently selected into the specified device context is used to determine the maximum allowable characters and the offsets.

Parameters

DC: A handle to a device context whose currently selected font's attributes are used in determining the text extents.

p2: A pointer to a null-terminated string whose text extents are to be retrieved.

p3: Specifies the size of the string pointed to by the p2 parameter, in bytes.

p4: Specifies the maximum allowable width of the output string on the device context in logical units.

p5: A pointer to an integer that will receive the maximum number of characters that will fit in the logical space on the specified device context as defined by the p4 parameter. If this parameter is set to NIL, the p4 parameter is ignored.

p6: A pointer to an array of integers that receive the individual character extents for each character in the string pointed to by the p2 parameter. Each entry in the array is associated with the character in the identical position in the string, and contains the offset from the beginning of the string to the origin of the character when it is drawn to the screen. This offset will always fall within the maximum width as specified by the p4 parameter. Although there should be as many array entries as there are characters in the p2 string, the function only fills array entries for the number of characters as received by the p5 parameter. This parameter can be set to NIL if individual character extents are not needed.

p7: A pointer to a TSize structure that receives the width and height of the specified string in logical units.

Return Value

If the function succeeds, it returns TRUE; otherwise, it returns FALSE. To get extended error information, call the GetLastError function.

See Also

GetTextExtentPoint32

Example

Listing 13-14: Programmatically justifying text

```
var
  Form1: TForm1;
```

Text Output Functions

```
implementation

{$R *.DFM}

procedure TForm1.PaintBox1Paint(Sender: TObject);
var
  TheString: PChar;        // holds the output string
  StrPointer: PChar;       // a pointer within the output string
  DisplayString: PChar;    // holds the actual displayed string
  MaxChars: Integer;       // receives the maximum displayable characters
  StringSize: TSize;       // receives the string dimensions
  LineNum: Integer;        // a line number counter
  ExtraSpace: Integer;     // holds the extra space to add
  NumBreaks: Integer;      // holds the number of spaces in a string
  Count: Integer;          // a general loop control variable
begin
  {erase the image on the paintbox canvas}
  with PaintBox1.Canvas do
  begin
    Brush.Color := clWhite;
    FillRect(ClipRect);
  end;

  {initialize the original string}
  TheString:='Delphi is the most awesome Windows development environment ever!';

  {initialize the line number and the string pointer}
  LineNum := 0;
  StrPointer := TheString;

  {retrieve enough memory for the displayed string}
  GetMem(DisplayString, Length(TheString));

  {loop through the string until the entire string is displayed}
  while Length(StrPointer)>0 do
  begin
    {retrieve the maximum number of characters that can fit on
     one line within the small paintbox}
    GetTextExtentExPoint(PaintBox1.Canvas.Handle, TheString,
                         Length(TheString), PaintBox1.Width, @MaxChars,
                         nil, StringSize);

    {if the remaining string is longer than what can be displayed on one line,
     and the last character to be displayed is not a space, continue
     decreasing the maximum displayable characters until we hit a space}
    while (Length(StrPointer)>MaxChars) and (StrPointer[MaxChars]<>' ') do
      Inc(MaxChars, -1);

    {copy only the computed amount of characters into the displayable string.
     this new string should fit within the paintbox without breaking any words}
    StrLCopy(DisplayString, StrPointer, MaxChars);

    {if the remaining string is longer that what can be displayed, move
     the string pointer beyond the end of the displayed string; otherwise,
     point the string pointer to an empty string}
    if Length(StrPointer)>MaxChars then
      StrPointer := @StrPointer[MaxChars+1];
```

```
    else
      StrPointer := #0;

    {retrieve the width and height of the string}
    GetTextExtentPoint32(PaintBox1.Canvas.Handle, DisplayString,
                    Length(DisplayString), StringSize);

    {to justify the text so that it fills the entire line, compute the amount
     of space left between the size of the string and the width of the
     paintbox}
    ExtraSpace := PaintBox1.Width - StringSize.cx;

    {count the number of break characters in the displayed string. note that
     this assumes that the break character is a space (' ')}
    NumBreaks := 0;
    for Count := 0 to Length(DisplayString)-1 do
      if DisplayString[Count] = ' ' then
        Inc(NumBreaks);

    {if there is at least one space, set the text justification. this will add
     the computed amount of extra space evenly among all of the spaces in the
     line, thus performing a full justification when the string is drawn to
     the device context}
    if NumBreaks>0 then
      SetTextJustification(PaintBox1.Canvas.Handle, ExtraSpace, NumBreaks);

    {draw the fully justified string to the paint box device context}
    TextOut(PaintBox1.Canvas.Handle, 0, LineNum*Stringsize.cy, DisplayString,
                    Length(DisplayString));

    {reset the text justification to its original value for the next pass}
    SetTextJustification(PaintBox1.Canvas.Handle, 0, 0);

    {track the current text line number}
    Inc(LineNum);
  end;

  {free the display string memory}
  FreeMem(DisplayString, Length(TheString));
end;
```

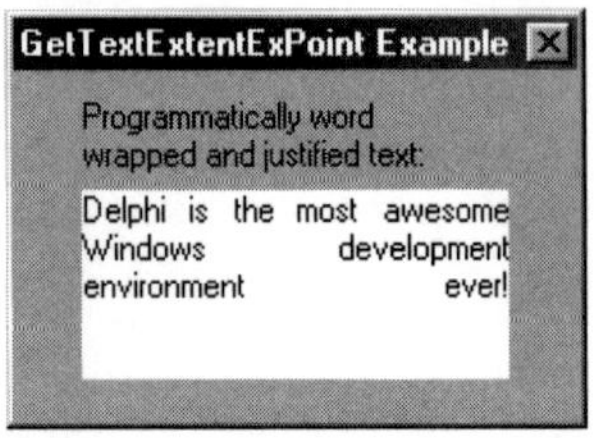

Figure 13-15:
The justified text

GetTextExtentPoint32   Windows.pas

Syntax

GetTextExtentPoint32(
DC: HDC;   {a handle to a device context}

```
Str: PChar;                  {a pointer to a string}
Count: Integer;              {the number of characters in the string}
var Size: TSize              {points to a TSize structure receiving the dimensions}
): BOOL;                     {returns TRUE or FALSE}
```

Description

This function retrieves the width and height of the string pointed to by the Str parameter, in logical units. The width and height are based on the attributes of the string currently selected into the device context identified by the DC parameter. The clipping region of the specified device context does not affect the computed dimensions. In instances where a string containing kerning pairs is output to a device supporting character kerning, the dimensions returned by this function may not match the sum of the individual character dimensions in the string.

Parameters

DC: A handle to the device context whose currently selected font is used to determine the string's width and height.

Str: A pointer to a string whose width and height are to be retrieved. This does not have to be a null-terminated string, as the Count parameter specifies the string length.

Count: Specifies the number of characters in the string pointed to by the Str parameter.

Size: A pointer to a TSize structure that receives the width and height of the specified string based on the attributes of the font selected into the specified device context.

Return Value

If the function succeeds, it returns TRUE; otherwise, it returns FALSE. To get extended error information, call the GetLastError function.

See Also

GetTabbedTextExtent, GetTextExtentExPoint, SetTextCharacterExtra

Example

See Listing 13-14 under GetTextExtentExPoint.

GetTextFace   Windows.pas

Syntax

```
GetTextFace(
DC: HDC;                     {a handle to a device context}
Count: Integer;              {the buffer length}
Buffer: PChar                {a buffer receiving the typeface name}
): Integer;                  {returns the number of characters copied}
```

Description

This function retrieves the typeface name of the font currently selected into the device context identified by the DC parameter.

Parameters

DC: A handle to the device context whose currently selected font's typeface name is to be retrieved.

Count: Specifies the size of the buffer pointed to by the Buffer parameter, in characters. If the retrieved typeface name string is longer than the value specified by this parameter, the string is truncated.

Buffer: A pointer to a null-terminated string buffer that receives the typeface name of the currently selected font. If this parameter is set to NIL, the function returns the size of the required buffer in characters, including the null terminator.

Return Value

If the function succeeds, it returns the number of characters copied to the buffer pointed to by the Buffer parameter. If the function fails, it returns zero. To get extended error information, call the GetLastError function.

See Also

EnumFontFamilies, EnumFontFamiliesEx, GetTextAlign, GetTextColor, GetTextMetrics

Example

See Listing 13-15 under GetTextMetrics.

GetTextMetrics   Windows.pas

Syntax

```
GetTextMetrics(
  DC: HDC;                  {a handle to a device context}
  var TM: TTextMetric       {a pointer to a TTextMetric structure}
): BOOL;                    {returns TRUE or FALSE}
```

Description

This function retrieves metric information, such as height, ascent, descent, and other physical measurements, for the currently selected font in the device context identified by the DC parameter.

Parameters

DC: A handle to the device context whose currently selected font's metric information is to be retrieved.

TM: A pointer to a TTextMetric data structure that receives the physical measurements and other attributes for the currently selected font of the specified device context. Note that all measurements are in logical units and are dependent on the mapping mode of the specified device context. The TTextMetric structure is defined as:

```
TTextMetric = record
    tmHeight: Longint;            {the height of a character}
    tmAscent: Longint;            {the ascent of a character}
```

```
    tmDescent: Longint;              {the descent of a character}
    tmInternalLeading: Longint;      {the internal leading}
    tmExternalLeading: Longint;      {the external leading}
    tmAveCharWidth: Longint;         {the average character width}
    tmMaxCharWidth: Longint;         {the maximum character width}
    tmWeight: Longint;               {the boldness value}
    tmOverhang: Longint;             {the overhang width}
    tmDigitizedAspectX: Longint;     {the horizontal aspect}
    tmDigitizedAspectY: Longint;     {the vertical aspect}
    tmFirstChar: AnsiChar;           {the first character}
    tmLastChar: AnsiChar;            {the last character}
    tmDefaultChar: AnsiChar;         {the default character}
    tmBreakChar: AnsiChar;           {the word break character}
    tmItalic: Byte;                  {the italics flag}
    tmUnderlined: Byte;              {the underlined flag}
    tmStruckOut: Byte;               {the strikeout flag}
    tmPitchAndFamily: Byte;          {the pitch and family flags}
    tmCharSet: Byte;                 {the character set}
end;
```

tmHeight: Specifies the height of characters within the font. The character height is measured as tmAscent+tmDescent.

tmAscent: Specifies the ascent of the characters within the font. The ascent is measured from the baseline to the top of the character, including the internal leading.

tmDescent: Specifies the descent of the characters within the font. The descent is measured from the baseline to the bottom of the character, and includes descenders for characters such as "g" or "y."

tmInternalLeading: Specifies the amount of space inside of the ascent for such things as accent and diacritical marks. The font designer may set this value to zero.

tmExternalLeading: Specifies the amount of extra space above the top of the font. This space is intended for added extra room between rows of text, and does not contain any marks. The font designer may set this value to zero.

tmAveCharWidth: Specifies the average width of characters within the font, excluding any overhang required for italic or bold characters.

tmMaxCharWidth: Specifies the width of the widest character within the font.

tmWeight: Specifies the boldness of the font. The value of this member can be in the range of 0-1000, or can be set to one value from Table 13-39.

tmOverhang: Specifies the extra width per string that is added when synthesizing bold or italic fonts. For bold fonts, this value indicates the overstrike offset. For italic fonts, this value indicates the shearing distance. Use the value returned by a call to the GetTextExtentPoint32 function on a single character minus the value of this member to determine the actual character width.

tmDigitizedAspectX: Specifies the horizontal aspect of the device for which the font was originally designed.

tmDigitizedAspectY: Specifies the vertical aspect of the device for which the font was originally designed.

tmFirstChar: Specifies the value of the first defined character.

tmLastChar: Specifies the value of the last defined character.

tmDefaultChar: Specifies the value of the default character. This character is used when text output with this font contains a character not defined within the font.

tmBreakChar: Specifies the value of the character used for word breaks and text justification.

tmItalic: Specifies the italics attribute for the font. If this member is set to TRUE, the font is italicized.

tmUnderlined: Specifies the underlining attribute for the font. If this member is set to TRUE, the font is underlined.

tmStruckOut: Specifies the strikeout attribute for the font. If this member is set to TRUE, the font is struck out.

tmPitchAndFamily: Specifies the font pitch and font family. The low-order 4 bits specify the pitch of the font, and can contain one or more values from the font pitch table (Table 13-40). The high-order 4 bits indicate the font family. Combining this member with a value of $F0 using the Boolean AND operator will retrieve a value matching one flag from the font family table (Table 13-41).

tmCharSet: Specifies the character set of the font. This member may contain one value from Table 13-42.

Return Value

If the function succeeds, it returns TRUE; otherwise, it returns FALSE. To get extended error information, call the GetLastError function.

See Also

EnumFontFamilies, EnumFontFamiliesEx, GetTextAlign, GetTextExtentExPoint, GetTextExtentPoint32, GetTextFace, SetTextJustification

Example

Listing 13-15: Retrieving font metric information

```
procedure TForm1.FormActivate(Sender: TObject);
var
  FontInfo: TTextMetric;              // holds the font metric information
  FaceName: array[0..255] of char;    // holds the font name
begin
  {retrieve the name of the currently selected font and display it}
  GetTextFace(Form1.Canvas.Handle, 256, FaceName);
  Label2.Caption := FaceName;

  {retrieve the physical attributes for the selected font}
  GetTextMetrics(Form1.Canvas.Handle, FontInfo);

  {clear the list box and begin displaying the physical font attributes}
  ListBox1.Items.Clear;
```

```
with FontInfo, ListBox1.Items do
begin
  {display the various font measurements}
  Label15.Caption := IntToStr(tmHeight);
  Label14.Caption := IntToStr(tmAscent);
  Label13.Caption := IntToStr(tmDescent);
  Label12.Caption := IntToStr(tmInternalLeading);
  Label11.Caption := IntToStr(tmExternalLeading);

  {display the average and maximum character width}
  Add('Average Char Width: '+IntToStr(tmAveCharWidth));
  Add('Max Char Width: '+IntToStr(tmMaxCharWidth));

  {display the boldness setting}
  case tmWeight of
    FW_DONTCARE:   Add('Weight: Don''t care');
    FW_THIN:       Add('Weight: Thin');
    FW_EXTRALIGHT: Add('Weight: Extra light');
    FW_LIGHT:      Add('Weight: Light');
    FW_NORMAL:     Add('Weight: Normal');
    FW_MEDIUM:     Add('Weight: Medium');
    FW_SEMIBOLD:   Add('Weight: Semibold');
    FW_BOLD:       Add('Weight: Bold');
    FW_EXTRABOLD:  Add('Weight: Extra bold');
    FW_HEAVY:      Add('Weight: Heavy');
  end;

  {display the overhang measurement}
  Add('Overhang: '+IntToStr(tmOverhang));

  {display the horizontal and vertical aspect.
   note: there is a bug in the GetTextMetrics function that causes these
   two values to be swapped.  the AspectX value is returned in the AspectY
   member, and vice versa}
  Add('Digitized Aspect X: '+IntToStr(tmDigitizedAspectY));
  Add('Digitized Aspect Y: '+IntToStr(tmDigitizedAspectX));

  {display the important font characters}
  Add('First Character: '+Char(tmFirstChar));
  Add('Last Char: '+Char(tmLastChar));
  Add('Default Char: '+Char(tmDefaultChar));
  Add('Break Char: '+Char(tmBreakChar));

  {indicate italic, underlined, or strikeout attributes}
  CheckBox1.Checked := (tmItalic>0);
  CheckBox2.Checked := (tmUnderlined>0);
  CheckBox3.Checked := (tmStruckOut>0);

  {display the font pitch}
  Add('Pitch: ');
  if ((tmPitchAndFamily and $0F) and TMPF_FIXED_PITCH)= TMPF_FIXED_PITCH then
    Add('     Fixed pitch');
  if ((tmPitchAndFamily and $0F) and TMPF_VECTOR) = TMPF_VECTOR then
    Add('     Vector');
  if ((tmPitchAndFamily and $0F) and TMPF_TRUETYPE) = TMPF_TRUETYPE then
    Add('     TrueType');
  if ((tmPitchAndFamily and $0F) and TMPF_DEVICE) = TMPF_DEVICE then
```

Chapter 13

```
            Add('    Device');
      if (tmPitchAndFamily and $0F) = 0 then
            Add('    Monospaced bitmap font');

      {display the font family}
      case (tmPitchAndFamily and $F0) of
         FF_DECORATIVE: Add('Family: Decorative');
         FF_DONTCARE:   Add('Family: Don''t care');
         FF_MODERN:     Add('Family: Modern');
         FF_ROMAN:      Add('Family: Roman');
         FF_SCRIPT:     Add('Family: Script');
         FF_SWISS:      Add('Family: Swiss');
      end;

      {display the character set}
      case tmCharSet of
         ANSI_CHARSET:        Add('Character set: ANSI');
         DEFAULT_CHARSET:     Add('Character set: Default');
         SYMBOL_CHARSET:      Add('Character set: Symbol');
         SHIFTJIS_CHARSET:    Add('Character set: ShiftJis');
         GB2312_CHARSET:      Add('Character set: GB2312');
         HANGEUL_CHARSET:     Add('Character set: Hangeul');
         CHINESEBIG5_CHARSET: Add('Character set: Chinese Big5');
         OEM_CHARSET:         Add('Character set: OEM');
      else
         Add('Windows 95 only character set');
      end;
   end;
end;
```

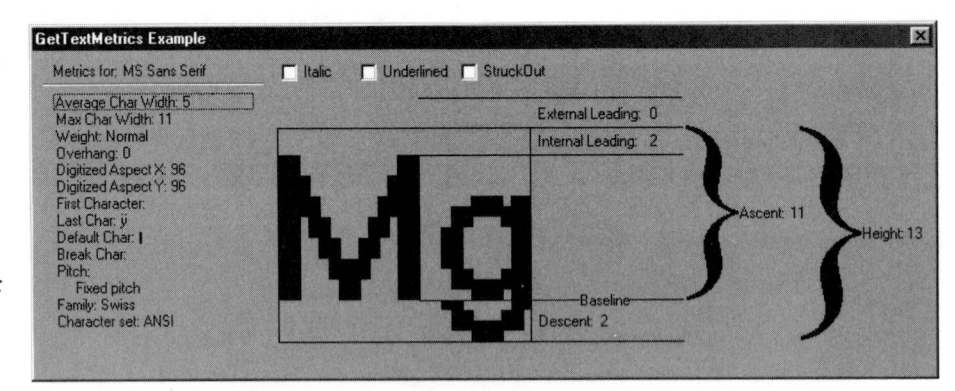

Figure 13-16: The current font metric information

Table 13-39: GetTextMetrics TM.tmWeight values

Value	Description
FW_THIN	Extra thin font weight (100).
FW_EXTRALIGHT	Thin font weight (200).
FW_LIGHT	Below average bolding (300).
FW_NORMAL	Normal bolding (400).
FW_MEDIUM	Above average bolding (500).
FW_SEMIBOLD	Light bolding (600).

Value	Description
FW_BOLD	Bolded font (700).
FW_EXTRABOLD	Extra bolding (800).
FW_HEAVY	Very heaving bolding (900).

Table 13-40: GetTextMetrics TM.tmPitchAndFamily font pitch values

Value	Description
TMPF_FIXED_PITCH	If this flag is present, the font is a variable pitch font. If this flag is not present, this font is a fixed pitch, or monospaced, font.
TMPF_VECTOR	Indicates a vector font.
TMPF_TRUETYPE	Indicates a TrueType font.
TMPF_DEVICE	Indicates a device font.

Table 13-41: GetTextMetrics TM.tmPitchAndFamily font family values

Value	Description
FF_DECORATIVE	Indicates a novelty or decorative font, such as Old English.
FF_DONTCARE	The general font style is unknown or unimportant.
FF_MODERN	Indicates a monospaced font with consistent stroke widths, with or without serifs, such as Courier New.
FF_ROMAN	Indicates a proportional font with variable stroke widths, containing serifs, such as Times New Roman.
FF_SCRIPT	Indicates a font resembling handwriting, such as Brush Script.
FF_SWISS	Indicates a proportional font with variable stroke widths, without serifs, such as Arial.

Table 13-42: GetTextMetrics TM.tmCharSet values

Value	Description
ANSI_CHARSET	The ANSI character set.
DEFAULT_CHARSET	The default character set.
SYMBOL_CHARSET	The symbol character set.
SHIFTJIS_CHARSET	The shiftjis character set.
GB2312_CHARSET	The GB2312 character set.
HANGEUL_CHARSET	The Korean character set.
CHINESEBIG5_CHARSET	The Chinese character set.
OEM_CHARSET	The original equipment manufacturer character set.
JOHAB_CHARSET	**Windows 95 and later:** The Johab character set.
HEBREW_CHARSET	**Windows 95 and later:** The Hebrew character set.
ARABIC_CHARSET	**Windows 95 and later:** The Arabic character set.
GREEK_CHARSET	**Windows 95 and later:** The Grecian character set.
TURKISH_CHARSET	**Windows 95 and later:** The Turkish character set.
VIETNAMESE_CHARSET	**Windows 95 and later:** The Vietnamese character set.

Value	Description
THAI_CHARSET	**Windows 95 and later:** The Thai character set.
EASTEUROPE_CHARSET	**Windows 95 and later:** The eastern Europe character set.
RUSSIAN_CHARSET	**Windows 95 and later:** The Russian character set.
MAC_CHARSET	**Windows 95 and later:** The Macintosh character set.
BALTIC_CHARSET	**Windows 95 and later:** The Baltic character set.

RemoveFontResource   *Windows.pas*

Syntax

```
RemoveFontResource(
p1: PChar        {the font resource filename}
): BOOL;         {returns TRUE or FALSE}
```

Description

This function removes the font resource contained in the specified font resource file from the internal system font tables. If the font is successfully removed, the application that removed the font should inform all other applications of the change. This is accomplished by sending the WM_FONTCHANGE message with the SendMessage function, specifying HWND_BROADCAST as the value of the hWnd parameter. The font resource will not actually be removed until it is no longer selected into any device context.

Parameters

p1: A pointer to a null-terminated string containing the name of the font resource file whose font resource is to be removed from the internal system font tables.

Return Value

If the function succeeds, it returns TRUE; otherwise, it returns FALSE. To get extended error information, call the GetLastError function.

See Also

AddFontResource, CreateScalableFontResource, GetFontData

Example

See Listing 13-4 under CreateScalableFontResource.

SetTextAlign   *Windows.pas*

Syntax

```
SetTextAlign(
DC: HDC;         {a handle to a device context}
Flags: UINT      {the text alignment flags}
): UINT;         {returns the previous alignment flags}
```

Description

This function sets the alignment used when drawing text on the specified device context. The alignment is based on a bounding rectangle surrounding all characters within the string. The string's bounding rectangle dimensions can be retrieved by calling the GetTextExtentPoint32 function. Text alignment is based on the starting point of the string, as defined by text output functions such as TextOut.

Parameters

DC: A handle to the device context whose text alignment is to be set.

Flags: A series of flags indicating the new text alignment for the specified device context. This parameter can be set to one or more values from the following table by combining them with the Boolean OR operator. However, only one flag each from those that modify horizontal or vertical alignment can be chosen, and only one flag from those that modify the current position can be chosen.

Return Value

If this function succeeds, it returns the previous text alignment flags; otherwise, it returns GDI_ERROR. To get extended error information, call the GetLastError function.

See Also

DrawText, DrawTextEx, GetTextAlign, TabbedTextOut, TextOut

Example

Listing 13-16: Manipulating text

```
var
  Form1: TForm1;
  HorzAlignmentValue: UINT;           // holds the horizontal alignment
  VertAlignmentValue: UINT;           // holds the vertical alignment
  IntercharacterSpacing: Integer;     // holds the intercharacter spacing

implementation

{$R *.DFM}

procedure TForm1.PaintBox1Paint(Sender: TObject);
var
  TextAlignment: UINT;   // holds the text alignment
begin
  {set the text alignment}
  SetTextAlign(PaintBox1.Canvas.Handle,
               HorzAlignmentValue or VertAlignmentValue);

  {set the intercharacter spacing}
  SetTextCharacterExtra(PaintBox1.Canvas.Handle, SpinEdit1.Value);

  {retrieve and display the current intercharacter spacing}
  Label7.Caption := IntToStr(GetTextCharacterExtra(PaintBox1.Canvas.Handle));

  {set the text color}
```

```
    SetTextColor(PaintBox1.Canvas.Handle, ColorGrid1.ForegroundColor);

    {retrieve and display the current text color}
    Label9.Caption := IntToHex(GetTextColor(PaintBox1.Canvas.Handle), 8);

    {draw some text (affected by alignment, spacing, and color) to
     the device context}
    TextOut(PaintBox1.Canvas.Handle, PaintBox1.Width div 2,
            PaintBox1.Height div 2, 'ABCabc', Length('ABCabc'));

    {retrieve the current text alignment}
    TextAlignment := GetTextAlign(PaintBox1.Canvas.Handle);

    {display the horizontal alignment}
    if (TextAlignment and (TA_LEFT or TA_CENTER or TA_RIGHT)) = TA_LEFT then
      Label2.Caption := 'Left';
    if (TextAlignment and (TA_LEFT or TA_CENTER or TA_RIGHT)) = TA_CENTER then
      Label2.Caption := 'Center';
    if (TextAlignment and (TA_LEFT or TA_CENTER or TA_RIGHT)) = TA_RIGHT then
      Label2.Caption := 'Right';

    {display the vertical alignment}
    if (TextAlignment and (TA_TOP or TA_BASELINE or TA_BOTTOM)) = TA_TOP then
      Label4.Caption := 'Top';
    if (TextAlignment and (TA_TOP or TA_BASELINE or TA_BOTTOM)) = TA_BASELINE then
      Label4.Caption := 'Baseline';
    if (TextAlignment and (TA_TOP or TA_BASELINE or TA_BOTTOM)) = TA_BOTTOM then
      Label4.Caption := 'Bottom';
end;

procedure TForm1.RadioButton1Click(Sender: TObject);
begin
  {indicate the selected horizontal alignment}
  HorzAlignmentValue := 0;
  case TRadioButton(Sender).Tag of
    1: HorzAlignmentValue := TA_LEFT;
    2: HorzAlignmentValue := TA_CENTER;
    3: HorzAlignmentValue := TA_RIGHT;
  end;

  {refresh the screen}
  PaintBox1.Refresh;
end;

procedure TForm1.RadioButton4Click(Sender: TObject);
begin
  {indicate the selected vertical alignment}
  VertAlignmentValue := 0;
  case TRadioButton(Sender).Tag of
    1: VertAlignmentValue := TA_TOP;
    2: VertAlignmentValue := TA_BASELINE;
    3: VertAlignmentValue := TA_BOTTOM;
  end;

  {refresh the screen}
  PaintBox1.Refresh;
end;
```

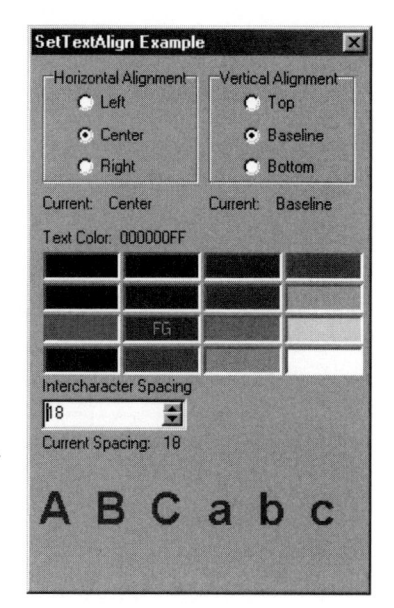

Figure 13-17: The effects of text alignment, color, and spacing

Table 13-43: SetTextAlign Flags values

Value	Description
TA_BASELINE	The starting point is on the text baseline.
TA_BOTTOM	The starting point is on the bottom of the bounding rectangle for the text.
TA_TOP	The starting point is on the top of the bounding rectangle for the text.
TA_CENTER	The starting point is the horizontal center of the bounding rectangle for the text.
TA_LEFT	The starting point is on the left of the bounding rectangle for the text.
TA_RIGHT	The starting point is on the right of the bounding rectangle for the text.
TA_RTLREADING	**Windows 95 only:** Indicates that the text is in a right-to-left reading order. This value is meaningful only when the selected font is either Hebrew or Arabic.
TA_NOUPDATECP	Does not update the current position after drawing text.
TA_UPDATECP	Updates the current position after drawing text.
VTA_BASELINE	**Vertical baseline fonts only:** The starting point is on the text baseline.
VTA_CENTER	**Vertical baseline fonts only:** The starting point is the vertical center of the bounding rectangle for the text.

SetTextCharacterExtra   Windows.pas

Syntax

```
SetTextCharacterExtra(
  DC: HDC;                    {a handle to a device context}
  CharExtra: Integer          {the extra character spacing amount}
): Integer;                   {returns the previous intercharacter spacing amount}
```

Description

This function sets the amount of extra space, in logical units, added between characters when drawing a line of text on the specified device context.

Parameters

DC: A handle to the device context whose extra character spacing value is to be set.

CharExtra: Specifies the amount of space to add between characters, in logical units. If the specified device context's current mapping mode is not set to MM_TEXT, this value will be translated for the current mapping mode and rounded to the nearest pixel.

Return Value

If the function succeeds, it returns the previous extra space; otherwise, it returns $80000000.

See Also

DrawText, DrawTextEx, GetTextCharacterExtra, TextOut

Example

See Listing 13-16 under SetTextAlign.

SetTextColor   Windows.pas

Syntax

```
SetTextColor(
  DC: HDC;                  {a handle to a device context}
  Color: COLORREF           {the new 32-bit text color specifier}
): COLORREF;                {returns the previous text color specifier}
```

Description

This function sets the current color used when drawing text on the device context identified by the DC parameter.

Parameters

DC: A handle to the device context whose text color is to be set.

Color: Specifies a 32-bit color specifier defining the new color in which to draw text. The actual color used is the closest matching color for the specified color in the currently realized palette of the specified device context.

Return Value

If the function succeeds, it returns the previous text color specifier; otherwise, it returns CLR_INVALID. To get extended error information, call the GetLastError function.

See Also

DrawText, DrawTextEx, GetTextColor, SetBkColor, SetBkMode, TabbedTextOut, TextOut

Example

See Listing 13-16 under SetTextAlign.

SetTextJustification   Windows.pas

Syntax

```
SetTextJustification(
DC: HDC;                   {a handle to a device context}
BreakExtra: Integer;       {the total extra space}
BreakCount: Integer        {the number of break characters}
): Integer;                {returns a zero or non-zero value}
```

Description

This function specifies the amount of extra space, in logical units, that should be added to each break character in a string of text when drawing the string on the specified device context. Most fonts define the break character as the space (" "), but some non-Latin fonts may define a different character. Use the GetTextMetrics function to retrieve any specific font's defined break character. The GetTextExtentPoint32 function can be used to retrieve the width of the output text so that the appropriate extra space can be determined. The TextOut function distributes the specified extra character space evenly among all break characters in an output line of text.

Parameters

DC: A handle to the device context whose extra space for justification is to be set.

BreakExtra: Specifies the total extra space that will be added to the output line of text, in logical units. If the specified device context's current mapping mode is not set to MM_TEXT, this value will be translated for the current mapping mode and rounding to the nearest pixel.

BreakCount: Specifies the total number of break characters in the string to be justified.

Return Value

If the function succeeds, it returns a non-zero value; otherwise, it returns zero. To get extended error information, call the GetLastError function.

See Also

DrawText, DrawTextEx, GetTextExtentExPoint, GetTextExtentPoint32, GetTextMetrics, TextOut

Example

See Listing 13-14 under GetTextExtentExPoint.

TabbedTextOut   Windows.pas

Syntax

```
TabbedTextOut(
hDC: HDC;                        {a handle to a device context}
X: Integer;                      {the horizontal text origin}
Y: Integer;                      {the vertical text origin}
lpString: PChar;                 {the string to be drawn onto the device context}
nCount: Integer;                 {the number of characters in the string}
nTabPositions: Integer;          {the number of entries in the tab stops array}
lpnTabStopPositions: Pointer;    {a pointer to an array of tab stop positions}
nTabOrigin: Integer              {the horizontal tab stop origin}
): Longint;                      {returns the string dimensions}
```

Description

This function outputs the specified string of text onto the device context identified by the hDC parameter, expanding any tab characters in the string to the tab stop positions indicated by the array of integers pointed to by the lpnTabStopPositions parameter. The tabs are expanded to the values in this array as they are encountered, with the first tab character in the string expanding to the position indicated by the first entry in the array, the second tab character expanding to the position indicated by the second entry in the array, and so on. The currently selected font in the specified device context is used when drawing the text. The function will not update the current position unless the SetTextAlign function has been called with the TA_UPDATECP flag specified.

Parameters

hDC: A handle to the device context upon which the text is drawn.

X: The horizontal coordinate of the output line of text, in logical units. If the current position is set to be updated, this parameter is ignored on subsequent calls.

Y: The vertical coordinate of the output line of text, in logical units. If the current position is set to be updated, this parameter is ignored on subsequent calls.

lpString: A pointer to the string containing tab characters that is to be drawn onto the specified device context. This does not have to be a null-terminated string, as the nCount parameter specifies the string length.

nCount: Specifies the number of characters in the string pointed to by the lpString parameter.

nTabPositions: Specifies the number of entries in the array of tab stops pointed to by the lpnTabStopPositions parameter.

lpnTabStopPositions: A pointer to an array of integers. Each integer entry in the array indicates a tab stop position, in device units. The tab stops must be arranged in an increasing order, with the smallest tab stop position as the first entry in the array and each tab stop position increasing thereafter. If this parameter is set to NIL and the nTabPositions parameter is set to zero, tab characters are expanded to eight times the average character width of the selected font.

Windows 95 only: A negative tab stop position indicates a right-aligned tab stop.

nTabOrigin: Specifies the horizontal coordinate from which to start expanding tabs, in logical units.

Return Value

If the function succeeds, it returns the dimensions of the output string in logical units, with the height of the string in the high-order word of the return value, and the width in the low-order word. If the function fails, it returns zero.

See Also

DrawText, DrawTextEx, GetTabbedTextExtent, GrayString, SetTextAlign, TextOut

Example

Listing 13-17: Outputting text like a table

```
{Whoops! Delphi incorrectly imports this function, so we must reimport it
 manually to obtain the full functionality of this function}
function TabbedTextOut(hDC: HDC; X, Y: Integer; lpString: PChar; nCount,
  nTabPositions: Integer; lpnTabStopPositions: Pointer; nTabOrigin: Integer):
  Longint; stdcall;

{Whoops!  Delphi incorrectly imports this function, so we must reimport it
 manually to obtain the full functionality of this function}
function GetTabbedTextExtent(hDC: HDC; lpString: PChar;
  nCount, nTabPositions: Integer; lpnTabStopPositions: Pointer): DWORD; stdcall;

var
  Form1: TForm1;

implementation

{$R *.DFM}

{reimport the function}
function GetTabbedTextExtent; external user32 name 'GetTabbedTextExtentA';

{reimport the function}
function TabbedTextOut; external user32 name 'TabbedTextOutA';

procedure TForm1.PaintBox1Paint(Sender: TObject);
const
  {define some static arrays of strings}
  NameCol: array[0..8] of string = ('Name', 'John', 'David', 'Larry', 'Phil',
                                    'Kenneth', 'Rod', 'Ovais', 'Mike');
  IDCol:   array[0..8] of string = ('ID Number', '100', '101', '102', '103',
                                    '104', '105', '106', '107');
  ScoreCol: array[0..8] of string = ('Score', '9,000,000', '8,345,678',
                                     '7,325,876', '8,324,689', '5,234,761',
                                     '5,243,864', '8,358,534', '6,538,324');
var
```

```
            TabStops: array[0..2] of Integer;  // holds the tab stops
            FontSize: TSize;                    // holds the font size
            Count: Integer;                     // a general loop control variable
          begin
            {define our tab stops}
            TabStops[0] := 10;
            TabStops[1] := PaintBox1.Width div 2;
            TabStops[2] := -PaintBox1.Width;         // a right aligned tab stop

            {retrieve the height of a string}
            GetTextExtentPoint32(PaintBox1.Canvas.Handle, 'ABC', Length('ABC'), FontSize);

            with PaintBox1.Canvas do
            begin
              {erase the last image}
              Brush.Color := clWhite;
              FillRect(ClipRect);

              {output the above string arrays, using tab stops to format the
               strings like a table}
              for Count := 0 to 8 do
                TabbedTextOut(Handle, 0, FontSize.cy*Count,
                          PChar(NameCol[Count]+#9+IDCol[Count]+#9+ScoreCol[Count]),
                          Length(NameCol[Count]+#9+IDCol[Count]+#9+ScoreCol[Count]),
                          3, @TabStops, 0);
            end;

            {retrieve the length of a string containing tabs, in pixels.  this value
             should equal the width of the paintbox.}
            Label3.Caption := IntToStr(LoWord(GetTabbedTextExtent(PaintBox1.Canvas.Handle,
                                  PChar(NameCol[0]+#9+IDCol[0]+#9+ScoreCol[0]),
                                  Length(NameCol[0]+#9+IDCol[0]+#9+ScoreCol[0]),
                                  3, @TabStops)));
          end;
```

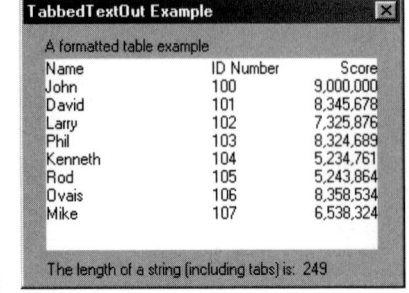

Figure 13-18:
Text output with tab stops

TextOut   Windows.pas

Syntax

TextOut(
DC: HDC;   {a handle to a device context}
X: Integer;   {the horizontal text origin}
Y: Integer;   {the vertical text origin}

Str: PChar;	{the string to be drawn onto the device context}
Count: Integer	{the number of characters in the string}
): BOOL;	{returns TRUE or FALSE}

Description

This function outputs the specified string of text onto the device context identified by the DC parameter. The currently selected font in the specified device context is used when drawing the text. The function will not update the current position unless the SetTextAlign function has been called with the TA_UPDATECP flag specified.

Parameters

DC: A handle to the device context upon which the text is drawn.

X: The horizontal coordinate of the output line of text in logical units. If the current position is set to be updated, this parameter is ignored on subsequent calls.

Y: The vertical coordinate of the output line of text in logical units. If the current position is set to be updated, this parameter is ignored on subsequent calls.

Str: A pointer to the string to be drawn onto the specified device context. This does not have to be a null-terminated string, as the Count parameter specifies the string length.

Count: Specifies the number of characters in the string pointed to by the Str parameter.

Return Value

If the function succeeds, it returns TRUE; otherwise, it returns FALSE. To get extended error information, call the GetLastError function.

See Also

DrawText, DrawTextEx, GetTextAlign, SetTextAlign, TabbedTextOut

Example

See Listing 13-2 under CreateFont, and other examples throughout this chapter.

Appendix A

Bibliography

There exists quite a large knowledge base on Windows programming in general and Delphi programming in particular. The information for this book is based in part on research and knowledge gleaned from the following books:

Beveridge and Wiener, *Multithreading Applications in Win32* [Addison-Wesley Developers Press, 1997]

Calvert, Charles, *Delphi 2 Unleashed* [Sams Publishing, 1996]

Cluts, Nancy, *Programming the Windows 95 User Interface* [Microsoft Press, 1995]

Cooke and Telles, *Windows 95 How-To* [Waite Group Press, 1996]

Frerking, Wallace, and Niddery, *Borland Delphi How-To* [Waite Group Press, 1995]

Jarol, Haygood, and Coppola, *Delphi 2 Multimedia Adventure Set* [Coriolis Group Books, 1996]

Konopka, Ray, *Developing Custom Delphi 3 Components* [Coriolis Group Books, 1997]

Lischner, Ray, *Secrets of Delphi 2* [Waite Group Press, 1996]

Miller, Powell, et. al., *Special Edition Using Delphi 3* [QUE, 1997]

Pacheco and Teixeira, *Delphi 2 Developers Guide* [Sams Publishing, 1996]

Petzold and Yao, *Programming Windows 95* [Microsoft Press, 1996]

Pietrek, Matt, *Windows 95 System Programming Secrets* [IDG Books, 1995]

Rector and Newcomer, *Win32 Programming* [Addison-Wesley Developers Press, 1997]

Richter, Jeffrey, *Advanced Windows,* [Microsoft Press, 1997]

Simon, Gouker, and Barnes, *Windows 95 Win32 Programming API Bible* [Waite Group Press, 1996]

Swan and Cogswell, *Delphi 32-Bit Programming Secrets* [IDG Books, 1996]

Thorpe, Danny, *Delphi Component Design* [Addison-Wesley Developers Press, 1997]

Wallace and Tendon, *Delphi 2 Developer's Solutions* [Waite Group Press, 1996]

Appendix B

Virtual Key Code Chart

Virtual Key Code	Decimal Value	Hex Value	Description
VK_LBUTTON	1	$1	Left mouse button
VK_RBUTTON	2	$2	Right mouse button
VK_CANCEL	3	$3	Ctrl+Break key combination
VK_MBUTTON	4	$4	Middle mouse button
VK_BACK	8	$8	Backspace
VK_TAB	9	$9	Tab
VK_CLEAR	12	$C	Numeric Keypad 5, NumLock off
VK_RETURN	13	$D	Enter
VK_SHIFT	16	$10	Shift
VK_CONTROL	17	$11	Ctrl
VK_MENU	18	$12	Alt
VK_PAUSE	19	$13	Pause
VK_CAPITAL	20	$14	Caps Lock
VK_ESCAPE	27	$1B	Esc
VK_SPACE	32	$20	Space bar
VK_PRIOR	33	$21	Page Up
VK_NEXT	34	$22	Page Down
VK_END	35	$23	End
VK_HOME	36	$24	Home
VK_LEFT	37	$25	Left cursor key
VK_UP	38	$26	Up cursor key
VK_RIGHT	39	$27	Right cursor key
VK_DOWN	40	$28	Down cursor key
VK_SNAPSHOT	44	$2C	Print Screen
VK_INSERT	45	$2D	Insert
VK_DELETE	46	$2E	Delete
VK_LWIN	91	$5B	Left Windows key on a Windows 95 compatible keyboard
VK_RWIN	92	$5C	Right Windows key on a Windows 95 compatible keyboard

Virtual Key Code	Decimal Value	Hex Value	Description
VK_APPS	93	$5D	Menu key on a Windows 95 compatible keyboard
VK_NUMPAD0	96	$60	Numeric keypad 0
VK_NUMPAD1	97	$61	Numeric keypad 1
VK_NUMPAD2	98	$62	Numeric keypad 2
VK_NUMPAD3	99	$63	Numeric keypad 3
VK_NUMPAD4	100	$64	Numeric keypad 4
VK_NUMPAD5	101	$65	Numeric keypad 5
VK_NUMPAD6	102	$66	Numeric keypad 6
VK_NUMPAD7	103	$67	Numeric keypad 7
VK_NUMPAD8	104	$68	Numeric keypad 8
VK_NUMPAD9	105	$69	Numeric keypad 9
VK_MULTIPLY	106	$6A	Numeric keypad multiply (*)
VK_ADD	107	$6B	Numeric keypad add (+)
VK_SUBTRACT	109	$6D	Numeric keypad subtract (−)
VK_DECIMAL	110	$6E	Numeric keypad decimal (.)
VK_DIVIDE	111	$6F	Numeric keypad divide (/)
VK_F1	112	$70	F1
VK_F2	113	$71	F2
VK_F3	114	$72	F3
VK_F4	115	$73	F4
VK_F5	116	$74	F5
VK_F6	117	$75	F6
VK_F7	118	$76	F7
VK_F8	119	$77	F8
VK_F9	120	$78	F9
VK_F10	121	$79	F10
VK_F11	122	$7A	F11
VK_F12	123	$7B	F12
VK_F13	124	$7C	F13
VK_F14	125	$7D	F14
VK_F15	126	$7E	F15
VK_F16	127	$7F	F16
VK_F17	128	$80	F17
VK_F18	129	$81	F18
VK_F19	130	$82	F19
VK_F20	131	$83	F20
VK_F21	132	$84	F21
VK_F22	133	$85	F22
VK_F23	134	$86	F23
VK_F24	135	$87	F24
VK_NUMLOCK	144	$90	Num Lock

Virtual Key Code	Decimal Value	Hex Value	Description
VK_SCROLL	145	$91	Scroll Lock
VK_LSHIFT	160	$A0	Left shift key
VK_RSHIFT	161	$A1	Right shift key
VK_LCONTROL	162	$A2	Left Ctrl key
VK_RCONTROL	163	$A3	Right Ctrl key
VK_LMENU	164	$A4	Left Alt key
VK_RMENU	165	$A5	Right Alt key

Appendix C

Tertiary Raster Operation Codes

ROP Code	Boolean Operation
$00000042	Result is all black
$00010289	NOT (brush OR source OR destination)
$00020C89	NOT (brush OR source) AND destination
$000300AA	NOT (brush OR source)
$00040C88	NOT (brush OR destination) AND source
$000500A9	NOT (brush OR destination)
$00060865	NOT (brush OR NOT(source XOR destination))
$000702C5	NOT (brush OR (source AND destination))
$00080F08	NOT brush AND source AND destination
$00090245	NOT (brush OR (source XOR destination))
$000A0329	NOT brush AND destination
$000B0B2A	NOT (brush OR (source AND NOT destination))
$000C0324	NOT brush AND source
$000D0B25	NOT (brush OR (NOT source AND destination))
$000E08A5	NOT (brush OR NOT (source OR destination))
$000F0001	NOT brush
$00100C85	brush AND NOT (source OR destination)
$001100A6	NOT (source OR destination)
$00120868	NOT (source OR NOT (brush XOR destination))
$001302C8	NOT (source OR (brush AND destination))
$00140869	NOT (destination OR NOT (brush XOR source))
$001502C9	NOT (destination OR (brush AND source))
$00165CCA	brush XOR (source XOR (destination AND NOT (brush AND source)))
$00171D54	NOT (source XOR ((source XOR brush) AND (source XOR destination)))
$00180D59	(brush XOR source) AND (brush XOR destination)
$00191CC8	NOT (source XOR (destination AND NOT (brush AND source)))
$001A06C5	brush XOR (destination OR (source AND brush))
$001B0768	NOT (source XOR (destination AND (brush XOR source)))
$001C06CA	brush XOR (source OR (brush AND destination))
$001D0766	NOT (destination XOR (source AND (brush XOR destination)))

ROP Code	Boolean Operation
$001E01A5	brush XOR (source OR destination)
$001F0385	NOT (brush AND (source OR destination))
$00200F09	brush AND NOT source AND destination
$00210248	NOT (source OR (brush XOR destination))
$00220326	NOT source AND destination
$00230B24	NOT (source OR (brush AND NOT destination))
$00240D55	(source XOR brush) AND (source XOR destination)
$00251CC5	NOT (brush XOR (destination AND NOT (source AND brush)))
$002606C8	source XOR (destination OR (brush AND source))
$00271868	source XOR (destination OR NOT (brush XOR source))
$00280369	destination AND (brush XOR source)
$002916CA	NOT (brush XOR (source XOR (destination OR (brush AND source))))
$002A0CC9	destination AND NOT (brush AND source)
$002B1D58	NOT (source XOR ((source XOR brush) AND (brush AND destination)))
$002C0784	source XOR (brush AND (source OR destination))
$002D060A	brush XOR (source OR NOT destination)
$002E064A	brush XOR (source OR (brush XOR destination))
$002F0E2A	NOT (brush AND (source OR NOT destination))
$0030032A	brush AND NOT source
$00310B28	NOT (source OR (NOT brush AND destination))
$00320688	source XOR (brush OR source OR destination)
$00330008	NOT source
$003406C4	source XOR (brush OR (source AND destination))
$00351864	source XOR (brush OR NOT (source XOR destination))
$003601A8	source XOR (brush OR destination)
$00370388	NOT (source AND (brush OR destination))
$0038078A	brush XOR (source AND (brush OR destination))
$00390604	source XOR (brush OR NOT destination)
$003A0644	source XOR (brush XOR (source OR destination))
$003B0E24	NOT (source AND (brush OR NOT destination))
$003C004A	brush XOR source
$003D18A4	source XOR (brush OR NOT (source OR destination))
$003E1B24	source XOR (brush OR (NOT source AND destination))
$003F00EA	NOT (brush AND source)
$00400F0A	brush AND source AND NOT destination
$00410249	NOT (destination OR (brush XOR source))
$00420D5D	(source XOR destination) AND (brush XOR destination)
$00431CC4	NOT (source XOR (brush AND NOT (source AND destination)))
$00440328	source AND NOT destination
$00450B29	NOT (destination OR (brush AND NOT source))
$004606C6	destination XOR (source OR (brush AND destination))
$0047076A	NOT (brush XOR (source AND (brush XOR destination)))

ROP Code	Boolean Operation
$00480368	source AND (brush XOR destination)
$004916C5	NOT (brush XOR (destination XOR (source OR (brush AND destination))))
$004A0789	destination XOR (brush AND (source OR destination))
$004B0605	brush XOR (NOT source OR destination)
$004C0CC8	source AND NOT (brush AND destination)
$004D1954	NOT (source XOR ((brush XOR source) OR (source XOR destination)))
$004E0645	brush XOR (destination OR (brush XOR source))
$004F0E25	NOT (brush AND (NOT source OR destination))
$00500325	brush AND NOT destination
$00510B26	NOT (destination OR (NOT brush AND source))
$005206C9	destination XOR (brush OR (source AND destination))
$00530764	NOT (source XOR (brush AND (source XOR destination)))
$005408A9	NOT (destination OR NOT (brush OR source))
$00550009	NOT destination
$005601A9	destination XOR (brush OR source)
$00570389	NOT (destination AND (brush OR source))
$00580785	brush XOR (destination AND (brush OR source))
$00590609	destination XOR (brush OR NOT source)
$005A0049	brush XOR destination
$005B18A9	destination XOR (brush OR NOT (source OR destination))
$005C0649	destination XOR (brush OR (source XOR destination))
$005D0E29	NOT (destination AND (brush OR NOT source))
$005E1B29	destination XOR (brush OR (source AND NOT destination))
$005F00E9	NOT (brush AND destination)
$00600365	brush AND (source XOR destination)
$006116C6	NOT (destination XOR (source XOR (brush OR (source AND destination))))
$00620786	destination XOR (source AND (brush OR destination))
$00630608	source XOR (NOT brush OR destination)
$00640788	source XOR (destination AND (brush OR source))
$00650606	destination XOR (NOT brush OR source)
$00660046	source XOR destination
$006718A8	source XOR (destination OR NOT (brush OR source))
$006858A6	NOT (destination XOR (source XOR (brush OR NOT (source OR destination))))
$00690145	NOT (brush XOR (source XOR destination))
$006A01E9	destination XOR (brush AND source)
$006B178A	NOT (brush XOR (source XOR (destination AND (source OR brush))))
$006C01E8	source XOR (brush AND destination)
$006D1785	NOT (brush XOR (destination XOR (source AND (brush OR destination))))
$006E1E28	source XOR (destination AND (brush OR NOT source))
$006F0C65	NOT (brush AND NOT (source XOR destination))
$00700CC5	brush AND NOT (source AND destination)
$00711D5C	NOT (source XOR ((source XOR destination) AND (brush XOR destination)))

ROP Code	Boolean Operation
$00720648	source XOR (destination OR (brush XOR source))
$00730E28	NOT (source AND (NOT brush OR destination))
$00740646	destination XOR (source OR (brush XOR destination))
$00750E26	NOT (destination AND (NOT brush OR source))
$00761B28	source XOR (destination OR (brush AND NOT source))
$007700E6	NOT (source AND destination)
$007801E5	brush XOR (source AND destination)
$00791786	NOT (destination XOR (source XOR (brush AND (source OR destination))))
$007A1E29	destination XOR (brush AND (source OR NOT destination))
$007B0C68	NOT (source AND NOT (brush XOR destination))
$007C1E24	source XOR (brush AND (NOT source OR destination))
$007D0C69	NOT(destination AND NOT (source XOR brush))
$007E0955	(brush XOR source) OR (source XOR destination)
$007F03C9	NOT (brush AND source AND destination)
$008003E9	brush AND source AND destination
$00810975	NOT ((brush XOR source) OR (source XOR destination))
$00820C49	NOT (brush XOR source) AND destination
$00831E04	NOT (source XOR (brush AND (NOT source OR destination)))
$00840C48	source AND NOT (brush XOR destination)
$00851E05	NOT (brush XOR (destination AND (NOT brush OR source)))
$008617A6	destination XOR (source XOR (brush AND (source OR destination)))
$008701C5	NOT (brush XOR (source and destination))
$008800C6	source AND destination
$00891B08	NOT (source XOR (destination OR (brush AND NOT source)))
$008A0E06	(NOT brush OR source) AND destination
$008B0666	NOT(destination XOR (source OR (brush OR destination)))
$008C0E08	source AND (NOT brush OR destination)
$008D0668	NOT (source XOR (destination OR (brush XOR source)))
$008E1D7C	source XOR ((source XOR destination AND (brush XOR destination))
$008F0CE5	NOT (brush AND NOT (source AND destination))
$00900C45	brush AND NOT (source XOR destination)
$00911E08	NOT (source XOR (destination AND (brush OR NOT source)))
$009217A9	destination XOR (brush XOR (source AND (brush OR destination)))
$009301C4	NOT (source XOR (brush AND destination))
$009417AA	brush XOR (source XOR (destination AND (brush OR source)))
$009501C9	NOT (destination XOR (brush AND source))
$00960169	brush XOR source XOR destination
$0097588A	brush XOR (source XOR (destination OR NOT (brush OR source)))
$00981888	NOT (source XOR (destination OR NOT (brush OR source)))
$00990066	NOT (source XOR destination)
$009A0709	(brush AND NOT source)XOR destination
$009B07A8	NOT (source XOR (destination AND (brush OR source)))

ROP Code	Boolean Operation
$009C0704	source XOR (brush AND NOT destination)
$009D07A6	NOT (destination XOR (source AND (brush OR destination)))
$009E16E6	(source XOR (brush OR (source AND destination)))XOR destination
$009F0345	NOT(brush AND (source XOR destination))
$00A000C9	brush AND destination
$00A11B05	NOT (brush XOR (destination OR (NOT brush AND source)
$00A20E09	(brush OR NOT source) AND destination
$00A30699	NOT (destination XOR (brush OR (source XOR destination)))
$00A41885	NOT (brush XOR (destination OR NOT (brush OR source)))
$00A50065	NOT (brush XOR destination)
$00A60706	(NOT brush AND source) XOR destination
$00A707A5	NOT (brush XOR (destination AND (brush OR source)))
$00A803A9	(brush OR source) AND destination
$00A90189	NOT ((brush OR source) XOR destination)
$00AA0029	destination
$00AB0889	NOT(brush OR source) OR destination
$00AC0744	source XOR (brush AND (source XOR destination))
$00AD06E9	NOT (destination XOR (brush OR (source AND destination)))
$00AE0B06	(NOT brush AND source) OR destination
$00AF0229	NOT brush OR destination
$00B00E05	brush AND (NOT source OR destination)
$00B10665	NOT (brush OR (destination OR (brush XOR source)))
$00B12974	source XOR ((brush XOR source) OR (source XOR destination))
$00B03CE8	NOT (source AND NOT (brush AND destination))
$00B4070A	brush XOR (source AND NOT destination)
$00B507A9	NOT (destination XOR (brush AND (source OR destination)))
$00B616E9	destination XOR (brush XOR (source OR (brush AND destination)))
$00B70348	NOT (source And (brush XOR destination))
$00B8074A	brush XOR (source AND (brush XOR destination))
$00B906E6	NOT (destination XOR (source OR (brush AND destination)))
$00BA0B09	(brush AND NOT source) OR destination
$00BB0226	NOT source OR destination
$00BC1CE4	source XOR (brush AND NOT (source AND destination))
$00BD0D7D	NOT ((brush XOR destination) AND (source XOR destination))
$00BE0269	(brush XOR source) OR destination
$00BF08C9	NOT (brush AND source) OR destination
$00C000CA	brush AND source
$00C11B04	NOT (source XOR (brush OR (NOT source AND destination)))
$00C21884	NOT (source XOR (brush OR NOT(source OR destination)))
$00C3006A	NOT (brush XOR source)
$00C40E04	source AND (brush OR NOT destination)
$00C50664	NOT (source XOR (brush OR (source XOR destination)))

Appendix C

ROP Code	Boolean Operation
$00C60708	source XOR (NOT brush AND destination)
$00C707AA	NOT (brush XOR (source AND (brush OR destination))
$00C803A8	source AND (brush OR destination)
$00C90184	NOT (source XOR (brush OR destination))
$00CA0749	destination XOR (brush AND (source XOR destination))
$00CB06E4	NOT (source XOR (brush OR (source AND destination))
$00CC0020	source
$00CD0888	source OR NOT (brush OR destination)
$00CE0B08	source OR (NOT brush AND destination)
$00CF0224	source OR NOT brush
$00D00E0A	brush AND (source OR NOT destination)
$00D1066A	NOT (brush XOR (source OR (brush XOR destination)))
$00D20705	brush XOR (NOT source AND destination)
$00D307A4	NOT (source XOR (brush AND (source OR destination)))
$00D41D78	source XOR ((brush XOR source AND (brush XOR destination))
$00D50CE9	NOT (destination AND NOT (brush AND source))
$00D616EA	brush XOR (source XOR (destination OR (brush AND source)))
$00D70349	NOT (destination AND (brush XOR source))
$00D80745	brush XOR (destination AND (brush XOR source))
$00D906E8	NOT (source XOR (destination OR (brush AND source)))
$00DA1CE9	destination XOR (brush AND NOT (source XOR destination))
$00DB0D75	NOT ((brush XOR source) AND (source XOR destination)
$00DC0B04	source OR (brush AND NOT destination)
$00DD0228	source OR NOT destination
$00DE0268	source OR (brush XOR destination)
$00DF08C8	source OR NOT (brush AND destination)
$00E003A5	brush AND (destination OR source)
$00E10185	NOT (brush XOR (source OR destination))
$00E20746	destination XOR (source AND (brush XOR destination))
$00E306EA	NOT (brush XOR (source OR (brush AND destination)))
$00E40748	source XOR (destination AND (brush XOR source))
$00E506E5	NOT (brush XOR (destination OR (brush AND source)
$00E61CE8	source XOR (destination AND NOT (brush AND source))
$00E70D79	NOT ((brush XOR source) AND (brush XOR destination))
$00E81D74	source XOR ((brush XOR source) AND (source XOR destination))
$00E95CE6	NOT (destination XOR (source XOR (brush AND NOT (source AND destination))))
$00EA02E9	(brush AND source) OR destination
$00EB0849	NOT (brush XOR source) OR destination
$00EC02E8	source OR (brush AND destination)
$00ED0848	source OR NOT (brush XOR destination)
$00EE0086	source OR destination
$00EF0A08	NOT brush OR source OR destination

ROP Code	Boolean Operation
$00F00021	brush
$00F10885	brush OR NOT (source OR destination)
$00F20B05	brush OR (NOT source AND destination)
$00F3022A	brush OR NOT source
$00F40B0A	brush OR (source AND NOT destination)
$00F50225	brush OR NOT destination
$00F60265	brush OR (source XOR destination)
$00F708C5	brush OR NOT (source AND destination)
$00F802E5	brush OR (source AND destination)
$00F90845	brush OR NOT (source XOR destination)
$00FA0089	brush OR destination
$00FB0A09	brush OR NOT source OR destination
$00FC008A	brush OR source
$00FD0A0A	brush OR source OR NOT destination
$00FE02A9	brush OR source OR destination
$00FF0062	Result is all white

Index

16-bit memory functions, 127

A
AbortPath, 462
AddFontResource, 619
allocating
    global memory, 135-136
    memory from the heap 147-148
    memory from the Process heap, 134-135
    virtual memory, 160-162
ANISOTROPIC, 339
application message loop, 57-58
Arc, 348-350
ASCII strings, *see* strings
ATOM, 2
attributes,
    child window identifier/menu handle, 10
    creation data, 11
    instance handle, 11
    window class, 10
    window name, 10
    window parent/owner, 10
    window position, 10
    window size, 10
    window style, 10
    window z-order, 10
audible error cues, 268

B
Beep, 270
BeginPaint, 351-352
BeginPath, 463
Bezier curves, *see* PolyBezier, PolyBezierTo
BitBlt, 539
bitmap operations, 530
bitmaps, 529
    copying, *see* BitBlt
    creating, 545, *see also* CreateCompatibleBitmap, CreateDIBitmap
    dimensions, *see* GetBitmapDimensionEx
    loading, 582
    scaling, 530
    see also HBITMAP
BOOL, 2
boolean operations, combining constants, 6
BroadcastSystemMessage, 63-64
brush,
    creating, 362, *see also* CreateBrushIndirect
    creating a hatch brush, *see* CreateHatchBrush
    creating a pattern brush, *see* CreatePatternBrush
    see also HBRUSH
brushes and pens, 346
BUTTON, 36
button styles, 38-39

C
callback functions, 5
calling
    the DLL from within a thread, 176-178
    the previous window procedure in a subclassed window, 66-68
calling conventions, 170
CallNextHookEx, 65
CallWindowProc, 66
ChangeDisplaySettings, 290-292
changing
    the brushes in an enhanced metafile, 568-569
    the display mode, 292-293
character dimensions, 611
character sets, 610,
    Unicode, 6
    see also fonts
child window identifier/menu handle, 10
child window type, 16
child windows, MDI, 21
Chord, 352-354
class device context, *see* device contexts, types
class

720 ■ Index

registering, *see* RegisterClass, RegisterClassEx, UnregisterClass
   window, 10
client area device contexts, 282
ClientToScreen, 294-295
clipping drawing to a defined region, 517-519
CloseEnhMetaFile, 541
CloseFigure, 463-464
closing an open figure in a path bracket, 464-465
color, background, *see* GetBkColor
COLORREF, 3
CombineRgn, 465-467
combining two regions to create a special effect, 466-467
combo box styles, 39-40
COMBOBOX, 36
common device context, *see* device contexts, types
communicating using a unique message identifier, 92-93
comparing two regions, 482
computer-based training, *see* hooks, computer-based training
constants, 4
   combining, 6
converting a path into a region, 507-509
converting coordinates between coordinate systems, 295-296
coordinate systems, 283
   converting, *see* ClientToScreen, ScreenToClient
CopyEnhMetaFile, 541-542
CopyImage, 542-543
CopyMemory, 132
CopyRect, 468
cosmetic pens, 346
CreateBitmap, 545-546
CreateBitmapIndirect, 548-549
CreateBrushIndirect, 354-355
CreateCompatibleBitmap, 550-551
CreateCompatibleDC, 296
CreateDIBitmap, 552-553
CreateDIBSection, 556-559
CreateEllipticRgn, 469
CreateEllipticRgnIndirect, 469-470
CreateEnhMetaFile, 562-563
CreateEvent, 194-195
CreateFont, 619
CreateFontIndirect, 626-628
CreateHatchBrush, 357-358

CreateMDIWindow, 26-27
CreateMutex, 197-198
CreateParams method, 23
CreatePatternBrush, 358-359
CreatePen, 360-361
CreatePenIndirect, 362-363
CreatePolygonRgn, 471
CreatePolyPolygonRgn, 474
CreateProcess, 200-204
CreateRectRgn, 476-477
CreateRectRgnIndirect, 477-478
CreateRoundRectRgn, 478-479
CreateScalableFontResource, 632
CreateSemaphore, 206-207
CreateSolidBrush, 364
CreateThread, 210-211
CreateWindowEx, 29-33
creating
   a bitmap, 546-547
   a bitmap compatible with the current display device, 551-552
   a device-dependent bitmap from a device-independent bitmap, 554-555
   a device-independent bitmap, 559-560
   a DIB from a device-dependent bitmap, 573-574
   a font indirectly, 628-629
   a form with a raised edge, 25
   a hatched brush, 358
   a message box, 47
   a monochrome image to perform a transparent copy, 543-544
   a multiple polygon region, 474-476
   a new pen, 361
   a pen indirectly, 363-364
   a rectangular region, 477
   a round window for an analog clock application, 523-524
   a rounded rectangular region, 479-480
   a semaphore to synchronize multiple processes, 207-208
   a solid brush, 364-365
   a star shaped region, 471-472
   a window, 11-12
   a window with a private device context, 281-282
   a window with extended window styles, 33-35
   an enhanced metafile, 563-564
   an event and waiting for it, 195-196
   an MDI application in Object Pascal, 18-21

and terminating a process, 245-246
and using a new brush, 355-356
MDI child windows, 17, 21
special text effects, 513-516
various fonts, 622-623
windows, the basic steps, 9
creation data, 11
critical sections, 190
   deleting, 211
   entering, 214
   initializing, 226
   leaving, 232

D

data types, 1-3
deadlocks, 189
debugging, *see* hooks, debug
default heaps, 126
DefFrameProc, 68-69
DefMDIChildProc, 73-74
DefWindowProc, 74-75
DeleteCriticalSection, 208
DeleteDC, 299
DeleteEnhMetaFile, 565-566
DeleteObject, 365-366
DestroyWindow, 45-46
device capabilities, *see* GetDeviceCaps
device contexts (DC), 280 *see also* HDC
   creating, *see* CreateCompatibleDC
   deleting, 299
   releasing, 328
   restoring, 329
   retrieving, *see* GetDC
   saving, 329
   scrolling, *see* ScrollDC
   types, 280
   windows, *see* GetWindowDC
device-dependent bitmaps, 530
device independence, 279
device-independent bitmaps (DIB), 530
dialog box styles, 40-41
DIBs and the GDI, 535
DisableThreadLibraryCalls, 172
DispatchMessage, 75-76
display settings, s*ee* ChangeDisplaySettings
displaying
   a bitmap with transparent pixels, 534
   the current position, 399-400

DLL
   calling from within a thread, 176-178
   freeing, 173, *see also* FreeLibraryAndExitThread
   handle, 179
   loading, 180, *see also* LoadLibraryEx
   module file name, 178
DLLMain, 171
DPtoLP, 299-300
DrawCaption, 366
DrawEdge, 367-368
DrawFocusRect, 370
DrawFrameControl, 371-372
drawing
   3-D edges, 368-369
   a Bezier curve, 431-432
   a chord, 354
   a focus rectangle, 371
   a foreground image only once, 483-485
   a pie wedge, 429
   a polygon outline, 433-434
   a rainbow, 350-351
   a rectangle with an animated fill, 439-440
   a rectangular frame, 392
   a rounded rectangle, 442
   an animated section rectangle, 422-423
   an unfilled polygon starting from the current position, 435
   Bezier curve, 430
   ellipses, 380
   formatted text, 635-636
   grayed text, 416-417
   images in a disabled state, 377-378
   multiple polygons, 436
   multiple unfilled polygons, 438
   only invalid region of a canvas, 419-420
   only the invalid rectangle of a canvas, 417-418
   paths with geometric pens, 385-386
   text with and without the background color, 394-395
   text with margins, 639-641
   the desktop onto a form, 426
   the outline of text, 527-528
   various frame controls, 372-374
DrawState, 375-377
DrawText, 634-635
DrawTextEx, 638-639
DuplicateHandle, 211-213
DWORD, 2

dynamically creating an elliptical region based on the form size, 470-471
dynamic-link library entry point function, 170

E

edges, *see* DrawEdge
EDIT, 37
edit control styles 41-42
Ellipse, 379-380
embedding Truetype fonts into a document, 613-617
emptying out a rectangle, 520-521
emulating a timer, 253-254
enabling and disabling window updating, 424
EndPaint, 380
EndPath, 480
enhanced metafiles, 537
   copying, *see* CopyEnhMetaFile
   creating, 562
   deleting, 565
   description, *see* GetEnhMetafileDescription
   opening, 575-578
   playing, 590
EnterCriticalSection, 214-215
EnumDisplaySettings, 300-302
EnumEnhMetaFile, 566-568
enumerating
   all available display modes for the current display, 302-303
   all pens in a device context, 382-383
   available fonts, 645-646
   only symbol fonts, 650-652
EnumFontFamExProc, 649
EnumFontFamilies, 642-645
EnumFontFamiliesEx, 647-651
EnumObjects, 381-382
EqualRect, 480-481
EqualRgn, 481-482
error codes, *see* GetLastError, SetLastError
error descriptions, 267
error trapping, 129
events, 191
   creating, 194
   name comparison, 194
   opening, 232
   pulse, 237
   resetting, 240
   setting, 241
example DLL, 184-185
example dynamic-link library, 174-176, 181-182
ExcludeClipRect, 482-483
exit codes, *see* GetExitCodeProcess, GetExitCodeThread
exiting
   a process, 215
   windows, 271-272
ExitProcess, 215-216
ExitThread, 216-217
ExitWindows, 271
ExitWindowsEx, 272-273
ExtCreatePen, 383-385
ExtCreateRegion, 485-487
extending functionality, 23
ExtFloodFill, 387
ExtSelectClipRgn, 483-488

F

FARPROC, 3
FatalAppExit, 273-274
fill mode, polygons, *see* GetPolyFillMode
filling
   a background, 589
   a path, 389
   a region with the current brush, 427
   an area, 388
FillMemory 133-134
FillPath, 388-389
FillRect, 389-390
FillRgn, 391
FlattenPath, 489
flood fill, *see* ExtFloodFill
font table, 611
fonts, 609
   adding, *see* AddFontResource
   creating, 619
   data, *see* GetFontData
   embedding, 612
   families, 609
   see also HFONT
FrameRect, 391-392
FrameRgn, 392-393
framing a region, 393-394
FreeLibrary, 173
FreeLibraryAndExitThread,174
functionality, extending, *see* extending functionality
functions,
   callback, *see* callback functions

Index ■ 723

calling conventions, 170
importing, *see* Windows functions, importing
importing/exporting, 169
memory allocation, *see* memory allocation functions, categories of
parameters, 6

G

geometric pens, 346, *see also* ExtCreatePen
GetBitMapBits, 569
GetBitmapDimensionEx, 571
GetBkColor, 394
GetBkMode, 395
GetBoundsRect, 395-396
GetBrushOrgEx, 397-398
GetCharABCWidths, 653-654
GetCharWidth, 655-656
GetClipBox, 489-90
GetClipRgn, 490
GetCurrentObject, 398
GetCurrentPositionEx, 399
GetCurrentProcess, 217
GetCurrentProcessId, 217-218
GetCurrentThread, 218
GetCurrentThreadId, 218-219
GetDC, 303-304
GetDCOrgEx, 304
GetDeviceCaps, 305
GetDIBits, 571-573
GetEnhMetaFile, 575
GetEnhMetafileDescription, 578
GetEnhMetaFileHeader, 579-581
GetExitCodeProcess, 219-220
GetExitCodeThread, 220
GetFontData, 656-657
GetGlyphOutline, 657-659
GetKerningPairs, 662
GetLastError, 274-275
GetMapMode, 313-314
GetMessage, 76-77
GetMessageExtraInfo, 79
GetMessagePos, 80-81
GetMessageTime, 81
GetMiterLimit, 400-403
GetModuleFileName, 178-179
GetModuleHandle, 179
GetObject, 401
GetObjectType, 405-406
GetOutlineTextMetrics, 664-668
GetPath, 491
GetPixel, 406-407
GetPolyFillMode, 407
GetPriorityClass, 221-222
GetProcAddress, 179-180
GetProcessHeap, 134-135
GetQueueStatus, 81-82
GetRasterizerCaps, 679
GetRegionData, 494
GetRgnBox, 494-495
GetROP2, 409
GetStockObject, 411-412
GetStretchBltMode, 581
GetSystemMetrics, 314-315
GetTabbedTextExtent, 680-681
GetTextAlign, 681-682
GetTextCharacterExtra, 682
GetTextColor, 683
GetTextExtentExPoint, 683-684
GetTextExtentPoint32, 686-687
GetTextFace, 687-688
GetTextMetrics, 688-690
GetThreadPriority, 223-224
GetTickCount, 259-260
GetUpdateRect, 413
GetUpdateRgn, 413-414
GetViewportExtEx, 319-320
GetViewportOrgEx, 320
GetWindowDC, 320-321
GetWindowExtEx, 322-323
GetWindowOrgEx, 323
GetWindowThreadProcessId, 225-226
global memory, *see* memory
GlobalAlloc, 135-136
GlobalDiscard, 136-137
GlobalFlags, 137-138
GlobalFree, 138
GlobalHandle, 138-139
GlobalLock, 139
GlobalMemoryStatus, 140-141
GlobalReAlloc, 142-144
GlobalSize, 145
GlobalUnlock, 145-146
graphical objects, 345
Graphics Device Interface (GDI), 279
GrayString, 414-416

H

handles, 3
   duplicating, 211
   instance, 11
   see also THandle
HBITMAP, 3
HBRUSH, 3
HCURSOR, 3
HDC, 3
HeapAlloc, 146-148
HeapCreate, 148-149
HeapDestroy, 150
HeapFree, 150-151
HeapReAlloc, 151-152
heaps, 126, 134
   allocating, 146, *see also* HeapReAlloc
   creating, 148
   destroying, 150
   freeing, 150
HeapSize, 152-153
HENHMETAFILE, 3
HFILE, 3
HFONT, 3
HGDIOBJ, 3
HGLOBAL, 2
HHOOK, 2
HICON, 3
HIENGLISH, 339
high-resolution timer, 257
HIMETRIC, 339
HINST, 3
HKL, 3
HLOCAL, 3
HMENU, 3
HMETAFILE, 3
HMODULE, 3
hooks,
   computer-based training, 107
   debug, 110
   idle thread, 111
   journal playback, 112
   journal recording, 114
   keyboard intercept, 116
   message intercepting, 106, 111, 117, 120
   mouse, 59-61
   setting, 103
   shell notification, 118
   unhooking, *see* UnhookWindowsHookEx
   Windows, 58
   see also CallNextHookEx, HHOOK
HPALETTE, 3
HPEN, 3
HRGN, 3
HRSRC, 3
HWND, 2

I

images, copying, 542
importing/exporting functions, 4, 169
   incorrectly, 5
indirectly creating a bitmap, 549-550
InflateRect, 495-496
InitializeCriticalSection, 226-227
initializing
   a memory block, 168
   buffer values, 134
InSendMessage, 83-84
installing a new TrueType font, 633-634
instance handle, 11
intercepting the Tab and Enter keys, 121-122
InterlockedExchange, 230-231
InterlockedDecrement, 228-229
InterlockedIncrement, 231
interprocess communication, 61
IntersectRect, 496-497
InvalidateRect, 417
InvalidateRgn, 419
inverting a rectangular portion of an image, 497-498
InvertRect, 497
InvertRgn, 498
IsBadCodePtr, 153-154
IsBadReadPtr, 154-155
IsBadStringPtr, 155-156
IsBadWritePtr, 156-157
ISOTROPIC, 339
IsRectEmpty, 498-499

K

kerning, *see* GetKerningPairs
keyboard intercept, *see* hooks, keyboard intercept
KillTimer, 260-261

L

LANGID, 2
launching and terminating a process, 235-236
LCID, 2
LeaveCriticalSection, 232

Index

LineDDA, 421-422
LineDDAProc, 421
LineTo, 423-424
list box styles, 42-43
LISTBOX, 37
LoadBitmap, 582
LoadImage, 585-586
loading
    a predefined bitmap, 582-584
    bitmap images from files, 586-587
    the example dynamic-link library, 182-183
LoadLibrary, 180-181
LoadLibraryEx, 183-184
LockWindowUpdate, 424
LOENGLISH, 339
logical coordinate systems, 283
    problems, 288
LOMETRIC, 339
LPARAM, 2
LPCSTR, 1
LPDWORD, 2
LPSTR, 1
LPtoDP, 323-324
LRESULT, 2

M

manipulating
    a DIB using GDI drawing functions, 535-537
    text, 695-697
mapping logical coordinates into device coordinates, 284
mapping modes, 284
    ANISOTROPIC, 339
    HIENGLISH, 339
    HIMETRIC, 339
    ISOTROPIC, 339
    LOENGLISH, 339
    LOMETRIC, 339
    retrieving, *see* GetMapMode
    setting, *see* SetMapMode
    TEXT, 339
    TWIPS, 339
MapWindowPoints, 324-325
MDI client styles, 43
MDICLIENT, 37
measuring function time using a high-resolution timer, 258

memory,
    16-bit memory functions, 127
    allocating, 135-136, *see* GlobalReAlloc
    copying, *see* CopyMemory
    discarding, 136
    emptying, *see* ZeroMemory
    error trapping, 129
    filling, *see* FillMemory
    freeing, 138
    global and local memory calls, 127
    heaps, 126
    initializing, 168
    moving, 157
    multiple heaps, 128
    retrieving the status, 141
    speed, 130
    states, 127
        committed, 128
        free, 128
        reserved, 128
    swap file, 128
    thread access, 129
    virtual, 127
memory allocation functions, categories of, 126
message processing functions, 62
message queue and message loop, 57
MessageBeep, 275-276
MessageBox, 46-47
messages,
    broadcasting, *see* BroadcastSystemMessage
    dispatching, *see* DispatchMessage
    hook, *see* hooks
    interprocess communication, 61
    parameters, *see* LPARAM, WPARAM
    position, *see* GetMessagePos
    posting, *see* PostMessage
    posting to a thread, *see* PostThreadMessage
    queue status, *see* GetQueueStatus
    registering, *see* RegisterWindowMessage
    replying, *see* ReplyMessage
    retrieving, *see* GetMessage
    sending, *see* SendMessage
    time, *see* GetMessageTime
    translating, 122
    waiting, *see* WaitMessage
    window procedure, 13
metafiles, 537, *see also* enhanced metafiles, HENHMETAFILE, HMETAFILE

modifying
   a variable in a thread-safe manner, 229-230
   the viewport and window extents and origins, 285-288
MoveMemory, 157-159
MoveToEx, 425
moving
   a region to produce special animation effects, 505-506
   memory from one array to another, 158-159
Multiple Document Interface (MDI), 17
multi-threaded applications, 187
mutex, 190
   creating, 197
   opening, 233
   releasing, 238

O

objects,
   current, *see* GetCurrentObject
   deleting, 365
   graphical, 345
   retrieving, *see* GetObject
   selecting, 442
   stock objects, *see* GetStockObject
   type, *see* GetObjectType
OffsetClipRgn, 499-500
OffsetRect, 501-502
OffsetRgn, 505
OffsetViewportOrgEx, 326-327
OffsetWindowOrgEx, 327-328
OpenEvent, 232-233
opening
   an event created in another process, 233
   enhanced metafiles, 575-578
OpenMutex, 233-234
OpenProcess, 234-235
OpenSemaphore, 236-237
outlining
   a path, 453-454
   and filling a path simultaneously, 452-453
outputting text like a table, 701-702
overlapped window type, 15

P

PaintDesktop, 425-426
painting, *see* BeginPaint, EndPaint
PaintRgn, 426
parameters, *see* functions, parameters

parent/owner window, 10
PatBlt, 588
paths, 458
   aborting, 462
   creating, *see* BeginPath, EndPath
   filling, 388, *see also* StrokeAndFillPath
   flattening, 489
   outlining, 453-454
   widening, 527
PathToRegion, 507
pausing a loop, 254
PBOOL, 2
PByte, 2
PDouble, 2
PDWORD, 2
PeekMessage, 84-85
pens and brushes, 346
pens, *see also* HPEN
   cosmetic, 346
   creating, 360, 383, *see also* CreatePenIndirect
   geometric, 346, *see also* GetMiterLimit, ExtCreatePen
pie, 427-429
PINT, 2
PInteger, 2
pixel, 529
PlayEnhMetaFile, 590
PlayEnhMetaFileRecord, 591
playing sounds, 274, *see also* Beep, MessageBeep
PLongint, 2
pointers, testing, *see* IsBadCodePtr, IsBadReadPtr, IsBadStringPtr, IsBadWritePtr
PolyBezier, 429-430
PolyBezierTo, 431
Polygon, 432-433
Polyline, 433-434
PolylineTo, 434-435
PolyPolygon, 435-436
PolyPolyline, 437-438
pop-up window type, 15
position, window, 10
posting
   a message to a thread, 90-91
   a message to a window's message queue, 87-89
PostMessage, 86-87
PostQuitMessage, 89
PostThreadMessage, 89-90
precise timing, 257

preventing an application from running more then
    once, 191-192
priority levels, 188
private device context, *see* device contexts, types
procedure, Windows, 51
process, 188
    creating, 200
    exiting, 215
    ID, *see* GetCurrentProcessId
    opening, 234
    terminating, 245
programmatically
    drawing a caption bar, 366-367
    justifying text, 684-686
providing default message handling in an MDI
    frame window, 69-73
PSingle, 2
PSmallInt, 2
PtInRect, 509
PtInRegion, 509-510
PtVisible, 510-511
PUCHAR, 2
PUINT, 2
PULONG, 2
PulseEvent, 237-238
PWORD, 2

Q

QueryPerformanceCounter, 262
QueryPerformanceFrequency, 263

R

raster font, *see* fonts
raster operations, 533, *see also* GetROP2, SetROP2
reallocating a global memory object, 142-144
Rectangle, 438-439
rectangle,
    bounds, *see* GetBoundsRect
    copying, *see* CopyRect
    drawing, *see* Rectangle
    empty, *see* IsRectEmpty
    filling, 389
    framing, *see* FrameRect
    intersecting, 496
    rounded, *see* RoundRect
    see also DrawFocusRect
    setting, *see* SetRect
    subtracting, 525
    union, 526

RectInRegion, 511
RectVisible, 511-512
regions, 455
    combining, *see* CombineRgn
    creating, *see* ExtCreateRegion
    elliptic, *see* CreateEllipticRgn,
        CreateEllipticRgnIndirect
    filling, 391
    framing, *see* FrameRgn
    polygon, *see* CreatePolygonRgn
    rectangle, *see* CreateRectRgn
    special effects, 458
    see also HRGN
RegisterClass, 49-51
RegisterClassEx, 53-55
RegisterWindowMessage, 91-92
ReleaseDC, 328
ReleaseMutex, 238-239
ReleaseSemaphore, 239-240
RemoveFontResource, 694
ReplyMessage, 93-94
ResetEvent, 240
RestoreDC, 329
ResumeThread, 240-241
retrieving
    a common device context for a window, 303-304
    a thread's exit code, 220-221
    ABC widths for all uppercase letters, 654-655
    bitmap color data, 570
    character widths for all uppercase letters, 656
    device capabilities, 305-310
    extra message information, 79-80
    font metric information, 690-692
    glyph bitmaps, 659-661
    information about an object, 404-405
    kerning pairs for the currently selected font, 663
    messages using PeekMessage, 85-86
    more information about a function failure, 268
    region information, 456-458
    specific item dimensions, 315-316
    the current high-resolution performance counter
        value, 260-261
    the current message queue status, 82-83
    the current process and thread identifiers, 218
    the high-resolution performance counter fre-
        quency, 263
    the memory status, 141

the number of milliseconds since Windows was started, 260
the points defining a flattened curve, 492-493
the window's thread and process identifiers, 226
TrueType font text metrics, 668-675
rich edit styles, 43
RICHEDIT_CLASS, 37
RoundRect, 440-442

S
SaveDC, 329-331
ScaleViewportExtEx, 330
ScaleWindowsExtEx, 334-335
scaling, 530
   viewports and windows, 331-334
screen device contexts, 282
ScreenToClient, 335-336
scroll bar styles, 43-44
SCROLLBAR, 37
ScrollDC, 336
scrolling an image inside of a viewing area, 337-338
SelectClipPath, 512-513
SelectClipRgn, 516-517
SelectObject, 442-443
semaphore sibling program, 208-209
semaphores, 190
   creating, 206
   opening, 236
   releasing, 239
sending
   a message and returning before it is processed, 98-100
   a message via SendNotifyMessage, 101-102
   a message with a callback function, 96-97
SendMessage , 94-95
SendMessageCallback, 95-96
SendMessageCallbackProc, 96
SendMessageTimeout, 97-98
SendNotifiyMessage, 100-101
SetBitmapBits, 592
SetBitmapDimensionEx, 594
SetBkColor, 443
SetBkMode, 444
SetBoundsRect, 444-445
SetBrushOrgEx, 446-447
SetDIBits, 594-596
SetDIBitsToDevice, 599-601
SetEvent, 241

SetLastError, 276-277
SetMapMode, 338-339
SetMessageExtraInfo, 102
SetMiterLimit, 446
SetPixel, 447-448
SetPixelV, 449
SetPolyFillMode, 449-450
SetPriorityClass, 241-242
SetRect, 519-520
SetRectEmpty, 520
SetRectRgn, 521-522
SetROP2, 450-451
SetStretchBltMode, 601-602
SetTextAlign, 694-695
SetTextCharacterExtra, 697-698
SetTextColor, 698-699
SetTextJustification, 699
SetThreadPriority, 243
SetTimer, 264-265
setting
   a global mouse hook, 59-61
   the bitmap bits, 592-593
   the image of a DDB from a DIB, 596-598
SetViewportExtEx, 339-340
SetViewportOrgEx, 340-341
SetWindowExtEx, 341-342
SetWindowOrgEx, 342-343
SetWindowRgn, 522-523
SetWindowsHookEx, 103-104
shell notification, *see* hooks, shell notification
SHORT, 2
size, window, 10
Sleep, 244
special effects, 458
speed, 130
static control styles, 44-45
STATIC, 37
StretchBlt, 602-603
StretchDIBits, 604-606
strings, 4
   grayed text, *see* GrayString
   see also LPSTR, LPCSTR, Unicode
StrokeAndFillPath, 452
StrokePath, 453-454
structures,
   TABC, 654
   TBitmap, 548
   TBitmapInfo, 553, 556, 572, 595, 600, 605

TBitmapInfoHeader, 553, 556, 573, 595, 600, 605
TCBTActivateStruct, 109
TCBTCreateWnd, 109
TClientCreateStruct, 32
TCreateParams, 23
TCreateStruct, 32
TCWPRetStruct, 106
TCWPStruct, 105
TDebugHookInfo, 110
TDeviceModeA, 290, 301
TDIBSection, 402
TDrawTextParams, 638
TEnhMetaHeader, 579
TEnhMetaRecords, 567, 591
TEnumLogFont, 643
TEnumLogFontEx, 645
TEventMsg, 113, 115
TExtLogPen, 403
TFixed, 659
TFontSignature, 650
TGlyphMetrics, 658
TKerningPair, 662
TLogBrush, 354, 384
TLogFont, 626, 644, 648
TLogPen, 362
TMat2, 658
TMemoryBasicInformation, 166
TMemoryStatus, 140
TMouseHookStruct, 109, 117
TMsg, 75, 76, 85, 112, 118, 120, 122
TNewTextMetric, 644, 649
TNewTextMetricEx, 649
TOutlineTextMetric, 664
TPaintStruct, 351, 381
TPanose, 666
TProcessInformation, 204
TRasterizerStatus, 679
TRGBQuad, 558, 573, 596, 600, 606
TRgnData, 486, 494
TRgnDataHeader, 486
TSize, 571
TStartupInfo, 201
TTextMetric, 665, 688
TWndClass, 49
TWndClassEx, 54
TXForm, 485

styles,
    button, 38-39
    combo box, 39-40
    dialog box, 40-41
    edit control, 41-42
    list box, 42-43
    MDI client, 43
    rich edit, 43
    scroll bar, 43-44
    window, 10
subtracting one rectangle from another, 525-526
SubtractRect, 525
SuspendThread, 244
swap file, 128
synchronizing
    a process with a mutex, 191
    and coordination, 188
    objects, 190

T
TabbedTextOut, 700-701
TABC, 654
TBitmap, 548
TBitmapInfo, 553, 556, 572, 595, 600, 605
TBitmapInfoHeader, 553, 556, 573, 595, 600, 605
TCBTActivateStruct, 109
TCBTCreateWnd, 109
TClientCreateStruct, 32
TCreateParams, 23
TCreateStruct, 32
TCWPRetStruct, 106
TCWPStruct, 105
TDebugHookInfo, 110
TDeviceModeA, 290, 301
TDIBSection, 402
TDrawTextParams, 638
TEnhMetaHeader, 579
TEnhMetaRecord, 567, 591
TEnumLogFont, 643
TEnumLogFontEx, 649
TerminateProcess, 245
TerminateThread, 246
terminating
    a thread prematurely, 246-247
    applications, 89, 274, *see also* PostQuitMessage
testing for read access
    at a specific memory address, 154
    to a range of memory, 155

to a string, 156
TEventMsg, 113, 115
TEXT, 339
text, drawing, 634
TExtLogPen, 402
TextOut, 702-703
TFixed, 659
TFontSignature, 650
TGlyphMetrics, 658
THandle, 2
thread access, 129
thread local storage, 188
    see also TlsAlloc, TlsFree, TlsGetValue,
       TlsSetValue
threads, 188
   creating, 210
   deadlocks, 189
   exiting, 214
   important concepts, 187
   multi-threaded applications, 187
   pausing, see Sleep
   priority, 221, see also SetThreadPriority
   priority class, 219, see also SetPriorityClass
   priority levels, 188
   resuming, 240
   suspending, 244
   synchronization and coordination, 188
   synchronization objects, 190
   terminating, 246
   thread-safe variables, see InterlockedDecrement,
      InterlockedIncrement
timeout intervals, see also synchronizing
timer
   killing, 260
   setting, 264
TimerProc, 265
timing, precise, 257, see also
   QueryPerformanceCounter,
   QueryPerformanceFrequency
TKerningPair, 662
TLogBrush, 354, 384
TLogFont, 626, 644, 648
TLogPen, 362
TlsAlloc, 247-250
TlsFree, 250
TlsGetValue, 250-251
TlsSetValue, 251
TMat2, 658

TMemoryBasicInformation, 166
TMemoryStatus, 140
TMouseHookStruct, 109, 117
TMsg, 75, 76, 85, 112, 118, 120, 122
TNewTextMetric, 644, 649
TNewTextMetricEx, 649
TOutlineTextMetric, 664
TPaintStruct, 351, 381
TPanose, 666
TProcessInformation, 204
TranslateMessage, 122-123
TRasterizerStatus, 679
TRGBQuad, 558, 573, 596, 600, 606
TRgnData, 486, 494
TRgnDataHeader, 486
TrueType font, see fonts
TSecurityAttributes, 194
TSize, 571
TStartupInfo, 201
TTextMetric, 665, 688
TWIPS, 339
TWndClass, 49
TWndClassEx, 54
TXForm, 485
types of windows, 15
   child, 16
   overlapped, 15
   pop-up, 15

U
UCHAR, 2
UINT, 2
ULONG, 2
UnhookWindowsHookEx, 123
Unicode, 6
UnionRect, 526-527
UnregisterClass, 55
using
   a bitmap as a brush pattern, 359-360
   a duplicated thread handle to resume a thread,
      213-214
   a mutex to synchronize thread execution, 198-199
   a stock object, 412
   critical sections to synchronize a thread within
      the process, 227-228
   memory device contexts for animation, 296-299
   the foreground mix mode to draw a dragable
      rectangle, 409-410

the WM_MDICREATE message with a Delphi form, 22-23
thread local storage to store string information, 248-249

V

vector font, *see* fonts
viewports
   offsetting, *see* OffsetViewportOrgEx
   scaling, *see* ScaleViewportExtEx
   see also GetViewportExtEx, GetViewportOrgEx
   setting, *see* SetViewportExtEx, SetViewportOrgEx
virtual memory, 127
   allocating, 159-162
   freeing, 163
virtual memory architecture, 125
VirtualAlloc, 159-160
VirtualFree, 163-164
VirtualProtect, 164-165
VirtualQuery, 166-167

W

wait functions, *see* synchronizing and coordination, 188
WaitForInputIdle, 251-252
WaitForSingleObject, 253
waiting
   for a message, 124
   for a process to load, 252
WaitMessage, 123-124
WH_CALLWNDPROC hook function, 105
WH_CALLWNDPROCRET hook function, 106
WH_CBT hook function, 107
WH_DEBUG hook function, 110-111
WH_FOREGROUNDIDLE hook function, 111
WH_GETMESSAGE hook function, 111-112
WH_JOURNALPLAYBACK hook function, 112-113
WH_JOURNALRECORD hook function, 114-115
WH_KEYBOARD hook function, 115-116
WH_MOUSE hook function, 116-117
WH_MSGFILTER hook function, 117-118
WH_SHELL hook function, 118-119
WH_SYSMSGFILTER hook function, 120-124
WidenPath, 525
Win32 virtual memory architecture, 125
window attributes, 10
   see also attributes, window parent/owner

window
   class, 10, *see also* RegisterClass, RegisterClassEx, UnregisterClass
   creating, 11-12, *see also* CreateWindowEx
   device contexts, 282
   destroying, *see* DestroyWindow
   handle, *see* HWND
   MDI styles, *see* MDI client styles
   MDI, *see* CreateMDIWindow
   name, 10
   position, 10
   procedure, 13, *see also* CallWindowProc, DefFrameProc, DefMDIChildProc, DefWindowProc
   size, 10
   styles, 10, 37-38
   types, 15,
   z-order, 10
WindowProc, 51
Windows
   application written entirely in Object Pascal, 13-15
   creation, 9
   data types, 1
   font table, 611
   functions, callback, 5
   functions, importing, 4, 5
   functions, parameters, 6
   hardcore programming, 13
   hooks, 58
   procedure, 51
   scaling, *see* ScaleWindowsExtEx
   styles, 35-36
WPARAM, 2

Z

ZeroMemory, 168
z-order, window, 10

Looking for more?

Check out Wordware's market-leading Delphi Developer's Library featuring the following new releases and upcoming titles.

Available Now:

Delphi Developer's Guide to XML

1-55622-812-0
$59.95
7½ x 9¼
544 pp.

The Tomes of Delphi: Developer's Guide to Troubleshooting

1-55622-816-3
$59.95
7½ x 9¼
568 pp.

Coming Soon:

Kylix Development

1-55622-774-4
$49.95
7½ x 9¼
600 pp.

Available December 2001

The Tomes of Kylix: The Linux API

1-55622-823-6
$59.95
7½ x 9¼
600 pp.

Available December 2001

The Tomes of Delphi: Win 32 Shell API— Windows 2000 Edition

1-55622-749-3
$59.95
7½ x 9¼
740 pp.

Available February 2002

Special Offer

30% off and free shipping*

* Continental U.S. only

Check out the complete Delphi Library online at
www.wordware.com

Extend Your Power.

Borland Solution Partner Resource Guide provides an opportunity for vendors of software products and services designed to extend the power of Borland developer tools and technologies to reach developers and IT professionals at the point of purchase.

The primary means of distribution of *Borland Solution Partner Resource Guide* is its placement into every North American box of Delphi (for both Linux and Windows), C++Builder, JBuilder, Application Server, VisiBroker, and AppCenter from Borland Software Corporation. In addition, Borland Software Corporation and Informant Communications Group will distribute *Borland Solution Partner Resource Guide* at a number of leading industry trade shows. When you advertise in *Borland Solution Partner Resource Guide*, you will also receive a FREE advertisement in the electronic version at www.BorlandSolutions.com. Traffic will be directed to this site from both the Borland and Informant Communications Group Web sites. Advertisements in the electronic version may be updated each month. Visitors to your online advertisement will be linked directly to your Web site. Your electronic advertisement will appear until the next edition of *Borland Solution Partner Resource Guide* is published.

No other publication will reach as many Borland development and IT professionals more quickly or efficiently.

2 Great Ways to Get Your Delphi Fix!

Delphi Informant Magazine: FREE Issue, FREE Web Site

Receive **one free issue** of **Delphi™ Informant® Magazine**, and a **FREE** 30-day **DelphiZine.com** Web site membership. If you choose to subscribe, you'll get 12 additional issues (13 in all) and a one-year Web site membership for the super low price of **$49.99**. If you don't, simply write "cancel" on the invoice and owe nothing.

With the first issue, you'll discover why **Delphi Informant Magazine** is the world's leading publication covering Delphi development. And you'll see why **DelphiZine.com** is the most comprehensive and valuable information resource on Delphi development in the world.

- ▶ Complete Delphi 6 coverage
- ▶ Ready-to-run code examples
- ▶ Real-world solutions
- ▶ Tips, tricks, and techniques
- ▶ Web and database development
- ▶ COM+, MTS, LDAP, and more

Delphi Informant Magazine Complete Works CD ROM

Get a jump on your Delphi skills with this comprehensive reference. The **Delphi Informant Magazine Complete Works CD-ROM** contains all content published in **Delphi Informant Magazine** from 1995-2000, including all supporting code and sample files. Order this unbelievable collection for only **$49.99** *(additional charges apply for shipping & handling)*.

The must-have ultimate reference source for Delphi developers *features*:

- ▶ Over 500 technical articles, product reviews, book reviews, and other content appearing in **Delphi Informant Magazine** from 1995 through 2000
- ▶ All supporting code, sample files, and utilities from each article
- ▶ Fast text searching across all articles contained on the CD-ROM
- ▶ Bookmarks for easy navigation
- ▶ ... And much more

(1995-2000)

CALL NOW!
YES! *I want to sharpen my Delphi™ programming skills...*

800-884-6367 x10   Outside the US dial (916) 686-6610

INFORMANT
COMMUNICATIONS GROUP

About the CD

The companion CD-ROM contains the code and compiled executables for every example in the book. The files are organized by chapter and listing, and are accessible using Windows Explorer.

For a comprehensive Windows Help file covering every function within the book, visit us online at **www.wordware.com/tomes**.

Warning: By opening the CD package, you accept the terms and conditions of the CD/Source Code Usage License Agreement on the following page.

Opening the CD package makes this book nonreturnable.

CD/Source Code Usage License Agreement

Please read the following CD/Source Code usage license agreement before opening the CD and using the contents therein:

1. By opening the accompanying software package, you are indicating that you have read and agree to be bound by all terms and conditions of this CD/Source Code usage license agreement.
2. The compilation of code and utilities contained on the CD and in the book are copyrighted and protected by both U.S. copyright law and international copyright treaties, and is owned by Wordware Publishing, Inc. Individual source code, example programs, help files, freeware, shareware, utilities, and evaluation packages, including their copyrights, are owned by the respective authors.
3. No part of the enclosed CD or this book, including all source code, help files, shareware, freeware, utilities, example programs, or evaluation programs, may be made available on a public forum (such as a World Wide Web page, FTP site, bulletin board, or Internet news group) without the express written permission of Wordware Publishing, Inc. or the author of the respective source code, help files, shareware, freeware, utilities, example programs, or evaluation programs.
4. You may not decompile, reverse engineer, disassemble, create a derivative work, or otherwise use the enclosed programs, help files, freeware, shareware, utilities, or evaluation programs except as stated in this agreement.
5. The software, contained on the CD and/or as source code in this book, is sold without warranty of any kind. Wordware Publishing, Inc. and the authors specifically disclaim all other warranties, express or implied, including but not limited to implied warranties of merchantability and fitness for a particular purpose with respect to defects in the disk, the program, source code, sample files, help files, freeware, shareware, utilities, and evaluation programs contained therein, and/or the techniques described in the book and implemented in the example programs. In no event shall Wordware Publishing, Inc., its dealers, its distributors, or the authors be liable or held responsible for any loss of profit or any other alleged or actual private or commercial damage, including but not limited to special, incidental, consequential, or other damages.
6. One (1) copy of the CD or any source code therein may be created for backup purposes. The CD and all accompanying source code, sample files, help files, freeware, shareware, utilities, and evaluation programs may be copied to your hard drive. With the exception of freeware and shareware programs, at no time can any part of the contents of this CD reside on more than one computer at one time. The contents of the CD can be copied to another computer, as long as the contents of the CD contained on the original computer are deleted.
7. You may not include any part of the CD contents, including all source code, example programs, shareware, freeware, help files, utilities, or evaluation programs in any compilation of source code, utilities, help files, example programs, freeware, shareware, or evaluation programs on any media, including but not limited to CD, disk, or Internet distribution, without the express written permission of Wordware Publishing, Inc. or the owner of the individual source code, utilities, help files, example programs, freeware, shareware, or evaluation programs.
8. You may use the source code, techniques, and example programs in your own commercial or private applications unless otherwise noted by additional usage agreements as found on the CD.

> **Warning:** By opening the CD package, you accept the terms and conditions of the CD/Source Code Usage License Agreement.
>
> Additionally, **opening the CD package makes this book non-returnable.**